Plays for the Theatre

Eleventh Edition

From the Wadsworth Series in Theatre

Plays for the Theatre

ELEVENTH EDITION

Oscar G. Brockett
University of Texas at Austin

Robert J. Ball
University of the Incarnate Word

With Revisions and Additional Material by
John Fleming
Texas State University

Andrew Carlson
University of Texas at Austin

WADSWORTH
CENGAGE Learning

Australia • Brazil • Japan • Korea • Mexico • Singapore • Spain • United Kingdom • United States

WADSWORTH
CENGAGE Learning·

Plays for the Theatre: A Drama Anthology, Eleventh Edition
Oscar G. Brockett and
Robert J. Ball
With revisions and additional material by John Fleming and Andrew Carlson

Senior Publisher: Lyn Uhl

Publisher: Michael Rosenberg

Development Editor:
Megan Garvey

Assistant Editor: Erin Bosco

Editorial Assistant:
Rebecca Donahue

Media Editor: Jessica Badiner

Brand Manager: Ben Rivera

Senior Marketing
Communications Manager:
Linda Yip

Content Project Manager:
Dan Saabye

Art Director: Linda May

Manufacturing Planner:
Doug Bertke

Rights Acquisition Specialist:
Mandy Groszko

Production Service: Integra

Text and Cover Designer:
Chris Miller

Cover Image:
Robbie Jack/© Corbis

Compositor: Integra

For product information and
technology assistance, contact us at **Cengage Learning Customer & Sales Support, 1-800-354-9706**

For permission to use material from this text or product, submit all requests online at **cengage.com/permissions**
Further permissions questions can be emailed to
permissionrequest@cengage.com

Library of Congress Control Number: 2013931126

Student Edition:

ISBN-13: 978-1-1333-1069-3

ISBN-10: 1-133-31069-9

Wadsworth
20 Channel Center Street
Boston, MA 02210
USA

Cengage Learning is a leading provider of customized learning solutions with office locations around the globe, including Singapore, the United Kingdom, Australia, Mexico, Brazil, and Japan. Locate your local office at **international.cengage.com/region**

Cengage Learning products are represented in Canada by Nelson Education, Ltd.

For your course and learning solutions, visit
www.cengage.com

Purchase any of our products at your local college store or at our preferred online store **www.ichapters.com**

Printed in the U.S.A.
1 2 3 4 5 6 7 17 16 15 14 13

Contents

Preface

The Eleventh edition OF *Plays for the Theatre* contains fourteen plays. Three of these plays are new to this collection: Sam Shepard's *True West*, an intense sibling drama; August Wilson's *Fences*, a Pulitzer Prize-winning exploration of an African American family; and Tony Kushner's *Angels in America*, a theatrical epic of 1980s America during the AIDS crisis. These three writers are among the most critically acclaimed American playwrights in recent decades.

Selecting plays for an anthology is always a problematic position. For each play chosen, many others, perhaps equally worthy, must be excluded as we seek to provide a broad selection of representative, exciting, and culturally diverse plays from the past and present.

The works included in this anthology come from many periods, representing the drama of ancient Greece, the Middle Ages, seventeenth-century England and France, late nineteenth-century Norway and England, and a wide range of twentieth- and twenty-first century American drama. As such, they provide a broad cultural perspective.

In addition to the new works, the collection includes plays by Sophocles, Shakespeare, Molière, Ibsen, Wilde, and Williams, as well as an anonymous author of a medieval mystery play. This edition also includes a Noh drama attributed to the Japanese master playwright Zeami, and an African drama by Nobel Prize–winner Wole Soyinka. As in previous editions, the anthology contains recent American plays chosen for their dramatic power as well as their cultural diversity and artistic excellence. These include plays by Pulitzer Prize–winning African American dramatist August Wilson, and a Pulitzer Prize–winning play by Paula Vogel. Each of these plays is discussed at some length in a companion book, *The Essential Theatre*, Eleventh Edition, also published by Wadsworth Cengage. This companion volume places each of the plays included in *Plays for the Theatre* within its historical and cultural context. Although each of these books can stand alone, together they provide a greater understanding of the plays than when used separately.

Acknowledgements

We would like to thank the reviewers who took time to provide insight and guidance on this project:

Tracy Angle, *Carolina Community College*
Laurie J Wolf, *College of William and Mary*

Finally, we thank the staff at Wadsworth: Michael Rosenberg, Publisher; Megan Garvey, Development Editor; Erin Bosco, Assistant Editor; Rebecca Donahue, Editorial Assistant, and Dan Saaybe, Content Jessica Badiner, Media Editor, and Matt Gauthier at Integra.

John Fleming
Andrew Carlson

Plays for the Theatre

ELEVENTH EDITION

Sophocles (495–406 B.C.)

Oedipus Rex
(C. 430 B.C.)

O EDIPUS *REX* was first performed in Athens at the City Dionysia (a major religious and civic festival held annually in honor of Dionysus, the god of wine and fertility) in competition with works by two other playwrights. Each dramatist presented three tragedies and one satyr play each time he competed before the audience of approximately fifteen thousand spectators. Sophocles was awarded first prize for the group of plays that included *Oedipus Rex*.

The most striking feature of Greek tragedy is the alternation of dramatic episodes with choral passages. In Sophocles's day, the tragic chorus included fifteen performers who sang (or recited) and danced the choral passages to musical accompaniment. Other typical features of Greek tragedy are the small number of individualized characters, the restriction of the action to a single place, the tightly unified plot, the serious and philosophic tone, and the poetic language.

The action of *Oedipus Rex* is extremely concentrated: A complete reversal of the protagonist's fortune takes place in a single day. The story follows Oedipus, king of Thebes, as he attempts to discover the murderer of Laïos, the former king, after an oracle declares that the plague now destroying the city will not be lifted until the guilty one is cast out. Oedipus's search gradually uncovers terrible truths about the past and his own origins. The initial suspicion that Oedipus himself may be the slayer of Laïos is rapidly followed by other electrifying moments (among them Iocastê's recognition that she is not only Oedipus's wife but also his mother), and the ultimate outcome: blindness, exile, and anguish for the once powerful king.

The Greek philosopher Aristotle thought that *Oedipus Rex* was an ideal example of the tragic form because Sophocles combined "recognition" (a sudden change from ignorance to knowledge) and reversal of fortune at the same moment. Oedipus recognizes the truth of who he is and what he has done, and in that moment his stature changes from king to pariah. Aristotle believed that this combination of recognition and reversal of fortune increased a tragedy's power to evoke a strong emotional reaction.

Sophocles is admired particularly for his skillful management of extensive plot materials: He accomplishes the gradual unveiling of mystery after mystery and a steady increase in dramatic tension with the utmost economy of means. Although, like most great plays, *Oedipus Rex* is open to many interpretations, most critics have agreed that a central concern is the uncertainty of fate and humanity's helplessness in the face of destiny.

Oedipus Rex
(C. 430 B.C.)

ENGLISH VERSION BY DUDLEY FITTS AND ROBERT FITZGERALD

Persons Represented

OEDIPUS

A PRIEST

CREON

TEIRESIAS

IOCASTÊ [JOCASTA]

MESSENGER

SHEPHERD OF LAÏOS

SECOND MESSENGER

CHORUS OF THEBAN ELDERS

THE SCENE———Before the palace of OEDIPUS, *King of Thebes. A central door and two lateral doors open onto a platform which runs the length of the façade. On the platform, right and left, are altars; and three steps lead down into the "orchestra," or chorus-ground. At the beginning of the action these steps are crowded by suppliants who have brought branches and chaplets of olive leaves and who lie in various attitudes of despair.* OEDIPUS *enters.*

PROLOGUE

OEDIPUS: My children, generations of the living
    In the line of Kadmos, nursed at his ancient hearth:
    Why have you strewn yourselves before these altars
    In supplication, with your boughs and garlands?
    The breath of incense rises from the city   5
    With a sound of prayer and lamentation.
                        Children,
    I would not have you speak through messengers,
    And therefore I have come myself to hear you—
    I, Oedipus, who bear the famous name.   10

      [*To a* PRIEST.]

    You, there, since you are eldest in the company,
    Speak for them all, tell me what preys upon you,
    Whether you come in dread, or crave some blessing:

Tell me, and never doubt that I will help you
In every way I can; I should be heartless   15
Were I not moved to find you suppliant here.
PRIEST: Great Oedipus, O powerful King of Thebes!
    You see how all the ages of our people
    Cling to your altar steps: here are boys
    Who can barely stand alone, and here are priests   20
    By weight of age, as I am a priest of God,
    And young men chosen from those yet unmarried;
    As for the others, all that multitude,
    They wait with olive chaplets in the squares,
    At the two shrines of Pallas, and where Apollo   25
    Speaks in the glowing embers.
                         Your own eyes,
    Must tell you: Thebes is tossed on a murdering sea
    And can not lift her head from the death surge.
    A rust consumes the buds and fruits of the earth;
    The herds are sick; children die unborn,   30
    And labor is vain. The god of plague and pyre
    Raids like detestable lightning through the city,
    And all the house of Kadmos is laid waste,
    All emptied, and all darkened; Death alone   35
    Battens upon the misery of Thebes.

    You are not one of the immortal gods, we know;
    Yet we have come to you to make our prayer
    As to the man surest in mortal ways
    And wisest in the ways of God. You saved us   40
    From the Sphinx, that flinty singer, and the tribute
    We paid to her so long; yet you were never
    Better informed than we, nor could we teach you:
    It was some god breathed in you to set us free.

    Therefore, O mighty King, we turn to you:
    Find us our safety, find us a remedy,   45
    Whether by counsel of the gods or men.
    A king of wisdom tested in the past
    Can act in a time of troubles, and act well.
    Noblest of men, restore   50
    Life to your city! Think how all men call you
    Liberator for your triumph long ago;
    Ah, when your years of kingship are remembered,
    Let them not say We rose, but later fell—
    Keep the State from going down in the storm!   55
    Once, years ago, with a happy augury,
    You brought us fortune; be the same again!
    No man questions your power to rule the land:
    But rule over men, not over a dead city!
    Ships are only hulls, citadels are nothing,   60
    When no life moves in the empty passageways.

OEDIPUS: Poor children! You may be sure I know
    All that you longed for in your coming here.
    I know that you are deathly sick; and yet,
    Sick as you are, not one is as sick as I. 65
    Each of you suffers in himself alone
    His anguish, not another's; but my spirit
    Groans for the city, for myself, for you.
    I was not sleeping, you are not waking me.
    No, I have been in tears for a long while 70
    And in my restless thought walked many ways.
    In all my search, I found one helpful course,
    And that I have taken: I have sent Creon,
    Son of Menoikeus, brother of the Queen,
    To Delphi, Apollo's place of revelation, 75
    To learn there, if he can,
    What act or pledge of mine may save the city.
    I have counted the days, and now, this very day,
    I am troubled, for he has overstayed his time.
    What is he doing? He has been gone too long. 80
    Yet whenever he comes back, I should do ill
    To scant whatever duty God reveals.
PRIEST: It is a timely promise. At this instant
    They tell me Creon is here.
OEDIPUS: O Lord Apollo! 85
    May his news be fair as his face is radiant!
PRIEST: It could not be otherwise: he is crowned with bay,
    The chaplet is thick with berries.
OEDIPUS: We shall soon know;
    He is near enough to hear us now. 90

    [*Enter* CREON.]

                    O Prince:
    Brother: son of Menoikeus:
    What answer do you bring us from the god?
CREON: A strong one. I can tell you, great afflictions
    Will turn out well, if they are taken well. 95
OEDIPUS: What was the oracle? These vague words
    Leave me still hanging between hope and fear.
CREON: Is it your pleasure to hear me with all these
    Gathered around us? I am prepared to speak,
    But should we not go in? 100
OEDIPUS: Let them all hear it.
    It is for them I suffer, more than for myself.
CREON: Then I will tell you what I heard at Delphi.
    In plain words
    The god commands us to expel from the land of Thebes 105
    An old defilement we are sheltering.
    It is a deathly thing, beyond cure;
    We must not let it feed upon us longer.

OEDIPUS: What defilement? How shall we rid ourselves of it?
CREON: By exile or death, blood for blood. It was   110
    Murder that brought the plague-wind on the city.
OEDIPUS: Murder of whom? Surely the god has named him?
CREON: My lord: long ago Laïos was our king,
    Before you came to govern us.
OEDIPUS: I know;   115
    I learned of him from others; I never saw him.
CREON: He was murdered; and Apollo commands us now
    To take revenge upon whoever killed him.
OEDIPUS: Upon whom? Where are they? Where shall we find a clue
    To solve that crime, after so many years?   120
CREON: Here in this land, he said.
                   If we make enquiry,
    We may touch things that otherwise escape us.
OEDIPUS: Tell me: Was Laïos murdered in his house,
    Or in the fields, or in some foreign country?   125
CREON: He said he planned to make a pilgrimage.
    He did not come home again.
OEDIPUS: And was there no one,
    No witness, no companion, to tell what happened?
CREON: They were all killed but one, and he got away   130
    So frightened that he could remember one thing only.
OEDIPUS: What was that one thing? One may be the key
    To everything, if we resolve to use it.
CREON: He said that a band of highwaymen attacked them,
    Outnumbered them, and overwhelmed the King.   135
OEDIPUS: Strange, that a highwayman should be so daring—
    Unless some faction here bribed him to do it.
CREON: We thought of that. But after Laïos' death
    New troubles arose and he had no avenger.
OEDIPUS: What troubles could prevent your hunting down the killers?   140
CREON: The riddling Sphinx's song
    Made us deaf to all mysteries but her own.
OEDIPUS: Then once more I must bring what is dark to light.
    It is most fitting that Apollo shows,
    As you do, this compunction for the dead.   145
    You shall see how I stand by you, as I should,
    To avenge the city and the city's god,
    And not as though it were for some distant friend,
    But for my own sake, to be rid of evil.
    Whoever killed King Laïos might—who knows?—   150
    Decide at any moment to kill me as well.
    By avenging the murdered king I protect myself.
    Come, then, my children: leave the altar steps,
    Lift up your olive boughs!
                 One of you go   155
    And summon the people of Kadmos to gather here.
    I will do all that I can; you may tell them that.

[*Exit a* PAGE.]

So, with the help of God,
We shall be saved—or else indeed we are lost.

PRIEST: Let us rise, children. It was for this we came,   160
And now the King has promised it himself.
Phoibos has sent us an oracle; may he descend
Himself to save us and drive out the plague.

[*Exeunt* OEDIPUS *and* CREON *into the palace by the central door. The* PRIEST
and the SUPPLIANTS *disperse R and L. After a short pause the* CHORUS *enters
the orchestra.*]

PARODOS

CHORUS: What is God singing in his profound   [STROPHE 1]
Delphi of gold and shadow?   165
What oracle for Thebes, the sunwhipped city?

Fear unjoints me, the roots of my heart tremble.

Now I remember, O Healer, your power, and wonder:
Will you send doom like a sudden cloud, or weave it
Like nightfall of the past?   170

Speak, speak to us, issue a holy sound:
Dearest to our expectancy: be tender!

Let me pray to Athenê, the immortal daughter of Zeus,
                                                                        [ANTISTROPHE 1]
And to Artemis her sister
Who keeps her famous throne in the market ring,   175
And to Apollo, bowman at the far butts of heaven-

O gods, descend! Like three streams leap against
The fires of our grief, the fires of darkness;
Be swift to bring us rest!

As in the old time from the brilliant house   180
Of air you stepped to save us, come again!

Now our afflictions have no end,   [STROPHE 2]
Now all our stricken host lies down
And no man fights off death with his mind;
The noble plowland bears no grain,   185
And groaning mothers can not bear—

See, how our lives like birds take wing,
Like sparks that fly when a fire soars,
To the shore of the god of evening.

The plague burns on; it is pitiless,   [ANTISTROPHE 2]   190
Though pallid children laden with death
Lie unwept in the stony ways,

And old gray women by every path
Flock to the strand about the altars

There to strike their breasts and cry   195
Worship of Phoibos in wailing prayers:
Be kind, God's golden child!

There are no swords in this attack by fire,   [STROPHE 3]
No shields, but we are ringed with cries.
Send the besieger plunging from our homes   200
Into the vast sea-room of the Atlantic
Or into the waves that foam eastward of Thrace—

For the day ravages what the night spares—

Destroy our enemy, lord of the thunder!
Let him be riven by lightning from heaven!   205

Phoibos Apollo, stretch the sun's bowstring,   [ANTISTROPHE 3]
That golden cord, until it sings for us,
Flashing arrows in heaven!
                    Artemis, Huntress,
Race with flaring lights upon our mountains!   210

O scarlet god, O golden-banded brow,
O Theban Bacchos in a storm of Maenads,

   [*Enter* OEDIPUS, *C.*]

Whirl upon Death, that all the Undying hate.
Come with blinding torches, come in joy!

SCENE I

OEDIPUS: Is this your prayer? It may be answered. Come,
    Listen to me, act as the crisis demands,
    And you shall have relief from all these evils.
    Until now I was a stranger to this tale,
    As I had been a stranger to the crime.   5
    Could I track down the murderer without a clue?

    But now, friends,
    As one who became a citizen after the murder,
    I make this proclamation to all Thebans:
    If any man knows by whose hand Laïos, son of Labdakos,   10

Met his death, I direct that man to tell me everything,
No matter what he fears for having so long withheld it.
Let it stand as promised that no further trouble
Will come to him, but he may leave the land in safety.

Moreover: If anyone knows the murderer to be foreign, 15
Let him not keep silent: he shall have his reward from me.
However, if he does conceal it; if any man
Fearing for his friend or for himself disobeys this edict,
Hear what I propose to do:

I solemnly forbid the people of this country, 20
Where power and throne are mine, ever to receive that man
Or speak to him, no matter who he is, or let him
Join in sacrifice, lustration, or in prayer.
I decree that he be driven from every house,
Being, as he is, corruption itself to us: the Delphic 25
Voice of Zeus has pronounced this revelation.
Thus I associate myself with the oracle
And take the side of the murdered king.

As for the criminal, I pray to God—
Whether it be a lurking thief, or one of a number— 30
I pray that that man's life be consumed in evil and wretchedness.
And as for me, this curse applies no less
If it should turn out that the culprit is my guest here,
Sharing my hearth.
                    You have heard the penalty. 35
I lay it on you now to attend to this
For my sake, for Apollo's, for the sick
Sterile city that heaven has abandoned.
Suppose the oracle had given you no command:
Should this defilement go uncleansed for ever? 40
You should have found the murderer: your king,
A noble king, had been destroyed!
                    Now I,
Having the power that he held for me,
Having his bed, begetting children there 45
Upon his wife, as he would have, had he lived—
Their son would have been my children's brother,
If Laïos had had luck in fatherhood!
(But surely ill luck rushed upon his reign)—
I say I take the son's part, just as though 50
I were his son, to press the fight for him
And see it won! I'll find the hand that brought
Death to Labdakos' and Polydoros' child,
Heir to Kadmos' and Agenor's line.
And as for those who fail me, 55
May the gods deny them the fruit of the earth,
Fruit of the womb, and may they rot utterly!
Let them be wretched as we are wretched, and worse!

For you, for loyal Thebans, and for all
who find my actions right, I pray the favor 60
Of justice, and of all the immortal gods.
CHORAGOS: Since I am under oath, my lord, I swear
I did not do the murder, I can not name
The murderer. Might not the oracle
That has ordained the search tell where to find him? 65
OEDIPUS: An honest question. But no man in the world
Can make the gods do more than the gods will.
CHORAGOS: There is one last expedient—
OEDIPUS: Tell me what it is.
Though it seem slight, you must not hold it back. 70
CHORAGOS: A lord clairvoyant to the lord Apollo,
As we all know, is the skilled Teiresias.
One might learn much about this from him, Oedipus.
OEDIPUS: I am not wasting time:
Creon spoke of this, and I have sent for him— 75
Twice, in fact; it is strange that he is not here.
CHORAGOS: The other matter—that old report—seems useless.
OEDIPUS: Tell me. I am interested in all reports.
CHORAGOS: The King was said to have been killed by highwaymen.
OEDIPUS: I know. But we have no witnesses to that. 80
CHORAGOS: If the killer can feel a particle of dread,
Your curse will bring him out of hiding!
OEDIPUS: No.
The man who dared that act will fear no curse.

[*Enter the blind seer* TEIRESIAS, *led by a* PAGE.]

CHORAGOS: But there is one man who may detect the criminal. 85
This is Teiresias, this is the holy prophet
In whom, alone of all men, truth was born.
OEDIPUS: Teiresias: seer: student of mysteries,
Of all that's taught and all that no man tells,
Secrets of Heaven and secrets of the earth: 90
Blind though you are, you know the city lies
Slick with plague; and from this plague, my lord,
We find that you alone can guard or save us.

Possibly you did not hear the messengers?
Apollo, when we sent to him, 95
Sent us back word that this great pestilence
Would lift, but only if we established clearly
The identity of those who murdered Laïos.
They must be killed or exiled.
                                      Can you use 100
Birdflight or any art of divination
To purify yourself, and Thebes, and me
From this contagion? We are in your hands.
There is no fairer duty
Than that of helping others in distress. 105
TEIRESIAS: How dreadful knowledge of the truth can be

When there's no help in truth! I knew this well,
But made myself forget. I should not have come.

OEDIPUS: What is troubling you? Why are your eyes so cold?

TEIRESIAS: Let me go home. Bear your own fate, and I'll   110
Bear mine. It is better so: trust what I say.

OEDIPUS: What you say is ungracious and unhelpful
To your native country. Do not refuse to speak.

TEIRESIAS: When it comes to speech, your own is neither temperate
Nor opportune. I wish to be more prudent.   115

OEDIPUS: In God's name, we all beg you—

TEIRESIAS: You are all ignorant.
No; I will never tell you what I know.
Now it is my misery; then, it would be yours.

OEDIPUS: What! You do know something, and will not tell us?   120
You would betray us all and wreck the State?

TEIRESIAS: I do not intend to torture myself, or you.
Why persist in asking? You will not persuade me.

OEDIPUS: What a wicked old man you are! You'd try a stone's
Patience! Out with it! Have you no feeling at all?   125

TEIRESIAS: You call me unfeeling. If you could only see
The nature of your own feelings. . .

OEDIPUS: Why,
Who would not feel as I do? Who could endure
Your arrogance toward the city?   130

TEIRESIAS: What does it matter!
Whether I speak or not, it is bound to come.

OEDIPUS: Then, if "it" is bound to come, you are bound to tell me.

TEIRESIAS: No, I will not go on. Rage as you please.

OEDIPUS: Rage? Why not!   135
                      And I'll tell you what I think:
You planned it, you had it done, you all but
Killed him with your own hands: if you had eyes,
I'd say the crime was yours, and yours alone.

TEIRESIAS: So? I charge you, then,   140
Abide by the proclamation you have made:
From this day forth
Never speak again to these men or to me;
You yourself are the pollution of this country.

OEDIPUS: You dare say that! Can you possibly think you have   145
Some way of going free, after such insolence?

TEIRESIAS: I have gone free. It is the truth sustains me.

OEDIPUS: Who taught you shamelessness? It was not your craft.

TEIRESIAS: You did. You made me speak. I did not want to.

OEDIPUS: Speak what? Let me hear it again more clearly.   150

TEIRESIAS: Was it not clear before? Are you tempting me?

OEDIPUS: I did not understand it. Say it again.

TEIRESIAS: I say that you are the murderer whom you seek.

OEDIPUS: Now twice you have spat out infamy. You'll pay for it!

TEIRESIAS: Would you care for more? Do you wish to be really angry?   155

OEDIPUS: Say what you will. Whatever you say is worthless.

TEIRESIAS: I say you live in hideous shame with those
    Most dear to you. You can not see the evil.
OEDIPUS: It seems you can go on mouthing like this for ever.
TEIRESIAS: I can, if there is power in truth.   160
OEDIPUS: There is:
    But not for you, not for you,
    You sightless, witless, senseless, mad old man!
TEIRESIAS: You are the madman. There is no one here
    who will not curse you soon, as you curse me.   165
OEDIPUS: You child of endless night! You can not hurt me
    Or any other man who sees the sun.
TEIRESIAS: True: it is not from me your fate will come.
    That lies within Apollo's competence.
    As it is his concern.   170
OEDIPUS: Tell me.
    Are you speaking for Creon, or for yourself?
TEIRESIAS: Creon is no threat. You weave your own doom.
OEDIPUS: Wealth, power, craft of statesmanship!
    Kingly position, everywhere admired!   175
    What savage envy is stored up against these,
    If Creon, whom I trusted, Creon my friend,
    For this great office which the city once
    Put in my hands unsought-if for this power
    Creon desires in secret to destroy me!   180

    He has bought this decrepit fortune-teller, this
    Collector of dirty pennies, this prophet fraud—
    Why, he is no more clairvoyant than I am!
                            Tell us.
    Has your mystic mummery ever approached the truth?   185
    When that hellcat the Sphinx was performing here,
    What help were you to these people?
    Her magic was not for the first man who came along:
    It demanded a real exorcist. Your birds—
    What good were they? or the gods, for the matter of that?   190
    But I came by,
    Oedipus, the simple man, who knows nothing—
    I thought it out for myself, no birds helped me!
    And this is the man you think you can destroy,
    That you may be close to Creon when he's king!   195
    Well, you and your friend Creon, it seems to me,
    Will suffer most. If you were not an old man,
    You would have paid already for your plot.
CHORAGOS: We can not see that his words or yours
    Have been spoken except in anger, Oedipus,   200
    And of anger we have no need. How can God's will
    Be accomplished best? That is what most concerns us.
TEIRESIAS: You are a king. But where argument's concerned
    I am your man, as much a king as you.
    I am not your servant, but Apollo's.   205

I have no need of Creon to speak for me.

Listen to me. You mock my blindness, do you?
But I say that you, with both your eyes, are blind:
You can not see the wretchedness of your life,
Nor in whose house you live, no, nor with whom.   210
Who are your father and mother? Can you tell me?
You do not even know the blind wrongs
That you have done them, on earth and in the world below.
But the double lash of your parents' curse will whip you
Out of this land some day, with only night   215
Upon your precious eyes.
Your cries then—where will they not be heard?
What fastness of Kithairon will not echo them?
And that bridal-descant of yours—you'll know it then,
The song they sang when you came here to Thebes   220
And found your misguided berthing.
All this, and more, that you can not guess at now,
Will bring you to yourself among your children.
Be angry, then. Curse Creon. Curse my words.
I tell you, no man that walks upon the earth   225
Shall be rooted out more horribly than you.

OEDIPUS: Am I to bear this from him?—Damnation
    Take you! Out of this place! Out of my sight!
TEIRESIAS: I would not have come at all if you had not asked me.
OEDIPUS: Could I have told that you'd talk nonsense, that   230
    You'd come here to make a fool of yourself, and of me?
TEIRESIAS: A fool? Your parents thought me sane enough.
OEDIPUS: My parents again!—Wait: who were my parents?
TEIRESIAS: This day will give you a father, and break your heart.
OEDIPUS: Your infantile riddles! Your damned abracadabra!   235
TEIRESIAS: You were a great man once at solving riddles.
OEDIPUS: Mock me with that if you like; you will find it true.
TEIRESIAS: It was true enough. It brought about your ruin.
OEDIPUS: But if it saved this town?
TEIRESIAS: [to the PAGE] Boy, give me your hand.   240
OEDIPUS: Yes, boy; lead him away.
    —While you are here
    We can do nothing. Go; leave us in peace.
TEIRESIAS: I will go when I have said what I have to say.
    How can you hurt me? And I tell you again: 245
    The man you have been looking for all this time,
    The damned man, the murderer of Laïos,
    That man is in Thebes. To your mind he is foreign-born,
    But it will soon be shown that he is Theban,
    A revelation that will fail to please.   250
                                        A blind man,
    Who has his eyes now; a penniless man, who is rich now;
    And he will go tapping the strange earth with his staff

To the children with whom he lives now he will be
Brother and father—the very same; to her   255
Who bore him, son and husband—the very same
Who came to his father's bed, wet with his father's blood.
Enough. Go think that over.
If later you find error in what I have said,
You may say that I have no skill in prophecy.   260

[*Exit* TEIRESIAS, *led by his* PAGE. OEDIPUS *goes into the palace.*]

ODE I

CHORUS: The Delphic stone of prophecies   [STROPHE 1]
    Remembers ancient regicide
    And a still bloody hand.
    That killer's hour of flight has come.
    He must be stronger than riderless   265
    Coursers of untiring wind,
    For the son of Zeus armed with his father's thunder
    Leaps in lightning after him;
    And the Furies follow him, the sad Furies.
    Holy Parnassos' peak of snow   [ANTISTROPHE 1]   270
    Flashes and blinds that secret man,
    That all shall hunt him down:
    Though he may roam the forest shade
    Like a bull wild from pasture
    To rage through glooms of stone.   275
    Doom comes down on him; flight will not avail him;
    For the world's heart calls him desolate,
    And the immortal Furies follow, forever follow.

    But now a wilder thing is heard   [STROPHE 2]
    From the old man skilled at hearing Fate in the wingbeat of a bird.   280
    Bewildered as a blown bird, my soul hovers and can not find
    Foothold in this debate, or any reason or rest of mind.
    But no man ever brought—none can bring
    Proof of strife between Thebes' royal house,
    Labdakos' line, and the son of Polybos;   285
    And never until now has any man brought word
    Of Laïos' dark death staining Oedipus the King.

    Divine Zeus and Apollo hold   [ANTISTROPHE 2]
    Perfect intelligence alone of all tales ever told;
    And well though this diviner works, he works in his own night;   290
    No man can judge that rough unknown or trust in second sight,
    For wisdom changes hands among the wise.
    Shall I believe my great lord criminal
    At a raging word that a blind old man let fall?

I saw him, when the carrion woman faced him of old,   295
Prove his heroic mind! These evil words are lies.

SCENE II

CREON: Men of Thebes:
   I am told that heavy accusations
   Have been brought against me by King Oedipus.

   I am not the kind of man to bear this tamely.

   If in these present difficulties   5
   He holds me accountable for any harm to him
   Through anything I have said or done—why, then,
   I do not value life in this dishonor.
   It is not as though this rumor touched upon
   Some private indiscretion. The matter is grave.   10
   The fact is that I am being called disloyal
   To the State, to my fellow citizens, to my friends.
CHORAGOS: He may have spoken in anger, not from his mind.
CREON: But did you not hear him say I was the one
   Who seduced the old prophet into lying?   15
CHORAGOS: The thing was said; I do not know how seriously.
CREON: But you were watching him! Were his eyes steady?
   Did he look like a man in his right mind?
CHORAGOS: I do not know.
   I can not judge the behavior of great men.   20
   But here is the King himself.

   [*Enter* OEDIPUS.]

OEDIPUS: So you dared come back.
   Why? How brazen of you to come to my house,
   You murderer!
                              Do you think I do not know   25
   That you plotted to kill me, plotted to steal my throne?
   Tell me, in God's name: am I coward, a fool,
   That you should dream you could accomplish this?
   A fool who could not see your slippery game?
   A coward, not to fight back when I saw it?   30
   You are the fool, Creon, are you not? hoping
   Without support or friends to get a throne?
   Thrones may be won or bought: you could do neither.
CREON: Now listen to me. You have talked; let me talk, too.
   You can not judge unless you know the facts.   35
OEDIPUS: You speak well: there is one fact; but I find it hard
   To learn from the deadliest enemy I have.
CREON: That above all I must dispute with you.
OEDIPUS: That above all I will not hear you deny.

CREON: If you think there is anything good in being stubborn   40
     Against all reason, then I say you are wrong.
OEDIPUS: If you think a man can sin against his own kind
     And not be punished for it, I say you are mad.
CREON: I agree. But tell me: what have I done to you?
OEDIPUS: You advised me to send for that wizard, did you not?   45
CREON: I did. I should do it again.
OEDIPUS: Very well. Now tell me:
     How long has it been since Laïos—
CREON: What of Laïos?
OEDIPUS: Since he vanished in that onset by the road?   50
CREON: It was long ago, a long time.
OEDIPUS: And this prophet,
     Was he practicing here then?
CREON: He was; and with honor, as now.
OEDIPUS: Did he speak of me at that time?   55
CREON: He never did:
     At least, not when I was present.
OEDIPUS: But . . . the enquiry?
     I suppose you held one?
CREON: We did, but we learned nothing.   60
OEDIPUS: Why did the prophet not speak against me then?
CREON: I do not know; and I am the kind of man
     Who holds his tongue when he has no facts to go on.
OEDIPUS: There's one fact that you know, and you could tell it.
CREON: What fact is that? If I know it, you shall have it.   65
OEDIPUS: If he were not involved with you, he could not say
     That it was I who murdered Laïos.
CREON: If he says that, you are the one that knows it!—
     But now it is my turn to question you.
OEDIPUS: Put your questions. I am no murderer.   70
CREON: First, then: You married my sister?
OEDIPUS: I married your sister.
CREON: And you rule the kingdom equally with her?
OEDIPUS: Everything that she wants she has from me.
CREON: And I am the third, equal to both of you?   75
OEDIPUS: That is why I call you a bad friend.
CREON: No. Reason it out, as I have done.
     Think of this first: Would any sane man prefer
     Power, with all a king's anxieties,
     To that same power and the grace of sleep?   80
     Certainly not I.
     I have never longed for the king's power—only his rights.
     Would any wise man differ from me in this?
     As matters stand, I have my way in everything
     With your consent, and no responsibilities.   85
     If I were king, I should be a slave to policy.

     How could I desire a scepter more
     Than what is now mine—untroubled influence?

No, I have not gone mad; I need no honors,
Except those with the perquisites I have now.   90
I am welcome everywhere; every man salutes me,
And those who want your favor seek my ear,
Since I know how to manage what they ask.
Should I exchange this case for that anxiety?
Besides, no sober mind is treasonable.   95
I hate anarchy
And never would deal with any man who likes it.

Test what I have said. Go to the priestess
At Delphi; ask if I quoted her correctly.
And as for this other thing: if I am found   100
Guilty of treason with Teiresias,
Then sentence me to death! You have my word
It is a sentence I should cast my vote for—
But not without evidence!
                                You do wrong   105
When you take good men for bad, bad men for good.
A true friend thrown aside—why, life itself
Is not more precious!
                        In time you will know this well:
For time, and time alone, will show the just man,   110
Though scoundrels are discovered in a day.
CHORAGOS: This is well said, and a prudent man would ponder it.
     Judgments too quickly formed are dangerous.
OEDIPUS: But is he not quick in his duplicity?
     And shall I not be quick to parry him?   115
     Would you have me stand still, hold my peace, and let
     This man win everything, through my inaction?
CREON: And you want—what is it, then? To banish me?
OEDIPUS: No, not exile. It is your death I want,
     So that all the world may see what treason means.   120
CREON: You will persist, then? You will not believe me?
OEDIPUS: How can I believe you?
CREON: Then you are a fool.
OEDIPUS: To save myself?
CREON: In justice, think of me.   125
OEDIPUS: You are evil incarnate.
CREON: But suppose that you are wrong?
OEDIPUS: Still I must rule.
CREON: But not if you rule badly.
OEDIPUS: O city, city!   130
CREON: It is my city, too!
CHORAGOS: Now, my lords, be still, I see the Queen,
     Iocastê, coming from her palace chambers;
     And it is time she came, for the sake of you both.
     This dreadful quarrel can be resolved through her.   135

          [*Enter* IOCASTÊ.]

IOCASTÊ: Poor foolish men, what wicked din is this?
     With Thebes sick to death, is it not shameful

That you should rake some private quarrel up?

[*To* OEDIPUS:]

Come into the house.

        —And you, Creon, go now: 140
Let us have no more of this tumult over nothing.
CREON: Nothing? No, sister: what your husband plans for me
    Is one of two great evils: exile or death.
OEDIPUS: He is right.
           Why, woman, I have caught him squarely   145
    Plotting against my life.
CREON: No! let me die
    Accurst if ever I have wished you harm!
IOCASTÊ: Ah, believe it, Oedipus!
    In the name of the gods, respect this oath of his   150
    For my sake, for the sake of these people here!   [STROPHE 1]

CHORAGOS: Open your mind to her, my lord, Be ruled by her, I beg you!
OEDIPUS: What would you have me do?
CHORAGOS: Respect Creon's word. He has never spoken like a fool,
    And now he has sworn an oath.   155
OEDIPUS: You know what you ask?
CHORAGOS: I do.
OEDIPUS: Speak on, then.
CHORAGOS: A friend so sworn should not be baited so,
    In blind malice, and without final proof.   160
OEDIPUS: You are aware, I hope, that what you say
    Means death for me, or exile at the least.
CHORAGOS: No, I swear by Helios, first in Heaven!
    May I die friendless and accurst,
    The worst of deaths, if ever I meant that!   165
    It is the withering fields
    That hurt my sick heart:
    Must we bear all these ills,
    And now your bad blood as well?
OEDIPUS: Then let him go. And let me die, if I must,   170
    Or be driven by him in shame from the land of Thebes.
    It is your unhappiness, and not his talk,
    That touches me.
           As for him—
    Wherever he goes, hatred will follow him.   175
CREON: Ugly in yielding, as you were ugly in rage!
    Natures like yours chiefly torment themselves.
OEDIPUS: Can you not go? Can you not leave me?
CREON: I can.
    You do not know me; but the city knows me,   180
    And in its eyes, I am just, if not in yours.

    [*Exit* CREON.]

                     [ANTISTROPHE 1]
CHORAGOS: Lady Iocastê, did you not ask the King to go to his chambers?

IOCASTÊ: First tell me what has happened.

CHORAGOS: There was suspicion without evidence: yet it rankled
    As even false charges will.   185

IOCASTÊ: On both sides?

CHORAGOS: On both.

IOCASTÊ: But what was said?

CHORAGOS: Oh let it rest, let it be done with!
    Have we not suffered enough?   190

OEDIPUS: You see to what your decency has brought you:
    You have made difficulties where my heart saw none.

CHORAGOS: Oedipus, it is not once only I have told you—   [ANTISTROPHE 2]
    You must know I should count myself unwise
    To the point of madness, should I now forsake you—   195
    You, under whose hand,
    In the storm of another time,
     Our dear land sailed out free.
    But now stand fast at the helm!

IOCASTÊ: In God's name, Oedipus, inform your wife as well: 200
    Why are you so set in this hard anger?

OEDIPUS: I will tell you, for none of these men deserves
    My confidence as you do. It is Creon's work,
    His treachery, his plotting against me.

IOCASTÊ: Go on, if you can make this clear to me.   205

OEDIPUS: He charges me with the murder of Laïos.

IOCASTÊ: Has he some knowledge? Or does he speak from hearsay?

OEDIPUS: He would not commit himself to such a charge,
    But he has brought in that damnable soothsayer
    To tell his story.   210

IOCASTÊ: Set your mind at rest.
    If it is a question of soothsayers, I tell you
    That you will find no man whose craft gives knowledge
    Of the unknowable.

                  Here is my proof.   215
    An oracle was reported to Laïos once
    (I will not say from Phoibos himself, but from
    His appointed ministers, at any rate)
    That his doom would be death at the hands of his own son—
    His son, born of his flesh and of mine!   220

    Now, you remember the story: Laïos was killed
    By marauding strangers where three highways meet.
    But his child had not been three days in this world
    Before the King had pierced the baby's ankles
    And left him to die on a lonely mountainside.   225

    Thus, Apollo never caused that child
    To kill his father, and it was not Laïos' fate
    To die at the hands of his son, as he had feared.
    This is what prophets and prophecies are worth!
    Have no dread of them.   230

It is God himself
Who can show us what he wills, in his own way.
OEDIPUS: How strange a shadowy memory crossed my mind,
Just now while you were speaking; it chilled my heart.
IOCASTÊ: What do you mean? What memory do you speak of?   235
OEDIPUS: If I understand you, Laïos was killed
At a place where three roads meet.
IOCASTÊ: So it was said;
We have no later story.
OEDIPUS: Where did it happen?   240
IOCASTÊ: Phokis, it is called: at a place where the Theban Way
Divides into the roads toward Delphi and Daulia.
OEDIPUS: When?
IOCASTÊ: We had the news not long before you came
And proved the right to your succession here.   245
OEDIPUS: Ah, what net has God been weaving for me?
IOCASTÊ: Oedipus! Why does this trouble you?
OEDIPUS: Do not ask me yet.
First, tell me how Laïos looked, and tell me
How old he was.   250
IOCASTÊ: He was tall, his hair just touched
With white; his form was not unlike your own.
OEDIPUS: I think that I myself may be accurst
By my own ignorant edict.
IOCASTÊ: You speak strangely.   255
It makes me tremble to look at you, my King.
OEDIPUS: I am not sure that the blind man can not see.
But I should know better if you were to tell me—
IOCASTÊ: Anything—though I dread to hear you ask it.
OEDIPUS: Was the King lightly escorted, or did he ride   260
With a large company, as a ruler should?
IOCASTÊ: There were five men with him in all: one was a herald,
And a single chariot, which he was driving.
OEDIPUS: Alas, that makes it plain enough!
But who—   265
Who told you how it happened?
IOCASTÊ: A household servant,
The only one to escape.
OEDIPUS: And is he still
A servant of ours?   270
IOCASTÊ: No; for when he came back at last
And found you enthroned in the place of the dead king,
He came to me, touched my hand with his, and begged
That I would send him away to the frontier district
Where only the shepherds go—   275
As far away from the city as I could send him.
I granted his prayer; for although the man was a slave,
He had earned more than this favor at my hands.
OEDIPUS: Can he be called back quickly?
IOCASTÊ: Easily.   280

        But why?
OEDIPUS: I have taken too much upon myself
    Without enquiry; therefore I wish to consult him.
IOCASTÊ: Then he shall come.
                     But am I not one also   285
    To whom you might confide these fears of yours?
OEDIPUS: That is your right; it will not be denied you,
    Now least of all; for I have reached a pitch
    Of wild foreboding. Is there anyone
    To whom I should sooner speak?   290

    Polybos of Corinth is my father.
    My mother is a Dorian: Meropê.
    I grew up chief among the men of Corinth
    Until a strange thing happened—
    Not worth my passion, it may be, but strange.   295

    At a feast, a drunken man maundering in his cups
    Cries out that I am not my father's son!

    I contained myself that night, though I felt anger
    And a sinking heart. The next day I visited
    My father and mother, and questioned them. They stormed,   300
    Calling it all the slanderous rant of a fool;
    And this relieved me. Yet the suspicion
    Remained always aching in my mind;
    I know there was talk; I could not rest;
    And finally, saying nothing to my parents,   305
    I went to the shrine at Delphi.
    The god dismissed my question without reply;
    He spoke of other things.
                  Some were clear,
    Full of wretchedness, dreadful, unbearable: 310
    As, that I should lie with my own mother, breed
    Children from whom all men would turn their eyes;
    And that I should be my father's murderer.

    I heard all this, and fled. And from that day
    Corinth to me was only in the stars   315
    Descending in that quarter of the sky,
    As I wandered farther and farther on my way
    To a land where I should never see the evil
    Sung by the oracle. And I came to this country
    Where, so you say, King Laïos was killed.   320

    I will tell you all that happened there, my lady.
    There were three highways
    Coming together at a place I passed;
    And there a herald came towards me, and a chariot
    Drawn by horses, with a man such as you describe   325

Seated in it. The groom leading the horses
Forced me off the road at his lord's command;
But as this charioteer lurched over towards me
I struck him in my rage. The old man saw me
And brought his double goad down upon my head   330
As I came abreast.

                He was paid back, and more!
Swinging my club in this right hand I knocked him
Out of his car, and he rolled on the ground.

                          I killed him.   335
I killed them all.
Now if that stranger and Laïos were—kin,
Where is a man more miserable than I?
More hated by the gods? Citizen and alien alike
Must never shelter me or speak to me—   340
I must be shunned by all.

                  And I myself
Pronounced this malediction upon myself!
Think of it: I have touched you with these hands,
These hands that killed your husband. What defilement!   345

Am I all evil, then? It must be so,
Since I must flee from Thebes, yet never again
See my own countrymen, my own country,
For fear of joining my mother in marriage
And killing Polybos, my father.   350

                    Ah,
If I was created so, born to this fate,
Who could deny the savagery of God?
O holy majesty of heavenly powers!
May I never see that day! Never!   355
Rather let me vanish from the race of men
Than know the abomination destined me!
CHORAGOS: We, too, my lord, have felt dismay at this.
    But there is hope: you have yet to hear the shepherd.
OEDIPUS: Indeed, I fear no other hope is left me.   360
IOCASTÊ: What do you hope from him when he comes?
OEDIPUS: This much:
    If his account of the murder tallies with yours,
    Then I am cleared.
IOCASTÊ: What was it that I said   365
    Of such importance?
OEDIPUS: Why, "marauders," you said,
    Killed the King, according to this man's story.
    If he maintains that still, if there were several,
    Clearly the guilt is not mine: I was alone.   370
    But if he says one man, singlehanded, did it,
    Then the evidence all points to me.
IOCASTÊ: You may be sure that he said there were several;
    And can he call back that story now? He can not.

The whole city heard it as plainly as I. 375
But suppose he alters some detail of it:
He can not ever show that Laïos' death
Fulfilled the oracle: for Apollo said
My child was doomed to kill him; and my child—
Poor baby!—it was my child that died first. 380
No. From now on, where oracles are concerned,
I would not waste a second thought on any.

OEDIPUS: You might be right.
But come: let someone go
For the shepherd at once. This matter must be settled. 385

IOCASTÊ: I will send for him.
I would not wish to cross you in anything,
And surely not in this.—Let us go in.

[*Exeunt into the palace.*]

ODE II

CHORUS: Let me be reverent in the ways of right, [STROPHE 1]
Lowly the paths I journey on; 390
Let all my words and actions keep
The laws of the pure universe
From highest Heaven handed down.
For Heaven is their bright nurse,
Those generations of the realms of light; 395
Ah, never of mortal kind were they begot,
Nor are they slaves of memory, lost in sleep;
Their Father is greater than Time, and ages not.

The tyrant is a child of Pride [ANTISTROPHE 1]
Who drinks from his great sickening cup 400
Recklessness and vanity,
Until from his high crest headlong
He plummets to the dust of hope.
That strong man is not strong.
But let no fair ambition be denied; 405
May God protect the wrestler for the State
In government, in comely policy,
Who will fear God, and on His ordinance wait.

Haughtiness and the high hand of disdain [STROPHE 2]
Tempt and outrage God's holy law; 410
And any mortal who dares hold
No immortal Power in awe
Will be caught up in a net of pain:
The price for which his levity is sold.
Let each man take due earnings, then, 415
And keep his hands from holy things,

And from blasphemy stand apart—
Else the crackling blast of heaven
Blows on his head, and on his desperate heart;
Though fools will honor impious men,   420
In their cities no tragic poet sings.

Shall we lose faith in Delphi's obscurities,   [ANTISTROPHE 2]
We who have heard the world's core
Discredited, and the sacred wood
Of Zeus at Elis praised no more?   425
The deeds and the strange prophecies
Must make a pattern yet to be understood.
Zeus, if indeed you are lord of all,
Throned in light over night and day,
Mirror this in your endless mind: 430
Our masters call the oracle
Words on the wind, and the Delphic vision blind!
Their hearts no longer know Apollo,
And reverence for the gods has died away.

SCENE III

[*Enter* IOCASTÊ.]

IOCASTÊ: Princes of Thebes, it has occurred to me
To visit the altars of the gods, bearing
These branches as a suppliant, and this incense.
Our King is not himself: his noble soul
Is overwrought with fantasies of dread,   5
Else he would consider
The new prophecies in the light of the old.
He will listen to any voice that speaks disaster,
And my advice goes for nothing.

                             To you, then, Apollo,   10
Lycean lord, since you are nearest, I turn in prayer.
Receive these offerings, and grant us deliverance
From defilement. Our hearts are heavy with fear
When we see our leader distracted, as helpless sailors
Are terrified by the confusion of their helmsman.   15

        [*Enter* MESSENGER.]

MESSENGER: Friends, no doubt you can direct me:
Where shall I find the house of Oedipus,
Or, better still, where is the King himself?
CHORAGOS: It is this very place, stranger; he is inside.
This is his wife and mother of his children.   20
MESSENGER: I wish her happiness in a happy house,
Blest in all the fulfillment of her marriage.

IOCASTÊ: I wish as much for you: your courtesy
　　　Deserves a like good fortune. But now, tell me:
　　　Why have you come? What have you to say to us?　　　　　　　　　25
MESSENGER: Good news, my lady, for your house and your husband.
IOCASTÊ: What news? Who sent you here?
MESSENGER:　　　　　　　　　　　　I am from Corinth.
　　　The news I bring ought to mean joy for you,
　　　Though it may be you will find some grief in it.　　　　　　　　　30
IOCASTÊ: What is it? How can it touch us in both ways?
MESSENGER: The word is that the people of the Isthmus
　　　Intend to call Oedipus to be their king.
IOCASTÊ: But old King Polybos—is he not reigning still?
MESSENGER: No. Death holds him in his sepulchre.　　　　　　　　　35
IOCASTÊ: What are you saying? Polybos is dead?
MESSENGER: If I am not telling the truth, may I die myself.
IOCASTÊ: [to a MAIDSERVANT] Go in, go quickly; tell this to your master.
　　　O riddlers of God's will, where are you now!
　　　This was the man whom Oedipus, long ago,　　　　　　　　　40
　　　Feared so, fled so, in dread of destroying him—
　　　But it was another fate by which he died.

　　　　　[*Enter* OEDIPUS.]

OEDIPUS: Dearest Iocastê, why have you sent for me?
IOCASTÊ: Listen to what this man says, and then tell me
　　　What has become of the solemn prophecies.　　　　　　　　　45
OEDIPUS: Who is this man? What is his news for me?
IOCASTÊ: He has come from Corinth to announce your father's death!
OEDIPUS: Is it true, stranger? Tell me in your own words.
MESSENGER: I can not say it more clearly: the King is dead.
OEDIPUS: Was it by treason? Or by an attack of illness?　　　　　　　50
MESSENGER: A little thing brings old men to their rest.
OEDIPUS: It was sickness, then?
MESSENGER:　　　　　　　　　Yes, and his many years.
OEDIPUS: Ah!
　　　Why should a man respect the Pythian hearth, or　　　　　　　55
　　　Give heed to the birds that jangle above his head?
　　　They prophesied that I should kill Polybos,
　　　Kill my own father; but he is dead and buried,
　　　And I am here—I never touched him, never,
　　　Unless he died of grief for my departure,　　　　　　　　　60
　　　And thus, in a sense, through me. No. Polybos
　　　Has packed the oracles off with him underground.
　　　They are empty words.
IOCASTÊ:　　　　　　　　　Had I not told you so?
OEDIPUS: You had; it was my faint heart that betrayed me.　　　　　65
IOCASTÊ: From now on never think of those things again.
OEDIPUS: And yet—must I not fear my mother's bed?
IOCASTÊ: Why should anyone in this world be afraid,
　　　Since Fate rules us and nothing can be foreseen?
　　　A man should live only for the present day.　　　　　　　　　70

Have no more fear of sleeping with your mother:
How many men, in dreams, have lain with their mothers!
No reasonable man is troubled by such things.
OEDIPUS: That is true; only—
    If only my mother were not still alive!   75
    But she is alive. I can not help my dread.
IOCASTÊ: Yet this news of your father's death is wonderful.
OEDIPUS: Wonderful. But I fear the living woman.
MESSENGER: Tell me, who is this woman that you fear?
OEDIPUS: It is Meropê, man; the wife of King Polybos.   80
MESSENGER: Meropê? Why should you be afraid of her?
OEDIPUS: An oracle of the gods, a dreadful saying.
MESSENGER: Can you tell me about it or are you sworn to silence?
OEDIPUS: I can tell you, and I will.
    Apollo said through his prophet that I was the man   85
    Who should marry his own mother, shed his father's blood
    With his own hands. And so, for all these years
    I have kept clear of Corinth, and no harm has come—
    Though it would have been sweet to see my parents again.
MESSENGER: And is this the fear that drove you out of Corinth?   90
OEDIPUS: Would you have me kill my father?
MESSENGER: As for that
    You must be reassured by the news I gave you.
OEDIPUS: If you could reassure me, I would reward you.
MESSENGER: I had that in mind, I will confess: I thought   95
    I could count on you when you returned to Corinth.
OEDIPUS: No: I will never go near my parents again.
MESSENGER: Ah, son, you still do not know what you are doing—
OEDIPUS: What do you mean? In the name of God tell me!
MESSENGER:—If these are your reasons for not going home.   100
OEDIPUS: I tell you, I fear the oracle may come true.
MESSENGER: And guilt may come upon you through your parents?
OEDIPUS: That is the dread that is always in my heart.
MESSENGER: Can you not see that all your fears are groundless?
OEDIPUS: How can you say that? They are my parents, surely?   105
MESSENGER: Polybos was not your father.
OEDIPUS: Not my father?
MESSENGER: No more your father than the man speaking to you.
OEDIPUS: But you are nothing to me!
MESSENGER: Neither was he.   110
OEDIPUS: Then why did he call me son?
MESSENGER: I will tell you:
    Long ago he had you from my hands, as a gift.
OEDIPUS: Then how could he love me so, if I was not his?
MESSENGER: He had no children, and his heart turned to you.   115
OEDIPUS: What of you? Did you buy me? Did you find me by chance?
MESSENGER: I came upon you in the crooked pass of Kithairon.
OEDIPUS: And what were you doing there?
MESSENGER: Tending my flocks.
OEDIPUS: A wandering shepherd?   120
MESSENGER: But your savior, son, that day.

OEDIPUS: From what did you save me?

MESSENGER: Your ankles should tell you that.

OEDIPUS: Ah, stranger, why do you speak of that childhood pain?

MESSENGER: I cut the bonds that tied your ankles together. 125

OEDIPUS: I have had the mark as long as I can remember.

MESSENGER: That was why you were given the name you bear.

OEDIPUS: God! Was it my father or my mother who did it?
    Tell me!

MESSENGER: I do not know. The man who gave you to me 130
    Can tell you better than I.

OEDIPUS: It was not you that found me, but another?

MESSENGER: It was another shepherd gave you to me.

OEDIPUS: Who was he? Can you tell me who he was?

MESSENGER: I think he was said to be one of Laïos' people. 135

OEDIPUS: You mean the Laïos who was king here years ago?

MESSENGER: Yes; King Laïos; and the man was one of his herdsmen.

OEDIPUS: Is he still alive? Can I see him?

MESSENGER: These men here
    Know best about such things. 140

OEDIPUS: Does anyone here
    Know this shepherd that he is talking about?
    Have you seen him in the fields, or in the town?
    If you have, tell me. It is time things were made plain.

CHORAGOS: I think the man he means is that same shepherd 145
    You have already asked to see. Iocastê perhaps
    Could tell you something.

OEDIPUS: Do you know anything
    About him, Lady? Is he the man we have summoned?
    Is that the man this shepherd means? 150

IOCASTÊ: Why think of him?
    Forget this herdsman. Forget it all.
    This talk is a waste of time.

OEDIPUS: How can you say that?
    When the clues to my true birth are in my hands? 155

IOCASTÊ: For God's love, let us have no more questioning!
    Is your life nothing to you?
    My own is pain enough for me to bear.

OEDIPUS: You need not worry. Suppose my mother a slave,
    And born of slaves: no baseness can touch you. 160

IOCASTÊ: Listen to me, I beg you: do not do this thing!

OEDIPUS: I will not listen; the truth must be made known.

IOCASTÊ: Everything that I say is for your own good!

OEDIPUS: My own good
    Snaps my patience, then; I want none of it. 165

IOCASTÊ: You are fatally wrong! May you never learn who you are!

OEDIPUS: Go, one of you, and bring the shepherd here.
    Let us leave this woman to brag of her royal name.

IOCASTÊ: Ah, miserable!
    That is the only word I have for you now. 170
    That is the only word I can ever have.

[*Exit into the palace.*]

CHORAGOS: Why has she left us, Oedipus? Why has she gone
In such a passion of sorrow? I fear this silence:
Something dreadful may come of it.
OEDIPUS: Let it come!   175
However base my birth, I must know about it.
The Queen, like a woman, is perhaps ashamed
To think of my low origin. But I
Am a child of Luck; I can not be dishonored.
Luck is my mother; the passing months, my brothers,   180
Have seen me rich and poor.
                                   If this is so,
How could I wish that I were someone else?
How could I not be glad to know my birth?

ODE III

CHORUS: If ever the coming time were known   [STROPHE I]   185
To my heart's pondering,
Kithairon, now by Heaven I see the torches
At the festival of the next full moon,
And see the dance, and hear the choir sing
A grace to your gentle shade: 190
Mountain where Oedipus was found,
O mountain guard of a noble race!
May the god who heals us lend his aid,
And let that glory come to pass
For our king's cradling-ground.   195

Of the nymphs that flower beyond the years,   [ANTISTROPHE I]
Who bore you, royal child,
To Pan of the hills or the timberline, Apollo,
Cold in delight where the upland clears,
Or Hermês for whom Kyllenê's heights are piled?   200
Or flushed as evening cloud,
Great Dionysos, roamer of mountains,
He—was it he who found you there,
And caught you up in his own proud
Arms from the sweet god-ravisher   205
Who laughed by the Muses' fountains?

SCENE IV

OEDIPUS: Sirs: though I do not know the man,
I think I see him coming, this shepherd we want:
He is old, like our friend here, and the men

Bringing him seem to be servants of my house.
But you can tell, if you have ever seen him.   5

[*Enter* SHEPHERD *escorted by servants.*]

CHORAGOS: I know him, he was Laïos' man. You can trust him.
OEDIPUS: Tell me first, you from Corinth: is this the shepherd
    We were discussing?
MESSENGER: This is the very man.
OEDIPUS: [*to* SHEPHERD] Come here. No, look at me. You must answer   10
    Everything I ask.—You belonged to Laïos?
SHEPHERD: Yes: born his slave, brought up in his house.
OEDIPUS: Tell me: what kind of work did you do for him?
SHEPHERD: I was a shepherd of his, most of my life.
OEDIPUS: Where mainly did you go for pasturage?   15
SHEPHERD: Sometimes Kithairon, sometimes the hills nearby.
OEDIPUS: Do you remember ever seeing this man out there?
SHEPHERD: What would he be doing there? This man?
OEDIPUS: This man standing here. Have you ever seen him before?
SHEPHERD: No. At least, not to my recollection.   20
MESSENGER: And that is not strange, my lord. But I'll refresh
    His memory: he must remember when we two
    Spent three whole seasons together, March to September,
    On Kithairon or thereabouts. He had two flocks;
    I had one. Each autumn I'd drive mine home   25
    And he would go back with his to Laïos' sheepfold.—
    Is this not true, just as I have described it?
SHEPHERD: True, yes; but it was all so long ago.
MESSENGER: Well, then: do you remember, back in those days,
    That you gave me a baby boy to bring up as my own?   30
SHEPHERD: What if I did? What are you trying to say?
MESSENGER: King Oedipus was once that little child.
SHEPHERD: Damn you, hold your tongue!
OEDIPUS: No more of that!
    It is your tongue needs watching, not this man's.   35
SHEPHERD: My King, my Master, what is it I have done wrong?
OEDIPUS: You have not answered his question about the boy.
SHEPHERD: He does not know. . .He is only making trouble. . .
OEDIPUS: Come, speak plainly, or it will go hard with you.
SHEPHERD: In God's name, do not torture an old man!   40
OEDIPUS: Come here, one of you; bind his arms behind him.
SHEPHERD: Unhappy king! What more do you wish to learn?
OEDIPUS: Did you give this man the child he speaks of?
SHEPHERD: I did.
    And I would to God I had died that very day.   45
OEDIPUS: You will die now unless you speak the truth.
SHEPHERD: Yet if I speak the truth, I am worse than dead.
OEDIPUS: Very well; since you insist upon delaying—
SHEPHERD: No! I have told you already that I gave him the boy.
OEDIPUS: Where did you get him? From your house? From somewhere else?   50

SHEPHERD: Not from mine, no. A man gave him to me.
OEDIPUS: Is that man here? Do you know whose slave he was?
SHEPHERD: For God's love, my King, do not ask me any more!
OEDIPUS: You are a dead man if I have to ask you again.
SHEPHERD: Then. . . Then the child was from the palace of Laïos.   55
OEDIPUS: A slave child? or a child of his own line?
SHEPHERD: Ah, I am on the brink of dreadful speech!
OEDIPUS: And I of dreadful hearing. Yet I must hear.
SHEPHERD: If you must be told, then. . .

                                     They said it was Laïos' child;   60
      But it is your wife who can tell you about that.
OEDIPUS: My wife!—Did she give it to you?
SHEPHERD: My lord, she did.
OEDIPUS: Do you know why?
SHEPHERD: I was told to get rid of it.   65
OEDIPUS: An unspeakable mother!
SHEPHERD: There had been prophecies. . .
OEDIPUS: Tell me.
SHEPHERD: It was said that the boy would kill his own father.
OEDIPUS: Then why did you give him over to this old man?   70
SHEPHERD: I pitied the baby, my King.
      And I thought that this man would take him far away
      To his own country.
                He saved him—but for what a fate!
      For if you are what this man says you are,   75
      No man living is more wretched than Oedipus.
OEDIPUS: Ah God!
      It was true!
          All the prophecies!
                    —Now,   80
      O, Light, may I look on you for the last time!
      I, Oedipus,
      Oedipus, damned in his birth, in his marriage damned,
      Damned in the blood he shed with his own hand!

      [*He rushes into the palace.*]

ODE IV

CHORUS: Alas for the seed of men.   [STROPHE 1]   85
      What measure shall I give these generations
      That breathe on the void and are void
      And exist and do not exist?

      Who bears more weight of joy
      Than mass of sunlight shifting in images,   90
      Or who shall make his thought stay on
      That down time drifts away?

Your splendor is all fallen.

O naked brow of wrath and tears,
O change of Oedipus!   95
I who saw your days call no man blest—
Your great days like ghosts gone.
That mind was a strong bow.   [ANTISTROPHE 1]

Deep, how deep you drew it then, hard archer,
At a dim fearful range,   100
And brought dear glory down!

You overcame the stranger—
The virgin with her hooking lion claws—
And though death sang, stood like a tower
To make pale Thebes take heart.   105

Fortress against our sorrow!

True king, giver of laws,
Majestic Oedipus!
No prince in Thebes had ever such renown,
No prince won such grace of power.   110

And now of all men ever known   [STROPHE 2]
Most pitiful is this man's story:
His fortunes are most changed, his state
Fallen to a low slave's
Ground under bitter fate.   115

O Oedipus, most royal one!
The great door that expelled you to the light
Gave at night—ah, gave night to your glory:
As to the father, to the fathering son.

All understood too late.   120

How could that queen whom Laïos won,
The garden that he harrowed at his height,
Be silent when that act was done?

But all eyes fail before time's eye,   [ANTISTROPHE 2]
All actions come to justice there.   125
Though never willed, though far down the deep past,
Your bed, your dread sirings,
Are brought to book at last.
Child by Laïos doomed to die,
Then doomed to lose that fortunate little death,   130
Would God you never took breath in this air
That with my wailing lips I take to cry:
For I weep the world's outcast.

I was blind, and now I can tell why:
Asleep, for you had given ease of breath   135
To Thebes, while the false years went by.

ÈXODUS

SECOND MESSENGER: Elders of Thebes, most honored in this land,
　　What horrors are yours to see and hear, what weight
　　Of sorrow to be endured, if, true to your birth,
　　You venerate the line of Labdakos!   140
　　I think neither Istros nor Phasis, those great rivers,
　　Could purify this place of the corruption
　　It shelters now, or soon must bring to light—
　　Evil not done unconsciously, but willed.

　　The greatest griefs are those we cause ourselves.   145
CHORAGOS: Surely, friend, we have grief enough already;
　　What new sorrow do you mean?
SECOND MESSENGER:　　　　　　　The Queen is dead.
CHORAGOS: Iocastê? Dead? But at whose hand?
SECOND MESSENGER:　　　　　　　　　Her own.   150
　　The full horror of what happened you can not know,
　　For you did not see it; but I, who did, will tell you
　　As clearly as I can how she met her death.

　　When she had left us,
　　In passionate silence, passing through the court,   155
　　She ran to her apartment in the house,
　　Her hair clutched by the fingers of both hands.
　　She closed the doors behind her; then, by that bed
　　Where long ago the fatal son was conceived—
　　That son who should bring about his father's death—   160
　　We hear her call upon Laïos, dead so many years,
　　And heard her wail for the double fruit of her marriage,
　　A husband by her husband, children by her child.

　　Exactly how she died I do not know:
　　For Oedipus burst in moaning and would not let us   165
　　Keep vigil to the end: it was by him
　　As he stormed about the room that our eyes were caught.
　　From one to another of us he went, begging a sword,
　　Cursing the wife who was not his wife, the mother
　　Whose womb had carried his own children and himself.   170
　　I do not know: it was none of us aided him,
　　But surely one of the gods was in control!
　　For with a dreadful cry
　　He hurled his weight, as though wrenched out of himself,
　　At the twin doors: the bolts gave, and he rushed in.   175
　　And there we saw her hanging, her body swaying

From the cruel cord she had noosed about her neck.
A great sob broke from him, heartbreaking to hear,
As he loosed the rope and lowered her to the ground.

I would blot out from my mind what happened next!   180
For the King ripped from her gown the golden brooches
That were her ornament, and raised them, and lunged them down
Straight into his own eyeballs, crying, "No more,
No more shall you look on the misery about me,
The horrors of my own doing! Too long you have known   185
The faces of those whom I should never have seen,
Too long been blind to those for whom I was searching!
From this hour, go in darkness!" And as he spoke,
He struck at his eyes—not once, but many times;
And the blood spattered his beard,   190
Bursting from his ruined sockets like red hail.

So from the unhappiness of two this evil has sprung,
A curse on the man and woman alike. The old
Happiness of the house of Labdakos
Was happiness enough: where is it today?   195
It is all wailing and ruin, disgrace, death—all
The misery of mankind that has a name—
And it is wholly and for ever theirs.
CHORAGOS: Is he in agony still? Is there no rest for him?
SECOND MESSENGER: He is calling for someone to lead him to the gates   200
So that all the children of Kadmos may look upon
His father's murderer, his mother's—no,
I can not say it!
                    And then he will leave Thebes,
Self-exiled, in order that the curse   205
Which he himself pronounced may depart from the house.
He is weak, and there is none to lead him,
So terrible is his suffering.
                    But you will see:
Look, the doors are opening; in a moment   210
You will see a thing that would crush a heart of stone.

[*The central door is opened;* OEDIPUS, *blinded, is led in.*]

CHORAGOS: Dreadful indeed for men to see.
         Never have my own eyes
         Looked on a sight so full of fear.

Oedipus!   215
What madness came upon you, what daemon
Leaped on your life with heavier
Punishment than a mortal man can bear?
No: I can not even
Look at you, poor ruined one.   220
And I would speak, question, ponder,

If I were able. No.
You make me shudder.
OEDIPUS: God. God.
    Is there a sorrow greater?   225
    Where shall I find harbor in this world?
    My voice is hurled far on a dark wind.
    What has God done to me?
CHORAGOS: Too terrible to think of, or to see.
OEDIPUS: O cloud of night,   [STROPHE 1]   230
    Never to be turned away: night coming on,
    I can not tell how: night like a shroud!
    My fair winds brought me here.
                  O God. Again
    The pain of the spikes where I had sight,   235
    The flooding pain
    Of memory, never to be gouged out.
CHORAGOS: This is not strange.
    You suffer it all twice over, remorse in pain,
    Pain in remorse.   240
OEDIPUS: Ah dear friend   [ANTISTROPHE 1]
    Are you faithful even yet, you alone?
    Are you still standing near me, will you stay here,
    Patient, to care for the blind?
                The blind man!   245
    Yet even blind I know who it is attends me,
    By the voice's tone—
    Though my new darkness hide the comforter.
CHORAGOS: Oh fearful act!
    What god was it drove you to rake black   250
    Night across your eyes?
OEDIPUS: Apollo. Apollo. Dear   [STROPHE 2]
    Children, the god was Apollo.
    He brought my sick, sick fate upon me.
    But the blinding hand was my own!   255
    How could I bear to see
    When all my sight was horror everywhere?
CHORAGOS: Everywhere; that is true.
OEDIPUS: And now what is left?
    Images? Love? A greeting even,   260
    Sweet to the senses? Is there anything?
    Ah, no, friends: lead me away.
    Lead me away from Thebes.
                Lead the great wreck
    And hell of Oedipus, whom the gods hate.   265
CHORAGOS: Your fate is clear, you are not blind to that.
    Would God you had never found it out!
OEDIPUS: Death take the man who unbound   [ANTISTROPHE 2]
    My feet on that hillside
    And delivered me from death to life! What life?   270
    If only I had died,

This weight of monstrous doom
Could not have dragged me and my darlings down.
CHORAGOS: I would have wished the same.
OEDIPUS: Oh never to have come here   275
     With my father's blood upon me! Never
     To have been the man they call his mother's husband!
     Oh accurst! Oh child of evil,
     To have entered that wretched bed—
                         the selfsame one!   280
     More primal than sin itself, this fell to me.
CHORAGOS: I do not know how I can answer you.
     You were better dead than alive and blind.
OEDIPUS: Do not counsel me any more. This punishment
     That I have laid upon myself is just.   285
     If I had eyes,
     I do not know how I could bear the sight
     Of my father, when I came to the house of Death,
     Or my mother: for I have sinned against them both
     So vilely that I could not make my peace   290
     By strangling my own life.
                 Or do you think my children,
     Born as they were born, would be sweet to my eyes?
     Ah never, never! Nor this town with its high walls,
     Nor the holy images of the gods.   295
              For I,
     Thrice miserable!—Oedipus, noblest of all the line
     Of Kadmos, have condemned myself to enjoy
     These things no more, by my own malediction
     Expelling that man whom the gods declared   300
     To be a defilement in the house of Laïos.
     After exposing the rankness of my own guilt,
     How could I look men frankly in the eyes?
     No, I swear it,
     If I could have stifled my hearing at its source,   305
     I would have done it and made all this body
     A tight cell of misery, blank to light and sound:
     So I should have been safe in a dark agony
     Beyond all recollection.
                 Ah Kithairon!   310
     Why did you shelter me? When I was cast upon you,
     Why did I not die? Then I should never
     Have shown the world my execrable birth.

     Ah Polybos! Corinth, city that I believed
     The ancient seat of my ancestors: how fair   315
     I seemed, your child! And all the while this evil
     Was cancerous within me!
               For I am sick
     In my daily life, sick in my origin.

     O three roads, dark ravine, woodland and way   320

Where three roads met: you, drinking my father's blood,
My own blood, spilled by my own hand: can you remember
The unspeakable things I did there, and the things
I went on from there to do?

            O marriage, marriage!   325
The act that engendered me, and again the act
Performed by the son in the same bed—

                Ah, the net
Of incest, mingling fathers, brothers, sons,
With brides, wives, mothers: the last evil   330
That can be known by men: no tongue can say
How evil!

      No. For the love of God, conceal me
Somewhere far from Thebes; or kill me; or hurl me
Into the sea, away from men's eyes for ever.   335

Come, lead me. You need not fear to touch me.
Of all men, I alone can bear this guilt.

    [*Enter* CREON.]

CHORAGOS: We are not the ones to decide; but Creon here
    May fitly judge of what you ask. He only
    Is left to protect the city in your place.   340
OEDIPUS: Alas, how can I speak to him? What right have I
    To beg his courtesy whom I have deeply wronged?
CREON: I have not come to mock you, Oedipus,
    Or to reproach you either.
        [*To* ATTENDANTS:]—You, standing there: 345
    If you have lost all respect for man's dignity,
    At least respect the flame of Lord Helios:
    Do not allow this pollution to show itself
    Openly here, an affront to the earth
    And Heaven's rain and the light of day. No, take him   350
    Into the house as quickly as you can.
    For it is proper
    That only the close kindred see his grief.
OEDIPUS: I pray you in God's name, since your courtesy
    Ignores my dark expectation, visiting   355
    With mercy this man of all men most execrable:
    Give me what I ask—for your good, not for mine.
CREON: And what is it that you would have me do?
OEDIPUS: Drive me out of this country as quickly as may be
    To a place where no human voice can ever greet me.   360
CREON: I should have done that before now—only,
    God's will had not been wholly revealed to me.
OEDIPUS: But his command is plain: the parricide
    Must be destroyed. I am that evil man.
CREON: That is the sense of it, yes; but as things are,   365
    We had best discover clearly what is to be done.
OEDIPUS: You would learn more about a man like me?
CREON: You are ready now to listen to the god.

OEDIPUS: I will listen. But it is to you   370
     That I must turn for help. I beg you, hear me.
     The woman in there—
     Give her whatever funeral you think proper:
     She is your sister.
               —But let me go, Creon!
     Let me purge my father's Thebes of the pollution   375
     Of my living here, and go out to the wild hills,
     To Kithairon, that has won such fame with me,
     The tomb my mother and father appointed for me,
     And let me die there, as they willed I should.
     And yet I know   380
     Death will not ever come to me through sickness
     Or in any natural way: I have been preserved
     For some unthinkable fate. But let that be.

     As for my sons, you need not care for them.
     They are men, they will find some way to live.   385
     But my poor daughters, who have shared my table,
     Who never before have been parted from their father—
     Take care of them. Creon; do this for me.
     And will you let me touch them with my hands
     A last time, and let us weep together?   390
     Be kind, my lord.
     Great prince, be kind!
               Could I but touch them,
     They would be mine again, as when I had my eyes.

    [*Enter* ANTIGONE *and* ISMENE, *attended.*]

     Ah, God!   395
     Is it my dearest children I hear weeping?
     Has Creon pitied me and sent my daughters?
CREON: Yes, Oedipus: I knew that they were dear to you
     In the old days, and know you must love them still.
OEDIPUS: May God bless you for this—and be a friendlier   400
     Guardian to you than he has been to me!
     Children, where are you?
     Come quickly to my hands: they are your brother's—
     Hands that have brought your father's once clear eyes
     To this way of seeing—   405
               Ah dearest ones,
     I had neither sight nor knowledge then, your father
     By the woman who was the source of his own life!
     And I weep for you—having no strength to see you—
     I weep for you when I think of the bitterness   410
     That men will visit upon you all your lives.
     What homes, what festivals can you attend
     Without being forced to depart again in tears?
     And when you come to marriageable age,
     Where is the man, my daughters, who would dare   415

Risk the bane that lies on all my children?
Is there any evil wanting? Your father killed
His father; sowed the womb of her who bore him;
Engendered you at the fount of his own existence!
That is what they will say of you   420
                                    Then, whom
Can you ever marry? There are no bridegrooms for you,
And your lives must wither away in sterile dreaming.

O Creon, son of Menoikeus!
You are the only father my daughters have,   425
Since we, their parents, are both of us gone for ever.
They are your own blood: you will not let them
Fall into beggary and loneliness;
You will keep them from the miseries that are mine!
Take pity on them; see, they are only children,   430
Friendless except for you. Promise me this,
Great Prince, and give me your hand in token of it.

        [CREON *clasps his right hand.*]

        Children:
I could say much, if you could understand me,
But as it is, I have only this prayer for you: 435
Live where you can, be as happy as you can—
Happier, please God, than God has made your father!
CREON: Enough. You have wept enough. Now go within.
OEDIPUS: I must; but it is hard.
CREON: Time eases all things.   440
OEDIPUS: But you must promise—
CREON: Say what you desire.
OEDIPUS: Send me from Thebes!
CREON: God grant that I may!
OEDIPUS: But since God hates me. . .   445
CREON: No, he will grant your wish.
OEDIPUS: You promise?
CREON: I can not speak beyond my knowledge.
OEDIPUS: Then lead me in.
CREON: Come now, and leave your children.   450
OEDIPUS: No! Do not take them from me!
CREON: Think no longer
That you are in command here, but rather think
How, when you were, you served your own destruction.

        [*Exeunt into the house all but the* CHORUS; *the* CHORAGOS *chants directly
        to the audience:*]

CHORAGOS: Men of Thebes: look upon Oedipus.   455

    This is the king who solved the famous riddle
    And towered up, most powerful of men.

No mortal eyes but looked on him with envy,
Yet in the end ruin swept over him.

Let every man in mankind's frailty   460
Consider his last day; and let none
Presume on his good fortune until he find
Life, at his death, a memory without pain.

The Shrine in the Fields
(15TH CENTURY)

THE SHRINE IN THE FIELDS represents one of the five basic types of Noh plays. A "woman play," it is based on episodes from a famous Japanese novel, *The Tale of the Genji* (c.1021). In the novel, Lord Genji is the lover of Lady Rokujo (she is called Miyasudokoro in the play) but after a time neglects her. At a festival, attendants on Lord Genji's wife publicly humiliate Lady Rokujo by pushing her carriage out of the procession and disabling it. Lady Rokujo then leaves the capital and goes to Nonomiya, where her daughter is being prepared to become priestess of Ise (the Sun Goddess). While at Nonomiya, Lady Rokujo is visited by Lord Genji, who begs her to return to him. Although she refuses, her love and humiliation keep drawing her back to Nonomiya even after her death.

The major influence on Noh is Zen Buddhism, which teaches that ultimate peace comes from overcoming individual desire in order to achieve union with all being. The protagonists of Noh are ghosts, demons, or obsessed humans whose souls cannot find rest because in life they became too devoted to love, honor, or other goals that pull them back into the physical world.

In Noh, each play occurs in a specific season of the year, and the mood throughout must be in keeping with that season. In this play, the season is autumn, and the mood is one of melancholy and bittersweet longing. The introductory scene drastically compresses time and place: the itinerant priest (the *waki*) travels almost instantaneously from the capital to Nonomiya. The ghost of Lady Rokujo (in the guise of a village girl) appears and, as the priest questions her, it becomes apparent that she is protecting some secret. Later she returns as herself, the Miyasudokoro (Lady Rokujo) of long ago. As she tells her story, the emotion builds until, as in all Noh plays, it finds expression in a dance. In the final scene, the pull between this and the next world are fully symbolized by the ghost of Miyasudokoro passing back and forth through the gate of the shrine. At the end, the freeing of the soul is indicated by rushing out of the "burning house," an image for the world, which, in Buddhist teaching, enlightened persons are counseled to flee as willingly as they would a burning building. Thus, at the end, we are asked to believe that Miyasudokoro has broken her attachment to the world. Overall, *The Shrine in the Fields* does not seek to tell a story or to develop a character so much as to capture a particular mood, to distill a powerful emotion, and to express an attitude about the physical world and human existence.

The Shrine in the Fields
(15TH CENTURY)

TRANSLATED BY H. PAUL VARLEY

Persons
A TRAVELING PRIEST
A VILLAGE GIRL
MIYASUDOKORO

PLACE————*Sagano in Yamashiro Province*

TIME————*Late autumn, the seventh day of the ninth month*

[*The stage assistant places a* torii *at the front of the stage. To either upright of the torii are attached short sections of fence made of brushwood twigs. The* PRIEST *enters. He carries a rosary in his hand. He stands at the naming-place.*]

PRIEST: I am an itinerant priest. Recently I have been staying in the Capital, where I have visited all the famous sites and relics of the past. Autumn is nearing its close and Sagano will be lovely now. I think I shall go there for a visit. [*He turns towards the torii, indicating that he has already arrived in Sagano.*] When I asked people about this wood they told me it is the ancient site of the Shrine in the Fields. I would like   5
to visit the place, though I am no more than a passing stranger.

[*He advances to stage center, still facing the* torii.]

I enter the wood and I see
A rustic log *torii*
And a fence of brushwood twigs.
Surely nothing has changed from the past!   10
But why should time have spared this place?
Be that as it may, how lucky I am
To have come at this lovely time of year
And be able to worship at such a place.

[*He kneels and presses his palms together.*]

40

The Great Shrine at Ise 15
Makes no distinction
Between gods and Buddhas:
The teachings of the Buddhist Law
Have guided me straight along the path,
And I have arrived at the Shrine. 20
My heart is pure in the evening light,
Pure in the clear evening light!

[*The* GIRL *enters. She wears the* fukai *mask and carries a branch of* sakaki. *She
stands at the* shite-*position and faces the musicians.*]

GIRL: Shrine in the Fields
Where I have lived with flowers;
Shrine in the Fields 25
Where I have lived with flowers—
What will be left when autumn has passed?

[*She faces front.*]

Now lonely autumn ends,
But still my sleeves
Wilt in a dew of tears; 30
The dusk racks my body,
And my heart of itself
Takes on the fading colors
Of the thousand flowers;
It withers, as all things, with neglect. 35
Each year on this day,
Unknown to anyone else,
I return to the old remains.
In the wood at the Shrine in the Fields
Autumn has drawn to a close 40
And the harsh winds blow;
Colors so brilliant
They pierced the senses
Have faded and vanished;
What remains now to recal 45
The memories of the past
What use was it to come here?

[*She takes a few steps to her right, then faces front.*]

Ahh—how I loathe the attachment
That makes me go back and forth,
Again and again on my journey 50
To this meaningless, fugitive world.

[*The* PRIEST *rises and faces her.*]

PRIEST: As I was resting in the shade of the trees, thinking about the past and refreshing my
mind, a charming young lady has suddenly appeared. Please tell me who you are.

GIRL: It would be appropriate if I had asked who you are. This is Nonomiya, the Shrine
in the Fields, where in ancient days the virgin designated as the Priestess of Ise was   55
temporarily lodged. The custom has fallen into disuse, but today, the seventh day of
the ninth month, is still a time for recalling the past. Each year, unknown to anyone
else, I come to sweep the shrine and to perform a service. I do not know where you
have come from, but your presence here is an intrusion. Please leave at once.

[*She takes two steps towards the* PRIEST.]

PRIEST: No, no. There can be no objection to my being here. I am only a wandering priest   60
who has renounced the uncertain world. But tell me, why should you return here,
to these old ruins, on this particular day each year in search of the past?
GIRL: This is the day when Genji the Shining One visited this place, the seventh day of the
ninth month. He brought with him a twig of *sakaki* and pushed it through the sacred
fence. Miyasudokoro at once composed this poem: 65
"This sacred enclosure
Has no cypress to mark the spot;[1]
By some error you have picked
A twig of *sakaki* wood."
It happened on this day!   70
PRIEST: That was truly a worthy poem.[2]
—And the *sakaki* branch
You hold in your hand
Is the same color it was in the past.
GIRL: The same color as in the past?   75
How clever to put it that way!
Only the *sakaki* stays green forever,
And in its unvarying shade
PRIEST: On the pathways through the wood,
The autumn deepens   80
GIRL: And leaves turn crimson only to scatter.
PRIEST: In the weed-grown fields

[*She goes to the* torii *and places the* sakaki *branch there. The* PRIEST *kneels.*]

CHORUS: The stalks and leaf tips wither;
Nonomiya, the Shrine in the Fields,
Stands amidst the desolation   85
Of withered stalks and leaves
The seventh day of the ninth month
Has returned again today
To this place of memories.

[*She moves to center stage.*]

How fragile it seemed at the time,   90
This little fence of brushwood twigs.

[*She gazes at the fence.*]

---

[1] Evergreen is associated with enduring love and devotion.
[2] The poem quoted is from *The Tale of Genji*, where it seems to mean that the visitor has come without invitation,
pretending to have been invited.

And the house that looked so temporary
Has now become the guardian's hut.

[*She turns towards the gazing-pillar.*]

A dim glow shines from inside:
I wonder if the longing within me   95
Reveals itself outwardly?
How lonely a place is this shrine,
How lonely a place is this palace!
PRIEST: Please tell me more of the story of Miyasudokoro.

[*The* GIRL *kneels at center stage.*]

CHORUS: The lady known as Miyasudokoro   100
        Became the wife of the former Crown Prince,
        The brother of Kiritsubo's Emperor,[3]
        A man at the height of his glory;
        They were like the color and perfume
        Of the same flower, indissolubly bound.   105
GIRL: They knew, of course, the truth
      That those who must meet part—
CHORUS: Why should it have surprised them?
        But it came so soon—like a nightmare—
        His death that left her alone.   110
GIRL: She could not remain in that state,
      Helpless and given to tears;
CHORUS: Soon Genji the Shining One
        Imposed his love and began
        Their clandestine meetings.   115
GIRL: How did their love affair end?

CHORUS: And why, after they separated,
        Did his love never turn to hate?
        With customary tenderness
        He made his way through the fields   120
        To distant Nonomiya.
        The autumn flowers had all withered,
        The voices of insects were sparse.
        Oh, the loneliness of that journey!
        Even the wind echoing in the pines   125
        Reminded him there is no end
        To the sadness of autumn.
        So the Prince visited her,
        And with the deepest affection
        Spoke his love in many ways;   130
        How noble and sensitive a man!
GIRL: Later, by the Katsura River,
      She performs cleansing rite,

---

[3] Kiritsubo was Genji's mother.

CHORUS: Setting the white-wrapped branches[4]
    Adrift on the river waves;   135
    Herself like a drifting weed,
    No roots or destination,
    She moved at the water's will.
    "Through the waves of the eighty rapids
    Of Suzuki River to Ise,   140
    Who will worry if the waves wet me or no?"
    She wrote this poem to describe her journey.
    Never before had a mother
    Escorted her daughter, the Virgin,
    All the way to the Také Palace.[5]   145
    Mother and daughter on the way
    Felt only the bitterness of regret.

       [*for* PRIEST]

    Now that I have heard your tale,
    I am sure that you are no ordinary woman.
    Please tell me your name.   150
GIRL: Revealing my name
    Would serve no purpose;
    In my helplessness
    I am ashamed of myself.
    Sooner or later   155
    My name will be known,
    It can't be helped;
    But now say a prayer for one nameless,
    And not of this world.
CHORUS: [*for* PRIEST] Not of this world?   160
    What strange words to hear!
    Then, have you died and departed
GIRL: This world, long ago,
    A name my only monument:
CHORUS: Miyasudokoro   165
GIRL: Is myself.
CHORUS: Autumn winds rise at dusk;

       [*She stands.*]

    Through the forest branches
    The evening moonlight shines

       [*She goes to the* shite-*position.*]

    Dimly illuminating,   170
    Under the trees,

       [*She looks at the* torii.]

---

[4] Streamers of paper or mulberry bark were inscribed with prayers and attached to *sakaki* branches, then tossed into the stream.
[5] The Virgin resided at Ise in the Také Palace.

The rustic logs of the *torii*.
She passes between the two pillars
And vanishes without a trace;
She has vanished without a trace.   175

> [*She slowly exits. A Villager then enters and performs the* kyōgen *interlude, a lengthy recapitulation of* MIYASUDOKORO'*s story. The* PRIEST *asks the Villager to tell what he knows, and then the two men agree that the* PRIEST *has just seen the ghost of* MIYASUDOKORO. *The* PRIEST *decides to stay and read the sutras and prayers for her. The Villager withdraws.*]

PRIEST: Alone I lie on the forest moss,
    A sleeve of my robe spread beneath me—
    Under forest trees, a mossy robe:
    My mat is grass of the same color.[6]
    Unfolding my memories   180
    I shall offer prayers all night long;
    I shall pray for her repose.

> [*The* GIRL, *now revealed as* MIYASUDOKORO, *enters and stands at the* shite-*position.*]

MIYASUDOKORO: In this carriage,
    Lovely as the autumn followers
    At Nonomiya,   185
    I too have returned to the past,
    To long ago.
PRIEST: How strange!
    In the faint moonlight
    The soft sounds   190
    Of an approaching carriage,
    A courtly carriage
    With reed blinds hanging—
    A sight of unimagined beauty!
    It must be you, Miyasudokoro!   195
    But what is the carriage you ride in?
MIYASUDOKORO: You ask me about my carriage?
    I remember now
    That scene of long ago—
    The Kamo Festival,   200
    The jostling carriages,
    No one could tell
    Who their owners were,
    But thick as dewdrops
PRIEST: The splendid ranks crowded the place.   205
MIYASUDOKORO: Pleasure carriages of every description,
    And one among them of special magnificence,
    The Princess Aoi's.

---

[6] A priest's robe was frequently called *kokegoromo*, literally meaning "moss robe." Here it also refers to moss and autumn grass that is faded like the priest's robe.

PRIET: "Make way for Her Highness's carriage!"
    The servants cried, clearing the crowd,   210
    And in the confusion
MIYASUDOKORO: I answered, "My carriage is small,
    I have nowhere else to put it."
    I stood my ground,
PRIEST: But around the carriage   215
MIYASUDOKORO: Men suddenly swarmed.

    [Her gestures suggest the actions described.]

CHORUS: Grasping the shafts,
    They pushed my carriage back
    Into the ranks of servants.
    My carriage had come for no purpose,   220
    My pleasure gone,
    And I knew my helplessness.
    I realized now
    That all that happened
    Was surely retribution   225
    For the sins of former lives.
    Even now I am in agony:
    Like the wheels of my carriage
    I return again and again—
    How long must I still keep returning?   230
    I beg you, dispel this delusion!
    I beg you, dispel this suffering!

    [She presses her palms together in supplication.]

MIYASUDOKORO: Remembering the vanished days
    I dance, waving at the moon
    My flowerlike sleeves,   235
CHORUS: As if begging it to restore the past.

    [She goes to the shite-*position and begins to dance. As her dance ends, the text resumes.]*

MIYASUDOKORO: Even the moon
    At the Shrine in the Fields
    Must remember the past;
CHORUS: Its light forlornly trickles   240
    Through the leaves to the forest dew.
    Through the leaves to the forest dew.
MIYASUDOKORO: This place, once my refuge,
    This garden, still lingers
CHORUS: Unchanged from long ago,   245
MIYASUDOKORO: A beauty nowhere else,
CHORUS: Though transient, insubstantial
MIYASUDOKORO: As this little wooden fence
CHORUS: From which he used to brush the dew.

    [She brushes the fence with her fan.]

I, whom he visited,   250
And he, my lover too,
The whole world turned to dreams,
To aging ruins;
Whom shall I pine for now?
The voices of the pine-crickets   255
Trill *rin, rin,*
The wind howls:

> [*She advances to stage front. She gazes at the* torii.]

How I remember
Nights at the Shrine in the Fields!

> [*Weeping, she withdraws to the area before the musicians and starts to dance.*
> *The text resumes when her dance has ended.*]

CHORUS: At this shrine we have always worshiped   260
The divine wind that blows from Ise,

> [*She goes before the* torii.]

The Inner and Outer Shrines.
As I pass to and fro through this *torii*
I seem to wander on the path of delusion:
I waver between life and death.   265

> [*She passes back and forth through the* torii.]

The gods will surely reject me!
Again she climbs in her carriage and rides out
The gate of the Burning House,
The gate of the Burning House.[7]

---

[7] The Burning House is an image for this world, which an enlightened person should flee as eagerly as from a burning house.

Noah and His Sons
(A.D. 1425–1450)

NOAH AND HIS SONS was presented at Wakefield (England), the third of the thirty-two short plays that together dramatized the biblical account of human existence from Creation to the Last Judgment. The entire cycle was presented outdoors during the Corpus Christi festival, a religious celebration of the sacrament of bread and wine (the body and blood of Christ), the union of the human and divine in the person of Christ, and the promise of redemption through His sacrifice.

The central feature of the Corpus Christi festival was a procession (which included representatives from every rank and profession) through the town with the consecrated bread and wine. This procession may have been the inspiration for the staging of the cycle: mounting plays on wagons and performing them at various stops along a processional route. Each play was assigned to a different trade guild that was then responsible for mounting and financing its play. The overall cycle was under the supervision of the town council, and the scripts had to be approved by the church.

Noah and His Sons is one of five plays identified as the work of the "Wakefield Master," works considered far superior to the other plays in the same cycle. *Noah* is noted in part for the variety achieved through the comic bickering of the title character and his wife. Unlike Latin liturgical drama (drama performed within the structure of a church service or liturgy), the Wakefield cycle was written in common English. The playwright, who may have remained anonymous rather than accept individual credit for a work written to promote the greater glory of God, invented scenes between Noah and his wife not present in the Bible. The play humanizes these biblical figures; we witness their arguments and hear each complain about the lot their sex is subjected to in married life. Noah's wife engages in everyday activities (she is busy spinning thread during their first scene together) and does not accept her husband's orders as unquestionable laws. Thus, both the language of the play and the relationship between Noah and his wife make the play readily accessible to an English medieval audience.

The play is short (558 lines), made up of sixty-two stanzas of nine lines each. The structure of the stanzas suggests a formalized delivery by the performers. The play is divided into three parts of approximately equal length: the opening expository scene with God and Noah establishing justification for the flood; two scenes of bickering between Noah and his wife; and the scenes showing first the building of the ark and then the time on board. It is clear, entertaining, and didactic.

Noah and His Sons
(A.D. 1425–1450)

Edited by Oscar G. Brockett

Characters

NOAH
GOD
NOAH'S WIFE
FIRST SON
SECOND SON
THIRD SON
FIRST WIFE
SECOND WIFE
THIRD WIFE

Note: Many obsolete words have been retained so as not to alter unduly the rhyme scheme. The first four lines of each nine-line stanza use both end and midline rhymes; the fifth and ninth lines rhyme, as do lines six through eight. To clarify obsolete words, modern equivalents have been placed in brackets immediately following the words they clarify.

NOAH: Mightful god veray [truly], Maker of all that is,
　　　Three persons, none say nay, one god in endless bliss,
　　　Thou made both night and day, beast, fowl, and fish,
　　　All creatures that live may, wrought thou at thy wish,
　　　　As thou well might;　　　　　　　　　　　　　　5
　　　The sun, the moon, verament [truly],
　　　Thou made; the firmament,
　　　The stars also, full fervent,
　　　　To shine thou made full bright.

　　　Angels thou made full even, all orders that is,　　10
　　　To have the bliss in heaven. This did thou more and less,
　　　Full marvelous to neven [tell]; yet was there unkindness,
　　　More by folds seven than I can well express;
　　　　For why?
　　　Of all angels in brightness　　　　　　　　　　15
　　　God gave Lucifer most lightness,
　　　Yet proudly he fled his dais,
　　　　And set him even Him by.
　　　He thought himself as worthy as Him that him made;
　　　In brightness, in beauty, therefore God did him degrade;　　20

50

Put him in a low degree soon after, in a brade [minute],
Him and all his menye [minions], where he may be unglad
  For ever.
Shall they never win away,
Hence unto doomsday,   25
But burn in hell for aye,
  Shall they depart never.

Soon after, that gracious lord in His likeness made man,
That place to be restored, even as he began,
Of the Trinity by accord, Adam and Eve, that woman,   30
To multiply without discord, in paradise put He them,
  And sayeth to both
Gave in commandment,
On the tree of life to lay no hand;
But yet the false fiend   35
  Made Him with man wroth,

Enticed man to gluttony, stirred him to sin in pride;
But in paradise securely might no sin abide,
And therefore man full hastily was put out, in that tide [time],
In woe and wretchedness for to be, in pains full cried,   40
  To know,
First on earth, and then in hell
With fiends for to dwell,
But He his mercy mell [dispenses]
  To those that will Him trow [swear allegiance].   45

Oil of mercy He has hight [promised], as I have heard said,
To every living wight that would love Him and dread;
But now before His sight every living leyde [person],
Most party day and night, sin in word and deed
  Full bold;   50
Some in pride, ire, and envy,
Some in covetousness and gluttony,
Some in sloth and lechery,
  And otherwise manifold.

Therefore I dread lest God on us will take vengeance   55
For sin is now allowed without any repentance;
Six hundred years and odd have I, without distance [dispute],
On earth, as any sod, lived with great grievance
  Always;
And now I wax old,   60
Sick, sorry, and cold,
As muck upon mold
  I wither away;

But yet will I cry for mercy and call;
Noah thy servant, am I, Lord over all!   65
Lest me and my fry shall also fall;

Save from villainy and bring to Thy hall
  In heaven;
And keep me from sin,
This world within;   70
Comely king of mankind,
  I pray Thee, hear my stevyn [voice]!

    [GOD *appears above.*]

GOD: Since I have made all thing that is liffand [living],
     Duke, emperor, and king, with mine own hand,
     For to have their liking by sea and by sand,   75
     Every man to my bidding should be bound
       Full fervent;
     That made man such a creature,
     Fairest of favor,
     Man must love me par-amour,   80
       By reason, and repent.

     Methought I showed man love when I made him to be
     All angels above, like to the Trinity;
     And now in great reproof full low lies he,
     On earth himself to stuff with sin that displeases me   85
       Most of all;
     Vengeance will I take,
     In earth for sin's sake,
     My anger thus will I wake,
       Both of great and small.   90

     I repent full sore that ever I made man,
     By me he sets no store, and I am his sovereign;
     I will destroy, therefore, both beast, man and woman,
     All shall perish, less and more; that bargain may they ban [regret],
       That ill has done.   95
     In earth I see right naught
     But sin that is unsought [unrepented];
     Of those that well has wrought
       Find I almost none.

     Therefore shall I undo [destroy] all this middle erd [earth] 100
     With floods that shall flow and run with hideous rerd [noise];
     I have good cause thereto: of me no man is afeard,
     As I say, shall I do: of vengeance draw my sword,
       And make end
     Of all that bears life,   105
     Save Noah and his wife,
     For they would never strive
       With me nor me offend.

     To him to great win [joy] hastily will I go,
     To Noah my servant, ere I blyn [stop] to warn him of his woe. 110
     In earth I see but sin running to and fro,

Among both more and min [less], each the other's foe;
  With all their intent;
They shall I forego [destroy]
With floods that shall flow,   115
I shall work them woe,
  That will not repent.

    [GOD *descends and comes to* NOAH.]

GOD: Noah, my friend, I thee command, from cares thee dispel,
A ship I do demand of nail and board full well.
Thou was e'er a trusty man, to me true as steel,   120
To my bidding obedient; friendship shall thou feel
  To mede [in reward].
Of length thy ship be
Three hundred cubits, warn I thee,
Of height even thirty,   125
  Of fifty also in brede [breadth].

Anoint thy ship with pitch and tar without and also within,
The water out to spar [keep] this is a helpful gyn [means];
Look no man thee mar. Three tiers of chambers begin,
Thou must spend many a spar, this work ere thou win   130
  To end fully.
Make in thy ship also,
Parlors one or two,
And other houses mo [more],
  For beasts that there must be.   135

One cubit in height a window shall thou make;
On the side a doore with slyght [skill] beneath shall thou take;
With thee shall no man fight, nor do thee any kind of hate.
When all is done thus right, thy wife, that is thy mate,
  Take in to thee;   140
Thy sons of good fame,
Shem, Japhet, and Ham,
Take in also them,
  Their wives also three.

For all shall be undone [destroyed] that live on land but ye, 145
With floods that from above shall fall, and that plentily;
It shall begin full soon to rain incessantly,
After seven days' twill come, and endure days forty,
  Without fail.
Take to thy ship also   150
Of each kind, beasts two,
Male and female, but no more,
  Ere thou pull up thy sail.

For they may thee avail when all this thing is wrought;
Stuff thy ship with victual, for hunger that ye perish nought; 155
Of beasts, fowl, and cattle, for them have thou in thought,

For them in my counsel, that some succor be sought,
  In haste;
They must have corn and hay,
And other meat alway;   160
Do now as I thee say,
  In the name of the Holy Ghost.

NOAH: Ah! Benedicite! What art thou that thus
    Tells afore that shall be? Thou art full marvelous!
    Tell me, for charity, thy name so gracious.   165
GOD: My name is of dignity and also full glorious
     To know.
    I am God most mighty,
    One God in Trinity,
    Made thee and each man to be;   170
     To love me well thou owe.

NOAH: I thank thee, lord so dear, that would vouch safe
    Thus low to appear to a simple knave;
    Bless us, lord, here, for charity I it crave,
    The better may we steer the ship that we shall have, 175
     Certain.
GOD: Noah, to thee and thy fry
    My blessing grant I;
    Ye shall wax and multiply,
     And fill the earth again,   180

    When all these floods are past and fully gone away.
NOAH: Lord, homeward will I haste as fast as that I may;
    My wife will I frast [ask] what she will say, [*Exit* GOD.]
    And I am aghast that we get some fray
     Betwixt us both;   185
    For she is full testy,
    For little oft angry,
    If anything wrong be,
     Soon is she wroth. [*He goes to his wife.*]

    God speed, dear wife, how fare ye?   190
WIFE: Now, as ever I might thrive, the worst is I see thee;
    Do tell me belife [quickly] where has thou thus long be?
    To death may we drive, or live for thee [for all you care],
     For want indeed.
    When we sweat or swink [labor],   195
    Thou does what thou think,
    Yet of meat and of drink
     Have we great need.

NOAH: Wife, we are hard stead with tidings new.
WIFE: But thou were worthy be clad in Stafford blue [*be beaten blue*]; 200
    For thou art always afraid, be it false or true;
    But God knows I am led, and that may I rue,
     For ill;

For I dare be thy borrow [pledge],
From even unto morrow,   205
Thou speaks ever of sorrow;
  God send thee once thy fill!

We women may wary [curse] all ill husbands;
I have one, by Mary, that loosed me of my bands;
If he be troubled I must tarry, how so ever it stands,   210
With semblance full sorry, wringing both my hands
  For dread.
But yet other while,
With pleasure and with guile,
I shall smite and smile,   215
  And quit him his mede [give him what he deserves].

NOAH: Well! hold thy tongue ram-skyt, or I shall thee still!
WIFE: By my thrift, if thou smite, I shall turn thee until!
NOAH: We shall assay as tight! Have at thee, Gill!
  Upon the bone shall it bite!   220
WIFE: Ah, so, marry! thou smitest ill!
  But I suppose
I shall not in thy debt,
Flee from this flett [floor]!
Take thee there a langett [thong]   225
  To tie up thy hose!

NOAH: A! wilt thou so? Marry, that is mine.
WIFE: Thou shall three for two, I swear by God's pain!
NOAH: And I shall return them though, in faith, ere syne [long].
WIFE: Out upon thee, ho!   230
NOAH: Thou can both bite and whine,
  with a rerd [noise];
For all if she strike,
Yet fast will she shriek,
In faith I hold none like   235
  In all middle-earth;

But I will keep charity, for I have work to do.
WIFE: Here shall no man tarry thee. I pray thee go to!
  Full well may we miss thee as ever have I ro [peace];
  To spin will I dress me.   240
NOAH: Well, farewell, lo!
  But wife,
Pray for me busily,
Till again I come unto thee.
WIFE: Even as thou prays for me,   245
  As ever might I thrive. [Exit WIFE.]

NOAH: I tarry full long from my work, I trow;
  Now my gear will I fang [take] and thitherward draw;
  I may full ill gang [go], the truth for to know,

But if God help not among, I may sit down daw [melancholy]   250
  To ken;
Now assay will I
How I can of wrightry [workmanship],
In nomine patris et filii, et spiritus sancti,
  Amen.   255

To begin of this tree, my bones will I bend,
I trust from the Trinity succor will be sent;
It fares full fair, think me, this work to my hand;
Now blessed be he that this can amend.
  Lo, here the length,   260
Three hundred cubits evenly,
Of breadth, lo, is it fifty,
The height is even thirty
  Cubits full strength.

Now my gown will I cast, and work in my coat,   265
Make will I the mast ere I shift one foot,
A! my back, I trow, will burst! This is a sorry note!
It is wonder that I last, such an old dote
  All dulled,
To begin such a work!   270
My bones are so stark [stiff],
No wonder if they wark [ache],
  For I am full old.

The top and the sail both will I make,
The helm and the castle also will I take;   275
To drive each single nail will I not forsake;
This gear may never fail, that dare I undertake
  At once.
This is a noble gin [device]
These nails so they run,   280
Through more and min [less],
  These boards each one;

Window and door, even as he said,
Three chief chambers, they are well made;
Pitch and tar full sure thereupon laid,   285
This will ever endure, thereof am I paid;
  for why?
It is better wrought
Than I could have thought;
Him that made all of nought   290
  I thank only.

Now will I hie me and nothing be lither [slow],
My wife and my meneye [family], to bring even hither.
Attend hither tidily wife, and consider,
Hence must us flee, all of us together,   295
  In haste.

WIFE: Why, sir, what ails you?
    Who is't that assails you?
    To flee it avails you,
      And ye be aghast [afraid].   300

NOAH: [*seeing his wife spinning*] There is yarn on the reel other, my dame.
WIFE: Tell me that each deal, else get ye blame.
NOAH: He that cares may keill [cool] blessed be his name!
    He has for our seyll [happiness] to shield us from shame,
      And said,   305
    All this world about
    With floods so stout,
    That shall run on a route,
      Shall be overlaid.

    He said all shall be slain but only we,   310
    Our sons that are bayn [obedient] and their wives three;
    A ship he bade me ordain, to save us and our fee [property],
    Therefore with all our main, thank we that free
      Healer of bayll [sorrow];
    Hie us fast, go we thither.   315
WIFE: I know never whither,
    I am dazed and I dither
      For fear of that tale.

NOAH: Be not afeard, have done. Pack up our gear,
    That we be there ere noon without more dere [hindrance].   320
FIRST SON: It shall be done full soon. Brothers, help to bear.
SECOND SON: Full long shall I not hoyne [delay] to do my share,
    Brother Shem.
THIRD SON: Without any yelp,
    With my might shall I help.
WIFE: Yet for dread of a skelp [blow]   325
    Help well thy dam.

NOAH: Now are we there as we should be;
    To get in our gear, our cattle and fee,
    In this vessel here, my children free.   330
WIFE: I was never shut up ere, as now might I be,
    In such an hostel as this,
    In faith I can not find
    Which is before, which is behind.
    But shall we here be confined,   335
      Noah, as have thou bliss?

NOAH: Dame, as it is skill [reason], here must us abide grace;
    Therefore, wife, with good will come into this place.
WIFE: Sir, for Jack nor for Jill will I turn my face
    Till I have on this hill spun a space
      on my rok [distaff];   340
    Well were he, might get me,
    Now will I down set me,

Yet reede [warn] I no man let me [stop me],
  For dread of a knock.   345

NOAH: Behold from the heaven the cararacts all,
  That are open full even, great and small,
  And the planets seven gone from their stall,
  These thunders and levyn [lightning] down make fall
    Full stout,   350
  Both halls and bowers,
  Castles and towers;
  Full sharp are these showers,
    That rain about;

  Therefore, wife, have done. Come into ship fast.   355
WIFE: Yea, Noah, go patch thy shone [shoes] the better will they last.
FIRST WIFE: Good mother, come in soon, for all is overcast,
  Both the sun and the moon.
SECOND WIFE: And many winds blast
    Full sharp.   360
  These floods so thay run,
  Therefore, mother, come in.
WIFE: In faith, yet will I spin;
  All in vain ye carp.

THIRD WIFE: If ye like ye may spin, Mother, in the ship.   365
NOAH: Now is this twice. Come in, dame, on my friendship.
WIFE: Whether I lose or I win, in faith, for thy fellowship
  Care I not a pin. This spindle will I slip
    Upon this hill,
  Ere I stir one foot.   370
NOAH: Peter! I trow we dote;
  Without any more note
    Come in if ye will.

WIFE: Yea, water nighs so near that I sit not dry;
  Into the ship with a byr [rush] therefore will I hie   375
  For dread that I drown here.
NOAH: Dame, securely,
  It be bought full dear, ye abode so long by
    Out of the ship.
WIFE: I will not, for thy bidding,   380
  Go from door to midding [dunghill; do whatever you demand].
NOAH: In faith, and for your long tarrying
  Ye shall taste of the whip.

WIFE: Spare me not, I pray thee, but even as thou think,
  These great words shall not flay me.   385
NOAH: Abide, dame, and drink,
  For beaten shall thou be, with this staff till thou stink;
  Are the strokes good? say me.
WIFE: What say ye, Wat Wynk?
NOAH: Speak!   390
  Cry me mercy, I say!

WIFE: Thereto say I nay.
NOAH: Unless thou do, by this day,
    Thy head shall I break.

    [to women in the audience]

WIFE: Lord, I were at rest and heartily full whole,   395
    Might I once have a mess of widow's coyll [fare];
    For thy soul, without jest, should I deal penny doyll [alms],
    So would more, no frese [fear], that I see in this sole [place]
      Of wives that are here
    For the life they have led   400
    Would their husbands were dead
    For, as ever ate I bread,
      So would I our sire were.

    [to men in the audience]

NOAH: Ye men who have wives whilst they are young,
    If you love your lives, chastise their tongue: 405
    Methinks my heart rives, both liver and lung,
    To see such strifes, wedmen among;
      But I,
    As have I bliss,
    Shall chastise this.   410
WIFE: Yet may you miss,
    Nicholl Neddy!

NOAH: I shall make thee still as stone, beginner of blunder!
    I shall beat thee back and bone and break all asunder.

    [They fight.]

WIFE: Oh, alas, I am gone! Out upon thee, man's wonder!   415
NOAH: See how she can groan, and I lie under!
      But, wife,
    In this haste let us ho [stop],
    For my back is near in two.
WIFE: And I am beat so blue   420
    That I may not thrive.

    [They enter the ark.]

FIRST SON: Ah! why fare ye thus? Father and mother both!
SECOND SON: Ye should not be so spitus [spiteful] standing in such a
    woth [danger].
THIRD SON: These weathers are so hidus [hideous] with many a cold   425
    coth [disease].
NOAH: We will do as ye bid us. We will no more be wroth,
    Dear bairns!
    Now to the helm will I hent [go],
    And to my ship tend.   430
WIFE: I see on the firmament,
    Methinks, the seven stars.

NOAH: This is a great flood, wife, take heed.
WIFE: So me thought, as I stood. We are in great dread;
    These waves are so wode [wild].   435
NOAH: Help, God, in this need!
    As thou art steerman good and best, as I rede [counsel],
      Of all;
    Thou rule us in this race,
    As thou me promised has.   440
WIFE: This is a perilous case:
    Help, God, when we call!

NOAH: Wife, attend the steer-tree, and I shall assay
    The deepness of the sea that we bear, if I may.
WIFE: That shall I do full wisely. Now go thy way,   445
    For upon this flood have we floated many a day,
      With pain.
NOAH: Now the water will I sound
    Ah! it is far to the ground;
    This travail I expound   450
    Had I to tyne [lose].

Above all hills bedeyn [completely] the water is risen late
Cubits fifteen, but in a higher state
It may not be, I ween, for this well I wate [know],
This forty days has rain been. It will therefore abate   455
    Full lele [loyal].
This water in haste,
Eft will I test;
Now am I aghast,
    It is waned a great deal.   460

Now are the weathers ceased and cataracts quit,
    Both the most and the least.
WIFE: Methink, by my wit,
    The sun shines in the east. Lo, is not yond it?
    We should have a good feast were these floods flit   465
      So spytus [malicious].
NOAH: We have been here, all we,
    Three hundred days and fifty.
WIFE: Yea, now wanes the sea;
    Lord, well is us!   470

NOAH: The third time will I prove [test] what deepness we bear.
WIFE: How long shall thou heave. Lay in thy line there.
NOAH: I may touch with my lufe [hand] the ground even here.
WIFE: Then begins to grufe [grow] to us merry cheer;
    But, husband,   475
          What ground may this be?
NOAH: The hills of Armenia.
WIFE: Now blessed be he
    That thus for us ordained!

NOAH: I see tops of hills he [high] many at a sight,   480
    Nothing to hinder me, the weather is so bright.
WIFE: These are of mercy, tokens full right.
NOAH: Dame, thou counsel me what fowl best might
      And cowth [could],
      With flight of wing   485
      Bring, without tarrying,
      Of mercy some tokening
        Either by north or south.

      For this is the first day of the tenth moon.
WIFE: The raven, dare I lay, will come again soon;   490
    As fast as thou may cast him forth, have done,
    He may happen to day come again ere noon
      Without delay.
NOAH: I will cast out also
      Doves one or two: 495
      Go your way, go,
        God send you some prey!

      Now are these fowls flown into separate country;
      Pray we fast each one, kneeling on our knee,
      To him that is alone worthiest of degree,   500
      That he would send anon our fowls some fee
        To glad us.
WIFE: They may not fail of land,
      The water is so wanand [waning].
NOAH: Thank we God all weldand [wielding],   505
      That lord that made us.

      It is a wondrous thing, me thinks soothly,
      They are so long tarrying, the fowls that we
      Cast out in the morning.
WIFE: Sir, it may be   510
      They tarry till they bring.
NOAH: The raven is a-hungry
      Alway;
      He is without any reason,
      If he find any carrion,   515
      As peradventure may befon [befall],
      He will not away;

      The dove is more gentle, her trust I unto,
      Like unto the turtle, for she is ay true.
WIFE: Hence but a little. She comes, lew, lew!   520
    She brings in her bill some novels [signs] new;
      Behold!
    It is of an olive tree
    A branch, thinkest me.
NOAH: It is so, perde [par dieu; by our God],   525
    Right so is it called.

Dove, bird full blest, fair might thee befall!
Thou art true for to trust as stone in the wall;
Full well I it wist [knew] thou would come to thy hall.
WIFE: A true token is't we shall be saved all;   530
    For why?
The water, since she come,
Of deepness plumb,
Is fallen a fathom,
    And more hardily [certainly].   535

FIRST SON: These floods are gone. Father, behold!
SECOND SON: There is left right none, and that be ye bold.
THIRD SON: As still as a stone, our ship is stalled.
NOAH: Upon land here anon that we were, fain I would;   540
    My childer dear,
Shem, Japhet, and Ham,
With glee and with gam [sport],
Come we all sam [together],
    We will no longer abide here.

WIFE: Here have we been, Noah, long enough,   545
    With trouble and with teyn [grief], and endured much woe.
NOAH: Behold on this green neither cart nor plough
    Is left, as I ween, neither tree nor bough,
      Nor other thing,
But all is away;   550
Many castles, I say,
Great towns of array,
    Flit [destroyed] has this flowyng [flood].

WIFE: These floods, not afright, all this world so wide
    Has moved with might, on sea and by side.   555
NOAH: To death are they dyght [gone], proudest of pride,
    Every wight that ever was spied,
      With sin,
All are they slain,
And put unto pain.   560
WIFE: From thence again
    May they never win.

NOAH: Win? no, I-wis, but He that might has
    Would remember their mys [misery] and admit them to
      grace;   565
As He in misfortune is bliss, I pray Him in this space,
In heaven high with His, to secure us a place,
    That we,
With His saints in sight,
And His angels bright,   570
May come to His light:
    Amen, for charity.

Hamlet, Prince of Denmark
(c. 1600–1601)

During the sixteenth century, after religious drama was forbidden, the groups that had financed and staged the cycle plays ceased their support of theatre, disapproving of the professional and commercial role that theatre had been forced to adopt in order to survive. The necessity of attracting a paying audience motivated acting companies to offer a different play each day (though the same play might be repeated at intervals during a season), and thus they created an ongoing demand for new plays. Partially for this reason, the years between 1585 and 1610 produced an exceptional number of outstanding English playwrights. Of these, William Shakespeare is universally acknowledged the greatest, and possibly the greatest playwright the world has known.

In addition to being a playwright, Shakespeare was an actor and a shareholder (part owner) both in his acting company and in the theatre in which the company performed. As the company's principal playwright, he wrote an average of two plays each season. Among his thirty-eight surviving plays, *Hamlet* is one of the most admired.

Hamlet, like *Oedipus Rex*, has as its protagonist a man who is charged with punishing the murderer of a king. But Shakespeare uses a much broader canvas than Sophocles does and includes within his drama more facets of his story, more characters, and a wider sweep of time and place. Shakespeare's play develops chronologically and places all important incidents on stage. The only important events that precede the play's opening (Claudius's seduction of his brother's wife and his murder of his brother) are replicated in the play-within-the-play. The rapid shifts in time and place are made possible by theatrical conventions that establish locale and other significant conditions through spoken passages ("spoken decor") that localize as needed the fixed facade against which the action occurred.

Hamlet is thematically rich: the pervasiveness of betrayal (brother of brother, wife of husband, parent of child, friend of friend); the opposing demands made on Hamlet (that he revenge his father's murder and that he adhere to Christian doctrine against murder); the nature of kingship and the need to rule oneself before ruling others; and several other themes. Shakespeare's dramatic poetry is generally conceded to be the finest in the English language. The basic medium is blank verse, which allows the flexibility of ordinary speech while elevating it through imagery and rhythm.

Because of its compelling story, powerful characters, and great poetry, *Hamlet* is one of the world's finest achievements in drama. Although it embodies many ideas typical of its time, it transcends the limitations of a particular era. It continues to move spectators in the theatre as it has since its first presentation over four hundred years ago.

William Shakespeare

Hamlet, Prince of Denmark
(c. 1600–1601)

Dramatis Personae

CLAUDIUS, *King of Denmark*
HAMLET, *son to the former and nephew to the present king*
POLONIUS, *Lord Chamberlain*
HORATIO, *friend to Hamlet*
LAERTES, *son to Polonius*

VOLTEMAND
CORNELIUS
ROSENCRANTZ
GUILDENSTERN } *courtiers*
OSRIC
A GENTLEMAN
A PRIEST
MARCELLUS
BERNARDO } *officers*
FRANCISCO, *a soldier*
REYNALDO, *servant to Polonius*
PLAYERS
TWO CLOWNS, *grave diggers*
FORTINBRAS, *prince of Norway*
A NORWEGIAN CAPTAIN
ENGLISH AMBASSADORS
GERTRUDE, *queen of Denmark, and mother of Hamlet*
OPHELIA, *daughter to Polonius*
GHOST *of Hamlet's father*
LORDS, LADIES, OFFICERS, SOLDIERS, **SAILORS, MESSENGERS,**
    AND ATTENDANTS

SCENE————*Denmark.*

ACT I

SCENE I————*Elsinore. The guard-platform of the Castle.*

[FRANCISCO *at his post. Enter to him* BERNARDO.]

˙indicates a note identified by line number. The textual reference is given in bold type, its clarification in roman type.

BERNARDO: Who's there?

FRANCISCO: Nay, answer me. Stand and unfold* yourself.

BERNARDO: Long live the king!

FRANCISCO: Bernardo?

BERNARDO: He.

FRANCISCO: You come most carefully upon your hour.   5

BERNARDO: 'Tis now struck twelve; get thee to bed, Francisco.

FRANCISCO: For this relief much thanks. 'tis bitter cold,
    And I am sick at heart.

BERNARDO: Have you had quiet guard?

FRANCISCO: Not a mouse stirring.   10

BERNARDO: Well; good night.
    If you do meet Horatio and Marcellus,
    The rivals* of my watch, bid them make haste.

[*Enter* HORATIO *and* MARCELLUS.]

FRANCISCO: I think I hear them. Stand, ho! Who is there?   15

HORATIO: Friends to this ground.

MARCELLUS: And liegemen to the Dane.*

FRANCISCO: Give you good night.

MARCELLUS: O, farewell, honest soldier!
    Who hath reliev'd you?   20

FRANCISCO: Bernardo hath my place.
    Give you good night.   [*Exit.*]

MARCELLUS: Holla, Bernardo!

BERNARDO: Say—
    What, is Horatio there?   25

HORATIO: A piece of him.

BERNARDO: Welcome, Horatio; welcome, good Marcellus.

HORATIO: What, has this thing appear'd again to-night?

BERNARDO: I have seen nothing.

MARCELLUS: Horatio says 'tis but our fantasy,   30
    And will not let belief take hold of him
    Touching this dreaded sight, twice seen of us;
    Therefore I have entreated him along
    With us to watch the minutes of this night,
    That, if again this apparition come,   35
    He may approve* our eyes and speak to it.

HORATIO: Tush, tush, 'twill not appear.

BERNARDO: Sit down awhile,
    And let us once again assail your ears,
    That are so fortified against our story,   40
    What we have two nights seen.

[1,2] **unfold** identify

[1] **rivals** companions

[17] **liegemen to the Dane** loyal subjects to the king of Denmark

[36] **approve** confirm

HORATIO: Well, sit we down,
 And let us hear Bernardo speak of this.
BERNARDO: Last night of all,
 When yond same star that's westward from the pole   45
 Had made his course t' illume that part of heaven
 Where now it burns, Marcellus and myself,
 The bell then beating one—

  [*Enter* GHOST.]

MARCELLUS: Peace, break thee off; look where it comes again.
BERNARDO: In the same figure, like the King that's dead.   50
MARCELLUS: Thou art a scholar; speak to it, Horatio.
BERNARDO: Looks 'a not like the King? Mark it, Horatio.
HORATIO: Most like. It harrows me with fear and wonder.
BERNARDO: It would be spoke to.
MARCELLUS: Question it, Horatio.   55
HORATIO: What art thou that usurp'st this time of night
 Together with that fair and warlike form
 In which the majesty of buried Denmark*
 Did sometimes march? By heaven I charge thee, speak!
MARCELLUS: It is offended.   60
BERNARDO: See, it stalks away.
HORATIO: Stay! speak, speak! I charge thee, speak!

  [*Exit* GHOST.]

MARCELLUS: 'Tis gone, and will not answer.
BERNARDO: How now, Horatio! You tremble and look pale.
 Is not this something more than fantasy?   65
 What think you on't?
HORATIO: Before my God, I might not this believe
 Without the sensible and true avouch*
 Of mine own eyes.
MARCELLUS: Is it not like the King?   70
HORATIO: As thou art to thyself:
 Such was the very armour he had on
 When he the ambitious Norway* combated;
 So frown'd he once when, in an angry parle,*
 He smote the sledded Polacks* on the ice.   75
 'Tis strange.
MARCELLUS: Thus twice before, and jump* at this dead hour,
 With martial stalk hath he gone by our watch.

---

⁵⁸ **buried Denmark** buried king of Denmark
⁶⁸ **avouch** proof
⁷³ **Norway** king of Norway
⁷⁴ **parle** parley
⁷⁵ **sledded Polacks** Poles on sleds
⁷⁷ **jump** just

HORATIO: In what particular thought to work I know not;
    But, in the gross and scope* of mine opinion,   80
    This bodes some strange eruption to our state.
MARCELLUS: Good now, sit down, and tell me, he that knows,
    Why this same strict and most observant watch
    So nightly toils the subject* of the land;
    And why such daily cast of brazen cannon,   85
    And foreign mart* for implements of war;
    Why such impress* of shipwrights, whose sore task
    Does not divide the Sunday from the week;
    What might be toward,* that this sweaty haste
    Doth make the night joint-labourer with the day: 90
    Who is't that can inform me?
HORATIO: That can I;
    At least, the whisper goes so. Our last King,
    Whose image even but now appear'd to us,
    Was, as you know, by Fortinbras of Norway,   95
    Thereto prick'd on by a most emulate pride,
    Dar'd to the combat; in which our valiant Hamlet—
    For so this side of our known world esteem'd him—
    Did slay this Fortinbras; who, by a seal'd compact,
    Well ratified by law and heraldry,*   100
    Did forfeit, with his life, all those his lands
    Which he stood seiz'd of,* to the conqueror;
    Against the which a moiety competent*
    Was gaged* by our King; which had return'd
    To the inheritance of Fortinbras,   105
    Had he been vanquisher; as, by the same comart*
    And carriage of the article design'd,*
    His fell to Hamlet. Now, sir, young Fortinbras,
    Of unimproved* mettle hot and full,
    Hath in the skirts* of Norway, here and there,   110
    Shark'd up a list of lawless resolutes,*
    For food and diet, to some enterprise
    That hath a stomach in't,* which is no other,
    As it doth well appear unto our state,

---

[80] **gross and scope** general drift
[84] **nightly toils the subject** citizens work by night (as well as by day)
[86] **mart** trade
[87] **impress** forced service
[89] **toward** in preparation
[100] **law and heraldry** heraldic law
[102] **seiz'd of** in possession of
[103] **moiety competent** like portion
[104] **gaged** pledged
[106] **comart** agreement
[107] **carriage of the article design'd** provisions of the pact
[109] **unimproved** unproved
[110] **skirts** borders, outskirts
[111] **Shark'd up a list of lawless resolutes** enlisted a force of desperate men
[113] **hath a stomach in't** requires courage

But to recover of us, by strong hand   115
And terms compulsatory, those foresaid lands
So by his father lost; and this, I take it,
Is the main motive of our preparations,
The source of this our watch, and the chief head*
Of this post-haste and romage* in the land.   120
BERNARDO: I think it be no other but e'en so.
     Well may it sort,* that this portentous figure
     Comes armed through our watch; so like the King
     That was and is the question of these wars.
HORATIO: A mote it is to trouble the mind's eye.   125
     In the most high and palmy state of Rome,
     A little ere the mightiest Julius fell,
     The graves stood tenantless, and the sheeted dead
     Did squeak and gibber in the Roman streets;
     As, stars with trains of fire, and dews of blood,   130
     Disasters* in the sun; and the moist star*
     Upon whose influence Neptune's empire* stands
     Was sick almost to doomsday with eclipse;
     And even the like precurse* of fear'd events,
     As harbingers preceding still the fates   135
     And prologue to the omen coming on,
     Have heaven and earth together demonstrated
     Unto our climatures* and countrymen.

     [*Reenter* GHOST.]

But, soft, behold! Lo, where it comes again!
I'll cross it,* though it blast me. Stay, illusion.   140

     [GHOST *spreads its arms.*]

If thou hast any sound or use of voice,
Speak to me.
If there be any good thing to be done,
That may to thee do ease and grace to me,
Speak to me.   145
If thou art privy to thy country's fate,
Which happily* foreknowing may avoid,
O, speak!
Or if thou hast uphoarded in thy life

---

¹¹⁹ **chief head** principal reason
¹²⁰ **romage** bustling activity
¹²² **sort** turn out
¹³¹ **Disasters** threatening signs
¹³¹ **moist star** the moon
¹³² **Neptune's empire** the ocean (the Roman god Neptune's domain)
¹³⁴ **precurse** foreshadowing
¹³⁸ **climatures** regions
¹⁴⁰ **cross it** cross its path
¹⁴⁷ **happily** haply, perhaps

Extorted treasure in the womb of earth,   150
For which, they say, you spirits oft walk in death,

[*The cock crows.*]

Speak of it. Stay, and speak. Stop it, Marcellus.
MARCELLUS: Shall I strike at it with my partisan?*
HORATIO: Do, if it will not stand.
BERNARDO: 'Tis here!   155
HORATIO: 'Tis here!
MARCELLUS: 'Tis gone!   [*Exit* GHOST.]
We do it wrong, being so majestical,
To offer it the show of violence;
For it is, as the air, invulnerable,   160
And our vain blows malicious mockery.
BERNARDO: It was about to speak, when the cock crew.
HORATIO: And then it started like a guilty thing
Upon a fearful summons. I have heard
The cock, that is the trumpet to the morn,   165
Doth with his lofty and shrill-sounding throat
Awake the god of day; and at his warning,
Whether in sea or fire, in earth or air,
Th' extravagant and erring* spirit hies
To his confine; and of the truth herein   170
This present object made probation.*
MARCELLUS: It faded on the crowing of the cock.
Some say that ever 'gainst* that season comes
Wherein our Saviour's birth is celebrated,
This bird of dawning singeth all night long;   175
And then, they say, no spirit dare stir abroad,
The nights are wholesome, then no planets strike,*
No fairy takes, nor witch hath power to charm,
So hallowed and so gracious is that time.
HORATIO: So have I heard, and do in part believe it.   180
But look, the morn, in russet mantle clad,
Walks o'er the dew of yon high eastward hill.
Break we our watch up; and, by my advice,
Let us impart what we have seen to-night
Unto young Hamlet; for, upon my life,   185
This spirit, dumb to us, will speak to him.
Do you consent we shall acquaint him with it,
As needful in our loves, fitting our duty?
MARCELLUS: Let's do't, I pray; and I this morning know
Where we shall find him most convenient.   190

[*Exeunt.*]

---

[153] **partisan** (weapon)
[169] **extravagant and erring** wandering outside its proper realm
[171] **made probation** gives proof
[173] **ever 'gainst** just before
[177] **strike** exert evil influence

SCENE II———*Elsinore. The Castle.*

[*Flourish.* * *Enter* CLAUDIUS KING OF DENMARK, GERTRUDE THE QUEEN, *and* COUNCILLORS, *including* POLONIUS, *his son* LAERTES, VOLTEMAND, CORNELIUS, *and* HAMLET.]

KING: Though yet of Hamlet our dear brother's death
     The memory be green; and that it us befitted
     To bear our hearts in grief, and our whole kingdom
     To be contracted in one brow of woe;
     Yet so far hath discretion fought with nature   5
     That we with wisest sorrow think on him,
     Together with remembrance of ourselves.
     Therefore our sometime sister,* now our queen,
     Th' imperial jointress* to this warlike state,
     Have we, as 'twere with a defeated joy,   10
     With an auspicious and a dropping eye,
     With mirth in funeral, and with dirge in marriage,
     In equal scale weighing delight and dole,
     Taken to wife; nor have we herein barr'd
     Your better wisdoms, which have freely gone   15
     With this affair along. For all, our thanks.
     Now follows that you know: young Fortinbras,
     Holding a weak supposal of our worth,
     Or thinking by our late dear brother's death
     Our state to be disjoint and out of frame,*   20
     Co-leagued with this dream of his advantage*—
     He hath not fail'd to pester us with message
     Importing the surrender of those lands
     Lost by his father, with all bands of law,
     To our most valiant brother. So much for him.   25
     Now for ourself, and for this time of meeting,
     Thus much the business is: we have here writ
     To Norway, uncle of young Fortinbras—
     Who, impotent and bed-rid, scarcely hears
     Of this his nephew's purpose—to suppress   30
     His further gait* herein, in that the levies,
     The lists, and full proportions,* are all made
     Out of his subject;* and we here dispatch
     You, good Cornelius, and you, Voltemand,
     For bearers of this greeting to old Norway;   35
     Giving to you no further personal power

I,ii (stage direction) **Flourish** trumpet fanfare
* **our sometime sister** my former sister-in-law
9 **jointress** joint ruler
20 **frame** order
21 **advantage** superior power
31 **gait** proceeding
32 **proportions** war supplies
33 **Out of his subject** out of the Norwegian king's subjects

To business with the King more than the scope
Of these dilated articles* allow.
Farewell; and let your haste commend your duty.
CORNELIUS: }
VOLTEMAND: } In that and in all things we will show our duty.   40
KING: We doubt it nothing; heartily farewell.

> [*Exeunt* VOLTEMAND *and* CORNELIUS.]

And now, Laertes, what's the news with you?
You told us of some suit; what is't, Laertes?
You cannot speak of reason to the Dane
And lose your voice.* What wouldst thou beg, Laertes,   45
That shall not be my offer, not thy asking?
The head is not more native* to the heart,
The hand more instrumental to the mouth,
Than is the throne of Denmark to thy father.
What wouldst thou have, Laertes?   50
LAERTES: My dread lord,
Your leave and favour to return to France;
From whence though willingly I came to Denmark
To show my duty in your coronation,
Yet now, I must confess, that duty done,   55
My thoughts and wishes bend again toward France,
And bow them to your gracious leave and pardon.
KING: Have you your father's leave? What says Polonius?
POLONIUS: 'A hath, my lord, wrung from me my slow leave
By laboursome petition; and at last   60
Upon his will I seal'd my hard consent.*
I do beseech you, give him leave to go.
KING: Take thy fair hour, Laertes; time be thine,
And thy best graces spend it at thy will!
But now, my cousin* Hamlet, and my son—   65
HAMLET: [*aside*] A little more than kin, and less than kind.
KING: How is it that the clouds* still hang on you?
HAMLET: Not so, my Lord; I am too much in the sun.
QUEEN: Good Hamlet, cast thy nighted colour off,
And let thine eye look like a friend on Denmark.   70
Do not for ever with thy vailed lids*
Seek for thy noble father in the dust.
Thou know'st 'tis common—all that lives must die,
Passing through nature to eternity.
HAMLET: Ay, madam, it is common.   75

---

38 **dilated articles** detailed documents
45 **lose your voice** waste your breath
47 **native** related
61 **hard consent** reluctantly gave consent
65 **cousin** kinsman
67 **clouds** grief; mourning dress
71 **vailed lids** lowered eyes

QUEEN: If it be,
    Why seems it so particular with thee?
HAMLET: Seems, madam! Nay, it is; I know not seems.
    'Tis not alone my inky cloak, good mother,
    Nor customary suits of solemn black,   80
    Nor windy suspiration* of forc'd breath,
    No, nor the fruitful river in the eye,
    Nor the dejected haviour of the visage,
    Together with all forms, moods, shapes of grief,
    That can denote me truly. These, indeed, seem;   85
    For they are actions that a man might play;
    But I have that within which passes show—
    These but the trappings and the suits of woe.
KING: 'Tis sweet and commendable in your nature, Hamlet,
    To give these mourning duties to your father;   90
    But you must know your father lost a father;
    That father lost, lost his; and the survivor bound,
    In filial obligation, for some term
    To do obsequious* sorrow. But to persever
    In obstinate condolement* is a course   95
    Of impious stubbornness; 'tis unmanly grief;
    It shows a will most incorrect to heaven,
    A heart unfortified, a mind impatient,
    An understanding simple and unschool'd;
    For what we know must be, and is as common   100
    As any the most vulgar thing to sense,
    Why should we in our peevish opposition
    Take it to heart? Fie! 'tis a fault to heaven,
    A fault against the dead, a fault to nature,
    To reason most absurd; whose common theme   105
    Is death of fathers, and who still hath cried,
    From the first corse* till he that died to-day,
    'This must be so.' We pray you throw to earth
    This unprevailing* woe, and think of us
    As of a father; for let the world take note   110
    You are the most immediate to our throne;
    And with no less nobility of love
    Than that which dearest father bears his son
    Do I impart toward you. For your intent
    In going back to school in Wittenberg,   115
    It is most retrograde* to our desire;
    And we beseech you bend you* to remain
    Here, in the cheer and comfort of our eye,

---

[81] **windy suspiration** heavy sighs
[94] **obsequious** funereal
[95] **condolement** mourning
[107] **corse** corpse
[109] **unprevailing** unavailing
[116] **retrograde** contrary
[117] **bend you** agree

Our chiefest courtier, cousin, and our son.
QUEEN: Let not thy mother lose her prayers, Hamlet: 120
    I pray thee stay with us; go not to Wittenberg.
HAMLET: I shall in all my best obey you, madam.
KING: Why, 'tis a loving and a fair reply.
    Be as ourself in Denmark. Madam, come;
    This gentle and unforc'd accord of Hamlet   125
    Sits smiling to my heart; in grace whereof,
    No jocund health that Denmark drinks to-day
    But the great cannon to the clouds shall tell
    And the King's rouse* the heaven shall bruit* again,
    Re-speaking earthly thunder. Come away.   130

    [Flourish. Exeunt all but HAMLET.]

HAMLET: O, that this too too solid flesh would melt,
    Thaw, and resolve itself into a dew!
    Or that the Everlasting had not fix'd
    His canon* 'gainst self-slaughter! O God! God!
    How weary, stale, flat, and unprofitable,   135
    Seem to me all the uses of this world!
    Fie on't! Ah, fie! 'tis an unweeded garden,
    That grows to seed; things rank and gross in nature
    Possess it merely.* That it should come to this!
    But two months dead! Nay, not so much, not two.   140
    So excellent a king that was to this
    Hyperion* to a satyr, so loving to my mother,
    That he might not beteem* the winds of heaven
    Visit her face too roughly. Heaven and earth!
    Must I remember? Why, she would hang on him   145
    As if increase of appetite had grown
    By what it fed on; and yet, within a month—
    Let me not think on't. Frailty, thy name is woman!—
    A little month, or ere those shoes were old
    With which she followed my poor father's body,   150
    Like Niobe,* all tears—why she, even she—
    O God! a beast that wants discourse of reason*
    Would have mourn'd longer—married with my uncle,
    My father's brother; but no more like my father
    Than I to Hercules. Within a month,   155
    Ere yet the salt of most unrighteous tears
    Had left the flushing in her galled eyes,
    She married. O, most wicked speed, to post*

---

[129] **rouse** drinking, carousing
[129] **bruit** noisily announce
[134] **canon** law
[139] **merely** completely
[142] **Hyperion** the sun god noted for beauty
[143] **beteem** permit
[151] **Niobe** mother in Greek mythology who wept without stopping for the death of her children
[152] **wants discourse of reason** lacks reasoning power
[158] **post** hasten

With such dexterity to incestuous* sheets!
It is not, nor it cannot come to good.   160
But break, my heart, for I must hold my tongue.

[*Enter* HORATIO, MARCELLUS, *and* BERNARDO.]

HORATIO: Hail to your lordship!
HAMLET: I am glad to see you well.
    Horatio—or I do forget myself.
HORATIO: The same, my lord, and your poor servant ever.   165
HAMLET: Sir, my good friend. I'll change* that name with you.
    And what make you from Wittenberg, Horatio?
    Marcellus?
MARCELLUS: My good lord!
HAMLET: I am very glad to see you. [*to* BERNARDO] Good even, sir.—   170
    But what, in faith, make you from Wittenberg?
HORATIO: A truant disposition, good my lord.
HAMLET: I would not hear your enemy say so;
    Nor shall you do my ear that violence,
    To make it truster* of your own report.   175
    Against yourself. I know you are no truant.
    But what is your affair in Elsinore?
    We'll teach you to drink deep ere you depart.
HORATIO: My lord, I came to see your father's funeral.
HAMLET: I prithee do not mock me, fellow-student;   180
    I think it was to see my mother's wedding.
HORATIO: Indeed, my lord, it followed hard upon.
HAMLET: Thrift, thrift, Horatio! The funeral bak'd-meats
    Did coldly furnish forth the marriage tables.
    Would I had met my dearest* foe in heaven   185
    Or ever I had seen that day, Horatio!
    My father—methinks I see my father.
HORATIO: Where, my lord?
HAMLET: In my mind's eye, Horatio.
HORATIO: I saw him once; 'a was a goodly king.   190
HAMLET: 'A* was a man, take him for all in all,
    I shall not look upon his like again.
HORATIO: My lord, I think I saw him yesternight.
HAMLET: Saw who?
HORATIO: My lord, the King your father.   195
HAMLET: The King my father!
HORATIO: Season your admiration* for a while
    With an attent ear, till I may deliver,
    Upon the witness of these gentlemen,
    This marvel to you.   200

---

[159] **incestuous** incestuous because the church considered a sister-in-law equivalent to being a sister
[166] **change** exchange
[175] **truster** believer
[185] **dearest** most hated
[191] **'A** he
[197] **Season your admiration** control your wonder

HAMLET: For God's love, let me hear.

HORATIO: Two nights together had these gentlemen,
    Marcellus and Bernardo, on their watch,
    In the dead waste and middle of the night,
    Been thus encount'red. A figure like your father,   205
    Armed at point exactly, cap-a-pe,*
    Appears before them, and with solemn march
    Goes slow and stately by them; thrice he walk'd
    By their oppress'd and fear-surprised eyes,
    Within his truncheon's length,* whilst they, distill'd*   210
    Almost to jelly with the act of fear,
    Stand dumb and speak not to him. This to me
    In dreadful* secrecy impart they did;
    And I with them the third night kept the watch;
    Where, as they had delivered, both in time,   215
    Form of the thing, each word made true and good,
    The apparition comes. I knew your father;
    These hands are not more like.

HAMLET: But where was this?

MARCELLUS: My lord, upon the platform where we watch.   220

HAMLET: Did you not speak to it?

HORATIO: My lord, I did;
    But answer made it none; yet once methought
    It lifted up its head and did address
    Itself to motion, like as it would speak;   225
    But even then the morning cock crew loud,
    And at the sound it shrunk in haste away
    And vanish'd from our sight.

HAMLET: 'Tis very strange.

HORATIO: As I do live, my honour'd lord, 'tis true;   230
    And we did think it writ down in our duty
    To let you know of it.

HAMLET: Indeed, indeed, sirs, but this troubles me.
    Hold you the watch to-night?

ALL: We do, my lord.   235

HAMLET: Arm'd, say you?

ALL: Arm'd, my lord.

HAMLET: From top to toe?

ALL: My lord, from head to foot.

HAMLET: Then saw you not his face?   240

HORATIO: O yes, my lord; he wore his beaver* up.

HAMLET: What, look'd he frowningly?

HORATIO: A countenance more in sorrow than in anger.

HAMLET: Pale or red?

HORATIO: Nay, very pale.   245

---

[206] **cap-a-pe** head to foot
[210] **truncheon's length** space of a short club
[210] **distill'd** reduced
[213] **dreadful** terrified
[241] **beaver** visor, face guard

HAMLET: And fix'd his eyes upon you?
HORATIO: Most constantly.
HAMLET: I would I had been there.
HORATIO: It would have much amaz'd you.
HAMLET: Very like, very like. Stay'd it long? 250
HORATIO: While one with moderate haste might tell* a hundred.
BOTH: Longer, longer.
HORATIO: Not when I saw't.
HAMLET: His beard was grizzl'd*—no?
HORATIO: It was, as I have seen it in his life, 255
    A sable silver'd.*
HAMLET: I will watch to-night;
    Perchance 'twill walk again.
HORATIO: I warr'nt it will.
HAMLET: If it assume my noble father's person. 260
    I'll speak to it, though hell itself should gape
    And bid me hold my peace, I pray you all,
    If you have hitherto conceal'd this sight,
    Let it be tenable* in your silence still;
    And whatsoever else shall hap to-night, 265
    Give it an understanding, but no tongue;
    I will requite your loves. So, fare you well—
    Upon the platform, 'twixt eleven and twelve,
    I'll visit you.
ALL: Our duty to your honour. 270
HAMLET: Your loves, as mine to you; farewell.

       [*Exeunt all but* HAMLET.]

My father's spirit in arms! All is not well.
I doubt* some foul play. Would the night were come!
Till then sit still, my soul. Foul deeds will rise,
Though all the earth o'erwhelm them, to men's eyes.   [*Exit.*] 275

      SCENE III————*Elsinore. The house of* POLONIUS.

    [*Enter* LAERTES *and* OPHELIA *his sister.*]

LAERTES: My necessaries are embark'd. Farewell.
    And, sister, as the winds give benefit
    And convoy* is assistant, do not sleep,
    But let me hear from you.
OPHELIA: Do you doubt that? 5
LAERTES: For Hamlet, and the trifling of his favour,

---

251 **tell** count
254 **grizzl'd** gray
256 **sable silver'd** black mixed with gray
264 **tenable** held
273 **doubt** suspect
1,iii,3 **convoy** conveyance

Hold it a fashion and a toy* in blood,
A violet in the youth of primy* nature,
Forward* not permanent, sweet not lasting,
The perfume and suppliance* of a minute;   10
No more.
OPHELIA: No more but so?
LAERTES: Think it no more;
For nature crescent* does not grow alone
In thews* and bulk, but as this temple* waxes,   15
The inward service of the mind and soul
Grows wide withal. Perhaps he loves you now,
And now no soil nor cautel* doth besmirch
The virtue of his will; but you must fear,
His greatness weigh'd,* his will is not his own;   20
For he himself is subject to his birth:
He may not, as unvalued* persons do,
Carve for himself; for on his choice depends
The sanity and health of this whole state;
And therefore must his choice be circumscrib'd   25
Unto the voice and yielding of that body
Whereof he is the head. Then if he says he loves you,
It fits your wisdom so far to believe it
As he in his particular act and place
May give his saying deed; which is no further   30
Than the main voice of Denmark goes withal.
Then weigh what loss your honour may sustain,
If with too credent* ear you list his songs,
Or lose your heart, or your chaste treasure open
To his unmast'red importunity.   35
Fear it, Ophelia, fear it, my dear sister;
And keep you in the rear of your affection,
Out of the shot and danger of desire.
The chariest maid is prodigal enough
If she unmask her beauty to the moon.   40
Virtue itself scapes not calumnious strokes;
The canker* galls the infants of the spring
Too oft before their buttons* be disclos'd;
And in the morn and liquid dew of youth

---

[7] **toy** idle fancy
[8] **primy** youthful, springlike
[9] **Forward** premature
[10] **suppliance** diversion
[14] **crescent** increasing
[15] **thews** sinews
[15] **temple** the body
[18] **cautel** deceit
[20] **greatness weigh'd** high rank considered
[22] **unvalued** of low rank
[33] **credent** credulous
[42] **canker** worm
[43] **buttons** buds

Contagious blastments are most imminent. 45
Be wary, then; best safety lies in fear:
Youth to itself rebels, though none else near.
OPHELIA: I shall the effect of this good lesson keep
As watchman to my heart. But, good my brother,
Do not, as some ungracious* pastors do, 50
Show me the steep and thorny way to heaven,
Whiles, like a puff'd and reckless libertine,
Himself the primrose path of dalliance treads
And recks not his own rede.*
LAERTES: O, fear me not! 55

[*Enter* POLONIUS.]

I stay too long. But here my father comes.
A double blessing is a double grace;
Occasion smiles upon a second leave.
POLONIUS: Yet here, Laertes! Aboard, aboard, for shame!
The wind sits in the shoulder of your sail, 60
And you are stay'd for. There—my blessing with thee!
And these few precepts in thy memory
Look thou character.* Give thy thoughts no tongue,
Nor any unproportion'd* thought his act.
Be thou familiar, but by no means vulgar. 65
Those friends thou hast, and their adoption tried,
Grapple them to thy soul with hoops of steel;
But do not dull thy palm with entertainment
Of each new-hatch'd, unfledg'd comrade. Beware
Of entrance to a quarrel; but, being in, 70
Bear't that th' opposed may beware of thee.
Give every man thy ear, but few thy voice;
Take each man's censure, but reserve thy judgment.
Costly thy habit as thy purse can buy,
But not express'd in fancy; rich, not gaudy; 75
For the apparel oft proclaims the man;
And they in France of the best rank and station
Are of a most select and generous choice in that.
Neither a borrower nor a lender be;
For loan oft loses both itself and friend, 80
And borrowing dulls the edge of husbandry.*
This above all—to thine own self be true,
And it must follow, as the night the day,
Thou canst not then be false to any man.
Farewell; my blessing season* this in thee! 85

---

[50] **ungracious** without themselves being in God's grace
[54] **recks not his own rede** doesn't heed his own advice
[63] **character** inscribe
[64] **unproportion'd** unconsidered
[81] **husbandry** thrift
[85] **season** make fruitful

LAERTES: Most humbly do I take my leave, my lord.

POLONIUS: The time invites you; go, your servants tend.*

LAERTES: Farewell, Ophelia; and remember well
>   What I have said to you.

OPHELIA: 'Tis in my memory lock'd,   90
>   And you yourself shall keep the key of it.

LAERTES: Farewell.

POLONIUS: What is't, Ophelia, he hath said to you?

OPHELIA: So please you, something touching the Lord Hamlet.

POLONIUS: Marry,* well bethought!   95
>   'Tis told me he hath very oft of late
>   Given private time to you; and you yourself
>   Have of your audience been most free and bounteous.
>   If it be so—as so 'tis put on me,
>   And that in way of caution—I must tell you   100
>   You do not understand yourself so clearly
>   As it behooves my daughter and your honour.
>   What is between you? Give me up the truth.

OPHELIA: He hath, my lord, of late made many tenders
>   Of his affection to me.   105

POLONIUS: Affection! Pooh! You speak like a green girl,
>   Unsifted* in such perilous circumstance.
>   Do you believe his tenders, as you call them?

OPHELIA: I do not know, my lord, what I should think.

POLONIUS: Marry, I will teach you: think yourself a baby   110
>   That you have ta'en these tenders for true pay
>   Which are not sterling. Tender yourself more dearly;
>   Or—not to crack the wind of the poor phrase,
>   Running it thus—you'll tender me a fool.*

OPHELIA: My lord, he hath importun'd me with love   115
>   In honourable fashion.

POLONIUS: Ay, fashion you may call it; go to, go to.

OPHELIA: And hath given countenance to his speech, my lord,
>   With almost all the holy vows of heaven.

POLONIUS: Ay, springes to catch woodcocks!* I do know,   120
>   When the blood burns, how prodigal the soul
>   Lends the tongue vows. These blazes, daughter,
>   Giving more light than heat—extinct in both,
>   Even in their promise, as it is a-making—
>   You must not take for fire. From this time   125
>   Be something scanter of your maiden presence;
>   Set your entreatments* at a higher rate
>   Than a command to parle. For Lord Hamlet,

---

[87] **tend** await

[95] **Marry** By the Virgin Mary

[107] **Unsifted** untried

[114] **tender me a fool** present me with a baby

[120] **springes to catch woodcocks** snares to catch unwary birds

[127] **entreatments** conversations

Believe so much in him, that he is young,
And with a larger tether may he walk   130
Than may be given you. In few, Ophelia,
Do not believe his vows; for they are brokers,*
Not of that dye* which their investments* show,
But mere implorators* of unholy suits,
Breathing like sanctified and pious bonds,*   135
The better to beguile. This is for all—
I would not, in plain terms, from this time forth
Have you so slander* any moment leisure
As to give words or walk with the Lord Hamlet.
Look to't, I charge you. Come your ways.   140
OPHELIA: I shall obey, my lord.   [*Exeunt.*]

SCENE IV———*Elsinore. The guard-platform of the Castle.*

[*Enter* HAMLET, HORATIO, *and* MARCELLUS.]

HAMLET: The air bites shrewdly;* it is very cold.
HORATIO: It is a nipping and an eager* air.
HAMLET: What hour now?
HORATIO: I think it lacks of twelve.
MARCELLUS: No, it is struck.   5
HORATIO: Indeed? I heard it not. It then draws near the season
    Wherein the spirit held his wont to walk.

[*A flourish of trumpets, and two pieces go off.*]

What does this mean, my lord?
HAMLET: The King doth wake* to-night and takes his rouse,*
    Keeps wassail, and the swagg'ring up-spring* reels,   10
    And, as he drains his draughts of Rhenish* down,
    The kettledrum and trumpet thus bray out
    The triumph of his pledge.*
HORATIO: Is it a custom?
HAMLET: Ay, marry, is't;   15
    But to my mind, though I am native here
    And to the manner born, it is a custom

---

[132] **brokers** procurers
[133] **dye** kind
[133] **investments** outer garments
[134] **implorators** solicitors
[135] **bonds** pledges
[138] **slander** disgrace
[I.iv.1] **shrewdly** bitterly
[2] **eager** sharp
[9] **wake** revel
[9] **rouse** carouses
[10] **up-spring** dance
[11] **Rhenish** Rhine wine
[13] **The triumph of his pledge** drinking a glass of wine in one draught

More honour'd in the breach than the observance.
This heavy-headed revel east and west
Makes us traduc'd and tax'd of* other nations;   20
They clepe* us drunkards, and with swinish phrase
Soil our addition,* and, indeed, it takes
From our achievements, though perform'd at height,
The pith and marrow of our attribute.*
So, oft it chances in particular men   25
That, for some vicious mole* of nature in them,
As in their birth, wherein they are not guilty,
Since nature cannot choose his origin;
By the o'ergrowth of some complexion,*
Oft breaking down the pales* and forts of reason;   30
Or by some habit that too much o'er-leavens*
The form of plausive* manners—that these men,
Carrying, I say, the stamp of one defect,
Being nature's livery or fortune's star,*
His virtues else, be they as pure as grace,   35
As infinite as man may undergo,
Shall in the general censure* take corruption
From that particular fault. The dram of eale
Doth all the noble substance of a doubt
To his own scandal.   40

      [*Enter* GHOST.]

HORATIO: Look, my lord, it comes.
HAMLET: Angels and ministers of grace defend us!
     Be thou a spirit of health* or goblin damn'd,
     Bring with thee airs from heaven or blasts from hell,
     Be thy intents wicked or charitable,   45
     Thou com'st in such a questionable* shape
     That I will speak to thee. I'll call thee Hamlet,
     King, father, royal Dane. O, answer me!
     Let me not burst in ignorance, but tell
     Why thy canoniz'd* bones, hearsed in death,   50
     Have burst their cerements;* why the sepulchre

---

[20] **tax'd of** accused by
[21] **clepe** call
[22] **addition** honor
[24] **attribute** reputation
[26] **mole** blemish
[29] **complexion** natural disposition
[30] **pales** walls
[31] **o'er-leavens** overdoes, corrupts
[32] **plausive** pleasing
[34] **nature's livery or fortune's star** determined by nature or by the stars
[37] **general censure** popular judgment
[43] **spirit of health** good spirit
[46] **questionable** of dubious identity
[50] **canoniz'd** buried according to church rules
[51] **cerements** burial garments

Wherein we saw thee quietly enurn'd
Have op'd his ponderous and marble jaws
To cast thee up again. What may this mean
That thou, dead corse, again in complete steel   55
Revisits thus the glimpses of the moon,
Making night hideous, and we fools of nature
So horridly to shake our disposition*
With thoughts beyond the reaches of our souls?
Say, why is this? wherefore? What should we do?   60

        [GHOST *beckons* HAMLET.]

HORATIO: It beckons you to go away with it,
    As if some impartment* did desire
    To you alone.
MARCELLUS: Look with what courteous action
    It waves you to a more removed ground.   65
    But do not go with it.
HORATIO: No, by no means.
HAMLET: It will not speak; then I will follow it.
HORATIO: Do not, my lord.
HAMLET: Why, what should be the fear?   70
    I do not set my life at a pin's fee;
    And for my soul, what can it do to that,
    Being a thing immortal as itself?
    It waves me forth again; I'll follow it.
HORATIO: What if it tempt you toward the flood, my lord,   75
    Or to the dreadful summit of the cliff
    That beetles* o'er his base into the sea,
    And there assume some other horrible form,
    Which might deprive your sovereignty of reason
    And draw you into madness? Think of it: 80
    The very place puts toys* of desperation,
    Without more motive, into every brain
    That looks so many fathoms to the sea
    And hears it roar beneath.
HAMLET: It waves me still.   85
    Go on; I'll follow thee.
MARCELLUS: You shall not go, my lord.
HAMLET: Hold off your hands.
HORATIO: Be rul'd; you shall not go.
HAMLET: My fate cries out,   90
    And makes each petty arture* in this body
    As hardy as the Nemean lion's nerve.* [GHOST *beckons.*]

---

58 **shake our disposition** unsettle our minds
62 **impartment** message to impart
77 **beetles** juts out
81 **toys** notions
91 **arture** artery
92 **Nemean lion's nerve** sinews of the mythical lion slain by Heracles

Still am I call'd. Unhand me, gentlemen.
By heaven, I'll make a ghost of him that lets* me.
I say, away! Go on; I'll follow thee.   95

> [*Exeunt* GHOST *and* HAMLET.]

HORATIO: He waxes desperate with imagination.
MARCELLUS: Let's follow; 'tis not fit thus to obey him.
HORATIO: Have after. To what issue will this come?
MARCELLUS: Something is rotten in the state of Denmark.
HORATIO: Heaven will direct it.   100
MARCELLUS: Nay, let's follow him.   [*Exeunt.*]

SCENE V———*Elsinore. The Battlements of the Castle.*

> [*Enter* GHOST *and* HAMLET.]

HAMLET: Whither wilt thou lead me? Speak. I'll go no further.
GHOST: Mark me.
HAMLET: I will.
GHOST: My hour is almost come,
    When I to sulph'rous and tormenting flames   5
    Must render up myself.
HAMLET: Alas, poor ghost!
GHOST: Pity me not, but lend thy serious hearing
    To what I shall unfold.
HAMLET: Speak; I am bound to hear.   10
GHOST: So art thou to revenge, when thou shalt hear.
HAMLET: What?
GHOST: I am thy father's spirit,
    Doom'd for a certain term to walk the night,
    And for the day confin'd to fast in fires,   15
    Till the foul crimes done in my days of nature
    Are burnt and purg'd away. But that I am forbid
    To tell the secrets of my prison-house,
    I could a tale unfold whose lightest word
    Would harrow up thy soul, freeze thy young blood,   20
    Make thy two eyes, like stars, start from their spheres,
    Thy knotted and combined locks to part,
    And each particular hair to stand an end,
    Like quills upon the fretful porpentine.*
    But this eternal blazon* must not be   25
    To ears of flesh and blood. List, list, O, list!
    If thou didst ever thy dear father love—
HAMLET: O God!
GHOST: Revenge his foul and most unnatural murder.
HAMLET: Murder!   30

---

[94] **lets** hinders
[I.v.24] **fretful porpentine** fearful porcupine
[25] **eternal blazon** revelation about eternity

GHOST: Murder most foul, as in the best it is;
    But this most foul, strange, and unnatural.
HAMLET: Haste me to know't, that I, with wings as swift
    As meditation or the thoughts of love,
    May sweep to my revenge. 35
GHOST: I find thee apt;
    And duller shouldst thou be than the fat weed
    That roots itself in ease on Lethe wharf,*
    Wouldst thou not stir in this. Now, Hamlet, hear:
    'Tis given out that, sleeping in my orchard, 40
    A serpent stung me; so the whole ear of Denmark
    Is by a forged process* of my death
    Rankly abus'd; but know, thou noble youth,
    The serpent that did sting thy father's life
    Now wears his crown. 45
HAMLET: O my prophetic soul!
    My uncle!
GHOST: Ay, that incestuous, that adulterate* beast,
    With witchcraft of his wits, with traitorous gifts—
    O wicked wit and gifts that have the power 50
    So to seduce—won to his shameful lust
    The will of my most seeming virtuous queen.
    O Hamlet, what a falling off was there,
    From me, whose love was of that dignity
    That it went hand in hand even with the vow 55
    I made to her in marriage; and to decline
    Upon a wretch whose natural gifts were poor
    To those of mine!
    But virtue, as it never will be moved,
    Though lewdness court it in a shape of heaven, 60
    So lust, though to a radiant angel link'd,
    Will sate itself in a celestial bed
    And prey on garbage.
    But soft! methinks I scent the morning air.
    Brief let me be. Sleeping within my orchard, 65
    My custom always of the afternoon,
    Upon my secure* hour thy uncle stole,
    With juice of cursed hebona* in a vial,
    And in the porches of my ears did pour
    The leperous distilment; whose effect 70
    Holds such an enmity with blood of man
    That swift as quicksilver it courses through
    The natural gates and alleys of the body;
    And with a sudden vigour it doth posset*

---

[38] **Lethe wharf** bank of the river of forgetfulness in Hades
[42] **forged process** false account
[48] **adulterate** adulterous
[67] **secure** unsuspecting
[68] **hebona** poisonous plant
[74] **posset** curdle

And curd, like eager* droppings into milk,   75
The thin and wholesome blood. So did it mine;
And a most instant tetter* bark'd about,
Most lazar-like,* with vile and loathsome crust,
All my smooth body.
Thus was I, sleeping, by a brother's hand   80
Of life, of crown, of queen, at once dispatch'd;
Cut off even in the blossoms of my sin,
Unhous'led, disappointed, unanel'd;*
No reck'ning made, but sent to my account
With all my imperfections on my head   85
O, horrible! O, horrible! most horrible!
If thou hast nature in thee, bear it not;
Let not the royal bed of Denmark be
A couch for luxury* and damned incest.
But howsoever thou pursuest this act,   90
Taint not thy mind, nor let thy soul contrive
Against thy mother aught; leave her to heaven,
And to those thorns that in her bosom lodge
To prick and sting her. Fare thee well at once.
The glowworm shows the matin* to be near,   95
And gins to pale his uneffectual fire.
Adieu, adieu, adieu! Remember me.   [*Exit.*]
HAMLET: O all you host of heaven! O earth! What else?
And shall I couple hell? O, fie! Hold, hold, my heart;
And you, my sinews, grow not instant old,   100
But bear me stiffly up. Remember thee!
Ay, thou poor ghost, whiles memory holds a seat
In this distracted globe.* Remember thee!
Yea, from the table* of my memory
I'll wipe away all trivial fond* records,   105
All saws* of books, all forms, all pressures* past,
That youth and observation copied there,
And thy commandment all alone shall live
Within the book and volume of my brain,
Unmix'd with baser matter. Yes, by heaven!   110
O most pernicious woman!
O villain, villain, smiling, damned villain!
My tables—meet it is I set it down

---

⁷⁵ **eager** acid
⁷⁷ **tetter** inflammation of the skin
⁷⁸ **lazar-like** leperlike
⁸³ **Unhous'led, disappointed, unanel'd** without the sacrament of communion, unabsolved of sin, without extreme unction
⁸⁹ **luxury** lust
⁹⁵ **matin** morning
¹⁰³ **globe** head
¹⁰⁴ **table** tablet
¹⁰⁵ **fond** foolish
¹⁰⁶ **saws** maxims
¹⁰⁶ **pressures** impressions

That one may smile, and smile, and be a villain;
At least I am sure it may be so in Denmark. [*writing*]   115
So, uncle, there you are. Now to my word:
It is 'Adieu, adieu! Remember me.'
I have sworn't.
HORATIO: [*within*] My lord, my lord!

[*Enter* HORATIO *and* MARCELLUS.]

MARCELLUS: Lord Hamlet!   120
HORATIO: Heavens secure him!
HAMLET: So be it!
MARCELLUS: Illo, ho, ho,* my lord!
HAMLET: Hillo, ho, ho, boy! Come, bird, come.
MARCELLUS: How is't, my noble lord?   125
HORATIO: What news, my lord?
HAMLET: O, wonderful!
HORATIO: Good my lord, tell it.
HAMLET: No; you will reveal it.
HORATIO: Not I, my lord, by heaven!   130
MARCELLUS: Nor I, my lord.
HAMLET: How say you, then; would heart of man once think it?
     But you'll be secret?
BOTH: Ay, by heaven, my lord!
HAMLET: There's never a villain dwelling in all Denmark   135
     But he's an arrant knave.
HORATIO: There needs no ghost, my lord, come from the grave
     To tell us this.
HAMLET: Why, right; you are in the right;
     And so, without more circumstance* at all,   140
     I hold it fit that we shake hands and part;
     You, as your business and desire shall point you—
     For every man hath business and desire,
     Such as it is; and for my own poor part,
     Look you, I will go pray.   145
HORATIO: These are but wild and whirling words, my lord.
HAMLET: I am sorry they offend you, heartily;
     Yes, faith, heartily.
HORATIO: There's no offence, my lord.
HAMLET: Yes, by Saint Patrick, but there is, Horatio,   150
     And much offence, too. Touching this vision here—
     It is an honest ghost,* that let me tell you.
     For your desire to know what is between us,
     O'ermaster't as you may. And now, good friends,
     As you are friends, scholars, and soldiers,   155
     Give me one poor request.
HORATIO: What is't, my lord? We will.
HAMLET: Never make known what you have seen to-night.

---

123 **Illo, ho, ho** falconer's call to his hawk
140 **circumstance** details
152 **honest ghost** true ghost of his father rather than a demon

BOTH: My lord, we will not.

HAMLET: Nay, but swear't.   160

HORATIO: In faith,
    My lord, not I.

MARCELLUS: Nor I, my lord, in faith.

HAMLET: Upon my sword.

MARCELLUS: We have sworn, my lord, already.   165

HAMLET: Indeed, upon my sword, indeed.

GHOST: [*cries under the stage*] Swear.

HAMLET: Ha, ha, boy! say'st thou so? Art thou there, true-penny?*
    Come on. You hear this fellow in the cellarage:
    Consent to swear.   170

HORATIO: Propose the oath, my lord.

HAMLET: Never to speak of this that you have seen,
    Swear by my sword.

GHOST: [*beneath*] Swear.

HAMLET: Hic et ubique?* Then we'll shift our ground.   175
    Come hither, gentlemen,
    And lay your hands again upon my sword.
    Swear by my sword
    Never to speak of this that you have heard.

GHOST: [*beneath*] Swear, by his sword.   180

HAMLET: Well said, old mole! Canst work i' th' earth so fast?
    A worthy pioneer!* Once more remove, good friends.

HORATIO: O day and night, but this is wondrous strange!

HAMLET: And therefore as a stranger give it welcome.
    There are more things in heaven and earth, Horatio,   185
    Than are dreamt of in your philosophy.
    But come.
    Here, as before, never, so help you mercy,
    How strange or odd soe'er I bear myself—
    As I perchance hereafter shall think meet   190
    To put an antic disposition* on—
    That you, at such times, seeing me, never shall,
    With arms encumb'red* thus, or this head-shake,
    Or by pronouncing of some doubtful phrase,
    As 'Well, well, we know' or 'We could, an if we would'   195
    Or, 'If we list to speak' or 'There be, an if they might'
    Or such ambiguous giving out, to note
    That you know aught of me—this do swear,
    So grace and mercy at your most need help you.

GHOST: [*beneath*] Swear.   200

HAMLET: Rest, rest, perturbed spirit! So, gentlemen,
    With all my love I do commend me* to you;

---

[168] **true-penny** honest fellow
[175] **Hic et ubique** here and everywhere
[182] **pioneer** miner
[191] **antic disposition** strange behavior
[193] **encumb'red** folded
[202] **commend me** entrust myself

And what so poor a man as Hamlet is
May do t'express his love and friending to you,
God willing, shall not lack. Let us go in together;   205
And still your fingers on your lips, I pray.
The time is out of joint. O cursed spite,
That ever I was born to set it right!
Nay, come, let's go together.   *[Exeunt.]*

ACT II

SCENE I———*Elsinore. The house of* POLONIUS.

[*Enter* POLONIUS *and* REYNALDO.]

POLONIUS: Give him this money and these notes, Reynaldo.
REYNALDO: I will, my lord.
POLONIUS: You shall do marvellous wisely, good Reynaldo,
    Before you visit him, to make inquire
    Of his behaviour.   5
REYNALDO: My lord, I did intend it.
POLONIUS: Marry, well said; very well said. Look you, sir,
    Enquire me first what Danskers* are in Paris;
    And how, and who, what means, and where they keep,*
    What company, at what expense; and finding   10
    By this encompassment and drift of question
    That they do know my son, come you more nearer
    Than your particular demands will touch it.
    Take you, as 'twere, some distant knowledge of him;
    As thus: 'I know his father and his friends,   15
    And in part him.' Do you mark this, Reynaldo?
REYNALDO: Ay, very well, my lord.
POLONIUS: 'And in part him—but' you may say 'not well;
    But if't be he I mean, he's very wild;
    Addicted so and so'; and there put on him   20
    What forgeries you please; marry, none so rank
    As may dishonour him; take heed of that;
    But, sir, such wanton, wild, and usual slips
    As are companions noted and most known
    To youth and liberty.   25
REYNALDO: As gaming, my lord.
POLONIUS: Ay, or drinking, fencing, swearing, quarrelling.
    Drabbing*—you may go so far.

II,i,8 **Danskers** Danes
9 **keep** dwell
28 **Drabbing** womanizing

REYNALDO: My lord, that would dishonour him.

POLONIUS: Faith, no; as you may season it in the charge.   30
    You must not put another scandal on him,
    That he is open to incontinency;
    That's not my meaning. But breathe his faults so quaintly*
    That they may seem the taints of liberty;
    The flash and outbreak of a fiery mind,   35
    A savageness in unreclaimed blood,
    Of general assault.*

REYNALDO: But, my good lord—

POLONIUS: Wherefore should you do this?

REYNALDO: Ay, my lord,   40
    I would know that.

POLONIUS: Marry, sir, here's my drift,
    And I believe it is a fetch of warrant:*
    You laying these slight sullies on my son,
    As 'twere a thing a little soil'd wi' th' working,   45
    Mark you,
    Your party in converse, him you would sound,
    Having ever seen in the prenominate crimes*
    The youth you breathe of guilty, be assur'd
    He closes with you in this consequence—*   50
    'Good sir' or so, or 'friend' or 'gentleman'
    According to the phrase or the addition*
    Of man and country.

REYNALDO: Very good, my lord.

POLONIUS: And then, sir, does 'a* this—'a does—What was   55
    I about to say? By the mass, I was about to say something;
    Where did I leave?

REYNALDO: At 'closes in the consequence,' at 'friend or so' and 'gentleman.'

POLONIUS: At 'closes in the consequence'—ay, marry,
    He closes thus: 'I know the gentleman;   60
    I saw him yesterday, or t'other day,
    Or then, or then; with such, or such; and, as you say,
    There was 'a gaming; there o'ertook in's rouse;
    There falling out at tennis'; or perchance
    'I saw him enter such a house of sale,'   65
    Videlicet,* a brothel, or so forth. See you now
    Your bait of falsehood take this carp of truth;
    And thus do we of wisdom and of reach,
    With windlasses and with assays of bias,*

---

[33] **quaintly** ingeniously
[37] **Of general assault** common to all men
[43] **fetch of warrant** justifiable device
[48] **Having . . . crimes** if he has ever seen the aforementioned crimes
[50] **He closes . . . this consequence** agrees with you
[52] **addition** title
[55] **'a** he
[66] **Videlicet** namely
[69] **windlasses . . . bias** indirect means

By indirections find directions out;   70
So, by my former lecture and advice,
Shall you my son. You have me, have you not?
REYNALDO: My lord, I have.
POLONIUS: God buy ye; fare ye well.
REYNALDO: Good my lord!   75
POLONIUS: Observe his inclination in yourself.*
REYNALDO: I shall, my lord.
POLONIUS: And let him ply his music.
REYNALDO: Well, my lord.
POLONIUS: Farewell!   [*Exit* REYNALDO.]   80

    [*Enter* OPHELIA.]

How now, Ophelia! What's the matter?
OPHELIA: O my lord, my lord, I have been so affrighted!
POLONIUS: With what, i' th' name of God?
OPHELIA: My lord, as I was sewing in my closet,*
    Lord Hamlet, with his doublet all unbrac'd,*   85
    No hat upon his head, his stockings fouled,
    Ungart'red and down-gyved* to his ankle;
    Pale as his shirt, his knees knocking each other,
    And with a look so piteous in purport
    As if he had been loosed out of hell   90
    To speak of horrors—he comes before me.
POLONIUS: Mad for thy love?
OPHELIA: My lord, I do not know,
    But truly I do fear it.
POLONIUS: What said he?   95
OPHELIA: He took me by the wrist, and held me hard;
    Then goes he to the length of all his arm,
    And, with his other hand thus o'er his brow,
    He falls to such a perusal of my face
    As 'a would draw it. Long stay'd he so.   100
    At last, a little shaking of mine arm,
    And thrice his head thus waving up and down,
    He rais'd a sigh so piteous and profound
    As it did seem to shatter all his bulk
    And end his being. That done, he lets me go,   105
    And, with his head over his shoulder turn'd,
    He seem'd to find his way without his eyes;
    For out adoors he went without their help
    And to the last bended their light on me.
POLONIUS: Come, go with me. I will go seek the King.   110
    This is the very ecstasy* of love,
    Whose violent property fordoes* itself,

---

[76] **in yourself** for yourself
[84] **closet** private room
[85] **doublet all unbrac'd** jacket entirely unlaced/open
[87] **down-gyved** hanging down
[111] **ecstasy** madness
[112] **property fordoes** quality destroys

And leads the will to desperate undertakings
As oft as any passion under heaven
That does afflict our natures. I am sorry— 115
What, have you given him any hard words of late?
OPHELIA: No, my good lord; but, as you did command,
I did repel his letters, and denied
His access to me.
POLONIUS: That hath made him mad. 120
I am sorry that with better heed and judgment
I had not quoted* him. I fear'd he did but trifle,
And meant to wreck thee; but beshrew my jealousy!*
By heaven, it is as proper to our age
To cast beyond ourselves in our opinions 125
As it is common for the younger sort
To lack discretion. Come, go we to the King.
This must be known; which, being kept close, might move
More grief to hide than hate to utter love.*
Come. [*Exeunt.*] 130

SCENE II————*Elsinore. The Castle.*

[*Flourish. Enter* KING, QUEEN, ROSENCRANTZ, GUILDENSTERN, *and attendants.*]

KING: Welcome, dear Rosencrantz and Guildenstern!
Moreover that we much did long to see you,
The need we have to use you did provoke
Our hasty sending. Something have you heard
Of Hamlet's transformation; so I call it, 5
Sith* nor th' exterior nor the inward man
Resembles that it was. What it should be,
More than his father's death, that thus hath put him
So much from th' understanding of himself,
I cannot deem of. I entreat you both 10
That, being of so* young days brought up with him,
And sith so neighboured to his youth and haviour,
That you vouchsafe your rest* here in our court
Some little time; so by your companies
To draw him on to pleasures, and to gather, 15
So much as from occasion you may glean,
Whether aught to us unknown afflicts him thus
That, open'd,* lies within our remedy.
QUEEN: Good gentlemen, he hath much talk'd of you;

---

[122] **quoted** noted
[123] **beshrew my jealousy** curse on my suspicions
[127–129] **Come, go . . . utter love** telling the king may anger him, but not telling him might anger him more
[II,ii,6] **Sith** since
[11] **of so** from such
[13] **vouchsafe your rest** consent to remain
[18] **open'd** revealed

And sure I am two men there is not living   20
To whom he more adheres. If it will please you
To show us so much gentry* and good will
As to expend your time with us awhile
For the supply and profit of our hope,
Your visitation shall receive such thanks   25
As fits a king's remembrance.
ROSENCRANTZ: Both your Majesties
    Might, by the sovereign power you have of us,
    Put your dread pleasures more into command
    Than to entreaty.   30
GUILDENSTERN: But we both obey,
    And here give up ourselves, in the full bent,*
    To lay our service freely at your feet,
    To be commanded.
KING: Thanks, Rosencrantz and gentle Guildenstern.   35
QUEEN: Thanks, Guildenstern and gentle Rosencrantz.
    And I beseech you instantly to visit
    My too much changed son. Go, some of you,
    And bring these gentlemen where Hamlet is.
GUILDENSTERN: Heavens make our presence and our practices   40
    Pleasant and helpful to him!
QUEEN: Aye amen! [*Exeunt* ROSENCRANTZ, GUILDENSTERN, *and some attendants.*]

    [*Enter* POLONIUS.]

POLONIUS: Th' ambassadors from Norway, my good lord,
    Are joyfully return'd.
KING: Thou still hast been the father of good news.   45
POLONIUS: Have I, my lord? I assure you, my good liege,
    I hold my duty, as I hold my soul,
    Both to my God and to my gracious King;
    And I do think—or else this brain of mine
    Hunts not the trail of policy so sure   50
    As it hath us'd to do—that I have found
    The very cause of Hamlet's lunacy.
KING: O, speak of that; that do I long to hear.
POLONIUS: Give first admittance to th' ambassadors;
    My news shall be the fruit to that great feast.   55
KING: Thyself do grace to them, and bring them in.

    [*Exit* POLONIUS.]

He tells me, my dear Gertrude, he hath found
The head and source of all your son's distemper.
QUEEN: I doubt it is no other but the main,
    His father's death and our o'erhasty marriage.   60
KING: Well, we shall sift him.

---

²² **gentry** courtesy
³² **in the full bent** entirely

[*Reenter* POLONIUS, *with* VOLTEMAND *and* CORNELIUS.]

    Welcome, my good friends!
    Say, Voltemand, what from our brother Norway?
VOLTEMAND: Most fair return of greetings and desires.
    Upon our first,* he sent out to suppress   65
    His nephew's levies; which to him appear'd
    To be a preparation 'gainst the Polack;
    But, better look'd into, he truly found
    It was against your Highness. Whereat griev'd,
    That so his sickness, age, and impotence,   70
    Was falsely borne in hand,* sends out arrests
    On Fortinbras; which he, in brief, obeys;
    Receives rebuke from Norway; and, in fine,
    Makes vow before his uncle never more
    To give th' assay of arms against your Majesty.   75
    Whereon old Norway, overcome with joy,
    Gives him threescore thousand crowns in annual fee,
    And his commission to employ those soldiers,
    So levied as before, against the Polack;
    With an entreaty, herein further shown, [*gives a paper*]   80
    That it might please you to give quiet pass
    Through your dominions for this enterprise,
    On such regards of safety and allowance
    As therein are set down.
KING: It likes us well;   85
    And at our more considered time we'll read,
    Answer, and think upon this business.
    Meantime we thank you for your well-took labour.
    Go to your rest; at night we'll feast together.
    Most welcome home!   [*Exeunt* AMBASSADORS *and attendants.*]   90
POLONIUS: This business is well ended.
    My liege, and madam, to expostulate
    What majesty should be, what duty is,
    Why day is day, night night, and time is time,
    Were nothing, but to waste night, day, and time.   95
    Therefore, since brevity is the soul of wit,
    And tediousness the limbs and outward flourishes,
    I will be brief. Your noble son is mad.
    Mad call I it; for, to define true madness,
    What is't but to be nothing else but mad?   100
    But let that go.
QUEEN: More matter with less art.
POLONIUS: Madam, I swear I use no art at all.
    That he's mad, 'tis true: 'Tis true 'is pity;
    And pity 'is 'tis true. A foolish figure!   105
    But farewell it, for I will use no art.
    Mad let us grant him, then; and now remains

---

[65] **first** first meeting
[71] **falsely borne in hand** deceived

That we find out the cause of this effect;
Or rather say the cause of this defect,
For this effect defective comes by cause. 110
Thus it remains, and the remainder thus.
Perpend.*
I have a daughter—have while she is mine—
Who in her duty and obedience, mark,
Hath given me this. Now gather, and surmise. [*reads*] 115

'*To the celestial, and my soul's idol, the most beautified Ophelia.*' That's an ill
phrase, a vile phrase; 'beautified' is a vile phrase. But you shall hear.
Thus: [*reads*]
'*In her excellent white bosom, these, &c.*'

QUEEN: Came this from Hamlet to her? 120
POLONIUS: Good madam, stay awhile; I will be faithful. [*reads*]
'*Doubt thou the stars are fire;*
Doubt that the sun doth move;
Doubt* truth to be a liar;
But never doubt I love. 125
'*O dear Ophelia, I am ill at these numbers.* I have not art to reckon my groans;*
but that I love thee best, O most best, believe it. Adieu.
'*Thine evermore, most dear lady, whilst*
this machine is to him,
Hamlet.' 130

This, in obedience, hath my daughter shown me;
And more above,* hath his solicitings,
As they fell out by time, by means, and place,
All given to mine ear.
KING: But how hath she 135
Receiv'd his love?
POLONIUS: What do you think of me?
KING: As of a man faithful and honourable.
POLONIUS: I would fain prove so. But what might you think,
When I had seen this hot love on the wing, 140
As I perceiv'd it, I must tell you that,
Before my daughter told me—what might you,
Or my dear Majesty your Queen here think,
If I had play'd the desk or table-book;*
Or given my heart a winking,* mute and dumb; 145
Or look'd upon this love with idle sight—
What might you think? No, I went round to work,
And my young mistress thus I did bespeak:
'Lord Hamlet is a prince out of thy star;
This must not be.' And then I prescripts gave her, 150

---

[112] **Perpend** consider carefully
[124] **Doubt** suspect
[126] **ill at these numbers** unskilled at versifying
[132] **above** besides
[144] **play'd the desk or table-book** been a passive receiver of secrets
[145] **winking** closed my eyes

That she should lock herself from his resort,
Admit no messengers, receive no tokens.
Which done, she took the fruits of my advice;
And he repelled, a short tale to make,
Fell into a sadness, then into a fast, 155
Thence to a watch,* thence into a weakness,
Thence to a lightness,* and, by this declension,
Into the madness wherein now he raves
And all we mourn for.
KING: Do you think 'tis this? 160
QUEEN: It may be, very like.
POLONIUS: Hath there been such a time—I would fain know that—
    That I have positively said ''tis so,'
    When it prov'd otherwise?
KING: Not that I know. 165
POLONIUS: Take this from this,* if this be otherwise.
    If circumstances lead me, I will find
    Where truth is hid, though it were hid indeed
    Within the centre.*
KING: How may we try it further? 170
POLONIUS: You may know sometimes he walks four hours together,
    Here in the lobby.
QUEEN: So he does, indeed.
POLONIUS: At such a time I'll loose my daughter to him.
    Be you and I behind an arras* then; 175
    Mark the encounter: if he love her not,
    And be not from his reason fall'n thereon,
    Let me be no assistant for a state,
    But keep a farm and carters.
KING: We will try it. 180

[*Enter* HAMLET, *reading on a book.*]

QUEEN: But look where sadly the poor wretch comes reading.
POLONIUS: Away, I do beseech you, both away:
    I'll board him presently.* O, give me leave.

[*Exeunt* KING *and* QUEEN.]

How does my good Lord Hamlet?
HAMLET: Well, God-a-mercy. 185
POLONIUS: Do you know me, my lord?
HAMLET: Excellent well; you are a fishmonger.*
POLONIUS: Not I, my lord.
HAMLET: Then I would you were so honest a man.

---

[156] **watch** wakefulness
[157] **lightness** mental derangement
[166] **this from this** (indicating by pointing) head from body
[169] **centre** center of the earth
[175] **arras** tapestry
[183] **board him presently** accost him at once
[187] **fishmonger** dealer in fish (slang for procurer)

POLONIUS: Honest, my lord! 190

HAMLET: Ay, sir; to be honest, as this world goes, is to be one man pick'd out of ten thousand.

POLONIUS: That's very true, my lord.

HAMLET: For if the sun breed maggots in a dead dog, being a good kissing carrion—Have you a daughter? 195

POLONIUS: I have, my lord.

HAMLET: Let her not walk i' th' sun. Conception* is a blessing. But as your daughter may conceive—friend, look to't.

POLONIUS: How say you by that? [aside] Still harping on my daughter. Yet he knew me not at first; 'a said I was a fishmonger. 'A is far gone, far gone. And truly in 200 my youth I suff'red much extremity for love. Very near this. I'll speak to him again.—What do you read, my lord?

HAMLET: Words, words, words.

POLONIUS: What is the matter, my lord?

HAMLET: Between who? 205

POLONIUS: I mean, the matter that you read, my lord.

HAMLET: Slanders, sir; for the satirical rogue says here that old men have grey beards; that their faces are wrinkled; their eyes purging thick amber and plum-tree gum; and that they have a plentiful lack of wit, together with most weak hams—all which, sir, though I most powerfully and potently believe, 210 yet I hold it not honesty to have it thus set down; for you yourself, sir, shall grow old as I am, if, like a crab, you could go backward.

POLONIUS: [aside] Though this be madness, yet there is method in't.—Will you walk out of the air, my lord?

HAMLET: Into my grave? 215

POLONIUS: Indeed, that's out of the air. [aside] How pregnant sometimes his replies are! a happiness that often madness hits on, which reason and sanity could not so prosperously be delivered of. I will leave him, and suddenly contrive the means of meeting between him and my daughter.—My lord. I will take my leave of you. 220

HAMLET: You cannot, sir, take from me anything that I will more willingly part withal—except my life, except my life, except my life.

[Enter ROSENCRANTZ and GUILDENSTERN.]

POLONIUS: Fare you well, my lord.

HAMLET: These tedious old fools!

POLONIUS: You go to seek the Lord Hamlet; there he is. 225

ROSENCRANTZ: [to POLONIUS] God save you, sir!

[Exit POLONIUS.]

GUILDENSTERN: My honour'd lord!

ROSENCRANTZ: My most dear lord!

HAMLET: My excellent good friends! How dost thou, Guildenstern? Ah, Rosencrantz! Good lads, how do you both? 230

ROSENCRANTZ: As the indifferent* children of the earth.

---

197 **Conception** understanding; becoming pregnant
231 **indifferent** ordinary

GUILDENSTERN: Happy in that we are not over-happy;
   On fortune's cap we are not the very button.
HAMLET: Nor the soles of her shoe?
ROSENCRANTZ: Neither, my lord.   235
HAMLET: Then you live about her waist, or in the middle of her favours?
GUILDENSTERN: Faith, her privates we.
HAMLET: In the secret parts of Fortune? O, most true; she is a strumpet. What
   news?
ROSENCRANTZ: None, my lord, but that the world's grown honest.   240
HAMLET: Then is doomsday near. But your news is not true. Let me question more
   in particular. What have you, my good friends, deserved at the hands of
   Fortune, that she sends you to prison hither?
GUILDENSTERN: Prison, my lord!
HAMLET: Denmark's a prison.   245
ROSENCRANTZ: Then is the world one.
HAMLET: A goodly one; in which there are many confines, wards, and dungeons,
   Denmark being one o' th' worst.
ROSENCRANTZ: We think not so, my lord.
HAMLET: Why, then, 'tis none to you; for there is nothing either good or bad, but   250
   thinking makes it so. To me it is a prison.
ROSENCRANTZ: Why, then your ambition makes it one; 'tis too narrow for your
   mind.
HAMLET: O God, I could be bounded in a nutshell and count myself a king of
   infinite space, were it not that I have bad dreams.   255
GUILDENSTERN: Which dreams indeed are ambition; for the very substance of the
   ambitious is merely the shadow of a dream.
HAMLET: A dream itself is but a shadow.
ROSENCRANTZ: Truly, and I hold ambition of so airy and light a quality that it is
   but a shadow's shadow.   260
HAMLET: Then are our beggars bodies, and our monarchs and oustretch'd heroes
   the beggars' shadows. Shall we to th' court? for, by my fay,* I cannot reason.
BOTH: We'll wait upon you.
HAMLET: No such matter. I will not sort you with the rest of my servants; for, to
   speak to you like an honest man, I am most dreadfully attended. But, in the   265
   beaten way of friendship, what make you at Elsinore?
ROSENCRANTZ: To visit you, my lord; no other occasion.
HAMLET: Beggar that I am, I am even poor in thanks; but I thank you; and sure,
   dear friends, my thanks are too dear a half-penny.* Were you not sent for?
   Is it your own inclining? It is a free visitation? Come, come, deal justly with   270
   me. Come, come; nay, speak.
GUILDENSTERN: What should we say, my lord?
HAMLET: Why, any thing. But to th' purpose: you were sent for; and there is a
   kind of confession in your looks, which your modesties have not craft
   enough to colour; I know the good King and Queen have sent for you.   275
ROSENCRANTZ: To what end, my lord?

---

[262] **fay** faith
[269] **too dear a half-penny** not worth a half-penny

HAMLET: That you must teach me. But let me conjure you by the rights of our
　　fellowship, by the consonancy of our youth, by the obligation of our ever-
　　preserved love, and by what more dear a better proposer can charge you
　　withal, be even and direct with me, whether you were sent for or no?　　　280
ROSENCRANTZ: [*aside to* GUILDENSTERN] What say you?
HAMLET: [*aside*] Nay, then, I have an eye of you.—If you love me, hold not off.
GUILDENSTERN: My lord, we were sent for.
HAMLET: I will tell you why; so shall my anticipation prevent your discovery,*
　　and your secrecy to the King and Queen moult no feather. I have of late—　285
　　but wherefore I know not—lost all my mirth, forgone all custom of exer-
　　cises; and indeed it goes so heavily with my disposition that this goodly
　　frame, the earth, seems to me a sterile promontory; this most excellent
　　canopy the air, look you, this brave o'er-hanging firmament, this majestical
　　roof fretted* with golden fire—why, it appeareth no other thing to me than a　290
　　foul and pestilent congregation of vapours. What a piece of work is man!
　　How noble in reason! how infinite in faculties! in form and moving, how
　　express* and admirable! in action, how like an angel! in apprehension, how
　　like a god! the beauty of the world! the paragon of animals! And yet, to me,
　　what is this quintessence of dust? Man delights not me—no, nor woman neither,　295
　　though by your smiling you seem to say so.
ROSENCRANTZ: My lord, there was no such stuff in my thoughts.
HAMLET: Why did ye laugh, then, when I said 'Man delights not me'?
ROSENCRANTZ: To think, my lord, if you delight not in man, what lenten enter-
　　tainment the players shall receive from you. We coted* them on the way;　300
　　and hither are they coming to offer you service.
HAMLET: He that plays the king shall be welcome—his Majesty shall have tri-
　　bute on me; the adventurous knight shall use his foil and target;* the lover
　　shall not sigh gratis; the humorous man shall end his part in peace; the
　　clown shall make those laugh whose lungs are tickle o' th' sere;* and the lady　305
　　shall say her mind freely, or the blank verse shall halt* for't. What players
　　are they?
ROSENCRANTZ: Even those you were wont to take such delight in—the tragedians
　　of the city.
HAMLET: How chances it they travel? Their residence, both in reputation and profit,　310
　　was better both ways.
ROSENCRANTZ: I think their inhibition* comes by the means of the late innovation.*
HAMLET: Do they hold the same estimation they did when I was in the city? Are
　　they so followed?
ROSENCRANTZ: No, indeed, are they not.　　　315
HAMLET: How comes it? Do they grow rusty?

---

[284] **prevent your discovery** forestall your disclosure
[290] **fretted** adorned
[293] **express** exact
[300] **coted** overtook
[303] **target** shield
[305] **tickle o' th' sere** on a hair trigger
[306] **halt** limp
[312] **inhibition** hindrance
[312] **innovation** probably a reference to the boys' theatre companies that were at this time offering serious competition to the adult companies

ROSENCRANTZ: Nay, their endeavour keeps in the wonted pace; but there is, sir, an eyrie* of children, little eyases that cry out on the top of question,* and are most tyrannically clapp'd* for't. These are now the fashion, and so berattle the common stages*—so they call them—that many wearing rapiers are afraid of goose quills* and dare scarce come thither.

HAMLET: What, are they children? Who maintains 'em? How are they escoted?* Will they pursue the quality* no longer than they can sing? Will they not say afterwards, if they should grow themselves to common players—as it is most like, if their means are no better—their writers do them wrong to make them exclaim against their own succession?*

ROSENCRANTZ: Faith, there has been much to-do on both sides; and the nation holds it no sin to tarre* them to controversy. There was for a while no money bid for argument,* unless the poet and the player went to cuffs in the question.

HAMLET: Is't possible?

GUILDENSTERN: O, there has been much throwing about of brains.

HAMLET: Do the boys carry it away?

ROSENCRANTZ: Ay, that they do, my lord—Hercules and his load,* too.

HAMLET: It is not very strange; for my uncle is King of Denmark, and those that would make mows at him while my father lived give twenty, forty, fifty, a hundred ducats apiece for his picture in little. 'Sblood, there is something in this more than natural, if philosophy could find it out.

[a flourish]

GUILDENSTERN: There are the players.

HAMLET: Gentlemen, you are welcome to Elsinore. Your hands, come then; th'appurtenance of welcome is fashion and ceremony. Let me comply* with you in this garb;* lest my extent* to the players, which, I tell you, must show fairly outwards, should more appear like entertainments than yours. You are welcome. But my uncle-father and aunt-mother are deceived.

GUILDENSTERN: In what, my dear lord?

HAMLET: I am but mad north-north-west; when the wind is southerly I know a hawk from a handsaw.

[Reenter POLONIUS.]

POLONIUS: Well be with you, gentlemen!

HAMLET: Hark you, Guildenstern, and you, too—at each ear a hearer: that great baby you see there is not yet out of his swaddling clouts.

---

318 **eyrie** nest
318 **little eyases . . . question** young hawks that cry shrilly above others in a debate
319 **tyrannically clapp'd** violently applauded
320 **berattle the common stages** put down the public theatres
321 **goose quills** pens (of those who satirize the public theatres and their audiences)
322 **escoted** financially supported
323 **quality** profession of acting
326 **succession** future profession
328 **tarre** incite
329 **argument** for a playscript
334 **Hercules and his load** reference to the Globe Theatre, whose sign showed Hercules carrying the globe on his shoulders
341 **comply** be courteous
342 **garb** outward show
342 **extent** behavior

320
325
330
335
340
345

ROSENCRANTZ: Happily* he is the second time come to them; for they say an old   350
    man is twice a child.

HAMLET: I will prophesy he comes to tell me of the players; mark it. You say
    right, sir: a Monday morning; 'twas then indeed.

POLONIUS: My lord, I have news to tell you.   355

HAMLET: My lord, I have news to tell you. When Roscius was an actor in
    Rome—

POLONIUS: The actors are come hither, my lord.

HAMLET: Buzz, buzz!

POLONIUS: Upon my honour—   360

HAMLET: They came each actor on his ass—

POLONIUS: The best actors in the world, either for tragedy, comedy, history,
    pastoral, pastoral-comical, historical-pastoral, tragical-historical, tragical-
    comical-historical-pastoral, scene individable, or poem unlimited. Seneca
    cannot be too heavy nor Plautus too light. For the law of writ and the liberty,*   365
    these are the only men.

HAMLET: O Jephthah, judge of Israel, what a treasure hadst thou!

POLONIUS: What a treasure had he, my lord?

HAMLET: Why—
> 'One fair daughter, and no more,   370
> The which he loved passing well.'

POLONIUS: [aside] Still on my daughter.

HAMLET: Am I not i' th' right, old Jephthah?

POLONIUS: If you call me Jephthah, my lord, I have a daughter that I love pass-
    ing well.   375

HAMLET: Nay, that follows not.

POLONIUS: What follows then, my lord?

HAMLET: Why—
> 'As by lot, God wot'

and then, you know,   380
> 'It came to pass, as most like it was.'

The first row of the pious chanson* will show you more; for look where my
abridgement* comes.

    [Enter the PLAYERS.]

You are welcome, masters; welcome all.—I am glad to see thee well.—
Welcome, good friends.—O, my old friend! Why thy face is valanc'd* since   385
I saw thee last; com'st thou to beard me in Denmark?—What, my young
lady* and mistress! By'r lady, your ladyship is nearer to heaven than when I
saw you last by the altitude of a chopine.* Pray God, your voice, like a piece
of uncurrent gold, be not crack'd within the ring.*—Masters, you are all

---

350 **Happily** perhaps
365 **law of writ and the liberty** sticking to the text and improvising
382 **first row of the pious chanson** first stanza of a religious song
383 **abridgement** interruption
385 **valanc'd** furnished with a beard
386–87 **young lady** boy who played female roles
388 **chopine** thick-soled shoe
389 **crack'd within the ring** comparing a boy's breaking voice with a cracked coin (which it was illegal to use)

welcome. We'll e'en to't like French falconers, fly at anything we see. We'll   390
have a speech straight. Come, give us a taste of your quality; come, a passionate speech.

FIRST PLAYER: What speech, my good lord?

HAMLET: I heard thee speak me a speech once, but it was never acted; or, if it was,
not above once; for the play, I remember, pleas'd not the million; 'twas   395
caviary to the general.* But it was—as I received it, and others whose judgments in such matters cried in the top of mine*—an excellent play, well
digested in the scenes, set down with as much modesty as cunning.* I
remember one said there were no sallets* in the lines to make the matter
savoury, nor no matter in the phrase that might indict the author of affec-   400
tation; but call'd it an honest method, as wholesome as sweet, and by very
much more handsome than fine.* One speech in it I chiefly lov'd; 'twas
Aeneas' tale to Dido; and thereabout of it especially where he speaks of
Priam's slaughter. If it live in your memory, begin at this line—let me see:
    *'The rugged Pyrrhus, like th' Hyrcanian beast,'**   405
'Tis not so; it begins with Pyrrhus.
    'The rugged Pyrrhus, he whose sable arms,*
    Black as his purpose, did the night resemble
    *When he lay couched in the ominous horse,**
    Hath now this dread and black complexion smear'd   410
    With heraldry more dismal; head to foot
    *Now is he total gules, horridly trick'd**
    With blood of fathers, mothers, daughters, sons,
    Bak'd and impasted with the parching streets,*
    That lend a tyrannous and damned light   415
    To their lord's murder. Roasted in wrath and fire,
    And thus o'er-sized with coagulate gore,*
    With eyes like carbuncles, the hellish Pyrrhus
    Old grandsire Priam seeks.'
So proceed you.   420

POLONIUS: Fore God, my lord, well spoken, with good accent and good discretion.

FIRST PLAYER: '*Anon he finds him*
    Striking too short at Greeks; his antique sword,
    Rebellious to his arm, lies where it falls,
    Repugnant to command. Unequal match'd,   425
    Pyrrhus at Priam drives, in rage strikes wide;
    But with the whiff and wind of his fell sword

---

[396] **caviary to the general** too rich for the common audience
[397] **top of mine** agreed with or exceeded mine
[398] **modesty as cunning** restraint as cleverness
[399] **sallets** salads (spicy jests)
[402] **more handsome than fine** well proportioned rather than ornamented
[405] **Hyrcanian beast** tiger
[407] **sable** black
[409] **ominous horse** the wooden horse used in taking Troy
[412] **total gules, horridly trick'd** entirely red, horridly adorned
[414] **impasted** encrusted
[417] **o'er-sized** smeared over

Th' unnerved father falls. Then senseless Ilium,*
Seeming to feel this blow, with flaming top
Stoops to his base,* and with a hideous crash   430
Takes prisoner Pyrrhus' ear. For, lo! his sword,
Which was declining on the milky head
Of reverend Priam, seem'd i' th' air to stick.
So, as a painted tyrant, Pyrrhus stood
And, like a neutral to his will and matter,   435
Did nothing.
But as we often see, against* some storm,
A silence in the heavens, the rack* stand still,
The bold winds speechless, and the orb below
As hush as death, anon the dreadful thunder   440
Doth rend the region; so, after Pyrrhus' pause,
A roused vengeance sets him new a-work;
And never did the Cyclops' hammers fall
On Mars' armour, forg'd for proof eterne,*
With less remorse than Pyrrhus' bleeding sword   445
Now falls on Priam.
Out, out, thou strumpet, Fortune! All you gods,
In general synod,* take away her power;
Break all the spokes and fellies* from her wheel,
And bowl the round nave* down the hill of heaven,   450
As low as to the fiends.'

POLONIUS: This is too long.
HAMLET: It shall to the barber's, with your beard. Prithee say on. He's for a jig,
   or a tale of bawdry, or he sleeps. Say on; come to Hecuba.
FIRST PLAYER: 'But who, ah, who had seen the mobled* queen—'   455
HAMLET: 'The mobled queen'?
POLONIUS: That's good; 'mobled queen' is good.
FIRST PLAYER: '*Run barefoot up and down, threat'ning the flames*
   With bisson rheum,* a clout* upon that head
   Where late the diadem stood, and for a robe,   460
   About her lank and all o'er-teemed loins,*
   A blanket, in the alarm of fear caught up—
   Who this had seen, with tongue in venom steep'd,
   'Gainst Fortune's state would treason have pronounc'd.
   But if the gods themselves did see her then,   465

---

[428] **Ilium** Troy
[430] **Stoops to his base** collapses
[437] **against** before
[438] **rack** clouds
[444] **proof eterne** to last forever
[448] **synod** council
[449] **fellies** rims
[450] **nave** hub
[455] **mobled** muffled
[459] **bisson rheum** blinding tears
[459] **clout** rag
[461] **o'er-teemed loins** exhausted with childbearing

> *When she saw Pyrrhus make malicious sport*
> *In mincing with his sword her husband's limbs,*
> *The instant burst of clamour that she made—*
> *Unless things mortal move them not at all—*
> *Would have made milch* the burning eyes of heaven,*　　　　　470
> *And passion in the gods.'*

POLONIUS: Look whe'er* he has not turn'd his colour, and has tears in 's eyes.
　　Prithee no more.

HAMLET: 'Tis well; I'll have thee speak out the rest of this soon.—Good my lord,
　　will you see the players well bestowed? Do you hear: let them be well used;　　475
　　for they are the abstract and brief chronicles of the time; after your death
　　you were better have a bad epitaph than their ill report while you live.

POLONIUS: My lord, I will use them according to their desert.

HAMLET: God's bodkins, man, much better. Use every man after his desert, and
　　who shall 'scape whipping? Use them after your own honour and dignity; the　　480
　　less they deserve, the more merit is in your bounty. Take them in.

POLONIUS: Come, sirs.

HAMLET: Follow him, friends. We'll hear a play to-morrow. Dost thou hear me,
　　old friend; can you play 'The Murder of Gonzago'?

FIRST PLAYER: Ay, my lord.　　485

HAMLET: We'll ha't to-morrow night. You could, for a need, study a speech of
　　some dozen or sixteen lines which I would set down and insert in't, could
　　you not?

FIRST PLAYER: Ay, my lord.

HAMLET: Very well. Follow that lord; and look you mock him not. [*Exeunt*　　490
　　POLONIUS *and* PLAYERS.] My good friends, I'll leave you till night.
　　You are welcome to Elsinore.

ROSENCRANTZ: Good my lord!

[*Exeunt* ROSENCRANTZ *and* GUILDENSTERN.]

HAMLET: Ay, so God buy to you! Now I am alone.
> O, what a rogue and peasant slave am I!　　495
> Is it not monstrous that this player here,
> But in a fiction, in a dream of passion,
> Could force his soul so to his own conceit*
> That from her working all his visage wann'd;
> Tears in his eyes, distraction in's aspect,　　500
> A broken voice, and his whole function* suiting
> With forms* to his conceit? And all for nothing!
> For Hecuba!
> What's Hecuba to him or he to Hecuba,
> That he should weep for her? What would he do,　　505
> Had he the motive and the cue for passion
> That I have? He would drown the stage with tears,
> And cleave the general ear with horrid speech;

---

⁴⁷⁰ **milch** moist
⁴⁷² **whe'er** whether
⁴⁹⁸ **conceit** imagination
⁵⁰¹ **function** action
⁵⁰² **forms** bodily expressions

Make mad the guilty, and appal the free,*
Confound the ignorant, and amaze indeed   510
The very faculties of eyes and ears.
Yet I,
A dull and muddy-mettl'd* rascal, peak,
Like John-a-dreams,* unpregnant of* my cause,
And can say nothing; no, not for a king   515
Upon whose property and most dear life
A damn'd defeat was made. Am I a coward?
Who calls me villain, breaks my pate across,
Plucks off my beard and blows it in my face,
Tweaks me by the nose, gives me the lie i' th' throat   520
As deep as to the lungs? Who does me this?
Ha!
'Swounds, I should take it; for it cannot be
But I am pigeon-liver'd* and lack gall
To make oppression bitter, or ere this   525
I should 'a fatted all the region kites*
With this slave's offal. Bloody, bawdy villain!
Remorseless, treacherous, lecherous, kindless* villain!
O, vengeance!
Why, what an ass am I! This is most brave,   530
That I, the son of a dear father murder'd,
Prompted to my revenge by heaven and hell,
Must, like a whore, unpack my heart with words,
And fall a-cursing like a very drab,*
A scullion!* Fie upon't! foh!   535
About,* my brains. Hum—I have heard
That guilty creatures, sitting at a play,
Have by the very cunning of the scene
Been struck so to the soul that presently*
They have proclaim'd their malefactions;   540
For murder, though it have no tongue, will speak
With most miraculous organ. I'll have these players
Play something like the murder of my father
Before mine uncle. I'll observe his looks;
I'll tent* him to the quick. If 'a do blench,*   545
I know my course. The spirit that I have seen

---

509 **appal the free** terrify the guiltless
513 **muddy-mettl'd** weak spirited
513–14 **peak, Like John-a-dreams** mope like a dreamer
514 **unpregnant of** unmoved by
524 **pigeon-liver'd** a coward
526 **kites** scavenger birds
528 **kindless** unnatural
534 **drab** prostitute
535 **scullion** kitchen servant
536 **About** to work
539 **presently** immediately
545 **tent** probe
545 **blench** blanch

May be a devil; and the devil hath power
T'assume a pleasing shape; yea and perhaps
Out of my weakness and my melancholy,
As he is very potent with such spirits,   550
Abuses me to damn me. I'll have grounds
More relative* than this. The play's the thing
Wherein I'll catch the conscience of the King.   [*Exit.*]

ACT III

SCENE I————*Elsinore. The Castle.*

[*Enter* KING, QUEEN, POLONIUS, OPHELIA, ROSENCRANTZ, *and* GUILDENSTERN.]

KING: And can you by no drift of conference*
    Get from him why he puts on this confusion,
    Grating so harshly all his days of quiet
    With turbulent and dangerous lunacy?
ROSENCRANTZ: He does confess he feels himself distracted,   5
    But from what cause 'a will by no means speak.
GUILDENSTERN: Nor do we find him forward to be sounded;*
    But, with a crafty madness, keeps aloof
    When we would bring him on to some confession
    Of his true state.   10
QUEEN: Did he receive you well?
ROSENCRANTZ: Most like a gentleman.
GUILDENSTERN: But with much forcing of his disposition.*
ROSENCRANTZ: Niggard of question; but of our demands
    Most free in his reply.   15
QUEEN: Did you assay* him
    To any pastime?
ROSENCRANTZ: Madam, it so fell out that certain players
    We o'er-raught* on the way. Of these we told him;
    And there did seem in him a kind of joy   20
    To hear of it. They are here about the court,
    And, as I think, they have already order
    This night to play before him.
POLONIUS: 'Tis most true;

---

552 **relative** certain
III,i,1 **conference** conversation
7 **forward to be sounded** willing to be questioned
13 **forcing of his disposition** effort
16 **assay** tempt
19 **o'er-raught** overtook

And he beseech'd me to entreat your Majesties   25
To hear and see the matter.
KING: With all my heart; and it doth much content me
To hear him so inclin'd.
Good gentlemen, give him a further edge,
And drive his purpose into these delights.   30
ROSENCRANTZ: We shall, my lord.

    [*Exeunt* ROSENCRANTZ *and* GUILDENSTERN.]

KING: Sweet Gertrude, leave us, too;
For we have closely* sent for Hamlet hither,
That he, as 'twere by accident, may here
Affront* Ophelia.   35
Her father and myself—lawful espials*—
Will so bestow ourselves that, seeing unseen,
We may of their encounter frankly judge,
And gather by him, as he is behav'd,
If 't be th' affliction of his love or no   40
That thus he suffers for.
QUEEN: I shall obey you;
And for your part, Ophelia, I do wish
That your good beauties be the happy cause
Of Hamlet's wildness; so shall I hope your virtues   45
Will bring him to his wonted way again,
To both your honours.
OPHELIA: Madam, I wish it may.   [*Exit* QUEEN.]
POLONIUS: Ophelia, walk you here.—Gracious, so please you,
We will bestow ourselves.—Read on this book;   50
That show of such an exercise may colour*
Your loneliness.—We are oft to blame in this:
'Tis too much prov'd, that with devotion's visage
And pious action we do sugar o'er
The devil himself.   55
KING: [aside] O, 'tis too true!
How smart a lash that speech doth give my conscience!
The harlot's cheek, beautied with plast'ring art,
Is not more ugly to the thing that helps it
Than is my deed to my most painted word.   60
O heavy burden!
POLONIUS: I hear him coming; let's withdraw, my lord.

    [*Exeunt* KING *and* POLONIUS.]

    [*Enter* HAMLET.]

---

[33] **closely** secretly
[35] **Affront** meet face to face
[36] **espials** observers
[51] **colour** give an excuse for

HAMLET: To be, or not to be—that is the question;
    Whether 'tis nobler in the mind to suffer
    The slings and arrows of outrageous fortune,   65
    Or to take arms against a sea of troubles,
    And by opposing end them? To die, to sleep—
    No more; and by a sleep to say we end
    The heart-ache and the thousand natural shocks
    That flesh is heir to. 'tis a consummation   70
    Devoutly to be wish'd. To die, to sleep;
    To sleep, perchance to dream. Ay, there's the rub;*
    For in that sleep of death what dreams may come,
    When we have shuffled off this mortal coil,*
    Must give us pause. There's the respect*   75
    That makes calamity of so long life;
    For who would bear the whips and scorns of time,
    Th' oppressor's wrong, the proud man's contumely,
    The pangs of despis'd love, the law's delay,
    The insolence of office, and the spurns   80
    That patient merit of th' unworthy takes,
    When he himself might his quietus* make
    With a bare bodkin?* Who would these fardels* bear,
    To grunt and sweat under a weary life,
    But that the dread of something after death—   85
    The undiscover'd country, from whose bourn*
    No traveller returns—puzzles the will,
    And makes us rather bear those ills we have
    Than fly to others that we know not of?
    Thus conscience does make cowards of us all;   90
    And thus the native hue of resolution
    Is sicklied o'er with the pale cast* of thought,
    And enterprises of great pitch and moment,
    With this regard, their currents turn awry
    And lose the name of action.—Soft you now!   95
    The fair Ophelia.—Nymph, in thy orisons*
    Be all my sins rememb'red.
OPHELIA: Good my lord,
    How does your honour for this many a day?
HAMLET: I humbly thank you; well, well, well.
OPHELIA: My lord, I have remembrance of yours   100
    That I have longed to re-deliver.
    I pray you now receive them.

---

72 **rub** impediment
74 **shuffled off this mortal coil** separated body from soul
75 **respect** consideration
82 **quietus** end
83 **bodkin** dagger
83 **fardels** burdens
86 **bourn** region
92 **cast** color
96 **orisons** prayers

HAMLET: No, not I;
    I never gave you aught.   105

OPHELIA: My honour'd lord, you know right well you did,
    And with them words of so sweet breath compos'd
    As made the things more rich; their perfume lost,
    Take these again; for to the noble mind
    Rich gifts wax poor when givers prove unkind.   110
    There, my lord.

HAMLET: Ha, Ha! Are you honest?*

OPHELIA: My lord?

HAMLET: Are you fair?

OPHELIA: What means your lordship?   115

HAMLET: That if you be honest and fair, your honesty should admit no discourse
    to your beauty.

OPHELIA: Could beauty, my lord, have better commerce than with honesty?

HAMLET: Ay, truly; for the power of beauty will sooner transform honesty from
    what it is to a bawd* than the force of honesty can translate beauty into his   120
    likeness. This was sometime a paradox, but now the time gives it proof. I
    did love you once.

OPHELIA: Indeed, my lord, you made me believe so.

HAMLET: You should not have believ'd me; for virtue cannot so inoculate our old
    stock but we shall relish of it.* I loved you not.   125

OPHELIA: I was the more deceived.

HAMLET: Get thee to a nunnery. Why wouldst thou be a breeder of sinners? I am
    myself indifferent honest,* but yet I could accuse me of such things that it
    were better my mother had not borne me: I am very proud, revengeful, ambi-
    tious; with more offences at my beck than I have thoughts to put them in,   130
    imagination to give them shape, or time to act them in. What should such
    fellows as I do crawling between earth and heaven? We are arrant knaves, all;
    believe none of us. Go thy ways to a nunnery. Where's your father?

OPHELIA: At home, my lord.

HAMLET: Let the doors be shut upon him, that he may play the fool nowhere but   135
    in's own house. Farewell.

OPHELIA: O, help him, you sweet heavens!

HAMLET: If thou dost marry, I'll give thee this plague for thy dowry: be thou as
    chaste as ice, as pure as snow, thou shalt not escape calumny. Get thee to a
    nunnery, go, farewell. Or, if thou wilt needs marry, marry a fool; for wise men   140
    know well enough what monsters* you make of them. To a nunnery go;
    and quickly, too. Farewell.

OPHELIA: O heavenly powers, restore him!

HAMLET: I have heard of your paintings, too, well enough; God hath given you
    one face, and you make yourselves another. You jig and amble, and you lisp,   145
    and nickname God's creatures, and make your wantonness your ignorance.*
    Go to, I'll no more on't; it hath made me mad. I say we will have no more

---

[112] **Are you honest?** are you modest; chaste; truthful
[120] **bawd** procurer
[124-25] **virtue cannot . . . relish of it** virtue cannot shield us from still desiring sinful pleasures
[128] **indifferent honest** modestly virtuous
[141] **monsters** cuckolds
[146] **make your wantonness your ignorance** excuse your wantonness by pretending ignorance

marriage: those that are married already, all but one, shall live; the rest shall keep as they are. To a nunnery, go.

[*Exit.*]

OPHELIA: O, what a noble mind is here o'erthrown!   150
    The courtier's, soldier's, scholar's, eye, tongue, sword;
    Th' expectancy and rose* of the fair state,
    The glass of fashion and the mould of form,*
    Th' observ'd of all observers—quite, quite down!
    And I, of ladies most deject and wretched,   155
    That suck'd the honey of his music vows,
    Now see that noble and most sovereign reason,
    Like sweet bells jangled, out of time and harsh;
    That unmatch'd form and feature of blown* youth
    Blasted with ecstasy.* O, woe is me   160
    T' have seen what I have seen, see what I see!

[*Reenter* KING *and* POLONIUS.]

KING: Love! His affections do not that way tend;
    Nor what he spake, though it lack'd form a little,
    Was not like madness. There's something in his soul
    O'er which his melancholy sits on brood;   165
    And I do doubt* the hatch and the disclose
    Will be some danger; which to prevent
    I have in quick determination
    Thus set it down: he shall with speed to England
    For the demand of our neglected tribute.   170
    Haply the seas and countries different,
    With variable objects, shall expel
    This something-settled matter in his heart
    Whereon his brains still beating puts him thus
    From fashion of himself. What think you on't?   175
POLONIUS: It shall do well. But yet do I believe
    The origin and commencement of his grief
    Sprung from neglected love. How now, Ophelia!
    You need not tell us what Lord Hamlet said;
    We heard it all. My lord, do as you please;   180
    But if you hold it fit, after the play
    Let his queen mother all alone entreat him
    To show his grief. Let her be round* with him;
    And I'll be placed, so please you, in the ear
    Of all their conference. If she find him not,*   185
    To England send him; or confine him where

---

[152] **expectancy and rose** hope
[153] **mould of form** pattern of excellent behavior
[159] **blown** blooming
[160] **ecstasy** madness
[166] **doubt** fear
[183] **round** blunt
[185] **find him not** doesn't find out what is bothering him

Your wisdom best shall think.

KING: It shall be so:

Madness in great ones must not unwatch'd go.

[*Exeunt.*]

SCENE II————*Elsinore. The Castle.*

[*Enter* HAMLET *and three of the* PLAYERS.]

HAMLET: Speak the speech, I pray you, as I pronounc'd it to you, trippingly on the tongue; but if you mouth it, as many of our players do, I had as lief the towncrier spoke my lines. Nor do not saw the air too much with your hand, thus, but use all gently; for in the very torrent, tempest, and, as I may say, whirlwind of your passion, you must acquire and beget a temperance that may 5 give it smoothness. O, it offends me to the soul to hear a robustious periwig-pated* fellow tear a passion to tatters, to very rags, to split the ears of the groundlings,* who, for the most part, are capable of nothing* but inexplicable dumb shows* and noise. I would have such a fellow whipp'd for o'erdoing Termagant; it out-herods Herod.* Pray you avoid it. 10

FIRST PLAYER: I warrant your honour.

HAMLET: Be not too tame neither, but let your own discretion be your tutor. Suit the action to the word, the word to the action; with this special observance, that you o'erstep not the modesty of nature; for anything so o'erdone is from* the purpose of playing, whose end, both at the first and now, was and 15 is to hold, as 'twere, the mirror up to nature; to show virtue her own feature, scorn her own image, and the very age and body of the time his form and pressure.* Now, this overdone or come tardy off, though it makes the un-skilful laugh, cannot but make the judicious grieve; the censure of the which one must, in your allowance, o'erweigh a whole theatre of others. O, there 20 be players that I have seen play—and heard others praise, and that highly— not to speak it profanely, that, neither having th' accent of Christians, nor the gait of Christian, pagan, nor man, have so strutted and bellowed that I have thought some of Nature's journeymen* had made men, and not made them well, they imitated humanity so abominably. 25

FIRST PLAYER: I hope we have reform'd that indifferently* with us, sir.

HAMLET: O, reform it altogether. And let those that play your clowns speak no more than is set down for them; for there be of them that will themselves laugh, to set on some quantity of barren spectators to laugh, too, though in the meantime some necessary question of the play be then to be considered. 30

III,ii,7 **periwig-pated** wig-wearing

8 **groundlings** spectators who stood in the space surrounding the stage; presumably the poorest and least-educated spectators

8 **are capable of nothing** understand nothing

9 **dumb shows** silent miming (used, as later in this scene, as prologues to plays)

10 **Termagant . . . Herod** exaggeratedly overacted roles in medieval mystery plays

15 **from** contrary to

18 **pressure** image

24 **journeymen** workers not yet masters of their craft

26 **indifferently** mostly

That's villainous, and shows a most pitiful ambition in the fool that uses it.
Go, make you ready.

[*Exeunt* PLAYERS.]

[*Enter* POLONIUS, ROSENCRANTZ, *and* GUILDENSTERN.]

How now, my lord! Will the King hear this piece of work?
POLONIUS: And the Queen, too, and that presently.
HAMLET: Bid the players make haste.   [*Exit* POLONIUS.]   35
     Will you two help to hasten them?
ROSENCRANTZ: Ay, my lord.   [*Exeunt they two.*]
HAMLET: What, ho, Horatio!

     [*Enter* HORATIO.]

HORATIO: Here, sweet lord, at your service.
HAMLET: Horatio, thou art e'en as just a man   40
     As e'er my conversation cop'd withal.*
HORATIO: O my dear lord!
HAMLET: Nay, do not think I flatter;
     For what advancement may I hope from thee,
     That no revenue hast but thy good spirits   45
     To feed and clothe thee? Why should the poor be flatter'd?
     No, let the candied* tongue lick absurd pomp,
     And crook the pregnant hinges of the knee*
     Where thrift* may follow fawning. Dost thou hear?
     Since my dear soul was mistress of her choice   50
     And could of men distinguish her election,
     S'hath seal'd thee* for herself; for thou hast been
     As one, in suff'ring all, that suffers nothing;
     A man that Fortune's buffets and rewards
     Hast ta'en with equal thanks; and blest are those   55
     Whose blood* and judgment are so well commingled
     That they are not a pipe for Fortune's finger
     To sound what stop she please. Give me that man
     That is not passion's slave, and I will wear him
     In my heart's core, ay, in my heart of heart,   60
     As I do thee. Something too much of this.
     There is a play to-night before the King;
     One scene of it comes near the circumstance
     Which I have told thee of my father's death.
     I prithee, when thou seest that act afoot,   65
     Even with the very comment* of thy soul

---

[41] **cop'd withal** met with
[47] **candied** sugared, flattering
[48] **pregnant hinges of the knee** quick to curtsy and kneel
[49] **thrift** profit
[52] **S'hath seal'd thee** my soul has chosen you
[56] **blood** feelings
[66] **very comment** deepest wisdom

Observe my uncle. If his occulted* guilt
Do not itself unkennel in one speech,
It is a damned ghost that we have seen,
And my imaginations are as foul   70
As Vulcan's stithy.* Give him heedful note;
For I mine eyes will rivet to his face;
And, after, we will both our judgments join
In censure of his seeming.*
HORATIO: Well, my lord.   75
If 'a steal aught the whilst this play is playing,
And 'scape detecting, I will pay the theft.

[*Enter trumpets and kettledrums. Danish march. Sound a flourish. Enter* KING,
QUEEN, POLONIUS, OPHELIA, ROSENCRANTZ, GUILDENSTERN, *and other*
LORDS *attendant, with the guard carrying torches.*]

HAMLET: They are coming to the play; I must be idle.*
Get you a place.
KING: How fares our cousin Hamlet?   80
HAMLET: Excellent, i' faith; of the chameleon's dish.* I eat the air promise-
cramm'd; you cannot feed capons so.
KING: I have nothing with this answer, Hamlet; these words are not mine.
HAMLET: No, nor mine now. [*to* POLONIUS] My lord, you play'd once in th' uni-
versity, you say?   85
POLONIUS: That did I, my lord, and was accounted a good actor.
HAMLET: What did you enact?
POLONIUS: I did enact Julius Caesar; I was kill'd i' th' Capitol; Brutus kill'd me.
HAMLET: It was a brute part of him to kill so capital a calf there. Be the players
ready?   90
ROSENCRANTZ: Ay, my lord; they stay upon your patience.
QUEEN: Come hither, my dear Hamlet, sit by me.
HAMLET: No, good mother; here's metal more attractive.*
POLONIUS: [*to the* KING] O, ho! do you mark that?
HAMLET: Lady, shall I lie in your lap? [*lying down at* OPHELIA's *feet*]   95
OPHELIA: No, my lord.
HAMLET: I mean, my head upon your lap?
OPHELIA: Ay, my lord.
HAMLET: Do you think I meant country matters?*
OPHELIA: I think nothing, my lord.   100
HAMLET: That's a fair thought to lie between maids' legs.
OPHELIA: What is, my lord?
HAMLET: Nothing.
OPHELIA: You are merry, my lord.
HAMLET: Who, I?   105

---

⁶⁷ **occulted** hidden
⁷¹ **Vulcan's stithy** forge of the Greek god
⁷⁴ **censure of his seeming** judgment on his response
⁷⁸ **be idle** play the fool
⁸¹ **chameleon's dish** air on which chameleons were thought to live
⁹³ **attractive** magnetic
⁹⁹ **country matters** a sexual innuendo

OPHELIA: Ay, my lord.

HAMLET: O God, your only jig-maker!* What should a man do but be merry?
For look you how cheerfully my mother looks, and my father died within's
two hours.

OPHELIA: Nay, 'tis twice two months, my lord.   110

HAMLET: So long? Nay then, let the devil wear black, for I'll have a suit of sables.
O heavens! die two months ago, and not forgotten yet? Then there's hope a
great man's memory may outlive his life half a year; but, by'r lady, 'a must
build churches, then; or else shall 'a suffer not thinking on, with the hobby-
horse,* whose epitaph is 'For O, for O, the hobby-horse is forgot!'   115

[*The trumpet sounds. Hautboys play. The Dumb Show enters.*]

[*Enter a* KING *and a* QUEEN, *very lovingly; the* QUEEN *embracing him and he her.
She kneels, and makes a show of protestation unto him. He takes her up, and declines his
head upon her neck. He lies him down upon a bank of flowers; she, seeing him asleep,
leaves him. Anon comes in a* FELLOW, *takes off his crown, kisses it, pours poison in the
sleeper's ears, and leaves him. The* QUEEN *returns; finds the* KING *dead, and makes
passionate action. The* POISONER, *with some two or three* MUTES, *comes in again,
seeming to condole with her. The dead body is carried away. The* POISONER *woos the*
QUEEN *with gifts: she seems harsh awhile, but in the end accepts his love. Exeunt.*]

OPHELIA: What means this, my lord?

HAMLET: Marry, this is miching mallecho;* it means mischief.

OPHELIA: Belike this show imports the argument* of the play.

[*Enter* PROLOGUE.]

HAMLET: We shall know by this fellow: the players cannot keep counsel; they'll
tell all.   120

OPHELIA: Will 'a tell us what this show meant?

HAMLET: Ay, or any show that you show him. Be not you asham'd to show, he'll
not shame to tell you what it means.

OPHELIA: You are naught, you are naught.* I'll mark the play.

PROLOGUE: *For us, and for our tragedy,*   125
Here stooping to your clemency,
We beg your hearing patiently.

[*Exit.*]

HAMLET: Is this a prologue, or the posy of a ring?*

OPHELIA: 'Tis brief, my lord.

HAMLET: As woman's love.   130

[*Enter the* PLAYER KING *and* QUEEN.]

---

[107] **jig-maker** composer of songs and dances (jigs were often performed as afterpieces in the theatre, and often
by the fool)

[114-15] **hobby-horse** mock horse worn by a performer in mummers' plays

[117] **miching mallecho** sneaky mischief

[118] **argument** plot

[124] **naught** naughty

[128] **posy of a ring** sentiment inscribed in a ring

PLAYER KING: *Full thirty times hath Phoebus' cart* gone round*
    Neptune's salt wash* and Tellus's* orbed ground,
    And thirty dozen moons with borrowed sheen
    About the world have times twelve thirties been,
    Since love our hearts and Hymen* did our hands 135
    Unite comutual in most sacred bands.

PLAYER QUEEN: *So many journeys may the sun and moon*
    Make us again count o'er ere love be done!
    But, woe is me, you are so sick of late,
    So far from cheer and from your former state, 140
    That I distrust* you. Yet, though I distrust,
    Discomfort you, my lord, it nothing must;
    For women fear too much even as they love,
    And women's fear and love hold quantity,
    In neither aught, or in extremity. 145
    Now, what my love is, proof hath made you know;
    And as my love is siz'd, my fear is so.
    Where love is great, the littlest doubts are fear;
    Where little fears grow great, great love grows there.

PLAYER KING: *Faith, I must leave thee, love, and shortly, too:* 150
    My operant* powers their functions leave to do;
    And thou shalt live in this fair world behind,
    Honour'd, belov'd; and haply one as kind
    For husband shalt thou—

PLAYER QUEEN: *O, confound the rest!* 155
    Such love must needs be treason in my breast.
    In second husband let me be accurst!
    None wed the second but who kill'd the first.

HAMLET: That's wormwood, wormwood.*

PLAYER QUEEN: *The instances* that second marriage move** 160
    Are base respects of thrift,* but none of love.
    A second time I kill my husband dead,
    When second husband kisses me in bed.

PLAYER KING: *I do believe you think what now you speak;*
    But what we do determine oft we break. 165
    Purpose is but the slave to memory,
    Of violent birth, but poor validity;*
    Which now, the fruit unripe, sticks on the tree;
    But fall unshaken when they mellow be.
    Most necessary 'tis that we forget 170

---

[131] **Phoebus' cart** the sun god's chariot
[132] **Neptune's salt wash** the sea
[132] **Tellus** Roman goddess of the Earth
[135] **Hymen** god of marriage
[141] **distrust** am anxious about
[151] **operant** active
[159] **wormwood** a bitter herb
[160] **instances** motives
[160] **move** induce
[161] **base respects of thrift** considerations of profit
[167] **validity** strength

To pay ourselves what to ourselves is debt.
What to ourselves in passion we propose,
The passion ending, doth the purpose lose,
The violence of either grief or joy
Their own enactures* with themselves destroy. 175
Where joy most revels grief doth most lament;
Grief joys, joy grieves, on slender accident.
This world is not for aye; nor 'tis not strange
That even our loves should with our fortunes change;
For 'tis a question left us yet to prove, 180
Whether love lead fortune or else fortune love.
The great man down, you mark his favourite flies;
The poor advanc'd makes friends of enemies.
And hitherto doth love on fortune tend;
For who not needs shall never lack a friend, 185
And who in want a hollow friend doth try,
Directly seasons* him his enemy.
But, orderly to end where I begun,
Our wills and fates do so contrary run
That our devices still are overthrown; 190
Our thoughts are ours, their ends none of our own.
So think thou wilt no second husband wed;
But die thy thoughts when thy first lord is dead.
PLAYER QUEEN: Nor earth to me give food, nor heaven light,
Sport and repose lock from me day and night, 195
To desperation turn my trust and hope,
An anchor's* cheer in prison be my scope,
Each opposite that blanks* the face of joy
Meet what I would have well, and it destroy,
Both here and hence pursue my lasting strife, 200
If, once a widow, ever I be wife!
HAMLET: If she should break it now!
PLAYER KING: 'Tis deeply sworn. Sweet, leave me here awhile;
My spirits grow dull, and fain I would beguile
The tedious day with sleep. [Sleeps.] 205
PLAYER QUEEN: Sleep rock thy brain,
And never come mischance between us twain!
HAMLET: Madam, how like you this play?
QUEEN: The lady doth protest too much, methinks.
HAMLET: O, but she'll keep her word. 210
KING: Have you heard the argument?* Is there no offence in't?
HAMLET: No, no; they do but jest, poison in jest; no offence i' th' world.
KING: What do you call the play?

---

[175] **enactures** acts
[187] **seasons** ripens him into
[197] **anchor's** anchorite, hermit
[198] **opposite that blanks** adverse thing that makes the face blanch
[211] **argument** plot

HAMLET: 'The Mouse-trap.' Marry, how? Tropically.* This play is the image of a murder done in Vienna: Gonzago is the duke's name; his wife, Baptista. You shall see anon. 'Tis a knavish piece of work; but what of that? Your Majesty, and we that have free* souls, it touches us not. Let the galled jade* wince, our withers are unwrung. 215

[*Enter* LUCIANUS.]

This is one Lucianus, nephew to the King.

OPHELIA: You are as good as a chorus, my lord. 220

HAMLET: I could interpret* between you and your love, if I could see the puppets dallying.

OPHELIA: You are keen, my lord, you are keen.

HAMLET: It would cost you a groaning to take off mine edge.*

OPHELIA: Still better, and worse. 225

HAMLET: So you mis-take* your husbands.—Begin, murderer; pox, leave thy damnable faces and begin. Come; the croaking raven doth bellow for revenge.

LUCIANUS: *Thoughts black, hands apt, drugs fit, and time agreeing;*
Confederate season, else no creature seeing;* 230
Thou mixture rank, of midnight weeds collected,
With Hecate's ban thrice blasted, thrice infected.*
*Thy natural magic and dire property**
On wholesome life usurps immediately.
[*Pours the poison in his ears.*]

HAMLET: 'A poisons him i' th' garden for his estate. His name's Gonzago. The story 235 is extant, and written in very choice Italian. You shall see anon how the murderer gets the love of Gonzago's wife.

OPHELIA: The King rises.

HAMLET: What, frighted with false fire!*

QUEEN: How fares my lord? 240

POLONIUS: Give o'er the play.

KING: Give me some light. Away!

POLONIUS: Lights, lights, lights!

[*Exeunt all but* HAMLET *and* HORATIO.]

HAMLET: Why, let the strucken deer go weep,
The hart ungalled play; 245
For some must watch, while some must sleep;
Thus runs the world away.

---

214 **Tropically** figuratively
217 **free** souls free of guilt
217 **galled jade** chafed horse
221 **interpret** explain like a puppet master if he could see the puppets playing wantonly
224 **cost . . . edge** a sexual reference
226 **mis-take** err in taking
230 **Confederate season** the opportunity offered me
232 **Hecate's ban** the goddess of sorcery's curse
233 **property** nature
239 **false fire** blank firing of a gun

Would not this, sir, and a forest of feathers*—if the rest of my fortunes turn
Turk* with me—with two Provincial roses on my raz'd shoes,* get me a fel-
lowship in a cry of players,* sir?   250
HORATIO: Half a share.
HAMLET: A whole one, I.
    For thou dost know, O Damon dear,
    This realm dismantled was
    Of Jove himself; and now reigns here   255
    A very, very—peacock.
HORATIO: You might have rhym'd.
HAMLET: O good Horatio, I'll take the ghost's word for a thousand pound. Didst
    perceive?
HORATIO: Very well, my lord.   260
HAMLET: Upon the talk of the poisoning.
HORATIO: I did very well note him.
HAMLET: Ah, ha! Come, some music. Come, the recorders.
    For if the King like not the comedy,
    Why, then, belike he likes it not, perdy.*   265

Come, some music.

    [*Reenter* ROSENCRANTZ *and* GUILDENSTERN.]

GUILDENSTERN: Good my lord, vouchsafe me a word with you.
HAMLET: Sir, a whole history.
GUILDENSTERN: The King, sir—
HAMLET: Ay, sir, what of him?   270
GUILDENSTERN: Is, in his retirement, marvellous distemp'red.
HAMLET: With drink, sir?
GUILDENSTERN: No, my lord, rather with choler.*
HAMLET: Your wisdom should show itself more richer to signify this to his doc-
    tor; for for me to put him to his purgation would perhaps plunge him into   275
    far more choler.
GUILDENSTERN: Good my lord, put your discourse into some frame,* and start
    not so wildly from my affair.
HAMLET: I am tame, sir. Pronounce.
GUILDENSTERN: The Queen, your mother, in most great affliction of spirit, hath   280
    sent me to you.
HAMLET: You are welcome.
GUILDENSTERN: Nay, good my lord, this courtesy is not of the right breed. If it
    shall please you to make me a wholesome answer, I will do your mother's
    commandment; if not, your pardon and my return shall be the end of my   285
    business.

---

[248] **forest of feathers** costume with feathers
[248–49] **turn Turk** go badly
[249] **raz'd shoes** shoes ornamented with slashes
[250] **cry of players** company of actors
[265] **perdy** by God (par dieu)
[273] **choler** anger
[277] **frame** order, control

HAMLET: Sir, I cannot.

ROSENCRANTZ: What, my lord?

HAMLET: Make you a wholesome* answer, my wit's diseas'd. But, sir, such answer
as I can make, you shall command: or rather, as you say, my mother.
Therefore no more, but to the matter: my mother, you say— 290

ROSENCRANTZ: Then thus she says: your behaviour hath struck her into amazement
and admiration.*

HAMLET: O wonderful son, that can so stonish a mother! But is there no sequel
at the heels of this mother's admiration? Impart. 295

ROSENCRANTZ: She desires to speak with you in her closet ere you go to bed.

HAMLET: We shall obey, were she ten times our mother. Have you any further trade
with us?

ROSENCRANTZ: My lord, you once did love me.

HAMLET: And do still, by these pickers and stealers.* 300

ROSENCRANTZ: Good my lord, what is your cause of distemper? You do surely bar
the door upon your own liberty, if you deny your griefs to your friend.

HAMLET: Sir, I lack advancement.*

ROSENCRANTZ: How can that be, when you have the voice of the King himself for
your succession in Denmark? 305

HAMLET: Ay, sir, but 'While the grass grows'—the proverb* is something musty.

[*Reenter the* PLAYERS, *with recorders.*]

O, the recorders! Let me see one. To withdraw* with you—why do you go
about to recover the wind of me,* as if you would drive me into a toil?*

GUILDENSTERN: O my lord, if my duty be too bold, my love is too unmannerly.*

HAMLET: I do not well understand that. Will you play upon this pipe? 310

GUILDENSTERN: My lord, I cannot.

HAMLET: I pray you.

GUILDENSTERN: Believe me, I cannot.

HAMLET: I do beseech you.

GUILDENSTERN: I know no touch of it, my lord. 315

HAMLET: It is as easy as lying: govern these ventages* with your fingers and
thumb, give it breath with your mouth, and it will discourse most eloquent
music. Look you, these are the stops.

GUILDENSTERN: But these cannot I command to any utterance of harmony; I
have not the skill. 320

HAMLET: Why, look you now, how unworthy a thing you make of me! You would
play upon me; you would seem to know my stops; you would pluck out the
heart of my mystery; you would sound me from my lowest note to the top of

---

289 **wholesome** sane
293 **admiration** wonder
300 **pickers and stealers** hands
303 **advancement** promotion
306 **proverb** (the rest of the proverb is "the horse starveth")
307 **withdraw** speak privately
308 **recover the wind of me** get on the windward side of me
308 **toil** snare
309 **duty . . . unmannerly** if I have seemed rude it is because my love for you leads me beyond good manners
316 **ventages** vents, stops on a musical instrument

my compass;* and there is much music, excellent voice, in this little organ,*
yet cannot you make it speak. 'Sblood, do you think I am easier to be play'd 325
on than a pipe? Call me what instrument you will, though you can fret me,
yet you cannot play upon me.

[*Reenter* POLONIUS.]

God bless you, sir!
POLONIUS: My lord, the Queen would speak with you, and presently.
HAMLET: Do you see yonder cloud that's almost in shape of a camel? 330
POLONIUS: By th' mass, and 'tis like a camel indeed.
HAMLET: Methinks it is like a weasel.
POLONIUS: It is back'd like a weasel.
HAMLET: Or like a whale?
POLONIUS: Very like a whale. 335
HAMLET: Then I will come to my mother by and by. [*aside*] They fool me to the
    top of my bent.*—I will come by and by.
POLONIUS: I will say so. [*Exit* POLONIUS.]
HAMLET: 'By and by' is easily said. Leave me, friends.

[*Exeunt all but* HAMLET.]

'Tis now the very witching time of night, 340
When churchyards yawn, and hell itself breathes out
Contagion to this world. Now could I drink hot blood,
And do such bitter business as the day
Would quake to look on. Soft! now to my mother.
O heart, lose not thy nature; let not ever 345
The soul of Nero* enter this firm bosom.
Let me be cruel, not unnatural:
I will speak daggers to her, but use none.
My tongue and soul in this be hypocrites—
How in my words somever she be shent,* 350
To give them seals* never, my soul, consent!

[*Exit.*]

SCENE III————*Elsinore. The Castle.*

[*Enter* KING, ROSENCRANTZ, *and* GUILDENSTERN.]

KING: I like him not; nor stands it safe with us
    To let his madness range. Therefore prepare you;
    I your commission will forthwith dispatch,

---

[324] **compass** range
[324] **organ** the recorder
[336-37] **fool me . . . my bent** they force me to play the fool to the fullest
[346] **Nero** Roman emperor who killed his mother
[350] **shent** rebuked
[351] **give them seals** confirm them with deeds

And he to England shall along with you.
The terms* of our estate may not endure   5
Hazard so near's as doth hourly grow
Out of his brows.
GUILDENSTERN: We will ourselves provide.
Most holy and religious fear it is
To keep those many many bodies safe   10
That live and feed upon your Majesty.
ROSENCRANTZ: The single and peculiar* life is bound
With all the strength and armour of the mind
To keep itself from noyance;* but much more
That spirit upon whose weal depends and rests   15
The lives of many. The cease of majesty
Dies not alone, but like a gulf* doth draw
What's near it with it. It is a massy wheel,
Fix'd on the summit of the highest mount,
To whose huge spokes ten thousand lesser things   20
Are mortis'd and adjoin'd; which when it falls,
Each small annexment, petty consequence,
Attends the boist'rous ruin. Never alone
Did the king sigh, but with a general groan.
KING: Arm* you, I pray you, to this speedy voyage;   25
For we will fetters put about this fear,
Which now goes too free-footed.
ROSENCRANTZ: We will haste us.

　　[*Exeunt* ROSENCRANTZ *and* GUILDENSTERN.]

　　[*Enter* POLONIUS.]

POLONIUS: My lord, he's going to his mother's closet.
Behind the arras I'll convey myself   30
To hear the process.* I'll warrant she'll tax him home;*
And, as you said, and wisely was it said,
'Tis meet that some more audience than a mother,
Since nature makes them partial, should o'erhear
The speech, of vantage.* Fare you well, my liege.   35
I'll call upon you ere you go to bed,
And tell you what I know.
KING: Thanks, dear my lord.   [*Exit* POLONIUS.]
O, my offence is rank, it smells to heaven;

III.iii.5 **terms** conditions
12 **peculiar** private
14 **noyance** injury
17 **gulf** whirlpool
25 **Arm** prepare
31 **process** proceedings
31 **tax him home** rebuke him sharply
35 **of vantage** from some advantageous place

It hath the primal eldest curse* upon't—   40
A brother's murder! Pray can I not,
Though inclination be as sharp as will.
My stronger guilt defeats my strong intent,
And, like a man to double business bound,
I stand in pause where I shall first begin,   45
And both neglect. What if this cursed hand
Were thicker than itself with brother's blood,
Is there not rain enough in the sweet heavens
To wash it white as snow? Whereto serves mercy
But to confront the visage of offence?   50
And what's in prayer but this twofold force,
To be forestalled ere we come to fall,
Or pardon'd being down? Then I'll look up;
My fault is past. But, O, what form of prayer
Can serve my turn? 'Forgive me my foul murder'!   55
That cannot be; since I am still possess'd
Of those effects* for which I did the murder—
My crown, mine own ambition, and my queen.
May one be pardon'd and retain th' offence?
In the corrupted currents of this world   60
Offence's gilded hand may shove by justice;
And oft 'tis seen the wicked prize itself
Buys out the law. But 'tis not so above:
There is no shuffling;* there the action lies
In his true nature; and we ourselves compell'd,   65
Even to the teeth and forehead of our faults,
To give in evidence. What then? What rests?*
Try what repentance can. What can it not?
Yet what can it when one cannot repent?
O wretched state! O bosom black as death!   70
O limed* soul, that, struggling to be free,
Art more engag'd!* Help, angels. Make assay:
Bow, stubborn knees; and, heart, with strings of steel,
Be soft as sinews of the new-born babe.
All may be well.   [*He kneels.*]   75

    [*Enter* HAMLET.]

HAMLET: Now might I do it pat, now 'a is a-praying;
    And now I'll do't—and so 'a goes to heaven,
    And so am I reveng'd. That would be scann'd.*

---

40 **primal eldest curse** oldest curse (Cain's murder of his brother Abel)
57 **effects** things gained
64 **shuffling** trickery
67 **rests** remains
71 **limed** trapped (birds were caught by liming tree limbs with a sticky substance)
72 **engag'd** entrapped
78 **would be scann'd** needs to be thought about

A villain kills my father; and for that,
I, his sole son, do this same villain send   80
To heaven.
Why, this is hire and salary, not revenge.
'A took my father grossly, full of bread,*
With all his crimes broad blown, as flush* as May;
And how his audit* stands who knows save heaven?   85
But in our circumstance and course of thought
'Tis heavy with him; and am I then reveng'd
To take him in the purging of his soul,
When he is fit and season'd for his passage?
No.   90
Up, sword, and know thou a more horrid hent.
When he is drunk asleep, or in his rage;
Or in th' incestuous pleasure of his bed;
At game, a-swearing, or about some act
That has no relish of salvation in't—   95
Then trip him, that his heels my kick at heaven,
And that his soul may be as damn'd and black
As hell, whereto it goes. My mother stays.
This physic* but prolongs thy sickly days.   [*Exit.*]
KING: [*rising*] My words fly up, my thoughts remain below.   100
Words without thoughts never to heaven go.   [*Exit.*]

SCENE IV————*The* QUEEN*'s closet.*

[*Enter* QUEEN *and* POLONIUS.]

POLONIUS: 'A will come straight. Look you lay home* to him;
   Tell him his pranks have been too broad* to bear with,
   And that your Grace hath screen'd and stood between
   Much heat and him. I'll silence me even here.
   Pray you be round with him.   5
HAMLET: [*within*] Mother, mother, mother!
QUEEN: I'll warrant you. Fear me not.
   Withdraw, I hear him coming.

                              [POLONIUS *goes behind the arras.*]

[*Enter* HAMLET.]

HAMLET: Now, mother, what's the matter?
QUEEN: Hamlet, thou hast thy father much offended.   10
HAMLET: Mother, you have my father much offended.

---

83 **full of bread** worldly gratifications
84 **crimes . . . flush** sins in full bloom as flowers in May
85 **audit** account
99 **physic** (to Claudius) this medicine (prayer)
III,iv,1 **lay home** rebuke him sharply
2 **broad** unrestrained

QUEEN: Come, come, you answer with an idle* tongue.
HAMLET: Go, go, you question with a wicked tongue.
QUEEN: Why, how now, Hamlet!
HAMLET: What's the matter now?   15
QUEEN: Have you forgot me?
HAMLET: No, by the rood,* not so:
    You are the Queen, your husband's brother's wife;
    And—would it were not so!—you are my mother.
QUEEN: Nay then, I'll set those to you that can speak.   20
HAMLET: Come, come, and sit you down; you shall not budge.
    You go not till I set you up a glass*
    Where you may see the inmost part of you.
QUEEN: What wilt thou do? Thou wilt not murder me?
    Help, help, ho!   25
POLONIUS: [behind] What, ho! help, help, help!
HAMLET: [draws] How now! a rat?
    Dead, for a ducat, dead!

      [kills POLONIUS with a pass through the arras]

POLONIUS: [behind] O, I am slain!
QUEEN: O me, what hast thou done?   30
HAMLET: Nay, I know not:
    Is it the King?
QUEEN: O, what a rash and bloody deed is this!
HAMLET: A bloody deed!—almost as bad, good mother,
    As kill a king and marry with his brother.   35
QUEEN: As kill a king!
HAMLET: Ay, lady, it was my word. [parting the arras]
    Thou wretched, rash, intruding fool, farewell!
    I took thee for thy better. Take thy fortune;
    Thou find'st to be too busy is some danger.   40
    Leave wringing of your hands. Peace; sit you down,
    And let me wring your heart; for so I shall,
    If it be made of penetrable stuff;
    If damned custom have not braz'd* it so
    That it be proof and bulwark against sense.*   45
QUEEN: What have I done that thou dar'st wag thy tongue
    In noise so rude against me?
HAMLET: Such an act
    That blurs the grace and blush of modesty;
    Calls virtue hypocrite; takes off the rose   50
    From the fair forehead of an innocent love,
    And sets a blister there,* makes marriage-vows

---

[12] **idle** foolish
[17] **rood** cross
[22] **glass** mirror
[44] **braz'd** hardened
[45] **proof . . . sense** armored against feeling
[52] **sets a blister** brands (as a harlot)

As false as dicers' oaths. O, such a deed
As from the body of contraction* plucks
The very soul, and sweet religion makes   55
A rhapsody* of words. Heaven's face does glow
O'er this solidity and compound mass
With heated visage, as against the doom—
Is thought-sick at the act.

QUEEN: Ay me, what act,   60
    That roars so loud and thunders in the index?*

HAMLET: Look here upon this picture and on this,
    The counterfeit presentment* of two brothers.
    See what a grace was seated on this brow;
    Hyperion's curls; the front* of Jove himself;   65
    An eye like Mars, to threaten and command;
    A station* like the herald Mercury
    New lighted on a heaven-kissing hill—
    A combination and a form indeed
    Where every god did seem to set his seal,   70
    To give the world assurance of a man.
    This was your husband. Look you now what follows:
    Here is your husband, like a mildew'd ear
    Blasting his wholesome brother. Have you eyes?
    Could you on this fair mountain leave to feed,   75
    And batten* on this moor? Ha! have you eyes?
    You cannot call it love; for at your age
    The heyday in the blood is tame, it's humble,
    And waits upon the judgment; and what judgment
    Would step from this to this? Sense, sure, you have,   80
    Else could you not have motion; but sure that sense
    Is apoplex'd;* for madness would not err,
    Nor sense to ecstasy* was ne'er so thrall'd
    But it reserv'd some quantity of choice
    To serve in such a difference. What devil was't   85
    That thus hath cozen'd you at hoodman-blind?*
    Eyes without feeling, feeling without sight.
    Ears without hands or eyes, smelling sans* all,
    Or but a sickly part of one true sense
    Could not so mope.* O shame! where is thy blush?   90
    Rebellious hell,

---

54 **contraction** marriage contract
56 **rhapsody** senseless string
61 **index** prologue
63 **counterfeit presentment** represented image
65 **front** forehead
67 **station** bearing
76 **batten** feed gluttonously
82 **apoplex'd** paralyzed
83 **ecstasy** madness
86 **hoodman-blind** cheated you at blindman's buff
88 **sans** without
90 **so mope** be so stupid

If thou canst mutine in a matron's bones,
To flaming youth let virtue be as wax
And melt in her own fire; proclaim no shame
When the compulsive ardour gives the charge,   95
Since frost itself as actively doth burn,
And reason panders will.*
QUEEN: O Hamlet, speak no more!
Thou turn'st my eyes into my very soul;
And there I see such black and grained spots   100
As will not leave their tinct.*
HAMLET: Nay, but to live
In the rank sweat of an enseamed* bed,
Stew'd in corruption, honeying and making love
Over the nasty sty!   105
QUEEN: O, speak to me no more!
These words like daggers enter in my ears;
No more, sweet Hamlet.
HAMLET: A murderer and a villain!
A slave that is not twentieth part the tithe*   110
Of your precedent lord; a vice* of kings;
A cutpurse of the empire and the rule,
That from a shelf the precious diadem stole
And put it in his pocket!
QUEEN: No more!   115

                [*Enter* GHOST.]

HAMLET: A king of shreds and patches—
Save me, and hover o'er me with your wings,
You heavenly guards! What would your gracious figure?
QUEEN: Alas, he's mad!
HAMLET: Do you not come your tardy son to chide,   120
That, laps'd in time and passion, lets go by
Th' important acting of your dread command?
O, say!
GHOST: Do not forget; this visitation
Is but to whet thy almost blunted purpose.   125
But look, amazement on thy mother sits.
O, step between her and her fighting soul!
Conceit* in weakest bodies strongest works.
Speak to her, Hamlet.
HAMLET: How is it with you, lady?   130
QUEEN: Alas, how is't with you,
That you do bend your eye on vacancy,

---

97 **reason panders will** reason acts as a panderer for desire
101 **tinct** color
103 **enseamed** rumpled
110 **tithe** tenth part
111 **vice** wicked character in medieval plays
128 **Conceit** imagination

And with th' incorporal* air do hold discourse?
Forth at your eyes and spirits wildly peep;
And, as the sleeping soldiers in th' alarm,   135
Your bedded* hairs like life in excrements*
Start up and stand an end. O gentle son,
Upon the heat and flame of thy distemper
Sprinkle cool patience! Whereon do you look?
HAMLET: On him, on him! Look you how pale he glares.   140
His form and cause conjoin'd, preaching to stones,
Would make them capable.*—Do not look upon me,
Lest with this piteous action you convert
My stern effects;* then what I have to do
Will want true colour—tears perchance for blood.   145
QUEEN: To whom do you speak this?
HAMLET: Do you see nothing there?
QUEEN: Nothing at all; yet all that is I see.
HAMLET: Nor did you nothing hear?
QUEEN: No, nothing but ourselves.   150
HAMLET: Why, look you there. Look how it steals away.
My father, in his habit* as he liv'd!
Look where he goes even now out at the portal.

[*Exit* GHOST.]

QUEEN: This is the very coinage of your brain.
This bodiless creation ecstasy   155
Is very cunning in.
HAMLET: Ecstasy!
My pulse as yours doth temperately keep time.
And makes as healthful music. It is not madness
That I have utt'red. Bring me to the test,   160
And I the matter will re-word which madness
Would gambol* from. Mother, for love of grace,
Lay not that flattering unction* to your soul,
That not your trespass but my madness speaks:
It will but skin and film the ulcerous place,   165
Whiles rank corruption, mining* all within,
Infects unseen. Confess yourself to heaven;
Repent what's past; avoid what is to come;
And do not spread the compost on the weeds,
To make them ranker. Forgive me this my virtue;   170
For in the fatness of these pursy* times

---

133 **incorporal** empty, bodiless
136 **bedded** flat-lying
136 **excrements** outgrowths
142 **capable** receptive
143-44 **convert my stern effects** divert my serious purpose
152 **habit** garment
162 **gambol** start away
163 **unction** ointment
166 **mining** undermining
171 **pursy** bloated

   Virtue itself of vice must pardon beg,
   Yea, curb* and woo for leave to do him good.
QUEEN: O Hamlet, thou hast cleft my heart in twain.
HAMLET: O, throw away the worser part of it,   175
   And live the purer with the other half.
   Good night—but go not to my uncle's bed;
   Assume a virtue, if you have it not.
   That monster custom, who all sense doth eat,
   Of habits devil, is angel yet in this,   180
   That to the use* of actions fair and good
   He likewise gives a frock or livery
   That aptly is put on. Refrain to-night;
   And that shall lend a kind of easiness
   To the next abstinence; the next more easy;   185
   For use almost can change the stamp of nature,
   And either curb the devil, or throw him out,
   With wondrous potency. Once more, good night;
   And when you are desirous to be blest,
   I'll blessing beg of you. For this same lord   190
   I do repent; but Heaven hath pleas'd it so,
   To punish me with this, and this with me,
   That I must be their scourge and minister.
   I will bestow him, and will answer well
   The death I gave him. So, again, good night.   195
   I must be cruel only to be kind;
   Thus bad begins and worse remains behind.
   One word more, good lady.
QUEEN: What shall I do?
HAMLET: Not this, by no means, that I bid you do: 200
   Let the bloat King tempt you again to bed;
   Pinch wanton on your cheek; call you his mouse;
   And let him, for a pair of reechy* kisses,
   Or paddling in your neck with his damn'd fingers,
   Make you to ravel all this matter out,   205
   That I essentially am not in madness,
   But mad in craft. 'Twere good you let him know;
   For who that's but a queen, fair, sober, wise,
   Would from a paddock,* from a bat, a gib,*
   Such dear concernings hide? Who would do so?   210
   No, in despite of sense and secrecy,
   Unpeg the basket on the house's top,
   Let the birds fly, and, like the famous ape,
   To try conclusions,* in the basket creep
   And break your own neck down.   215

---

[173] **curb** bow low
[181] **use** practice
[203] **reechy** foul
[209] **paddock** toad
[209] **gib** tomcat
[214] **try conclusions** make experiments

QUEEN: Be thou assur'd, if words be made of breath
  And breath of life, I have no life to breathe
  What thou hast said to me.
HAMLET: I must to England; you know that?
QUEEN: Alack,   220
  I had forgot. 'Tis so concluded on.
HAMLET: There's letters seal'd; and my two school-fellows,
  Whom I will trust as I will adders fang'd—
  They bear the mandate;* they must sweep my way
  And marshal me to knavery. Let it work;   225
  For 'tis the sport to have the engineer
  Hoist with his own petar;* and't shall go hard
  But I will delve one yard below their mines
  And blow them at the moon, O, 'tis most sweet
  When in one line two crafts* directly meet.   230
  This man shall set me packing.
  I'll lug the guts into the neighbour room.
  Mother, good night. Indeed, this counsellor
  Is now most still, most secret, and most grave,
  Who was in life a foolish prating knave.   235
  Come, sir, to draw toward an end with you.
  Good night, mother.

    [*Exeunt severally;* HAMLET *tugging in* POLONIUS.]

ACT IV

SCENE I———*Elsinore. The Castle.*

   [*Enter* KING, QUEEN, ROSENCRANTZ, *and* GUILDENSTERN.]

KING: There's matter in these sighs, these profound heaves,
  You must translate; 'tis fit we understand them.
  Where is your son?
QUEEN: Bestow this place on us a little while.

   [*Exeunt* ROSENCRANTZ *and* GUILDENSTERN.]

  Ah, mine own lord, what have I seen to-night!   5
KING: What, Gertrude? How does Hamlet?
QUEEN: Mad as the sea and wind, when both contend
  Which is the mightier. In his lawless fit,

---

[224] **mandate** command
[227] **petar** bomb
[230] **crafts** intrigues

Behind the arras hearing something stir,
Whips out his rapier, cries 'A rat, a rat!'   10
And in this brainish apprehension* kills
The unseen good old man.

KING: O heavy deed!
It had been so with us had we been there.
His liberty is full of threats to all—   15
To you yourself, to us, to every one.
Alas, how shall this bloody deed be answer'd?
It will be laid to us, whose providence*
Should have kept short, restrain'd, and out of haunt,*
This mad young man. But so much was our love,   20
We would not understand what was most fit;
But, like the owner of a foul disease,
To keep it from divulging, let it feed
Even on the pith of life. Where is he gone?

QUEEN: To draw apart the body he hath kill'd;   25
O'er whom his very madness, like some ore
Among a mineral of metals base,*
Shows itself pure: 'a weeps for what is done.

KING: O Gertrude, come away!
The sun no sooner shall the mountains touch   30
But we will ship him hence; and this vile deed
We must with all our majesty and skill
Both countenance and excuse. Ho Guildenstern!

[*Reenter* ROSENCRANTZ *and* GUILDENSTERN.]

Friends, both go join you with some further aid:
Hamlet in madness hath Polonius slain,   35
And from his mother's closet hath he dragg'd him;
Go seek him out; speak fair, and bring the body
Into the chapel. I pray you haste in this.

[*Exeunt* ROSENCRANTZ *and* GUILDENSTERN.]

Come, Gertrude, we'll call up our wisest friends
And let them know both what we mean to do   40
And what's untimely done; so haply slander—
Whose whisper o'er the world's diameter,
As level as the cannon to his blank,*
Transports his pois'ned shot—may miss our name,
And hit the woundless* air. O, come away!   45
My soul is full of discord and dismay.   [*Exeunt.*]

IV,i,11 **brainish apprehension** mad imagination
18 **providence** foresight
19 **out of haunt** away from association with others
26–27 **ore . . . base** like gold among baser metals
43 **blank** white center of a target
45 **woundless** invulnerable

SCENE II————Elsinore. The Castle.

[*Enter* HAMLET.]

HAMLET: Safely stow'd.
GENTLEMEN: [*within*] Hamlet! Lord Hamlet!
HAMLET: But soft! What noise? Who calls on Hamlet? O, here they come!

[*Enter* ROSENCRANTZ *and* GUILDENSTERN.]

ROSENCRANTZ: What have you done, my lord, with the dead body?
HAMLET: Compounded it with dust, whereto 'tis kin.   5
ROSENCRANTZ: Tell us where 'tis, that we may take it thence. And bear it to the
    chapel.
HAMLET: Do not believe it.
ROSENCRANTZ: Believe what?
HAMLET: That I can keep your counsel, and not mine own. Besides, to be demanded   10
    of* a sponge—what replication* should be made by the son of a king?
ROSENCRANTZ: Take you me for a sponge, my lord?
HAMLET: Ay, sir; that soaks up the King's countenance,* his rewards, his authorities.
    But such officers do the King best service in the end: he keeps them like an ape   15
    an apple in the corner of his jaw; first mouth'd to be last swallowed;
    when he needs what you have glean'd, it is but squeezing you and, sponge,
    you shall be dry again.
ROSENCRANTZ: I understand you not, my lord.
HAMLET: I am glad of it; a knavish speech sleeps in a foolish ear.   20
ROSENCRANTZ: My lord, you must tell us where the body is, and go with us to
    the King.
HAMLET: The body is with the King, but the King is not with the body. The King
    is a thing—
GUILDENSTERN: A thing, my lord!   25
HAMLET: Of nothing. Bring me to him. Hide fox, and all after.*   [*Exeunt.*]

SCENE III————Elsinore. The Castle.

[*Enter* KING, *attended.*]

KING: I have sent to seek him, and to find the body.
    How dangerous is it that this man goes loose!
    Yet must not we put the strong law on him:
    He's lov'd of the distracted* multitude,
    Who like not in their judgment but their eyes;   5

IV,ii,10–11 **demanded of** questioned by
[11] **replication** reply
[14] **countenance** favor
[26] **Hide fox, and all after** call in game (as in hide-and-seek)
IV,iii,4 **distracted** confused

And where 'tis so, th' offender's scourge is weigh'd,
But never the offence. To bear* all smooth and even,
This sudden sending him away must seem
Deliberate pause.* Diseases desperate grown
By desperate appliance are reliev'd,   10
Or not at all.

> [*Enter* ROSENCRANTZ.]

How now! what hath befall'n?
ROSENCRANTZ: Where the dead body is bestow'd, my lord,
    We cannot get from him.
KING: But where is he?   15
ROSENCRANTZ: Without, my lord; guarded, to know your pleasure.
KING: Bring him before us.
ROSENCRANTZ: Ho, Guildenstern! bring in the lord.

> [*Enter* HAMLET *and* GUILDENSTERN.]

KING: Now, Hamlet, where's Polonius?
HAMLET: At supper.   20
KING: At supper! Where?
HAMLET: Not where he eats, but where 'a is eaten; a certain convocation of
    politic* worms are e'en at him. Your worm is your only emperor for diet: we
    fat all creatures else to fat us, and we fat ourselves for maggots; your fat king
    and your lean beggar is but variable service*—two dishes, but to one table.   25
    That's the end.
KING: Alas, alas!
HAMLET: A man may fish with the worm that hath eat of a king, and eat of the fish
    that hath fed of that worm.
KING: What dost thou mean by this?   30
HAMLET: Nothing but to show you how a king may go a progress through the
    guts of a beggar.
KING: Where is Polonius?
HAMLET: In heaven; send thither to see; if your messenger find him not there,
    seek him i' th' other place yourself. But if, indeed, you find him not within   35
    this month, you shall nose him as you go up the stairs into the lobby.
KING: [*to attendants*] Go seek him there.
HAMLET: 'A will stay till you come.   [*Exeunt attendants.*]
KING: Hamlet, this deed, for thine especial safety—
    Which we do tender,* as we dearly grieve   40
    For that which thou hast done—must send thee hence
    With fiery quickness. Therefore prepare thyself;
    The bark is ready, and the wind at help,
    Th' associates tend,* and everything is bent
    For England.   45

---

[7] **bear** carry out
[9] **pause** planning
[23] **politic** statesmanlike
[25] **variable service** different courses
[40] **tender** hold dear
[44] **tend** wait

HAMLET: For England!

KING: Ay, Hamlet.

HAMLET: Good!

KING: So is it, if thou knew'st our purposes.

HAMLET: I see a cherub that sees them. But, come; for England! Farewell, dear   50
    mother.

KING: Thy loving father, Hamlet.

HAMLET: My mother: father and mother is man and wife; man and wife is one flesh;
    and so, my mother. Come, for England.   [*Exit.*]

KING: Follow him at foot;* tempt him with speed aboard;   55
    Delay it not; I'll have him hence to-night.
    Away! for everything is seal'd and done
    That else leans* on th' affair. Pray you make haste.

      [*Exeunt all but the* KING.]

    And, England, if my love thou hold'st at aught—
    As my great power thereof may give thee sense,   60
    Since yet thy cicatrice* looks raw and red
    After the Danish sword, and thy free awe*
    Pays homage to us—thou mayst not coldly set
    Our sovereign process;* which imports at full,
    By letters congruing to that effect,   65
    The present* death of Hamlet. Do it, England:
    For like the hectic* in my blood he rages,
    And thou must cure me. Till I know 'tis done,
    Howe'er my haps,* my joys were ne'er begun.   [*Exit.*]

        SCENE IV———*A plain in Denmark.*

      [*Enter* FORTINBRAS *with his army over the stage.*]

FORTINBRAS: Go, Captain, from me greet the Danish king.
    Tell him that by his license Fortinbras
    Craves the conveyance of a promis'd march
    Over his kingdom. You know the rendezvous.
    If that his Majesty would aught with us,   5
    We shall express our duty in his eye;*
    And let him know so.

CAPTAIN: I will do't, my lord.

---

55 **at foot** closely

58 **leans** depends

61 **cicatrice** scar

62 **free awe** uncompelled submission

63–64 **coldly set our sovereign process** disregard our royal command

66 **present** immediate

67 **hectic** fever

69 **haps** fortunes

IV,iv,6 **in his eye** in his presence

FORTINBRAS: Go softly* on.   [*Exeunt all but the* CAPTAIN.]
    [*Enter* HAMLET, ROSENCRANTZ, GUILDENSTERN, *and others.*]
HAMLET: Good sir, whose powers are these?   10
CAPTAIN: They are of Norway, sir.
HAMLET: How purpos'd, sir, I pray you?
CAPTAIN: Against some part of Poland.
HAMLET: Who commands them, sir?
CAPTAIN: The nephew to old Norway, Fortinbras.   15
HAMLET: Goes it against the main* of Poland, sir,
    Or for some frontier?
CAPTAIN: Truly to speak, and with no addition,
    We go to gain a little patch of ground
    That hath in it no profit but the name.
    To pay five ducats, five, I would not farm it;   20
    Nor will it yield to Norway or the Pole
    A ranker* rate should it be sold in fee.*
HAMLET: Why, then the Polack never will defend it.
CAPTAIN: Yes, it is already garrison'd.   25
HAMLET: Two thousand souls and twenty thousand ducats
    Will not debate* the question of this straw.
    This is th' imposthume* of much wealth and peace,
    That inward breaks, and shows no cause without
    Why the man dies. I humbly thank you, sir.   30
CAPTAIN: God buy you, sir.
ROSENCRANTZ: Will't please you go, my lord?
HAMLET: I'll be with you straight. Go a little before.

      [*Exeunt all but* HAMLET.]

    How all occasions do inform against me,
    And spur my dull revenge! What is a man,   35
    If his chief good and market* of his time
    Be but to sleep and feed? A beast, no more!
    Sure he that made us with such large discourse,*
    Looking before and after, gave us not
    That capability and godlike reason   40
    To fust* in us unus'd. Now, whether it be
    Bestial oblivion, or some craven scruple
    Of thinking too precisely on th' event—
    A thought which, quarter'd, hath but one part wisdom
    And ever three parts coward—I do not know   45
    Why yet I live to say 'This thing's to do,'

---

⁹ **softly** slowly
¹⁶ **main** main part
²³ **ranker** higher
²³ **in fee** outright
²⁷ **debate** settle
²⁸ **imposthume** ulcer
³⁶ **market** profit
³⁸ **discourse** understanding
⁴¹ **fust** grow moldy

Sith I have cause, and will, and strength, and means,
To do't. Examples gross* as earth exhort me:
Witness this army, of such mass and charge,*
Led by a delicate and tender prince,   50
Whose spirit, with divine ambition puff'd,
Makes mouths at the invisible event,*
Exposing what is mortal and unsure
To all that fortune, death, and danger dare,
Even for an egg-shell. Rightly to be great   55
Is not to stir without great argument,*
But greatly* to find quarrel in a straw,
When honour's at the stake. How stand I, then,
That have a father kill'd, a mother stain'd,
Excitements* of my reason and my blood,   60
And let all sleep, while to my shame I see
The imminent death of twenty thousand men
That, for a fantasy and trick of fame,
Go to their graves like beds, fight for a plot
Whereon the numbers cannot try the cause,   65
Which is not tomb enough and continent*
To hide the slain? O, from this time forth,
My thoughts be bloody, or be nothing worth!   [*Exit.*]

SCENE V———*Elsinore. The Castle.*

[*Enter* QUEEN, HORATIO, *and a* GENTLEMAN.]

QUEEN: I will not speak with her.
GENTLEMAN: She is importunate, indeed distract.
   Her mood will needs be pitied.
QUEEN: What would she have?
GENTLEMAN: She speaks much of her father; says she hears   5
   There's tricks i' th' world, and hems, and beats her heart;
   Spurns enviously at straws;* speaks things in doubt,*
   That carry but half sense. Her speech is nothing,
   Yet the unshaped use of it doth move
   The hearers to collection;* they yawn* at it,   10
   And botch the words up fit to their own thoughts;
   Which, as her winks and nods and gestures yield them,

---

[48] **gross** large
[49] **charge** expense
[52] **Makes mouths . . . event** scorns the outcome
[56] **argument** reason
[57] **greatly** nobly
[60] **Excitements** incentives
[66] **continent** container
[IV,v,7] **Spurns . . . straws** objects to insignificant matters
[7] **in doubt** uncertainly
[10] **collection** gather and listen
[10] **yawn** gape

Indeed would make one think there might be thought,
Though nothing sure, yet much unhappily.

HORATIO: 'Twere good she were spoken with; for she may strew   15
Dangerous conjectures in ill-breeding minds.

QUEEN: Let her come in.   [*Exit* GENTLEMAN.]

[*aside*] To my sick soul, as sin's true nature is,

Each toy seems prologue to some great amiss.*
So full of artless jealousy* is guilt,   20
It spills* itself in fearing to be spilt.

[*Enter* OPHELIA *distracted.*]

OPHELIA: Where is the beauteous Majesty of Denmark?
QUEEN: How now, Ophelia!
OPHELIA: [*sings*]

> How should I your true love know
>> From another one?   25
> By his cockle hat and staff,
>> And his sandal shoon.*

QUEEN: Alas, sweet lady, what imports this song?
OPHELIA: Say you? Nay, pray you, mark.   [*sings*]

> He is dead and gone, lady,   30
>> He is dead and gone;
> At his head a grass-green turf,
>> At his heels a stone.

O, ho!

QUEEN: Nay, but, Ophelia—   35
OPHELIA: Pray you, mark.   [*sings*]

> White his shroud as the mountain snow—

[*Enter* KING.]

QUEEN: Alas, look here, my lord.
OPHELIA: Larded* with sweet flowers;
> Which bewept to the grave did not go   40
>> With true-love showers.

KING: How do you, pretty lady?
OPHELIA: Well, God dild* you! They say the owl was a baker's daughter. Lord,
we know that we are, but know not what we may be. God be at your table!
KING: Conceit* upon her father.   45
OPHELIA: Pray let's have no words of this; but when they ask you what it means,
say you this: [*sings*]

> To-morrow is Saint Valentine's day,
> All in the morning betime,

---

[19] **amiss** misfortune
[20] **artless jealousy** crude suspicion
[21] **spills** destroys
[27] **shoon** shoes
[39] **Larded** decorated
[43] **dild** reward
[45] **Conceit** brooding

> *And I a maid at your window,*   50
> *To be your Valentine.*
> *Then up he rose, and donn'd his clothes,*
> *And dupp'd* the chamber-door;*
> *Let in the maid, that out a maid*
> *Never departed more.*   55

KING: Pretty Ophelia!

OPHELIA: Indeed, la, without an oath, I'll make an end on't.   [*sings*]

> *By Gis* and by Saint Charity,*
> *Alack, and fie for shame!*
> *Young men will do't, if they come to't;*   60
> *By Cock, they are to blame.*
> *Quoth she 'Before you tumbled me,*
> *You promis'd me to wed.'*

He answers:

> *'So would I 'a done, by yonder sun,*   65
> *An thou hadst not come to my bed.'*

KING: How long hath she been thus?

OPHELIA: I hope all will be well. We must be patient; but I cannot choose but weep to think they would lay him i' th' cold ground. My brother shall know of it; and so I thank you for your good counsel. Come, my coach! Good   70
night, ladies; good night, sweet ladies, good night, good night.

> [*Exit.*]

KING: Follow her close; give her good watch, I pray you.

> [*Exit* HORATIO.]

O, this is the poison of deep grief; it springs
All from her father's death. And now behold—
O Gertrude, Gertrude!   75
When sorrows come, they come not single spies,
But in battalions! First, her father slain;
Next, your son gone, and he most violent author
Of his own just remove; the people muddied,*
Thick and unwholesome in their thoughts and whispers   80
For good Polonius' death; and we have done but greenly*
In hugger-mugger* to inter him; poor Ophelia
Divided from herself and her fair judgment,
Without the which we are pictures, or mere beasts;
Last, and as much containing as all these,   85
Her brother is in secret come from France;
Feeds on his wonder,* keeps himself in clouds,

---

⁵³ **dupp'd** opened
⁵⁸ **Gis** Jesus
⁷⁹ **muddied** confused
⁸¹ **greenly** foolishly
⁸² **hugger-mugger** secret haste
⁸⁷ **wonder** suspicion

And wants not buzzers* to infect his ear
With pestilent speeches of his father's death;
Wherein necessity, of matter beggar'd,*   90
Will nothing stick* our person to arraign
In ear and ear. O my dear Gertrude, this,
Like to a murd'ring piece,* in many places
Gives me superfluous death.   [*a noise within*]
QUEEN: Alack, what noise is this?   95
KING: Attend!

      [*Enter a* GENTLEMAN.]

Where are my Switzers!* Let them guard the door.
What is the matter?
GENTLEMAN: Save yourself, my lord:
The ocean, overpeering of his list,*   100
Eats not the flats with more impetuous haste
Than young Laertes, in a riotous head,*
O'erbears your officers. The rabble call him lord;
And, as the world were now but to begin,
Antiquity forgot, custom not known,   105
The ratifiers and props of every word,
They cry 'Choose we; Laertes shall be king.'
Caps, hands, and tongues, applaud it to the clouds,
'Laertes shall be king, Laertes king.'
QUEEN: How cheerfully on the false trail they cry!   110
      [*noise within*]
O, this is counter, you false Danish dogs!
KING: The doors are broke. [*Enter* LAERTES, *with others, in arms.*]
LAERTES: Where is this king?—Sirs, stand you all without.
ALL: No, let's come in.
LAERTES: I pray you give me leave.   115
ALL: We will, we will.
      [*Exeunt.*]
LAERTES: I thank you. Keep the door.—O thou vile king,
Give me my father!
QUEEN: Calmly, good Laertes.
LAERTES: That drop of blood that's calm proclaims me bastard;   120
Cries cuckold to my father; brands the harlot
Even here, between the chaste unsmirched brow
Of my true mother.
KING: What is the cause, Laertes,
That thy rebellion looks so giant-like?   125

---

88 **buzzers** tale bearers
90 **beggar'd** lacking facts
91 **Will nothing stick** will not hesitate
93 **murd'ring piece** cannon
97 **Switzers** Swiss guards
100 **list** shore
102 **in a riotous head** with a rebellious mob

Let him go, Gertrude; do not fear our person:
There's such divinity doth hedge a king
That treason can but peep to what it would,
Acts little of his will. Tell me, Laertes,
Why thou art thus incens'd. Let him go, Gertrude. 130
Speak, man.

LAERTES: Where is my father?

KING: Dead.

QUEEN: But not by him.

KING: Let him demand his fill. 135

LAERTES: How came he dead? I'll not be juggled with.
To hell, allegiance! Vows, to the blackest devil!
Conscience and grace, to the profoundest pit!
I dare damnation. To this point I stand,
That both the worlds I give to negligence,* 140
Let come what comes; only I'll be reveng'd
Most thoroughly for my father.

KING: Who shall stay you?

LAERTES: My will, not all the world's.
And for my means, I'll husband them* so well 145
They shall go far with little.

KING: Good Laertes,
If you desire to know the certainty
Of your dear father, is't writ in your revenge
That, swoopstake,* you will draw both friend and foe, 150
Winner and loser?

LAERTES: None but his enemies.

KING: Will you know them, then?

LAERTES: To his good friends thus wide I'll ope my arms
And, like the kind life-rend'ring pelican, 155
Repast* them with my blood.

KING: Why, now you speak
Like a good child and a true gentleman.
That I am guiltless of your father's death,
And am most sensibly in grief for it, 160
It shall as level to your judgment 'pear'
As day does to your eye.   [*A noise within:* 'Let her come in.']

LAERTES: How now! What noise is that?
[*Reenter* OPHELIA.]
O, heat dry up my brains! tears seven times salt
Burn out the sense and virtue* of mine eye! 165
By heaven, thy madness shall be paid with weight
Till our scale turn the beam.* O rose of May!

---

140 **both the worlds . . . negligence** I care not what may happen to me in this world or the next
145 **husband them** use them economically
150 **swoopstake** in a full sweep
155–56 **pelican, repast** (pelicans were thought to use their own blood to feed their young)
165 **virtue** power
167 **scale turn the beam** weigh down the balance of a scale

Dear maid, kind sister, sweet Ophelia!
O heavens! is't possible a young maid's wits
Should be as mortal as an old man's life?　　　　　　　　　　170
Nature is fine* in love; and where 'tis fine
It sends some precious instance* of itself
After the thing it loves.

OPHELIA: [*sings*]

> They bore him barefac'd on the bier;
> Hey non nonny, nonny, hey nonny;　　　　　　　　　　175
> And in his grave rain'd many a tear—
> Fare you well, my dove!

LAERTES: Hadst thou thy wits, and didst persuade revenge,
　　It could not move thus.
OPHELIA: You must sing 'A-down, a-down,' an you call him a-down-a. O, how the　　180
　　wheel becomes it! It is the false steward, that stole his master's daughter.
LAERTES: This nothing's more than matter.*
OPHELIA: There's rosemary, that's for remembrance; pray you, love, remember.
　　And there is pansies, that's for thoughts.
LAERTES: A document* in madness—thoughts and remembrance fitted.　　　　185
OPHELIA: There's fennel for you, and columbines. There's rue for you; and here's
　　some for me. We may call it herb of grace a Sundays. O, you must wear your
　　rue with a difference. There's a daisy. I would give you some violets, but they
　　wither'd all when my father died. They say 'a made a good end.
　　[*sings*] For bonny sweet Robin is all my joy.　　　　　　　190
LAERTES: Thought and affliction, passion, hell itself,
　　She turns to favour* and to prettiness.
OPHELIA: [*sings*]

> And will 'a not come again
> And will 'a not come again?
> No, no, he is dead,　　　　　　　　　　195
> Go to thy death-bed,
> He never will come again.
> His beard was as white as snow,
> All flaxen was his poll;*
> He is gone, he is gone,　　　　　　　　　　200
> And we cast away moan:
> God-a-mercy on his soul!

And of all Christian souls, I pray God. God buy you.

　　[*Exit.*]

LAERTES: Do you see this, O God?
KING: Laertes, I must commune with your grief,　　　　　　　205

---

¹⁷¹ **fine** refined
¹⁷² **instance** sample
¹⁸² **nothing's . . . matter** this nonsense contains more meaning than does a statement of great matter
¹⁸⁵ **document** lesson
¹⁹² **favour** to beauty
¹⁹⁹ **flaxen was his poll** his hair was white

Or you deny me right. Go but apart,
Make choice of whom your wisest friends you will,
And they shall hear and judge 'twixt you and me.
If by direct or by collateral* hand
They find us touch'd,* we will our kingdom give,   210
Our crown, our life, and all that we call ours,
To you in satisfaction; but if not,
Be you content to lend your patience to us,
And we shall jointly labour with your soul
To give it due content.   215
LAERTES: Let this be so.
His means of death, his obscure funeral—
No trophy, sword, nor hatchment,* o'er his bones,
No noble rite nor formal ostentation*—
Cry to be heard, as 'twere from heaven to earth,   220
That I must call't in question.
KING: So you shall;
And where th' offence is, let the great axe fall.
I pray you go with me.   [*Exeunt.*]

SCENE VI———*Elsinore. The Castle.*

[*Enter* HORATIO *with an* ATTENDANT.]

HORATIO: What are they that would speak with me?
ATTENDANT: Sea-faring men, sir; they say they have letters for you.
HORATIO: Let them come in.   [*Exit* ATTENDANT.]
      I do not know from what part of the world
      I should be greeted, if not from Lord Hamlet.   5

[*Enter* SAILORS.]

SAILOR: God bless you, sir.
HORATIO: Let Him bless thee, too.
SAILOR: 'A shall, sir, an't please Him. There's a letter for you, sir; it came from
      th'ambassador that was bound for England—if your name be Horatio, as I
      am let to know it is.   10
HORATIO: [*reads*] 'Horatio, when thou shalt have overlook'd* this, give these
      fellows some means to the King: they have letters for him. Ere we were two
      days old at sea, a pirate of very warlike appointment gave us chase. Finding
      ourselves too slow of sail, we put on a compelled valour; and in the grapple
      I boarded them. On the instant they got clear of our ship; so I alone became   15
      their prisoner. They have dealt with me like thieves of mercy; but they knew
      what they did; I am to do a good turn for them. Let the King have the letters
      I have sent; and repair thou to me with as much speed as thou wouldest fly

---

²⁰⁹ **collateral** indirect
²¹⁰ **touch'd** implicated
²¹⁸ **hatchment** stone bearing coat of arms
²¹⁹ **ostentation** ceremony
^{IV,vi,11} **overlook'd** read

death. I have words to speak in thine ear will make thee dumb; yet are they
much too light for the bore of the matter. These good fellows will bring thee   20
where I am. Rosencrantz and Guildenstern hold their course for England; of
them I have much to tell thee. Farewell.

He that thou knowest thine, Hamlet.'

Come, I will give you way for these your letters,
And do't the speedier that you may direct me   25
To him from whom you brought them.   [*Exeunt.*]

SCENE VII———Elsinore. The Castle.

[*Enter* KING *and* LAERTES.]

KING: Now must your conscience my acquittance seal,
 And you must put me in your heart for friend,
 Sith you have heard, and with a knowing ear,
 That he which hath your noble father slain
 Pursu'd my life.   5
LAERTES: It well appears. But tell me
 Why you proceeded not against these feats,
 So crimeful and so capital* in nature,
 As by your safety, wisdom, all things else,
 You mainly were stirr'd up.   10
KING: O, for two special reasons,
 Which may to you, perhaps, seem much unsinew'd,*
 But yet to me th' are strong. The Queen his mother
 Lives almost by his looks; and for myself,
 My virtue or my plague, be it either which—   15
 She is so conjunctive* to my life and soul
 That, as the star moves not but in his sphere,
 I could not but by her. The other motive,
 Why to a public count I might not go,
 Is the great love the general gender* bear him;   20
 Who, dipping all his faults in their affection,
 Work like the spring that turneth wood to stone,
 Convert his gyves* to graces; so that my arrows,
 Too slightly timber'd* for so loud a wind,
 Would have reverted to my bow again,   25
 But not where I have aim'd them.
LAERTES: And so have I a noble father lost;
 A sister driven into desp'rate terms,
 Whose worth, if praises may go back again,
 Stood challenger on mount of all the age   30
 For her perfections. But my revenge will come.

IV,vii,8 **capital** deserving death
[12] **unsinew'd** weak
[16] **conjunctive** closely united
[20] **general gender** common people
[23] **gyves** fetters
[24] **timber'd** shafted

KING: Break not your sleeps for that. You must not think
    That we are made of stuff so flat and dull
    That we can let our beard be shook with danger,
    And think it pastime. You shortly shall hear more   35
    I lov'd your father, and we love our self;
    And that, I hope, will teach you to imagine—

    [*Enter a* MESSENGER *with letters.*]

    How now! What news?
MESSENGER: Letters, my lord, from Hamlet:
    These to your Majesty; this to the Queen.   40
KING: From Hamlet! Who brought them?
MESSENGER: Sailors, my lord, they say; I saw them not.
    They were given me by Claudio; he receiv'd them
    Of him that brought them.
KING: Laertes, you shall hear them.   45
    Leave us   [*Exit* MESSENGER.]
    [*reads*] 'High and Mighty. You shall know I am set naked* on your kingdom.
    To-morrow shall I beg leave to see your kingly eyes; when I shall, first asking
    your pardon thereunto, recount the occasion of my sudden and more
    strange return.   50
                     Hamlet.'

    What should this mean? Are all the rest come back?
    Or is it some abuse,* and no such thing?
LAERTES: Know you the hand?
KING: 'Tis Hamlet's character. 'Naked'!   55
    And in a postscript here, he says 'alone.'
    Can you devise* me?
LAERTES: I am lost in it, my lord. But let him come;
    It warms the very sickness in my heart
    That I shall live and tell him to his teeth   60
    'Thus didest thou.'
KING: If it be so, Laertes—
    As how should it be so, how otherwise?—
    Will you be rul'd by me?
LAERTES: Ay, my lord;   65
    So you will not o'errule me to a peace.
KING: To thine own peace. If he be now return'd,
    As checking at* his voyage, and that he means
    No more to undertake it, I will work him
    To an exploit now ripe in my device,   70
    Under the which he shall not choose but fall;
    And for his death, no wind of blame shall breathe;
    But even his mother shall uncharge the practice
    And call it accident.

---

47 **naked** destitute
53 **abuse** deception
57 **devise** advise
68 **checking at** abandoning

LAERTES: My lord, I will be rul'd 75
  The rather, if you could devise it so
  That I might be the organ.
KING: It falls right.
  You have been talk'd of since your travel much,
  And that in Hamlet's hearing, for a quality 80
  Wherein they say you shine. Your sum of parts
  Did not together pluck such envy from him
  As did that one; and that, in my regard,
  Of the unworthiest siege.*
LAERTES: What part is that, my lord? 85
KING: A very riband in the cap of youth,
  Yet needful, too; for youth no less becomes
  The light and careless livery that it wears
  Than settled age his sables and his weeds,*
  Importing health and graveness. Two months since 90
  Here was a gentleman of Normandy—
  I have seen myself, and serv'd against, the French,
  And they can well on horseback; but this gallant
  Had witchcraft in't; he grew into his seat,
  And to such wondrous doing brought his horse, 95
  As had he been incorps'd and demi-natur'd
  With the brave beast. So far he topp'd my thought,
  That I, in forgery* of shapes and tricks,
  Come short of what he did.
LAERTES: A Norman was't?
                                            100
KING: A Norman.
LAERTES: Upon my life, Lamord.
KING: The very same.
LAERTES: I know him well. He is the brooch* indeed
  And gem of all the nation. 105
KING: He made confession* of you;
  And gave you such a masterly report
  For art and exercise in your defence,
  And for your rapier most especial,
  That he cried out 'twould be a sight indeed 110
  If one could match you. The scrimers* of their nation
  He swore had neither motion, guard, nor eye,
  If you oppos'd them. Sir, this report of his
  Did Hamlet so envenom with his envy
  That he could nothing do but wish and beg 115
  Your sudden coming o'er, to play with you.
  Now out of this—

---

[84] **siege** rank
[89] **weeds** sober attire
[98] **forgery** invention
[104] **brooch** ornament
[106] **confession** report
[111] **scrimers** fencers

LAERTES: What out of this, my lord?
KING: Laertes, was your father dear to you?
    Or are you like the painting of a sorrow,   120
    A face without a heart?
LAERTES: Why ask you this?
KING: Not that I think you did not love your father;
    But that I know love is begun by time,
    And that I see, in passages of proof,*   125
    Time qualifies* the spark and fire of it.
    There lives within the very flame of love
    A kind of wick or snuff that will abate it;
    And nothing is at a like goodness still;
    For goodness, growing to a pleurisy,*   130
    Dies in his own too much. That we would do,
    We should do when we would; for this 'would' changes,
    And hath abatements and delays as many
    As there are tongues, are hands, are accidents;
    And then this 'should' is like a spendthrift's sigh   135
    That hurts by easing. But to the quick* of th' ulcer:
    Hamlet comes back; what would you undertake
    To show yourself in deed your father's son
    More than in words?
LAERTES: To cut his throat i' th' church.   140
KING: No place, indeed, should murder sanctuarize;*
    Revenge should have no bounds. But, good Laertes,
    Will you do this? Keep close within your chamber.
    Hamlet return'd shall know you are come home.
    We'll put on those shall praise your excellence,   145
    And set a double varnish on the fame
    The Frenchman gave you; bring you, in fine,* together,
    And wager on your heads. He, being remiss,
    Most generous, and free from all contriving,
    Will not peruse the foils; so that with ease   150
    Or with a little shuffling, you may choose
    A sword unbated,* and, in a pass of practice,*
    Requite him for your father.
LAERTES: I will do't;
    And for that purpose I'll anoint my sword.   155
    I bought an unction of a mountebank,
    So mortal that but dip a knife in it,
    Where it draws blood no cataplasm* so rare,

---

[125] **passages of proof** proved cases
[126] **qualifies** diminishes
[130] **pleurisy** excess
[136] **quick** sensitive part
[141] **sanctuarize** protect
[147] **in fine** finally
[152] **unbated** not blunted
[152] **pass of practice** treacherous thrust
[158] **cataplasm** poultice   .

Collected from all simples* that have virtue
Under the moon, can save the thing from death   160
That is but scratch'd withal. I'll touch my point
With this contagion, that, if I gall him slightly,
It may be death.

KING: Let's further think of this;
Weigh what convenience both of time and means   165
May fit us to our shape.* If this should fail,
And that our drift look through* our bad performance,
'Twere better not assay'd, therefore this project
Should have a back or second, that might hold
If this did blast in proof.* Soft! let me see.   170
We'll make a solemn wager on your cunnings—
I ha't.
When in your motion you are hot and dry—
As make your bouts more violent to that end—
And that he calls for drink, I'll have preferr'd him   175
A chalice for the nonce,* whereon but sipping,
If he by chance escape your venom'd stuck,*
Our purpose may hold there. But stay; what noise?

[*Enter* QUEEN.]

QUEEN: One woe doth tread upon another's heel,
So fast they follow. Your sister's drown'd, Laertes.   180
LAERTES: Drown'd? O, where?
QUEEN: There is a willow grows aslant the brook
That shows his hoar* leaves in the glassy stream;
Therewith fantastic garlands did she make
Of crowflowers, nettles, daisies, and long purples   185
That liberal* shepherds give a grosser name,
But our cold maids do dead men's fingers call them.
There, on the pendent boughs her coronet weeds
Clamb'ring to hang, an envious sliver broke;
When down her weedy trophies and herself   190
Feel in the weeping brook. Her clothes spread wide
And, mermaid-like, awhile they bore her up;
Which time she chanted snatches of old lauds,*
As one incapable* of her own distress,
Or like a creature native and indued*   195

---

[159] **simples** medicinal herbs
[166] **shape** role
[167] **drift look through** purpose show through
[170] **blast in proof** fail in performance
[176] **nonce** occasion
[177] **stuck** thrust
[183] **hoar** silver gray
[186] **liberal** coarse-mouthed
[193] **lauds** hymns
[194] **incapable** unaware
[195] **indued** in harmony with

Unto that element; but long it could not be
Till that her garments, heavy with their drink,
Pull'd the poor wretch from her melodious lay
To muddy death.
LAERTES: Alas, then she is drown'd!   200
QUEEN: Drown'd, drown'd.
LAERTES: Too much of water hast thou, poor Ophelia,
And therefore I forbid my tears; but yet
It is our trick,* nature her custom holds,
Let shame say what it will. When these are gone,   205
The woman* will be out. Adieu, my lord.
I have a speech o' fire that fain would blaze
But that this folly douts it.   [*Exit.*]
KING: Let's follow, Gertrude.
How much I had to do to calm his rage!   210
Now fear I this will give it start again;
Therefore let's follow.   [*Exeunt.*]

ACT V

SCENE I———*Elsinore. A churchyard.*

[*Enter two* CLOWNS *with spades and picks.*]

FIRST CLOWN: Is she to be buried in Christian burial when she wilfully seeks her
    own salvation?
SECOND CLOWN: I tell thee she is; therefore make her grave straight.* The
    crowner* hath sat on her, and finds it Christian burial.
FIRST CLOWN: How can that be, unless she drown'd herself in her own defence?   5
SECOND CLOWN: Why, 'tis found so.
FIRST CLOWN: It must be 'se offendendo';* it cannot be else. For here lies the
    point: if I drown myself wittingly, it argues an act; and an act hath three
    branches—it is to act, to do, to perform; argal,* she drown'd herself
    wittingly.   10
SECOND CLOWN: Nay, but hear you, Goodman Delver.
FIRST CLOWN: Give me leave. Here lies the water; good. Here stands the man;
    good. If the man go to this water and drown himself, it is, will he, nill he,
    he goes—mark you that; but if the water come to him and drown him, he
    drowns not himself. Argal, he that is not guilty of his own death shortens not   15
    his own life.

---

[204] **trick** way
[206] **woman** womanly part
[V,i,3] **straight** straight way
[4] **crowner** coroner
[7] **se offendendo** false latin, instead of "se defendendo" meaning "in self-defense"
[9] **argal** false Latin for "ergo" ("therefore")

SECOND CLOWN: But is this law?

FIRST CLOWN: Ay, marry is't; crowner's quest* law.

SECOND CLOWN: Will you ha' the truth an't? If this had not been a gentlewoman,   20
she should have been buried out a Christian burial.

FIRST CLOWN: Why, there thou say'st; and the more pity that great folk should
have count'nance* in this world to drown or hang themselves more than
their even Christen.* Come, my spade. There is no ancient gentlemen but
gard'ners, ditchers, and grave-makers; they hold up* Adam's profession.

SECOND CLOWN: Was he a gentleman?   25

FIRST CLOWN: 'A was the first that ever bore arms.*

SECOND CLOWN: Why, he had none.

FIRST CLOWN: What, art a heathen? How dost thou understand the Scripture?
The Scripture says Adam digg'd. Could he dig without arms? I'll put another
question to thee. If thou answerest me not to the purpose, confess   30
thyself—

SECOND CLOWN: Go to.

FIRST CLOWN: What is he that builds stronger than either the mason, the shipwright, or the carpenter?

SECOND CLOWN: The gallows-maker; for that frame outlives a thousand tenants.   35

FIRST CLOWN: I like thy wit well; in good faith the gallows does well; but how
does it well? It does well to those that do ill. Now thou dost ill to say the
gallows is built stronger than the church; argal, the gallows may do well to
thee. To't again, come.

SECOND CLOWN: Who builds stronger than a mason, a shipwright, or a carpenter?   40

FIRST CLOWN: Ay, tell me that, and unyoke.*

SECOND CLOWN: Marry, now I can tell.

FIRST CLOWN: To't.

SECOND CLOWN: Mass, I cannot tell.

[*Enter* HAMLET *and* HORATIO, *afar off.*]

FIRST CLOWN: Cudgel thy brains no more about it, for your dull ass will not   45
mend his pace with beating, and when you are ask'd this question next, say
'a grave-maker': the house he makes lasts till doomsday. Go, get thee to
Yaughan; fetch me a stoup* of liquor.   [*Exit* SECOND CLOWN.]

[*digs and sings*]

In youth, when I did love, did love
Methought it was very sweet,   50
*To contract-o-the time for-a my behove,**
O, methought there-a-was nothing-a meet.

HAMLET: Has this fellow no feeling of his business, that 'a sings in grave-making?

---

¹⁸ **crowner's quest** coroner's inquest

²² **count'nance** privilege

²³ **even Christen** fellow Christian

²⁴ **hold up** keep up

²⁶ **bore arms** had a coat of arms

⁴¹ **unyoke** quit work for the day

⁴⁸ **stoup** tankard

⁵¹ **behove** advantage

HORATIO: Custom hath made it in him a property of easiness.*
HAMLET: 'Tis e'en so; the hand of little employment hath the daintier sense.   55
FIRST CLOWN: [sings]

> But age, with his stealing steps,
> Hath clawed me in his clutch,
> And hath shipped me intil the land,
> As if I had never been such.

[throws up a skull]

HAMLET: That skull had a tongue in it, and could sing once. How the knave jowls*   60
it to the ground, as if 'twere Cain's jawbone, that did the first murder! This
might be the pate of a politician, which this ass now o'erreaches; one that
would circumvent God, might it not?
HORATIO: It might, my lord.
HAMLET: Or of a courtier; which could say 'Good morrow, sweet lord! How dost   65
thou, sweet lord?' This might be my Lord Such-a-one, that praised my Lord
Such-a-one's horse, when 'a meant to beg it—might it not?
HORATIO: Ay, my lord.
HAMLET: Why, e'en so; and now my Lady Worm's, chapless,* and knock'd about
the mazard* with a sexton's spade. Here's fine revolution, an we had the   70
trick to see't. Did these bones cost no more the breeding but to play at loggats*
with them? Mine ache to think on't.
FIRST CLOWN: [sings]

> A pick-axe and a spade, a spade
> For and a shrouding sheet:
> O, a pit of clay for to be made   75
> For such a guest is meet.

[throws up another skull]

HAMLET: There's another. Why may not that be the skull of a lawyer? Where be
his quiddities* now, his quillets,* his cases, his tenures,* and his tricks? Why
does he suffer this rude knave now to knock him about the sconce* with a
dirty shovel, and will not tell him of his action of battery? Hum! This fellow   80
might be in's time a great buyer of land, with his statutes, his recognizances,
his fines,* his double vouchers, his recoveries. Is this the fine* of his fines,
and the recovery of his recoveries, to have his fine pate full of fine dirt? Will
his vouchers vouch him no more of his purchases, and double ones, too, than
the length and breadth of a pair of indentures?* The very conveyances of his   85
lands will scarcely lie in this box; and must th' inheritor himself have no
more, ha?

---

54 **Custom . . . easiness** constant practice has made it easy
60 **jowls** hurls
69 **chapless** missing the lower jaw
70 **mazard** head
71 **loggats** a game involving throwing at objects
78 **quiddities, quillets, tenures** legal terms
79 **sconce** head
82 **fines, fine** play on words for documents, death, and so on
85 **indentures** contracts

HORATIO: Not a jot more, my lord.

HAMLET: Is not parchment made of sheep-skins?

HORATIO: Ay, my lord, and of calves' skins, too.   90

HAMLET: They are sheep and calves which seek out assurance in that. I will speak
to this fellow. Whose grave's this, sirrah?

FIRST CLOWN: Mine, sir.   [*sings*]

> O, a pit of clay for to be made
> For such a guest is meet.   95

HAMLET: I think it be thine indeed, for thou liest in't.

FIRST CLOWN: You lie out on't, sir, and therefore 'tis not yours. For my part, I do
not lie in't, yet it is mine.

HAMLET: Thou dost lie in't, to be in't and say it is thine; 'tis for the dead, not for
the quick; therefore thou liest.   100

FIRST CLOWN: 'Tis a quick lie, sir; 'twill away again from me to you.

HAMLET: What man dost thou dig it for?

FIRST CLOWN: For no man, sir.

HAMLET: What woman, then?

FIRST CLOWN: For none neither.   105

HAMLET: Who is to be buried in't?

FIRST CLOWN: One that was a woman, sir; but, rest her soul, she's dead.

HAMLET: How absolute* the knave is! We must speak by the card,* or equivoca-
tion will undo us. By the Lord, Horatio, this three years I have took note of
it: the age is grown so picked* that the toe of the peasant comes so near the   110
heel of the courtier, he galls his kibe.* How long hast thou been a gravemaker?

FIRST CLOWN: Of all the days i' th' year, I came to't that day that our last King
Hamlet overcame Fortinbras.

HAMLET: How long is that since?

FIRST CLOWN: Cannot you tell that? Every fool can tell that: it was that very day   115
that young Hamlet was born—he that is mad, and sent into England.

HAMLET: Ay, marry, why was he sent into England?

FIRST CLOWN: Why, because 'a was mad: 'a shall recover his wits there; or, if 'a do
not, 'tis no great matter there.

HAMLET: Why?   120

FIRST CLOWN: 'Twill not be seen in him there: there the men are as mad as he.

HAMLET: How came he mad?

FIRST CLOWN: Very strangely, they say.

HAMLET: How strangely?

FIRST CLOWN: Faith, e'en with losing his wits.   125

HAMLET: Upon what ground?

FIRST CLOWN: Why, here in Denmark. I have been sexton here, man and boy,
thirty years.

HAMLET: How long will a man lie i' th' earth ere he rot?

---

[108] **absolute** positive, certain
[108] **card** exactly
[110] **picked** refined
[111] **kibe** sore on the heel

FIRST CLOWN: Faith, if 'a be not rotten before 'a die—as we have many pocky   130
corses* now-a-days that will scarce hold the laying in—'a will last you some
eight year or nine year. A tanner will last you nine year.

HAMLET: Why he more than another?

FIRST CLOWN: Why, sir, his hide is so tann'd with his trade that 'a will keep out
water a great while; and your water is a sore decayer of your whoreson dead   135
body. Here's a skull now; this skull has lien you i' th' earth three and twenty
years.

HAMLET: Whose was it?

FIRST CLOWN: A whoreson mad fellow's it was. Whose do you think it was?

HAMLET: Nay, I know not.   140

FIRST CLOWN: A pestilence on him for a mad rogue! 'A poured a flagon of Rhenish on my head once. This same skull, sir, was, sir, Yorick's skull, the King's
jester.

HAMLET: This?

FIRST CLOWN: E'en that.   145

HAMLET: Let me see. [*takes the skull*] Alas, poor Yorick! I knew him, Horatio: a
fellow of infinite jest, of most excellent fancy; he hath borne me on his back
a thousand times. And now how abhorred in my imagination it is! My gorge
rises at it. Here hung those lips that I have kiss'd I know not how oft. Where
be your gibes now, your gambols, your songs, your flashes of merriment   150
that were wont to set the table on a roar? Not one now to mock your own
grinning—quite chap-fall'n?* Now get you to my lady's chamber, and tell
her, let her paint an inch thick, to this favour* she must come; make her
laugh at that. Prithee, Horatio, tell me one thing.

HORATIO: What's that, my lord?   155

HAMLET: Dost thou think Alexander look'd o' this fashion i' th' earth?

HORATIO: E'en so.

HAMLET: And smelt so? Pah   [*throws down the skull*]

HORATIO: E'en so, my lord.

HAMLET: To what base uses we may return, Horatio! Why may not imagination   160
trace the noble dust of Alexander till 'a find it stopping a bung-hole?

HORATIO: 'Twere to consider too curiously* to consider so.

HAMLET: No, faith, not a jot; but to follow him thither with modesty enough, and
likelihood to lead it, as thus: Alexander died, Alexander was buried, Alexander returneth to dust; the dust is earth; of earth we make loam, and why of   165
that loam whereto he was converted might they not stop a beer-barrel?

Imperious Caesar, dead and turn'd to clay,
Might stop a hole to keep the wind away.
O, that that earth which kept the world in awe
Should patch a wall t' expel the winter's flaw!   170

But soft! but soft! awhile. Here comes the King.

[*Enter the* KING, QUEEN, LAERTES, *in funeral procession after the coffin, with*
PRIEST *and* LORDS *attendant.*]

130–31 **pocky corses** corpses of those with syphilis
152 **chap-fall'n** jawless (down in the mouth)
153 **favour** appearance, condition
162 **curiously** minutely
170 **flaw** gust

The Queen, the courtiers. Who is this they follow?
And with such maimed* rites? This doth betoken
The corse they follow did with desperate hand
Fordo it own life. 'Twas of some estate.*   175
Couch* we awhile and mark.   [*retiring with* HORATIO]
LAERTES: What ceremony else?
HAMLET: That is Laertes, a very noble youth. Mark.
LAERTES: What ceremony else?
PRIEST: Her obsequies have been so far enlarg'd   180
    As we have warrantise. Her death was doubtful;
    And, but that great command o'ersways the order,
    She should in ground unsanctified have lodg'd
    Till the last trumpet; for charitable prayers,
    Shards, flints, and pebbles, should be thrown on her;   185
    Yet here she is allow'd her virgin crants,*
    Her maiden strewments, and the bringing home
    Of bell and burial.
LAERTES: Must there no more be done?
PRIEST: No more be done.   190
    We should profane the service of the dead
    To sing sage requiem and such rest to her
    As to peace-parted souls.
LAERTES: Lay her i' th' earth;
    And from her fair and unpolluted flesh   195
    May violets spring! I tell thee, churlish priest,
    A minist'ring angel shall my sister be
    When thou liest howling.
HAMLET: What, the fair Ophelia!
QUEEN: Sweets to the sweet; farewell! [*scattering flowers*]   200
    I hop'd thou shouldst have been my Hamlet's wife;
    I thought thy bride-bed to have deck'd, sweet maid,
    And not have strew'd thy grave.
LAERTES: O, treble woe
    Fall ten times treble on that cursed head   205
    Whose wicked deed thy most ingenious sense*
    Depriv'd thee of! Hold off the earth awhile,
    Till I have caught her once more in mine arms.

      [*leaps into the grave*]

Now pile your dust upon the quick and dead,
Till of this flat a mountain you have made   210
T' o'er-top old Pelion or the skyish head
Of blue Olympus.

---

[173] **maimed** curtailed
[175] **estate** high rank
[176] **Couch** hide
[186] **crants** garlands
[206] **ingenious sense** finely endowed mind

HAMLET: [*advancing*] What is he whose grief
    Bears such an emphasis, whose phrase of sorrow
    Conjures the wand'ring stars, and makes them stand   215
    Like wonder-wounded hearers? This is I,
    Hamlet, the Dane.   [*leaps into the grave*]
LAERTES: The devil take thy soul! [*grappling with him*]
HAMLET: Thou pray'st not well.
    I prithee take thy fingers from my throat;   220
    For, though I am not splenitive* and rash,
    Yet have I in me something dangerous,
    Which let thy wiseness fear. Hold off thy hand.
KING: Pluck them asunder.
QUEEN: Hamlet! Hamlet!   225
ALL: Gentlemen!
HORATIO: Good my lord, be quiet.

    [*The attendants part them, and they come out of the grave.*]

HAMLET: Why, I will fight with him upon this theme
    Until my eyelids will no longer wag.
QUEEN: O my son, what theme?   230
HAMLET: I lov'd Ophelia: forty thousand brothers
    Could not, with all their quantity of love
    Make up my sum. What wilt thou do for her?
KING: O, he is mad, Laertes.
QUEEN: For love of God, forbear him.   235
HAMLET: 'Swounds, show me what th'owt do:
    Woo't weep, woo't fight, woo't fast, woo't tear thyself,
    Woo't drink up eisel,* eat a crocodile?
    I'll do't. Dost come here to whine?
    To outface me with leaping in her grave?   240
    Be buried quick with her, and so will I;
    And, if thou prate of mountains, let them throw
    Millions of acres on us, till our ground,
    Singeing his pate against the burning zone,*
    Make Ossa like a wart! Nay, an thou'lt mouth,   245
    I'll rant as well as thou.
QUEEN: This is mere madness;
    And thus awhile the fit will work on him;
    Anon, as patient as the female dove
    When that her golden couplets are disclos'd*   250
    His silence will sit drooping.
HAMLET: Hear you, sir:
    What is the reason that you use me thus?

---

[221] **splenitive** fiery spirited
[238] **eisel** vinegar
[244] **burning zone** the sun
[250] **golden couplets are disclos'd** doves were thought to lay only two eggs; here the reference is to young, just-hatched doves

I lov'd you ever. But it is no matter.
Let Hercules himself do what he may, 255
The cat will mew, and dog will have his day. [*Exit.*]
KING: I pray thee, good Horatio, wait upon him.

[*Exit* HORATIO.]

[*to* LAERTES] Strengthen your patience in our last night's speech;
We'll put the matter to the present push.*—
Good Gertrude, set some watch over your son.— 260
This grave shall have a living* monument.
An hour of quiet shortly shall we see;
Till then in patience our proceeding be. [*Exeunt.*]

SCENE II———*Elsinore. The Castle.*

[*Enter* HAMLET *and* HORATIO.]

HAMLET: So much for this, sir; now shall you see the other.
You do remember all the circumstance?
HORATIO: Remember it, my lord!
HAMLET: Sir, in my heart there was a kind of fighting
That would not let me sleep. Methought I lay 5
Worse than the mutines in the bilboes.* Rashly,
And prais'd be rashness for it—let us know,
Our indiscretion sometime serves us well,
When our deep plots do pall,* and that should learn us
There's a divinity that shapes our ends, 10
Rough-hew them how we will.
HORATIO: That is most certain.
HAMLET: Up from my cabin,
My sea-gown scarf'd about me, in the dark
Grop'd to find out them; had my desire; 15
Finger'd* their packet, and in fine withdrew
To mine own room again, making so bold,
My fears forgetting manners, to unseal
Their grand commission; where I found, Horatio,
Ah, royal knavery! an exact command, 20
Larded* with many several sorts of reasons,
Importing Denmark's health and England's, too,
With, ho! such bugs and goblins in my life*—

---

259 **present push** immediate test
261 **living** lasting
V.ii,6 **mutines in the bilboes** mutineers in chains
9 **pall** fail
16 **Finger'd** stole
21 **Larded** enriched
23 **bugs . . . my life** imagined terrors if were allowed to live

That, on the supervise,* no leisure bated,*
No, not to stay the grinding of the axe,   25
My head should be struck off.
HORATIO: Is't possible?
HAMLET: Here's the commission; read it at more leisure.
But wilt thou hear now how I did proceed?
HORATIO: I beseech you.   30
HAMLET: Being thus benetted round with villainies—
Ere I could make a prologue to my brains,
They had begun the play—I sat me down;
Devis'd a new commission; wrote it fair.
I once did hold it, as our statists* do,   35
A baseness to write fair,* and labour'd much
How to forget that learning; but sir, now
It did me yeoman's service. Wilt thou know
Th' effect* of what I wrote?
HORATIO: Ay, good my lord.   40
HAMLET: An earnest conjuration from the King,
As England was his faithful tributary,
As love between them like the palm might flourish,
As peace should still her wheaten garland wear
And stand a comma* tween their amities,   45
And many such like as's of great charge,
That, on the view and knowing of these contents,
Without debatement further more or less,
He should those bearers put to sudden death,
Not shriving-time* allow'd.   50
HORATIO: How was this seal'd?
HAMLET: Why, even in that was heaven ordinant.*
I had my father's signet in my purse,
Which was the model of that Danish seal;
Folded the writ up in the form of th' other;   55
Subscrib'd it, gave't th' impression, plac'd it safely,
The changeling never known. Now, the next day
Was our sea-fight; and what to this was sequent
Thou knowest already.
HORATIO: So Guildenstern and Rosencrantz go to't.   60
HAMLET: Why, man, they did make love to this employment;
They are not near my conscience; their defeat
Does by their own insinuation* grow:
'tis dangerous when the baser nature comes

---

24 **supervise** reading
24 **leisure bated** delay allowed
35 **statists** statesmen
36 **fair** clearly
39 **effect** purport
45 **comma** link
50 **shriving-time** time to be absolved of sin
52 **ordinant** on my side
63 **insinuation** meddling

Between the pass and fell* incensed points   65
   Of mighty opposites.
HORATIO: Why, what a king is this!
HAMLET: Does it not, think thee, stand me now upon*—
   He that hath kill'd my king and whor'd my mother,
   Popp'd in between th' election* and my hopes;   70
   Thrown out his angle for my proper life,*
   And with such coz'nage*—is't not perfect conscience
   To quit* him with this arm? And is't not to be damn'd
   To let this canker of our nature come
   In further evil?   75
HORATIO: It must be shortly known to him from England
   What is the issue of the business there.
HAMLET: It will be short; the interim is mine.
   And a man's life's no more than to say 'one.'
   But I am very sorry, good Horatio,   80
   That to Laertes I forgot myself;
   For by the image of my cause I see
   The portraiture of his. I'll court his favours.
   But sure the bravery of his grief did put me
   Into a tow'ring passion.   85
HORATIO: Peace; who comes here?

   [*Enter young* OSRIC.]

OSRIC: Your lordship is right welcome back to Denmark.
HAMLET: I humbly thank you, sir. [*aside to* HORATIO] Dost know this water-fly?
HORATIO: [*aside to* HAMLET] No, my good lord.
HAMLET: [*aside to* HORATIO] Thy state is the more gracious; for 'tis a vice to know   90
   him. He hath much land, and fertile. Let a beast be lord of beasts, and
   his crib shall stand at the king's mess!* 'Tis a chough,* but, as I say,
   spacious* in the possession of dirt.
OSRIC: Sweet lord, if your lordship were at leisure, I should impart a thing to you
   from his Majesty.   95
HAMLET: I will receive it, sir, with all diligence of spirit. Put your bonnet to his
   right use, 'tis for the head.
OSRIC: I thank your lordship; it is very hot.
HAMLET: No, believe me, 'tis very cold; the wind is northerly.
OSRIC: It is indifferent cold, my lord, indeed.   100
HAMLET: But yet methinks it is very sultry and hot for my complexion.*
OSRIC: Exceedingly, my lord; it is very sultry, as 'twere—I cannot tell how. But,

---

⁶⁵ **pass and fell** thrust and cruel
⁶⁸ **stand me now upon** became incumbent on me
⁷⁰ **election** selection to be king
⁷¹ **angle for my proper life** tried to end my own life
⁷² **coz'nage** trickery
⁷³ **quit** pay back
⁹² **mess** table
⁹² **chough** chatterer
⁹³ **spacious** well off
¹⁰¹ **complexion** temperament

my lord, his Majesty bade me signify to you that 'a has laid a great wager
on your head. Sir, this is the matter—
HAMLET: I beseech you, remember.   105

[HAMLET *moves him to put on his hat.*]

OSRIC: Nay, good my lord; for my ease, in good faith. Sir, here is newly come to
court Laertes; believe me, an absolute gentleman, full of most excellent differences,* of very soft society and great showing. Indeed, to speak feelingly
of him, he is the card* or calendar of gentry, for you shall find in him the
continent* of what part a gentleman would see.   110
HAMLET: Sir, his definement* suffers no perdition* in you; though, I know, to
divide him inventorially would dozy* th' arithmetic of memory, and yet but
yaw neither in respect of his quick sail. But, in the verity of extolment, I take
him to be a soul of great article, and his infusion of such dearth and rareness,
as to make true diction of him, his semblable is his mirror, and who else would   115
trace him, his umbrage, nothing more.
OSRIC: Your lordship speaks most infallibly of him.
HAMLET: The concernancy,* sir? Why do we wrap the gentleman in our more
rawer breath?
OSRIC: Sir?   120
HORATIO: [*aside to* HAMLET] Is't not possible to understand in another tongue?
You will to't, sir, really.
HAMLET: What imports the nomination of this gentleman?
OSRIC: Of Laertes?
HORATIO: [*aside*] His purse is empty already; all's golden words are spent.   125
HAMLET: Of him, sir.
OSRIC: I know you are not ignorant—
HAMLET: I would you did, sir; yet, in faith, if you did, it would not much approve*
me. Well, sir.
OSRIC: You are not ignorant of what excellence Laertes is—   130
HAMLET: I dare not confess that, lest I should compare with him in excellence;
but to know a man well were to know himself.
OSRIC: I mean, sir, for his weapon; but in the imputation* laid on him by them,
in his meed* he's unfellowed.
HAMLET: What's his weapon?   135
OSRIC: Rapier and dagger.
HAMLET: That's two of his weapons—but well.
OSRIC: The King, sir, hath wager'd him with six Barbary horses; against the
which he has impon'd,* as I take it, six French rapiers and poniards, with

---

[107] **differences** distinguishing characteristics
[109] **card** model
[110] **continent** summary
[111] **definement** description
[111] **perdition** loss (this entire speech mocks Osric's use of overblown language)
[112] **dozy** dizzy
[118] **concernancy** meaning
[128] **approve** commend
[133] **imputation** reputation
[134] **meed** merit
[139] **impon'd** wagered

their assigns,* as girdle, hangers, and so—three of the carriages, in faith, are 140
very dear to fancy, very responsive to the hilts, most delicate carriages, and
of very liberal conceit.

HAMLET: What call you the carriages?

HORATIO: [*aside to* HAMLET] I knew you must be edified by the margent* ere you
had done. 145

OSRIC: The carriages, sir, are the hangers.

HAMLET: The phrase would be more germane to the matter if we could carry a
cannon by our sides. I would it might be hangers till then. But on: six Barbary horses against six French swords, their assigns, and three liberal conceited carriages; that's the French bet against the Danish. Why is this all 150
impon'd, as you call it?

OSRIC: The King, sir, hath laid, sir, that in a dozen passes between yourself and
him he shall not exceed you three hits; he hath laid on twelve for nine, and it
would come to immediate trial if your lordship would vouchsafe the answer.

HAMLET: How if I answer no? 155

OSRIC: I mean, my lord, the opposition of your person in trial.

HAMLET: Sir, I will walk here in the hall. If it please his Majesty, it is the breathing time of day* with me; let the foils be brought, the gentlemen willing, and
the King hold his purpose, I will win for him an I can; if not, I will gain nothing but my shame and the odd hits. 160

OSRIC: Shall I redeliver you e'en so?

HAMLET: To this effect, sir, after what flourish your nature will.

OSRIC: I commend my duty to your lordship.

HAMLET: Yours, yours. [*Exit* OSRIC.] He does well to commend it himself; there
are no tongues else for's turn. 165

HORATIO: This lapwing runs away with the shell on his head.

HAMLET: 'A did comply, sir, with his dug before 'a suck'd it.* Thus has he, and
many more of the same bevy, that I know the drossy age dotes on, only got
the tune of the time and outward habit of encounter*—a kind of yesty* collection, which carries them through and through the most fann'd and win- 170
nowed opinions; and do but blow them to their trial, the bubbles are out.*

[*Enter a* LORD.]

LORD: My lord, his Majesty commended him to you by young Osric, who brings
back to him that you attend him in the hall. He sends to know if your pleasure hold to play with Laertes, or that you will take longer time.

HAMLET: I am constant to my purposes; they follow the king's pleasure: if his fitness 175
speaks, mine is ready now—or whensoever, provided I be so able as now.

LORD: The King and Queen and all are coming down.

HAMLET: In happy time.

---

¹⁴⁰ **assigns** accompaniments
¹⁴⁴ **margent** exaggerated terminology
¹⁵⁷⁻⁵⁸ **breathing time of day** time when I do my exercises
¹⁶⁷ **'A did comply . . . suck'd it** He was ceremoniously polite to his mother's breast before he sucked it
¹⁶⁹ **habit of encounter** superficial way of talking to people
¹⁶⁹ **yesty** frothy
¹⁷¹ **blow them . . . bubbles are out** question them and they are at a loss

LORD: The Queen desires you to use some gentle entertainment* to Laertes before   180
you fall to play.
HAMLET: She well instructs me.   [*Exit* LORD.]
HORATIO: You will lose this wager, my lord.
HAMLET: I do not think so; since he went into France I have been in continual
practice. I shall win at the odds. But thou wouldst not think how ill all's here   185
about my heart; but it is no matter.
HORATIO: Nay, good my lord—
HAMLET: It is but foolery; but it is such a kind of gaingiving* as would perhaps
trouble a woman.
HORATIO: If your mind dislike anything, obey it. I will forestall their repair hither,   190
and say you are not fit.
HAMLET: Not a whit, we defy augury: there is a special providence in the fall of
a sparrow. If it be now, 'tis not to come; if it be not to come, it will be now;
if it be not now, yet it will come—the readiness is all. Since no man owes of
aught he leaves, what is't to leave betimes?* Let be.   195

[*A table prepared. Trumpets, drums, and officers with cushions, foils, and daggers.
Enter* KING, QUEEN, LAERTES, *and all the state.*]

KING: Come, Hamlet, come, and take this hand from me.

[*The* KING *puts* LAERTES' *hand into* HAMLET'S.]

HAMLET: Give me your pardon, sir. I have done you wrong;
But pardon't, as you are a gentleman.
This presence* knows,
And you must needs have heard how I am punish'd   200
With a sore distraction. What I have done
That might your nature, honour, and exception,*
Roughly awake, I here proclaim was madness.
Was't Hamlet wrong'd Laertes? Never Hamlet.
If Hamlet from himself be ta'en away,   205
And when he's not himself does wrong Laertes,
Then Hamlet does it not, Hamlet denies it.
Who does it, then? His madness. If't be so,
Hamlet is of the faction* that is wrong'd;
His madness is poor Hamlet's enemy.   210
Sir, in this audience,
Let my disclaiming from a purpos'd evil
Free me so far in your most generous thoughts
That I have shot my arrow o'er the house
And hurt my brother.   215

---

180 **gentle entertainment** be courteous
188 **gaingiving** misgiving
195 **betimes** early
199 **presence** assembly
202 **exception** disapproval
209 **faction** group

LAERTES: I am satisfied in nature,
    Whose motive in this case should stir me most
    To my revenge; but in my terms of honour
    I stand aloof, and will no reconcilement
    Till by some elder masters of known honour   220
    I have a voice and precedent of peace
    To keep my name ungor'd—but till that time
    I do receive your offer'd love like love,
    And will not wrong it.
HAMLET: I embrace it freely;   225
    And will this brother's wager frankly play.
    Give us the foils. Come on.
LAERTES: Come, one for me.
HAMLET: I'll be your foil, Laertes; in mine ignorance
    Your skill shall, like a star i' th' darkest night,   230
    Stick fiery off* indeed.
LAERTES: You mock me, sir.
HAMLET: No, by this hand.
KING: Give them the foils, young Osric. Cousin Hamlet,
    You know the wager?   235
HAMLET: Very well, my lord;
    Your Grace has laid the odds a' th' weaker side.
KING: I do not fear it: I have seen you both;
    But since he's better'd,* we have therefore odds.
LAERTES: This is too heavy; let me see another.   240
HAMLET: This likes me well. These foils have all a length?

    [*They prepare to play.*]

OSRIC: Ay, my good lord.
KING: Set me the stoups of wine upon that table.
    If Hamlet give the first or second hit,
    Or quit in answer of the third exchange,   245
    Let all the battlements their ordnance fire;
    The King shall drink to Hamlet's better breath,
    And in the cup an union* shall he throw,
    Richer than that which four successive kings
    In Denmark's crown have worn. Give me the cups;   250
    And let the kettle* to the trumpet speak,
    The trumpet to the cannoneer without,
    The cannons to the heavens, the heaven to earth,
    'Now the King drinks to Hamlet.' Come, begin—
    And you, the judges, bear a wary eye.   255
HAMLET: Come on, sir.

---

[231] **stick fiery off** stand out brilliantly
[239] **better'd** improved
[248] **union** pearl
[251] **kettle** kettledrum

LAERTES: Come, my lord.   [*They play.*]
HAMLET: One.
LAERTES: No.
HAMLET: Judgment?   260
OSRIC: A hit, a very palpable hit.
LAERTES: Well, again.
KING: Stay, give me drink. Hamlet, this pearl is thine;
    Here's to thy health. [*drum, trumpets, and shot*] Give him the cup.
HAMLET: I'll play this bout first; set it by awhile.   265
    Come. [*They play.*] Another hit; what say you?
LAERTES: A touch, a touch, I do confess't.
KING: Our son shall win.
QUEEN: He's fat,* and scant of breath.
    Here, Hamlet, take my napkin, rub thy brows.   270
    The Queen carouses to thy fortune, Hamlet.
HAMLET: Good madam!
KING: Gertrude, do not drink.
QUEEN: I will, my lord; I pray you pardon me.
KING: [*aside*] It is the poison'd cup; it is too late.   275
HAMLET: I dare not drink yet, madam; by and by.
QUEEN: Come, let me wipe thy face.
LAERTES: My lord, I'll hit him now.
KING: I do not think't.
LAERTES: [*aside*] And yet it is almost against my conscience.   280
HAMLET: Come, for the third. Laertes, you do but dally;
    I pray you pass with your best violence;
    I am afeard you make a wanton* of me.
LAERTES: Say you so? Come on.   [*They play.*]
OSRIC: Nothing, neither way.   285
LAERTES: Have at you now!

    [LAERTES *wounds* HAMLET; *then, in scuffling, they change rapiers, and* HAMLET
    wounds LAERTES.]

KING: Part them; they are incens'd.
HAMLET: Nay, come again.   [*The* QUEEN *falls.*]
OSRIC: Look to the Queen there, ho!
HORATIO: They bleed on both sides. How is it, my lord?   290
OSRIC: How is't, Laertes?
LAERTES: Why, as a woodcock, to mine own springe,* Osric;
    I am justly kill'd with mine own treachery.
HAMLET: How does the Queen?
KING: She swoons to see them bleed.   295
QUEEN: No, no, the drink, the drink! O my dear Hamlet!
    The drink, the drink! I am poison'd.   [*dies*]
HAMLET: O, villainy! Ho! let the door be lock'd.
    Treachery! Seek it out.   [LAERTES *falls.*]

---

²⁶⁹ **fat** sweaty
²⁸³ **wanton** spoiled child
²⁹² **springe** snare

LAERTES: It is here, Hamlet. Hamlet, thou art slain;   300
    No med'cine in the world can do thee good;
    In thee there is not half an hour's life;
    The treacherous instrument is in thy hand,
    Unbated and envenom'd. The foul practice*
    Hath turn'd itself on me; lo, here I lie,   305
    Never to rise again. Thy mother's poison'd.
    I can no more. The King, the King's to blame.
HAMLET: The point envenom'd, too!
    Then, venom, to thy work.   *[stabs the* KING]
ALL: Treason! treason!   310
KING: O, yet defend me, friends; I am but hurt.
HAMLET: Here, thou incestuous, murd'rous, damned Dane,
    Drink off this potion. Is thy union here?
    Follow my mother.   [KING *dies.*]
LAERTES: He is justly serv'd: 315
    It is a poison temper'd* by himself.
    Exchange forgiveness with me, noble Hamlet.
    Mine and my father's death come not upon thee,
    Nor thine on me!   [*dies*]
HAMLET: Heaven make thee free of it! I follow thee.   320
    I am dead, Horatio. Wretched Queen, adieu!
    You that look pale and tremble at this chance,
    That are but mutes or audience to this act,
    Had I but time, as this fell sergeant Death
    Is strict in his arrest, O, I could tell you—   325
    But let it be. Horatio, I am dead:
    Thou livest; report me and my cause aright
    To the unsatisfied.
HORATIO: Never believe it.
    I am more an antique Roman* than a Dane;   330
    Here's yet some liquor left.
HAMLET: As th'art a man,
    Give me the cup. Let go. By heaven, I'll ha't.
    O good Horatio, what a wounded name,
    Things standing thus unknown, shall live behind me!   335
    If thou didst ever hold me in thy heart,
    Absent thee from felicity awhile,
    And in this harsh world draw thy breath in pain,
    To tell my story. [*march afar off, and shot within*] What warlike noise
        is this?   340
OSRIC: Young Fortinbras, with conquest come from Poland,
    To th'ambassadors of England gives
    This warlike volley.
HAMLET: O, I die, Horatio!

---

[304] **foul practice** deception
[316] **temper'd** mixed
[330] **antique Roman** given to suicide

The potent poison quite o'er-crows* my spirit.   345
I cannot live to hear the news from England,
But I do prophesy th' election lights
On Fortinbras; he has my dying voice.
So tell him, with th' occurrents,* more and less,
Which have solicited*—the rest is silence.   [*dies*]   350
HORATIO: Now cracks a noble heart. Good night, sweet prince,
   And flights of angels sing thee to thy rest!   [*march within*]
   Why does the drum come hither?

   [*Enter* FORTINBRAS *and* ENGLISH AMBASSADORS, *with drum, colours, and*
   attendants.]

FORTINBRAS: Where is this sight?
HORATIO: What is it you would see?   355
   If aught of woe or wonder, cease your search.
FORTINBRAS: This quarry* cries on havoc.* O proud death,
   What feast is toward* in thine eternal cell
   That thou so many princes at a shot
   So bloodily hast struck?   360
FIRST AMBASSADOR: The sight is dismal;
   And our affairs from England come too late:
   The ears are senseless that should give us hearing
   To tell him his commandment is fulfill'd
   That Rosencrantz and Guildenstern are dead.   365
   Where should we have our thanks?
HORATIO: Not from his* mouth,
   Had it th' ability of life to thank you:
   He never gave commandment for their death.
   But since, so jump* upon this bloody question,   370
   You from the Polack wars, and you from England,
   And here arrived, give order that these bodies
   High on a stage* be placed to the view;
   And let me speak to th' yet unknowing world
   How these things came about. So shall you hear   375
   Of carnal, bloody, and unnatural acts;
   Of accidental judgments, casual* slaughters;
   Of deaths put on by cunning and forc'd cause;
   And, in this upshot, purposes mistook
   Fall'n on th' inventors' heads—all this can I   380
   Truly deliver.

---

[345] **o'er-crows** overpowers
[349] **occurrents** occurrences
[350] **solicited** incited
[357] **quarry** heap of slain bodies
[357] **cries on havoc** proclaims general slaughter
[358] **toward** in preparation
[367] **his** Claudius'
[370] **jump** precisely
[373] **stage** platform
[377] **casual** unplanned

FORTINBRAS: Let us haste to hear it,
          And call the noblest to the audience.
          For me, with sorrow I embrace my fortune;
          I have some rights of memory* in this kingdom,   385
          Which now to claim my vantage doth invite me.
HORATIO: Of that I shall have also cause to speak,
          And from his mouth whose voice will draw on more.*
          But let this same be presently perform'd,
          Even while men's minds are wild, lest more mischance   390
          On* plots and errors happen.
FORTINBRAS: Let four captains
          Bear Hamlet like a soldier to the stage;
          For he was likely, had he been put on,
          To have prov'd most royal; and for his passage*   395
          The soldier's music and the rite of war
          Speak loudly for him.
          Take up the bodies. Such a sight as this
          Becomes the field, but here shows much amiss.
          Go, bid the soldiers shoot.   400

     [*Exeunt marching. A peal of ordnance shot off.*]

---

[385] **rights of memory** past claims
[388] **voice will draw on more** vote will influence others
[391] **On** on top of earlier
[395] **passage** death

Tartuffe
(1664, 1667, 1669)

While English drama of Shakespeare's time owed much to medieval conventions, French dramatists after the 1630s looked back to Greece and Rome for their standards. This conscious imitation of the classics gave rise to a set of literary standards summed up in the term *neoclassicism*. These included the unities of time, place, and action; strict distinction between tragedy and comedy, with no intermingling of the two; the use of universalized character types; and the demand that drama teach moral lessons. Many of the plays written in compliance with these demands now seem lifeless, but the tragedies of Racine and the comedies of Molière, written in France during the last half of the seventeenth century, reached a peak of artistry in the neoclassical mode. Unlike plays of earlier eras, these were written for the proscenium arch stage and for perspective settings composed of wings, drops, and borders.

Molière is one of the most skillful and inventive comic dramatists of all time, and *Tartuffe* is one of his most admired plays. Within the restricted frame of one room, one day, and one main story, using a limited number of characters and little physical action, Molière creates an excellent comedy of character. The action of *Tartuffe*, divided into five acts, develops through five stages: the demonstration of Tartuffe's complete hold over Orgon; the unmasking of Tartuffe; Tartuffe's attempted revenge; the foiling of Tartuffe's plan; and the happy resolution. Molière has been criticized for delaying Tartuffe's first appearance until the third act, but he makes skillful use of this delay by having all the other characters establish his hypocrisy and Orgon's gullibility in trusting Tartuffe. The resolution, in which Tartuffe is suddenly discovered to be a notorious criminal, has also been criticized as overly contrived, but it is emotionally satisfying because it punishes Tartuffe and reestablishes the norm.

In *Tartuffe* Molière uses the verse form that by that time had become standard in French tragedy—the alexandrine (twelve-syllable lines, with each pair of adjacent lines rhyming). The translation used here was written by Christopher Hampton for the Royal Shakespeare Company in 1983. For ease of speaking in performance, Hampton rendered his translation in blank verse.

When *Tartuffe* was written in 1664, it was immediately denounced as an attack on religious piety. The controversy was so intense that Louis XIV forbade the play's production. Molière rewrote it in 1667, only to have it banned once more. Finally, in 1669 he was able to gain permission for its production. It has remained in the repertory continuously since that time. It is still performed more often than any other play by Molière.

Tartuffe
(1664, 1667, 1669)

TRANSLATED BY CHRISTOPHER HAMPTON

Characters
MME. PERNELLE, *Orgon's mother*
ORGON, *Elmire's husband*
ELMIRE, *Orgon's wife*
DAMIS, *Orgon's son, Elmire's stepson*
MARIANE, *Orgon's daughter, Elmire's stepdaughter, in love with Valère*
VALÈRE, *in love with Mariane*
CLÉANTE, *Orgon's brother-in-law*
TARTUFFE, *a hypocrite*
DORINE, *Mariane's lady's-maid*
M. LOYAL, *a bailiff*
A POLICE OFFICER
FLIPOTE, *Mme. Pernelle's maid*

The scene throughout: ORGON'S *house in Paris*

--- ACT I ---

SCENE I

MADAME PERNELLE, *her maidservant* FLIPOTE, ELMIRE, MARIANE, DORINE, DAMIS, CLÉANTE.

MADAME PERNELLE: Come, come, Flipote; it's time I left this place.
ELMIRE: I can't keep up, you walk at such a pace.
MADAME PERNELLE: Don't trouble, child; no need to show me out.
    It's not your manners I'm concerned about.
MME PERNELLE: Come on, Flipote, let's go, I can't stay here.   5
ELMIRE: Why are you in such a rush? We can't keep up.
MME PERNELLE: Then leave me, dear, don't take another step.
    I'm sure I never asked for all this fuss.
ELMIRE: I think we know our duty and we'll do it.
    But what is it that's made you run away?   10
MME PERNELLE: I can't bear all the turmoil in this house.
    Nobody cares a button for my feelings.

It's been a most unedifying visit:
nobody listens to a word I say;
there's no respect, everyone shouts at once,   15
it's like some frightful Parliament of Apes.
DORINE: If . . .
MME PERNELLE: You, my girl, are nothing but a maid
    with far too much to say and most of that
    impertinent; we don't need your opinion.   20
DAMIS: But . . .
MME PERNELLE: There's a word for you, my boy:
                                        buffoon.
    Yes, I'm your grandmother and I should know.
    And if I've told your father once, I've told him   25
    a hundred times, I think you're a bad lot,
    who'll never give him anything but heartache.
MARIANE: I think . . .
MME PERNELLE: Good Lord, the quiet one's found
                        her voice,   30
    sweetness and light, the sister meek and mild;
    but still waters run deep, they always say,
    and deep down you're as bad as all the rest.
ELMIRE: But, mother . . .
MME PERNELLE: Now, dear, don't take this   35
                      amiss,
    but everything you do is simply wrong.
    You ought to set these two a good example,
    as their late mother never failed to do.
    You spend too much, I must say it upsets me,   40
    the way you go round dressed like a princess.
    A woman who wants just to please her husband
    has no business parading like a clothes-horse.
CLÉANTE: But, after all, Madame . . .
MME PERNELLE: And as for you,   45
    it's not that I don't like you and respect you,
    but if I were my son's wife, even if
    you were my brother, you'd be barred the
                  house:
    spouting your endless theories about life,   50
    which no one in their right mind would accept.
    Perhaps I've been too frank; but I'm like that,
    I never could conceal what's on my mind.
DAMIS: I'm sure your Monsieur Tartuffe would be
                  pleased . . .   55
MME PERNELLE: He's a good man, who must be listened to,
    and if I have to hear a fool like you
    attacking him, I may get very cross.
DAMIS: Some sanctimonious faker seizes power,
    and I'm supposed to lie back and enjoy it,   60
    and no one is allowed the simplest pleasure
    without permission from this turkey-cock!
DORINE: If what he says is anything to go by,

you move and you commit a mortal sin:
his beady critic's eye is watching you. 65
MME PERNELLE: And everything he watches must be watched.
He's trying to lead you up the path to Heaven,
and my son ought to force you all to love him.
DAMIS: No, listen to me, grandmother, no father,
no anyone could make me wish him well. 70
If I said otherwise, I would be lying.
The way he carries on infuriates me.
There's only one way out of this, I tell you,
I and that peasant can't but come to blows.
DORINE: You can't deny it's scandalous to see 75
a stranger taking over here, a beggar
who, when he came, had nothing on his feet
and whose whole wardrobe wasn't worth a
fiver,
going so far as to forget his place, 80
lording it over us and finding fault.
MME PERNELLE: Good gracious me, you'd all be better off,
if you submitted to his pious will!
DORINE: You have this fantasy that he's a saint,
when everything he does proves he's a fraud. 85
MME PERNELLE: Be quiet!
DORINE: I'd need a written guarantee,
before I'd trust him or his man Laurent.
MME PERNELLE: I can't vouch for his servant, but Tartuffe
—you have my guarantee he's a good man. 90
The only reason you object to him
is that his criticisms are all true.
What makes him angry is your sinfulness,
his sole criterion is what's good for Heaven.
DORINE: I know, but why, especially recently, 95
is he so very down on visitors?
He makes so much fuss, it gives you a
headache.
What harm's a courtesy visit do to Heaven?
You want my explanation? Keep it quiet, 100

(*She turns to* ELMIRE.)

but I'm convinced he's jealous of your friends.
MME PERNELLE: You shut your mouth and think before you
speak.
He's not the only one who disapproves:
it's all the fuss your visitors bring with them, 105
carriages always blocking up the gates,
vast quantities of footmen milling round,
making a noise and upsetting the neighbours.
I'm willing to believe nothing goes on;
but people talk, and that's to be avoided. 110
CLÉANTE: And how do you propose to stop them talking?
Life would be pretty miserable if,

for fear of what some imbecile might say,
you had to give up all your closest friends.
And even if you did decide to do that,   115
you think you'd put a stop to all the rumours?
There's no defence against malicious talk.
So let's pay no attention to it, please,
let's live as blamelessly as we can manage
and leave the gossips to say what they like.   120
DORINE: I know who runs us down behind our backs,
    it's Daphné, next door, and the dwarf, her
                                  husband.
It's always the most ludicrously guilty,
who are the first in line accusing others.   125
They never miss an opportunity
to batten on the slightest hint of friendship,
twist it to suit their purposes and then
gleefully spread the news to everyone.
They think they justify their own misconduct   130
by painting others' deeds in lurid colours,
and hope, in vain, to whitewash their intrigues,
or to sidestep the general condemnation
which weighs them down and redistribute it.
MME PERNELLE: Your arguments are quite irrelevant.   135
    Orante, who's well known for her model life
and pious dedication, says, I hear,
she strongly disapproves of your salon.
DORINE: Well, she's a fine example, I must say!
    She may personify austerity,   140
but what inspires her zeal is called old age.
She's virtuous because she has no choice.
As long as she was still at all attractive,
she made the most of everything she had;
but now the sparkle in her eye has dimmed,   145
she's registering withdrawal from the world
before it casts her off, and trying to hide
the sorry remnants of her faded beauty
behind an ornate veil of good behaviour.
These are the standard wiles of ageing flirts.   150
It's hard for them to watch their beaux
                             disperse.
And so the only outlet for their suffering
is to take virtue up professionally;
and the puritan code of these good ladies   155
implacably finds fault with everything.
They disapprove of everybody's life,
not from benevolence but spurred by envy:
they just can't tolerate the thought of pleasures,
which the onset of age denies to them.   160
MME PERNELLE: (*To* ELMIRE)
    You all enjoy these fairytales, I see.
In your house no one gets a word in edgeways,

because of madam holding forth all day;
well, now I've got a chance to speak at last,   165
I'm telling you, the wisest thing my son
has ever done is to install Tartuffe,
whom God has sent here, just when he was
                                 needed,
to save your souls, when you had gone astray;   170
listen to what he says, it's for your good,
everything he condemns deserves condemning.
These visitors, these dances, these discussions
—all of them are inventions of the devil;
you never hear a word about religion,   175
just idle chatter, songs, that sort of nonsense,
often as not demolishing your neighbours
and spreading slanders left and right, until
sensible people's heads are spinning with it,
dozens of rumours whipped up out of nothing,   180
and as a friend of mine, theologist,
put it so pithily the other day:
in the Tower of Babel, babble's what you get,
and he went on to illustrate his point . . .

      (*She indicates* CLÉANTE.)

I don't know what he's sniggering about.   185
Go to an asylum if you want to laugh
and don't . . .

      (*To* ELMIRE)

                  I'll say no more. Goodbye, my
                                 dear,
I take a very poor view of all this.   190
You won't be seeing me for quite some time.

      (*She slaps* FLIPOTE.)

Well, come along, wake up, don't gawk at me!
My goodness me, I'll box your ears for you.
Get on with you, you slut!

SCENE II

CLÉANTE, DORINE.

CLÉANTE: I'm staying put,   195
      I don't want her to start on me again.
      Silly old . . .
DORINE: What a shame she isn't here
      to comment on your turn of phrase: I know
      she'd tell you you're the one who's being silly   200
      and that no one could ever call her old.
CLÉANTE: She got annoyed with us for no good reason,

and she seems quite besotted with Tartuffe!
DORINE: I promise you her son is even worse
    and if you saw him you would be appalled.   205
    During the troubles he was very brave,
    enhanced his reputation with the King,
    but ever since he's fallen for Tartuffe,
    he's gone around like someone in a daze.
    He loves the man: a hundred times as much as   210
    his wife, his son, his daughter or his mother;
    he calls him brother, whispers all his secrets
    to him alone and has appointed him
    the watchful overseer of his conduct.
    He pampers him, caresses him: I'd say   215
    you couldn't be more loving to a mistress.
    He sits him at the top end of the table,
    enjoys watching him eat enough for six;
    you have to serve him all the tastiest bits,
    and even when he burps, he says: 'God bless   220
                        you!'
    In short, he's mad about him; he's his hero,
    his everything, admired in every way
    and quoted on all possible occasions,
    his slightest action is miraculous   225
    and every word he says is like an oracle.
    The fact is, he's a man can spot a victim
    and knows how to exploit and dazzle him
    with every bogus swindle in the book.
    He wheedles money when he feels like it,   230
    by turning on his sanctimonious cant
    and doesn't hesitate to pick on us.
    Even his servant orders us about,
    gives himself airs and preaches wild-eyed sermons
    and throws away our rouge and beauty spots.   235
    The other day the brute found my lace bib
    between two pages of *The Lives of the Saints*
    and ripped it up, saying it was a crime
    to stain what's holy with the devil's frills.

SCENE III

ELMIRE, MARIANE, DAMIS, CLÉANTE, DORINE.

ELMIRE: (*To* CLÉANTE)   240
    You're very wise to have stayed here, you
                    missed
    her lecture at the gate. My husband's here:
    he hasn't seen me and I'd rather wait
    for him upstairs.   245
CLÉANTE: I'll wait and catch him here,
    I've really only time to say hello.

DAMIS: Ask him about my sister's wedding, will you?
    I have a feeling Tartuffe is against it
    and forcing him to make these long delays.   250
    It's important to me as well, you know.
    My sister loves Valère and he loves her:
    but, as you know, I'm in love with his sister,
    and if . . .
DORINE: He's coming.   255

SCENE IV

ORGON, CLÉANTE, DORINE.

ORGON: Ah, Cléante, hello!
CLÉANTE: I was just on my way, I'm glad I caught you.
    Nothing much out yet, is there, in the country?
ORGON: Dorine . . .

    (*To* CLÉANTE)

        You must excuse me, just a minute,   260
    you don't mind if I find out what's been
                    happening
    and put my mind at rest?

    (*To* DORINE)

          Everything fine?
    What's everybody up to? Are they well?   265
DORINE: Two days ago the mistress had a fever
    and a strange nagging headache all day long.
ORGON: And Tartuffe?
DORINE: Tartuffe's in the best of health,
    big, fat and blooming, with his nice red mouth.   270
ORGON: Poor boy!
DORINE: She felt quite nauseous all evening
    and couldn't touch a mouthful of her dinner,
    her headache was so painful.
ORGON: And Tartuffe?   275
DORINE: He sat in front of her and ate alone,
    swallowing, most religiously, a brace
    of partridge, followed by a leg of mutton.
ORGON: Poor boy!
DORINE: She never closed her eyes all night,   280
    she had hot flushes, which kept her awake,
    we had to sit up with her till the dawn.
ORGON: And Tartuffe?
DORINE: He was struck down by a kind
                   of   285
    pleasantly weary feeling and repaired
    directly from the table to his room,

        where he collapsed into his nice warm bed
        and slumbered dreamlessly until the morning.
ORGON: Poor boy!   290
DORINE: We finally persuaded her
        to be bled, and she felt better at once.
ORGON: And Tartuffe?
DORINE: Put his bravest face on it,
        and, bracing himself against the blows of fate,   295
        to make up for the blood the mistress lost,
        drank four large tumblersful of wine for
                                        breakfast.
ORGON: Poor boy!
DORINE: At any rate they're now quite well,   300
        and I must go upstairs and tell the mistress
        how interested you've been in her recovery.

SCENE V

ORGON, CLÉANTE.

CLÉANTE: She's making fun of you, you must have
                                        noticed;
        and I don't want to make you angry, but,   305
        quite frankly, it's no more than you deserve.
        I've never heard of such grotesque behaviour:
        how can this man have cast a spell and made
                                        you
        oblivious to everybody else?   310
        So that as well as saving him from poverty,
        you've gone as far as to . . .
ORGON: That's quite
                            enough!
        How can you talk about him, you don't know   315
                            him.
CLÉANTE: Certainly I don't know him, but to guess
        the kind of man he is, you only need to . . .
ORGON: No, you'd be captivated by him, and
        your ecstasy would know no bounds. You see,   320
        this is a man, who . . . well . . . a man in
                            fact . . .
        er, to sum up, a man. You listen to him
        and you enjoy the deepest peace of mind
        and see the world for what it is: a dunghill.   325
        Oh, yes, I've quite changed under his
                            instruction:
        he teaches me to cast aside affection
        and clear my mind of any trace of love;
        now I could watch my mother or my brother,   330
        my wife and children die, and not give that.
CLÉANTE: I see, he's a humanitarian.

ORGON: Ah, if you'd only been there when we met,
    you'd feel as warm towards him as I do.
    He'd arrive every day in church and kneel,   335
    meekly, right next to me and never fail
    to capture the whole congregation's notice
    with the enthusiasm of his praying; –
    he'd groan and sigh and throw himself around
    and humbly kiss the ground, time and again,   340
    and when I left, he'd hurry on ahead
    to hand me the holy water at the door.
    His servant, who was like his mirror image,
    told me about him, who he was, his poverty:
    I gave him money; but, restrained as ever,   345
    he always tried to give some back to me.
    'Too much,' he'd say, 'I don't need half this
                               much,
    What makes you think I should deserve your
                               pity?'   350
    When I'd refuse to take it back, he'd go
    and share it with the poor, in front of me.
    Finally I was inspired to bring him here,
    since when it seems that all of us have
                           flourished.   355
    He disapproves of everything, of course,
    and keeps a very close watch on my wife,
    just to protect my honour; gives me names
    of all the people who make eyes at her;
    he's far more jealous than I've ever been.   360
    You've no idea, the fervour of the man:
    he sees the slightest failing as a sin,
    he's scandalized by what we'd hardly notice;
    recently he was full of self-reproach
    for having caught a flea while he was praying   365
    and killed it with excessive savagery.
CLÉANTE: What is this, are you making fun of me?
    You must be mad, you think this
                         pantomime . . .
ORGON: Now, what you're saying smacks of atheism.   370
    You're tainted with it, and if I've told you
                         once,
    I've told you fifty times, that's the best way
    to get yourself into quite serious trouble.
CLÉANTE: I know, that's what you people always say.   375
    You want us all to be as blind as you are.
    Good eyesight is a sign of atheism,
    and anyone who doesn't worship idols
    has no respect and no religious faith.
    Nothing you say can frighten me: God sees   380
    into my heart and I know what I mean.
    You can't make me a slave of affectation:
    false piety's as common as false courage,

and just as on the battlefield you find
that those who make the loudest noise are not   385
the truly brave, the truly pious, whose
example we should follow, equally,
are not the ones who pull the holiest faces.
Can it be true you don't make a distinction
between hypocrisy and piety?   390
And do you really class them both together,
respect the mask as highly as the face,
consider sham the equal of sincerity,
confuse appearance and reality,
value a ghost as much as someone living   395
and forgeries no less than genuine coin?
Men are peculiar creatures, most of them!
They never seem to hit the happy medium.
Reason's too limited, they burst its bounds,
and often what's most admirable's ruined   400
through sheer exaggeration and excess.
I only thought I'd mention this in passing.
ORGON: Yes, I see, you're a most distinguished genius,
repository of universal knowledge,
uniquely brilliant and uniquely wise,   405
an oracle, a Cato of our time,
compared to whom the rest of us are fools.
CLÉANTE: No, I am not a most distinguished genius,
repository of universal knowledge:
but there's one thing I do know how to do,   410
that's tell the difference between true and false.
And while there's no one I approve of more
than genuinely religious men, and nothing
nobler or more uplifting in the world
than the enthusiasm of true belief,   415
equally, there is nothing more disgraceful
than specious fervour laid on with a trowel,
and no one worse than those downright
                               impostors,
those worshippers in public, whose deceit   420
and sacreligious antics go unpunished,
while they pervert and make a mockery of
everything human beings hold most sacred;
those career mystics, businessmen on their
                               knees,   425
trying to notch up credit and prestige,
by screwing up their eyes and throwing fits;
those abnormally zealous ones, I mean,
chasing their fortunes via the road to Heaven,
who make demands between each ardent   430
                               prayer,
and make sure they are well installed at Court
before they preach withdrawal from the world,
whose faith's adjustable to fit their vices,

who are disloyal, fleet, vindictive, cunning,   435
and, when the time comes to destroy an enemy,
can brazenly disguise their fierce resentments
behind a cover of what's good for Heaven;
doubly dangerous because the weapons
they turn against us in their bitterness   440
are so respected, and because the passion,
for which they are so genuinely admired,
aims at our hearts a consecrated sword.
This faking is becoming far too common;
meanwhile our age has shown us, very often,   445
glorious examples of true piety,
easily recognizable as such.
Look at Ariston, look at Périandre,
Oronte, Alcidamas, Polydore, Clitandre:
no one disputes their genuineness, and yet   450
none of them ever boasts about his virtue
or displays such intolerable pride,
their religion is flexible and humane.
They're not censorious, because that would
                                        show   455
an arrogance they'd rather leave to others,
if they reproach us, then it's through their
                                        actions.
They don't judge by appearances, instead
their inclination's to think well of others.   460
They don't form cliques, they don't approve of
                                        plotting:
their only aim is to live righteously.
They have no animosity against sinners,
reserving all their hatred for the sin,   465
and no urge to pursue the Church's interests
more violently than it would itself.
They're the ones I approve of, that's the way,
that's the example one should set oneself.
Frankly, your man is quite another species;   470
I'm sure you sing his praises in good faith,
but I believe you're blinded by mere show.
ORGON: Is that all?
CLÉANTE: Yes.
ORGON: Then perhaps you would   475
                                        excuse me?

(*He makes to go.*)

CLÉANTE: Oh, just one minute, please: I'll change the
                                        subject.
You have promised Valère your daughter's
                                        hand?   480
ORGON: Yes.
CLÉANTE: And you'd even given them a date?
ORGON: That's right.

CLÉANTE:	Then why have you postponed the	
	wedding?	485

ORGON: I've no idea.

CLÉANTE: Have you perhaps changed your
mind?

ORGON: Possibly.

CLÉANTE: Are you going to break your word? 490

ORGON: I didn't say that.

CLÉANTE: I just can't imagine
what could prevent you honouring your promise.

ORGON: Depends.

CLÉANTE: What is all this evasiveness? 495
Valère has asked me to see you about it.

ORGON: Well, that is nice.

CLÉANTE: But what am I to tell him?

ORGON: You tell him what you like.

CLÉANTE: But then I have to 500
know what you have in mind: what are your
plans?

ORGON: To do God's will.

CLÉANTE: Be serious, will you? Look:
Valère has had your promise: will you keep it? 505

ORGON: Goodbye.

CLÉANTE: (*Alone*)
I fear the worst for his engagement.
I have to warn him of what's going on.

ACT II

SCENE I

ORGON, MARIANE.

ORGON: Mariane.

MARIANE: Yes, father.

ORGON: Come here, I'd like
a word with you in private.

MARIANE: What's in there? 5

(**ORGON** *is looking into a closet.*)

ORGON: Nothing, I'm only checking no one's there,
I wouldn't like us to be overheard.
No, that's all right. Well, Mariane, I've always
appreciated your obedience,
and you've always been very dear to me. 10

MARIANE: I'm very grateful, father, that you love me.

ORGON: Well said, my dear. And if I'm to continue,

your only worry need be to provide me
with what I want.
MARIANE: I take a pride in it.   15
ORGON: Good. What do you think of our guest,
                                        Tartuffe?

MARIANE: Who, me?
ORGON: You. Now, be careful what you say.
MARIANE: Oh, dear. Well, I'll say anything you like.   20
ORGON: How very sensible. Well, then, my dear,
    why don't you say he's wholly excellent,
    he's reached your heart and it would make you
                                        happy
    if I agreed to let him marry you?   25
    Mm?

    (MARIANE *steps back, surprised.*)

MARIANE: Mm?
ORGON: What is it?
MARIANE: Sorry?
ORGON: What?   30
MARIANE: I don't
    think I caught what you said.
ORGON: What do you
                                        mean?
MARIANE: Who is it that you wanted me to say   35
    had reached my heart? And it would make me
                                        happy
    if you agreed to let me marry whom?
ORGON: Tartuffe
MARIANE: But, look, it wouldn't, not at all.   40
    Why should you want to make me tell a lie?
ORGON: What I want is for it to be the truth;
    that's my decision, what more do you need?
MARIANE: You mean you want . . .
ORGON: Yes, my dear, I   45
                                        intend
    to make Tartuffe a member of the family.
    He's going to be your husband, it's all settled,
    and since I have the power to insist . . .

SCENE II

DORINE, ORGON, MARIANE.
ORGON *notices* DORINE.

ORGON: What are you doing? Eavesdropping again?   50
    Suffering from chronic curiosity?
DORINE: I heard somebody mentioning this marriage,
    and I couldn't decide if it was rumour,
    with some basis in fact, or pure invention:

the one obvious thing was it was nonsense.   55
ORGON: You find it unbelievable?
DORINE: So much so,
   I wouldn't believe it, even if you told me.
ORGON: I think I know a way to make you, though.
DORINE: I know, you're telling us a fairy story.   60
ORGON: I'm telling you exactly what will happen.
DORINE: Rubbish!
ORGON: Now, this is serious, Mariane.
DORINE: Get on with you, your father doesn't mean it,
   he's joking.   65
ORGON: Will you listen . . . ?
DORINE: No, no good,
   we don't believe you.
ORGON: I'm starting to get
   annoyed.   70
DORINE: All right, we do believe you, then.
   In which case, shame on you. You look quite
                                   normal,
   that big beard in the middle of your face,
   and yet you mean you're mad enough to . . .   75
ORGON: Listen:
   you've taken certain liberties today
   which I don't like one little bit: I warn you . . .
DORINE: Let's try and keep our temper, shall we, sir?
   I still think this is some elaborate joke.   80
   Your daughter isn't cut out for a bigot,
   and he should have other things on his mind.
   And anyway, what possible advantage
   could such a marriage bring you? And why
                                   choose   85
   a beggar for a son-in-law with all
   your money . . . ?
ORGON: That's enough. If he has
                             nothing,
   all the more reason to admire him.   90
   His poverty is honest poverty:
   it lifts him higher than the great, he's poor
   through voluntary renunciation and
   his pure indifference to temporal things
   and his commitment to eternity.   95
   I intend to provide him with some means,
   free him from want and re-acquire his lands,
   properties highly thought of where he comes
                             from;
   even as he stands, it's obvious he's a   100
                             gentleman.
DORINE: So he keeps saying, and that kind of pride
   doesn't quite fit with his religiousness.
   You wouldn't think a man who'd chosen
                             sainthood   105

would need to boast about his name and rank;
the self-effacing rules of piety
hardly accommodate rampant ambition.
What is the purpose of his vanity . . .?
This is upsetting you: let's leave his   110
       background
and talk about his personality.
Could you really, without the least remorse,
hand a girl like her to a man like him?
Can't you foresee how such a marriage would   115
turn out, have you no sense of decency?
If you force any girl to take a husband
against her will, you're gambling with her
        virtue;
she may intend to lead a life of honour,   120
but that depends on who you've chosen for her,
and those whose wives are famously unfaithful
have often driven them to that condition.
And after all it's quite hard to be faithful
to certain husbands cast in a certain mould;   125
and anyone who gives a girl away
to a man she can't stand is answerable
before God for whatever she might do.
So think what danger your plan puts you in.
ORGON: Do I need her to teach me how to live?   130
DORINE: If you've got any sense, you'll listen to me.
ORGON: Let us not waste our time, dear, on this
       nonsense:
I am your father and I know what's best.
It's true, I had promised you to Valère;   135
but he's been seen more than once playing
       cards,
and I suspect he may be a freethinker;
I haven't seen a lot of him in church.
DORINE: Why should he go exactly when you do?   140
  He's not, like others, just there to be seen.
ORGON: I don't need your opinion. I just know
  Heaven smiles on Tartuffe and that's an asset
  second to none. This marriage will fulfil
  your wildest dreams, a series of sweet   145
       pleasures.
You'll live together, faithfully in love,
like two true children, like two turtle-doves.
You'll never quarrel, and you'll find that you
can turn him into anything you please.   150
DORINE: A cuckold, for example, which is all
  she'll want to turn him into.
ORGON: That's enough!
DORINE: It's written all over him, it's in his stars;
  not all your daughter's virtue could resist it.   155
ORGON: Will you stop interrupting me? Shut up,

keep your nose out of other people's business.
DORINE: I'm only trying to help.

(*From now on, she interrupts him every time he turns away to speak to his daughter.*)

ORGON: Well, don't; be quiet.
DORINE: It's only because we love you . . .   160
ORGON: I don't want
to be loved.
DORINE: Even so, I want to love you.
ORGON: Ah!
DORINE: See, your reputation is important   165
to me, I hate to see you lay yourself
open to general ridicule.
ORGON: Shut up!
DORINE: How could I let you contract such a marriage,
in all conscience?   170
ORGON: Will you be quiet, snake,
before I . . .
DORINE: I thought you were supposed to be
religious.
ORGON: So I am, but all this jabber   175
is making my blood boil and I insist
you hold your tongue.
DORINE: Certainly. I won't say
another word. But you can't stop me thinking.
ORGON: Think all you like; just concentrate on not   180
speaking to me, or . . . Enough.

(*He turns to his daughter.*)

                              In my wisdom,
after mature consideration . . .
DORINE: (*Aside*)
                              It's   185
infuriating not to be allowed
to speak.

(*She stops talking, as soon as he turns to her.*)

ORGON: While not exactly very pretty,
Tartuffe is . . .
DORINE: (*Aside*)   190
                 Off the side of Notre Dame!
ORGON: Even if you could find no sympathy
for all his gifts . . .
DORINE: (*Aside*)
                    This *is* your lucky day!   195

(ORGON *turns to face* DORINE; *he watches her, listening, with his arms folded.*)

If I was in her place, I'm telling you,
no man would marry me against my will;

or soon after the wedding he'd find out
there's one way women can revenge
                       themselves.   200
ORGON: (*To* DORINE)
    I see, you're just ignoring what I said.
DORINE: What's the matter? I'm not speaking to you.
ORGON: What are you doing?
DORINE: Talking to myself.   205
ORGON: I see. (*Aside.*) I've never heard such insolence,
    she deserves a good smack and here it comes.

      (*He gets in a position to slap her; every time he glances at her,* DORINE *is
      standing up straight, in silence.*)

My dear, you must agree to my suggestion . . .
The husband I have . . . chosen for you is . . .

      (*To* DORINE)

Well, speak up!   210
DORINE: I have nothing else to say.
ORGON: Surely there's something?
DORINE: No, don't feel like it.
ORGON: But I've been waiting.
DORINE: You think I'm a fool?   215
ORGON: Well, anyway, I insist on your obedience
    and your complete acceptance of my choice.
DORINE: (*Running for it*)
    I wouldn't be seen dead with such a husband.

      (*He tries to slap her and misses.*)

ORGON: That girl's a pest, I can't put up with her   220
    without surrendering to sinful rage.
    I really can't go on with our discussion;
    her insolence has goaded me to frenzy,
    I need some air to calm me down a bit.

SCENE III

DORINE, MARIANE.

DORINE: Well, have you lost your tongue, am I supposed   225
    to play your part in this? How can you let
    someone propose this idiotic plan,
    without saying a single word against it?
MARIANE: What could I say? A father's power is absolute.
DORINE: Anything to stave off a threat like this.   230
MARIANE: What?
DORINE: Tell him you can't love at second hand.
    Tell him you're marrying for your sake, not his.
    Since you're the centre of attention here,

it's you, not him, your husband must appeal to; 235
and if he thinks Tartuffe is so attractive,
he's quite welcome to marry him himself.
MARIANE: I've never had the strength to raise a protest
against father's authority, I admit.
DORINE: Just a minute. Valère has made his move: 240
tell me, do you love him or do you not?
MARIANE: How can you be so unfair to my love,
Dorine? How can you ask me such a question?
Haven't I always confided in you,
and told you fifty times how much I love him? 245
DORINE: How do I know if all of that was true,
and whether you feel genuinely about him?
MARIANE: Dorine, it's very wrong of you to doubt it,
you know I've never hidden my true feelings.
DORINE: So then, you love him? 250
MARIANE: Yes, passionately.
DORINE: By all appearances, he loves you too?
MARIANE: I think he does.
DORINE: And both of you are most
impatient to get married? 255
MARIANE: Yes, we are.
DORINE: So what d'you plan to do about this business?
MARIANE: If they force me, I'm going to kill myself.
DORINE: That's wonderful. I hadn't thought of that;
'course, if you die, you'll avoid all these 260
                              problems.
What a brilliant way out! It makes me angry
to have to listen to this kind of talk.
MARIANE: There's no need to get in a huff, Dorine.
You have no sympathy for people's suffering. 265
DORINE: I have no sympathy for empty threats,
or crumbling without putting up a fight.
MARIANE: What d'you expect? I can't help being timid . . .
DORINE: But perseverance should be part of love.
MARIANE: And I have persevered: I love Valère. 270
Isn't it up to him to win my hand
from father?
DORINE: What, when father is this clown,
who's utterly besotted with Tartuffe,
and breaks his firm agreement on the marriage, 275
you think the blame should be put on Valère?
MARIANE: Would it be right to show, by flat refusal
or wild defiance, how much I'm in love?
However fine he is, should I abandon
my sex's modesty, my daughter's duty? 280
Do you think I should publicize my love . . .?
DORINE: No, no, I wouldn't want that. Now I see,
you want to marry Tartuffe after all,
and now I stop to think, I was quite wrong
to try to dissuade you. What right had I 285

        to quarrel with your wishes? He's a most
        eligible match is that Monsieur Tartuffe.
        Oh, no, he's nothing to be sneezed at, is he?
        I mean, you can't deny Monsieur Tartuffe's
        a man who knows his backside from his elbow.   290
        To be his better half, that's no small honour.
        He's generally admired, he's of good birth,
        at least he says he is, sort of well-built,
        those red ears and that nice florid face:
        the only danger is you'll be too happy.   295
MARIANE: Oh, God! . . .
DORINE: Can you imagine the elation?
        To be the wife of such a handsome man!
MARIANE: Oh, stop it, please, and find some way to help.
        I give up now, I'll do whatever you say.   300
DORINE: No, no, a daughter must obey her father,
        even if he wants to marry her to an ape.
        You're very lucky, why are you complaining?
        You'll take the coach back to his little town,
        and you'll meet all his uncles and his cousins,   305
        you're certain to enjoy their conversation.
        You'll be taken to all the best addresses
        and welcomed there by all the dignitaries,
        the bailiff's wife, the wife of the JP,
        they'll get out their spare canvas chair for you.   310
        Then there's the village fête to look forward to,
        there'll be a ball, with a great orchestra,
        consisting of a pair of bagpipers,
        and, as a special treat, an organ-grinder,
        and those amusing Punch and Judy shows.   315
        And if your husband . . .
MARIANE: Do you want to kill
                       me?
        Better if you could find some way to help.
DORINE: You mustn't ask me that.   320
MARIANE: Oh, please,
                     Dorine . . .
DORINE: No, it must go ahead now, you deserve it.
MARIANE: Dorine.
DORINE: No.   325
MARIANE: What I've told you . . .
DORINE: Nothing
                    doing
        Tartuffe's your man, you won't escape him
                 now.   330
MARIANE: You know I've always told you everything;
        now help me . . .
DORINE: No. You're going to be
                tartuffed.
MARIANE: I see. Well, since you're unmoved by my fate,   335
        you'd best abandon me to my despair:

and let it be my ready consolation;
I know there's one sure way out of my
                                    troubles.
DORINE: All right, come back: I'll try not to be angry.   340
   In spite of everything, I can't help feeling
   sorry for you.
MARIANE: If I'm to undergo
   this cruel martyrdom, you see, Dorine,
   I know it's going to be the death of me.   345
DORINE: Don't worry: I'm sure there's some clever
                                    way . . .
   But here's Valère himself.

SCENE IV

VALÈRE, MARIANE, DORINE.

VALÈREL: I have just heard
   the most extraordinary piece of news.   350
MARIANE: What's that?
VALÈRE: That you are marrying Tartuffe.
MARIANE: It's true my father wants me to.
VALÈRE: Your father . . .
MARIANE: Has changed his mind. He's just this minute
                                    told me.   355
VALÈRE: What, seriously?
MARIANE: Yes, seriously; he seems
   determined I should marry him.
VALÈRE: And what   360
   do you intend to do now?
MARIANE: I don't know.
VALÈRE: Well, there's an honest answer. You don't
                                    know?
MARIANE: No.   365
VALÈRE: No?
MARIANE: What's your advice?
VALÈRE: Oh, my advice
   is to accept.
MARIANE: That's your advice?   370
VALÈRE: It is.
MARIANE: You mean it?
VALÈRE: Certainly, I mean it, it's
   a handsome offer, well worth your attention.
MARIANE: Well, then, I'd better follow your advice.   375
VALÈRE: I don't think that will be too hard for you.
MARIANE: No harder than it was for you to give it.
VALÈRE: I did so in the hope of giving pleasure.
MARIANE: Whereas I shall now follow it to please you.

   (DORINE *withdraws upstage.*)

DORINE: Well, let's see how they can get out of this.   380
VALÈRE: Is this what love is? Was it just deceit
    when you…?
MARIANE: I'd rather not discuss that,
                      please
    You said quite openly that I should marry   385
    the husband I've been offered: I'm announcing
    that I intend to do so, following
    your excellent advice.
VALÈRE: You shouldn't use
    my stand as an excuse: you'd already   390
    decided, and you're grasping at this silly
    pretext to justify breaking your word.
MARIANE: It's true, you put it very well.
VALÈRE: I'm sure;
    you never really loved me.   395
MARIANE: You're entitled
    to your opinion.
VALÈRE: Yes, I am entitled;
    and I may manage to forestall your plan,
    by taking my proposal somewhere else.   400
MARIANE: I wouldn't be surprised; you're so
                good-looking . . .
VALÈRE: God, let's leave my looks out of it, shall we?
    They can't be that good, as you've just yourself
    demonstrated. But there is somebody,   405
    who feels kindly for me and, now I'm free,
    won't be ashamed to remedy my loss.
MARIANE: Your loss seems far from great, I'm sure you'll
                have
    no difficulty finding consolation.   410
VALÈRE: You may be confident I'll do my best.
    Being abandoned puts us on our mettle;
    we must make every effort to forget
    the person who's responsible, and even
    if we can't quite succeed, we must pretend to: 415
    to show oneself in love with someone faithless
    would be the most unpardonable weakness.
MARIANE: What an exalted, lofty sentiment.
VALÈRE: I don't think anyone could disapprove.
    I suppose you think that I should keep my love   420
    for you alive and burning endlessly,
    watching you fall into someone else's arms,
    without the right to find some new allegiance
    for the heart you've rejected?
MARIANE: Not at all;   425
    that sounds the best idea, I wish you'd done it
    already.
VALÈRE: Is that what you wish?
MARIANE: It is.
VALÈRE: Right, I'm not staying here to be insulted,   430

I'll do you a good turn by leaving.

(*He starts to go, but doesn't get very far.*)

MARIANE: Fine.
VALÈRE: (*Coming back*)
    You should at least remember that it's you
    who's driving me to this extreme.   435
MARIANE: I will.
VALÈRE: And that this plan is only following your
    example.
MARIANE: Following my example, yes.
VALÈRE: (*Leaving*)   440
    Well, that's enough: I'm leaving, like you said.
MARIANE: I'm pleased to hear it.
VALÈRE: (*Coming back again*)
                      This time it's for good.
MARIANE: Wonderful!   445

(VALÈRE *sets off again; when he reaches the door, he turns back.*)

VALÈRE: What?
MARIANE: You what?
VALÈRE: Did you say
                            something?
MARIANE: Me? You're imagining things.   450
VALÈRE: Right then, I'm
                            off
    Goodbye.

(*He moves slowly off.*)

MARIANE: Goodbye.
DORINE: (*To* MARIANE)   455
                  Have you gone off your
                      head?
    I've left you this long just to see how far
    you'd go. Hey, Monsieur Valère!

(*She takes hold of his arm.* VALÈRE *pretends to struggle furiously.*)

VALÈRE: What d'you   460
                            want,
    Dorine?
DORINE: Come here.
VALÈRE: No, no, I'm too upset.
    It's what she wanted, so don't try and talk me   465
    out of it.
DORINE: Stop it.
VALÈRE: No, look, it's all settled.
DORINE: Ah!
MARIANE: (*Aside*)   470
    He can't bear the sight of me, he's only
    leaving because I'm here, I'd better go
    instead.

(DORINE *leaves* VALÈRE *and runs after* MARIANE.)

DORINE: Oh, now it's her! Where are you off to?
MARIANE: Let go.   475
DORINE: Come back.
MARIANE: No, Dorine, it's no good.
VALÈRE: (*Aside*)
    I see my presence is a torment to her,
    the best course is to free her of it now.   480

(DORINE *leaves* MARIANE *and runs after* VALÈRE.)

DORINE: What, again? No, damned if I'm going to let
                             you!
    Stop this nonsense and come here, both of you.

(*She tugs at them both.*)

VALÈRE: (*To* DORINE)
    What do you want?   485
MARIANE: (*To* DORINE)
                What are you trying to do?
DORINE: Bring you together and get you out of this.

(*To* VALÈRE)

    Have you gone mad to start this kind of row?
VALÈRE: Didn't you hear the way she spoke to me?   490
DORINE: (*To* MARIANE)
    And you, have you gone mad, losing your
                        temper?
MARIANE: Didn't you see the way he treated me?
DORINE: (*To* VALÈRE)   495
    You're both as stupid as each other. All
    she wants is to be yours, I know that's true.

(*To* MARIANE)

    He loves no one but you, all he wants is
    to marry you: I'll stake my life on it.   500
MARIANE: (*To* VALÈRE)
    Well, then, why did you give me that advice?
VALÈRE: Why did you ask me for it, I'd like to know?
DORINE: You are both mad. Here, each give me a hand.

(*To* VALÈRE)

    Come on.

(VALÈRE *gives* DORINE *his hand.*)

VALÈRE: My hand, what for?   505
DORINE: (*To* MARIANE)
                    And you as well.

(MARIANE *also gives* DORINE *her hand.*)

MARIANE: What use will that be?

DORINE: My God, come here,
quick.   510
You love each other far more than you think.

(VALÈRE *and* MARIANE *hold hands for a while without*

looking at each other. Then VALÈRE *turns to* MARIANE
VALÈRE: Don't be so grudging, give us a friendly look.

(MARIANE *turns to* VALÈRE *and gives a little smile.*)

DORINE: Of course, it's well known lovers are quite mad.

VALÈRE: (*To* MARIANE)   515
Don't you think I have some grounds for
complain
You must admit, it wasn't very nice
to take such pleasure in upsetting me.

MARIANE: Aren't you the most ungrateful man alive....?   520

DORINE: Can we leave this discussion for the moment
and concentrate on fending off this wedding?

MARIANE: Tell us what we should do.

DORINE: Try everything.
Your father can't be serious with this nonsense.   525
All the same, you should react to his ravings
by giving an impression of consent,
so that in an emergency it'd be
easier for you to spin out the engagement.
The key thing in all this is playing for time.   530
You can develop sudden illnesses
to cause delay, or come across bad omens:
an argument with someone who's then died,
a broken mirror, dreams of muddy water.
The main thing is that they can't marry you   535
to him, or anyone, till you say, 'I do.'
Also, I'd say, to be on the safe side,
it's an idea not to be seen together.

(*To* VALÈRE)

So don't waste time, and get your friends to start
pressuring him to keep his promise to you.   540

(*To* MARIANE)

We must get your stepmother on our side
and ask her brother to keep trying. 'Bye.

VALÈRE: (*To* MARIANE)
To tell the truth, whatever we may try,
it's you I'm counting on.   545

MARIANE: (*To* VALÈRE)
Well, I can't answer
for what my father wants, but I know I'll
never belong to anyone but you.

VALÈRE: That's a great comfort! So whatever they . . .   550
DORINE: Lovers can't get enough of all this blather.
    Now, will you go . . .

      (VALÈRE *takes a step and then turns back.*)

VALÈRE: Just one thing . . .
DORINE: No
                                     more chat!   555

     (*She pushes them both by the shoulder.*)

    Now, you go this way, and you, you go that.

ACT III

SCENE I

DAMIS, DORINE.

DAMIS: I deserve to be struck dead on the spot
    and treated like a miserable nothing
    if I don't think up some brilliant idea,
    and when I do no power on earth will stop me!
DORINE: Oh, please, there's no need to exaggerate;   5
    it's only a suggestion of your father's.
    Not every resolution's carried out,
    there's many a slip.
DAMIS: I must scotch this swine's
                              plots,   10
    there's two words I must whisper in his ear.
DORINE: Now, take it easy! Let your stepmother
    deal with him as she's dealing with your father.
    She has some kind of influence on Tartuffe;
    she can say what she likes and he's always   15
    indulgent, perhaps he's even smitten with her.
    I hope to God he is! That would be fun.
    In fact, she's summoned him on your behalf;
    she wants to sound him out about this marriage
    that's worrying you so much, she wants to know   20
    the way he feels about it, and explain
    to him the difficulties it would cause
    if he was to encourage this idea.
    His servant says I can't see him, he's praying;
    but he also told me he'd be down soon.   25
    So please go now and let me wait for him.
DAMIS: Why shouldn't I just be here while they're
                           talking?
DORINE: No. They must be alone.

DAMIS: I wouldn't say   30
    a word to him.
DORINE: You're joking: we all know
    what a short fuse you're on, that's just the
                                way
    to ruin everything. Now off you go.   35
DAMIS: No, I can watch without losing my temper.
DORINE: You're so annoying! Go on, here he comes.

SCENE II

TARTUFFE, LAURENT, DORINE.

TARTUFFE: (*Noticing* DORINE)
    My hair shirt, Laurent, please put it away
    next to my birch, and I want you to pray   40
    for Heaven's eternal guidance. If there are
    visitors, tell them I'll be at the prison,
    distributing what few small coins I have.
DORINE: (*Aside*)
    Posturing humbug!   45
TARTUFFE: Yes, what do you want?
DORINE: To tell you . . .

       (TARTUFFE *pulls a handkerchief out of his pocket.*)

TARTUFFE: Oh, my goodness, just a
                         moment,
    before you say another word, take this.   50
DORINE: What for?
TARTUFFE: Cover your breasts, I shouldn't have
    to be exposed to them, that kind of thing
    does damage to the soul and can give rise
    to guilty thoughts.   55
DORINE: You're very vulnerable
    to temptation, I didn't know that flesh
    made such a big impression on your senses.
    I can't see why you should get overheated;
    I mean, I'm not so easy to arouse: 60
    for instance, I could look at you stark-naked,
    and not be tempted by a single inch.
TARTUFFE: If you don't show a little modesty,
    I'll be obliged to leave you.
DORINE: No, you won't,   65
    it's me who's going, so you can calm down;
    the only thing I have to say is this:
    Madame is on her way, she'd like a word.
TARTUFFE: By all means!
DORINE: (*Aside*)   70
        Ah, that's cheered him up! I
                    think
    I must be right.

TARTUFFE:	Will she be long?	
DORINE:	I think	75

that's her now, yes, it is, I'll leave you to it.

SCENE III

ELMIRE, TARTUFFE.

TARTUFFE: May God in all His infinite goodness grant you
    perpetual health in body and in soul,
    and bless you: that's His humblest suppliant's
                        prayer! 80

ELMIRE: I'm very grateful for your pious wishes.
    Sit down, let's make ourselves more
                    comfortable.

TARTUFFE: (*Sitting down*)
    I hope you've quite recovered from your illness. 85

ELMIRE: (*Sitting down*)
    Oh, yes, thank you, the fever didn't last.

TARTUFFE: My prayers are scarcely worthy of attracting
    grace from on high; but I must say their sole
    object has been your speedy convalescence. 90

ELMIRE: I really think you show too much desire
    for my welfare.

TARTUFFE: Your health is very precious;
    to bring it back I'd sacrifice my own.

ELMIRE: That's taking Christian charity to its limits; 95
    I do appreciate your kindness, really.

TARTUFFE: I do far less for you than you deserve.

ELMIRE: I've been wanting to talk to you in private,
    I'm glad that we're alone together here.

TARTUFFE: Yes, I'm delighted, it is such a pleasure 100
    to be alone with you for the first time:
    an opportunity I've often prayed for.

ELMIRE: I thought we could just have a conversation
    in which you'd feel you might confide in me.

    (*Without showing himself,* DAMIS *half-opens the door of the closet, in which
    he's been hiding, in order to listen to the conversation.*)

TARTUFFE: And I want nothing better than the chance, 105
    the privilege of baring my soul to you,
    and of assuring you that the protests
    I made against your visitors were nothing
    personal, they were prompted by my zeal
    and by an impulse to . . . 110

ELMIRE: So I assumed,
    I know my welfare was your main concern.

    (TARTUFFE *squeezes the ends of her fingers.*)

TARTUFFE: Of course it was, and such was my desire . . .
ELMIRE: Ow, that hurts!
TARTUFFE: It's just over-eagerness.   115
   I never meant to hurt you, I'd much rather

(*He puts his hand on her knee.*)

ELMIRE: What are you doing?
TARTUFFE: Just feeling your dress
   Isn't it velvety?
ELMIRE: Oh, no, please, don't.   120
   I'm very ticklish.

(*She moves her chair back, and* TARTUFFE *moves his chair closer. He starts
feeling the lace on* ELMIRE*'s bodice.*)

TARTUFFE: What workmanship!
   It's wonderful the things they do these days.
   My word, I've never seen anything like it.
ELMIRE: I'm sure. But can we get back to the point?   125
   I've heard my husband wants to break his
                                        promise
   and give his daughter to you. Is that true?
TARTUFFE: He said something about it; but, quite frankly,
   that's not the happiness I'm pining for;   130
   all my desires are concentrated on
   a different set of wonderful attractions.
ELMIRE: You mean you have no time for earthly
                                        matters.
TARTUFFE: My heart is not entirely made of stone.   135
ELMIRE: I know your aspirations are toward Heaven,
   that down here nothing can distract your will.
TARTUFFE: The love we feel for the eternal beauties
   doesn't preclude a love for what is temporal,
   and our senses can easily succumb   140
   under the spell of God's perfect creations.
   His glories are reflected in your sex,
   but in your case it's more than that, He's
                                        revealed
   His rarest wonders and lavished such beauties   145
   on you, we're dazzled, we're carried away;
   and I can't look at you, you perfect creature,
   without admiring the Almighty in you,
   struck to the heart with blazing love in front of
   God's loveliest self-portrait. Oh, at first,   150
   I was afraid this secret passion was
   a cunning subterfuge of the Prince of Darkness;
   and I even determined to avoid you,
   thinking you might jeopardize my salvation.
   But finally I realized, my sweet beauty: 155
   in such a feeling there could be no guilt,
   it could be reconciled with purity,

and that's when I surrendered myself to it.
I confess, it is very bold of me
to dare to offer you my love like this; 160
but I'm relying wholly on your kindness,
rather than on my own unworthiness.
My hopes, my well-being, my peace of mind
are in your hands, my suffering or my bliss
depend on you, and only you can make me 165
happy or unhappy, just as you choose.
ELMIRE: Well, that's a very gallant declaration,
if, to be honest, somewhat unexpected.
It seems to me you ought to have reflected
a little and held back from such a step. 170
A man whose reputation as a saint . . .
TARTUFFE: Why should a saint be any the less human?
Confronted with your heavenly attractions,
a man just gives way, how can he reflect?
It may seem strange for me to say such things; 175
but after all, Madame, I'm not an angel,
and if my declaration is blameworthy,
the real culprit is your enchanting beauty.
Ever since I first saw its superhuman,
radiant glory, you have ruled my heart. 180
The indescribable tenderness of your
divine expression broke down my resistance,
overcame all my fasting, prayers and weeping
and concentrated all my hopes on you.
I'm only voicing what you must have guessed 185
when I so often looked at you and sighed.
If you could bring yourself to show some favour
to your unworthy servant's tribulations,
if you would deign to stoop down to my level
and out of kindness offer me relief, 190
delicious prodigy, I guarantee
my eternal, unparalleled devotion.
Your reputation would be safe with me,
you'd run no risk of notoriety.
These libertines the ladies so admire 195
at court are ostentatious and loud-mouthed,
always bragging of conquests, of whose favours
no detail is too intimate to reveal;
their indiscretions and abuse of trust
degrade the very object of their worship. 200
People like us know how to love discreetly,
and how to keep it permanently secret.
Our own concern for our good character
acts as a guarantee for those we love,
and once you've given way, you'll find we offer 205
love without scandal, pleasure without fear.
ELMIRE: I've heard you out now, and your eloquence
is unambiguous enough, I think.

But aren't you worried that I might decide
to tell my husband about this proposal? 210
And that if he were told about your hopes
it might do damage to his friendship for you?
TARTUFFE: I know that you're too generous for that,
and that you will forgive my recklessness;
the violence of a passion which offends you 215
you will exonerate as human weakness,
and, bearing in mind your looks, you will
                                acknowledge
that I'm not blind and men are flesh and blood.
ELMIRE: Others might take another line perhaps, 220
but I prefer to exercise discretion.
I shall say nothing of this to my husband;
but in return I'd like something from you:
I want you to support quite openly,
without beating about the bush, Valère's 225
marriage to Mariane, and to give up
your unfair influence and your desire
to enrich yourself with someone else's money,
and . . .

SCENE IV

ELMIRE, DAMIS, TARTUFFE.
DAMIS *emerges from the closet in which he's been hiding.*

DAMIS: No, no, everyone must know about this. 230
I was in there and I heard everything;
it's as if Heaven led me there to crush
the hubris of a treacherous enemy,
and give me the potential for revenge
against his insolent hypocrisy, 235
the means to disabuse my father and
expose this monster's attempt to seduce you.
ELMIRE: No, Damis, it's enough he should improve
and try to be worthy of my reprieve.
I've given my promise, please don't make me 240
                                break it.
It isn't in my nature to make trouble;
a woman laughs off foolishness like this
and wouldn't dream of worrying her husband.
DAMIS: You have your reasons for that attitude 245
and I have mine for disagreeing with it.
I think to let him off would be a joke;
his insolence and sanctimoniousness
have got the better of my justified
protests too often and have caused too many 250
upheavals in this house. This liar has led
my father by the nose for far too long,

and done his best to undermine my love
as well as Valère's. Now Heaven has offered
an easy way of unmasking the traitor,   255
I have to take the opportunity,
it's far too providential to be missed;
to have it in my hand and let it go
would mean I would deserve to lose this
                              chance.   260

ELMIRE: Damis . . .
DAMIS: No, please, I have to trust my
                            judgement.
    I couldn't be happier, and you won't persuade
                          me   265
    to forgo all the pleasures of revenge.
    I have what I need to conclude this business;
    and here's the man who'll put my mind at rest.

SCENE V

ORGON, DAMIS, TARTUFFE, ELMIRE.

DAMIS: Now, listen, father, this should cheer you up,
    something's just happened which may startle   270
                        you.
    It's a reward for all your kindnesses,
    acknowledged by this man with a fat payment.
    He's just been showing his great love for you,
    which doesn't even draw the line at making   275
    a cuckold of you; I've just caught him here
    making a proposition to your wife.
    You know her gentleness and her discretion;
    she wanted very much to keep it secret,
    but I just can't indulge his shamelessness: 280
    I think it would be quite wrong not to tell you.
ELMIRE: It's true, I don't think one should ever ruin
    a husband's peace of mind for trivial reasons;
    honour is not affected, it's enough
    for us to know how to defend ourselves.   285
    That's how I feel; and if I'd had the slightest
    influence on you, you would have kept quiet.

SCENE VI

ORGON, DAMIS, TARTUFFE.

ORGON: My God, can it be possible, what they say?
TARTUFFE: Yes, brother, I am evil, I am guilty,
    a wicked sinner sunk in iniquity,   290
    the greatest criminal that ever lived.
    Each second of my life is stained with filth,

it's one huge seething rubbish heap of vice,
and Heaven's clearly seized upon this chance
to humiliate me as a punishment. 295
I wouldn't have the arrogance to deny
whatever sin it is that I'm accused of.
So fuel your anger, believe what they say,
and throw me on the street like some
                                        delinquent. 300
However great the shame you pile upon me,
it couldn't be as much as I deserve.

ORGON: (*To* DAMIS)
    You wretch, how dare you fabricate this lie
    and try to blot his purity and virtue? 305

DAMIS: You mean this hypocritical surrender
    could make you doubt . . . ?

ORGON: Be quiet, you little
                                        pest!

TARTUFFE: No, let him speak; it's wrong of you to blame 310
                                        him,
    you'd do better to believe what he says.
    Why should you favour me in this dispute?
    After all, how do you know what I might
    be capable of? Do you trust mere show? 315
    You think I'm better just because I seem so?
    No, no, you're letting yourself be tricked by
    appearances and, I'm sorry to say,
    I'm not at all the man I'm thought to be.
    Everyone takes me for a good man, but 320
    the simple truth is I'm entirely worthless.

    (*He turns to* DAMIS.)

    Come on, my boy, speak up: call me a traitor,
    a lost soul, a degenerate, a thief,
    a murderer; crush me with viler names;
    I won't deny them, I've deserved them all, 325
    and on my knees I welcome this disgrace
    in expiation of my life of crime.

ORGON: (*To* TARTUFFE)
    You go too far.

    (*To* DAMIS)

                        Aren't you ashamed, you 330
                                        wretch?

DAMIS: You mean you're taken in by this . . .?

ORGON: Be quiet,
    you gallows-bird!

    (*To* TARTUFFE)

                        Oh, please, brother, get up! 335

    (*To* DAMIS)

Scum!

DAMIS: Maybe . . .
ORGON: Shut up!
DAMIS: This is too much,
                              I . . .   340
ORGON: If you say one more word, I'll break your arms.
TARTUFFE: For God's sake, brother, please don't lose your
                                        temper.
    I'd rather suffer any punishment
    than see him take a scratch on my account.   345
ORGON: (*To* DAMIS)
    You upstart!
TARTUFFE: Leave him be. If necessary,
    I'll ask you to forgive him on my knees . . .
ORGON: (*To* TARTUFFE)   350
    You can't be serious!

      (*To* DAMIS)

          See how kind he is,
    you louse!
DAMIS: But . . .
ORGON: Silence!   355
DAMIS: What? I . . .
ORGON: I said,
                                  silence

    I know your motives for attacking him:
    all of you hate him and I've had to watch   360
    my wife, my children and my servants hound
                                   him
    No method is too brazen when it comes
    to driving this good person from my house.
    But the more you try to get rid of him,   365
    the better ways I'll find to keep him here;
    and to annihilate my family's arrogance,
    I'm going to give my daughter to him, soon.
DAMIS: You're going to force her to accept his hand?
ORGON: Yes, wretch, and, to spite you, this very   370
                              evening
    Ha, I defy you all, I'm going to teach you
    that I'm in charge here and I'll be obeyed.
    So take back what you said this minute, liar,
    down on your knees and ask him to forgive you!   375
DAMIS: Who, me? Me ask this unscrupulous fake . . . ?
ORGON: So you refuse, you ruffian, and insult him?
    A stick, bring me my stick!

      (*To* TARTUFFE)

          And you let go!

      (*To* DAMIS)

    Out of my house, and don't you dare come   380
                              back

DAMIS: All right, all right, I'm leaving . . .
ORGON: Get out,
                                      now
      I hereby disinherit you, you gaolbird;   385
      the only thing I'll give you is my curse.

SCENE VII

ORGON, TARTUFFE.

ORGON: What a way to insult a man of God!
TARTUFFE: Oh, Lord, forgive his trespasses against me!

      (*To* ORGON)

      Ah, if you only knew how much it hurts
      when people try to blacken me in your eyes . . .   390
ORGON: Don't!
TARTUFFE: Just to think of the ingratitude
      is such a cruel torment to my soul . . .
      The horror of it . . . My heart is so heavy,
      I can't speak, this will be the death of me.   395

      (ORGON *bursts into tears, and runs to the door through which he has
      driven* DAMIS.)

ORGON: You louse! I'm sorry I restrained myself,
      I should have knocked you senseless there and
                                          then.
      Calm down, now, brother, don't get so upset.
TARTUFFE: It's time we put an end to these dissensions.   400
      I know I've been a cause of trouble here,
      I can see no alternative to my leaving.
ORGON: You can't be serious!
TARTUFFE: They hate me here,
      they're trying to make you doubt my integrity.   405
ORGON: So what? You think I'm going to listen to
                                          them?
TARTUFFE: They won't give up attacking, that's for sure,
      and accusations which you now reject
      are bound to take their toll eventually.   410
ORGON: Impossible.
TARTUFFE: Brother, you know a wife
      can easily delude her husband.
ORGON: No,
      never.   415
TARTUFFE: If I were to leave here forthwith,
      they'd have no grounds for these attacks; so let
                                          me.
ORGON: No, you must stay, my life depends on it.
TARTUFFE: Well, in that case, I'll have to sacrifice   420
      myself. And yet . . .

ORGON: What?
TARTUFFE: No, we'll say no
                                                          more
    I know what's necessary. Honour is   425
    a fragile plant and our friendship obliges
    me to prevent this rumour and suspicion
    by avoiding your wife. I won't be seen . . .
ORGON: No, I defy them all, you'll spend time with her,
    my greatest pleasure is to make them angry,   430
    I want you to be seen with her constantly.
    And that's not all: to show them what I think,
    I'll make you my sole heir and waste no time
    in handing over all my worldly goods.
    You're my friend, you will be my son-in-law,   435
    dearer to me by far than my own son,
    my wife or my relations. Won't you please
    accept my offer?
TARTUFFE: Well, God's will be done!
ORGON: Poor boy! Come on, let's go and draft the   440
                                                          papers,
    and let that jealous lot gag on their own spite!

ACT IV

SCENE I

CLÉANTE, TARTUFFE.

CLÉANTE: Yes, everyone's discussing it, believe
    me, and the verdict's not to your advantage;
    I'm pleased to have this opportunity
    to give you my opinion in a few words.
    I don't propose to get into the details;   5
    forget all that and let's assume the worst.
    Suppose Damis has behaved badly and
    falsely accused you, would it not be Christian
    to overlook the sin and to suppress
    any desire for vengeance? Ought you to   10
    allow a son to be driven out of
    his father's house because of a dispute
    with you? I tell you frankly, I repeat,
    people of every class are shocked by this.
    If you take my advice, you'll make peace here   15
    and not let matters be pushed to extremes.
    Forget your anger, offer it up to God
    and reconcile a father with his son.
TARTUFFE: As far as I'm concerned, I would like nothing
    better, I have no animus against him.   20

I forgive him, I don't blame him at all,
I would do anything I could for him;
but from God's point of view, it's just not on,
and if he comes back, I shall have to leave.
After his unprecedented behaviour,   25
any contact between us would invite
scandal: God knows what might not be
                                        inferred!
I'd be accused of pure expedience,
and everyone would say that, out of guilt,   30
I was pretending to forgive my enemy,
that I was afraid of him and hoped I could
in some clandestine way pay for his silence.
CLÉANTE: These are just so many specious excuses.
Your reasoning is far too tortuous.   35
Why should you fret about God's point of view?
Does He need your help to chastise the guilty?
Leave it to Him to wreak His own revenges;
He tells us to forgive sinners, remember,
and not to take account of human judgements   40
when following His sovereign commands.
This weak concern for what people might think
surely can't be allowed to override
the majesty of doing good? No, no;
let's follow God's commandments every time,   45
and not confuse ourselves with other concepts.
TARTUFFE: I've already explained that I forgive him,
and therefore I am following God's
                                    commandments;
but after this scandal and today's insults,   50
there's no commandment says I have to live
                                        with him.
CLÉANTE: And is there a commandment says you should
acquiesce in this mad whim of his father's,
and accept his gift to you of a fortune   55
on which justice must tell you you've no claim?
TARTUFFE: Those who know me would never dream of
                                            thinking
that this is a result of my self-seeking.
The riches of this world have very little   60
appeal to me, I'm not one to be dazzled
by their illusory glow; and if Orgon
wants me to have this gift and I decide
to take it, it will only be because
otherwise, to be honest, I'd be worried   65
in case all of that money were to fall
into the wrong hands; and end up with people
who'd use their share for evil purposes,
rather than keeping it, as I intend to,
for God's glory and the welfare of my   70
                                    neighbour.

CLÉANTE: Oh, spare yourself these dainty inhibitions,
    which are offensive to the rightful heir.
    Let him come into his inheritance
    at his own risk, and don't distress yourself;   75
    just think, better for him to squander it,
    than for you to be charged with cheating him.
    I'm only startled that you seem to be
    quite unembarrassed by this proposition;
    I mean, is there some old religious maxim   80
    says thou shalt plunder the legitimate heir?
    And if God really has implanted in you
    this inability to live with Damis,
    which can't be overcome, would it not be
    better to show discretion and withdraw   85
    than to allow this quite unreasonable
    hounding out of a son on your account?
    Now that would be a sign of character . . .
TARTUFFE: You must excuse me now, it's half-past three,
    and I'm required upstairs to fulfil   90
    certain religious duties, much as I hate
    to leave you.
CLÉANTE: (*Alone*)
        Ha!

SCENE II

ELMIRE, MARIANE, DORINE, CLÉANTE.

DORINE: (*To* CLÉANTE)   95
                Please, sir, help us to help
                      her:
    she's in a dreadful state and this agreement
    her father's fixed up for this evening has
    driven her to despair. Look, here he comes: 100
    let's try our best, by cunning or brute force,
    to frustrate this abominable plan.

SCENE III

ORGON, ELMIRE, MARIANE, CLÉANTE, DORINE.

ORGON: Oh, good! I'm glad I've found you all together.

    (*To* MARIANE)

    Now here is something which should raise a
                    smile: 105
    this contract—you must know what it's about.
MARIANE: (*On her knees*)
    God knows how painful this is, and for His
                 sake,

by anything that's capable of touching   110
your heart, relax your father's rights a little,
exempt my love from having to obey you.
Don't impose this harsh law and so reduce me
to wish to God that I were not your daughter;
and please don't ruin my life for me, father,   115
this life you gave me. If you must forbid me
to belong to the man I love and thwart
the hopes that I have been allowed to cherish,
at least, I beg you on my knees, be kind
and don't condemn me to belong to a man   120
I loathe: don't exercise your power on me
and drive me to do something desperate.

ORGON: (*Feeling himself weaken*)
    Now, come on, steel yourself, no human
                    weakness!   125

MARIANE: I have nothing against your feeling for him,
    display it all you like, give him your money,
    and if that's not enough, add mine as well.
    I'd agree happily, it's yours, but can't you
    just draw the line at offering him my body?   130
    Let me use up my sad remaining days
    in the austere enclosure of a convent.

ORGON: I see, you're one of those who turns religious
    at the first setback to your amorous plans!
    On your feet! The more repulsive you find him,   135
    the more improving it will be for you.
    Use this marriage to mortify your senses,
    now that's all, I don't want any more nagging.

DORINE: But what . . . ?

ORGON: And you shut up, mind your   140
                    own business:
    don't you dare speak, I utterly forbid it.

CLÉANTE: If you'd allow just one word of advice . . .

ORGON: Yes, your advice is always admirable,
    well argued, and I do value it greatly;   145
    but you won't mind if this time I ignore it.

ELMIRE: (*To* ORGON)
    I don't know what to say about all this,
    I'm staggered by your blindness. You must be
    infatuated and obsessed with him,   150
    to overlook what's happened here today.

ORGON: Seeing's believing, with all due respect.
    I know how indulgent you are towards my son,
    and that you were afraid to contradict him,
    when he tried playing that trick on the poor   155
                    boy.
    You were too calm to be believable,
    you would have looked a good deal more upset.

ELMIRE: Need we react quite so ferociously
    when someone just declares his love for us?   160
    Are blazing eyes and spitting out insults

the only possible response to it?
My way is just to laugh at these approaches,
I get no pleasure out of melodrama.
I think we should be calm and sensible,   165
and I've no time for those rampaging prudes
whose virtue's red in tooth and claw, and who
would scratch your eyes out at the first excuse;
Heaven preserve us from such saintliness!
I'm for integrity without shrewishness,   170
I think a chilly and discreet refusal
is as effective a rebuff as any.

ORGON: I know my mind and I'm not changing it.

ELMIRE: Again, I'm staggered by this curious weakness.
But how would it affect your unbelief,   175
if I could show you we were telling the truth?

ORGON: Show me?

ELMIRE: Yes.

ORGON: Rubbish!

ELMIRE: Suppose I found a   180
                                                way
to prove it beyond any doubt?

ORGON: Absurd!

ELMIRE: What a man! Won't you answer me at least?
I don't ask you to take our word for it;   185
suppose we found a place somewhere round
                                                here,
where you could see and hear quite clearly,
                                        then
what would you have to say about this good   190
                                        man?

ORGON: In that case, I'd say . . . no, no, I'd say
                                        nothing,
because it couldn't happen.

ELMIRE: This delusion   195
has lasted far too long, and I am tired
of being accused of lying. It's high time
I gave myself the satisfaction of
showing you everything we've said is true.

ORGON: All right, I'll take you at your word. Let's see   200
you keep your promise.

ELMIRE: (*To* DORINE)
                        Bring him here to me.

DORINE: (*To* ELMIRE)
He's cunning and he may not be so easy   205
to catch out.

ELMIRE: No; in love, deceit is easy,
vanity leads people to fool themselves.
Bring him downstairs.

        (*She turns to* CLÉANTE *and* MARIANE.)

                        And you two'd better   210
                                go.

SCENE IV

ELMIRE, ORGON.

ELMIRE: Let's move this table, you get underneath.
ORGON: You what?
ELMIRE: It's quite important you're well
                                        hidden.   215
ORGON: But why under this table?
ELMIRE: Oh, my God!
    Do what you're told, I have my plan, you'll see.
    Come on, get under it, and when you're there,
    keep quiet and make sure you can't be seen.   220
ORGON: I must say, this is really very silly,
    but I can't wait to see you prove your point.
ELMIRE: I don't believe you'll have any complaints.

        (*He's now under the table.*)

    You mustn't be surprised if I sound strange,
    or be at all shocked. Whatever I say,   225
    remember I have promised to convince you,
    and must be given free rein. I shall coax,
    since I'm reduced to this, this hypocrite
    to take his mask off, and I shall encourage
    his insolent desires and stimulate   230
    his recklessness. Since all this is for you,
    this pretence of responding to him with
    the intention of fooling him, I'll only
    stop it when you acknowledge you were wrong,
    so things will go as far as you allow them.   235
    It's up to you to interrupt his ardour,
    when you consider they've gone far enough;
    protect your wife and don't expose me to
    any more than you need to be convinced.
    It's your business and you're in charge and . . .   240
                                        Here
he comes; stay there and mind he doesn't see
                                        you.

SCENE V

TARTUFFE, ELMIRE, ORGON, *hidden under the table.*

TARTUFFE: I'm told you asked to see me in this room.
ELMIRE: Yes, there's a secret I must tell you. But,   245
    before I do, would you please close the door,
    and make sure no one's likely to surprise us.

        (**TARTUFFE** *goes to close the door and comes back.*)

We don't want a repeat of what just happened
for anything, I've never been so shocked.
Damis gave me a dreadful fright, on your   250
behalf, and, as you saw, I did my best
to calm him down and frustrate his intentions.
It's true I was so worried that it never
occurred to me to contradict his story;
but, thank God, for that very reason things   255
turned out much better and less dangerously.
Your reputation soon dispelled the storm,
my husband couldn't think badly of you;
and to show his contempt for crude suspicions,
he wants us to spend lots of time together;   260
and that's why I can be alone with you
here, without any fear of being judged,
and what allows me to reveal to you
what I should perhaps keep back a little longer:
that I'm prepared to entertain your suit.   265
TARTUFFE: I'm not quite sure I follow you, Madame,
    just now you gave a very different answer.
ELMIRE: Oh, well, if my refusal put you off,
    you must know very little about women!
    You're no good at interpreting what's meant   270
by such an obviously weak defence.
On these occasions modesty is bound
to be in conflict with our tender feelings.
However right yielding to love may feel,
it's always slightly shaming to admit it.   275
At first we fight against it; but the way
we do so is a sign of our surrender;
our voice, for virtue's sake, protesting feebly
against our instincts, gives the kind of no
which promises you everything. Well, now,   280
I suppose that's a pretty damning confession,
I haven't paid much heed to modesty;
but, since it's in the open now at last,
would I have tried so hard to silence Damis?
I ask you, would I have so quietly listened   285
to that long declaration of your love?
Would I have taken it the way I did
unless something about it gave me pleasure?
And when I tried to blackmail you myself
not to accept this newly arranged wedding,   290
what did my urgency suggest to you,
if not that you now meant a lot to me,
and that this proposed marriage would upset
                me,
by, at the very least, making me share   295
a love I wanted for myself alone?
TARTUFFE: To hear such words from such a lovely mouth
    is exquisitely pleasurable, Madame;
    their honey sends unprecedented sweetness

flowing in long draughts through my entire 300
                                         system.
My main concern is to be fortunate
enough to please you and my greatest blessing
will be to fulfil your desires: but
forgive me if I take the liberty 305
of casting some small doubt on my good
                                         fortune.
What you say might be a straightforward trick
to make me break off this impending marriage;
And, to be brutally honest, I shan't trust
these delicious suggestions you have made 310
until I get a taste of what I crave
to reassure me there's been no mistake
and instil in me lasting confidence
in just how generous you mean to be. 315

(ELMIRE *coughs to alert* ORGON.)

ELMIRE: Surely you don't have to move quite so fast
        and exhaust all the possibilities
        in one go? To make such an intimate
        confession to you practically killed me:
        and now I find it's not enough for you. 320
        You mean you won't be satisfied until
        this thing has gone as far as it can go?
TARTUFFE: An undeserving man can never quite
        rely on hope. And conversation's not
        a firm basis for love. It's all too easy 325
        to have one's doubts about a glorious future:
        once I've enjoyed it, then I'll believe in it.
        You see, I don't think I deserve your kindness,
        I can't accept my boldness has paid off,
        I won't believe it, not until you find 330
        some realistic method to convince me.
ELMIRE: My God, now you're behaving like a tyrant,
        and plunging me into a strange confusion!
        Your love has taken passionate control,
        and your desire's so violently demanding! 335
        Is there no way out? Won't you give a girl
        a breathing space? And is it right to make
        such mercilessly rigorous demands,
        and take advantage so insistently
        of this weakness you know I have for you? 340
TARTUFFE: But why, if you approve of my advances,
        refuse me the definitive credential?
ELMIRE: But how can I agree to what you want
        without, as you would say, offending God?
TARTUFFE: If God is all you're worrying about, 345
        leave it to me to deal with that problem,
        you mustn't let that hold you back at all.
ELMIRE: We're always told we must fear Heaven's
                                         judgements!

TARTUFFE: I can dispel these ludicrous alarms,   350
    I know the art of freeing inhibitions.
    It's true that certain pleasures are forbidden
    by God; but there are ways of getting round
                            this.
    Depending on one's needs, there is a method   355
    of loosening the fetters of one's conscience,
    setting the purity of our intentions
    against the evil of the deed itself.
    I'll explain these mysteries some other time;
    all you need do for now is what I tell you.   360
    Don't be afraid to fulfil my desires;
    I'll be responsible for everything
    and take the sin upon myself, Madame.

      (ELMIRE *coughs louder.*)

    That is a bad cough.
ELMIRE: Yes, it's misery.   365

      (TARTUFFE *offers* ELMIRE *a twist of paper.*)

TARTUFFE: Perhaps it would help to suck a piece of
                         liquorice?
ELMIRE: This cold has clung on, I can't seem to shift it,
    I don't think it would help much to suck
                    anything.   370
TARTUFFE: Well, that is trying.
ELMIRE: Yes, unspeakably.
TARTUFFE: Anyway, I can easily remove
    your scruples: this will be completely secret,
    I can assure you, and the only evil   375
    is to make a great noise about things. What
    constitutes the offence is public scandal.
    Sinning in silence is no sin at all.

    (*Another bout of coughing from* ELMIRE.)

ELMIRE: All right, I see there's no alternative
    but to submit and give you what you want;   380
    clearly you can't be happy with a promise,
    and nothing less will do. I can't deny,
    I don't want to go this far and I do it
    against my better judgement; all the same,
    since you insist on making me and won't   385
    believe in my assurances and need
    more palpable corroboration, I
    must grit my teeth and try to keep you happy.
    And if agreeing to it is a crime,
    so much the worse for the man who's behind it,   390
    forcing me to it, it won't be my fault.
TARTUFFE: Yes, you leave it to me, Madame, you'll find . . .
ELMIRE: Just open that door, will you, and make sure
    my husband isn't in the gallery.

TARTUFFE: Why worry about him? Between ourselves,   395
    he's very easy to manipulate.
    He takes a pride in our relationship,
    I've got him so that he wouldn't believe it
    even if he saw us . . .
ELMIRE: Never mind, just go,   400
    and have a really good look round out there.

SCENE VI

ORGON, ELMIRE.
ORGON *emerges from underneath the table.*

ORGON: So you were right, what an appalling man!
    I can't get over it, it's such a shock.
ELMIRE: What, already? There must be some mistake.
    Get back under the tablecloth, you're early;   405
    wait till he's finished, to be on the safe side,
    I don't think you should make unfair
                       assumptions.
ORGON: He's worse than any devil out of Hell.
ELMIRE: Good God, now, don't go jumping to   410
                     conclusions!
    Before you change your mind, I think you
                   should
    be properly convinced, so don't be hasty,
    I wouldn't want you to make a mistake.   415

      (*She hides* ORGON *behind her.*)

SCENE VII

TARTUFFE, ELMIRE, ORGON.

TARTUFFE: (*Without seeing* ORGON)
    Nothing can stop me being happy now:
    I've checked all round, there's no one, my
                 delight . . .
ORGON: (*Stopping him*)   420
    Slow down! You're letting your desire run
                 rampant,
    I wouldn't let yourself get too excited.
    So, my good man, you thought you could
                 deceive me!   425
    When you decide to give in to temptation,
    no one could say you do the thing by halves!
    Marrying my daughter, lusting for my wife!
    I couldn't believe that it was really happening.
    I kept waiting for you to change your tune;   430
    but I think now we've had quite enough proof:

I'm satisfied in my mind, that's all I need.

ELMIRE: (*To* TARTUFFE)
I did all this against my better judgement;
I couldn't think of an alternative.   435

TARTUFFE: You mean you think . . .?

ORGON: Oh, please, let's have
                                                   no fuss.

Take yourself off without further ado.

TARTUFFE: I never meant . . .   440

ORGON: There's no point in all this;
Will you, this minute, get out of my house!

TARTUFFE: No, you get out, because it's my house now:
it won't do you the slightest good to grub up
these cheap excuses to get rid of me;   445
attacking me's more dangerous than you think,
I have a way of punishing impostors,
avenging this insult to God and making
people who try to throw me out repent.

SCENE VIII

ELMIRE, ORGON.

ELMIRE: What does he mean?   450

ORGON: My God, what shall I do?
This could be serious.

ELMIRE: Why?

ORGON: What he just said:
I fear that deed of gift was a mistake.   455

ELMIRE: What deed of gift?

ORGON: It's all signed, I'm afraid.
But something else he said disturbed me more.

ELMIRE: What?

ORGON: I'll explain; but first of all, let's see   460
if that attaché case is still upstairs.

──────────── **ACT V** ────────────

SCENE I

ORGON, CLÉANTE.

CLÉANTE: Where are you off to?

ORGON: Oh, I wish I knew.

CLÉANTE: It seems to me the first thing we must do
is to discuss the possibilities.

ORGON: My main worry is the attaché case;   5 it's much more serious than all the rest.

CLÉANTE: Is what's in this attaché case a secret?

ORGON: Argas, that friend of mine who was in trouble,
　　　left it with me in strictest confidence.
　　　He sought me out before he fled abroad; 　　　　　　　　　　10
　　　from what he said, I gather it contains
　　　essential private and financial papers.

CLÉANTE: Why did you hand it over to Tartuffe?

ORGON: To ease my conscience. I went straight to him,
　　　that traitor, and confided in him; he 　　　　　　　　　　　15
　　　persuaded me to give the case to him,
　　　on the grounds that, if anybody asked,
　　　I could deny I had it and still keep
　　　my conscience clear of any perjury.

CLÉANTE: I'd say things looked black for you; and, to be 　　　20
　　　　　　　　　　　　　　　　　　frank,
　　　this indiscretion and the deed of gift
　　　were undertaken by you much too lightly.
　　　You've put yourself in pawn to him; and since
　　　he does have such great power over you, 　　　　　　　　　25
　　　provoking him was desperately unwise,
　　　you ought to have tried harder to placate him.

ORGON: Who could imagine that devout façade
　　　could hide such double-dealing wickedness?
　　　To think I took him in when he had nothing . . . 　　　　30
　　　Well, he's the last religious man I'll trust;
　　　in future I'll recoil from them in horror,
　　　and never miss a chance to be their scourge.

CLÉANTE: Oh, not another of your tantrums, please!
　　　You don't know what a happy medium is; 　　　　　　　35
　　　your reason never coincides with reason,
　　　you always lurch from one excess to another.
　　　You realize your mistake, that you were
　　　　　　　　　　　　　　　　duped
　　　by a false piety, but what's the point 　　　　　　　　　40
　　　of trying to make up for it by falling
　　　into an even bigger trap and not
　　　seeing the difference between men of honour
　　　and this contemptible degenerate?
　　　Just because one thief has, with his veneer 　　　　　　45
　　　of hypocritical austerity,
　　　brazenly cheated you, you then assume
　　　everyone is like that and genuinely
　　　religious people don't exist today!
　　　Leave senseless thoughts like that to atheists; 　　　　50
　　　learn to distinguish virtue and its semblance,
　　　don't be too careless with your admiration,
　　　and show a necessary moderation.
　　　If possible, don't fall for hypocrites;
　　　but, equally, don't attack true devotion, 　　　　　　　55
　　　and, if you can't help going to extremes,
　　　better to make the same mistake again.

SCENE II

DAMIS, ORGON, CLÉANTE.

DAMIS: Is it true that this wretch is threatening you,
    father, forgetting all your kindness to him,
    and that with vile, infuriating pride,   60
    he's turned your generosity against you?
ORGON: Yes, my son, and I've never suffered so much.
DAMIS: Leave it to me, I'm going to cut his ears off.
    There's no point holding back against that kind
                               of   65
    shamelessness; yes, I'll get you out of this,
    there's only one answer: I'll beat his head in.
CLÉANTE: The voice of youth. Now, will you please calm
                      down!
    We're living in an age and in a kingdom   70
    where violence is never a solution.

SCENE III

MADAME PERNELLE, MARIANE, ELMIRE, DORINE, DAMIS, ORGON, CLÉANTE.

MME PERNELLE: What's happening? What are these dreadful
                      rumours?
ORGON: Unprecedented things, which I have witnessed,
    the rewards of my generosity.   75
    I take a poor man in most willingly;
    I put him up and treat him like my brother;
    I load him with new blessings every day;
    I offer him my daughter and my money;
    and all the while this criminal, this pig   80
    nurtures a black plot to seduce my wife;
    and not even content with that disgrace,
    he dares to threaten me with my own gifts
    and wants to use the weapons, with which my
    foolish kindness has armed him, to destroy me,   85
    to take the money I've transferred to him
    and bring me down to what he was: a beggar.
DORINE: Poor boy!
MME PERNELLE: My dear, I really can't believe
    he could possibly do something so wicked.   90
ORGON: What did you say?
MME PERNELLE: People are always jealous
    of a really good man.
ORGON: What can you mean?
MME PERNELLE: This is a strange household and it's well known   95
    how much he's hated.

ORGON: Hated? What's that to
                                do
   with what I've just been saying?
MME PERNELLE: When you   100
                                were
   a little boy, I told you fifty times:
   in this world, virtue's always persecuted;
   the envious may die, but envy, never.
ORGON: But what has this to do with what's just   105
                                happened?
MME PERNELLE: I expect they've made up all sorts of stories.
ORGON: I've already explained, I saw it all.
MME PERNELLE: There's nothing so ingenious as a gossip.
ORGON: I'll swing for you yet, mother. Will you listen?   110
   I saw him do these wicked things myself.
MME PERNELLE: There's always poison spread by idle tongues,
   no one on earth can get away from that.
ORGON: This conversation is ridiculous.
   I saw him, understand, I saw him, saw him   115
   with my own eyes, what I did is described
   as seeing. How many more times must I
   repeat myself, must I shout myself hoarse?
MME PERNELLE: Appearances deceive, often as not,
   you mustn't always go by what you see.   120
ORGON: I'm going mad.
MME PERNELLE: Suspicion's human nature,
   and good is often mistaken for evil.
ORGON: I'm to suppose the urge to kiss my wife
   has some religious motive?   130
MME PERNELLE: It's as well
   not to accuse people without just cause;
   You should have waited, to make really certain.
ORGON: Good God, was there a way to be more certain?
   I should have waited till, in front of me,   135
   he . . . no, you'll make me say things I regret.
MME PERNELLE: No, he's too pure, too much in love with virtue,
   I simply can't bring myself to believe
   he'd do the things that you accuse him of.
ORGON: You're making me so angry, I just don't   140
   know what I would say, if you weren't my
                                mother.
DORINE: (*To* ORGON)
   That's how it goes, sir, and it serves you right:
   you wouldn't listen and neither will she.   145
CLÉANTE: We're wasting time with all this nonsense,
                                which
   we should be using to draw up some plans.
   We can't afford to dream, these are real
                                threats.   150
DAMIS: You really think he'd dare to see them through?

ELMIRE: He wouldn't have the face to bring
                                                                      proceedings,
    he would seem just too blatantly ungrateful.
CLÉANTE: (*To* ORGON)   155
    I wouldn't bank on it: he'll work out ways
    to justify his handiwork against you;
    and I've seen people caught in a labyrinth,
    once the religious clique is down on them,
    on much less evidence. And, as I said,   160
    knowing his power, you shouldn't have
                                                                      provoked him.
ORGON: You're right; but how could I help it? How
                                                                      could I
    control my fury at his arrogance?   165
CLÉANTE: I wish there was some way of building a
    negotiated settlement between you.
ELMIRE: If I'd known he was so well armed against us,
    I'd never have given him fresh ammunition,
    I'm so . . .   170

        (ORGON *sees* MONSIEUR LOYAL *approaching.*)

ORGON: (*To* DORINE)
              What does that man want? Go and
                                                                      ask him.
    A visitor just now is all I need!

SCENE IV

MONSIEUR LOYAL, MADAME PERNELLE, ORGON, DAMIS, MARIANE, DORINE,
ELMIRE, CLÉANTE.
M. LOYAL, *still upstage, speaks to* DORINE.

M. LOYAL: Good afternoon, dear sister. May I speak   175
    to Monsieur Orgon?
DORINE: He has company.
    I doubt he can see anyone right now.
M. LOYAL: I'm not here to make a nuisance of myself.
    I don't think he'll have cause to regret my   180
    visit; I'm here to do him a good turn.
DORINE: What name is it?
M. LOYAL: Just tell him that I'm here
    for his own good, on Monsieur Tartuffe's
                                                                      behalf.   185
DORINE: (*To* ORGON)
    He's quite polite. He's here on Monsieur
                                                                      Tartuffe's
    behalf—he says he's doing you a favour.
CLÉANTE: (*To* ORGON)   190
    You must see who he is and what he wants.
ORGON: Perhaps he's come to make a settlement.

How ought I to behave?

CLÉANTE: Don't show your
                                        anger;   195
    and if he talks peace, you must listen to him.

M. LOYAL: (*To* ORGON)
    How do you do, sir. God protect you from
    your enemies and grant you all I'd wish you!

ORGON: (*Quietly to* CLÉANTE)   200
    That's a good start, it confirms my impression,
    I think it does imply a settlement.

M. LOYAL: I've always been devoted to your family,
    I was once in your father's service.

ORGON: Sir,   205
    I'm ashamed to admit, you must forgive me,
    I don't know who you are or what your name

                                        is.

M. LOYAL: My name is Loyal, I'm from Normandy,
    I hold the much respected post of bailiff.   210
    For forty years I've been so fortunate,
    thank God, as to discharge my task with

                                        honour;
    and I am here, with your permission, sir,
    to serve you with this writ . . .   215

ORGON: You mean
                            you've come...?

M. LOYAL: Now, let's not have a scene, sir: all I have
    is this summons here, this eviction order,
    which says you must forthwith, without delay,   220
    remove yourself, your family, your effects . . .

ORGON: What! Move out, me?

M. LOYAL: Yes, sir, if you don't
                                        mind.

    As you're no doubt aware, there is no question   225
    that at the present moment this house here
    belongs to our revered Monsieur Tartuffe.
    From now on he is lord and master of
    your possessions, by virtue of a contract,
    legally drawn up, incontestable,   230
    which I happen to have about my person.

DAMIS: (*To* M. LOYAL)
    You've got a nerve.

M. LOYAL: I'm not obliged to deal
    with you, sir; this is Monsieur Orgon's   235
                                        business:
    and he's a reasonable sort of chap,
    who knows full well a man must do his duty
    and wouldn't ever want to obstruct justice.

ORGON: But . . .   240

M. LOYAL: Yes, I know, sir, you would never
                                        dream

of playing up, and, as an honest man,
you'll let me carry out my orders here.

DAMIS: You're heading the right way to feel my stick   245
    laid right across your black gown, Monsieur
                                bailiff.

M. LOYAL: (*To* ORGON)
    Tell your son to shut up or go away;
    I'd hate to find it necessary to make   250
    a reference to this in my report.

DORINE: (*Aside*)
    Monsieur Loyal: he's not very well-named.

M. LOYAL: I always have been very well-disposed
    towards men of good will; and that's the reason   255
    I volunteered for this particular job,
    to comfort you and help you out and make sure
    they didn't send a man who, lacking my
    personal sympathy for you, might have
    approached the matter less respectfully.   260

ORGON: What's so respectful about turning people
    out on the streets?

M. LOYAL: You'll have plenty of time.
    I'll suspend execution of the writ
    until tomorrow. Oh, there's just one thing: 265
    I'll have to spend the night here with about
    ten of my men. There'll be no noise, no trouble.
    I will need, and before you go to bed, please,
    it's only a formality, the keys.
    I guarantee your sleep won't be disturbed,   270
    and there'll be no unnecessary suffering.
    You just be ready, first thing in the morning,
    to clear out every last household utensil.
    My men will help you, every one's hand-picked
    to render you assistance with the move.   275
    I don't think one can say fairer than that;
    and as I've been so lenient with you,
    I would request a corresponding temperance
    on your part, as I go about my duties.

ORGON: (*Quietly*)   280
    I'd willingly give up my last few coins
    this minute in return for the great pleasure
    of punching this buffoon hard on the nose.

CLÉANTE: (*Quietly, to* ORGON)
    Don't spoil everything.   285

DAMIS: But this is unheard-of,
    my knuckles itch, you'd better hold me back.

DORINE: You've such a good broad back, Monsieur
                            Loyal,
    a really good hiding might suit you nicely.   290

M. LOYAL: That kind of talk is actionable, dear,
    women are liable to prosecution,
    like anybody else.

CLÉANTE: Right, that's enough;
    give us your piece of paper and be off.   295
M. LOYAL: I'll see you very soon. God bless you all!
ORGON: And may He damn you and the man who sent
                                   you!

SCENE V

ORGON, CLÉANTE, MARIANE, ELMIRE, MADAME PERNELLE, DORINE, DAMIS.

ORGON: Well, mother, am I right? Look at this writ.
    Now do you understand that he's a traitor?   300
MME PERNELLE: I'm thunderstruck and discombobulated.
DORINE: (*To* ORGON)
    I think you're being rather hard on him,
    this is a confirmation of his goodness,
    the final proof of his love for his neighbour: 305
    he knows that money frequently corrupts,
    and purely out of charity he wants
    to take away this threat to your salvation.
ORGON: Be quiet: how many more times must I tell
                              you?   310
CLÉANTE: Come on, now, let's go and discuss the options.
ELMIRE: If you were to expose his insolence,
    surely the contract would be declared null;
    his treachery would be seen as too black
    for him to be allowed to profit by it.   315

SCENE VI

VALÈRE, ORGON, CLÉANTE, ELMIRE, MARIANE, MADAME PERNELLE,
DAMIS, DORINE.

VALÈRE: I'm sorry to impose on you like this;
    an urgent danger made me feel obliged to.
    A very close friend of mind, who's aware
    of my connection with you, for my sake,
    has breached the confidentiality   320
    owed to the State and passed on information,
    which gives you no choice but to run away.
    An hour ago, that swine who for so long
    has cheated you, denounced you to the King,
    and, among other accusations, gave him   325
    a case belonging to an enemy
    of the State, whose secrets, he said, you kept,
    so neglecting your duty as a subject.
    I don't know the exact crime you're accused of;
    but orders have gone out for your arrest,   330
    and Tartuffe has been told to come as well
    to help the officer who's been sent to fetch you.

CLÉANTE: That's how the traitor's trying to reinforce
    his claim to take over all your possessions.
ORGON: It's true, he really is an evil monster! 335
VALÈRE: The slightest hesitation could be fatal.
    Here is a thousand louis I have brought you,
    my carriage is waiting for you at the gate.
    Don't let's waste time; this is a thunderbolt,
    the kind of thing you simply can't escape, 340
    unless you run. I'll take you to a safe place
    and stay with you until you've got away.
ORGON: I don't know how to thank you for this
                       kindness!
    I'll have to wait before I can repay you, 345
    and I ask God to help me to express
    one day my true gratitude for this rescue.
    Goodbye; take care, all of you . . .
CLÉANTE: Hurry up;
    we'll try to do whatever's necessary. 350

SCENE VII

AN OFFICER, TARTUFFE, VALÈRE, ORGON, ELMIRE, MARIANE,
CLÉANTE, MADAME PERNELLE, DAMIS, DORINE.

TARTUFFE: (*Stopping* ORGON)
    All right, all right, not quite so fast, my friend;
    it's not so very far to where you're going.
    in the name of the King you're under arrest.
ORGON: You traitor, you've been saving this till last! 355
    A criminal, delivering the death-blow,
    the culmination of all your betrayals.
TARTUFFE: I am impervious to your insults; I'm
    trained to be tolerant in the sight of God.
CLÉANTE: How admirably self-controlled of you. 360
DAMIS: How insolently he takes the name of God!
TARTUFFE: I'm completely unmoved by your resentment,
    all I'm attempting is to do my duty.
MARIANE: You think this will enhance your reputation?
    You believe this is honourable conduct? 365
TARTUFFE: Conduct suggested by the power that sent me
    surely can't help but be exemplary.
ORGON: Have you forgotten that my charity
    rescued you from a life of poverty?
TARTUFFE: No, I am well aware of how you helped me; 370
    but my first duty must be to the King;
    the rightful power of this sacred duty
    has stifled all the gratitude in my heart;
    to these commitments I would sacrifice
    my friends, my wife, my parents or myself. 375
ELMIRE: Impostor!

DORINE: He's so treacherously clever
    at making use of what we most respect!
CLÉANTE: But if this sense of duty which drives you
    and which you're so proud of is so consuming,   380
    how come it held off making its appearance
    until he caught you molesting his wife?
    Why didn't you think of accusing him
    until he felt compelled to throw you out?
    He's just made you a gift of all his money,   385
    and I don't bring this up as a red herring;
    I just wonder, since you think he's so guilty,
    how you could condescend to be his heir.
TARTUFFE: (*To the* OFFICER)
    Why don't you put an end to all this whining   390
    and be so good as to obey your orders?
OFFICER: Yes, I suppose I've waited far too long,
    and what you say is a timely reminder;
    I will obey them: follow me at once,
    I'm taking you immediately to prison.   395
TARTUFFE: Who, me, sir?
OFFICER: Yes, you sir.
TARTUFFE: But why to prison?
OFFICER: I don't have to explain myself to you.

    (*To* ORGON)

    Calm yourself, sir. You're living in the reign   400
    of a King who's declared war on deceit,
    a King whose eyes can see into your heart,
    whom no impostor's cunning can mislead.
    The sharp perceptiveness of that great mind
    sees everything in its proper perspective.   405
    He's too intelligent to be swayed by passion
    or to fall into any kind of excess.
    He's always paid tribute to real goodness,
    without letting enthusiasm blind him,
    and his love for the genuine has never   410
    closed his mind to the horrors of bad faith.
    He's seen through more effective traps than this
    man set, he never really stood a chance.
    His perspicacity discerned at once.
    the wickedness of this man's secret heart.   415
    He came to denounce you and betrayed
                                    himself:
    by a supremely fitting stroke of justice,
    he let slip something which allowed the King
    to identify him as a wanted man,   420
    whose long record, under another name
    would fill a book with lists of vicious crimes.
    His Majesty also despises his vile
    disloyalty and ingratitude to you
    in addition to all the other horrors,   425

and only made me his subordinate
to see how far his shamelessness would go
before we made him make full restitution.
The King wants me to strip him, in your
                                 presence,   430
of all your papers, which he claims to own,
and exercises his prerogative
to break the contract which you signed to give
                                 him
all that you own, and finally he pardons   435
the crime your friend's exile made you commit,
as a reward for your support for him
during the troubles, just to demonstrate
that he knows the time to pay back a favour
is when you least expect it, and that he   440
cherishes the deserving and prefers
remembering the good to bearing grudges.
DORINE: Thank God!
MME PERNELLE: What a relief.
ELMIRE: A happy end.   445
MARIANE: Who would have thought it could turn out this
                                    way?

(**ORGON** *turns to* **TARTUFFE**, *as the* **OFFICER** *leads him away.*)

ORGON: What about this, then, traitor?
CLÉANTE: No, no, stop it,
don't stoop to mere abuse. Just let him go,   450
poor wretch, to his unhappy fate, and don't
add to the guilt which must be crippling him.
Better to hope this may encourage him
to return gladly to the paths of virtue,
to turn against his evil and repent   455
and cause our great King to temper his justice.
Meanwhile, you must go on your knees to him
and show how grateful you are for his lenience.
ORGON: That's well said, yes. Let's go and kiss his feet
and praise him for the goodness of his heart;   460
and that duty acquitted, we must meet
another necessary obligation
and reward a sincere and generous love
by celebrating your wedding, Valère.

A Doll's House
(1879)

Ibsen's early plays (beginning in 1850) were poetic dramas about Norwegian legend or history. In the 1870s, Ibsen deliberately abandoned his earlier approach to write prose plays about contemporary life. *A Doll's House* and *Ghosts* made Ibsen the most controversial playwright in Europe, for the former was thought to attack the institution of marriage and the family, and the latter brought the taboo subject of venereal disease to the stage. Ibsen's prose plays epitomize realism, a new movement then under way. Because his realist plays challenged traditional views and values, Ibsen is often called the founder of modern drama.

Undergirding *A Doll's House* is the basic assumption that hereditary and environmental forces determine character and action. What each character is and does is explained by information about background, upbringing, and experience. During the course of the action, we learn enough about all the characters to understand how they have arrived at where they are. Ibsen could have made his play melodramatic by depicting Krogstad as villain and Nora as persecuted heroine. Instead, all of the characters strive for what they consider right. Thus instead of a type, each character appears to be a complex, fallible human being.

A Doll's House is usually read today as a play about the status of women in the late nineteenth century. It pleases Torvald to think of Nora as incapable of making decisions, even about what she should wear to a party. The play also shows that women were legally reduced to the state of childhood (or doll) because a wife was required to have her husband's consent in almost all matters, whereas her husband could act wholly independently, even disposing of property originally hers without her consent or knowledge. The ending of the play shocked audiences and critics not because the play's potential villain relents and saves Nora and Torvald from public disgrace—that type of sentimental resolution was all too common—but because Nora insists on discussing what has happened with her husband and their roles as husband and wife. At the end of the play, Nora's alienation is not only from her husband but also from society in general. She chooses to leave her husband and children because, finding herself in disagreement with both law and public opinion and not yet certain of her own convictions, she does not believe herself ready to meet her responsibilities as a wife and mother. It was this ending that made the play so controversial, for it challenged the status quo.

A Doll's House could serve as a model of cause-to-effect dramatic structure. The first act sets up masterfully and with seeming naturalness all of the conditions out of which the subsequent action grows logically and seemingly inevitably.

Henrik Ibsen

A Doll's House
(1879)

Translated by William Archer
(with emendations by Oscar G. Brockett)

Characters

TORVALD HELMER
NORA, *his wife*
DOCTOR RANK
MRS. LINDE
NILS KROGSTAD
THE HELMERS' THREE YOUNG CHILDREN
ANNE, *their nurse*
A HOUSEMAID
A PORTER

The action of the play takes place in the Helmers' house.

ACT I

SCENE———*A room furnished comfortably and tastefully but not extravagantly. At the back, a door to the right leads to the entrance-hall, another to the left leads to* HELMER'*s study. Between the doors stands a piano. In the middle of the left-hand wall is a door, and beyond it a window. Near the window are a round table, armchairs, and a small sofa. In the right-hand wall, at the farther end, another door; and on the same side, nearer the footlights, a stove, two easy chairs, and a rocking chair; between the stove and the door, a small table. Engravings on the walls; a cabinet with china and other small objects; a small book-case with well-bound books. The floors are carpeted, and a fire burns in the stove. It is winter.*

A bell rings in the hall; shortly afterwards the door is heard to open. Enter NORA, *humming a tune and in high spirits. She is in out-door dress and carries a number of parcels; these she lays on the table to the right. She leaves the outer door open after her, and through it is seen a* PORTER *who is carrying a Christmas tree and a basket, which he gives to the* MAID, *who has opened the door.*

222

NORA: Hide the Christmas tree carefully, Helen. Be sure the children don't see it till this evening, when it is trimmed. [*to the* PORTER *taking out her purse*] How much?

PORTER: A half-crown.

NORA: There's a crown. No, keep the change. [*The* PORTER *thanks her, and goes out.* NORA *the door. She is laughing to herself, as she takes off her hat and coat. She takes a packet of macaroons from her pocket and eats one or two; then goes cautiously to her husband's door and listens.*] Yes, he is in. [*Still humming, she goes to the table on the right.*]

HELMER: [*calls out from his room*] Is that my little lark twittering out there?

NORA: [*busy opening some of the parcels*] Yes, it is!

HELMER: Is it my little squirrel bustling about?

NORA: Yes!

HELMER: When did my squirrel come home?

NORA: Just now. [*puts the bag of macaroons into her pocket and wipes her mouth*] Come in here, Torvald, and see what I have bought.

HELMER: Don't disturb me. [*A little later he opens the door and looks into the room, pen in hand.*] Bought, did you say? All these things? Has my little spendthrift been wasting money again?

NORA: Yes, but, Torvald, this year we really can let ourselves go a little. This is the first Christmas that we have not needed to economize.

HELMER: Still, you know, we can't spend money recklessly.

NORA: Yes, Torvald, we may be a wee bit more reckless now, mayn't we? Just a tiny wee bit! You are going to have a big salary and earn lots and lots of money.

HELMER: Yes, after the New Year; but then it will be a whole quarter before the salary is due.

NORA: Pooh! We can borrow till then.

HELMER: Nora! [*goes up to her and takes her playfully by the ear*] The same little featherhead! Suppose, now, that I borrowed one thousand crowns to-day, and you spent it all in the Christmas week, and then on New Year's Eve a roof tile fell on my head and killed me, and—

NORA: [*putting her hands over his mouth*] Oh! don't say such horrid things.

HELMER: Still, suppose that happened—what then?

NORA: If that were to happen, I don't suppose I should care whether I owed money or not.

HELMER: Yes, but what about the people who had lent it?

NORA: They? Who would care about them? I wouldn't know who they were.

HELMER: How like a woman! But seriously, Nora, you know what I think about that. No debt, no borrowing. There can be no freedom or beauty about a home that depends on borrowing and debt. We two have kept bravely on the straight road so far, and we will go on the same way for the short time left.

NORA: [*moving towards the stove*] As you please, Torvald.

HELMER: [*following her*] Come, come, my little skylark must not droop her wings. What is this! Is my little squirrel sulking? [*taking out his purse*] Nora, what do you think I've got here?

NORA: [*turning round quickly*] Money!

HELMER: There you are. [*gives her some money*] Do you think I don't know what a lot is needed for housekeeping at Christmas-time?

NORA: [*counting*] One-two-three! Thank you, thank you, Torvald; that will keep me going for a long time.

HELMER: Indeed it must.

NORA: Yes, yes, it will. But come here and let me show you what I have bought. And all so cheap! Look, here is a new suit for Ivar, and a sword; and a horse and trumpet for Bob;

and a doll and a doll's bed for Emmy—they are very plain, but anyway she'll soon break them. And here are dress materials and handkerchiefs for the maids; old Anne ought really to have something better.

HELMER: And what is in this parcel? 55

NORA: [*crying out*] No, no! You mustn't see that till this evening.

HELMER: Very well. But now tell me, you extravagant little person, what would you like for yourself?

NORA: For myself? Oh, I'm sure I don't want anything.

HELMER: Yes, but you must. Tell me something reasonable that you would particularly like 60 to have.

NORA: No, I really can't think of anything—unless, Torvald—

HELMER: Well?

NORA: [*playing with his coat buttons, and without raising her eyes to his*] if you really want to give me something, you might—you might— 65

HELMER: Well, out with it!

NORA: [*speaking quickly*] You might give me money, Torvald. Only just as much as you can afford; and then one of these days I will buy something with it.

HELMER: But, Nora—

NORA: Oh, do! dear Torvald; please, please do! Then I will wrap it up in beautiful gold 70 paper and hang it on the Christmas tree. Wouldn't that be fun?

HELMER: What are little people called that are always wasting money?

NORA: Spendthrifts—I know. Let's do what you suggest, Torvald, and then I shall have time to think what I need most. That is a very sensible plan, isn't it?

HELMER: [*smiling*] Indeed it is—that is to say, if you were really to save out of the money 75 I give you, and then really buy something for yourself. But if you spend it all on the housekeeping and any number of unnecessary things, then I merely have to pay up again.

NORA: Oh but, Torvald—

HELMER: You can't deny it, my dear little Nora. [*puts his arm around her waist*] It's a sweet 80 little spendthrift, but she uses up a lot of money. One would hardly believe how expensive such little persons are!

NORA: It's a shame to say that. I do really save all I can.

HELMER: [*laughing*] That's very true—all you can. But you can't save anything!

NORA: [*smiling quietly and happily*] You haven't any idea how many expenses we skylarks 85 and squirrels have, Torvald.

HELMER: You are an odd little soul. Very like your father. You always find some new way of wheedling money out of me, and, as soon as you have got it, it seems to melt in your hands. You never know where it has gone. Still, one must take you as you are. It is in the blood; for indeed it is true that you can inherit these things, Nora. 90

NORA: Ah, I wish I had inherited many of papa's qualities.

HELMER: And I would not wish you to be anything but just what you are, my sweet little skylark. But, do you know, it strikes me that you are looking rather—what shall I say—rather guilty to-day?

NORA: Do I? 95

HELMER: You do, really. Look straight at me.

NORA: [*looks at him*] Well?

HELMER: [*wagging his finger at her*] Hasn't Miss Sweet-Tooth been breaking rules in town to-day?

NORA: No; what makes you think that? 100

HELMER: Hasn't she paid a visit to the pastry shop?

NORA: No, I assure you, Torvald—

HELMER: Not been nibbling sweets?

NORA: No, certainly not.

HELMER: Not even taken a bite at a macaroon or two?   105

NORA: No, Torvald, I assure you really—

HELMER: There, there, of course I was only joking.

NORA: [*going to the table on the right*] I wouldn't think of going against your wishes.

HELMER: No, I am sure of that; besides, you gave me your word—[*going up to her*] Keep
    your little Christmas secrets to yourself, my darling. They will all be revealed tonight   110
    when the Christmas tree is lit, no doubt.

NORA: Did you remember to invite Doctor Rank?

HELMER: No. But there is no need; he will come to dinner with us as he always does.
    However, I will ask him when he comes in this morning. I have ordered some good
    wine. Nora, you can't think how I am looking forward to this evening.   115

NORA: So am I! And how the children will enjoy themselves, Torvald!

HELMER: It is splendid to feel that one has a secure job and a big enough income. It's
    delightful to think of, isn't it?

NORA: It's wonderful.

HELMER: Do you remember last Christmas? For a full three weeks beforehand you shut   120
    yourself up every evening till long after midnight, making ornaments for the Christ-
    mas tree and all the other fine things that were to be a surprise to us. It was the dullest
    three weeks I ever spent!

NORA: I didn't find it dull.

HELMER: [*smiling*] But there was precious little to show for it, Nora.   125

NORA: Oh, you shouldn't tease me about that again. How could I help the cat's getting in
    and tearing everything to pieces?

HELMER: Of course you couldn't, poor little girl. You had the best of intentions to please
    us all, and that's the main thing. But it is a good thing that our hard times are over.

NORA: Yes, it is really wonderful.   130

HELMER: This time I needn't be all alone and bored and you needn't ruin your dear eyes
    and your pretty little hands—

NORA: [*clapping her hands*] No, Torvald, I don't have to any longer, do I! It's wonderful
    to hear you say so! [*taking his arm*] Now I will tell you how I have been thinking we
    ought to arrange things, Torvald. As soon as Christmas is over—[*A bell rings in the*   135
    hall.] There's the doorbell. [*She tidies the room a little.*] There's someone at the door.
    What a nuisance!

HELMER: If it is a caller, remember I am not at home.

MAID: [*in the doorway*] A lady to see you, ma'am—a stranger.

NORA: Ask her to come in.   140

MAID: [*to* HELMER] The doctor came at the same time, sir.

HELMER: Did he go straight into my study?

MAID: Yes, sir.

> [HELMER *goes into his room. The* MAID *ushers in* MRS. LINDE, *who is in travelling*
> *clothes and shuts the door.*]

MRS. LINDE: [*in a dejected and timid voice*] How do you do, Nora?

NORA: [*doubtfully*] How do you do—   145

MRS. LINDE: You don't recognise me, I suppose.

NORA: No, I'm afraid—yes, to be sure, I seem to—[*suddenly*] Yes! Christine! Is it really you?

MRS. LINDE: Yes, it is I.

NORA: Christine! To think of my not recognising you! And yet how could I—[*in a gentle voice*] How you've changed, Christine! 150

MRS. LINDE: Yes, I have indeed. In nine, ten long years—

NORA: Is it so long since we met? I suppose it is. The last eight years have been a happy time for me, I can tell you. And so now you have come into town, and have taken this long journey in winter—that was brave of you.

MRS. LINDE: I arrived by boat this morning. 155

NORA: To have some fun at Christmas-time, of course. How delightful! We will have such fun together! But take off your things. You are not cold, I hope. [*helps her*] Now we will sit down by the stove, and be comfortable. No, take this armchair; I will sit here in the rocking chair. [*takes her hands*] Now you look like your old self again; it was only the first moment—You are a little paler, Christine, and perhaps a little thinner. 160

MRS. LINDE: And much, much older, Nora.

NORA: Perhaps a little older; very, very little; certainly not much. [*stops suddenly and speaks seriously*] What a thoughtless creature I am, chattering away like this. My poor, dear Christine, do forgive me.

MRS. LINDE: What do you mean, Nora? 165

NORA: [*gently*] Poor Christine, you are a widow.

MRS. LINDE: Yes; it is three years ago now.

NORA: Yes, I know; I saw it in the papers. I assure you, Christine, I meant to write to you at the time, but I always put it off and something always prevented me.

MRS. LINDE: I quite understand, dear. 170

NORA: It was very bad of me, Christine. Poor thing, how you must have suffered. And he left you nothing?

MRS. LINDE: No.

NORA: And no children?

MRS. LINDE: No. 175

NORA: Nothing at all, then?

MRS. LINDE: Not even sorrow or grief to live upon.

NORA: [*looking incredulously at her*] But, Christine, is that possible?

MRS. LINDE: [*smiles sadly and strokes her hair*] It sometimes happens, Nora.

NORA: So you are quite alone. How dreadfully sad that must be. I have three lovely children. You can't see them just now, for they are out with their nurse. But now you must tell me everything. 180

MRS. LINDE: No, no; I want to hear about you.

NORA: No, you must begin. I mustn't be selfish to-day; to-day I must only think of your affairs. But there is one thing I must tell you. Have you heard about our great piece of good luck? 185

MRS. LINDE: No, what is it?

NORA: Just imagine, my husband has been made manager of the Bank!

MRS. LINDE: Your husband? What good luck!

NORA: Yes, tremendous! A lawyer's profession is such an uncertain thing, especially if he won't undertake unsavoury cases; and naturally Torvald has never been willing to do that, and I quite agree with him. You may imagine how pleased we are! He'll begin his job in the Bank at the New Year, and then he'll have a big salary and lots of commissions. For the future we can live quite differently—we can do just as we like. I feel so relieved and so happy, Christine! It will be splendid to have heaps of money and not need to have any anxiety, won't it? 190 195

MRS. LINDE: Yes, anyhow I think it would be delightful to have what one needs.

NORA: No, not only what one needs, but heaps and heaps of money.

MRS. LINDE: [*smiling*] Nora, Nora, haven't you learnt sense yet? In our schooldays you were a great spendthrift. 200

NORA: [*laughing*] Yes, that is what Torvald says now. [*wags her finger at her*] But "Nora, Nora" isn't so silly as you think. We have not been in a position for me to waste money. We have both had to work.

MRS. LINDE: You, too!

NORA: Yes; odds and ends, needlework, crochetings, embroidery, and that kind of thing. 205 [*dropping her voice*] And other things as well. You know Torvald left his office when we were married? There was no prospect of promotion there, and he had to try and earn more than before. But during the first year he overworked himself dreadfully. You see, he had to make money every way he could, and he worked early and late; but he couldn't stand it, and fell dreadfully ill, and the doctors said it was necessary 210 for him to go south.

MRS. LINDE: You spent a whole year in Italy, didn't you?

NORA: Yes. It was no easy matter to get away, I can tell you. It was just after Ivar was born; but naturally we had to go. It was a wonderfully beautiful trip and it saved Torvald's life. But it cost a tremendous lot of money, Christine. 215

MRS. LINDE: So I should think.

NORA: It cost about forty-eight hundred crowns. That's a lot, isn't it?

MRS. LINDE: Yes, and in emergencies like that it is lucky to have the money.

NORA: We got the money from papa.

MRS. LINDE: Oh, I see. It was just about that time that he died, wasn't it? 220

NORA: Yes; and just think of it, I couldn't go and nurse him. I was expecting little Ivar's birth every day and I had my poor sick Torvald to look after. My dear, kind father— I never saw him again, Christine. That was the saddest time I have known since our marriage.

MRS. LINDE: I know how fond you were of him. And then you went off to Italy? 225

NORA: Yes; you see, we had money then, and the doctors insisted on our going, so we started a month later.

MRS. LINDE: And your husband came back quite well?

NORA: As sound as a bell!

MRS. LINDE: But—the doctor? 230

NORA: What doctor?

MRS. LINDE: I thought your maid said the gentleman who arrived here just as I did, was the doctor?

NORA: Yes, that was Doctor Rank, but he doesn't come here professionally. He is our closest friend, and comes in at least once every day. No, Torvald has not had an hour's 235 illness since then, and our children are strong and healthy and so am I. [*jumps up and claps her hands*] Christine! Christine! it's good to be alive and happy! But how horrid of me; I am talking of nothing but my own affairs. [*sits on a stool near her, and rests her arms on her knees*] You mustn't be angry with me. Tell me, is it really true that you did not love your husband? Why did you marry him? 240

MRS. LINDE: My mother was alive then, and was bedridden and helpless, and I had to provide for my two younger brothers; so I didn't think I was justified in refusing his offer.

NORA: No, perhaps you were quite right. He was rich at that time, then?

MRS. LINDE: I believe he was quite well off. But his business was a precarious one; and, when he died, it all went to pieces and there was nothing left. 245

NORA: And then?—

MRS. LINDE: Well, I had to turn my hand to anything I could find—first a small shop, then a small school, and so on. The last three years have seemed like one long working-day, with no rest. Now it is at an end, Nora. My poor mother needs me no more, for she is gone; and the boys don't need me either; they have got jobs and can shift for themselves.   250

NORA: What a relief you must feel—

MRS. LINDE: No, indeed; I only feel my life unspeakably empty. No one to live for any more. [gets up restlessly] That was why I could not stand the life in my little backwater any longer. I hope it may be easier here to find something which will busy me and occupy my thoughts. If only I could have the good luck to get some regular work— office work of some kind—   255

NORA: But, Christine, that is so frightfully tiring, and you look tired out now. You had far better go away to some watering-place.

MRS. LINDE: [walking to the window] I have no father to give me money for a journey,   260
Nora.

NORA: [rising] Oh, don't be angry with me.

MRS. LINDE: [going up to her] It is you that mustn't be angry with me, dear. The worst of a position like mine is that it makes one so bitter. No one to work for, and yet obliged to be always on the look-out for chances. One must live, and so one becomes selfish.   265
When you told me of the happy turn your fortunes have taken—you will hardly believe it—I was delighted not so much on your account as on my own.

NORA: How do you mean?—Oh, I understand. You mean that perhaps Torvald could get you something to do.

MRS. LINDE: Yes, that was what I was thinking of.   270

NORA: He must, Christine. Just leave it to me; I will broach the subject very cleverly—I will think of something that will please him very much. It will make me so happy to be of some use to you.

MRS. LINDE: How kind you are, Nora, to be so anxious to help me! It is doubly kind in you, for you know so little of the burdens and troubles of life.   275

NORA: I—? I know so little of them?

MRS. LINDE: [smiling] My dear! Small household cares and that sort of thing! You are a child, Nora.

NORA: [tosses her head and crosses the stage] You ought not to be so superior.

MRS. LINDE: No!   280

NORA: You are just like the others. They all think that I am incapable of anything really serious—

MRS. LINDE: Come, come—

NORA: —that I have gone through nothing in this world of cares.

MRS. LINDE: But, my dear Nora, you have just told me all your troubles.   285

NORA: Pooh!—Those were trifles. [lowering her voice] I have not told you the important thing.

MRS. LINDE: The important thing! What do you mean?

NORA: You look down on me, Christine—but you shouldn't. You are proud, aren't you, of having worked so hard and so long for your mother?   290

MRS. LINDE: Indeed, I don't look down on any one. But it is true that I am proud and glad to think that I was privileged to make the end of my mother's life almost free from care.

NORA: And you are proud to think of what you have done for your brothers.

MRS. LINDE: I think I have the right to be.   295

NORA: I think so, too. But now, listen to this; I, too, have something to be proud and glad of.

MRS. LINDE: I have no doubt you have. But what do you refer to?

NORA: Speak low. Suppose Torvald were to hear! He mustn't on any account—no one in the world must know, Christine, except you. 300

MRS. LINDE: But what is it?

NORA: Come here. [*pulls her down on the sofa beside her*] Now I'll show you that I also have something to be proud and glad of. It was I who saved Torvald's life.

MRS. LINDE: "Saved"? How?

NORA: I told you about our trip to Italy. Torvald would never have recovered if he had not 305 gone there—

MRS. LINDE: Yes, but your father gave you the necessary funds.

NORA: [*smiling*] Yes, that is what Torvald and all the others think, but—

MRS. LINDE: But—

NORA: Papa didn't give us a crown. It was I who procured the money. 310

MRS. LINDE: You? All that large sum?

NORA: Forty-eight hundred crowns. What do you think of that?

MRS. LINDE: But, Nora, how could you possibly do it? Did you win a prize in the Lottery?

NORA: [*contemptuously*] In the Lottery? There would have been no credit in that. 315

MRS. LINDE: But where did you get it then?

NORA: [*humming and smiling with an air of mystery*] Hm, hm! Aha!

MRS. LINDE: Because you couldn't have borrowed it.

NORA: Couldn't I? Why not?

MRS. LINDE: No, a wife cannot borrow without her husband's consent. 320

NORA: [*tossing her head*] Oh, if it's a wife who has any head for business—a wife who has the wit to be a little bit clever—

MRS. LINDE: I don't understand it at all, Nora.

NORA: There is no need you should. I never said I had borrowed the money. I may have got it some other way. [*lies back on the sofa*] Perhaps I got it from some admirer. 325 When you're as attractive as I am—

MRS. LINDE: You're mad.

NORA: Now, you know you're full of curiosity, Christine.

MRS. LINDE: Listen to me, Nora dear. Haven't you been a little bit foolish?

NORA: [*sits up straight*] Is it foolish to save your husband's life? 330

MRS. LINDE: It seems to me foolish without his knowledge, to—

NORA: But it was absolutely necessary that he not know! My goodness, can't you understand that? It was necessary he should have no idea what a dangerous condition he was in. It was to me that the doctors came and said that his life was in danger, and that the only thing to save him was to live in the south. Do you suppose I didn't try, 335 first of all, to get what I wanted as if it were for myself? I told him how much I should love to travel abroad like other young wives; I tried tears and entreaties with him; I told him that he ought to remember the condition I was in, and that he ought to be kind and indulgent to me; I even hinted that he might raise a loan. That nearly made him angry, Christine. He said I was thoughtless, and that it was his duty as my 340 husband not to indulge me in my whims and caprices—as I believe he called them. Very well, I thought, you must be saved—and that was how I came to devise a way out of the difficulty—

MRS. LINDE: And did your husband never find out from your father that the money hadn't come from him? 345

NORA: No, never. Papa died just at that time. I had meant to let him into the secret and beg him never to reveal it. But he was so ill then—unfortunately there was no need to tell him.

MRS. LINDE: And since then have you never told your secret to your husband?

NORA: Good Heavens, no! How could you think that? A man who has such strong opinions about these things! And besides, how painful and humiliating it would be for Torvald, with his male pride, to know that he owed me anything! It would upset our relationship altogether; our beautiful happy home would no longer be the same.   350

MRS. LINDE: Do you mean never to tell him about it?

NORA: [*meditatively, and with a half smile*] Yes—some day, perhaps, after many years, when I'm no longer as attractive as I am now. Don't laugh at me! I mean, of course, when Torvald is no longer as devoted to me as he is now; when my dancing and dressing-up and reciting have palled on him; then it may be a good thing to have something in reserve—[*breaking off*] What nonsense! That time will never come. Now, what do you think of my great secret, Christine? Do you still think I am of no use? I can tell you, too, that this affair has caused me a lot of worry. It has been by no means easy for me to meet my payments punctually. I may tell you that there is something that is called, in business, quarterly interest, and another thing called payment in installments, and it is always so dreadfully difficult to manage them. I have had to save a little here and there, where I could, you understand. I have not been able to put aside much from my housekeeping money, for Torvald must have a good table. I couldn't let my children be shabbily dressed; I have felt obliged to use up all he gave me for them, the sweet little darlings!   355   360   365

MRS. LINDE: So it has all had to come out of your own expenses, poor Nora?

NORA: Of course. Besides, I was the one responsible for it. Whenever Torvald has given me money for new dresses and such things, I have never spent more than half of it; I have always bought the simplest and cheapest things. Thank Heaven, any clothes look good on me, and so Torvald has never noticed it. But it was often very hard on me, Christine—because it is delightful to be really well dressed, isn't it?   370

MRS. LINDE: Quite so.   375

NORA: Well, then I have found other ways of earning money. Last winter I was lucky enough to get a lot of copying to do; so I locked myself up and sat writing every evening until quite late at night. Many a time I was desperately tired; but all the same it was a tremendous pleasure to sit there working and earning money. It was like being a man.   380

MRS. LINDE: How much have you been able to pay off in that way?

NORA: I can't tell you exactly. You see, it is very difficult to keep an account of a business matter of that kind. I only know that I have paid every penny that I could scrape together. Many a time I was at my wits' end. [*smiles*] Then I used to sit here and imagine that a rich old gentleman had fallen in love with me—   385

MRS. LINDE: What! Who was it?

NORA: —that he had died; and that when his will was opened it contained, written in big letters, the instruction: "The lovely Mrs. Nora Helmer is to have all I possess paid over to her at once in cash."

MRS. LINDE: But, my dear Nora—who could the man be!   390

NORA: Good gracious, can't you understand? There was no old gentleman at all; it was only something that I used to sit here and imagine, when I couldn't think of any way of getting money. But it's all the same now; the tiresome old person can stay where he is, as far as I am concerned; I don't care about him or his will, either, for I am free from care now. [*jumps up*] My goodness, it's delightful to think of, Christine! Free from care! To be able to be free from care, quite free from care; to be able to play and romp with the children; to be able to keep the house beautifully and have everything just as Torvald likes it! And, think of it, soon the spring will come and the big blue   395 sky! Perhaps we shall be able to take a little trip—perhaps I shall see the sea again! Oh, it's a wonderful thing to be alive and be happy. [*a bell is heard in the hall*] 400

MRS. LINDE: [*rising*] There's the doorbell; perhaps I had better go.

NORA: No, don't go; no one will come in here; it is sure to be for Torvald.

SERVANT: [at the hall door] Excuse me, ma'am—there is a gentleman to see the master, and as the doctor is with him—

NORA: Who is it? 405

KROGSTAD: [*at the door*] It is I, Mrs. Helmer. [MRS. LINDE *starts, trembles, and turns to the window.*]

NORA: [*takes a step towards him, and speaks in a strained, low voice*] You? What is it? What do you want to see my husband about?

KROGSTAD: Bank business—in a way. I have a small post in the Bank, and I hear your 410 husband is to be our chief now—

NORA: Then it is—

KROGSTAD: Nothing but dry business matters, Mrs. Helmer; absolutely nothing else.

NORA: Be so good as to go into the study, then. [*She bows indifferently to him and shuts the door into the hall; then comes back and makes up the fire in the stove.*] 415

MRS. LINDE: Nora—who was that man?

NORA: A lawyer named Krogstad.

MRS. LINDE: Then it really was he.

NORA: Do you know the man?

MRS. LINDE: I used to—many years ago. At one time he was a solicitor's clerk in our town. 420

NORA: Yes, he was.

MRS. LINDE: He is greatly altered.

NORA: He made a very unhappy marriage.

MRS. LINDE: He is a widower now isn't he?

NORA: With several children. There now, it's burning. [*shuts the door of the stove and moves* 425 *the rocking chair aside*]

MRS. LINDE: They say he carried on various kinds of business.

NORA: Really! Perhaps he does; I don't know anything about it. But don't let's think of business: it is so boring.

DOCTOR RANK: [*comes out of* HELMER's *study. Before he shuts the door he calls to him.*] No, 430 my dear fellow, I won't disturb you; I would rather go in to your wife for a little while. [*shuts the door and sees* MRS. LINDE] I beg your pardon; I'm afraid I'm disturbing you, too.

NORA: No, not at all. [*introducing him*] Doctor Rank, Mrs. Linde.

RANK: I have often heard Mrs. Linde's name mentioned here. I think I passed you on the 435 stairs when I arrived, Mrs. Linde?

MRS. LINDE: Yes, I go up very slowly; I can't manage stairs well.

RANK: Ah! Some slight internal weakness?

MRS. LINDE: No, the fact is I have been overworking myself.

RANK: Nothing more than that? Then I suppose you have come to town to amuse yourself 440 with our entertainments?

MRS. LINDE: I have come to look for work.

RANK: Is that a good cure for overwork?

MRS. LINDE: One must live, Doctor Rank.

RANK: Yes, the general opinion seems to be that it's necessary. 445

NORA: Look here, Doctor Rank—you know you want to live.

RANK: Certainly. However wretched I may feel, I want to prolong the agony as long as possible. All my patients are like that. And so are those who are morally sick—one of them, and a bad case, too, is at this very moment with Helmer—

MRS. LINDE: [*sadly*] Ah! 450

NORA: Whom do you mean?

RANK: A lawyer, Krogstad, a fellow you don't know at all. He suffers from a diseased moral character, Mrs. Helmer; but even he began talking about it being highly important that he should live.

NORA: Did he? What did he want to speak to Torvald about?   455

RANK: I have no idea; I only heard that it was something about the Bank.

NORA: I didn't know this—what's his name—Krogstad had anything to do with the Bank.

RANK: Yes, he has some sort of appointment there. [*to* MRS. LINDE] I don't know whether you find also in your part of the world that there are certain people who go zealously   460
sniffing about to smell out moral corruption, and, as soon as they have found some, put the person concerned into some lucrative position where they can keep their eye on him. Healthy natures are left out in the cold.

MRS. LINDE: Still I think the sick are those who most need taking care of.

RANK: [*shrugging his shoulders*] Yes, there you are. That is the sentiment that is turning   465
Society into a hospital.

> [NORA, *who has been absorbed in her thoughts, breaks out into smothered laughter and claps her hands.*]

RANK: Why do you laugh at that? Have you any notion what Society really is?

NORA: What do I care about tiresome Society? I am laughing at something quite different, something extremely amusing. Tell me, Doctor Rank, are all the people who are employed in the Bank dependent on Torvald now?   470

RANK: Is that what you find so extremely amusing?

NORA: [*smiling and humming*] That's my affair! [*walking about the room*] It's perfectly glorious to think that we have—that Torvald has so much power over so many people. [*takes the packet from her pocket*] Doctor Rank, what do you say to a macaroon?

RANK: What, macaroons? I thought they were forbidden here.   475

NORA: Yes, but these are some Christine gave me.

MRS. LINDE: What! I?

NORA: Oh, well, don't be alarmed! You couldn't know that Torvald had forbidden them. I must tell you that he's afraid they will spoil my teeth. But—once in a while—That's so, isn't it, Doctor Rank? Here [*puts a macaroon into his mouth*] you must have one,   480
too, Christine. And I shall have one, just a little one—or at most two. [*walking about*] I am tremendously happy. There is just one thing in the world now that I should dearly love to do.

RANK: Well, what is that?

NORA: It's something I should dearly love to say so Torvald could hear me.   485

RANK: Well, why can't you say it?

NORA: No, I daren't; it's so shocking.

MRS. LINDE: Shocking?

RANK: Well, I should not advise you to say it. Still, with us you might. What is it you would so much like to say so Torvald could hear?   490

NORA: I should just love to say—Well, I'm damned!

RANK: Are you mad?

MRS. LINDE: Nora, dear—!

RANK: Say it, here he is!

NORA: [*hiding the packet*] Hush! Hush! Hush! [HELMER *comes out of his room, with his coat*   495
over his arm and his hat in his hand.]

NORA: Well, Torvald dear, have you got rid of him?

HELMER: Yes, he's gone.

NORA: Let me introduce you—this is Christine, who has come to town.

HELMER: Christine—? Excuse me, but I don't know— 500

NORA: Mrs. Linde, dear; Christine Linde.

HELMER: Of course. A school friend of my wife, I presume?

MRS. LINDE: Yes, we've known each other since then.

NORA: And just think, she's taken a long journey in order to see you.

HELMER: What do you mean? 505

MRS. LINDE: No, really I—

NORA: Christine is tremendously clever at office work and she's frightfully anxious to work under some clever man, so as to improve—

HELMER: Very sensible, Mrs. Linde.

NORA: And when she heard you had been appointed manager of the Bank—the news was 510 telegraphed, you know—she travelled here as quick as she could, Torvald, I'm sure you will be able to do something for Christine, for my sake, won't you?

HELMER: Well, it is not altogether impossible. I presume you are a widow, Mrs. Linde?

MRS. LINDE: Yes.

HELMER: And have had some experience of office work? 515

MRS. LINDE: Yes, a fair amount.

HELMER: Ah! well, it's very likely I may be able to find something for you.

NORA: [clapping her hands] What did I tell you? What did I tell you?

HELMER: You have just come at a fortunate moment, Mrs. Linde.

MRS. LINDE: How am I to thank you? 520

HELMER: There's no need. [puts on his coat] But to-day you must excuse me—

RANK: Wait a minute, I'll come with you. [brings his fur coat from the hall and warms it at the fire]

NORA: Don't be long away, Torvald dear.

HELMER: About an hour, not more. 525

NORA: Are you going, too, Christine?

MRS. LINDE: [putting on her cloak] Yes, I must go and look for a room.

HELMER: Oh, well then, we can walk together.

NORA: [helping her] What a pity it is we are so short of space here; I am afraid it is impossible for us— 530

MRS. LINDE: Please don't think of it! Good-bye, Nora dear, and many thanks.

NORA: Good-bye for the present. Of course you will come back this evening. And you, too, Doctor Rank. What do you say? If you are well enough? Oh, you must be! Wrap yourself up well. [They go to the door all talking together. Children's voices are heard on the staircase.] 535

NORA: There they are. There they are! [She runs to open the door. The NURSE comes in with the children.] Come in! Come in! [stoops and kisses them] Oh, you sweet blessings! Look at them, Christine! Aren't they darlings?

RANK: Don't let's stand here in the draught.

HELMER: Come along, Mrs. Linde; the place will only be bearable for a mother now! 540 [RANK, HELMER, and MRS. LINDE go downstairs. The NURSE comes forward with the children; NORA shuts the hall door.]

NORA: How fresh and well you look! Such red cheeks!—like apples and roses. [The children all talk at once while she speaks to them.] Have you had great fun? That's splendid! What, you pulled both Emmy and Bob along on the sled?—both at once?—that was 545 good. You are a clever boy, Ivar. Let me take her for a little, Anne. My sweet little baby doll! [takes the baby from the MAID and dances it up and down] Yes, yes, mother will dance with Bob, too. What! Have you been snowballing? I wish I had been there, too! No, no, I will take their things off, Anne; please let me do it, it's such fun. Go in now, you look half frozen. There's some hot coffee for you on the stove.   550

[*The* NURSE *goes into the room on the left.* NORA *takes off the children's things and throws them about, while they all talk to her at once.*]

NORA: Really! Did a big dog run after you? But it didn't bite you? No, dogs don't bite nice little dolly children. You mustn't look at the parcels, Ivar. What are they? Ah, I daresay you would like to know. No, no—it's something nasty! Come, let us have a game! What shall we play? Hide-and-Seek? Yes, we'll play Hide-and-Seek. Bob shall hide first. Must I hide? Very well, I'll hide first. [*She and the children laugh and shout, and* 555 *romp in and out of the room; at last* NORA *hides under the table, the children rush in and look for her, but do not see her; they hear her smothered laughter, run to the table, lift up the cloth and find her. Shouts of laughter. She crawls forward and pretends to frighten them. Fresh laughter. Meanwhile there has been a knock at the hall door, but none of them has noticed it. The door is half opened, and* KROGSTAD *appears. He waits* 560 *a little; the game goes on.*]

KROGSTAD: Excuse me, Mrs. Helmer.

NORA: [*with a stifled cry, turns round and gets up on to her knees*] Ah! What do you want?

KROGSTAD: Excuse me, the outer door was ajar; I suppose someone forgot to shut it.

NORA: [*rising*] My husband is out, Mr. Krogstad.   565

KROGSTAD: I know that.

NORA: What do you want here, then?

KROGSTAD: A word with you.

NORA: With me?—[*to the children, gently*] Go in to nurse. What? No, the strange man won't do mother any harm. When he's gone we will have another game. [*She takes* 570 *the children into the room on the left, and shuts the door after them.*] You want to speak to me?

KROGSTAD: Yes, I do.

NORA: To-day? It is not the first of the month yet.

KROGSTAD: No, it is Christmas Eve, and it will depend on yourself what sort of a Christmas 575 you will spend.

NORA: What do you want? To-day it is absolutely impossible for me—

KROGSTAD: We won't talk about that till later on. This is something different. I presume you can give me a moment?

NORA: Yes—yes, I can—although—   580

KROGSTAD: Good. I was in Olsen's Restaurant and saw your husband going down the street—

NORA: Yes?

KROGSTAD: With a lady.

NORA: What then?   585

KROGSTAD: May I make so bold as to ask if it was a Mrs. Linde?

NORA: It was.

KROGSTAD: Just arrived in town?

NORA: Yes, to-day.

KROGSTAD: She's a great friend of yours, isn't she?   590

NORA: She is. But I don't see—

KROGSTAD: I knew her, too, once upon a time.

NORA: I'm aware of that.

KROGSTAD: Are you? So you know all about it; I thought as much. Then I can ask you, without beating about the bush—is Mrs. Linde to have an appointment in the Bank? 595

NORA: What right have you to question me, Mr. Krogstad?—You, one of my husband's subordinates! But since you ask, you shall know. Yes, Mrs. Linde *is* to have an appointment. And it was I who pleaded her cause, Mr. Krogstad, let me tell you that.

KROGSTAD: I was right in what I thought, then.

NORA: [*walking up and down*] Sometimes one has a tiny little bit of influence, I should   600
hope. Because one is a woman, it doesn't necessarily follow that—. When anyone is in a subordinate position, Mr. Krogstad, they should really be careful to avoid offending anyone who—who—

KROGSTAD: Who has influence?

NORA: Exactly.   605

KROGSTAD: [*changing his tone*] Mrs. Helmer, you will be so good as to use your influence on my behalf.

NORA: What? What do you mean?

KROGSTAD: You will be so kind as to see that I am allowed to keep my subordinate position in the Bank.   610

NORA: What do you mean by that? Who proposes to take your post away from you?

KROGSTAD: Oh, there is no necessity to keep up the pretence of ignorance. I can quite understand that your friend is not very anxious to expose herself to the chance of rubbing shoulders with me; and I quite understand, too, whom I have to thank for being discharged.   615

NORA: But I assure you—

KROGSTAD: Very likely; but, to come to the point, the time has come when I should advise you to use your influence to prevent that.

NORA: But, Mr. Krogstad, I *have* no influence.

KROGSTAD: Haven't you? I thought you said yourself just now—   620

NORA: Naturally I didn't mean you to put that construction on it. I! What should make you think I have any influence of that kind with my husband?

KROGSTAD: Oh, I have known your husband from our student days. I don't suppose he's any more unassailable than other husbands.

NORA: If you speak slightingly of my husband, I shall turn you out of the house.   625

KROGSTAD: You are bold, Mrs. Helmer.

NORA: I'm not afraid of you any longer. As soon as the New Year comes, I shall in a very short time be free of the whole thing.

KROGSTAD: [*controlling himself*] Listen to me, Mrs. Helmer. If necessary, I am prepared to fight for my small post in the Bank as if I were fighting for my life.   630

NORA: So it seems.

KROGSTAD: It's not only for the sake of the money; indeed, that weighs least with me in the matter. There's another reason—well, I may as well tell you. My position is this. I daresay you know, like everybody else, that once, many years ago, I was guilty of an indiscretion.   635

NORA: I think I've heard something of the kind.

KROGSTAD: The matter never came into court; but every way seemed to be closed to me after that. So I took to the business that you know of. I had to do something; and, honestly, I don't think I've been one of the worst. But now I must cut myself free from all that. My sons are growing up; for their sake I must try and win back as much   640
respect as I can in the town. This post in the Bank was like the first step up for me— and now your husband is going to kick me downstairs again into the mud.

NORA: But you must believe me, Mr. Krogstad; it's not in my power to help you at all.

KROGSTAD: Then it's because you haven't the will; but I have means to compel you.

NORA: You don't mean that you will tell my husband that I owe you money?   645

KROGSTAD: Hm!—Suppose I were to tell him?

NORA: It would be shameful of you. [*sobbing*] To think of his learning my secret, which has been my joy and pride, in such an ugly, clumsy way—that he should learn it from you! And it would put me in a horribly disagreeable position—

KROGSTAD: Only disagreeable? 650

NORA: [*impetuously*] Well, do it, then!—and it will be the worse for you. My husband will see for himself what a blackguard you are, and you certainly won't keep your post then.

KROGSTAD: I asked you if it was only a disagreeable scene at home that you were afraid of?

NORA: If my husband does get to know of it, of course he will at once pay you what is still owing, and we shall have nothing more to do with you. 655

KROGSTAD: [*coming a step nearer*] Listen to me, Mrs. Helmer. Either you have a very bad memory or you know very little of business. I shall be obliged to remind you of a few details.

NORA: What do you mean?

KROGSTAD: When your husband was ill, you came to me to borrow forty-eight hundred crowns. 660

NORA: I didn't know any one else to go to.

KROGSTAD: I promised to get you that amount—

NORA: Yes, and you did so.

KROGSTAD: I promised to get you that amount, on certain conditions. Your mind was so taken up with your husband's illness, and were so anxious to get the money for your journey, that you seem to have paid no attention to the conditions of our bargain. Therefore it will not be amiss if I remind you of them. Now, I promised to get the money on the security of a bond which I drew up. 665

NORA: Yes, and which I signed. 670

KROGSTAD: Good. But below your signature there were a few lines constituting your father a surety for the money; those lines your father should have signed.

NORA: Should? He did sign them.

KROGSTAD: I had left the date blank; that is to say your father should himself have inserted the date on which he signed the paper. Do you remember that? 675

NORA: Yes, I think I remember—

KROGSTAD: Then I gave you the bond to send by post to your father. Is that not so?

NORA: Yes.

KROGSTAD: And you naturally did so at once, because five or six days afterwards you brought me the bond with your father's signature. And then I gave you the money. 680

NORA: Well, haven't I been paying it off regularly?

KROGSTAD: Fairly so, yes. But—to come back to the matter in hand—that must have been a very trying time for you, Mrs. Helmer?

NORA: It was, indeed.

KROGSTAD: Your father was very ill, wasn't he? 685

NORA: He was very near his end.

KROGSTAD: And died soon afterwards?

NORA: Yes.

KROGSTAD: Tell me, Mrs. Helmer, can you by any chance remember what day your father died?—on what day of the month, I mean. 690

NORA: Papa died on the 29th of September.

KROGSTAD: That is correct; I have ascertained it for myself. And, as that is so, there is a discrepancy [*taking a paper from his pocket*] which I cannot account for.

NORA: What discrepancy? I don't know—

KROGSTAD: The discrepancy consists, Mrs. Helmer, in the fact that your father signed this bond three days after his death. 695

NORA: What do you mean? I don't understand—

KROGSTAD: Your father died on the 29th of September. But, look here; your father has dated his signature the 2nd of October. It is a discrepancy, isn't it? [NORA *is silent.*] Can you explain it to me? [NORA *is still silent.*] It is a remarkable thing, too, that the words "2nd of October," as well as the year, are not written in your father's handwriting but in one that I think I know. Well, of course it can be explained; your father may have forgotten to date his signature, and someone else may have dated it before they knew of his death. There is no harm in that. It all depends on the signature of the name; and *that* is genuine, I suppose, Mrs. Helmer? It was your father himself who signed his name here?

NORA: [*after a short pause, throws her head up and looks defiantly at him*] No, it was not. It was I that wrote papa's name.

KROGSTAD: Are you aware that is a dangerous confession?

NORA: In what way? You'll have your money soon.

KROGSTAD: Let me ask you a question; why did you not send the paper to your father?

NORA: It was impossible; papa was so ill. If I'd asked him for his signature, I should have had to tell him what the money was to be used for; and when he was so ill himself I couldn't tell him that my husband's life was in danger—it was impossible.

KROGSTAD: It would have been better for you if you had given up your trip abroad.

NORA: No, that was impossible. That trip was to save my husband's life; I couldn't give that up.

KROGSTAD: But did it never occur to you that you were committing a fraud on me?

NORA: I couldn't take that into account; I didn't trouble myself about you at all. I couldn't bear you, because you put so many heartless difficulties in my way, although you knew what a dangerous condition my husband was in.

KROGSTAD: Mrs. Helmer, you evidently do not realize clearly what it is that you have been guilty of. But I can assure you that my one false step, which lost me all my reputation, was nothing more or nothing worse than what you have done.

NORA: You? Do you ask me to believe that you were brave enough to run a risk to save your wife's life?

KROGSTAD: The law cares nothing about motives.

NORA: Then it must be a very foolish law.

KROGSTAD: Foolish or not, it is the law by which you will be judged, if I produce this paper in court.

NORA: I don't believe it. Is a daughter not to be allowed to spare her dying father anxiety and care? Is a wife not to be allowed to save her husband's life? I don't know much about law; but I am certain that there must be laws permitting such things as that. Have you no knowledge of such laws—you who are a lawyer? You must be a very poor lawyer, Mr. Krogstad.

KROGSTAD: Maybe. But matters of business—such business as you and I have had together—do you think I don't understand that? Very well. Do as you please. But let me tell you this—if I lose my position a second time, you shall lose yours with me. [*He bows, and goes out through the hall.*]

NORA: [*appears buried in thought for a short time, then tosses her head*] Nonsense! Trying to frighten me like that!—I am not so silly as he thinks. [*begins to busy herself putting the children's things in order*] And yet—? No, it's impossible! I did it for love's sake.

THE CHILDREN: [*in the doorway on the left*] Mother, the stranger has gone out through the gate.

NORA: Yes, dears, I know. But, don't tell anyone about the stranger. Do you hear? Not even papa.

CHILDREN: No, mother; but will you come and play again?

NORA: No, no—not now.

CHILDREN: But, mother, you promised.

NORA: Yes, but I can't now. Go in; I have such a lot to do. Go in, my sweet little darlings. 750
[*She gets them into the room by degrees and shuts the door on them; then sits down on the sofa, takes up a piece of needlework and sews a few stitches, but soon stops.*] No! [*throws down the work, gets up, goes to the hall door and calls out*] Helen! bring the tree in. [*goes to the table on the left, opens a drawer, and stops again*] No, no! it is quite impossible! 755

MAID: [*coming in with the tree*] Where shall I put it, ma'am?

NORA: Here, in the middle of the floor.

MAID: Shall I get you anything else?

NORA: No, thank you. I have all I want.

[Exit MAID.]

NORA: [*begins dressing the tree*] A candle here—and flowers here—. The horrible man! It's 760
all nonsense—there's nothing wrong. The tree shall be splendid! I'll do everything I can think of to please you, Torvald!—I'll sing for you, dance for you—[HELMER *comes in with some papers under his arm.*] Oh! are you back already?

HELMER: Yes. Has anyone been here?

NORA: Here? No. 765

HELMER: That's strange. I saw Krogstad going out of the gate.

NORA: Did you? Oh yes, I forgot, Krogstad was here for a moment.

HELMER: Nora, I can see from your manner that he has been here begging you to say a good word for him.

NORA: Yes. 770

HELMER: And you were to appear to do it of your own accord; you were to conceal from me the fact of his having been here; didn't he beg that of you, too?

NORA: Yes, Torvald, but—

HELMER: Nora, Nora, and you would be a party to that sort of thing? To have any talk with a man like that, and give him any sort of promise? And to tell me a lie into the 775
bargain?

NORA: A lie—?

HELMER: Didn't you tell me no one had been here? [*shakes his finger at her*] My little song-bird must never do that again. A song-bird must have a clean beak to chirp with—no false notes! [*puts his arm round her waist*] That's so, isn't it? Yes, I'm sure it is. [*lets her* 780
go] We will say no more about it. [*sits down by the stove*] How warm and snug it is here! [*turns over his papers*]

NORA: [*after a short pause, during which she busies herself with the Christmas tree*] Torvald!

HELMER: Yes.

NORA: I am looking forward tremendously to the fancy dress ball at the Stenborgs' the day 785
after to-morrow.

HELMER: And I'm tremendously curious to see what you're going to surprise me with.

NORA: It was very silly of me to want to do that.

HELMER: What do you mean?

NORA: I can't hit upon anything that will do; everything I think of seems so silly and 790
insignificant.

HELMER: Does my little Nora acknowledge that at last?

NORA: [*standing behind his chair with her arms on the back of it*] Are you very busy, Torvald?

HELMER: Well—

NORA: What are all those papers? 795

HELMER: Bank business.

NORA: Already?

HELMER: I have got authority from the retiring manager to undertake the necessary changes in the staff and in the reorganization of the work; and I must make use of the Christmas week for that, so as to have everything in order for the new year. 800

NORA: Then that was why this poor Krogstad—

HELMER: Hm!

NORA: [*leans against the back of his chair and strokes his hair*] If you hadn't been so busy I should have asked you a tremendously big favour, Torvald.

HELMER: What's that? Tell me. 805

NORA: There is no one has such good taste as you. And I do so want to look nice at the costume ball. Torvald, couldn't you take me in hand and decide what I shall go as, and what sort of a dress I shall wear?

HELMER: Aha! So my obstinate little woman is obliged to get someone to come to her rescue? 810

NORA: Yes, Torvald, I can't get along at all without your help.

HELMER: Very well, I'll think it over, we shall manage to hit on something.

NORA: That is nice of you. [*goes to the Christmas tree. A short pause.*] How pretty the red flowers look—. But, tell me, was it really something very bad that this Krogstad was guilty of? 815

HELMER: He forged someone's name. Have you any idea what that means?

NORA: Isn't it possible that he was driven to do it by necessity?

HELMER: Yes; or, as in so many cases, by imprudence. I am not so heartless as to condemn a man altogether because of a single false step of that kind.

NORA: No, you wouldn't, would you, Torvald? 820

HELMER: Many a man has been able to retrieve his character, if he has openly confessed his fault and taken his punishment.

NORA: Punishment—?

HELMER: But Krogstad did nothing of that sort; he got himself out of it by a cunning trick, and that is why he has gone under altogether. 825

NORA: But do you think it would—?

HELMER: Just think how a guilty man like that has to lie and play the hypocrite with everyone, how he has to wear a mask in the presence of those near and dear to him, even before his own wife and children. And about the children—that's the most terrible part of it all, Nora.

NORA: How? 830

HELMER: Because such an atmosphere of lies infects and poisons the whole life of a home. Each breath the children take in such a house is full of the germs of evil.

NORA: [*coming nearer him*] Are you sure of that?

HELMER: My dear, I have often seen it in the course of my life as a lawyer. Almost everyone who has gone to the bad early in life has had a deceitful mother. 835

NORA: Why do you only say—mother?

HELMER: It seems most commonly to be the mother's influence, though naturally a bad father's would have the same result. Every lawyer is familiar with the fact. This Krogstad, now, has been persistently poisoning his own children with lies and dissimulation; that's why I say he has lost all moral character. [*holds out his hands to her*] That's why 840 my sweet little Nora must promise me not to plead his cause. Give me your hand on it. Come, come, what's this? Give me your hand. There now, that's settled. I assure you it would be quite impossible for me to work with him; I literally feel physically ill when I am in the company of such people.

NORA: [*takes her hand out of his and goes to the opposite side of the Christmas tree*] How hot 845 it is in here; and I have such a lot to do.

HELMER: [*getting up and putting his papers in order*] Yes, and I must try and read through some of these before dinner; and I must think about your costume, too. And it's just possible I may have something ready in gold paper to hang up on the tree. [*puts his hand on her head*] My precious little singing-bird! [*He goes into his room and shuts the   850 door after him.*]

NORA: [*after a pause, whispers*] No, no—it isn't true. It's impossible; it must be impossible.

[*The* NURSE *opens the door on the left.*]

NURSE: The little ones are begging so hard to be allowed to come in to mamma.

NORA: No, no, no! Don't let them come in to me! You stay with them, Anne.

NURSE: Very well, ma'am. [*shuts the door*]   855

NORA: [*pale with terror*] Deprave my little children? Poison my home? [*A short pause. Then she tosses her head.*] It's not true. It can't possibly be true.

ACT II

THE SAME SCENE————*The Christmas tree is in the corner by the piano, stripped of its ornaments and with burnt-down candle-ends on its disheveled branches.* NORA's *cloak and hat are lying on the sofa. She is alone in the room, walking about uneasily. She stops by the sofa and takes up her cloak.*

NORA: [*drops the cloak*] Someone is coming now! [*goes to the door and listens*] No—it's no one. Of course, no one will come to-day, Christmas Day—nor to-morrow, either. But, perhaps—[*opens the door and looks out*] No, nothing in the mail box; it's quite empty. [*comes forward*] What rubbish! Of course he can't be in earnest about it. Such a thing couldn't happen; it's impossible—I have three little children.   5

[*Enter the* NURSE *from the room on the left, carrying a big cardboard box.*]

NURSE: At last I've found the box with the fancy dress.

NORA: Thanks; put it on the table.

NURSE: [*doing so*] But it's very much in want of mending.

NORA: I should like to tear it into a hundred thousand pieces.

NURSE: What an idea! It can easily be put in order—just a little patience.   10

NORA: Yes, I'll go and get Mrs. Linde to come and help me with it.

NURSE: What, out again? In this horrible weather? You'll catch cold, ma'am, and make yourself ill.

NORA: Well, worse than that might happen. How are the children?

NURSE: The poor little souls are playing with their Christmas presents, but—   15

NORA: Do they ask much for me?

NURSE: You see, they're so accustomed to have their mamma with them.

NORA: Yes, but nurse, I shan't be able to be so much with them now as I was before.

NURSE: Oh well, young children easily get accustomed to anything.

NORA: Do you think so? Do you think they would forget their mother if she went away   20 altogether?

NURSE: Good heavens!—went away altogether?

NORA: Nurse, I want you to tell me something I have often wondered about—how could you have the heart to put your own child out among strangers?

NURSE: I was obliged to, if I wanted to be little Nora's nurse. 25

NORA: Yes, but how could you be willing to do it?

NURSE: What, when I was going to get such a good place by it? A poor girl who has got into trouble should be glad to. Besides, that wicked man didn't do a single thing for me.

NORA: But I suppose your daughter has quite forgotten you.

NURSE: No, indeed she hasn't. She wrote to me when she was confirmed, and when she 30 was married.

NORA: [*putting her arms around her neck*] Dear old Anne, you were a good mother to me when I was little.

NURSE: Little Nora, poor dear, had no other mother but me.

NORA: And if my little ones had no other mother, I'm sure you would—. What nonsense 35 I'm talking! [*opens the box*] Go in to them. Now I must—. You will see to-morrow how charming I'll look.

NURSE: I'm sure there will be no one at the ball so charming as you, ma'am. [*goes into the room on the left*]

NORA: [*begins to unpack the box, but soon pushes it away from her*] If only I dared go out. If 40 only no one would come. If only I could be sure nothing would happen here in the meantime. Stuff and nonsense! No one will come. Only I mustn't think about it. I'll brush my muff. What lovely, lovely gloves! Out of my thoughts, out of my thoughts! One, two, three, four, five, six—[*screams*] Ah! there is someone coming—. [*makes a movement towards the door, but stands irresolute*] 45

[*Enter* MRS. LINDE *from the hall, where she has taken off her cloak and hat.*]

NORA: Oh, it's you, Christine. There is no one else out there, is there? How good of you to come!

MRS. LINDE: I heard you were up asking for me.

NORA: Yes, I was passing by. As a matter of fact, it's something you could help me with. Let us sit down here on the sofa. Look here. To-morrow evening there is to be a costume 50 ball at the Stenborgs', who live above us; and Torvald wants me to go as a Neapolitan fisher-girl, and dance the Tarantella that I learned on Capri.

MRS. LINDE: I see; you're going to perform a character.

NORA: Yes, Torvald wants me to. Look, here's the dress; Torvald had it made for me there, but now it's all so torn, and I haven't any idea—. 55

MRS. LINDE: We'll easily put that right. It's only some of the trimming come unsewn here and there. Needle and thread? Now then, that's all we need.

NORA: It *is* nice of you.

MRS. LINDE: [*sewing*] So you're going to be dressed up to-morrow, Nora. I'll tell you what—I'll come in for a moment and see you in your fine feathers. But I have com- 60 pletely forgotten to thank you for a delightful evening yesterday.

NORA: [*gets up, and crosses the stage*] Well, I don't think yesterday was as pleasant as usual. You ought to have come to town a little earlier, Christine. Certainly Torvald does understand how to make a house attractive.

MRS. LINDE: And so do you, it seems to me; you are not your father's daughter for nothing. 65 But tell me, is Doctor Rank always as depressed as he was yesterday?

NORA: No; yesterday it was very noticeable. I must tell you that he suffers from a very dangerous disease. He has tuberculosis of the spine, poor creature. His father was a horrible man who committed all sorts of excesses; and that's why his son was sickly from childhood, do you understand? 70

MRS. LINDE: [*dropping her sewing*] But my dearest Nora, how do you know anything about such things?

NORA: [*walking about*] Pooh! When you have three children, you get visits now and then from—from married women, who know something of medical matters, and they talk about one thing and another. 75

MRS. LINDE: [*goes on sewing. A short silence*] Does Doctor Rank come here every day?

NORA: Every day regularly. He's Torvald's best friend, and a great friend of mine, too. He's just like one of the family.

MRS. LINDE: But tell me this—is he perfectly sincere? I mean, isn't he the kind of man that is very anxious to make himself agreeable? 80

NORA: Not in the least. What makes you think that?

MRS. LINDE: When you introduced him to me yesterday, he declared he had often heard my name mentioned in this house; but afterwards I noticed that your husband hadn't the slightest idea who I was. So how could Doctor Rank—?

NORA: That's quite right, Christine. Torvald is so absurdly fond of me that he wants me 85 absolutely to himself, as he says. At first he used to seem almost jealous if I mentioned any of my friends back home, so naturally I gave up doing so. But I often talk about such things with Doctor Rank, because he likes hearing about them.

MRS. LINDE: Listen to me, Nora. You are still very like a child in many things, and I'm older than you in many ways and have a little more experience. Let me tell you this— 90 you ought to make an end of it with Doctor Rank.

NORA: What ought I to make an end of?

MRS. LINDE: Of two things, I think. Yesterday you talked some nonsense about a rich admirer who was to leave you money—

NORA: An admirer who doesn't exist, unfortunately! But what then? 95

MRS. LINDE: Is Doctor Rank well off?

NORA: Yes, he is.

MRS. LINDE: And has no one to provide for?

NORA: No, no one; but—

MRS. LINDE: And comes here every day? 100

NORA: Yes, I told you so.

MRS. LINDE: But how can this well-bred man be so tactless?

NORA: I don't understand you at all.

MRS. LINDE: Don't pretend, Nora. Do you suppose I don't guess who lent you the forty-eight hundred crowns? 105

NORA: Are you out of your senses? How can you think of such a thing! A friend of ours, who comes here every day! Do you realize what a horribly painful position that would be?

MRS. LINDE: Then it really isn't he?

NORA: No certainly not. It would never have entered my head for a moment. Besides, he had no money to lend then; he came into his money afterwards. 110

MRS. LINDE: Well, I think that was lucky for you, my dear Nora.

NORA: No, it would never have come into my head to ask Doctor Rank. Although I am quite sure that if I had asked him—

MRS. LINDE: But of course you won't.

NORA: Of course not. I have no reason to think it could possibly be necessary. But I'm 115 quite sure that if I told Doctor Rank—

MRS. LINDE: Behind your husband's back?

NORA: I must make an end of it with the other one, and that will be behind his back, too. I must make an end of it with him.

MRS. LINDE: Yes, that's what I told you yesterday, but— 120

NORA: [*walking up and down*] A man can put a thing like that straight much easier than a woman—

MRS. LINDE: One's husband, yes.

NORA: Nonsense! [*standing still*] When you pay off a debt you get your bond back, don't you?   125

MRS. LINDE: Yes, as a matter of course.

NORA: And can tear it into a hundred thousand pieces, and burn it—the nasty dirty paper!

MRS. LINDE: [*looks hard at her, lays down her sewing and gets up slowly*] Nora, you are keeping something from me.

NORA: Do I look as if I were?   130

MRS. LINDE: Something has happened to you since yesterday morning. Nora, what is it?

NORA: [*going nearer to her*] Christine! [*listens*] Hush! There's Torvald come home. Do you mind going in to the children for the present? Torvald can't bear to see dressmaking going on. Let Anne help you.

MRS. LINDE: [*gathering some of the things together*] Certainly—but I'm not leaving till we've   135
had it out with one another. [*She goes into the room on the left, as* HELMER *comes in from the hall.*]

NORA: [*going up to* HELMER] I have wanted you so much, Torvald dear.

HELMER: Was that the dressmaker?

NORA: No, it was Christine; she is helping me to put my costume in order. You will see I   140
shall look quite smart.

HELMER: Wasn't that a happy thought of mine, now?

NORA: Splendid! But don't you think it's nice of me, too, to do as you wish?

HELMER: Nice?—because you do as your husband wishes? Well, well, you little rogue, I'm
sure you did not mean it in that way. But I'm not going to disturb you; you will want   145
to be trying on your costume, I expect.

NORA: I suppose you're going to work.

HELMER: Yes. [*shows her a bundle of papers*] Look at that. I have just been to the Bank.
[*turns to go into his room*]

NORA: Torvald.   150

HELMER: Yes.

NORA: If your little squirrel were to ask you something very, very prettily—?

HELMER: What then?

NORA: Would you do it?

HELMER: I should like to hear what it is, first.   155

NORA: Your squirrel would run about and do all her tricks if you would be nice, and do
what she wants.

HELMER: Speak plainly.

NORA: Your skylark would chirp about in every room, with her song rising and falling—

HELMER: Well, my skylark does that anyhow.   160

NORA: I'd be a fairy and dance for you in the moonlight, Torvald.

HELMER: Nora—you surely don't mean that request you made of me this morning?

NORA: [*going near him*] Yes, Torvald, I beg you so earnestly—

HELMER: Have you really the nerve to bring up that question again?

NORA: Yes, dear, you *must* do as I ask; you *must* let Krogstad keep his post in the Bank.   165

HELMER: My dear Nora, it is his post that I have arranged for Mrs. Linde to have.

NORA: Yes, you've been awfully kind about that; but you could just as well dismiss some
other clerk instead of Krogstad.

HELMER: This is simply incredible obstinacy! Because you chose to give him a thoughtless
promise that you would speak for him, I am expected to—   170

NORA: That isn't the reason, Torvald. It is for your own sake. This fellow writes in the most
scurrilous newspapers; you've told me so yourself. He can do you an unspeakable
amount of harm. I am frightened to death of him—

HELMER: Ah, I understand; it is recollections of the past that scare you.

NORA: What do you mean? 175

HELMER: Naturally you are thinking of your father.

NORA: Yes—yes, of course. Just recall in your mind what these malicious creatures wrote in the papers about papa, and how horribly they slandered him. I believe they would have procured his dismissal if the Department had not sent you over to inquire into it, and if you had not been so kindly disposed and helpful to him. 180

HELMER: My little Nora, there is an important difference between your father and me. Your father's reputation as a public official was not above suspicion. Mine is, and I hope it will continue to be so, as long as I hold my office.

NORA: You never can tell what mischief these men may contrive. We ought to be so well off, so snug and happy here in our peaceful home, and have no cares—you and I and 185 the children, Torvald! That's why I beg you so earnestly—

HELMER: And it's just by interceding for him that you make it impossible for me to keep him. It's already known at the Bank that I mean to dismiss Krogstad. Is it to get about now that the new manager has changed his mind at his wife's bidding—

NORA: And what if it did? 190

HELMER: Of course!—if only this obstinate little person can get her way! Do you suppose I'm going to make myself ridiculous before my entire staff, to let people think that I am a man to be swayed by all sorts of outside influence? I should very soon feel the consequences of that, I can tell you! And besides, there is something that makes it quite impossible for me to have Krogstad in the Bank as long as I am manager. 195

NORA: Whatever is that?

HELMER: His moral failings I might perhaps have overlooked, if necessary—

NORA: Yes, you could—couldn't you?

HELMER: And I hear he is a good worker, too. But I knew him when we were boys. It was one of those rash friendships that so often prove an embarrassment later in life. I may 200 as well tell you plainly, we were once on first-name terms with one another. But this tactless fellow lays no restraint on himself when other people are present. On the contrary, he thinks it gives him the right to adopt a familiar tone with me, and every minute it is "I say, Helmer, old fellow!" and that sort of thing. It's extremely painful for me. He would make my position in the Bank intolerable. 205

NORA: Torvald, I don't believe you mean that.

HELMER: Don't you? Why not?

NORA: Because it is such a petty way of looking at things.

HELMER: What are you saying? Petty? Do you think I'm petty?

NORA: No, just the opposite, dear—it's exactly for that reason. 210

HELMER: It's the same thing. You say my point of view is petty, so I must be so, too. Petty. Very well—I must put an end to this. [*goes to the hall door and calls*] Helen!

NORA: What are you going to do?

HELMER: [*looking among his papers*] Settle it. [*Enter* MAID.] Look here; take this letter and go downstairs with it at once. Find a messenger and tell him to deliver it, and be 215 quick. The address is on it, and here is the money.

MAID: Very well, sir. [*exit with the letter*]

HELMER: [*putting his papers together*] Now then, little Miss Obstinate.

NORA: [*breathless*] Torvald—what was that letter?

HELMER: Krogstad's dismissal. 220

NORA: Call her back, Torvald! There is still time. Oh Torvald, call her back! Do it for my sake—for your own sake—for the children's sake! Do you hear me, Torvald? Call her back! You don't know what that letter can bring upon us.

HELMER: It's too late.

NORA: Yes, it's too late.   225

HELMER: My dear Nora, I can forgive the anxiety you are in, although really it is an insult to me. It is, indeed. Isn't it an insult to think that I should be afraid of a starving journalist's vengeance? But I forgive you nevertheless, because it's such eloquent witness to your great love for me. [*takes her in his arms*] And that's as it should be, my own darling Nora. Come what will, you may be sure I'll have both courage and strength if they be 230 needed. You'll see I am man enough to take everything upon myself.

NORA: [*in a horror-stricken voice*] What do you mean by that?

HELMER: Everything, I say

NORA: [*recovering herself*] You'll never have to do that.

HELMER: That's right. Well, we'll share it, Nora, as man and wife should. That's how it 235 should be. [*caressing her*] Are you happy now? There, there!—not these frightened dove's eyes! The whole thing is only the wildest fantasy—Now, you must go and play through the Tarantella and practice with your tambourine. I'll go into the inner office and shut the door, and I'll hear nothing, you can make as much noise as you please. [*turns back at the door*] And when Rank comes, tell him where he can find me. 240 [*nods to her, takes his papers and goes into his room and shuts the door after him*]

NORA: [*bewildered with anxiety, stands as if rooted to the spot, and whispers*] He was capable of doing it. He will do it. He will do it in spite of everything—No, not that! Never, never! Anything rather than that! Oh, for some help, some way out of it! [*the doorbell rings*] Doctor Rank! Anything rather than that—anything, whatever it is! [*She puts 245 her hands over her face, pulls herself together, goes to the door and opens it.* RANK *is standing without, hanging up his coat. During the following dialogue it begins to grow dark.*]

NORA: Good-day, Doctor Rank. I knew your ring. But you mustn't go into Torvald now; I think he is busy with something.   250

RANK: And you?

NORA: [*brings him in and shuts the door after him*] Oh, you know very well I always have time for you.

RANK: Thank you. I shall make use of as much of it as I can.

NORA: What do you mean by that? As much of it as you can?   255

RANK: Well, does that alarm you?

NORA: It was such a strange way of putting it. Is anything likely to happen?

RANK: Nothing but what I've long been prepared for. But I certainly didn't expect it to happen so soon.

NORA: [*gripping him by the arm*] What have you found out? Doctor Rank, you must tell me. 260

RANK: [*sitting down by the stove*] It's all up with me. And it can't be helped.

NORA: [*with a sigh of relief*] Is it about yourself?

RANK: Who else? It's no use lying to one's self. I am the most wretched of all my patients, Mrs. Helmer. Lately I've been taking stock of my internal economy. Bankrupt! Probably within a month I shall lie rotting in the churchyard.   265

NORA: What an ugly thing to say!

RANK: The thing itself is cursedly ugly, and the worst of it is that I'll have to face so much more that is ugly before that. I'll only make one more examination of myself; when I have done that, I'll know pretty certainly when the horrors of dissolution will begin. There's something I want to tell you. Helmer's sensitivity makes him disgusted at 270 everything that is ugly; I won't have him in my sickroom.

NORA: Oh, but, Doctor Rank—

RANK: I won't have him there. Not on any account. I bar my door to him. As soon as I'm quite certain that the worst has come, I'll send you my card with a black cross on it, and then you will know that the loathsome end has begun.   275

NORA: You are quite absurd to-day. And I wanted you so much to be in a really good humour.

RANK: With death stalking beside me?—To have to pay this penalty for another man's sin! Is there any justice in that? And in every single family, in one way or another, some such inexorable retribution is being exacted— 280

NORA: [*putting her hands over her ears*] Rubbish! Do talk of something cheerful.

RANK: Oh, it's a mere laughing matter, the whole thing. My poor innocent spine has to suffer for my father's youthful amusements.

NORA: [*sitting at the table on the left*] I suppose you mean that he was too partial to asparagus and paté de foie gras, don't you? 285

RANK: Yes, and to truffles.

NORA: Truffles, yes. And oysters, too, I suppose?

RANK: Oysters, of course, that goes without saying.

NORA: And heaps of port and champagne. It is sad that all these nice things should take their revenge on our bones. 290

RANK: Especially that they should revenge themselves on the unlucky bones of those who have not had the satisfaction of enjoying them.

NORA: Yes, that's the saddest part of it all.

RANK: [*with a searching look at her*] Hm!—

NORA: [*after a short pause*] Why did you smile? 295

RANK: No, it was you that laughed.

NORA: No, it was you that smiled, Doctor Rank!

RANK: [*rising*] You're a bigger tease than I thought.

NORA: I'm in a silly mood to-day.

RANK: So it seems. 300

NORA: [*putting her hands on his shoulders*] Dear, dear Doctor Rank, death mustn't take you away from Torvald and me.

RANK: It's a loss you would easily recover from. Those who are gone are soon forgotten.

NORA: [*looking at him anxiously*] Do you believe that?

RANK: People form new ties, and then— 305

NORA: Who will form new ties?

RANK: Both you and Helmer, when I'm gone. You yourself are already on the high road to it, I think. What did Mrs. Linde want here last night?

NORA: Oho!—you don't mean to say you're jealous of poor Christine?

RANK: Yes, I am. She'll be my successor in this house. When I'm done for, this woman will— 310

NORA: Hush! don't speak so loud. She's in that room.

RANK: To-day again. There, you see.

NORA: She's only come to sew my costume for me. Bless my soul, how unreasonable you are! [*sits down on the sofa*] Be nice now, Doctor Rank, and to-morrow you will see 315 how beautifully I shall dance, and you can imagine I'm doing it all for you—and for Torvald, too, of course. [*takes various things out of the box*] Doctor Rank, come and sit down here, and I'll show you something.

RANK: [*sitting down*] What is it?

NORA: Just look at those! 320

RANK: Silk stockings.

NORA: Flesh-coloured. Aren't they lovely? It is so dark here now, but to-morrow—. No, no, no! you must only look at the feet. Oh well, you may have leave to look at the legs, too.

RANK: Hm!— 325

NORA: Why are you looking so critical? Don't you think they will fit me?

RANK: I have no means of forming an opinion about that.

NORA: [*looks at him for a moment*] For shame! [*hits him lightly on the ear with the stockings*] That's to punish you. [*folds them up again*]

RANK: And what other nice things am I to be allowed to see? 330

NORA: Not a single thing more, for being so naughty. [*She looks among the things, humming to herself.*]

RANK: [*after a short silence*] When I'm sitting here, talking to you as intimately as this, I can't imagine for a moment what would have become of me if I had never come into this house. 335

NORA: [*smiling*] I believe you do feel thoroughly at home with us.

RANK: [*in a lower voice, looking straight in front of him*] And to be obliged to leave it all—

NORA: Nonsense, you're not going to leave it.

RANK: [*as before*] And not be able to leave behind one the slightest token of one's gratitude, scarcely even a fleeting regret—nothing but an empty place which the first comer can fill as well as any other. 340

NORA: And if I asked you now for a—? No!

RANK: For what?

NORA: For a big proof of your friendship—

RANK: Yes, yes! 345

NORA: I mean a tremendously big favour—

RANK: Would you really make me so happy for once?

NORA: Ah, but you don't know what it is yet.

RANK: No—but tell me.

NORA: I really can't, Doctor Rank. It's something out of all reason; it means advice, and help, and a favour— 350

RANK: The bigger the better. I can't conceive what it is you mean. Do tell me. Haven't I your confidence?

NORA: More than anyone else. I know you are my truest and best friend, and so I'll tell you what it is. Well, Doctor Rank, it's something you must help me to prevent. You know how devotedly, how inexpressibly deeply Torvald loves me; he would never for a moment hesitate to give his life for me. 355

RANK: [*leaning towards her*] Nora—do you think he is the only one—?

NORA: [*with a slight start*] The only one—?

RANK: The only one who would gladly give his life for your sake. 360

NORA: [*sadly*] Is that it?

RANK: I was determined you should know it before I went away, and there'll never be a better opportunity than this. Now you know it, Nora. And now you know, too, that you can trust me as you would trust no one else.

NORA: [*rises, deliberately and quietly*] Let me pass. 365

RANK: [*makes room for her to pass him, but sits still*] Nora!

NORA: [*at the hall door*] Helen, bring in the lamp. [*goes over to the stove*] Dear Doctor Rank, that was really horrid of you.

RANK: To have loved you as much as anyone else does? Was that horrid?

NORA: No, but to go and tell me so. There was really no need— 370

RANK: What do you mean? Did you know—? [MAID *enters with lamp, puts it down on the table, and goes out.*] Nora—Mrs. Helmer—tell me, had you any idea of this?

NORA: Oh, how do I know whether I had or whether I hadn't? I really can't tell you—To think you could be so clumsy, Doctor Rank! We were getting on so nicely.

RANK: Well, at all events you know now that you can command me, body and soul. So won't you speak out? 375

NORA: [*looking at him*] After what happened?

RANK: I beg you to let me know what it is.

NORA: I can't tell you anything now.

RANK: Yes, yes. You mustn't punish me in that way. Let me have permission to do for you   380
whatever a man may do.

NORA: You can do nothing for me now. Besides, I really don't need any help at all. You will
find the whole thing is merely fancy on my part. It really is so—of course it is! [*Sits
down in the rocking chair, and looks at him with a smile.*] You are a nice man, Doctor
Rank!—don't you feel ashamed of yourself, now the lamp has come!   385

RANK: Not a bit. But perhaps I had better go—for ever?

NORA: No, indeed, you shall not. Of course you must come here just as before. You know
very well Torvald can't do without you.

RANK: Yes, but you?

NORA: Oh I'm always tremendously pleased when you come.   390

RANK: It's just that, that put me on the wrong track. You are a riddle to me. I've often
thought that you'd almost as soon be in my company as in Helmer's.

NORA: Yes—you see there are some people one loves best, and others whom one would
almost always rather have as companions.

RANK: Yes, there is something in that.   395

NORA: When I was at home, of course I loved papa best. But I always thought it tremendous fun if I could steal down into the maids' room, because they never moralised at
all, and talked to each other about such entertaining things.

RANK: I see—it is their place I have taken.

NORA: [*jumping up and going to him*] Oh, dear, nice Doctor Rank, I never meant that at   400
all. But surely you can understand that being with Torvald is a little like being with
papa—

[*Enter* MAID *from the hall.*]

MAID: If you please, ma'am. [*whispers and hands her a card*]

NORA: [*glancing at the card*] Oh! [*puts it in her pocket*]

RANK: Is there anything wrong?   405

NORA: No, no, not in the least. It's only something—it's my new dress—

RANK: What? Your dress is lying there.

NORA: Oh, yes, that one; but this is another. I ordered it. Torvald mustn't know about
it—

RANK: Oho! Then that was the great secret.   410

NORA: Of course. Just go in to him; he is sitting in the inner room. Keep him as long
as—

RANK: Make your mind easy; I won't let him escape. [*goes into* HELMER'*s room*]

NORA: [*to the* MAID] And he's waiting in the kitchen?

MAID: Yes; he came up the back stairs.   415

NORA: But didn't you tell him no one was in?

MAID: Yes, but it was no good.

NORA: He won't go away?

MAID: No; he says he won't until he has seen you, ma'am.

NORA: Well, let him come in—but quietly. Helen, you mustn't say anything about it to   420
anyone. It's a surprise for my husband.

MAID: Yes, ma'am, I quite understand. [*exit*]

NORA: This dreadful thing is going to happen! It will happen in spite of me! No, no, no,
it can't happen—it shan't happen! [*She bolts the door of* HELMER'*s room. The* MAID
opens the hall door for KROGSTAD *and shuts it after him. He is wearing a fur coat, high*   425
boots, and a fur cap.]

NORA: [*advancing towards him*] Speak low—my husband is at home.

KROGSTAD: No matter about that!

NORA: What do you want of me?

KROGSTAD: An explanation.

NORA: Make haste then. What is it?

KROGSTAD: You know, I suppose, that I've got my dismissal.

NORA: I couldn't prevent it, Mr. Krogstad. I fought as hard as I could on your side, but it was no good.

KROGSTAD: Does your husband love you so little, then? He knows what I can expose you to, and yet he ventures—

NORA: How can you suppose that he has any knowledge of the sort?

KROGSTAD: I didn't suppose so at all. It would not be the least like our dear Torvald Helmer to show so much courage—

NORA: Mr. Krogstad, a little respect for my husband, please.

KROGSTAD: Certainly—all the respect he deserves. But since you have kept the matter so carefully to yourself, I make bold to suppose that you have a little clearer idea, than you had yesterday, of what it actually is that you have done?

NORA: More than you could ever teach me.

KROGSTAD: Yes, bad lawyer that I am.

NORA: What is it you want of me?

KROGSTAD: Only to see how you were, Mrs. Helmer. I have been thinking about you all day long. A mere cashier, hackwriter, a—well, a man like me—even he has a little of what is called feeling, you know.

NORA: Show it, then; think of my little children.

KROGSTAD: Have you and your husband thought of mine? But never mind about that. I only wanted to tell you that you need not take this matter too seriously. In the first place there will be no accusation made on my part.

NORA: No, of course not; I was sure of that.

KROGSTAD: The whole thing can be arranged amicably; there is no reason why anyone should know anything about it. It will remain a secret between us three.

NORA: My husband must never get to know anything about it.

KROGSTAD: How will you be able to prevent it? Am I to understand that you can pay the balance that's owing?

NORA: No, not just at present.

KROGSTAD: Or perhaps that you have some means of raising the money soon?

NORA: None that I mean to make use of.

KROGSTAD: Well, in any case, it would've been of no use to you now. If you stood there with ever so much money in your hand, I would never part with your bond.

NORA: Tell me what purpose you mean to put it to.

KROGSTAD: I shall only preserve it—keep it in my possession. No one who is not concerned in the matter shall have the slightest hint of it. So that if the thought of it has driven you to any desperate resolution—

NORA: It has.

KROGSTAD: If you had it in your mind to run away from your home—

NORA: I had.

KROGSTAD: Or even something worse—

NORA: How could you know that?

KROGSTAD: Give up the idea.

NORA: How did you know I had thought of *that*?

KROGSTAD: Most of us think of that at first. I did, too—but I hadn't the courage.

NORA: [*faintly*] No more had I.

KROGSTAD: [*in a tone of relief*] No, that's it, isn't it—you hadn't the courage, either?

NORA: No, I haven't—I haven't.

KROGSTAD: Besides, it would have been a great piece of folly. Once the first storm at home is over—. I have a letter for your husband in my pocket. 480

NORA: Telling him everything?

KROGSTAD: In as lenient a manner as I possibly could.

NORA: [*quickly*] He mustn't get that letter. Tear it up. I will find some means of getting money. 485

KROGSTAD: Excuse me, Mrs. Helmer, but I think I told you just now—

NORA: I am not speaking of what I owe you. Tell me what sum you are asking my husband for, and I will get the money.

KROGSTAD: I am not asking your husband for a penny.

NORA: What do you want, then? 490

KROGSTAD: I will tell you. I want to rehabilitate myself, Mrs. Helmer; I want to get on; and in that your husband must help me. For the last year and a half I have not had a hand in anything dishonourable, and all that time I have been struggling in most restricted circumstances. I was content to work my way up step by step. Now I'm turned out, and I'm not going to be satisfied with merely being taken into favour 495 again. I want to get on, I tell you. I want to get into the Bank again, in a higher position. Your husband must make a place for me—

NORA: That he will never do!

KROGSTAD: He will; I know him; he dare not protest. And as soon as I'm in there again with him, then you will see! Within a year I shall be the manager's right hand. It will 500 be Nils Krogstad and not Torvald Helmer who manages the Bank.

NORA: That's a thing you will never see!

KROGSTAD: Do you mean that you will—?

NORA: I have courage enough for it now.

KROGSTAD: Oh, you can't frighten me. A fine, spoilt lady like you— 505

NORA: You'll see, you'll see.

KROGSTAD: Under the ice, perhaps? Down into the cold, coal-black water? And then, in the spring, to float up to the surface, all horrible and unrecognisable, with your hair fallen out—

NORA: You can't frighten me. 510

KROGSTAD: Nor you me. People don't do such things, Mrs. Helmer. Besides, what use would it be? I should have him completely in my power all the same.

NORA: Afterwards? When I am no longer—

KROGSTAD: Have you forgotten that it is I who have the keeping of your reputation? [*Nora stands speechlessly looking at him.*] Well, now, I've warned you. Don't do any- 515 thing foolish. When Helmer has received my letter, I shall expect a message from him. And be sure you remember that it's your husband himself who has forced me into such ways as this again. I'll never forgive him for that. Good-bye, Mrs. Helmer. [*exit through the hall*]

NORA: [*goes to the hall door, opens it slightly and listens*] He's going. He's not putting the 520 letter in the box. Oh no, no! that's impossible! [*opens the door by degrees*] What's that? He's standing outside. He's not going downstairs. Is he hesitating? Can he—? [*A letter drops into the box; then* KROGSTAD's *footsteps are heard, till they die away as he goes downstairs.* NORA *utters a stifled cry, and runs across the room to the table by the sofa. A short pause.*] 525

NORA: In the mail box. [*steals across to the hall door*] There it lies—Torvald, Torvald, there is no hope for us now!

[MRS. LINDE *comes in from the room on the left, carrying the dress.*]

MRS. LINDE: There, I can't see anything more to mend now. Would you like to try it on—?

NORA: [*in a hoarse whisper*] Christine, come here.   530

MRS. LINDE: [*throwing the dress down on the sofa*] What's the matter with you? You look so upset.

NORA: Come here. Do you see that letter? There, look—you can see it through the glass in the box.

MRS. LINDE: Yes, I see it.   535

NORA: That letter is from Krogstad.

MRS. LINDE: Nora—it was Krogstad who lent you the money!

NORA: Yes, and now Torvald will know all about it.

MRS. LINDE: Believe me, Nora, that's the best thing for both of you.

NORA: You don't know all. I forged a name.   540

MRS. LINDE: Good heavens—!

NORA: I only want to say this to you, Christine—you must be my witness.

MRS. LINDE: Your witness? What do you mean? What am I to—?

NORA: If I should go out of my mind—and it might easily happen—

MRS. LINDE: Nora!   545

NORA: Or if anything else should happen to me—anything, for instance, that might prevent my being here—

MRS. LINDE: Nora! Nora! You're quite out of your mind.

NORA: And if it should happen that there were someone who wanted to take all the responsibility, all the blame, you understand—   550

MRS. LINDE: Yes, yes—but how can you suppose—?

NORA: Then you must be my witness, that it's not true, Christine. I'm not out of my mind at all. I'm in my right senses now, and I tell you no one else has known anything about it; I, and I alone, did the whole thing. Remember that.

MRS. LINDE: I will, indeed. But I don't understand all this.   555

NORA: How should you understand it? A miracle is going to happen.

MRS. LINDE: A miracle?

NORA: Yes, a miracle.—But it's so terrible, Christine; it *mustn't* happen, not for all the world.

MRS. LINDE: I will go at once and see Krogstad.

NORA: Don't go to him; he will do you some harm.   560

MRS. LINDE: There was a time when he would gladly do anything for my sake.

NORA: He?

MRS. LINDE: Where does he live?

NORA: How should I know—? Yes [*feeling in her pocket*] here is his card. But the letter, the letter—!   565

HELMER: [*calls from his room, knocking at the door*] Nora!

NORA: [*cries out anxiously*] Oh, what's that? What do you want?

HELMER: Don't be so frightened. We are not coming in; you have locked the door. Are you trying on your dress?

NORA: Yes, that's it. I look so nice, Torvald.   570

MRS. LINDE: [*who has read the card*] I see he lives at the corner here.

NORA: Yes, but it's no use. It's hopeless. The letter is lying there in the box.

MRS. LINDE: And your husband keeps the key?

NORA: Yes, always.

MRS. LINDE: Krogstad must ask for his letter back unread, he must find some pretence—   575

NORA: But it's just at this time that Torvald generally—

MRS. LINDE: You must delay him. Go in to him in the meantime. I'll come back as soon as I can. [*She goes out hurriedly through the hall door.*]

NORA: [*goes to* HELMER's *door, opens it and peeps in*] Torvald!

HELMER: [*from the inner room*] Well? May I venture at last to come into my own room   580
again? Come along, Rank, now you'll see—[*halting in the doorway*] But what is this?
NORA: What is what, dear?
HELMER: Rank led me to expect a splendid transformation.
RANK: [*in the doorway*] I understood so, but evidently I was mistaken.
NORA: Yes, nobody is to have the chance of admiring me in my costume until to-morrow.   585
HELMER: But, my dear Nora, you look so worn out. Have you been practising too much?
NORA: No, I have not practised at all.
HELMER: But you will need to—
NORA: Yes, indeed I shall, Torvald. But I can't get on a bit without you to help me; I have
absolutely forgotten the whole thing.   590
HELMER: Oh, we'll soon work it up again.
NORA: Yes, help me, Torvald. Promise that you will! I'm so nervous about it—all the people.
You must give yourself up to me entirely this evening. Not the tiniest bit of business—
you mustn't even take a pen in your hand. Will you promise, Torvald dear?
HELMER: I promise: This evening I'll be wholly and absolutely at your service, you helpless   595
little thing. But, first of all I'll just—[*goes towards the hall door*]
NORA: What are you going to do there?
HELMER: Only see if any letters have come.
NORA: No, no! Don't do that, Torvald!
HELMER: Why not?   600
NORA: Torvald, please don't. There is nothing there.
HELMER: Well, let me look. [*Turns to go to the letterbox.* NORA, *at the piano, plays the first
bars of the Tarantella.* HELMER *stops in the doorway.*] Aha!
NORA: I can't dance to-morrow if I don't practise with you.
HELMER: [*going up to her*] Are you really so afraid of it, dear?   605
NORA: Yes, so dreadfully afraid of it. Let me practise at once; there is time now, before we
go to dinner. Sit down and play for me, Torvald dear; coach me, and correct me as
you play.
HELMER: With great pleasure, if you wish me to. [*sits down at the piano*]
NORA: [*Takes out of the box a tambourine and a long variegated shawl. She hastily drapes the   610
shawl round her. Then she springs to the front of the stage and calls out.*] Now play for
me! I'm going to dance!

[HELMER *plays and* NORA *dances.* RANK *stands by the piano behind* HELMER,
and looks on.]

HELMER: [*as he plays*] Slower, slower!
NORA: I can't do it any other way.
HELMER: Not so violently, Nora!   615
NORA: This is the way.
HELMER: [*stops playing*] No, no—that's not a bit right.
NORA: [*laughing and swinging the tambourine*] Didn't I tell you so?
RANK: Let me play for her.
HELMER: [*getting up*] Yes, do. I can correct her better then.   620

[RANK *sits down at the piano and plays.* NORA *dances more and more wildly.*
HELMER *has taken up a position beside the stove, and during her dance gives her
frequent instructions. She does not seem to hear him; her hair comes down and
falls over her shoulders; she pays no attention to it, but goes on dancing. Enter*
MRS. LINDE.]

MRS. LINDE: [*standing as if spellbound in the doorway*] Oh!—

NORA: [*as she dances*] Such fun, Christine!

HELMER: My dear darling Nora, you are dancing as if your life depended on it.

NORA: So it does.

HELMER: Stop, Rank; this is sheer madness. Stop, I tell you! [RANK *stops playing, and*   625
NORA *suddenly stands still.* HELMER *goes up to her.*] I could never have believed it.
You have forgotten everything I taught you.

NORA: [*throwing away the tambourine*] There, you see.

HELMER: You'll want a lot of coaching.

NORA: Yes, you see how much I need it. You must coach me up to the last minute. Promise   630
me that, Torvald!

HELMER: You can depend on me.

NORA: You must not think of anything but me, either to-day or to-morrow; you mustn't
open a single letter—not even open the mail box—

HELMER: Ah, you're still afraid of that fellow—   635

NORA: Yes, indeed I am.

HELMER: Nora, I tell from your looks that there is a letter from him lying there.

NORA: I don't know; I think there is; but you must not read anything of that kind now.
Nothing horrid must come between us till this is all over.

RANK: [*whispers to* HELMER] You mustn't contradict her.   640

HELMER: [*taking her in his arms*] The child shall have her way. But to-morrow night, after
you've danced—

NORA: Then you will be free. [*The* MAID *appears in the doorway to the right.*]

MAID: Dinner is served, ma'am.

NORA: We will have champagne, Helen.   645

MAID: Very good, ma'am. [*exit*]

HELMER: Hullo!—are we going to have a banquet?

NORA: Yes, a champagne banquet till the small hours. [*calls out*] And a few macaroons,
Helen—lots, just for once!

HELMER: Come, come, don't be so wild and nervous. Be my own little skylark.   650

NORA: Yes, dear, I will. But go in now and you, too, Doctor Rank. Christine, you must
help me to do up my hair.

RANK: [*whispers to* HELMER *as they go out*] I suppose there's nothing—she is not expecting
anything?

HELMER: Far from it, my dear fellow; it is simply nothing more than this childish nervous-   655
ness I was telling you of. [*They go into the right-hand room.*]

NORA: Well!

MRS. LINDE: Gone out of town.

NORA: I could tell from your face.

MRS. LINDE: He's coming home to-morrow evening. I wrote a note for him.   660

NORA: You should have let it alone; you must prevent nothing. After all, it is splendid to
be waiting for a wonderful thing to happen.

MRS. LINDE: What is it that you are waiting for?

NORA: Oh, you wouldn't understand. Go in to them, I will come in a moment. [MRS.
LINDE *goes into the dining room.* NORA *stands still for a little while, as if to compose*   665
herself. Then she looks at her watch.] Five o'clock. Seven hours till midnight; and then
twenty-four hours till the next midnight. Then the Tarantella will be over. Twenty-
four and seven? Thirty-one hours to live.

HELMER: [*from the doorway on the right*] Where's my little skylark?

NORA: [*going to him with her arms outstretched*] Here she is!   670

———————————   ACT III   ———————————

THE SAME SCENE——*The table has been placed in the middle of the stage, with chairs round it. A lamp is burning on the table. The door into the hall stands open. Dance music is heard in the room above.* MRS. LINDE *is sitting at the table idly turning over the leaves of a book she tries to read, but does not seem able to collect her thoughts. Every now and then she listens intently for a sound at the outer door.*

MRS. LINDE: [*looking at her watch*] Not yet—and the time is nearly up. If only he doesn't—. [*listens again*] Ah, there he is. [*Goes into the hall and opens the outer door carefully. Light footsteps are heard on the stairs. She whispers.*] Come in. There's no one here.

KROGSTAD: [*in the doorway*] I found a note from you at home. What does this mean?

MRS. LINDE: It's absolutely necessary that I have a talk with you.   5

KROGSTAD: Really! And is it absolutely necessary that it should be here?

MRS. LINDE: It's impossible where I live; there's no private entrance to my rooms. Come in; we're quite alone. The maid's asleep and the Helmers are at the dance upstairs.

KROGSTAD: [*coming into the room*] Are the Helmers really at a dance to-night?

MRS. LINDE: Yes, why not?   10

KROGSTAD: Certainly—why not?

MRS. LINDE: Now, Nils, let's have a talk.

KROGSTAD: Can we two have anything to talk about.

MRS. LINDE: We have a great deal to talk about.

KROGSTAD: I shouldn't have thought so.   15

MRS. LINDE: No, you have never properly understood me.

KROGSTAD: Was there anything else to understand except what was obvious to all the world—a heartless woman jilts a man when a better catch turns up.

MRS. LINDE: Do you believe I'm as absolutely heartless as all that? And do you believe that I did it with a light heart?   20

KROGSTAD: Didn't you?

MRS. LINDE: Nils, did you really think that?

KROGSTAD: If it were as you say, why did you write to me as you did at that time?

MRS. LINDE: I could do nothing else. As I had to break with you, it was my duty also to put an end to all that you felt for me.   25

KROGSTAD: [*wringing his hands*] So that was it. And all this—only for the sake of money!

MRS. LINDE: You must not forget that I had a helpless mother and two little brothers. We couldn't wait for you, Nils; your prospects seemed hopeless then.

KROGSTAD: That may be so, but you had no right to throw me over for any one else's sake.

MRS. LINDE: Indeed I don't know. Many a time did I ask myself if I had the right to do it.   30

KROGSTAD: [*more gently*] When I lost you, it was as if all the solid ground went from under my feet. Look at me now—I'm a shipwrecked man clinging to a bit of wreckage.

MRS. LINDE: But help may be near.

KROGSTAD: It *was* near; but then you came and stood in my way.

MRS. LINDE: Unintentionally, Nils. It was only to-day that I learned it was your place I was going to take in the Bank.   35

KROGSTAD: I believe you, if you say so. But now that you know it, are you not going to give it up to me?

MRS. LINDE: No, because that would not benefit you in the least.

KROGSTAD: Oh, benefit, benefit—I would have done it whether or no.   40

MRS. LINDE: I have learned to act prudently. Life, and hard, bitter necessity have taught me that.

KROGSTAD: And life has taught me not to believe in fine speeches.

MRS. LINDE: Then life has taught you something very reasonable. But deeds you must believe in? 45

KROGSTAD: What do you mean by that?

MRS. LINDE: You said you were like a shipwrecked man clinging to some wreckage.

KROGSTAD: I had good reason to say so.

MRS. LINDE: Well, I am like a shipwrecked woman clinging to some wreckage—no one to mourn for, no one to care for. 50

KROGSTAD: It was your own choice.

MRS. LINDE: There was no other choice—then.

KROGSTAD: Well, what now?

MRS. LINDE: Nils, how would it be if we two shipwrecked people could join forces?

KROGSTAD: What are you saying? 55

MRS. LINDE: Two on the same piece of wreckage would stand a better chance than each on their own.

KROGSTAD: Christine!

MRS. LINDE: What do you suppose brought me to town?

KROGSTAD: Do you mean that you gave me a thought? 60

MRS. LINDE: I couldn't endure life without work. All my life, as long as I can remember, I have worked, and it's been my greatest and only pleasure. But now I'm quite alone in the world—my life is so dreadfully empty and I feel so forsaken. There is not the least pleasure in working for one's self. Nils, give me someone and something to work for.

KROGSTAD: I don't trust that. It's nothing but a woman's overstrained sense of generosity 65 that prompts you to make such an offer of yourself.

MRS. LINDE: Have you ever noticed anything of the sort in me?

KROGSTAD: Could you really do it? Tell me—do you know all about my past life?

MRS. LINDE: Yes.

KROGSTAD: And do you know what they think of me here? 70

MRS. LINDE: You seemed to me to imply that with me you might have been quite another man.

KROGSTAD: I'm certain of it.

MRS. LINDE: Is it too late now?

KROGSTAD: Christine, are you saying this deliberately? Yes, I'm sure you are. I see it in 75 your face. Have you really the courage, then—?

MRS. LINDE: I want to be a mother to someone, and your children need a mother. We two need each other. Nils, I have faith in your real character—I can dare anything together with you.

KROGSTAD: [grasps her hand] Thanks, thanks, Christine! Now I shall find a way to clear 80 myself in the eyes of the world. Ah, but I forgot—

MRS. LINDE: [listening] Hush! The Tarantella! Go, go!

KROGSTAD: Why? What is it?

MRS. LINDE: Do you hear them up there? When that is over, we may expect them back.

KROGSTAD: Yes, yes—I will go. But it's all no use. Of course you're not aware what steps 85 I've taken in the matter of the Helmers.

MRS. LINDE: Yes, I know all about that.

KROGSTAD: And in spite of that have you the courage to—?

MRS. LINDE: I understand very well to what lengths a man like you might be driven by despair. 90

KROGSTAD: If I could only undo what I've done!

MRS. LINDE: You cannot. Your letter is lying in the mail box now.

KROGSTAD: Are you sure of that?

MRS. LINDE: Quite sure, but—

KROGSTAD: [*with a searching look at her*] Is that what it all means?—that you want to save 95
your friend at any cost? Tell me frankly. Is that it?

MRS. LINDE: Nils, a woman who has once sold herself for another's sake, doesn't do it a
second time.

KROGSTAD: I'll ask for my letter back.

MRS. LINDE: No, no. 100

KROGSTAD: Yes, of course I will. I'll wait here till Torvald comes; I will tell him he must give
me my letter back—that it only concerns my dismissal—that he's not to read it.

MRS. LINDE: No, Nils, you must not recall your letter.

KROGSTAD: But, tell me, wasn't it for that very purpose that you asked me to meet you
here? 105

MRS. LINDE: In my first moment of fright, it was. But twenty-four hours have elapsed
since then, and in that time I've witnessed incredible things in this house. Torvald
must know all about it. This unhappy secret must be disclosed; they must have a
complete understanding between them, which is impossible with all this conceal-
ment and falsehood going on. 110

KROGSTAD: Very well, if you will take the responsibility. But there's one thing I can do in
any case, and I shall do it at once.

MRS. LINDE: [*listening*] You must be quick and go! The dance is over; we are not safe a
moment longer.

KROGSTAD: I'll wait for you below. 115

MRS. LINDE: Yes, do. You must see me back to my door.

KROGSTAD: I have never had such an amazing piece of good fortune in my life! [*goes out
through the outer door. The door between the room and the hall remains open.*]

MRS. LINDE: [*tidying up the room and laying her hat and cloak ready*] What a difference!
What a difference! Someone to work for and live for—a home to bring comfort into. 120
That I will do, indeed. I wish they would be quick and come—[*listens*] Ah, there
they are now. I must put on my things. [*Takes up her hat and cloak.* HELMER's *and*
NORA's *voices are heard outside; a key is turned, and* HELMER *brings* NORA *almost
by force into the hall. She is in an Italian costume with a large black shawl around her;
he is in evening dress, and a black cloak which is flying open.*] 125

NORA: [*hanging back in the doorway, and struggling with him*] No, no, no!—don't take me
in. I want to go upstairs again; I don't want to leave so early.

HELMER: But, my dearest Nora—

NORA: Please, Torvald dear—please, *please*—only an hour more.

HELMER: Not a single minute, my sweet Nora. You know that was our agreement. Come 130
along into the room; you are catching cold standing there. [*He brings her gently into
the room, in spite of her resistance.*]

MRS. LINDE: Good-evening.

NORA: Christine!

HELMER: You here, so late, Mrs. Linde? 135

MRS. LINDE: Yes, you must excuse me; I was so anxious to see Nora in her dress.

NORA: Have you been sitting here waiting for me?

MRS. LINDE: Yes, unfortunately I came too late; you had already gone upstairs, and I
thought I couldn't go away again without having seen you.

HELMER: [*taking off* NORA's *shawl*] Yes, take a good look at her. I think she's worth look- 140
ing at. Isn't she charming, Mrs. Linde?

MRS. LINDE: Yes, indeed she is.

HELMER: Doesn't she look remarkably pretty? Everyone thought so at the dance. But she
is terribly self-willed, this sweet little person. What are we to do with her? You will
hardly believe that I had almost to bring her away by force. 145

NORA: Torvald, you will repent not having let me stay, even if it were only for half an hour.

HELMER: Listen to her, Mrs. Linde! She had danced her Tarantella, and it had been a tremendous success, as it deserved—although possibly the performance was a trifle too realistic—a little more so, I mean, than was strictly compatible with propriety. But never mind about that! The chief thing is, she had made a success—she had made a tremendous success. Do you think I was going to let her remain there after that, and spoil the effect? No, indeed! I took my charming little Capri maiden—my capricious little Capri maiden, I should say—on my arm; took one quick turn around the room; a curtsy on either side, and, as they say in novels, the beautiful apparition disappeared. An exit ought always to be effective, Mrs. Linde; but that's what I cannot make Nora understand. Pooh! this room is hot. [*throws his cloak on a chair, and opens the door of his room*] Hullo! it's all dark in here. Oh, of course—excuse me—[*He goes in, and lights some candles.*]

NORA: [*in a hurried and breathless whisper*] Well?

MRS. LINDE: [*in a low voice*] I have had a talk with him.

NORA: Yes, and—

MRS. LINDE: Nora, you must tell your husband all about it.

NORA: [*in an expressionless voice*] I knew it.

MRS. LINDE: You have nothing to be afraid of as far as Krogstad is concerned; but you must tell him.

NORA: I won't tell him.

MRS. LINDE: Then the letter will.

NORA: Thank you, Christine. Now I know what I must do. Hush—!

HELMER: [*coming in again*] Well, Mrs. Linde, have you admired her?

MRS. LINDE: Yes, and now I will say good-night.

HELMER: What, already? Is this yours, this knitting?

MRS. LINDE: [*taking it*] Yes, thank you, I had very nearly forgotten it.

HELMER: So you knit?

MRS. LINDE: Of course.

HELMER: Do you know, you ought to embroider.

MRS. LINDE: Really? Why?

HELMER: Yes, it's far more becoming. Let me show you. You hold the embroidery thus in your left hand, and use the needle with the right—like this—with a long, easy sweep. Do you see?

MRS. LINDE: Yes, perhaps.

HELMER: But in the case of knitting—that can never be anything but ungraceful; look here—the arms close together, the knitting-needles going up and down—it has a sort of Chinese effect. That was really excellent champagne they gave us.

MRS. LINDE: Well—good-night, Nora, and don't be stubborn any more.

HELMER: That's right, Mrs. Linde.

MRS. LINDE: Good-night, Mr. Helmer.

HELMER: [*accompanying her to the door*] Good-night, good-night. I hope you'll get home all right. I should be very happy to—but you haven't any great distance to go. Good-night, good-night. [*She goes out; he shuts the door after her, and comes in again.*] Ah!—at last we have got rid of her. She is a frightful bore, that woman.

NORA: Aren't you very tired, Torvald?

HELMER: No, not in the least.

NORA: Nor sleepy?

HELMER: Not a bit. On the contrary, I feel extraordinarily lively. And you?—you really 195
look both tired and sleepy.

NORA: Yes, I'm very tired. I want to go to sleep at once.

HELMER: There, you see it was quite right of me not to let you stay there any longer.

NORA: Everything you do is quite right, Torvald.

HELMER: [*kissing her on the forehead*] Now my little skylark is speaking reasonably. Did 200
you notice what good spirits Rank was in this evening?

NORA: Really? Was he? I didn't speak to him at all.

HELMER: And I very little, but I haven't seen him in such good form for a long time. [*looks
for a while at her and then goes nearer to her*] It's delightful to be at home by ourselves
again, to be all alone with you—you fascinating, charming little darling! 205

NORA: Don't look at me like that, Torvald.

HELMER: Why shouldn't I look at my dearest treasure?—at all the beauty that's mine, all
mine?

NORA: [*going to the other side of the table*] You mustn't say things like that to me to-night.

HELMER: [*following her*] You have still got the Tarantella in your blood, I see. And it makes 210
you more captivating than ever. Listen—the guests are beginning to leave now. [*in a
lower voice*] Nora—soon the whole house will be quiet.

NORA: Yes, I hope so.

HELMER: Yes, my own darling Nora. Do you know when I'm out at a party with you like
this, why I speak so little to you, keep away from you, and only send a stolen glance 215
in your direction now and then?—do you know why I do that? It's because I make
believe that we are secretly in love, and you are my secretly promised bride, and that
no one suspects there is anything between us.

NORA: Yes, yes—I know very well you're thinking about me all the time.

HELMER: And when we are leaving, and I am putting the shawl over your beautiful young 220
shoulders—on your lovely neck—then I imagine that you are my bride and that
we have just come from the wedding, and I am bringing you for the first time into
our home—to be alone with you for the first time—quite alone with my shy little
darling! All this evening I have longed for nothing but you. When I watched the
seductive figures of the Tarantella, my blood was on fire; I could endure it no longer, 225
and that was why I brought you down so early—

NORA: Go away, Torvald! You must let me go. I won't—

HELMER: What's that? You're teasing, my little Nora! You won't—you won't? Am I not your
husband? [*A knock is heard at the outer door.*]

NORA: [*starting*] Did you hear—? 230

HELMER: [*going into the hall*] Who is it?

RANK: [*outside*] It is I. May I come in for a moment?

HELMER: [*in a fretful whisper*]. Oh, what does he want now? [*aloud*] Wait a minute!
[*unlocks the door*] Come, that's kind of you not to pass by our door.

RANK: I thought I heard your voice, and felt as if I should like to look in. [*with a swift* 235
glance round] Ah, yes!—these dear familiar rooms. You are very happy and cozy in
here, you two.

HELMER: It seems to me that you looked after yourself pretty well upstairs, too.

RANK: Excellently. Why shouldn't I? Why shouldn't one enjoy everything in this world?—
at any rate as much as one can, and as long as one can. The wine was capital— 240

HELMER: Especially the champagne.

RANK: So you noticed that, too? It's almost incredible how much I managed to put away!

NORA: Torvald drank a great deal of champagne to-night, too.

RANK: Did he?

NORA: Yes, and he is always in such good spirits afterwards. 245

RANK: Well, why should one not enjoy a merry evening after a well-spent day?

HELMER: Well spent: I'm afraid I can't take credit for that.

RANK: [*clapping him on the back*] But I can, you know!

NORA: Doctor Rank, you must have been occupied with some scientific investigation today. 250

RANK: Exactly.

HELMER: Just listen!—little Nora talking about scientific investigations!

NORA: And may I congratulate you on the result?

RANK: Indeed you may.

NORA: Was it favourable, then? 255

RANK: The best possible, for both doctor and patient—certainty.

NORA: [*quickly and searchingly*] Certainty?

RANK: Absolute certainty. So wasn't I entitled to make a merry evening of it after that?

NORA: Yes, you certainly were, Doctor Rank.

HELMER: I think so, too, so long as you don't have to pay for it in the morning. 260

RANK: Oh well, one can't have anything in this life without paying for it.

NORA: Doctor Rank—are you fond of masked balls?

RANK: Yes, if there's a fine lot of pretty costumes.

NORA: Tell me—what shall we two wear at the next?

HELMER: Little featherbrain!—are you thinking of the next already? 265

RANK: We two? Yes. I can tell you. You shall go as a good fairy—

HELMER: Yes, but what do you suggest as an appropriate costume for that?

RANK: Let your wife go dressed just as she is in everyday life.

HELMER: That was really very prettily turned. But can't you tell us what you'll be?

RANK: Yes, my dear friend, I have quite made up my mind about that. 270

HELMER: Well?

RANK: At the next fancy-dress ball I shall be invisible.

HELMER: That's a good joke!

RANK: There is a big black hat—have you never heard of hats that make you invisible? If you put one on, no one can see you. 275

HELMER: [*suppressing a smile*] Yes, you're quite right.

RANK: But I am clean forgetting what I came for. Helmer, give me a cigar—one of the dark Havanas.

HELMER: With the greatest pleasure. [*offers him his case*]

RANK: [*takes a cigar and cuts off the end*] Thanks. 280

NORA: [*striking a match*] Let me give you a light.

RANK: Thank you. [*She holds the match for him to light his cigar.*] And now good-bye!

HELMER: Good-bye, good-bye, dear old man!

NORA: Sleep well, Doctor Rank.

RANK: Thank you for that wish. 285

NORA: Wish me the same.

RANK: You? Well, if you want me to sleep well! And thanks for the light. [*He nods to them both and goes out.*]

HELMER: [*in a subdued voice*] He has drunk more than he ought.

NORA: [*absently*] Maybe. [HELMER *takes a bunch of keys out of his pocket and goes into the hall.*] Torvald! what are you going to do there? 290

HELMER: Empty the mail box; it's quite full; there will be no room for the newspaper, to-morrow morning.

NORA: Are you going to work to-night?

HELMER: You know quite well I'm not. What is this? Some one has been at the lock.

NORA: At the lock—?   295

HELMER: Yes, someone has. What can it mean? I should never have thought the maid—.
Here is a broken hairpin. Nora, it is one of yours.

NORA: [*quickly*] Then it must have been the children—

HELMER: Then you must get them out of those ways. There, at last I have got it open.
[*takes out the contents of the mail box, and calls to the kitchen*] Helen! Helen, put out   300
the light over the front door. [*goes back into the room and shuts the door into the hall.
He holds out his hand full of letters.*] Look at that—look what a heap of them there
are. [*turning them over*] What on earth is that?

NORA: [*at the window*] The letter—No! Torvald, no!

HELMER: Two cards—of Rank's.   305

NORA: Of Doctor Rank's?

HELMER: [*looking at them*] Doctor Rank. They were on the top. He must have put them
in when he went out.

NORA: Is there anything written on them?

HELMER: There is a black cross over the name. Look there—what an uncomfortable idea!   310
It looks as if he were announcing his own death.

NORA: It's just what he's doing.

HELMER: What? Do you know anything about it? Has he said anything to you?

NORA: Yes. He told me that when the cards came it would be his leave-taking from us. He
means to shut himself up and die.   315

HELMER: My poor old friend. Certainly I knew we should not have him very long with
us. But so soon! And so he hides himself away like a wounded animal.

NORA: If it has to happen, it's best it should be without a word—don't you think so,
Torvald?

HELMER: [*walking up and down*] He had so grown into our lives. I can't think of him as   320
having gone out of them. He, with his sufferings and his loneliness, was like a cloudy
background to our sunlit happiness. Well, perhaps it's best so. For him, anyway.
[*standing still*] And perhaps for us, too, Nora. We two are thrown quite upon each
other now. [*puts his arms round her*] My darling wife, I don't feel as if I could hold
you tight enough. Do you know, Nora, I've often wished that you might be threatened   325
by some great danger, so I might risk my life's blood, and everything, for your sake.

NORA: [*disengages herself, and says firmly and decidedly*] Now you must read your letters,
Torvald.

HELMER: No, no; not to-night. I want to be with you, my darling wife.

NORA: With the thought of your friend's death—   330

HELMER: You are right, it has affected us both. Something ugly has come between us—the
thought of the horrors of death. We must try and rid our minds of that. Until then—
we'll each go to our own room.

NORA: [*hanging on his neck*] Good-night, Torvald—Good-night!

HELMER: [*kissing her on the forehead*] Good-night, my little singing-bird. Sleep sound,   335
Nora. Now I'll read my letters through. [*He takes his letters and goes into his room,
shutting the door after him.*]

NORA: [*gropes distractedly about, seizes* HELMER'*s cloak, throws it round her, while she says in
quick, hoarse, spasmodic whispers*] Never to see him again. Never! Never! [*puts
her shawl over her head*] Never to see my children again, either—never again. Never!   340
Never!—Ah! the icy, black water—the unfathomable depths—if only it were over!

He has got it now—now he is reading it. Good-bye, Torvald and my children! [*She is about to rush out through the hall, when* HELMER *opens his door hurriedly and stands with an open letter in his hand.*]

HELMER: Nora!   345

NORA: Ah!—

HELMER: What's this? Do you know what's in this letter?

NORA: Yes, I know. Let me go! Let me get out!

HELMER: [*holding her back*] Where are you going?

NORA: [*trying to get free*] You shan't save me, Torvald!   350

HELMER: [*reeling*] True? Is this true, that I read here? Horrible! No, no—it's impossible that it can be true.

NORA: It's true. I have loved you above everything else in the world.

HELMER: Oh, don't let us have any silly excuses.

NORA: [*taking a step towards him*] Torvald—!   355

HELMER: Miserable creature—what have you done?

NORA: Let me go. You shall not suffer for my sake. You shall not take it upon yourself.

HELMER: No tragedy airs, please. [*locks the hall door*] Here you shall stay and give me an explanation. Do you understand what you've done? Answer me? Do you understand what you've done?   360

NORA: [*looks steadily at him and says with a growing look of coldness in her face*] Yes, now I am beginning to understand thoroughly.

HELMER: [*walking about the room*] What a horrible awakening! All these eight years—she who was my joy and pride—a hypocrite, a liar—worse, worse—a criminal! The unutterable ugliness of it all!—For shame! For shame! [NORA *is silent and looks* 365 *steadily at him. He stops in front of her.*] I ought to have suspected that something of the sort would happen. I ought to have foreseen it. All your father's lack of principle—be silent!—all your father's lack of principle has come out in you. No religion, no morality, no sense of duty—. How I'm punished for having winked at what he did! I did it for your sake, and this is how you repay me.   370

NORA: Yes, that's just it.

HELMER: Now you have destroyed all my happiness. You've ruined my entire future. It is horrible to think of! I'm in the power of an unscrupulous man; he can do what he likes with me, ask anything he likes of me, give me any orders he pleases—I dare not refuse. And I must sink to such miserable depths because of a silly woman!   375

NORA: When I'm out of the way, you'll be free.

HELMER: No fine speeches, please. Your father had always plenty of those ready, too. What good would it be to me if you were out of the way, as you say? Not the slightest. He can make the affair known everywhere; and if he does, I may be falsely suspected of having been a party to your criminal action. Very likely people will think I was 380 behind it all—that it was I who prompted you! and I have to thank you for all this— you whom I have cherished during the whole of our married life. Do you understand now what it is you have done to me?

NORA: [*coldly and quietly*] Yes.

HELMER: It's so incredible that I can't take it in. But we must come to some understanding. 385 Take off that shawl. Take it off, I tell you. I must try and appease him some way or another. The matter must be hushed up at any cost. And as for you and me, it must appear as if everything between us were just as before—but naturally only in the eyes of the world. You will still remain in my house, that is a matter of course. But I shall not allow you to bring up the children; I dare not trust them to you. To 390 think that I should be obliged to say so to one whom I have loved dearly, and whom I still—. No, that's all over. From this moment happiness is not the question; all that concerns us is to save the remains, the fragments, the appearance—

[*A ring is heard at the front-door bell.*]

HELMER: [*with a start*] What's that? So late? Can the worst—? Can he—? Hide yourself, Nora. Say you are ill.   395

[NORA *stands motionless.* HELMER *goes and unlocks the hall door.*]

MAID: [*half-dressed, comes to the door*] A letter for the mistress.

HELMER: Give it to me. [*takes the letter, and shuts the door*] Yes, it's from him. You shall not have it; I will read it myself.

NORA: Yes, read it.

HELMER: [*standing by the lamp*] I scarcely have the courage to do it. It may mean ruin for   400
both of us. No, I must know. [*tears open the letter, runs his eye over a few lines, looks at a paper enclosed, and gives a shout of joy*] Nora! [*She looks at him questioningly.*] Nora!—No, I must read it once again—. Yes, it's true! I'm saved! Nora, I'm saved!

NORA: And I?

HELMER: You, too, of course; we are both saved, both you and I. Look, he sends you your   405
bond back. He says he regrets and repents—that a happy change in his life—never mind what he says! We are saved, Nora! No one can do anything to you. Oh, Nora, Nora!—no, first I must destroy these hateful things. Let me see—. [*takes a look at the bond*] No, no, I won't look at it. The whole thing shall be nothing but a bad dream to me. [*tears up the bond and both letters, throws them all into the stove, and watches   410
them burn*] There—now it doesn't exist any longer. He says that since Christmas Eve you—. These must have been three dreadful days for you, Nora.

NORA: I have fought a hard fight these three days.

HELMER: And suffered agonies, and seen no way out but—. No, we won't call any of the horrors to mind. We'll only shout with joy, and keep saying, "It's all over! It's all   415
over!" Listen to me, Nora. You don't seem to realise that it is all over. What is this?—such a cold, set face! My poor little Nora, I quite understand; you don't feel that I have forgiven you. But it's true, Nora, I swear it; I've forgiven you everything. I know that what you did, you did out of love for me.

NORA: That's true.   420

HELMER: You have loved me as a wife ought to love her husband. Only you hadn't sufficient knowledge to judge of the means you used. But do you suppose you are any the less dear to me, because you don't understand how to act on your own responsibility? No, no; only lean on me; I will advise you and direct you. I should not be a man if this womanly helplessness did not just give you a double attractiveness in my eyes.   425
You mustn't think any more about the hard things I said in my first moment of consternation, when I thought everything was going to overwhelm me. I've forgiven you, Nora; I swear to you I've forgiven you.

NORA: Thank you for your forgiveness. [*She goes out through to the door to the right.*]

HELMER: No, don't go—[*looks in*] What are you doing in there?   430

NORA: [*from within*] Taking off my costume.

HELMER: [*standing at the open door*] Yes, do. Try and calm yourself, and make your mind easy again, my frightened little singing-bird. Be at rest, and feel secure; I have broad wings to shelter you under. [*walks up and down by the door*] How warm and cozy our home is, Nora. Here is shelter for you; here I'll protect you like a hunted dove that   435
I have saved from a hawk's claws: I'll bring peace to your poor beating heart. It will come, little by little, Nora, believe me. To-morrow morning you will look upon it all

quite differently; soon everything will be just as it was before. Very soon you won't
need me to assure you that I've forgiven you; you will feel the certainty that I've done
so. Can you suppose I should ever think of such a thing as repudiating you, or even   440
reproaching you? You have no idea what a true man's heart is like, Nora. There is
something so indescribably sweet and satisfying, to a man, in the knowledge that he
has forgiven his wife—forgiven her freely, and with all his heart. It seems as if that
had made her, as it were, doubly his own; he has given her a new life, so to speak;
and she has in a way become both wife and child to him. So you shall be for me   445
after this, my little scared, helpless darling. Have no anxiety about anything, Nora;
only be frank and open with me, and I'll serve as will and conscience both to you—.
What's this? Not gone to bed? Have you changed your clothes?
NORA: [*in everyday dress*] Yes, Torvald, I have changed my clothes now.
HELMER: But what for?—so late as this.   450
NORA: I shall not sleep to-night.
HELMER: But, my dear Nora—
NORA: [*looking at her watch*] It's not so very late. Sit down here, Torvald. You and I have
much to say to one another. [*She sits down at one side of the table.*]
HELMER: Nora—what's this?—this cold, set face!   455
NORA: Sit down. It'll take some time; I have a lot to talk over with you.
HELMER: [*sits down at the opposite side of the table*] You alarm me, Nora!—and I don't
understand you.
NORA: No, that's just it. You don't understand me, and I've never understood you either—
before to-night. No, you mustn't interrupt me. You must simply listen to what I say.   460
Torvald, this is a settling of accounts.
HELMER: What do you mean by that?
NORA: [*after a short silence*] Isn't there any thing that strikes you as strange in our sitting
here like this?
HELMER: What is that?   465
NORA: We've been married now eight years. Doesn't it occur to you that this is the first
time we two, you and I, husband and wife, have had a serious conversation?
HELMER: What do you mean by "serious"?
NORA: In all these eight years—longer than that—from the beginning of our acquaintance,
we've never exchanged a word on any serious subject.   470
HELMER: Was it likely that I would be continually and for ever telling you about worries
that you couldn't help me with?
NORA: I'm not speaking about business matters. I say that we have never sat down in earnest
together to try and get at the bottom of anything.
HELMER: But, dearest Nora, would it have been any good to you?   475
NORA: That's just it; you've never understood me. I have been greatly wronged, Torvald—
first by papa and then by you.
HELMER: What! By us two—by us two, who've loved you better than anyone else in the
world?
NORA: [*shaking her head*] You've never loved me. You've only thought it pleasant to be in   480
love with me.
HELMER: Nora, what do I hear you saying?
NORA: It's perfectly true, Torvald. When I was at home with papa, he told me his opinion
about everything, and so I had the same opinions; and if I differed from him I con-
cealed the fact, because he wouldn't have liked it. He called me his doll-child, and he   485
played with me just as I used to play with my dolls. And when I came to live with
you—
HELMER: What sort of an expression is that to use about our marriage?

NORA: [*undisturbed*] I mean that I was simply transferred from papa's hands into yours. You arranged everything according to your own taste, and so I got the same tastes as you—or else I pretended to. I'm really not quite sure which—I think sometimes the one and sometimes the other. When I look back on it, it seems to me as if I'd been living here like a poor woman—just from hand to mouth. I've existed merely to perform tricks for you, Torvald. But you would have it so. You and papa have committed a great sin against me. It's your fault that I have made nothing of my life. 490

HELMER: How unreasonable and how ungrateful you are, Nora! Have you not been happy here?

NORA: No, I have never been happy. I thought I was, but it's never really been so.

HELMER: Not—not happy!

NORA: No, only merry. And you've always been so kind to me. But our home has been nothing but a playroom. I've been your doll-wife, just as at home I was papa's doll-child; and here the children have been my dolls. I thought it great fun when you played with me, just as they thought it great fun when I played with them. That's what our marriage has been, Torvald. 500

HELMER: There is some truth in what you say—exaggerated and strained as your view of it is. But for the future it'll be different. Playtime shall be over, and lesson-time shall begin. 505

NORA: Whose lessons? Mine, or the children's?

HELMER: Both yours and the children's, my darling Nora.

NORA: Alas, Torvald, you're not the man to educate me into being a proper wife for you. 510

HELMER: And you can say that?

NORA: And I—how am I fitted to bring up the children?

HELMER: Nora!

NORA: Didn't you say so yourself a little while ago—that you dare not trust me to bring them up? 515

HELMER: In a moment of anger! Why do you pay any heed to that?

NORA: Indeed, you were perfectly right. I'm not fit for the task. There is another task I must undertake first. I must try and educate myself—you're not the man to help me in that. I must do that for myself. And that's why I'm going to leave you now.

HELMER: [*springing up*] What do you say? 520

NORA: I must stand quite alone, if I'm to understand myself and everything about me. It's for that reason that I cannot remain with you any longer.

HELMER: Now, Nora!

NORA: I'm going away from here now, at once. I'm sure Christine will take me in for the night— 525

HELMER: You're out of your mind! I won't allow it! I forbid you!

NORA: It's no use forbidding me anything any longer. I'll take with me what belongs to myself. I'll take nothing from you, either now or later.

HELMER: What sort of madness is this!

NORA: To-morrow I'll go home—I mean, to my old home. It will be easiest for me to find something to do there. 530

HELMER: You blind, foolish woman!

NORA: I must try and get some sense, Torvald.

HELMER: To desert your home, your husband, and your children! And you don't consider what people will say! 535

NORA: I can't consider that at all. I only know that it is necessary for me.

HELMER: It's shocking. This is how you would neglect your most sacred duties.

NORA: What do you consider my most sacred duties?

HELMER: Do I need to tell you that? Are they not your duties to your husband and your children?   540

NORA: I have other duties just as sacred.

HELMER: That you have not. What duties could those be?

NORA: Duties to myself.

HELMER: Before all else, you are a wife and a mother.

NORA: I don't believe that any longer. I believe that before all else I'm a reasonable human   545
being, just as you are—or, at all events, that I must try and become one. I know
quite well, Torvald, that most people would think you right, and that views of that
kind are to be found in books; but I can no longer content myself with what most
people say, or with what's found in books. I must think over things for myself and
get to understand them.   550

HELMER: Can't you understand your place in your own home? Haven't you a reliable guide
in such matters as that?—have you no religion?

NORA: I'm afraid, Torvald, I do not exactly know what religion is.

HELMER: What're you saying?

NORA: I know nothing but what the clergyman said, when I went to be confirmed. He   555
told us that religion was this, and that, and the other. When I'm away from all this,
and am alone, I'll look into that matter, too. I'll see if what the clergyman said is true,
or at all events if it is true for me.

HELMER: This is unheard of in a woman of your age! But if religion cannot touch you, let
me try and awaken your conscience. I suppose you have some moral sense? Or—   560
answer me—am I to think you have none?

NORA: I assure you, Torvald, that is not an easy question to answer. I really don't know.
The thing puzzles me altogether. I only know that you and I look at it in quite a
different light. I'm learning, too, that the law is quite another thing from what I
supposed; but I find it impossible to convince myself that the law is right. According   565
to it a woman has no right to spare her old dying father, or to save her husband's
life. I can't believe that.

HELMER: You talk like a child. You don't understand the conditions of the world in which
you live.

NORA: No, I don't. But now I'm going to try. I'm going to see if I can make out who is   570
right, the world or I.

HELMER: You're ill, Nora; you're delirious; I almost think you're out of your mind.

NORA: I've never felt my mind so clear and certain as to-night.

HELMER: And is it with a clear and certain mind that you forsake your husband and your
children?   575

NORA: Yes, it is.

HELMER: Then there is only one possible explanation.

NORA: What is that?

HELMER: You don't love me any more.

NORA: No, that's just it.   580

HELMER: Nora!—and you can say that?

NORA: It gives me great pain, Torvald, for you have always been so kind to me, but I can't
help it. I don't love you any more.

HELMER: [*regaining his composure*] Is that a clear and certain conviction, too?

NORA: Yes, absolutely clear and certain. That's the reason why I'll not stay here any longer.   585

HELMER: And can you tell me what I've done to forfeit your love?

NORA: Yes, indeed I can. It was to-night, when the wonderful thing did not happen; then
I saw you were not the man I had thought you.

HELMER: Explain yourself better—I don't understand you.

NORA: I've waited so patiently for eight years; for, goodness knows, I knew very well that   590
wonderful things don't happen every day. Then this horrible misfortune came upon
me; and then I felt quite certain that the wonderful thing was going to happen at last.
When Krogstad's letter was lying out there, never for a moment did I imagine that
you would consent to accept this man's conditions. I was so absolutely certain that you
would say to him: Publish the thing to the whole world. And when that was done—   595

HELMER: Yes, what then?—when I had exposed my wife to shame and disgrace?

NORA: When that was done, I was so absolutely certain, you would come forward and take
everything upon yourself, and say I'm the guilty one.

HELMER: Nora—!

NORA: You mean that I would never have accepted such a sacrifice on your part? No, of   600
course not. But what would my assurances have been worth against yours? That was
the wonderful thing which I hoped for and feared; and it was to prevent that, that
I wanted to kill myself.

HELMER: I would gladly work night and day for you, Nora—bear sorrow and want for
your sake. But no man would sacrifice his honour for the one he loves.   605

NORA: Millions of women have done it.

HELMER: Oh, you think and talk like a heedless child.

NORA: Maybe. But you neither think nor talk like the man I could bind myself to. As soon
as your fear was over—and it was not fear for what threatened me, but for what
might happen to you—when the whole thing was past, as far as you were concerned   610
it was exactly as if nothing at all had happened. Exactly as before, I was your little
skylark, your doll, which you would in future treat with doubly gentle care, because
it was so brittle and fragile. [*getting up*] Torvald—it was then it dawned on me that
for eight years I'd been living here with a strange man, and had borne him three
children—. Oh, I can't bear to think of it! I could tear myself into little bits!   615

HELMER: [*sadly*] I see, I see. An abyss has opened between us—there's no denying it. But,
Nora, wouldn't it be possible to fill it up?

NORA: As I am now, I'm no wife for you.

HELMER: I have it in me to become a different man.

NORA: Perhaps—if your doll is taken away from you.   620

HELMER: But to part!—to part from you! No, no. Nora, I can't understand that idea.

NORA: [*going out to the right*] That makes it all the more certain that it must be done. [*She
comes back with her cloak and hat and a small bag, which she puts on a chair by the
table.*]

HELMER: Nora, Nora, not now! Wait till to-morrow.   625

NORA: [*putting on her cloak*] I can't spend the night in a strange man's room.

HELMER: But can't we live here like brother and sister?

NORA: [*putting on her hat*] You know very well that wouldn't last long. [*puts the shawl round
her*] Good-bye, Torvald. I won't see the little ones. I know they are in better hands
than mine. As I am now, I can be of no use to them.   630

HELMER: But some day, Nora—some day?

NORA: How can I tell? I have no idea what is going to become of me.

HELMER: But you are my wife, whatever becomes of you.

NORA: Listen, Torvald. I have heard that when a wife deserts her husband's house, as I'm
doing now, he is legally freed from all obligations towards her. In any case I set you   635
free from all your obligations. You're not to feel yourself bound in the slightest way,
any more than I shall. There must be perfect freedom on both sides. See, here is your
ring back. Give me mine.

HELMER: That, too?

NORA: That, too.

HELMER: Here it is.

NORA: That's right. Now it's all over. I've put the keys here. The maids know all about everything in the house—better than I do. To-morrow, after I've left her, Christine will come here and pack up my own things that I brought with me from home. I'll have them sent to me.

HELMER: All over! all over!—Nora, shall you never think of me again?

NORA: I know I'll often think of you and the children and this house.

HELMER: May I write to you, Nora?

NORA: No—never. You must not do that.

HELMER: But at least let me send you—

NORA: Nothing—nothing—

HELMER: Let me help you if you're in want.

NORA: No. I can receive nothing from a stranger.

HELMER: Nora—can I never be anything more than a stranger to you?

NORA: [*taking her bag*] Ah, Torvald, the most miraculous thing of all would have to happen.

HELMER: Tell me what that would be!

NORA: Both you and I would have to be so changed that—Oh, Torvald, I don't believe any longer in miracles happening.

HELMER: But I will believe in it. Tell me? So changed that—?

NORA: That our life together would be a real wedlock. Good-bye. [*She goes out through the hall.*]

HELMER: [*sinks down on a chair at the door and buries his face in his hands*] Nora! Nora! [*looks round, and rises*] Empty. She is gone. [*A hope flashes across his mind.*] The most miraculous thing of all—?

[*The sound of a door shutting is heard from below.*]

The Importance of Being Earnest (1895)

Late-nineteenth- and early-twentieth-century movements in art and literature (symbolism, expressionism, and surrealism, for example) valued the subjective vision of artists and writers to interpret subjects rather than to reproduce them realistically. Many of these movements innovatively used abstraction and distortion to create evocative impressions or effects. In England, Walter Pater set forth the basic ideas of English aestheticism, which advocated the liberation of art from any function except to live life intensely and to provide sensuous pleasure ("art for art's sake"). But it was Oscar Wilde who became English aestheticism's best-known playwright and its most eloquent spokesman. In his 1889 essay, "The Decay of Lying," Wilde expresses the imaginative power of art to create independent of reality:

> [Art] is a veil, rather than a mirror. She has flowers that no forests know of, birds that no woodland possesses. She makes and unmakes many worlds, and can draw the moon from heaven with a scarlet thread. Hers are the 'forms more real than living man,'. . . . Lying, the telling of beautiful untrue things, is the proper aim of art.

The Importance of Being Earnest is Wilde's most successful play. Whereas some critics have seen the play as a flimsy farce that serves as an excuse for Wilde's witty epigrams, others have seen it as a penetratingly insightful social comedy. Wilde's earlier plays were somewhat conventional domestic comedies, featuring a secret being hidden from polite society, typified characters, somewhat clichéd dramatic situations, and sensational last-minute revelations. Although *The Importance of Being Earnest* uses these same devices, it lifts them to ridiculous levels.

The characters are obsessed with surface appearances, and Wilde both celebrates and satirizes their shallowness. He pokes fun at the pillars of society, the nobility, and the clergy (Lady Bracknell and Canon Chasuble) and exposes their moral standards as dull and hypocritical. Wilde contrasts these figures with delightful characters who "tell beautiful untrue things," which later become true.

Algernon invents a friend named "Bunbury," so that he may have an excuse to avoid dull social responsibilities. Jack invents a wicked brother named "Ernest" for much the same purpose and lives as Ernest in London, where he has become engaged to Gwendolen. Jack's ward Cecily invents (in her diary) a romance, engagement, break-up, and reconciliation with the irresistibly wicked Ernest, whom she has never met. Her fiction so appeals to her that when she meets Algernon, pretending to be Ernest, she accepts the events that she imagined as actually having taken place. When Gwendolen meets Cecily at Jack's country estate, confusion arises over who is engaged to "Ernest." Upon discovering that neither man is truly "Ernest," the women refuse to wed them until they are appropriately rechristened. By a delightfully contrived turn of events, Jack eventually proves to be named Ernest. The imagination's power to create models for life to imitate (rather than art imitating life) is clearly portrayed as the deceptions in the play, superior to truths, become true.

The Importance of Being Earnest
(1895)

Characters

JOHN WORTHING, J.P.[1]

LADY BRACKNELL

ALGERNON MONCRIEFF

HON. GWENDOLEN FAIRFAX[2]

REV. CANON CHASUBLE, D.D.[3]

CECILY CARDEW

MERRIMAN, *butler*

MISS PRISM, *governess*

LANE, *manservant*

ACT I ALGERNON MONCRIEFF'S *Flat in Half-Moon Street, W.*
ACT II *The Garden at the Manor House, Woolton*
ACT III *Drawing-Room of the Manor House, Woolton*

--------------------------------- ACT I ---------------------------------

SCENE———*Morning-room in* ALGERNON'S *flat in Half-Moon Street. The room is luxuriously and artistically furnished. The sound of a piano is heard in the adjoining room.* LANE *is arranging afternoon tea on the table, and after the music has ceased,* ALGERNON *enters.*

ALGERNON: Did you hear what I was playing, Lane?

LANE: I didn't think it polite to listen, sir.

ALGERNON: I'm sorry for that, for your sake. I don't play accurately—anyone can play accurately—but I play with wonderful expression. As far as the piano is concerned, sentiment is my forte. I keep science for Life.

LANE: Yes, sir.

ALGERNON: And, speaking of the science of Life, have you got the cucumber sandwiches cut for Lady Bracknell?

LANE: Yes, sir. [*hands them on a salver*]

5

---

[1] **J.P.** Justice of the Peace; indicates a country gentleman with extensive property.

[2] **Hon. Gwendolen Fairfax** identifies her as nobility and her father as a peer. Although "Bracknell" is the family, her surname is Fairfax.

[3] **Rev. Canon Chasuble, D.D.** identifies him as Rector of an Anglo-Catholic church with a Doctorate in theology.

ALGERNON: [*inspects them, takes two, and sits down on the sofa*] Oh! . . . by the way, Lane, I see   10
from your book that on Thursday night, when Lord Shoreman and Mr. Worthing were
dining with me, eight bottles of champagne are entered as having been consumed.

LANE: Yes, sir; eight bottles and a pint.

ALGERNON: Why is it that at a bachelor's establishment the servants invariably drink the
champagne? I ask merely for information.   15

LANE: I attribute it to the superior quality of the wine, sir. I have often observed that in
married households the champagne is rarely of a first-rate brand.

ALGERNON: Good heavens! Is marriage so demoralizing as that?

LANE: I believe it *is* a very pleasant state, sir. I have had very little experience of it myself
up to the present. I have only been married once. That was in consequence of a   20
misunderstanding between myself and a young woman.

ALGERNON: [*languidly*] I don't know that I am much interested in your family life, Lane.

LANE: No, sir; it is not a very interesting subject. I never think of it myself.

ALGERNON: Very natural, I am sure. That will do, Lane, thank you.

LANE: Thank you, sir. [LANE *goes out.*]   25

ALGERNON: Lane's views on marriage seem somewhat lax. Really, if the lower orders don't
set us a good example, what on earth is the use of them? They seem, as a class, to
have absolutely no sense of moral responsibility.

[*Enter* LANE.]

LANE: Mr. Ernest Worthing.

[*Enter* JACK. LANE *goes out.*]

ALGERNON: How are you, my dear Ernest? What brings you up to town?   30

JACK: Oh, pleasure, pleasure! What else should bring one anywhere? Eating as usual, I see,
Algy!

ALGERNON: [*stiffly*] I believe it is customary in good society to take some slight refresh-
ment at five o'clock. Where have you been since last Thursday?

JACK: [*sitting down on the sofa*] In the country.   35

ALGERNON: What on earth do you do there?

JACK: [*pulling off his gloves*] When one is in town one amuses oneself. When one is in the
country one amuses other people. It is excessively boring.

ALGERNON: And who are the people you amuse?

JACK: [*airily*] Oh, neighbors, neighbors.   40

ALGERNON: Got nice neighbors in your part of Shropshire?

JACK: Perfectly horrid! Never speak to one of them.

ALGERNON: How immensely you must amuse them! [*goes over and takes sandwich*] By the
way, Shropshire is your county, is it not?

JACK: Eh? Shropshire? Yes, of course. Hallo! Why all these cups? Why cucumber sand-   45
wiches? Why such reckless extravagance in one so young? Who is coming to tea?

ALGERNON: Oh! merely Aunt Augusta and Gwendolen.

JACK: How perfectly delightful!

ALGERNON: Yes, that is all very well; but I am afraid Aunt Augusta won't quite approve
of your being here.   50

JACK: May I ask why?

ALGERNON: My dear fellow, the way you flirt with Gwendolen is perfectly disgraceful. It
is almost as bad as the way Gwendolen flirts with you.

JACK: I am in love with Gwendolen. I have come up to town expressly to propose to her.

ALGERNON: I thought you had come up for pleasure? . . . I call that business.   55

JACK: How utterly unromantic you are!

ALGERNON: I really don't see anything romantic in proposing. It is very romantic to be in love. But there is nothing romantic about a definite proposal. Why, one may be accepted. One usually is, I believe. Then the excitement is all over. The very essence of romance is uncertainty. If ever I get married, I'll certainly try to forget the fact.   60

JACK: I have no doubt about that, dear Algy. The Divorce Court was specially invented for people whose memories are so curiously constituted.

ALGERNON: Oh! there is no use speculating on that subject. Divorces are made in Heaven—[JACK *puts out his hand to take a sandwich,* ALGERNON *at once interferes.*] Please don't touch the cucumber sandwiches. They are ordered specially for Aunt   65
Augusta. [*takes one and eats it*]

JACK: Well, you have been eating them all the time.

ALGERNON: That is quite a different matter. She is my aunt. [*takes plate from below*] Have some bread and butter. The bread and butter is for Gwendolen. Gwendolen is devoted to bread and butter.   70

JACK: [*advancing to table and helping himself*] And very good bread and butter it is too.

ALGERNON: Well, my dear fellow, you need not eat as if you were going to eat it all. You behave as if you were married to her already. You are not married to her already, and I don't think you will ever be.

JACK: Why on earth do you say that?   75

ALGERNON: Well, in the first place girls never marry the men they flirt with. Girls don't think it right.

JACK: Oh, that is nonsense!

ALGERNON: It isn't. It is a great truth. It accounts for the extraordinary number of bachelors that one sees all over the place. In the second place, I don't give my consent.   80

JACK: Your consent!

ALGERNON: My dear fellow, Gwendolen is my first cousin. And before I allow you to marry her, you will have to clear up the whole question of Cecily. [*rings bell*]

JACK: Cecily! What on earth do you mean? What do you mean, Algy, by Cecily? I don't know anyone of the name of Cecily.   85

[*Enter* LANE.]

ALGERNON: Bring me that cigarette case Mr. Worthing left in the smoking-room the last time he dined here.

LANE: Yes, sir. [LANE *goes out.*]

JACK: Do you mean to say you have had my cigarette case all this time? I wish to goodness you had let me know. I have been writing frantic letters to Scotland Yard about it. I   90
was very nearly offering a large reward.

ALGERNON: Well, I wish you would offer one. I happen to be more than usually hard up.

JACK: There is no good offering a large reward now that the thing is found.

[*Enter* LANE *with the cigarette case on a salver.* ALGERNON *takes it at once.* LANE *goes out.*]

ALGERNON: I think that is rather mean of you, Ernest, I must say. [*opens case and examines it*] However, it makes no matter, for, now that I look at the inscription, I find that   95
the thing isn't yours after all.

JACK: Of course it's mine. [*moving to him*] You have seen me with it a hundred times, and you have no right whatsoever to read what is written inside. It is a very ungentlemanly thing to read a private cigarette case.

ALGERNON: Oh! it is absurd to have a hard-and-fast rule about what one should read and   100
what one shouldn't. More than half of modern culture depends on what one shouldn't read.

JACK: I am quite aware of the fact, and I don't propose to discuss modern culture. It isn't the sort of thing one should talk of in private. I simply want my cigarette case back.

ALGERNON: Yes; but this isn't your cigarette case. This cigarette case is a present from   105
someone of the name of Cecily, and you said you didn't know anyone of that name.

JACK: Well, if you want to know, Cecily happens to be my aunt.

ALGERNON: Your aunt!

JACK: Yes. Charming old lady she is, too. Lives at Tunbridge Wells. Just give it back to
me, Algy.   110

ALGERNON: [*retreating to back of sofa*] But why does she call herself little Cecily if she is
your aunt and lives at Tunbridge Wells? [*reading*] "From little Cecily with her fondest love."

JACK: [*moving to sofa and kneeling upon it*] My dear fellow, what on earth is there in that?
Some aunts are tall, some aunts are not tall. That is a matter that surely an aunt may   115
be allowed to decide for herself. You seem to think that every aunt should be exactly
like your aunt! That is absurd! For Heaven's sake give me back my cigarette case.

[*follows* ALGERNON *round the room*]

ALGERNON: Yes. But why does your aunt call you her uncle? "From little Cecily, with her
fondest love to her dear Uncle Jack." There is no objection, I admit, to an aunt being   120
a small aunt, but why an aunt, no matter what her size may be, should call her own
nephew her uncle, I can't quite make out. Besides, your name isn't Jack at all; it's
Ernest.

JACK: It isn't Ernest; it's Jack.

ALGERNON: You have always told me it was Ernest. I have introduced you to everyone as   125
Ernest. You answer to the name of Ernest. You look as if your name was Ernest. You
are the most earnest-looking person I ever saw in my life. It is perfectly absurd your
saying that your name isn't Ernest. It's on your cards. Here is one of them. [*taking
it from case*] "Mr. Ernest Worthing, B 4, The Albany." I'll keep this as a proof your
name is Ernest if ever you attempt to deny it to me, or to Gwendolen, or to anyone   130
else. [*puts the card in his pocket*]

JACK: Well, my name is Ernest in town and Jack in the country, and the cigarette case was
given to me in the country.

ALGERNON: Yes, but that does not account for the fact that your small Aunt Cecily, who
lives at Tunbridge Wells, calls you her dear uncle. Come, old boy, you had much   135
better have the thing out at once.

JACK: My dear Algy, you talk exactly as if you were a dentist. It is very vulgar to talk like a
dentist when one isn't a dentist. It produces a false impression.

ALGERNON: Well, that is exactly what dentists always do. Now, go on! Tell me the whole
thing. I may mention that I have always suspected you of being a confirmed and   140
secret Bunburyist; and I am quite sure of it now.

JACK: Bunburyist? What on earth do you mean by a Bunburyist?

ALGERNON: I'll reveal to you the meaning of that incomparable expression as soon as you
are kind enough to inform me why you are Ernest in town and Jack in the country.

JACK: Well, produce my cigarette case first.   145

ALGERNON: Here it is. [*hands cigarette case*] Now produce your explanation, and pray
make it improbable. [*sits on sofa*]

JACK: My dear fellow, there is nothing improbable about my explanation at all. In fact it's
perfectly ordinary. Old Mr. Thomas Cardew, who adopted me when I was a little boy,
made me in his will guardian to his grand-daughter, Miss Cecily Cardew. Cecily, who   150

addresses me as her uncle from motives of respect that you could not possibly appreciate, lives at my place in the country under the charge of her admirable governess, Miss Prism.

ALGERNON: Where is that place in the country, by the way?

JACK: That is nothing to you, dear boy. You are not going to be invited. . . . I may tell you   155
candidly that the place is not in Shropshire.

ALGERNON: I suspected that, my dear fellow! I have Bunburyed all over Shropshire on two
separate occasions. Now, go on. Why are you Ernest in town and Jack in the country?

JACK: My dear Algy, I don't know whether you will be able to understand my real   160
motives. You are hardly serious enough. When one is placed in the position of
guardian, one has to adopt a very high moral tone on all subjects. It's one's duty
to do so. And as a high moral tone can hardly be said to conduce very much to
either one's health or one's happiness, in order to get up to town I have always
pretended to have a younger brother of the name of Ernest, who lives in the
Albany, and gets into the most dreadful scrapes. That, my dear Algy, is the whole   165
truth pure and simple.

ALGERNON: The truth is rarely pure and never simple. Modern life would be very tedious
if it were either, and modern literature a complete impossibility!

JACK: That wouldn't be at all a bad thing.

ALGERNON: Literary criticism is not your forte, my dear fellow. Don't try it. You should   170
leave that to people who haven't been at a University. They do it so well in the daily
papers. What you really are is a Bunburyist. I was quite right in saying you were a
Bunburyist. You are one of the most advanced Bunburyists I know.

JACK: What on earth do you mean?

ALGERNON: You have invented a very useful younger brother called Ernest, in order that   175
you may be able to come up to town as often as you like. I have invented an invaluable
permanent invalid called Bunbury, in order that I may be able to go down
into the country whenever I choose. Bunbury is perfectly invaluable. If it wasn't for
Bunbury's extraordinary bad health, for instance, I wouldn't be able to dine with
you at Willis' to-night, for I have been really engaged to Aunt Augusta for more than   180
a week.

JACK: I haven't asked you to dine with me anywhere to-night.

ALGERNON: I know. You are absurdly careless about sending out invitations. It is very
foolish of you. Nothing annoys people so much as not receiving invitations.

JACK: You had much better dine with your Aunt Augusta.   185

ALGERNON: I haven't the smallest intention of doing anything of the kind. To begin with,
I dined there on Monday, and once a week is quite enough to dine with one's own
relatives. In the second place, whenever I do dine there I am always treated as a
member of the family, and sent down with either no woman at all, or two. In the
third place, I know perfectly well whom she will place me next to, to-night. She will   190
place me next Mary Farquhar, who always flirts with her own husband across the
dinner-table. That is not very pleasant. Indeed, it is not even decent . . . and that
sort of thing is enormously on the increase. The amount of women in London who
flirt with their own husbands is perfectly scandalous. It looks so bad. It is simply
washing one's clean linen in public. Besides, now that I know you to be a con-   195
firmed Bunburyist I naturally want to talk to you about Bunburying. I want to tell
you the rules.

JACK: I'm not a Bunburyist at all. If Gwendolen accepts me, I am going to kill my brother.
Indeed, I think I'll kill him in any case. Cecily is a little too much interested in him.
It is rather a bore. So I am going to get rid of Ernest. And I strongly advise you to   200
do the same with Mr. . . . with your invalid friend who has the absurd name.

ALGERNON: Nothing will induce me to part with Bunbury, and if you ever get married, which seems to me extremely problematic, you will be very glad to know Bunbury. A man who marries without knowing Bunbury has a very tedious time of it.

JACK: That is nonsense. If I marry a charming girl like Gwendolen, and she is the only girl I ever saw in my life that I would marry, I certainly won't want to know Bunbury. 205

ALGERNON: Then your wife will. You don't seem to realize, that in married life three is company and two is none.

JACK: [*sententiously*] That, my dear young friend, is the theory that the corrupt French Drama[4] has been propounding for the last fifty years. 210

ALGERNON: Yes; and that the happy English home has proved in half the time.

JACK: For heaven's sake, don't try to be cynical. It's perfectly easy to be cynical.

ALGERNON: My dear fellow, it isn't easy to be anything now-a-days. There's such a lot of beastly competition about. [*The sound of an electric bell is heard.*] Ah! that must be Aunt Augusta. Only relatives, or creditors, ever ring in that Wagnerian[5] manner. 215 Now, if I get her out of the way for ten minutes, so that you can have an opportunity for proposing to Gwendolen, may I dine with you to-night at Willis'?

JACK: I suppose so, if you want to.

ALGERNON: Yes, but you must be serious about it. I hate people who are not serious about meals. It is so shallow of them. 220

[*Enter* LANE.]

LANE: Lady Bracknell and Miss Fairfax.

[ALGERNON *goes forward to meet them. Enter* LADY BRACKNELL *and* GWENDOLEN.]

LADY BRACKNELL: Good afternoon, dear Algernon, I hope you are behaving very well.

ALGERNON: I'm feeling very well, Aunt Augusta.

LADY BRACKNELL: That's not quite the same thing. In fact the two things rarely go together. [*Sees* JACK *and bows to him with icy coldness.*] 225

ALGERNON: [*to* GWENDOLEN] Dear me, you are smart![6]

GWENDOLEN: I am always smart! Aren't I, Mr. Worthing?

JACK: You're quite perfect, Miss Fairfax.

GWENDOLEN: Oh! I hope I am not that. It would leave no room for developments, and I intend to develop in many directions. 230

[GWENDOLEN *and* JACK *sit down together in the corner.*]

LADY BRACKNELL: I'm sorry if we are a little late, Algernon, but I was obliged to call on dear Lady Harbury. I hadn't been there since her poor husband's death. I never saw a woman so altered; she looks quite twenty years younger. And now I'll have a cup of tea, and one of those nice cucumber sandwiches you promised me.

ALGERNON: Certainly, Aunt Augusta. [*goes over to tea-table*] 235

LADY BRACKNELL: Won't you come and sit here, Gwendolen?

GWENDOLEN: Thanks, mamma, I'm quite comfortable where I am.

---

[4] **corrupt French Drama** the French were less adamant in censoring plays dealing with sexual misconduct than were the English
[5] **Wagnerian** pertaining to the operas of Richard Wagner (1813–1883), sometimes musically characterized as heavily dramatic and perhaps even imperious
[6] **smart** stylishly dressed

ALGERNON: [*picking up empty plate in horror*] Good heavens! Lane! Why are there no cucumber sandwiches? I ordered them specially.

LANE: [*gravely*] There were no cucumbers in the market this morning, sir. I went down twice. 240

ALGERNON: No cucumbers!

LANE: No, sir. Not even for ready money.

ALGERNON: That will do, Lane, thank you.

LANE: Thank you, sir. [*goes out*]

ALGERNON: I am greatly distressed, Aunt Augusta, about there being no cucumbers, not 245
even for ready money.

LADY BRACKNELL: It really makes no matter, Algernon. I had some crumpets with Lady Harbury, who seems to me to be living entirely for pleasure now.

ALGERNON: I hear her hair has turned quite gold from grief.

LADY BRACKNELL: It certainly has changed its color. From what cause I, of course, cannot 250
say. [ALGERNON *crosses and hands tea.*] Thank you. I've quite a treat for you to-night, Algernon. I am going to send you down with Mary Farquhar. She is such a nice woman, and so attentive to her husband. It's delightful to watch them.

ALGERNON: I am afraid, Aunt Augusta, I shall have to give up the pleasure of dining with you to-night after all. 255

LADY BRACKNELL: [*frowning*] I hope not, Algernon. It would put my table completely out.[7] Your uncle would have to dine upstairs. Fortunately he is accustomed to that.

ALGERNON: It is a great bore, and, I need hardly say, a terrible disappointment to me, but the fact is I have just had a telegram to say that my poor friend Bunbury is very ill again. [*He exchanges glances with* JACK.] They seem to think I should be with him. 260

LADY BRACKNELL: It is very strange. This Mr. Bunbury seems to suffer from curiously bad health.

ALGERNON: Yes; poor Bunbury is a dreadful invalid.

LADY BRACKNELL: Well, I must say, Algernon, that I think it is high time that Mr. Bunbury made up his mind whether he was going to live or to die. This shilly-shallying with 265
the question is absurd. Nor do I in any way approve of the modern sympathy with invalids. I consider it morbid. Illness of any kind is hardly a thing to be encouraged in others. Health is the primary duty of life. I am always telling that to your poor uncle, but he never seems to take much notice . . . as far as any improvement in his ailments goes. I should be much obliged if you would ask Mr. Bunbury, from me, 270
to be kind enough not to have a relapse on Saturday, for I rely on you to arrange my music for me. It is my last reception and one wants something that will encourage conversation, particularly at the end of the season when everyone has practically said whatever they had to say, which, in most cases, was probably not much.

ALGERNON: I'll speak to Bunbury, Aunt Augusta, if he is still conscious, and I think I can 275
promise you he'll be all right by Saturday. Of course the music is a great difficulty. You see, if one plays good music, people don't listen, and if one plays bad music people don't talk. But I'll run over the program I've drawn out, if you will kindly come into the next room for a moment.

LADY BRACKNELL: Thank you, Algernon. It is very thoughtful of you. [*rising, and following* 280
ALGERNON] I'm sure the program will be delightful, after a few expurgations. French songs I cannot possibly allow. People always seem to think that they are improper, and either look shocked, which is vulgar, or laugh, which is worse. But German sounds a thoroughly respectable language, and indeed, I believe is so. Gwendolen, you will accompany me. 285

---

[7] **put my table completely out** ruin the symmetry of the seating arrangements by creating an uneven number of men and women at the table

GWENDOLEN: Certainly, mamma.

[LADY BRACKNELL *and* ALGERNON *go into the music-room,* GWENDOLEN *remains behind.*]

JACK: Charming day it has been, Miss Fairfax.

GWENDOLEN: Pray don't talk to me about the weather, Mr. Worthing. Whenever people talk to me about the weather, I always feel quite certain that they mean something else. And that makes me so nervous.   290

JACK: I do mean something else.

GWENDOLEN: I thought so. In fact, I am never wrong.

JACK: And I would like to be allowed to take advantage of Lady Bracknell's temporary absence . . .

GWENDOLEN: I would certainly advise you to do so. Mamma has a way of coming back   295
suddenly into a room that I have often had to speak to her about.

JACK: [*nervously*] Miss Fairfax, ever since I met you I have admired you more than any girl . . . I have ever met since . . . I met you.

GWENDOLEN: Yes, I am quite aware of the fact. And I often wish that in public, at any rate, you had been more demonstrative. For me you have always had an irresistible   300
fascination. Even before I met you I was far from indifferent to you. [JACK *looks at her in amazement.*] We live, as I hope you know, Mr. Worthing, in an age of ideals. The fact is constantly mentioned in the more expensive monthly magazines, and has reached the provincial pulpits I am told: and my ideal has always been to love some one of the name of Ernest. There is something in that name that inspires absolute   305
confidence. The moment Algernon first mentioned to me that he had a friend called Ernest, I knew I was destined to love you.

JACK: You really love me, Gwendolen?

GWENDOLEN: Passionately!

JACK: Darling! You don't know how happy you've made me.   310

GWENDOLEN: My own Ernest!

JACK: But you don't really mean to say that you couldn't love me if my name wasn't Ernest?

GWENDOLEN: But your name is Ernest.

JACK: Yes, I know it is. But supposing it was something else? Do you mean to say you   315
couldn't love me then?

GWENDOLEN: [*glibly*] Ah! that is clearly a metaphysical speculation, and like most meta-physical speculations has very little reference at all to the actual facts of real life, as we know them.

JACK: Personally, darling, to speak quite candidly, I don't much care about the name of   320
Ernest . . . I don't think the name suits me at all.

GWENDOLEN: It suits you perfectly. It is a divine name. It has a music of its own. It pro-duces vibrations.

JACK: Well, really, Gwendolen, I must say that I think there are lots of other much nicer names. I think Jack, for instance, a charming name.   325

GWENDOLEN: Jack? . . . No, there is very little music in the name Jack, if any at all, indeed. It does not thrill. It produces absolutely no vibrations . . . I have known several Jacks, and they all, without exception, were more than usually plain. Besides, Jack is a notorious domesticity for John! And I pity any woman who is married to a man called John. She would probably never be allowed to know the entrancing   330
pleasure of a single moment's solitude. The only really safe name is Ernest.

JACK: Gwendolen, I must get christened at once—I mean we must get married at once. There is no time to be lost.

GWENDOLEN: Married, Mr. Worthing?

JACK: [*astounded*] Well . . . surely. You know that I love you, and you led me to believe,   335
Miss Fairfax, that you were not absolutely indifferent to me.

GWENDOLEN: I adore you. But you haven't proposed to me yet. Nothing has been said at
all about marriage. The subject has not even been touched on.

JACK: Well . . . may I propose to you now?

GWENDOLEN: I think it would be an admirable opportunity. And to spare you any pos-   340
sible disappointment, Mr. Worthing, I think it only fair to tell you quite frankly
beforehand that I am fully determined to accept you.

JACK: Gwendolen!

GWENDOLEN: Yes, Mr. Worthing, what have you got to say to me?

JACK: You know what I have got to say to you.   345

GWENDOLEN: Yes, but you don't say it.

JACK: Gwendolen, will you marry me? [*goes on his knees*]

GWENDOLEN: Of course I will, darling. How long you have been about it! I am afraid you
have had very little experience in how to propose.

JACK: My own one, I have never loved anyone in the world but you.   350

GWENDOLEN: Yes, but men often propose for practice. I know my brother Gerald does.
All my girl-friends tell me so. What wonderfully blue eyes you have, Ernest! They are
quite, quite blue. I hope you will always look at me just like that, especially when
there are other people present.

[*Enter* LADY BRACKNELL.]

LADY BRACKNELL: Mr. Worthing! Rise, sir, from this semi-recumbent posture. It is most   355
indecorous.

GWENDOLEN: Mamma! [*He tries to rise; she restrains him.*] I must beg you to retire. This
is no place for you. Besides, Mr. Worthing has not quite finished yet.

LADY BRACKNELL: Finished what, may I ask?

GWENDOLEN: I am engaged to Mr. Worthing, mamma. [*They rise together.*]   360

LADY BRACKNELL: Pardon me, you are not engaged to anyone. When you do become
engaged to someone, I, or your father, should his health permit him, will inform you
of the fact. An engagement should come on a young girl as a surprise, pleasant or
unpleasant, as the case may be. It is hardly a matter that she could be allowed to
arrange for herself. . . . And now I have a few questions to put to you, Mr. Worthing.   365
While I am making these inquiries, you, Gwendolen, will wait for me below in the
carriage.

GWENDOLEN: [*reproachfully*] Mamma!

LADY BRACKNELL: In the carriage, Gwendolen! [GWENDOLEN *goes to the door. She and*
JACK *blow kisses to each other behind* LADY BRACKNELL's *back.* LADY BRACKNELL   370
*looks vaguely about as if she could not understand what the noise was. Finally turns
round.*] Gwendolen, the carriage!

GWENDOLEN: Yes, mamma. [*goes out, looking back at* JACK]

LADY BRACKNELL: [*sitting down*] You can take a seat, Mr. Worthing. [*looks in her pocket
for note-book and pencil*]   375

JACK: Thank you, Lady Bracknell, I prefer standing.

LADY BRACKNELL: [*pencil and note-book in hand*] I feel bound to tell you that you are not
down on my list of eligible young men, although I have the same list as the dear
Duchess of Bolton has. We work together, in fact. However, I am quite ready to enter
your name, should your answers be what a really affectionate mother requires. Do   380
you smoke?

JACK: Well, yes, I must admit I smoke.

LADY BRACKNELL: I am glad to hear it. A man should always have an occupation of some kind. There are far too many idle men in London as it is. How old are you?

JACK: Twenty-nine.   385

LADY BRACKNELL: A very good age to be married at. I have always been of opinion that a man who desires to get married should know either everything or nothing. Which do you know?

JACK: [*after some hesitation*] I know nothing, Lady Bracknell.

LADY BRACKNELL: I am pleased to hear it. I do not approve of anything that tampers with   390
natural ignorance. Ignorance is like a delicate exotic fruit; touch it and the bloom is gone. The whole theory of modern education is radically unsound. Fortunately in England, at any rate, education produces no effect whatsoever. If it did, it would prove a serious danger to the upper classes, and probably lead to acts of violence in Grosvenor Square. What is your income?   395

JACK: Between seven and eight thousand a year.

LADY BRACKNELL: [*makes a note in her book*] In land, or in investments?

JACK: In investments, chiefly.

LADY BRACKNELL: That is satisfactory. What between the duties expected of one during one's lifetime, and the duties[8] exacted from one after one's death, land has ceased to   400
be either a profit or a pleasure. It gives one position, and prevents one from keeping it up. That's all that can be said about land.

JACK: I have a country house with some land, of course, attached to it, about fifteen hundred acres, I believe; but I don't depend on that for my real income. In fact, as far as I can make out, the poachers are the only people who make anything out of it.   405

LADY BRACKNELL: A country house! How many bedrooms? Well, that point can be cleared up afterwards. You have a town house, I hope? A girl with a simple, unspoiled nature, like Gwendolen, could hardly be expected to reside in the country.

JACK: Well, I own a house in Belgrave Square, but it is let by the year to Lady Bloxham. Of course, I can get it back whenever I like, at six months' notice.   410

LADY BRACKNELL: Lady Bloxham? I don't know her.

JACK: Oh, she goes about very little. She is a lady considerably advanced in years.

LADY BRACKNELL: Ah, now-a-days that is no guarantee of respectability of character. What number in Belgrave Square?

JACK: 149.   415

LADY BRACKNELL: [*shaking her head*] The unfashionable side. I thought there was something. However, that could easily be altered.

JACK: Do you mean the fashion, or the side?

LADY BRACKNELL: [*sternly*] Both, if necessary, I presume. What are your politics?

JACK: Well, I am afraid I really have none. I am a Liberal Unionist.[9]   420

LADY BRACKNELL: Oh, they count as Tories. They dine with us. Or come in the evening, at any rate. Now to minor matters. Are your parents living?

JACK: I have lost both my parents.

LADY BRACKNELL: Both? . . . That seems like carelessness. Who was your father? He was evidently a man of some wealth. Was he born in what the Radical papers call the   425
purple of commerce, or did he rise from the ranks of the aristocracy?

JACK: I am afraid I really don't know. The fact is, Lady Bracknell, I said I had lost my parents. It would be nearer the truth to say that my parents seem to have lost me . . . I don't actually know who I am by birth. I was . . . well, I was found.

[8] **duties estate taxes**; Wilde uses "duties" to set the two meanings of the word [responsibilities and taxes] off against each other
[9] **Liberal Unionist** member of the Liberal Party who opposed its leader, Gladstone, on many of his policies; therefore acceptable to the opposition party, the Tories

LADY BRACKNELL: Found!

JACK: The late Mr. Thomas Cardew, an old gentleman of a very charitable and kindly disposition, found me, and gave me the name of Worthing, because he happened to have a first-class ticket for Worthing in his pocket at the time. Worthing is a place in Sussex. It is a seaside resort.

LADY BRACKNELL: Where did the charitable gentleman who had a first-class ticket for this seaside resort find you?

JACK: [*gravely*] In a hand-bag.[10]

LADY BRACKNELL: A hand-bag?

JACK: [*very seriously*] Yes, Lady Bracknell. I was in a hand-bag—a somewhat large, black leather hand-bag, with handles to it—an ordinary hand-bag in fact.

LADY BRACKNELL: In what locality did this Mr. James, or Thomas, Cardew come across this ordinary hand-bag?

JACK: In the cloak-room at Victoria Station. It was given to him in mistake for his own.

LADY BRACKNELL: The cloak-room at Victoria Station?

JACK: Yes. The Brighton line.

LADY BRACKNELL: The line is immaterial. Mr. Worthing, I confess I feel somewhat bewildered by what you have just told me. To be born, or at any rate bred, in a hand-bag, whether it had handles or not, seems to me to display a contempt for the ordinary decencies of family life that remind one of the worst excesses of the French Revolution. And I presume you know what that unfortunate movement led to? As for the particular locality in which the hand-bag was found, a cloak-room at a railway station might serve to conceal a social indiscretion—has probably, indeed, been used for that purpose before now—but it could hardly be regarded as an assured basis for a recognized position in good society.

JACK: May I ask you then what you would advise me to do? I need hardly say I would do anything in the world to ensure Gwendolen's happiness.

LADY BRACKNELL: I would strongly advise you, Mr. Worthing, to try and acquire some relations as soon as possible, and to make a definite effort to produce at any rate one parent, of either sex, before the season is quite over.

JACK: Well, I don't see how I could possibly manage to do that. I can produce the hand-bag at any moment. It is in my dressing-room at home. I really think that should satisfy you, Lady Bracknell.

LADY BRACKNELL: Me, sir! What has it to do with me? You can hardly imagine that I and Lord Bracknell would dream of allowing our only daughter—a girl brought up with the utmost care—to marry into a cloak-room, and form an alliance with a parcel? Good morning, Mr. Worthing! [LADY BRACKNELL *sweeps out in majestic indignation.*]

JACK: Good morning!

[ALGERNON, *from the other room, strikes up the Wedding March.* JACK *looks perfectly furious and goes to the door.*]

JACK: For goodness' sake don't play that ghastly tune, Algy! How idiotic you are!

[*The music stops and* ALGERNON *enters cheerily.*]

ALGERNON: Didn't it go off all right, old boy? You don't mean to say Gwendolen refused you? I know it is a way she has. She is always refusing people. I think it is most ill-natured of her.

[10] **hand-bag** refers to a medium-size traveling bag (not a lady's small purse)

JACK: Oh, Gwendolen is as right as a trivet.[11] As far as she is concerned, we are engaged. Her mother is perfectly unbearable. Never met such a Gorgon . . . .[12] I don't really know what a Gorgon is like, but I am quite sure that Lady Bracknell is one. In any case, she is a monster, without being a myth, which is rather unfair. . . . I beg your   475 pardon, Algy, I suppose I shouldn't talk about your aunt in that way before you.

ALGERNON: My dear boy, I love hearing my relations abused. It is the only thing that makes me put up with them at all. Relations are simply a tedious pack of people, who haven't got the remotest knowledge of how to live, nor the smallest instinct about when to die.   480

JACK: Oh, that is nonsense!

ALGERNON: It isn't!

JACK: Well, I won't argue about the matter. You always want to argue about things.

ALGERNON: That is exactly what things were originally made for.

JACK: Upon my word, if I thought that, I'd shoot myself . . . . [*a pause*] You don't think there   485 is any chance of Gwendolen becoming like her mother in about a hundred and fifty years, do you, Algy?

ALGERNON: All women become like their mothers. That is their tragedy. No man does. That's his.

JACK: Is that clever?   490

ALGERNON: It is perfectly phrased! and quite as true as any observation in civilized life should be.

JACK: I am sick to death of cleverness. Everybody is clever now-a-days. You can't go anywhere without meeting clever people. The thing has become an absolute public nuisance. I wish to goodness we had a few fools left.   495

ALGERNON: We have.

JACK: I should extremely like to meet them. What do they talk about?

ALGERNON: The fools? Oh! about the clever people, of course.

JACK: What fools!

ALGERNON: By the way, did you tell Gwendolen the truth about your being Ernest in   500 town, and Jack in the country?

JACK: [*in a very patronizing manner*] My dear fellow, the truth isn't quite the sort of thing one tells to a nice, sweet, refined girl. What extraordinary ideas you have about the way to behave to a woman!

ALGERNON: The only way to behave to a woman is to make love to her, if she is pretty,   505 and to someone else if she is plain.

JACK: Oh, that is nonsense.

ALGERNON: What about your brother? What about the profligate Ernest?

JACK: Oh, before the end of the week I shall have got rid of him. I'll say he died in Paris of apoplexy. Lots of people die of apoplexy, quite suddenly, don't they?   510

ALGERNON: Yes, but it's hereditary, my dear fellow. It's a sort of thing that runs in families. You had much better say a severe chill.

JACK: You are sure a severe chill isn't hereditary, or anything of that kind?

ALGERNON: Of course it isn't!

JACK: Very well, then. My poor brother Ernest is carried off suddenly in Paris, by a severe   515 chill. That gets rid of him.

---

[11] **right as a trivet** perfectly fine; stable and reliable
[12] **Gorgon** in Greek mythology, the Gorgons were three sisters so hideous that to look upon any one of them turned a man into stone

ALGERNON: But I thought you said that . . . Miss Cardew was a little too much interested in your poor brother Ernest? Won't she feel his loss a good deal?

JACK: Oh, that is all right. Cecily is not a silly, romantic girl, I am glad to say. She has got a capital appetite, goes for long walks, and pays no attention at all to her lessons.   520

ALGERNON: I would rather like to see Cecily.

JACK: I will take very good care you never do. She is excessively pretty, and she is only just eighteen.

ALGERNON: Have you told Gwendolen yet that you have an excessively pretty ward who is only just eighteen?   525

JACK: Oh! one doesn't blurt these things out to people. Cecily and Gwendolen are perfectly certain to be extremely great friends. I'll bet you anything you like that half an hour after they have met, they will be calling each other sister.

ALGERNON: Women only do that when they have called each other a lot of other things first. Now, my dear boy, if we want to get a good table at Willis', we really must go   530 and dress. Do you know it is nearly seven?

JACK: [irritably] Oh! it always is nearly seven.

ALGERNON: Well, I'm hungry.

JACK: I never knew you when you weren't . . . .

ALGERNON: What shall we do after dinner? Go to a theatre?   535

JACK: Oh, no! I loathe listening.

ALGERNON: Well, let us go to the Club?

JACK: Oh, no! I hate talking.

ALGERNON: Well, we might trot round to the Empire[13] at ten?

JACK: Oh, no! I can't bear looking at things. It is so silly.   540

ALGERNON: Well, what shall we do?

JACK: Nothing!

ALGERNON: It is awfully hard work doing nothing. However, I don't mind hard work where there is no definite object of any kind.

[*Enter* LANE.]

LANE: Miss Fairfax.   545

[*Enter* GWENDOLEN. LANE *goes out.*]

ALGERNON: Gwendolen, upon my word!

GWENDOLEN: Algy, kindly turn your back. I have something very particular to say to Mr. Worthing.

ALGERNON: Really, Gwendolen, I don't think I can allow this at all.

GWENDOLEN: Algy, you always adopt a strictly immoral attitude towards life. You are not   550 quite old enough to do that.

[ALGERNON *retires to the fireplace.*]

JACK: My own darling!

GWENDOLEN: Ernest, we may never be married. From the expression on mamma's face I fear we never shall. Few parents now-a-days pay any regard to what their children say to them. The old-fashioned respect for the young is fast dying out. Whatever influ-   555 ence I ever had over mamma, I lost at the age of three. But although she may prevent

---

[13] **Empire** theatre specializing in popular music and farce

us from becoming man and wife, and I may marry someone else, and marry often, nothing that she can possibly do can alter my eternal devotion to you.

JACK: Dear Gwendolen!

GWENDOLEN: The story of your romantic origin, as related to me by mamma, with 560 unpleasing comments, has naturally stirred the deeper fibers of my nature. Your Christian name[14] has an irresistible fascination. The simplicity of your character makes you exquisitely incomprehensible to me. Your town address at the Albany I have. What is your address in the country?

JACK: The Manor House, Woolton, Hertfordshire. 565

[ALGERNON, *who has been carefully listening, smiles to himself, and writes the address on his shirt-cuff. Then picks up the Railway Guide.*]

GWENDOLEN: There is a good postal service, I suppose? It may be necessary to do something desperate. That, of course, will require serious consideration. I will communicate with you daily.

JACK: My own one!

GWENDOLEN: How long do you remain in town? 570

JACK: Till Monday.

GWENDOLEN: Good! Algy, you may turn round now.

ALGERNON: Thanks, I've turned round already.

GWENDOLEN: You may also ring the bell.

JACK: You will let me see you to your carriage, my own darling? 575

GWENDOLEN: Certainly.

JACK: [*to* LANE, *who now enters.*] I will see Miss Fairfax out.

LANE: Yes, sir.

[JACK *and* GWENDOLEN *go off.* LANE *presents several letters on a salver to* ALGERNON. *It is to be surmised that they are bills, as* ALGERNON, *after looking at the envelopes, tears them up.*]

ALGERNON: A glass of sherry, Lane.

LANE: Yes, sir.

ALGERNON: To-morrow, Lane, I'm going Bunburying. 580

LANE: Yes, sir.

ALGERNON: I shall probably not be back till Monday. You can put up my dress clothes, my smoking jacket, and all the Bunbury suits . . .

LANE: Yes, sir. [*handing sherry*] 585

ALGERNON: I hope to-morrow will be a fine day, Lane.

LANE: It never is, sir.

ALGERNON: Lane, you're a perfect pessimist.

LANE: I do my best to give satisfaction, sir.

[*Enter* JACK. LANE *goes off.*]

JACK: There's a sensible, intellectual girl! the only girl I ever cared for in my life. [ALGERNON 590 *is laughing immoderately.*] What on earth are you so amused at?

ALGERNON: Oh, I'm a little anxious about poor Bunbury, that's all.

JACK: If you don't take care, your friend Bunbury will get you into a serious scrape some day.

---

[14] **Your Christian name** first name given in the sacrament of baptism (christening)

ALGERNON: I love scrapes. They are the only things that are never serious.

JACK: Oh, that's nonsense, Algy. You never talk anything but nonsense. 595

ALGERNON: Nobody ever does.

> [JACK *looks indignantly at him, and leaves the room.* ALGERNON *lights a ciga-rette, reads his shirt-cuff, and smiles.*]

CURTAIN

ACT II

SCENE————*Garden at the Manor House. A flight of gray stone steps leads up to the house. The garden, an old-fashioned one, full of roses. Time of year, July. Basket chairs, and a table covered with books, are set under a large yew tree.* MISS PRISM *discovered seated at the table.* CECILY *is at the back watering flowers.*

MISS PRISM: [*calling*] Cecily, Cecily! Surely such a utilitarian occupation as the watering of flowers is rather Moulton's duty than yours? Especially at a moment when intellectual pleasures await you. Your German grammar is on the table. Pray open it at page fifteen. We will repeat yesterday's lesson.

CECILY: [*coming over very slowly*] But I don't like German. It isn't at all a becoming language. 5 I know perfectly well that I look quite plain after my German lesson.

MISS PRISM: Child, you know how anxious your guardian is that you should improve yourself in every way. He laid particular stress on your German, as he was leaving for town yesterday. Indeed, he always lays stress on your German when he is leaving for town.

CECILY: Dear Uncle Jack is so very serious! Sometimes he is so serious that I think he 10 cannot be quite well.

MISS PRISM: [*drawing herself up*] Your guardian enjoys the best of health, and his gravity of demeanor is especially to be commended in one so comparatively young as he is. I know no one who has a higher sense of duty and responsibility.

CECILY: I suppose that is why he often looks a little bored when we three are together. 15

MISS PRISM: Cecily! I am surprised at you. Mr. Worthing has many troubles in his life. Idle merriment and triviality would be out of place in his conversation. You must remember his constant anxiety about that unfortunate young man, his brother.

CECILY: I wish Uncle Jack would allow that unfortunate young man, his brother, to come down here sometimes. We might have a good influence over him, Miss Prism. I am 20 sure you certainly would. You know German, and geology, and things of that kind influence a man very much. [CECILY *begins to write in her diary.*]

MISS PRISM: [*shaking her head*] I do not think that even I could produce any effect on a character that, according to his own brother's admission, is irretrievably weak and vacillating. Indeed, I am not sure that I would desire to reclaim him. I am not in 25 favor of this modern mania for turning bad people into good people at a moment's notice. As a man sows so let him reap. You must put away your diary, Cecily. I really don't see why you should keep a diary at all.

CECILY: I keep a diary in order to enter the wonderful secrets of my life. If I didn't write them down I should probably forget all about them. 30

MISS PRISM: Memory, my dear Cecily, is the diary that we all carry about with us.

CECILY: Yes, but it usually chronicles the things that have never happened, and couldn't possibly have happened. I believe that Memory is responsible for nearly all the three-volume novels that Mudie[15] sends us.

MISS PRISM: Do not speak slightingly of the three-volume novel, Cecily. I wrote one 35
myself in earlier days.

CECILY: Did you really, Miss Prism? How wonderfully clever you are! I hope it did not end happily? I don't like novels that end happily. They depress me so much.

MISS PRISM: The good ended happily, and the bad unhappily. That is what Fiction means. 40

CECILY: I suppose so. But it seems very unfair. And was your novel ever published?

MISS PRISM: Alas! no. The manuscript unfortunately was abandoned. I use the word in the sense of lost or mislaid. To your work, child, these speculations are profitless.

CECILY: [*smiling*] But I see dear Dr. Chasuble coming up through the garden.

MISS PRISM: [*rising and advancing*] Dr. Chasuble! This is indeed a pleasure. 45

[*Enter* CANON CHASUBLE.]

CHASUBLE: And how are we this morning? Miss Prism, you are, I trust, well?

CECILY: Miss Prism has just been complaining of a slight headache. I think it would do her so much good to have a short stroll with you in the park, Dr. Chasuble.

MISS PRISM: Cecily, I have not mentioned anything about a headache.

CECILY: No, dear Miss Prism, I know that, but I felt instinctively that you had a headache. 50
Indeed I was thinking about that, and not about my German lesson when the Rector came in.

CHASUBLE: I hope, Cecily, you are not inattentive.

CECILY: Oh, I am afraid I am.

CHASUBLE: That is strange. Were I fortunate enough to be Miss Prism's pupil, I would 55
hang upon her lips. [MISS PRISM *glares*.] I spoke metaphorically.—My metaphor was drawn from bees. Ahem! Mr. Worthing, I suppose, has not returned from town yet?

MISS PRISM: We do not expect him till Monday afternoon.

CHASUBLE: Ah yes, he usually likes to spend his Sunday in London. He is not one of those whose sole aim is enjoyment, as, by all accounts, that unfortunate young man, 60
his brother, seems to be. But I must not disturb Egeria[16] and her pupil any longer.

MISS PRISM: Egeria? My name is Lætitia, Doctor.

CHASUBLE: [*bowing*] A classical allusion merely, drawn from the Pagan authors. I shall see you both no doubt at Evensong.

MISS PRISM: I think, dear Doctor, I will have a stroll with you. I find I have a headache 65
after all, and a walk might do it good.

CHASUBLE: With pleasure, Miss Prism, with pleasure. We might go as far as the schools and back.

MISS PRISM: That would be delightful. Cecily, you will read your Political Economy in my absence. The chapter on the Fall of the Rupee you may omit. It is somewhat too 70
sensational. Even these metallic problems have their melodramatic side. [*goes down the garden with* DR. CHASUBLE]

---

[15] **Mudie** popular lending-library service of the day
[16] **Egeria** according to Roman legend, a water-nymph goddess who inspired and guided Numa Pompilius (the successor of Romulus) in the kingship of Rome; she taught him wise legislation

CECILY: [*picks up books and throws them back on table*] Horrid Political Economy! Horrid Geography! Horrid, horrid German!

[*Enter* MERRIMAN *with a card on a salver.*]

MERRIMAN: Mr. Ernest Worthing has just driven over from the station. He has brought   75
his luggage with him.

CECILY: [*takes the card and reads it*] "Mr. Ernest Worthing, B 4, The Albany, W." Uncle Jack's brother! Did you tell him Mr. Worthing was in town?

MERRIMAN: Yes, Miss. He seemed very much disappointed. I mentioned that you and Miss Prism were in the garden. He said he was anxious to speak to you privately for   80
a moment.

CECILY: Ask Mr. Ernest Worthing to come here. I suppose you had better talk to the housekeeper about a room for him.

MERRIMAN: Yes, Miss. [MERRIMAN *goes off.*]

CECILY: I have never met any really wicked person before. I feel rather frightened. I am so   85
afraid he will look just like everyone else.

[*Enter* ALGERNON, *very gay and debonair.*]

He does!

ALGERNON: [*raising his hat*] You are my little Cousin Cecily, I'm sure.

CECILY: You are under some strange mistake. I am not little. In fact, I am more than usually tall for my age. [ALGERNON *is rather taken aback.*] But I am your Cousin Cecily.   90
You, I see from your card, are Uncle Jack's brother, my Cousin Ernest, my wicked Cousin Ernest.

ALGERNON: Oh! I am not really wicked at all, Cousin Cecily. You mustn't think that I am wicked.

CECILY: If you are not, then you have certainly been deceiving us all in a very inexcusable   95
manner. I hope you have not been leading a double life, pretending to be wicked and being really good all the time. That would be hypocrisy.

ALGERNON: [*looks at her in amazement*] Oh! Of course I have been rather reckless.

CECILY: I am glad to hear it.

ALGERNON: In fact, now you mention the subject, I have been very bad in my own small   100
way.

CECILY: I don't think you should be so proud of that, though I am sure it must have been very pleasant.

ALGERNON: It is much pleasanter being here with you.

CECILY: I can't understand how you are here at all. Uncle Jack won't be back till Monday   105
afternoon.

ALGERNON: That is a great disappointment. I am obliged to go up by the first train on Monday morning. I have a business appointment that I am anxious . . . to miss.

CECILY: Couldn't you miss it anywhere but in London?

ALGERNON: No; the appointment is in London.   110

CECILY: Well, I know, of course, how important it is not to keep a business engagement, if one wants to retain any sense of the beauty of life, but still I think you had better wait till Uncle Jack arrives. I know he wants to speak to you about your emigrating.

ALGERNON: About my what?

CECILY: Your emigrating. He has gone up to buy your outfit.   115

ALGERNON: I certainly wouldn't let Jack buy my outfit. He has no taste in neckties at all.

CECILY: I don't think you will require neckties. Uncle Jack is sending you to Australia.

ALGERNON: Australia! I'd sooner die.

CECILY: Well, he said at dinner on Wednesday night, that you would have to choose
between this world, the next world, and Australia.   120

ALGERNON: Oh, well! The accounts I have received of Australia and the next world, are
not particularly encouraging. This world is good enough for me, Cousin Cecily.

CECILY: Yes, but are you good enough for it?

ALGERNON: I'm afraid I'm not that. That is why I want you to reform me. You might
make that your mission, if you don't mind, Cousin Cecily.   125

CECILY: I'm afraid I've not time, this afternoon.

ALGERNON: Well, would you mind my reforming myself this afternoon?

CECILY: That is rather quixotic of you. But I think you should try.

ALGERNON: I will. I feel better already.

CECILY: You are looking a little worse.   130

ALGERNON: That is because I am hungry.

CECILY: How thoughtless of me. I should have remembered that when one is going to lead
an entirely new life, one requires regular and wholesome meals. Won't you come in?

ALGERNON: Thank you. Might I have a buttonhole[17] first? I never have any appetite unless
I have a buttonhole first.   135

CECILY: A Maréchal Niel?[18] [*picks up scissors*]

ALGERNON: No, I'd sooner have a pink rose.

CECILY: Why? [*cuts a flower*]

ALGERNON: Because you are like a pink rose, Cousin Cecily.

CECILY: I don't think it can be right for you to talk to me like that. Miss Prism never says   140
such things to me.

ALGERNON: Then Miss Prism is a short-sighted old lady. [CECILY *puts the rose in his buttonhole.*] You are the prettiest girl I ever saw.

CECILY: Miss Prism says that all good looks are a snare.

ALGERNON: They are a snare that every sensible man would like to be caught in.   145

CECILY: Oh! I don't think I would care to catch a sensible man. I shouldn't know what to
talk to him about.

[*They pass into the house.* MISS PRISM *and* DR. CHASUBLE *return.*]

MISS PRISM: You are too much alone, dear Dr. Chasuble. You should get married. A misanthrope I can understand—a womanthrope,[19] never!

CHASUBLE: [*with a scholar's shudder*] Believe me, I do not deserve so neologistic a phrase. The   150
precept as well as the practice of the Primitive Church was distinctly against matrimony.

MISS PRISM: [*sententiously*] That is obviously the reason why the Primitive Church has not
lasted up to the present day. And you do not seem to realize, dear Doctor, that by
persistently remaining single, a man converts himself into a permanent public temptation. Men should be careful; this very celibacy leads weaker vessels astray.   155

CHASUBLE: But is a man not equally attractive when married?

MISS PRISM: No married man is ever attractive except to his wife.

CHASUBLE: And often, I've been told, not even to her.

MISS PRISM: That depends on the intellectual sympathies of the woman. Maturity can always
be depended on. Ripeness can be trusted. Young women are green. [CHASUBLE *starts.*]   160
I spoke horticulturally. My metaphor was drawn from fruits. But where is Cecily?

CHASUBLE: Perhaps she followed us to the schools.

---

[17] **buttonhole** flower worn in the lapel
[18] **Maréchal Niel** pale yellow rose named in honor of a French general
[19] **Womanthrope** Ms. Prism's word for one who hates women; a "misanthrope" hates all human kind

[*Enter* JACK *slowly from the back of the garden. He is dressed in the deepest mourning, with crape hat-band and black gloves.*]

MISS PRISM: Mr. Worthing!

CHASUBLE: Mr. Worthing?

MISS PRISM: This is indeed a surprise. We did not look for you till Monday afternoon.   165

JACK: [*Shakes* MISS PRISM's *hand in a tragic manner.*] I have returned sooner than I expected. Dr. Chasuble, I hope you are well?

CHASUBLE: Dear Mr. Worthing, I trust this garb of woe does not betoken some terrible calamity?

JACK: My brother.   170

MISS PRISM: More shameful debts and extravagance?

CHASUBLE: Still leading his life of pleasure?

JACK: [*shaking his head*] Dead.

CHASUBLE: Your brother Ernest dead?

JACK: Quite dead.   175

MISS PRISM: What a lesson for him! I trust he will profit by it.

CHASUBLE: Mr. Worthing, I offer you my sincere condolence. You have at least the consolation of knowing that you were always the most generous and forgiving of brothers.

JACK: Poor Ernest! He had many faults, but it is a sad, sad blow.

CHASUBLE: Very sad indeed. Were you with him at the end?   180

JACK: No. He died abroad; in Paris, in fact. I had a telegram last night from the manager of the Grand Hotel.

CHASUBLE: Was the cause of death mentioned?

JACK: A severe chill, it seems.

MISS PRISM: As a man sows, so shall he reap.   185

CHASUBLE: [*raising his hand*] Charity, dear Miss Prism, charity! None of us are perfect. I myself am peculiarly susceptible to draughts. Will the interment take place here?

JACK: No. He seems to have expressed a desire to be buried in Paris.

CHASUBLE: In Paris! [*shakes his head*] I fear that hardly points to any very serious state of mind at the last. You would no doubt wish me to make some slight allusion to this   190
tragic domestic affliction next Sunday. [JACK *presses his hand convulsively.*] My sermon on the meaning of the manna[20] in the wilderness can be adapted to almost any occasion, joyful, or, as in the present case, distressing. [*All sigh.*] I have preached it at harvest celebrations, christenings, confirmations, on days of humiliation and festal days. The last time I delivered it was in the Cathedral, as a charity sermon on   195
behalf of the Society for the Prevention of Discontent among the Upper Orders. The Bishop, who was present, was much struck by some of the analogies I drew.

JACK: Ah, that reminds me, you mentioned christenings I think, Dr. Chasuble? I suppose you know how to christen all right? [CHASUBLE *looks astounded.*] I mean, of course, you are continually christening, aren't you?   200

MISS PRISM: It is, I regret to say, one of the Rector's most constant duties in this parish. I have often spoken to the poorer classes on the subject. But they don't seem to know what thrift is.

CHASUBLE: But is there any particular infant in whom you are interested, Mr. Worthing? Your brother was, I believe, unmarried, was he not?   205

JACK: Oh, yes.

---

[20] **manna** miraculous "bread from heaven" (Exodus 16)

MISS PRISM: [*bitterly*] People who live entirely for pleasure usually are.

JACK: But it is not for any child, dear Doctor. I am very fond of children. No! the fact is, I would like to be christened myself, this afternoon, if you have nothing better to do.

CHASUBLE: But surely, Mr. Worthing, you have been christened already? 210

JACK: I don't remember anything about it.

CHASUBLE: But have you any grave doubts on the subject?

JACK: I certainly intend to have. Of course, I don't know if the thing would bother you in any way, or if you think I am a little too old now.

CHASUBLE: Not at all. The sprinkling, and, indeed, the immersion of adults is a perfectly 215 canonical practice.

JACK: Immersion!

CHASUBLE: You need have no apprehensions. Sprinkling is all that is necessary, or indeed I think advisable. Our weather is so changeable. At what hour would you wish the ceremony performed? 220

JACK: Oh, I might trot round about five if that would suit you.

CHASUBLE: Perfectly, perfectly! In fact I have two similar ceremonies to perform at that time. A case of twins that occurred recently in one of the outlying cottages on your own estate. Poor Jenkins the carter, a most hard-working man.

JACK: Oh! I don't see much fun in being christened along with other babies. It would be 225 childish. Would half-past five do?

CHASUBLE: Admirably! Admirably! [*takes out watch*] And now, dear Mr. Worthing, I will not intrude any longer into a house of sorrow. I would merely beg you not to be too much bowed down by grief. What seem to us bitter trials at the moment are often blessings in disguise. 230

MISS PRISM: This seems to me a blessing of an extremely obvious kind.

[*Enter* CECILY *from the house.*]

CECILY: Uncle Jack! Oh, I am pleased to see you back. But what horrid clothes you have on! Do go and change them.

MISS PRISM: Cecily!

CHASUBLE: My child! My child! 235

[CECILY *goes towards* JACK; *he kisses her brow in a melancholy manner.*]

CECILY: What is the matter, Uncle Jack? Do look happy! You look as if you had a toothache and I have such a surprise for you. Who do you think is in the dining-room? Your brother!

JACK: Who?

CECILY: Your brother Ernest. He arrived about half an hour ago. 240

JACK: What nonsense! I haven't got a brother.

CECILY: Oh, don't say that. However badly he may have behaved to you in the past, he is still your brother. You couldn't be so heartless as to disown him. I'll tell him to come out. And you will shake hands with him, won't you, Uncle Jack? [*runs back into the house*]

CHASUBLE: These are very joyful tidings.

MISS PRISM: After we had all been resigned to his loss, his sudden return seems to me 245 peculiarly distressing.

JACK: My brother is in the dining-room? I don't know what it all means. I think it is perfectly absurd.

[*Enter* ALGERNON *and* CECILY *hand in hand. They come slowly up to* JACK.]

JACK: Good heavens! [*motions* ALGERNON *away*] 250

ALGERNON: Brother John, I have come down from town to tell you that I am very sorry for all the trouble I have given you, and that I intend to lead a better life in the future.

[JACK *glares at him and does not take his hand.*]

CECILY: Uncle Jack, you are not going to refuse your own brother's hand?

JACK: Nothing will induce me to take his hand. I think his coming down here disgraceful. 255
He knows perfectly well why.

CECILY: Uncle Jack, do be nice. There is some good in everyone. Ernest has just been tell-ing me about his poor invalid friend Mr. Bunbury, whom he goes to visit so often. And surely there must be much good in one who is kind to an invalid, and leaves the pleasures of London to sit by a bed of pain. 260

JACK: Oh! he has been talking about Bunbury, has he?

CECILY: Yes, he has told me all about poor Mr. Bunbury, and his terrible state of health.

JACK: Bunbury! Well, I won't have him talk to you about Bunbury or about anything else. It is enough to drive one perfectly frantic.

ALGERNON: Of course I admit that the faults were all on my side. But I must say that I 265
think that Brother John's coldness to me is peculiarly painful. I expected a more enthusiastic welcome, especially considering it is the first time I have come here.

CECILY: Uncle Jack, if you don't shake hands with Ernest I will never forgive you.

JACK: Never forgive me?

CECILY: Never, never, never! 270

JACK: Well, this is the last time I shall ever do it. [*shakes hands with* ALGERNON *and glares*]

CHASUBLE: It's pleasant, is it not, to see so perfect a reconciliation? I think we might leave the two brothers together.

MISS PRISM: Cecily, you will come with us. 275

CECILY: Certainly, Miss Prism. My little task of reconciliation is over.

CHASUBLE: You have done a beautiful action to-day, dear child.

MISS PRISM: We must not be premature in our judgments.

CECILY: I feel very happy.

[*They all go off except* JACK *and* ALGERNON.]

JACK: You young scoundrel, Algy, you must get out of this place as soon as possible. I don't 280
allow any Bunburying here.

[*Enter* MERRIMAN.]

MERRIMAN: I have put Mr. Ernest's things in the room next to yours, sir. I suppose that is all right?

JACK: What?

MERRIMAN: Mr. Ernest's luggage, sir. I have unpacked it and put it in the room next to 285
your own.

JACK: His luggage?

MERRIMAN: Yes, sir. Three portmanteaus, a dressing-case, two hat-boxes, and a large luncheon-basket.

ALGERNON: I am afraid I can't stay more than a week this time. 290

JACK: Merriman, order the dog-cart[21] at once. Mr. Ernest has been suddenly called back to town.

MERRIMAN: Yes, sir. [*goes back into the house*]

---

[21] **dog-cart** small, horse-drawn open carriage

ALGERNON: What a fearful liar you are, Jack. I have not been called back to town at all.

JACK: Yes, you have. 295

ALGERNON: I haven't heard anyone call me.

JACK: Your duty as a gentleman calls you back.

ALGERNON: My duty as a gentleman has never interfered with my pleasures in the smallest degree.

JACK: I can quite understand that. 300

ALGERNON: Well, Cecily is a darling.

JACK: You are not to talk of Miss Cardew like that. I don't like it.

ALGERNON: Well, I don't like your clothes. You look perfectly ridiculous in them. Why on earth don't you go up and change? It is perfectly childish to be in deep mourning for a man who is actually staying for a whole week with you in your house as a guest. 305 I call it grotesque.

JACK: You are certainly not staying with me for a whole week as a guest or anything else. You have got to leave . . . by the four-five train.

ALGERNON: I certainly won't leave you so long as you are in mourning. It would be most unfriendly. If I were in mourning you would stay with me, I suppose. I should think 310 it very unkind if you didn't.

JACK: Well, will you go if I change my clothes?

ALGERNON: Yes, if you are not too long. I never saw anybody take so long to dress, and with such little result.

JACK: Well, at any rate, that is better than being always over-dressed as you are. 315

ALGERNON: If I am occasionally a little over-dressed, I make up for it by being always immensely over-educated.

JACK: Your vanity is ridiculous, your conduct an outrage, and your presence in my garden utterly absurd. However, you have got to catch the four-five, and I hope you will have a pleasant journey back to town. This Bunburying, as you call it, has not been 320 a great success for you. [goes into the house]

ALGERNON: I think it has been a great success. I'm in love with Cecily, and that is everything.

[Enter CECILY at the back of the garden. She picks up the can and begins to water the flowers.]

But I must see her before I go, and make arrangements for another Bunbury. Ah, there she is.

CECILY: Oh, I merely came back to water the roses. I thought you were with Uncle Jack. 325

ALGERNON: He's gone to order the dog-cart for me.

CECILY: Oh, is he going to take you for a nice drive?

ALGERNON: He's going to send me away.

CECILY: Then have we got to part?

ALGERNON: I am afraid so. It's a very painful parting. 330

CECILY: It is always painful to part from people whom one has known for a very brief space of time. The absence of old friends one can endure with equanimity. But even a momentary separation from anyone to whom one has just been introduced is almost unbearable.

ALGERNON: Thank you. 335

[Enter MERRIMAN.]

MERRIMAN: The dog-cart is at the door, sir.

[ALGERNON looks appealingly at CECILY.]

CECILY: It can wait, Merriman . . . for . . . five minutes.

MERRIMAN: Yes, Miss. [Exit MERRIMAN.]

ALGERNON: I hope, Cecily, I shall not offend you if I state quite frankly and openly that you
    seem to me to be in every way the visible personification of absolute perfection.   340

CECILY: I think your frankness does you great credit, Ernest. If you will allow me I will
    copy your remarks into my diary. [*goes over to table and begins writing in diary*]

ALGERNON: Do you really keep a diary? I'd give anything to look at it. May I?

CECILY: Oh, no. [*puts her hand over it*] You see, it is simply a very young girl's record of
    her own thoughts and impressions, and consequently meant for publication. When   345
    it appears in volume form I hope you will order a copy. But pray, Ernest, don't stop.
    I delight in taking down from dictation. I have reached "absolute perfection." You
    can go on. I am quite ready for more.

ALGERNON: [*somewhat taken aback*] Ahem! Ahem!

CECILY: Oh, don't cough, Ernest. When one is dictating one should speak fluently and not   350
    cough. Besides, I don't know how to spell a cough. [*writes as* ALGERNON *speaks*]

ALGERNON: [*speaking very rapidly*] Cecily, ever since I first looked upon your wonderful
    and incomparable beauty, I have dared to love you wildly, passionately, devotedly,
    hopelessly.

CECILY: I don't think that you should tell me that you love me wildly, passionately, devotedly,   355
    hopelessly. Hopelessly doesn't seem to make much sense, does it?

ALGERNON: Cecily!

    [*Enter* MERRIMAN.]

MERRIMAN: The dog-cart is waiting, sir.

ALGERNON: Tell it to come round next week, at the same hour.

MERRIMAN: [*looks at* CECILY, *who makes no sign*] Yes, sir. [MERRIMAN *retires*]   360

CECILY: Uncle Jack would be very much annoyed if he knew you were staying on till next
    week, at the same hour.

ALGERNON: Oh, I don't care about Jack. I don't care for anybody in the whole world but
    you. I love you, Cecily. You will marry me, won't you?

CECILY: You silly boy! Of course. Why, we have been engaged for the last three months.   365

ALGERNON: For the last three months?

CECILY: Yes, it will be exactly three months on Thursday.

ALGERNON: But how did we become engaged?

CECILY: Well, ever since dear Uncle Jack first confessed to us that he had a younger brother
    who was very wicked and bad, you of course have formed the chief topic of conver-   370
    sation between myself and Miss Prism. And of course a man who is much talked
    about is always very attractive. One feels there must be something in him after all. I
    daresay it was foolish of me, but I fell in love with you, Ernest.

ALGERNON: Darling! And when was the engagement actually settled?

CECILY: On the 14th of February last. Worn out by your entire ignorance of my existence,   375
    I determined to end the matter one way or the other, and after a long struggle with
    myself I accepted you under this dear old tree here. The next day I bought this little
    ring in your name, and this is the little bangle with the true lovers' knot I promised
    you always to wear.

ALGERNON: Did I give you this? It's very pretty, isn't it?   380

CECILY: Yes, you've wonderfully good taste, Ernest. It's the excuse I've always given for your
    leading such a bad life. And this is the box in which I keep all your dear letters.
    [*kneels at table, opens box, and produces letters tied up with blue ribbon*]

ALGERNON: My letters! But my own sweet Cecily, I have never written you any letters.

CECILY: You need hardly remind me of that, Ernest. I remember only too well that I was forced   385
    to write your letters for you. I wrote always three times a week, and sometimes oftener.

ALGERNON: Oh, do let me read them, Cecily?

CECILY: Oh, I couldn't possibly. They would make you far too conceited. [*replaces box*] The three you wrote me after I had broken off the engagement are so beautiful, and so badly spelled, that even now I can hardly read them without crying a little.   390

ALGERNON: But was our engagement ever broken off?

CECILY: Of course it was. On the 22nd of last March. You can see the entry if you like. [*shows diary*] "To-day I broke off my engagement with Ernest. I feel it is better to do so. The weather still continues charming."

ALGERNON: But why on earth did you break it off? What had I done? I had done nothing   395
at all. Cecily, I am very much hurt indeed to hear you broke it off. Particularly when the weather was so charming.

CECILY: It would hardly have been a really serious engagement if it hadn't been broken off at least once. But I forgave you before the week was out.

ALGERNON: [*crossing to her, and kneels*] What a perfect angel you are, Cecily.   400

CECILY: You dear romantic boy. [*He kisses her, she puts her fingers through his hair.*] I hope your hair curls naturally, does it?

ALGERNON: Yes, darling, with a little help from others.

CECILY: I am so glad.

ALGERNON: You'll never break off our engagement again, Cecily?   405

CECILY: I don't think I could break it off now that I have actually met you. Besides, of course, there is the question of your name.

ALGERNON: [*nervously*] Yes, of course.

CECILY: You must not laugh at me, darling, but it had always been a girlish dream of mine to love someone whose name was Ernest.   410

[ALGERNON *rises*, CECILY *also.*]

There is something in that name that seems to inspire absolute confidence. I pity any poor married woman whose husband is not called Ernest.

ALGERNON: But, my dear child, do you mean to say you could not love me if I had some other name?

CECILY: But what name?   415

ALGERNON: Oh, any name you like—Algernon, for instance . . . .

CECILY: But I don't like the name of Algernon.

ALGERNON: Well, my own dear, sweet, loving little darling, I really can't see why you should object to the name of Algernon. It is not at all a bad name. In fact, it is rather an aristocratic name. Half of the chaps who get into the Bankruptcy Court are called Algernon.   420
But seriously, Cecily . . . [*moving to her*] . . . if my name was Algy, couldn't you love me?

CECILY: [*rising*] I might respect you, Ernest, I might admire your character, but I fear that I should not be able to give you my undivided attention.

ALGERNON: Ahem! Cecily! [*picking up hat*] Your Rector here is, I suppose, thoroughly experienced in the practice of all the rites and ceremonials of the Church?   425

CECILY: Oh, yes. Dr. Chasuble is a most learned man. He has never written a single book, so you can imagine how much he knows.

ALGERNON: I must see him at once on a most important christening—I mean on most important business.

CECILY: Oh!   430

ALGERNON: I shan't be away more than half an hour.

CECILY: Considering that we have been engaged since February the 14th, and that I only met you to-day for the first time, I think it is rather hard that you should leave me for so long a period as half an hour. Couldn't you make it twenty minutes?

ALGERNON: I'll be back in no time. [*kisses her and rushes down the garden*]   435

CECILY: What an impetuous boy he is! I like his hair so much. I must enter his proposal in my diary.

       [*Enter* MERRIMAN.]

MERRIMAN: A Miss Fairfax has just called to see Mr. Worthing. On very important business, Miss Fairfax states.

CECILY: Isn't Mr. Worthing in his library?   440

MERRIMAN: Mr. Worthing went over in the direction of the Rectory some time ago.

CECILY: Pray ask the lady to come out here; Mr. Worthing is sure to be back soon. And you can bring tea.

MERRIMAN: Yes, Miss. [*goes out*]

CECILY: Miss Fairfax! I suppose one of the many good elderly women who are associated   445
with Uncle Jack in some of his philanthropic work in London. I don't quite like women who are interested in philanthropic work. I think it is so forward of them.

       [*Enter* MERRIMAN.]

MERRIMAN: Miss Fairfax.

       [*Enter* GWENDOLEN. *Exit* MERRIMAN.]

CECILY: [*advancing to meet her*] Pray let me introduce myself to you. My name is Cecily Cardew.   450

GWENDOLEN: Cecily Cardew? [*moving to her and shaking hands*] What a very sweet name! Something tells me that we are going to be great friends. I like you already more than I can say. My first impressions of people are never wrong.

CECILY: How nice of you to like me so much after we have known each other such a comparatively short time. Pray sit down.   455

GWENDOLEN: [*still standing up*] I may call you Cecily, may I not?

CECILY: With pleasure!

GWENDOLEN: And you will always call me Gwendolen, won't you?

CECILY: If you wish.

GWENDOLEN: Then that is all quite settled, is it not?   460

CECILY: I hope so. [*a pause; they both sit down together*]

GWENDOLEN: Perhaps this might be a favorable opportunity for my mentioning who I am. My father is Lord Bracknell. You have never heard of papa, I suppose?

CECILY: I don't think so.

GWENDOLEN: Outside the family circle, papa, I am glad to say, is entirely unknown. I   465
think that is quite as it should be. The home seems to me to be the proper sphere for the man. And certainly once a man begins to neglect his domestic duties he becomes painfully effeminate, does he not? And I don't like that. It makes men so very attractive. Cecily, mamma, whose views on education are remarkably strict, has brought me up to be extremely short-sighted; it is part of her system; so do you mind my   470
looking at you through my glasses?

CECILY: Oh! not at all, Gwendolen. I am very fond of being looked at.

GWENDOLEN: [*after examining* CECILY *carefully through a lorgnette*²²] You are here on a short visit, I suppose.   475

CECILY: Oh, no, I live here.

GWENDOLEN: [*severely*] Really? Your mother, no doubt, or some female relative of advanced years, resides here also?

---

²² **lorgnette** opera glasses mounted on a handle

CECILY: Oh, no. I have no mother, nor, in fact, any relations.

GWENDOLEN: Indeed?

CECILY: My dear guardian, with the assistance of Miss Prism, has the arduous task of looking after me. 480

GWENDOLEN: Your guardian?

CECILY: Yes, I am Mr. Worthing's ward.

GWENDOLEN: Oh! It is strange he never mentioned to me that he had a ward. How secretive of him! He grows more interesting hourly. I am not sure, however, that the news 485 inspires me with feelings of unmixed delight. [*rising and going to her*] I am very fond of you, Cecily; I have liked you ever since I met you. But I am bound to state that now that I know that you are Mr. Worthing's ward, I cannot help expressing a wish you were—well, just a little older than you seem to be—and not quite so very alluring in appearance. In fact, if I may speak candidly— 490

CECILY: Pray do! I think that whenever one has anything unpleasant to say, one should always be quite candid.

GWENDOLEN: Well, to speak with perfect candor, Cecily, I wish that you were fully forty-two, and more than usually plain for your age. Ernest has a strong upright nature. He is the very soul of truth and honor. Disloyalty would be as impossible to him as 495 deception. But even men of the noblest possible moral character are extremely susceptible to the influence of the physical charms of others. Modern, no less than Ancient History, supplies us with most painful examples of what I refer to. If it were not so, indeed, History would be quite unreadable.

CECILY: I beg your pardon, Gwendolen, did you say Ernest? 500

GWENDOLEN: Yes.

CECILY: Oh, but it is not Mr. Ernest Worthing who is my guardian. It is his brother—his elder brother.

GWENDOLEN: [*sitting down again*] Ernest never mentioned to me that he had a brother.

CECILY: I am sorry to say they have not been on good terms for a long time. 505

GWENDOLEN: Ah! that accounts for it. And now that I think of it I have never heard any man mention his brother. The subject seems distasteful to most men. Cecily, you have lifted a load from my mind. I was growing almost anxious. It would have been terrible if any cloud had come across a friendship like ours, would it not? Of course you are quite, quite sure that it is not Mr. Ernest Worthing who is your guardian? 510

CECILY: Quite sure. [*a pause*] In fact, I am going to be his.

GWENDOLEN: [*enquiringly*] I beg your pardon?

CECILY: [*rather shy and confidingly*] Dearest Gwendolen, there is no reason why I should make a secret of it to you. Our little county newspaper is sure to chronicle the fact next week. Mr. Ernest Worthing and I are engaged to be married. 515

GWENDOLEN: [*quite politely, rising*] My darling Cecily, I think there must be some slight error. Mr. Ernest Worthing is engaged to me. The announcement will appear in the 'Morning Post' on Saturday at the latest.

CECILY: [*very politely, rising*] I am afraid you must be under some misconception. Ernest proposed to me exactly ten minutes ago. [*shows diary*] 520

GWENDOLEN: [*examines diary through her lorgnette carefully*] It is certainly very curious, for he asked me to be his wife yesterday afternoon at 5:30. If you would care to verify the incident, pray do so. [*produces diary of her own*] I never travel without my diary. One should always have something sensational to read in the train. I am so sorry, dear Cecily, if it is any disappointment to you, but I am afraid *I* have the 525 prior claim.

CECILY: It would distress me more than I can tell you, dear Gwendolen, if it caused you any mental or physical anguish, but I feel bound to point out that since Ernest proposed to you he clearly has changed his mind.

GWENDOLEN: [*meditatively*] If the poor fellow has been entrapped into any foolish prom-   530
ise I shall consider it my duty to rescue him at once, and with a firm hand.

CECILY: [*thoughtfully and sadly*] Whatever unfortunate entanglement my dear boy may
have got into, I will never reproach him with it after we are married.

GWENDOLEN: Do you allude to me, Miss Cardew, as an entanglement? You are presumptuous. On an occasion of this kind it becomes more than a moral duty to speak one's   535
mind. It becomes a pleasure.

CECILY: Do you suggest, Miss Fairfax, that I entrapped Ernest into an engagement? How
dare you? This is no time for wearing the shallow mask of manners. When I see a
spade I call it a spade.

GWENDOLEN: [*satirically*] I am glad to say that I have never seen a spade. It is obvious that   540
our social spheres have been widely different.

> [*Enter* MERRIMAN, *followed by the footman. He carries a salver, tablecloth, and
> plate stand.* CECILY *is about to retort. The presence of the servants exercises a
> restraining influence, under which both girls chafe.*]

MERRIMAN: Shall I lay tea here as usual, Miss?

CECILY: [*sternly, in a calm voice*] Yes, as usual.

> [MERRIMAN *begins to clear and lay cloth. A long pause.* CECILY *and* GWENDO-
> LEN *glare at each other.*]

GWENDOLEN: Are there many interesting walks in the vicinity, Miss Cardew?

CECILY: Oh, yes, a great many. From the top of one of the hills quite close one can see five   545
counties.

GWENDOLEN: Five counties! I don't think I should like that. I hate crowds.

CECILY: [*sweetly*] I suppose that is why you live in town?

> [GWENDOLEN *bites her lip, and beats her foot nervously with her parasol.*]

GWENDOLEN: [*looking round*] Quite a well-kept garden this is, Miss Cardew.

CECILY: So glad you like it, Miss Fairfax.   550

GWENDOLEN: I had no idea there were any flowers in the country.

CECILY: Oh, flowers are as common here, Miss Fairfax, as people are in London.

GWENDOLEN: Personally I cannot understand how anybody manages to exist in the country,
if anybody who is anybody does. The country always bores me to death.

CECILY: Ah! This is what the newspapers call agricultural depression, is it not? I believe the   555
aristocracy are suffering very much from it just at present. It is almost an epidemic
amongst them, I have been told. May I offer you some tea, Miss Fairfax?

GWENDOLEN: [*with elaborate politeness*] Thank you. [*aside*] Detestable girl! But I require tea!

CECILY: [*sweetly*] Sugar?

GWENDOLEN: [*superciliously*] No, thank you. Sugar is not fashionable any more.   560

> [CECILY *looks angrily at her, takes up the tongs and puts four lumps of sugar into
> the cup.*]

CECILY: [*severely*] Cake or bread and butter?

GWENDOLEN: [*in a bored manner*] Bread and butter, please. Cake is rarely seen at the best
houses nowadays.

CECILY: [*cuts a very large slice of cake, and puts it on the tray*] Hand that to Miss Fairfax.

> [MERRIMAN *does so, and goes out with footman.* GWENDOLEN *drinks the tea
> and makes a grimace. Puts down cup at once, reaches out her hand to the bread and
> butter, looks at it, and finds it is cake. Rises in indignation.*]

GWENDOLEN: You have filled my tea with lumps of sugar, and though I asked most dis-   565
    tinctly for bread and butter, you have given me cake. I am known for the gentleness
    of my disposition, and the extraordinary sweetness of my nature, but I warn you,
    Miss Cardew, you may go too far.

CECILY: [*rising*] To save my poor, innocent, trusting boy from the machinations of any
    other girl there are no lengths to which I would not go.   570

GWENDOLEN: From the moment I saw you I distrusted you. I felt that you were false and
    deceitful. I am never deceived in such matters. My first impressions of people are
    invariably right.

CECILY: It seems to me, Miss Fairfax, that I am trespassing on your valuable time. No doubt
    you have many other calls of a similar character to make in the neighborhood.   575

       [*Enter* JACK.]

GWENDOLEN: [*catching sight of him*] Ernest! My own Ernest!

JACK: Gwendolen! Darling! [*offers to kiss her*]

GWENDOLEN: [*drawing back*] A moment! May I ask if you are engaged to be married to
    this young lady? [*points to* CECILY]

JACK: [*laughing*] To dear little Cecily! Of course not! What could have put such an idea   580
    into your pretty little head?

GWENDOLEN: Thank you. You may. [*offers her cheek*]

CECILY: [*very sweetly*] I knew there must be some misunderstanding, Miss Fairfax.
    The gentleman whose arm is at present around your waist is my dear guardian,
    Mr. John Worthing.   585

GWENDOLEN: I beg your pardon?

CECILY: This is Uncle Jack.

GWENDOLEN: [*receding*] Jack! Oh!

       [*Enter* ALGERNON.]

CECILY: Here is Ernest.

ALGERNON: [*Goes straight over to* CECILY *without noticing anyone else.*] My own love!   590
    [*offers to kiss her*]

CECILY: [*drawing back*] A moment, Ernest! May I ask you—are you engaged to be married
    to this young lady?

ALGERNON: [*looking round*] To what young lady? Good heavens! Gwendolen!

CECILY: Yes, to good heavens, Gwendolen, I mean to Gwendolen.   595

ALGERNON: [*laughing*] Of course not! What could have put such an idea into your pretty
    little head?

CECILY: Thank you. [*presenting her cheek to be kissed*] You may. [ALGERNON *kisses her.*]

GWENDOLEN: I felt there was some slight error, Miss Cardew. The gentleman who is now
    embracing you is my cousin, Mr. Algernon Moncrieff.   600

CECILY: [*breaking away from* ALGERNON] Algernon Moncrieff! Oh! [*The two girls move
    towards each other and put their arms round each other's waist as if for protection.*] Are
    you called Algernon?

ALGERNON: I cannot deny it.

CECILY: Oh!   605

GWENDOLEN: Is your name really John?

JACK: [*standing rather proudly*] I could deny it if I liked. I could deny anything if I liked.
    But my name certainly is John. It has been John for years.

CECILY: [*to* GWENDOLEN] A gross deception has been practiced on both of us.

GWENDOLEN: My poor wounded Cecily!   610

CECILY: My sweet wronged Gwendolen!

GWENDOLEN: [*slowly and seriously*] You will call me sister, will you not? [*They embrace.* JACK *and* ALGERNON *groan and walk up and down.*]

CECILY: [*rather brightly*] There is just one question I would like to be allowed to ask my guardian. 615

GWENDOLEN: An admirable idea! Mr. Worthing, there is just one question I would like to be permitted to put to you. Where is your brother Ernest? We are both engaged to be married to your brother Ernest, so it is a matter of some importance to us to know where your brother Ernest is at present.

JACK: [*slowly and hesitatingly*] Gwendolen—Cecily—it is very painful for me to be forced 620 to speak the truth. It is the first time in my life that I have ever been reduced to such a painful position, and I am really quite inexperienced in doing anything of the kind. However, I will tell you quite frankly that I have no brother Ernest. I have no brother at all. I never had a brother in my life, and I certainly have not the smallest intention of ever having one in the future. 625

CECILY: [*surprised*] No brother at all?

JACK: [*cheerily*] None!

GWENDOLEN: [*severely*] Had you never a brother of any kind?

JACK: [*pleasantly*] Never. Not even of any kind.

GWENDOLEN: I am afraid it is quite clear, Cecily, that neither of us is engaged to be married 630 to anyone.

CECILY: It is not a very pleasant position for a young girl suddenly to find herself in. Is it?

GWENDOLEN: Let us go into the house. They will hardly venture to come after us there.

CECILY: No, men are so cowardly, aren't they?

[*They retire into the house with scornful looks.*]

JACK: This ghastly state of things is what you call Bunburying, I suppose? 635

ALGERNON: Yes, and a perfectly wonderful Bunbury it is. The most wonderful Bunbury I have ever had in my life.

JACK: Well, you've no right whatsoever to Bunbury here.

ALGERNON: That is absurd. One has a right to Bunbury anywhere one chooses. Every serious Bunburyist knows that. 640

JACK: Serious Bunburyist! Good heavens!

ALGERNON: Well, one must be serious about something, if one wants to have any amusement in life. I happen to be serious about Bunburying. What on earth you are serious about I haven't got the remotest idea. About everything, I should fancy. You have such an absolutely trivial nature. 645

JACK: Well, the only small satisfaction I have in the whole of this wretched business is that your friend Bunbury is quite exploded. You won't be able to run down to the country quite so often as you used to do, dear Algy. And a very good thing too.

ALGERNON: Your brother is a little off color, isn't he, dear Jack? You won't be able to disappear to London quite so frequently as your wicked custom was. And not a bad thing either. 650

JACK: As for your conduct towards Miss Cardew, I must say that your taking in a sweet, simple, innocent girl like that is quite inexcusable. To say nothing of the fact that she is my ward.

ALGERNON: I can see no possible defense at all for your deceiving a brilliant, clever, thoroughly experienced young lady like Miss Fairfax. To say nothing of the fact that she 655 is my cousin.

JACK: I wanted to be engaged to Gwendolen, that is all. I love her.

ALGERNON: Well, I simply wanted to be engaged to Cecily. I adore her.

JACK: There is certainly no chance of your marrying Miss Cardew.

ALGERNON: I don't think there is much likelihood, Jack, of you and Miss Fairfax being   660
    united.

JACK: Well, that is no business of yours.

ALGERNON: If it was my business, I wouldn't talk about it. [*begins to eat muffins*] It is very
    vulgar to talk about one's business. Only people like stockbrokers do that, and then
    merely at dinner parties.   665

JACK: How can you sit there, calmly eating muffins, when we are in this horrible trouble,
    I can't make out. You seem to me to be perfectly heartless.

ALGERNON: Well, I can't eat muffins in an agitated manner. The butter would probably
    get on my cuffs. One should always eat muffins quite calmly. It is the only way to
    eat them.   670

JACK: I say it's perfectly heartless your eating muffins at all, under the circumstances.

ALGERNON: When I am in trouble, eating is the only thing that consoles me. Indeed,
    when I am in really great trouble, as anyone who knows me intimately will tell you,
    I refuse everything except food and drink. At the present moment I am eating muf-
    fins because I am unhappy. Besides, I am particularly fond of muffins. [*rising*]   675

JACK: [*rising*] Well, that is no reason why you should eat them all in that greedy way. [*takes
    muffins from* ALGERNON]

ALGERNON: [*offering tea-cake*] I wish you would have tea-cake instead. I don't like tea-cake.

JACK: Good heavens! I suppose a man may eat his own muffins in his own garden.

ALGERNON: But you have just said it was perfectly heartless to eat muffins.   680

JACK: I said it was perfectly heartless of you, under the circumstances. That is a very dif-
    ferent thing.

ALGERNON: That may be. But the muffins are the same. [*He seizes the muffin-dish from*
    JACK.]

JACK: Algy, I wish to goodness you would go.   685

ALGERNON: You can't possibly ask me to go without having some dinner. It's absurd. I
    never go without my dinner. No one ever does, except vegetarians and people like
    that. Besides I have just made arrangements with Dr. Chasuble to be christened at a
    quarter to six under the name of Ernest.

JACK: My dear fellow, the sooner you give up that nonsense the better. I made arrangements   690
    this morning with Dr. Chasuble to be christened myself at 5:30, and I naturally will
    take the name of Ernest. Gwendolen would wish it. We can't both be christened
    Ernest. It's absurd. Besides, I have a perfect right to be christened if I like. There
    is no evidence at all that I ever have been christened by anybody. I should think it
    extremely probable I never was, and so does Dr. Chasuble. It is entirely different in   695
    your case. You have been christened already.

ALGERNON: Yes, but I have not been christened for years.

JACK: Yes, but you have been christened. That is the important thing.

ALGERNON: Quite so. So I know my constitution can stand it. If you are not quite sure
    about your ever having been christened, I must say I think it rather dangerous your   700
    venturing on it now. It might make you very unwell. You can hardly have forgotten
    that someone very closely connected with you was very nearly carried off this week
    in Paris by a severe chill.

JACK: Yes, but you said yourself that a severe chill was not hereditary.

ALGERNON: It usen't to be, I know—but I daresay it is now. Science is always making   705
    wonderful improvements in things.

JACK: [*picking up the muffin-dish*] Oh, that is nonsense; you are always talking nonsense.

ALGERNON: Jack, you are at the muffins again! I wish you wouldn't. There are only two
    left. [*takes them*] I told you I was particularly fond of muffins.

JACK: But I hate tea-cake.   710

ALGERNON: Why on earth then do you allow tea-cake to be served up for your guests? What ideas you have of hospitality!

JACK: Algernon! I have already told you to go. I don't want you here. Why don't you go?

ALGERNON: I haven't quite finished my tea yet, and there is still one muffin left.

[JACK *groans, and sinks into a chair.* ALGERNON *continues eating.*]

CURTAIN

---------- **ACT III** ----------

SCENE————*Morning-room at the Manor House.* GWENDOLEN *and* CECILY *are at the window, looking out into the garden.*

GWENDOLEN: The fact that they did not follow us at once into the house, as anyone else would have done, seems to me to show that they have some sense of shame left.

CECILY: They have been eating muffins. That looks like repentance.

GWENDOLEN: [*after a pause*] They don't seem to notice us at all. Couldn't you cough?

CECILY: But I haven't a cough.   5

GWENDOLEN: They're looking at us. What effrontery!

CECILY: They're approaching. That's very forward of them.

GWENDOLEN: Let us preserve a dignified silence.

CECILY: Certainly. It's the only thing to do now.

[*Enter* JACK *followed by* ALGERNON. *They whistle some dreadful popular air from a British Opera.*]

GWENDOLEN: This dignified silence seems to produce an unpleasant effect.   10

CECILY: A most distasteful one.

GWENDOLEN: But we will not be the first to speak.

CECILY: Certainly not.

GWENDOLEN: Mr. Worthing, I have something very particular to ask you. Much depends on your reply.   15

CECILY: Gwendolen, your common sense is invaluable. Mr. Moncrieff, kindly answer me the following question. Why did you pretend to be my guardian's brother?

ALGERNON: In order that I might have an opportunity of meeting you.

CECILY: [*to* GWENDOLEN] That certainly seems a satisfactory explanation, does it not?

GWENDOLEN: Yes, dear, if you can believe him.   20

CECILY: I don't. But that does not affect the wonderful beauty of his answer.

GWENDOLEN: True. In matters of grave importance, style, not sincerity is the vital thing. Mr. Worthing, what explanation can you offer to me for pretending to have a brother? Was it in order that you might have an opportunity of coming up to town to see me as often as possible?   25

JACK: Can you doubt it, Miss Fairfax?

GWENDOLEN: I have the gravest doubts upon the subject. But I intend to crush them. This is not the moment for German skepticism.[23] [*moving to* CECILY] Their explanations appear to be quite satisfactory, especially Mr. Worthing's. That seems to me to have the stamp of truth upon it.   30

CECILY: I am more than content with what Mr. Moncrieff said. His voice alone inspires one with absolute credulity.

GWENDOLEN: Then you think we should forgive them?

CECILY: Yes. I mean no.

GWENDOLEN: True! I had forgotten. There are principles at stake that one cannot surrender. Which of us should tell them? The task is not a pleasant one.   35

CECILY: Could we not both speak at the same time?

GWENDOLEN: An excellent idea! I nearly always speak at the same time as other people. Will you take the time from me?

CECILY: Certainly. [GWENDOLEN *beats time with uplifted finger.*]   40

GWENDOLEN AND CECILY: [*speaking together*] Your Christian names are still an insuperable barrier. That is all!

JACK AND ALGERNON: [*speaking together*] Our Christian names! Is that all? But we are going to be christened this afternoon.

GWENDOLEN: [*to* JACK] For my sake you are prepared to do this terrible thing?   45

JACK: I am.

CECILY: [*to* ALGERNON] To please me you are ready to face this fearful ordeal?

ALGERNON: I am.

GWENDOLEN: How absurd to talk of the equality of the sexes! Where questions of self-sacrifice are concerned, men are infinitely beyond us.   50

JACK: We are. [*clasps hands with* ALGERNON]

CECILY: They have moments of physical courage of which we women know absolutely nothing.

GWENDOLEN: [*to* JACK] Darling!

ALGERNON: [*to* CECILY] Darling!   55

[*They fall into each other's arms. Enter* MERRIMAN. *When he enters he coughs loudly, seeing the situation.*]

MERRIMAN: Ahem! Ahem! Lady Bracknell!

JACK: Good heavens!

[*Enter* LADY BRACKNELL. *The couples separate in alarm. Exit* MERRIMAN.]

LADY BRACKNELL: Gwendolen! What does this mean?

GWENDOLEN: Merely that I am engaged to be married to Mr. Worthing, mamma.

LADY BRACKNELL: Come here. Sit down. Sit down immediately. Hesitation of any kind   60
is a sign of mental decay in the young, of physical weakness in the old. [*turns to* JACK] Apprised, sir, of my daughter's sudden flight by her trusty maid, whose confidence I purchased by means of a small coin, I followed her at once by a luggage train. Her unhappy father is, I am glad to say, under the impression that she is attending a more than usually lengthy lecture by the University Extension Scheme   65
on the influence of a permanent income on thought. I do not propose to undeceive him. Indeed I have never undeceived him on any question. I would consider it wrong. But of course, you will clearly understand that all communication between

---

[23] **German skepticism** nineteenth-century German philosophical movements which called into question the first principles of religion and ethics

yourself and my daughter must cease immediately from this moment. On this point,   70
as indeed on all points, I am firm.

JACK: I am engaged to be married to Gwendolen, Lady Bracknell!

LADY BRACKNELL: You are nothing of the kind, sir. And now, as regards Algernon. . . .
Algernon!

ALGERNON: Yes, Aunt Augusta.

LADY BRACKNELL: May I ask if it is in this house that your invalid friend Mr. Bunbury   75
resides?

ALGERNON: [*stammering*] Oh, Bunbury doesn't live here. Bunbury is somewhere else at
present. In fact, Bunbury is dead.

LADY BRACKNELL: Dead! When did Mr. Bunbury die? His death must have been
extremely sudden.   80

ALGERNON: [*airily*] Oh, I killed Bunbury this afternoon. I mean poor Bunbury died this
afternoon.

LADY BRACKNELL: What did he die of?

ALGERNON: Bunbury? Oh, he was quite exploded.

LADY BRACKNELL: Exploded! Was he the victim of a revolutionary outrage? I was not   85
aware that Mr. Bunbury was interested in social legislation. If so, he is well punished
for his morbidity.

ALGERNON: My dear Aunt Augusta, I mean he was found out! The doctors found out that
Bunbury could not live, that is what I mean—so Bunbury died.

LADY BRACKNELL: He seems to have had great confidence in the opinion of his physicians.   90
I am glad, however, that he made up his mind at the last to some definite course
of action, and acted under proper medical advice. And now that we have finally
got rid of this Mr. Bunbury, may I ask, Mr. Worthing, who is that young person
whose hand my nephew Algernon is now holding in what seems to me a peculiarly
unnecessary manner?   95

JACK: That lady is Miss Cecily Cardew, my ward.

[LADY BRACKNELL *bows coldly to* CECILY.]

ALGERNON: I am engaged to be married to Cecily, Aunt Augusta.

LADY BRACKNELL: I beg your pardon?

CECILY: Mr. Moncrieff and I are engaged to be married, Lady Bracknell.

LADY BRACKNELL: [*with a shiver, crossing to the sofa and sitting down*] I do not know   100
whether there is anything peculiarly exciting in the air in this particular part of
Hertfordshire, but the number of engagements that go on seems to me considerably
above the proper average that statistics have laid down for our guidance. I think
some preliminary enquiry on my part would not be out of place. Mr. Worthing, is
Miss Cardew at all connected with any of the larger railway stations in London? I   105
merely desire information. Until yesterday I had no idea that there were any families
or persons whose origin was a Terminus.

[JACK *looks perfectly furious, but restrains himself.*]

JACK: [*in a clear, cold voice*] Miss Cardew is the granddaughter of the late Mr. Thomas
Cardew of 149, Belgrave Square, S.W.; Gervase Park, Dorking, Surrey; and the
Sporran, Fifeshire, N.B.[24]   110

LADY BRACKNELL: That sounds not unsatisfactory. Three addresses always inspire confidence, even in tradesmen. But what proof have I of their authenticity?

---

[24] **N.B.** North Britain, a snobbish English term for Scotland

JACK: I have carefully preserved the Court Guides of the period. They are open to your inspection, Lady Bracknell.

LADY BRACKNELL: [*grimly*] I have known strange errors in that publication.   115

JACK: Miss Cardew's family solicitors are Messrs. Markby, Markby, and Markby.

LADY BRACKNELL: Markby, Markby, and Markby! A firm of the very highest position in their profession. Indeed I am told that one of the Mr. Markbys is occasionally to be seen at dinner parties. So far I am satisfied.

JACK: [*very irritably*] How extremely kind of you, Lady Bracknell! I have also in my pos-   120
session, you will be pleased to hear, certificates of Miss Cardew's birth, baptism, whooping cough, registration, vaccination, confirmation, and the measles; both the German and the English variety.

LADY BRACKNELL: Ah! A life crowded with incident, I see; though perhaps somewhat too exciting for a young girl. I am not myself in favor of premature experiences. [*rises,*   125
looks at her watch] Gwendolen! the time approaches for our departure. We have not a moment to lose. As a matter of form, Mr. Worthing, I had better ask you if Miss Cardew has any little fortune?

JACK: Oh, about a hundred and thirty thousand pounds in the Funds.[25] That is all. Good-
bye, Lady Bracknell. So pleased to have seen you.   130

LADY BRACKNELL: [*sitting down again*] A moment, Mr. Worthing. A hundred and thirty thousand pounds! And in the Funds! Miss Cardew seems to me a most attractive young lady, now that I look at her. Few girls of the present day have any really solid qualities, any of the qualities that last, and improve with time. We live, I regret to say, in an age of surfaces. [*to* CECILY] Come over here, dear. [CECILY *goes across.*]   135
Pretty child! your dress is sadly simple, and your hair seems almost as Nature might have left it. But we can soon alter all that. A thoroughly experienced French maid produces a really marvelous result in a very brief space of time. I remember recom-
mending one to young Lady Lancing, and after three months her own husband did not know her.   140

JACK: [*to himself*] And after six months nobody knew her.

LADY BRACKNELL: [*Glares at* JACK *for a few moments. Then bends, with a practiced smile, to*
CECILY.] Kindly turn round, sweet child. [CECILY *turns completely round.*] No, the side view is what I want. [CECILY *presents her profile.*] Yes, quite as I expected. There are distinct social possibilities in your profile. The two weak points in our age are   145
its want of principle and its want of profile. The chin a little higher, dear. Style largely depends on the way the chin is worn. They are worn very high, just at present. Algernon!

ALGERNON: Yes, Aunt Augusta!

LADY BRACKNELL: There are distinct social possibilities in Miss Cardew's profile.   150

ALGERNON: Cecily is the sweetest, dearest, prettiest girl in the whole world. And I don't care two-pence about social possibilities.

LADY BRACKNELL: Never speak disrespectfully of society, Algernon. Only people who can't get into it do that. [*to* CECILY] Dear child, of course you know that Algernon has nothing but his debts to depend upon. But I do not approve of mercenary marriages.   155
When I married Lord Bracknell I had no fortune of any kind. But I never dreamed for a moment of allowing that to stand in my way. Well, I suppose I must give my consent.

ALGERNON: Thank you, Aunt Augusta.

---

[25] **a hundred and thirty thousand pounds in the Funds** tremendous sum of money held in conservative government bonds

LADY BRACKNELL: Cecily, you may kiss me!   160
CECILY: [*kisses her*] Thank you, Lady Bracknell.
LADY BRACKNELL: You may also address me as Aunt Augusta for the future.
CECILY: Thank you, Aunt Augusta.
LADY BRACKNELL: The marriage, I think, had better take place quite soon.
ALGERNON: Thank you, Aunt Augusta.   165
CECILY: Thank you, Aunt Augusta.
LADY BRACKNELL: To speak frankly, I am not in favor of long engagements. They give
    people the opportunity of finding out each other's character before marriage, which
    I think is never advisable.
JACK: I beg your pardon for interrupting you, Lady Bracknell, but this engagement is quite   170
    out of the question. I am Miss Cardew's guardian, and she cannot marry without my
    consent until she comes of age. That consent I absolutely decline to give.
LADY BRACKNELL: Upon what grounds, may I ask? Algernon is an extremely, I may
    almost say an ostentatiously, eligible young man. He has nothing, but he looks
    everything. What more can one desire?   175
JACK: It pains me very much to have to speak frankly to you, Lady Bracknell, about your
    nephew, but the fact is that I do not approve at all of his moral character. I suspect
    him of being untruthful.

    [ALGERNON *and* CECILY *look at him in indignant amazement.*]

LADY BRACKNELL: Untruthful! My nephew Algernon? Impossible! He is an Oxonian.[26]
JACK: I fear there can be no possible doubt about the matter. This afternoon, during my   180
    temporary absence in London on an important question of romance, he obtained
    admission to my house by means of the false pretense of being my brother. Under
    an assumed name he drank, I've just been informed by my butler, an entire pint
    bottle of my Perrier-Jouet, Brut, '89; a wine I was specially reserving for myself.
    Continuing his disgraceful deception, he succeeded in the course of the afternoon   185
    in alienating the affections of my only ward. He subsequently stayed to tea, and
    devoured every single muffin. And what makes his conduct all the more heartless is,
    that he was perfectly well aware from the first that I have no brother, that I never had
    a brother, and that I don't intend to have a brother, not even of any kind. I distinctly
    told him so myself yesterday afternoon.   190
LADY BRACKNELL: Ahem! Mr. Worthing, after careful consideration I have decided
    entirely to overlook my nephew's conduct to you.
JACK: That is very generous of you, Lady Bracknell. My own decision, however, is unalter-
    able. I decline to give my consent.
LADY BRACKNELL: [*to* CECILY] Come here, sweet child. [CECILY *goes over*] How old are   195
    you, dear?
CECILY: Well, I am really only eighteen, but I always admit to twenty when I go to evening
    parties.
LADY BRACKNELL: You are perfectly right in making some slight alteration. Indeed, no
    woman should ever be quite accurate about her age. It looks so calculating. . . . [*in a*   200
    meditative manner] Eighteen, but admitting to twenty at evening parties. Well, it will
    not be very long before you are of age and free from the restraints of tutelage. So I
    don't think your guardian's consent is, after all, a matter of any importance.
JACK: Pray excuse me, Lady Bracknell, for interrupting you again, but it is only fair to tell
    you that according to the terms of her grandfather's will Miss Cardew does not come   205
    legally of age till she is thirty-five.

---

[26] **Oxonian** Oxford graduate

LADY BRACKNELL: That does not seem to me to be a grave objection. Thirty-five is a very attractive age. London society is full of women of the very highest birth who have, of their own free choice, remained thirty-five for years. Lady Dumbleton is an instance in point. To my own knowledge she has been thirty-five ever since she arrived at the age of forty, which was many years ago now. I see no reason why our dear Cecily should not be even still more attractive at the age you mention than she is at present. There will be a large accumulation of property.   210

CECILY: Algy, could you wait for me till I was thirty-five?

ALGERNON: Of course I could, Cecily. You know I could.   215

CECILY: Yes, I felt it instinctively, but I couldn't wait all that time. I hate waiting even five minutes for anybody. It always makes me rather cross. I am not punctual myself, I know, but I do like punctuality in others, and waiting, even to be married, is quite out of the question.

ALGERNON: Then what is to be done, Cecily?   220

CECILY: I don't know, Mr. Moncrieff.

LADY BRACKNELL: My dear Mr. Worthing, as Miss Cardew states positively that she cannot wait till she is thirty-five—a remark which I am bound to say seems to me to show a somewhat impatient nature—I would beg of you to reconsider your decision.

JACK: But my dear Lady Bracknell, the matter is entirely in your own hands. The moment   225
you consent to my marriage with Gwendolen, I will most gladly allow your nephew to form an alliance with my ward.

LADY BRACKNELL: [*rising and drawing herself up*] You must be quite aware that what you propose is out of the question.

JACK: Then a passionate celibacy is all that any of us can look forward to.   230

LADY BRACKNELL: That is not the destiny I propose for Gwendolen. Algernon, of course, can choose for himself. [*pulls out her watch*] Come dear; [GWENDOLEN *rises.*] we have already missed five, if not six, trains. To miss any more might expose us to comment on the platform.

[*Enter* CHASUBLE.]

CHASUBLE: Everything is quite ready for the christenings.   235

LADY BRACKNELL: The christenings, sir! Is not that somewhat premature?

CHASUBLE: [*looking rather puzzled, and pointing to* JACK *and* ALGERNON] Both these gentlemen have expressed a desire for immediate baptism.

LADY BRACKNELL: At their age? The idea is grotesque and irreligious! Algernon, I forbid you to be baptized. I will not hear of such excesses. Lord Bracknell would be highly   240
displeased if he learned that that was the way in which you wasted your time and money.

CHASUBLE: Am I to understand then that there are to be no christenings at all this afternoon?

JACK: I don't think that, as things are now, it would be of much practical value to either of   245
us, Dr. Chasuble.

CHASUBLE: I am grieved to hear such sentiments from you, Mr. Worthing. They savor of the heretical views of the Anabaptists,[27] views that I have completely refuted in four of my unpublished sermons. However, as your present mood seems to be one peculiarly secular, I will return to the church at once. Indeed, I have just been informed   250
by the pew-opener that for the last hour and a half Miss Prism has been waiting for me in the vestry.

LADY BRACKNELL: [*starting*] Miss Prism! Did I hear you mention a Miss Prism?

---

[27] **Anabaptists** Christian sect advocating adult baptism even for those already baptized as infants

CHASUBLE: Yes, Lady Bracknell. I am on my way to join her.

LADY BRACKNELL: Pray allow me to detain you for a moment. This matter may prove to 255
be one of vital importance to Lord Bracknell and myself. Is this Miss Prism a female
of repellent aspect, remotely connected with education?

CHASUBLE: [*somewhat indignantly*] She is the most cultivated of ladies, and the very picture of respectability.

LADY BRACKNELL: It is obviously the same person. May I ask what position she holds in 260
your household?

CHASUBLE: [*severely*] I am a celibate, madam.

JACK: [*interposing*] Miss Prism, Lady Bracknell, has been for the last three years Miss
Cardew's esteemed governess and valued companion.

LADY BRACKNELL: In spite of what I hear of her, I must see her at once. Let her be sent for. 265

CHASUBLE: [*looking off*] She approaches; she is nigh.

[*Enter* MISS PRISM *hurriedly.*]

MISS PRISM: I was told you expected me in the vestry, dear Canon. I have been waiting for
you there for an hour and three-quarters. [*Catches sight of* LADY BRACKNELL, *who
has fixed her with a stony glare.* MISS PRISM *grows pale and quails. She looks
anxiously round as if desirous to escape.*] 270

LADY BRACKNELL: [*in a severe, judicial voice*] Prism! [MISS PRISM *bows her head in shame.*]
Come here, Prism! [MISS PRISM *approaches in a humble manner.*] Prism! Where is
that baby?

[*General consternation. The* CANON *starts back in horror.* ALGERNON *and*
JACK *pretend to be anxious to shield* CECILY *and* GWENDOLEN *from hearing
the details of a terrible public scandal.*]

Twenty-eight years ago, Prism, you left Lord Bracknell's house, Number 104, Upper
Grosvenor Street, in charge of a perambulator that contained a baby of the male 275
sex. You never returned. A few weeks later, through the elaborate investigations of
the Metropolitan police, the perambulator was discovered at midnight, standing by
itself in a remote corner of Bayswater. It contained the manuscript of a three-volume
novel of more than usually revolting sentimentality. [MISS PRISM *starts in involuntary
indignation.*] But the baby was not there! [*Everyone looks at* MISS PRISM.] Prism, 280
where is that baby? [*a pause*]

MISS PRISM: Lady Bracknell, I admit with shame that I do not know. I only wish I did.
The plain facts of the case are these. On the morning of the day you mention, a day
that is forever branded on my memory, I prepared as usual to take the baby out in
its perambulator. I had also with me a somewhat old, but capacious hand-bag in 285
which I had intended to place the manuscript of a work of fiction that I had written
during my few unoccupied hours. In a moment of mental abstraction, for which I
never can forgive myself, I deposited the manuscript in the bassinette, and placed
the baby in the hand-bag.

JACK: [*who has been listening attentively*] But where did you deposit the hand-bag? 290

MISS PRISM: Do not ask me, Mr. Worthing.

JACK: Miss Prism, this is a matter of no small importance to me. I insist on knowing where
you deposited the hand-bag that contained that infant.

MISS PRISM: I left it in the cloak-room of one of the larger railway stations in London.

JACK: What railway station? 295

MISS PRISM: [*quite crushed*] Victoria. The Brighton line. [*sinks into a chair*]

JACK: I must retire to my room for a moment. Gwendolen, wait here for me.

GWENDOLEN: If you are not too long, I will wait here for you all my life.

[*Exit* JACK *in great excitement.*]

CHASUBLE: What do you think this means, Lady Bracknell?

LADY BRACKNELL: I dare not even suspect, Dr. Chasuble. I need hardly tell you that in   300
families of high position strange coincidences are not supposed to occur. They are
hardly considered the thing.

[*Noises heard overhead as if someone was throwing trunks about. Everyone looks up.*]

CECILY: Uncle Jack seems strangely agitated.

CHASUBLE: Your guardian has a very emotional nature.

LADY BRACKNELL: This noise is extremely unpleasant. It sounds as if he was having   305
an argument. I dislike arguments of any kind. They are always vulgar, and often
convincing.

CHASUBLE: [*looking up*] It has stopped now. [*The noise is redoubled.*]

LADY BRACKNELL: I wish he would arrive at some conclusion.

GWENDOLEN: This suspense is terrible. I hope it will last.   310

[*Enter* JACK *with a hand-bag of black leather in his hand.*]

JACK: [*rushing over to* MISS PRISM] Is this the hand-bag, Miss Prism? Examine it carefully
before you speak. The happiness of more than one life depends on your answer.

MISS PRISM: [*calmly*] It seems to be mine. Yes, here is the injury it received through the
upsetting of a Gower Street omnibus in younger and happier days. Here is the stain
on the lining caused by the explosion of a temperance beverage, an incident that   315
occurred at Leamington. And here, on the lock, are my initials. I had forgotten that
in an extravagant mood I had had them placed there. The bag is undoubtedly mine.
I am delighted to have it so unexpectedly restored to me. It has been a great incon-
venience being without it all these years.

JACK: [*in a pathetic voice*] Miss Prism, more is restored to you than this hand-bag. I was   320
the baby you placed in it.

MISS PRISM: [*amazed*] You?

JACK: [*embracing her*] Yes . . . mother!

MISS PRISM: [*recoiling in indignant astonishment*] Mr. Worthing! I am unmarried!

JACK: Unmarried! I do not deny that is a serious blow. But after all, who has the right to   325
cast a stone against one who has suffered? Cannot repentance wipe out an act of
folly? Why should there be one law for men, and another for women? Mother, I
forgive you. [*tries to embrace her again*]

MISS PRISM: [*Still more indignant*] Mr. Worthing, there is some error. [*pointing to* LADY
BRACKNELL] There is the lady who can tell you who you really are.   330

JACK: [*after a pause*] Lady Bracknell, I hate to seem inquisitive, but would you kindly
inform me who I am?

LADY BRACKNELL: I am afraid that the news I have to give you will not altogether please
you. You are the son of my poor sister, Mrs. Moncrieff, and consequently Algernon's
elder brother.   335

JACK: Algy's elder brother? Then I have a brother after all. I knew I had a brother! I always
said I had a brother! Cecily—how could you have ever doubted that I had a brother?
[*seizes hold of* ALGERNON] Dr. Chasuble, my unfortunate brother. Miss Prism, my
unfortunate brother. Gwendolen, my unfortunate brother. Algy, you young scoundrel, you will have to treat me with more respect in the future. You have never   340
behaved to me like a brother in all your life.

ALGERNON: Well, not till to-day, old boy, I admit. I did my best, however, though I was
out of practice. [*shakes hands*]

GWENDOLEN: [*to* JACK] My own! But what own are you? What is your Christian name, now that you have become someone else? 345

JACK: Good heavens! . . . I had quite forgotten that point. Your decision on the subject of my name is irrevocable, I suppose?

GWENDOLEN: I never change, except in my affections.

CECILY: What a noble nature you have, Gwendolen!

JACK: Then the question had better be cleared up at once. Aunt Augusta, a moment. At 350 the time when Miss Prism left me in the hand-bag, had I been christened already?

LADY BRACKNELL: Every luxury that money could buy, including christening, had been lavished on you by your fond and doting parents.

JACK: Then I was christened! That is settled. Now, what name was I given? Let me know the worst. 355

LADY BRACKNELL: Being the eldest son you were naturally christened after your father.

JACK: [*irritably*] Yes, but what was my father's Christian name?

LADY BRACKNELL: [*meditatively*] I cannot at the present moment recall what the General's Christian name was. But I have no doubt he had one. He was eccentric, I admit. But only in later years. And that was the result of the Indian climate, and marriage, and 360 indigestion, and other things of that kind.

JACK: Algy! Can't you recollect what our father's Christian name was?

ALGERNON: My dear boy, we were never even on speaking terms. He died before I was a year old.

JACK: His name would appear in the Army Lists of the period, I suppose, Aunt Augusta? 365

LADY BRACKNELL: The General was essentially a man of peace, except in his domestic life. But I have no doubt his name would appear in any military directory.

JACK: The Army Lists of the last forty years are here. These delightful records should have been my constant study. [*rushes to bookcase and tears the books out*] M. Generals . . . Mallam, Maxbohm, Magley, what ghastly names they have—Markby, Migsby, Moss, 370 Moncrieff! Lieutenant 1840, Captain, Lieutenant-Colonel, Colonel, General 1869, Christian names, Ernest John. [*puts book very quietly down and speaks quite calmly*] I always told you, Gwendolen, my name was Ernest, didn't I? Well, it is Ernest after all. I mean it naturally is Ernest.

LADY BRACKNELL: Yes, I remember that the General was called Ernest. I knew I had some 375 particular reason for disliking the name.

GWENDOLEN: Ernest! My own Ernest! I felt from the first that you could have no other name!

JACK: Gwendolen, it is a terrible thing for a man to find out suddenly that all his life he has been speaking nothing but the truth. Can you forgive me? 380

GWENDOLEN: I can. For I feel that you are sure to change.

JACK: My own one!

CHASUBLE: [*to* MISS PRISM] Lætitia! [*embraces her*]

MISS PRISM: [*enthusiastically*] Frederick! At last!

ALGERNON: Cecily! [*embraces her*] At last! 385

JACK: Gwendolen! [*embraces her*] At last!

LADY BRACKNELL: My nephew, you seem to be displaying signs of triviality.

JACK: On the contrary, Aunt Augusta, I've now realized for the first time in my life the vital Importance of Being Earnest.

[*tableau*]

CURTAIN

Cat on a Hot Tin Roof
(1955)

For several years following World War II, the most successful American plays were written in a style that can be called modified realism. Influenced by modernism and by the "New Stagecraft," a design style popularized by Robert Edmond Jones, these plays sought to capture the psychological truth of characters and situations in suggestive rather than scrupulously realistic settings. Tennessee Williams helped to popularize this style with *The Glass Menagerie* (1944), in which scenes and characters are called up out of the narrator-character's memory. The emphasis in *Cat on a Hot Tin Roof* and in Williams's *A Streetcar Named Desire* (1947), both of which won Pulitzer Prizes, is on characters who are struggling to distinguish truth from illusion.

The action in *Cat on a Hot Tin Roof* takes place over the course of a single evening in a bed-sitting room in a large plantation house in Mississippi. Within this restricted time and space, the characters are engulfed in mendacity—deception both of themselves and others. Big Daddy and Brick are forced to face truths that threaten the very core of their being. Big Daddy faces the truth that he is actually dying of cancer even though he has been told he is free of it. Brick faces the truth that he drove his friend Skipper into an early grave when he refused to discuss Skipper's true feelings for him.

Brick's wife, Maggie, and his brother, Gooper (along with Gooper's wife, Mae), are primarily concerned with gaining control over Big Daddy's estate. Maggie, who comes from a far less wealthy family than Brick, describes herself as "consumed with envy an' eaten up with longing." Her description of her position as that of "a cat on a hot tin roof" gives the play its title. In Act Three Maggie falsely announces to the family that she is pregnant because she believes a child will help overcome doubts about Brick's reliability as Big Daddy's heir—doubts raised by his alcoholism. In a desperate bid to make this lie true, Maggie hides all of the alcohol from Brick, promising to return it only after he has slept with her. Her final line of the play asserts her love for Brick, as does Big Mama's last line to Big Daddy. Both Big Daddy and Brick respond to these declarations of love by saying, "Wouldn't it be funny if that was true," thereby underscoring the difficulty of knowing the truth in a world so full of mendacity.

With its powerful psychological portraits, compelling conflicts, and its insights into a world dominated by self-interest, *Cat on a Hot Tin Roof* is an excellent example of postwar modified realism.

Cat on a Hot Tin Roof
(1955)

Characters

MARGARET

BRICK

MAE, *sometimes called Sister Woman*

BIG MAMA

DIXIE, *a little girl*

BIG DADDY

REVEREND TOOKER

GOOPER, *sometimes called Brother Man*

DOCTOR BAUGH, *pronounced "Baw"*

LACEY, *a Negro servant*

SOOKEY, *another Negro servant*

Another little girl and two small boys

The set is the bed-sitting room of a plantation house in the Mississippi Delta. It is along an upstairs gallery that probably runs around the entire house; it has two pairs of very wide doors opening onto the gallery, showing white balustrades against a fair summer sky that fades into dusk and night during the course of the play. . . . The bathroom door, showing only pale-blue tile and silver towel racks, is in one side wall; the hall door in the opposite wall. Two articles of furniture need mention: a big double bed . . . ; and against the wall space between the two huge double doors upstage . . . a huge console combination of radio-phonograph (hi-fi with three speakers), TV set, and liquor cabinet, bearing and containing many glasses and bottles. . . . The walls below the ceiling should dissolve mysteriously into air; the set should be roofed by the sky. . . .

An evening in summer. The action is continuous, with two intermissions.

ACT I

At the rise of the curtain someone is taking a shower in the bathroom, the door of which is half open. A pretty young woman, with anxious lines in her face, enters the bedroom and crosses to the bathroom door.

MARGARET: [*shouting above roar of water*] One of those no-neck monsters hit me with a hot buttered biscuit so I have t' change!

> [MARGARET'*s voice is both rapid and drawling. In her long speeches she has the vocal tricks of a priest delivering a liturgical chant, the lines are almost sung, always continuing a little beyond her breath so she has to gasp for another. Sometimes she intersperses the lines with a little wordless singing, such as "DA-DA-DAAAA!"*]

[*Water turns off and* BRICK *calls out to her, but is still unseen. A tone of politely feigned interest, masking indifference, or worse, is characteristic of his speech with* MARGARET.]

BRICK: Wha'd you say, Maggie? Water was on s' loud I couldn't hearya. . . .

MARGARET: Well, I!—just remarked that!—one of th' no-neck monsters messed up m' lovely lace dress so I got t'—cha-a-ange. . . .

    5

    [*She opens and kicks shut drawers of the dresser.*]

BRICK: Why d'ya call Gooper's kiddies "no-neck monsters"?

MARGARET: Because they've got no necks! Isn't that a good enough reason?

BRICK: Don't they have any necks?

MARGARET: None visible. Their fat little heads are set on their fat little bodies without a bit of connection.

    10

BRICK: That's too bad.

MARGARET: Yes, it's too bad because you can't wring their necks if they've got no necks to wring! Isn't that right, honey?

    [*She steps out of her dress, stands in a slip of ivory satin and lace.*]

Yep, they're no-neck monsters, all no-neck people are monsters. . . .

    [*Children shriek downstairs.*]

Hear them? Hear them screaming? I don't know where their voice boxes are located since they don't have necks. I tell you I got so nervous at that table tonight I thought I would throw back my head and utter a scream you could hear across the Arkansas border an' parts of Louisiana an' Tennessee. I said to your charming sister-in-law, Mae, honey, couldn't you feed those precious little things at a separate table with an oilcloth cover? They make such a mess an' the lace cloth looks so pretty! She made enormous eyes at me and said, "Ohhh, noooooo! On Big Daddy's birthday? Why, he would never forgive me!" Well, I want you to know, Big Daddy hadn't been at the table two minutes with those five no-neck monsters slobbering and drooling over their food before he threw down his fork an' shouted, "Fo' God's sake, Gooper, why don't you put them pigs at a trough in th' kitchen?"—Well, I swear, I simply could have di-ieed!

    15

    20

    25

       Think of it, Brick, they've got five of them and number six is coming. They've brought the whole bunch down here like animals to display at a county fair. Why they have those children doin' tricks all the time! "Junior, show Big Daddy how you do this, show Big Daddy how you do that, say your little piece fo' Big Daddy, Sister. Show your dimples, Sugar. Brother, show Big Daddy how you stand on your head!"—It goes on all the time along, with constant little remarks and innuendos about the fact that you and I have not produced any children, are totally childless, and therefore totally useless!—Of course it's comical but it's also disgusting since it's so obvious what they're up to!

    30

    35

BRICK: [*without interest*] What are they up to, Maggie?

MARGARET: Why, you know what they're up to!

BRICK: [*appearing*] No, I don't know what they're up to.

[*He stands there in the bathroom doorway drying his hair with a towel and hanging onto the towel rack because one ankle is broken, plastered and bound. He is still slim and firm as a boy. His liquor hasn't started tearing him down outside. He has the additional charm of that cool air of detachment that people have who*] *have given up the struggle. But now and then, when disturbed, something flashes behind it, like lightning in a fair sky, which shows that at some deeper level he is far from peaceful. Perhaps in a stronger light he would show some signs of deliquescence, but the fading, still warm, light from the gallery treats him gently.]*

MARGARET: I'll tell you what they're up to, boy of mine!—They're up to cutting you out of your father's estate, and—   40

[*She freezes momentarily before her next remark. Her voice drops as if it were somehow a personally embarrassing admission.*]

—Now we know that Big Daddy's dyin' of—*cancer. . . .*

[*There are voices on the lawn below: long-drawn calls across distance.* MARGARET *raises her lovely bare arms and powders her armpits with a light sigh.*]

[*She adjusts the angle of a magnifying mirror to straighten an eyelash, then rises fretfully saying:*]

There's so much light in the room it—

BRICK: [*softly but sharply*] Do we?

MARGARET: Do we what?

BRICK: Know Big Daddy's dyin' of cancer?   45

MARGARET: Got the report today.

BRICK: Oh . . .

MARGARET: [*letting down bamboo blinds which cast long, gold-fretted shadows over the room*] Yep, got th' report just now . . . It didn't surprise me, Baby. . . .

[*Her voice has range and music; sometimes it drops low as a boy's and you have a sudden image of her playing boy's games as a child.*]

I recognized the symptoms soon's we got here last spring and I'm willin' to bet you   50
that Brother Man and his wife were pretty sure of it, too. That more than likely explains why their usual summer migration to the coolness of the Great Smokies was passed up this summer in favor of—hustlin' down here ev'ry whipstitch with their whole screamin' tribe! And why so many allusions have been made to Rainbow Hill lately. You know what Rainbow Hill is? Place that's famous for treatin' alcoholics   55
an' dope fiends in the movies!

BRICK: I'm not in the movies.

MARGARET: No, and you don't take dope. Otherwise you're a perfect candidate for Rainbow Hill, Baby, and that's where they aim to ship you—over my dead body! Yep, over my dead body they'll ship you there, but nothing would please them better. Then Brother   60
Man could get a-hold of the purse strings and dole out remittances to us, maybe get power of attorney and sign checks for us and cut off our credit wherever, whenever he wanted! Son-of-a-bitch!—How'd you like that, Baby?—Well, you've been doin' just about ev'rything in your power to bring it about, you've just been doin' ev'rything you can think of to aid and abet them in this scheme of theirs! Quittin'   65
work, devoting yourself to the occupation of drinkin'!—Breakin' your ankle last night on the high school athletic field: doin' what? Jumpin' hurdles? At two or three in the morning? Just fantastic! Got in the paper. *Clarksdale Register* carried a nice little item about it, human interest story about a well-known former athlete stagin' a one-man track meet on the Glorious Hill High School athletic field last night, but   70
was slightly out of condition and didn't clear the first hurdle! Brother Man Gooper claims he exercised his influence t' keep it from goin' out over AP or UP or every goddam "P."

But, Brick? You still have one big advantage!

[*During the above swift flood of words,* BRICK *has reclined with contrapuntal leisure on the snowy surface of the bed and has rolled over carefully on his side or belly.*]

BRICK: [*wryly*] Did you say something, Maggie? 75

MARGARET: Big Daddy dotes on you, honey. And he can't stand Brother Man and Brother Man's wife, that monster of fertility, Mae; she's downright odious to him! Know how I know? By little expressions that flicker over his face when that woman is holding fo'th on one of her choice topics such as—how she refused twilight sleep!—when the twins were delivered! Because she feels motherhood's an experience that a woman 80 ought to experience fully!—in order to fully appreciate the wonder and beauty of it! HAH!

[*This loud "HAH!" is accompanied by a violent action such as slamming a drawer shut.*]

—and how she made Brother Man come in an' stand beside her in the delivery room so he would not miss out on the "wonder and beauty" of it, either!—producin' those no-neck monsters. . . . 85

[*A speech of this kind would be antipathetic from almost anybody but* MARGARET; *she makes it oddly funny, because her eyes constantly twinkle and her voice shakes with laughter which is basically indulgent.*]

—Big Daddy shares my attitude toward those two! As for me, well—I give him a laugh now and then and he tolerates me. In fact!—I sometimes suspect that Big Daddy harbors a little unconscious "lech" fo' me. . . .

BRICK: What makes you think that Big Daddy has a lech for you, Maggie?

MARGARET: Way he always drops his eyes down my body when I'm talkin' to him, drops 90 his eyes to my boobs an' licks his old chops! Ha ha!

BRICK: That kind of talk is disgusting.

MARGARET: Did anyone ever tell you that you're an ass-aching Puritan, Brick? I think it's mighty fine that that ole fellow, on the doorstep of death, still takes in my shape with what I think is deserved appreciation! 95
　　And you wanta know something else? Big Daddy didn't know how many little Maes and Goopers had been produced! "How many kids have you got?" he asked at the table, just like Brother Man and his wife were new acquaintances to him! Big Mama said he was jokin', but that old boy wasn't jokin', Lord, no!
　　And when they infawmed him that they had five already and were turning out 100 number six!—the news seemed to come as a sort of unpleasant surprise. . . .

[*Children yell below.*]

Scream, monsters!

[*Turns to* BRICK *with a sudden, gay, charming smile which fades as she notices that he is not looking at her but into fading gold space with a troubled expression.*]

[*It is constant rejection that makes her humor "bitchy."*]

Yes, you should of been at that supper table, Baby.

[*Whenever she calls him "Baby" the word is a soft caress.*]

Y'know, Big Daddy, bless his ole sweet soul, he's the dearest ole thing in the world, but he does hunch over his food as if he preferred not to notice anything else. Well, 105 Mae an' Gooper were side by side at the table, direckly across from Big Daddy, watchin' his face like hawks while they jawed an' jabbered about the cuteness an' brilliance of th' no-neck monsters!

[*She giggles with a hand fluttering at her throat and her breast and her long throat arched.*]

[*She comes downstage and re-creates the scene with voice and gesture.*]

And the no-neck monsters were ranged around the table, some in high chairs and some on th' *Books of Knowledge,* all in fancy little paper caps in honor of Big Daddy's birthday, and all through dinner, well, I want you to know that Brother Man an' his partner never once, for one moment, stopped exchanging pokes an' pinches an' kicks an' signs an' signals!—Why, they were like a couple of cardsharps fleecing a sucker.—Even Big Mama, bless her ole sweet soul, she isn't th' quickest an' brightest thing in the world, she finally noticed, at last, an' said to Gooper, "Gooper, what are you an' Mae makin' all these signs at each other about?"—I swear t' goodness, I nearly choked on my chicken! 110 115

[MARGARET, *back at the dressing table, still doesn't see* BRICK. *He is watching her with a look that is not quite definable—Amused? shocked? contemptuous?— part of those and part of something else.*]

Y'know—your brother Gooper still cherishes the illusion he took a giant step up on the social ladder when he married Miss Mae Flynn of the Memphis Flynns.

[MARGARET, *moves about the room as she talks, stops before the mirror, moves on.*]

But I have a piece of Spanish news for Gooper. The Flynns never had a thing in this world but money and they lost that, they were nothing at all but fairly successful climbers. Of course, Mae Flynn came out in Memphis eight years before I made my debut in Nashville, but I had friends at Ward-Belmont who came from Memphis and they used to come to see me and I used to go to see them for Christmas and spring vacations, and so I know who rates an' who doesn't rate in Memphis society. Why, y'know ole Papa Flynn, he barely escaped doing time in the federal pen for shady manipulations on th' stock market when his chain stores crashed, and as for Mae having been a cotton carnival queen, as they remind us so often, lest we forget, well, that's one honor that I don't envy her for!—Sit on a brass throne on a tacky float an' ride down Main Street, smilin', bowin', and blowin' kisses to all the trash on the street— 120 125 130

[*She picks out a pair of jeweled sandals and rushes to the dressing table.*]

Why, year before last, when Susan McPheeters was singled out fo' that honor, y'know what happened to her? Y'know what happened to poor little Susie McPheeters?
BRICK: [*absently*] No. What happened to little Susie McPheeters?
MARGARET: Somebody spit tobacco juice in her face. 135
BRICK: [*dreamily*] Somebody spit tobacco juice in her face?
MARGARET: That's right, some old drunk leaned out of a window in the Hotel Gayoso and yelled, "Hey, Queen, hey, hey, there, Queenie!" Poor Susie looked up and flashed him a radiant smile and he shot out a squirt of tobacco juice right in poor Susie's face.
BRICK: Well, what d'you know about that. 140
MARGARET: [*gaily*] What do I know about it? I was there, I saw it!
BRICK: [*absently*] Must have been kind of funny.
MARGARET: Susie didn't think so. Had hysterics. Screamed like a banshee. They had to stop th' parade an' remove her from her throne an' go on with—

[*She catches sight of him in the mirror, gasps slightly, wheels about to face him. Count ten.*]

—*Why are you looking at me like that?*   145

BRICK: [*whistling softly, now*] Like what, Maggie?

MARGARET: [*intensely, fearfully*] The way y' were looking at me just now, befo' I caught
your eye in the mirror and you started t' whistle! I don't know how t' describe it but
it froze my blood!—I've caught you lookin' at me like that so often lately. What are
you thinkin' of when you look at me like that?   150

BRICK: I wasn't conscious of lookin' at you, Maggie.

MARGARET: Well, I was conscious of it! What were you thinkin'?

BRICK: I don't remember thinking of anything, Maggie.

MARGARET: Don't you think I know that—? Don't you—?—Think I know that—?

BRICK: [*coolly*] Know *what*, Maggie?   155

MARGARET: [*struggling for expression*] That I've gone through this—*hideous!*—*transformation*,
become—*hard! Frantic!*

[*Then she adds, almost tenderly:*]

—*cruel!!*

That's what you've been observing in me lately. How could y' help but observe it?
That's all right. I'm not—thin-skinned any more, can't afford t' be thin-skinned   160
any more.

[*She is now recovering her power.*]

—But Brick? Brick?

BRICK: Did you say something?

MARGARET: I was *goin'* t' say something: that I get—lonely. Very!

BRICK: Ev'rybody gets that. . . .   165

MARGARET: Living with someone you love can be lonelier—than living entirely *alone!*—if
the one that y' love doesn't love you. . . .

[*There is a pause.* BRICK *hobbles downstage and asks, without looking at her:*]

BRICK: Would you like to live alone, Maggie?

[*Another pause: then—after she has caught a quick, hurt breath:*]

MARGARET: No!—*God!—I wouldn't!*

[*Another gasping breath. She forcibly controls what must have been an impulse to
cry out. We see her deliberately, very forcibly, going all the way back to the world in
which you can talk about ordinary matters.*]

Did you have a nice shower?   170

BRICK: Uh-huh.

MARGARET: Was the water cool?

BRICK: No.

MARGARET: But it made y' feel fresh, huh?

BRICK: Fresher. . . .   175

MARGARET: I know something would make y' feel *much* fresher!

BRICK: What?

MARGARET: An alcohol rub. Or cologne, a rub with cologne!

BRICK: That's good after a workout but I haven't been workin' out, Maggie.

MARGARET: You've kept in good shape, though.   180

BRICK: [*indifferently*] You think so, Maggie?

MARGARET: I always thought drinkin' men lost their looks, but I was plainly mistaken.

BRICK: [*wryly*] Why; thanks, Maggie.

MARGARET: You're the only drinkin' man I know that it never seems t' put fat on.

BRICK: I'm gettin' softer, Maggie.   185

MARGARET: Well, sooner or later it's bound to soften you up. It was just beginning to soften up Skipper when—

[*She stops short.*]

I'm sorry. I never could keep my fingers off a sore—I wish you would lose your looks. If you did it would make the martyrdom of Saint Maggie a little more bearable. But no such goddam luck. I actually believe you've gotten better looking since   190 you've gone on the bottle. Yeah, a person who didn't know you would think you'd never had a tense nerve in your body or a strained muscle.

[*There are sounds of croquet on the lawn below: the click of mallets, light voices, near and distant.*]

Of course, you always had that detached quality as if you were playing a game without much concern over whether you won or lost, and now that you've lost the game, not lost but just quit playing, you have that rare sort of charm that usually   195 only happens in very old or hopelessly sick people, the charm of the defeated.—You look so cool, so cool, so enviably cool.

[*Music is heard.*]

They're playing croquet. The moon has appeared and it's white, just beginning to turn a little bit yellow. . . .

You were a wonderful lover. . . .   200

Such a wonderful person to go to bed with, and I think mostly because you were really indifferent to it. Isn't that right? Never had any anxiety about it, did it naturally, easily, slowly, with absolute confidence and perfect calm, more like opening a door for a lady or seating her at a table than giving expression to any longing for her. Your indifference made you wonderful at lovemaking—*strange?*—but true. . . .   205

You know, if I thought you would never, never, never make love to me again— I would go downstairs to the kitchen and pick out the longest and sharpest knife I could find and stick it straight into my heart, I swear that I would!

But one thing I don't have is the charm of the defeated, my hat is still in the ring, and I am determined to win!   210

[*There is the sound of croquet mallets hitting croquet balls.*]

—What is the victory of a cat on a hot tin roof?—I wish I knew. . . . Just staying on it, I guess, as long as she can. . . .

[*more croquet sounds*]

Later tonight I'm going to tell you I love you an' maybe by that time you'll be drunk enough to believe me. Yes, they're playing croquet. . . .

Big Daddy is dying of cancer. . . .   215

What were you thinking of when I caught you looking at me like that? Were you thinking of Skipper?

[BRICK *takes up his crutch, rises.*]

Oh, excuse me, forgive me, but laws of silence don't work! No, laws of silence don't work. . . .

[BRICK *crosses to the bar, takes a quick drink, and rubs his head with a towel.*]

Laws of silence don't work. . . .   220
   When something is festering in your memory or your imagination, laws of
silence don't work, it's just like shutting a door and locking it on a house on fire in hope
of forgetting that the house is burning. But not facing a fire doesn't put it out. Silence
about a thing just magnifies it. It grows and festers in silence, becomes malignant. . . .
Get dressed, Brick.   225

   [*He drops his crutch.*]

BRICK: I've dropped my crutch.

   [*He has stopped rubbing his hair dry but still stands hanging onto the towel rack in
   a white towel-cloth robe.*]

MARGARET: Lean on me.
BRICK: No, just give me my crutch.
MARGARET: Lean on my shoulder.
BRICK: I don't want to lean on your shoulder, I want my crutch!   230

   [*This is spoken like sudden lightning.*]

Are you going to give me my crutch or do I have to get down on my knees on the
floor and—
MARGARET: Here, here, take it, take it!

   [*She has thrust the crutch at him.*]

BRICK: [*hobbling out*] Thanks. . . .
MARGARET: We mustn't scream at each other, the walls in this house have ears. . . .   235

   [*He hobbles directly to liquor cabinet to get a new drink.*]

—but that's the first time I've heard you raise your voice in a long time, Brick. A
crack in the wall?—Of composure?
—I think that's a good sign. . . .
A sign of nerves in a player on the defensive!

   [BRICK *turns and smiles at her coolly over his fresh drink.*]

BRICK: It just hasn't happened yet, Maggie.   240
MARGARET: What?
BRICK: The click I get in my head when I've had enough of this stuff to make me
  peaceful. . . .
  Will you do me a favor?
MARGARET: Maybe I will. What favor?   245
BRICK: Just, just keep your voice down!
MARGARET: [*in a hoarse whisper*] I'll do you that favor, I'll speak in a whisper, if not shut
  up completely, if *you* will do *me* a favor and make that drink your last one till after
  the party.
BRICK: What party?   250
MARGARET: Big Daddy's birthday party.
BRICK: Is this Big Daddy's birthday?
MARGARET: You know this is Big Daddy's birthday!
BRICK: No, I don't, I forgot it.

MARGARET: Well, I remembered it for you. . . .   255

> [*They are both speaking as breathlessly as a pair of kids after a fight, drawing deep exhausted breaths and looking at each other with faraway eyes, shaking and panting together as if they had broken apart from a violent struggle.*]

BRICK: Good for you, Maggie.
MARGARET: You just have to scribble a few lines on this card.
BRICK: You scribble something, Maggie.
MARGARET: It's got to be your handwriting; it's your present, I've given him my present;   260
it's got to be your handwriting!

> [*The tension between them is building again, the voices becoming shrill once more.*]

BRICK: I didn't get him a present.
MARGARET: I got one for you.
BRICK: All right. You write the card, then.
MARGARET: And have him know you didn't remember his birthday?
BRICK: I didn't remember his birthday.   265
MARGARET: You don't have to prove you didn't!
BRICK: I don't want to fool him about it.
MARGARET: Just write "Love, Brick!" for God's—
BRICK: No.
MARGARET: You've *got* to!   270
BRICK: I don't have to do anything I don't want to do. You keep forgetting the conditions
on which I agreed to stay on living with you.
MARGARET: [*out before she knows it*] I'm not living with you. We occupy the same cage.
BRICK: You've got to remember the conditions agreed on.
MARGARET: They're impossible conditions!   275
BRICK: Then why don't you—?
MARGARET: HUSH! Who is out there? Is somebody at the door?

> [*There are footsteps in hall.*]

MAE: [*outside*] May I enter a moment?
MARGARET: Oh, you! Sure. Come in, Mae.

> [MAE *enters bearing aloft the bow of a young lady's archery set.*]

MAE: Brick, is this thing yours?   280
MARGARET: Why, Sister Woman—that's my Diana Trophy. Won it at the intercollegiate
archery contest on the Ole Miss campus.
MAE: It's a mighty dangerous thing to leave exposed round a house full of nawmal rid-
blooded children attracted t' weapons.
MARGARET: "Nawmal rid-blooded children attracted t' weapons" ought t' be taught to   285
keep their hands off things that don't belong to them.
MAE: Maggie, honey, if you had children of your own you'd know how funny that is. Will
you please lock this up and put the key out of reach?
MARGARET: Sister Woman, nobody is plotting the destruction of your kiddies.—Brick
and I still have our special archers' license. We're goin' deer-huntin' on Moon Lake   290
as soon as the season starts. I love to run with dogs through chilly woods, run, run
leap over obstructions—

> [*She goes into the closet carrying the bow.*]

MAE: How's the injured ankle, Brick?

BRICK: Doesn't hurt. Just itches.

MAE: Oh my! Brick—Brick, you should've been downstairs after supper! Kiddies put on a 295
show. Polly played the piano, Buster an' Sonny drums, an' then they turned out the
lights an' Dixie an' Trixie puhfawmed a toe dance in fairy costume with *spahkluhs!*
Big Daddy just beamed! He just beamed!

MARGARET: [*from the closet with a sharp laugh*] Oh, I bet. It breaks my heart that we
missed it! 300

[*She reenters.*]

But Mae? Why did y'give dawgs' names to all your kiddies?

MAE: Dogs' names?

[MARGARET *has made this observation as she goes to raise the bamboo blinds,
since the sunset glare has diminished. In crossing she winks at* BRICK.]

MARGARET: [*sweetly*] Dixie, Trixie, Buster, Sonny, Polly!—Sounds like four dogs and a
parrot . . . animal act in a circus!

MAE: Maggie? 305

[MARGARET *turns with a smile.*]

Why are you so catty?

MARGARET: 'Cause I'm a cat! But why can't you take a joke, Sister Woman?

MAE: Nothin' pleases me more than a joke that's funny. You know the real names of our
kiddies. Buster's real name is Robert. Sonny's real name is Saunders. Trixie's real name
is Marlene and Dixie's— 310

[*Someone downstairs calls for her.* "HEY, MAE!"—*She rushes to door, saying:*]

Intermission is over!

MARGARET: [*as* MAE *closes door*] I wonder what Dixie's real name is?

BRICK: Maggie, being catty doesn't help things any. . . .

MARGARET: I know! *WHY!*—Am I so catty?—'Cause I'm consumed with envy an' eaten
up with longing?—Brick, I've laid out your beautiful Shantung silk suit from Rome 315
and one of your monogrammed silk shirts. I'll put your cuff links in it, those lovely
star sapphires I get you to wear so rarely. . . .

BRICK: I can't get trousers on over this plaster cast.

MARGARET: Yes, you can, I'll help you.

BRICK: I'm not going to get dressed, Maggie. 320

MARGARET: Will you just put on a pair of white silk pajamas?

BRICK: Yes, I'll do that, Maggie.

MARGARET: Thank you, thank you *so much!*

BRICK: Don't mention it.

MARGARET: Oh, Brick! How long does it have t' go on? This punishment? Haven't I done 325
time enough, haven't I served my term, can't I apply for a—pardon?

BRICK: Maggie, you're spoiling my liquor. Lately your voice always sounds like you'd been
running upstairs to warn somebody that the house was on fire!

MARGARET: Well, no wonder, no wonder. Y'know what I feel like, Brick?

[*Children's and grown-ups' voices are blended, below, in a loud-but-uncertain
rendition of "My Wild Irish Rose."*]

I feel all the time like a cat on a hot tin roof! 330

BRICK: Then jump off the roof, jump off it, cats can jump off roofs and land on their four
feet uninjured!

MARGARET: Oh, yes!

BRICK: Do it!—Fo' God's sake, do it. . . .

MARGARET: Do what?   335

BRICK: Take a lover!

MARGARET: I can't see a man but you! Even with my eyes closed, I just see you!
Why don't you get ugly, Brick, why don't you please get fat or ugly or something so
I could stand it?

[*She rushes to hall door, opens it, listens.*]

The concert is still going on! Bravo, no-necks, bravo!   340

[*She slams and locks door fiercely.*]

BRICK: What did you lock the door for?

MARGARET: To give us a little privacy for a while.

BRICK: You know better, Maggie.

MARGARET: No, I don't know better. . . .

[*She rushes to gallery doors, draws the rose-silk drapes across them.*]

BRICK: Don't make a fool of yourself.   345

MARGARET: I don't mind makin' a fool of myself over you!

BRICK: I mind, Maggie. I feel embarrassed for you.

MARGARET: Feel embarrassed! But don't continue my torture. I can't live on and on under
these circumstances.

BRICK: You agreed to—   350

MARGARET: I know but—

BRICK: Accept that condition!

MARGARET: I CAN'T! CAN'T! CAN'T!

[*She seizes his shoulder.*]

BRICK: Let go!

[*He breaks away from her and seizes the small boudoir chair and raises it like a
lion-tamer facing a big circus cat.*]

[*Count five. She stares at him with her fist pressed to her mouth, then bursts into
shrill, almost hysterical laughter. He remains grave for a moment, then grins and
puts the chair down.*]

[BIG MAMA *calls through closed door.*]

BIG MAMA: Son? Son? Son?   355

BRICK: What is it, Big Mama?

BIG MAMA: [*outside*] Oh, son! We got the most wonderful news about Big Daddy. I just
had t' run up an' tell you right this—

[*She rattles the knob.*]

—What's this door doin', locked, faw? You all think there's robbers in the house?

MARGARET: Big Mama, Brick is dressin', he's not dressed yet.   360

BIG MAMA: That's all right, it won't be the first time I've seen Brick not dressed. Come on,
open this door!

[MARGARET, *with a grimace, goes to unlock and open the hall door, as* BRICK *hobbles rapidly to the bathroom and kicks the door shut.* BIG MAMA *has disappeared from the hall.*]

MARGARET: Big Mama?

[BIG MAMA *appears through the opposite gallery doors behind* MARGARET, *huffing and puffing like an old bulldog. She is a short, stout woman; her sixty years and 170 pounds have left her somewhat breathless most of the time; she's always tensed like a boxer, or rather, a Japanese wrestler. Her "family" was maybe a little superior to* BIG DADDY's, *but not much. She wears a black or silver lace dress and at least half a million in flashy gems. She is very sincere.*]

BIG MAMA: [*loudly, startling* MARGARET] Here—I come through Gooper's and Mae's gall'ry door. Where's Brick? *Brick*—Hurry on out of there, son, I just have a second and want to give you the news about Big Daddy.—I hate locked doors in a house. . . .   365

MARGARET: [*with affected lightness*] I've noticed you do, Big Mama, but people have got to have *some* moments of privacy, don't they?

BIG MAMA: No, ma'am, not in *my* house. [*without pause*] Whacha took off you' dress faw? I thought that little lace dress was so sweet on yuh, honey.   370

MARGARET: I thought it looked sweet on me, too, but one of m' cute little table partners used it for a napkin so—!

BIG MAMA: [*picking up stockings on floor*] What?

MARGARET: You know, Big Mama, Mae and Gooper's so touchy about those children—   375
thanks, Big Mama . . .

[BIG MAMA *has thrust the picked-up stockings in* MARGARET's *hand with a grunt.*]

—that you just don't dare to suggest there's any room for improvement in their—

BIG MAMA: Brick, hurry out!—Shoot, Maggie, you just don't like children.

MARGARET: I do SO like children! Adore them!—well brought up!

BIG MAMA: [*gentle—loving*] Well, why don't you have some and bring them up well, then,   380
instead of all the time pickin' on Gooper's an' Mae's?

GOOPER: [*shouting up the stairs*] Hey, hey, Big Mama, Betsy an' Hugh got to go, waitin' t' tell yuh g'by!

BIG MAMA: Tell 'em to hold their hawses, I'll be right down in a jiffy!

[*She turns to the bathroom door and calls out.*]

Son? Can you hear me in there?   385

[*There is a muffled answer.*]

We just got the full report from the laboratory at the Ochsner Clinic, completely negative, son, ev'rything negative, right on down the line! Nothin' a-tall's wrong with him but some little functional thing called a spastic colon. Can you hear me, son?

MARGARET: He can hear you, Big Mama.

BIG MAMA: Then why don't he say something? God Almighty, a piece of news like that   390
should make him shout. It made me shout, I can tell you. I shouted and sobbed and fell right down on my knees!—Look!

[*She pulls up her skirt.*]

See the bruises where I hit my kneecaps? Took both doctors to haul me back on my feet!

[*She laughs—she always laughs like hell at herself.*]

Big Daddy was furious with me! But ain't that wonderful news?   395

[*Facing bathroom again, she continues:*]

After all the anxiety we been through to git a report like that on Big Daddy's birth-day? Big Daddy tried to hide how much of a load that news took off his mind, but didn't fool *me*. He was mighty close to crying about it *himself!*

[*Goodbyes are shouted downstairs, and she rushes to door.*]

Hold those people down there, don't let them go!—Now, git dressed, we're all comin' up to this room fo' Big Daddy's birthday party because of your ankle.—How's his   400
ankle, Maggie?
MARGARET: Well, he broke it, Big Mama.
BIG MAMA: I know he broke it.

[*A phone is ringing in hall. A Negro voice answers:* "Mistuh Polly's res'dence."]

I mean does it hurt him much still.
MARGARET: I'm afraid I can't give you that information, Big Mama. You'll have to ask   405
Brick if it hurts much still or not.
SOOKEY: [*in the hall*] It's Memphis, Mizz Polly, it's Miss Sally in Memphis.
BIG MAMA: Awright, Sookey.

[**BIG MAMA** *rushes into the hall and is heard shouting on the phone:*]

Hello, Miss Sally. How are you, Miss Sally?—Yes, well, I was just gonna call you
about it. *Shoot!*—   410

[*She raises her voice to a bellow.*]

Miss Sally? Don't ever call me from the Gayoso Lobby, too much talk goes on in that hotel lobby, no wonder you can't hear me! Now listen, Miss Sally. They's nothin' serious wrong with Big Daddy. We got the report just now, they's nothin' wrong but a thing called a—spastic! *SPASTIC!*—colon. . . .

[*She appears at the hall door and calls to* MARGARET.]

—Maggie, come out here and talk to that fool on the phone. I'm shouted breathless!   415
MARGARET: [*goes out and is heard sweetly at phone*] Miss Sally? This is Brick's wife, Maggie.
So nice to hear your voice. Can you hear mine? Well, good!—Big Mama just wanted
you to know that they've got the report from the Ochsner Clinic and what Big
Daddy has is a spastic colon. Yes. Spastic colon, Miss Sally. That's right, spastic colon.
G'bye, Miss Sally, hope I'll see you real soon!   420

[*Hangs up a little before* MISS SALLY *was probably ready to terminate the talk.
She returns through the hall door.*]

She heard me perfectly. I've discovered with deaf people the thing to do is not shout
at them but just enunciate clearly. My rich old Aunt Cornelia was deaf as the dead
but I could make her hear me just by sayin' each word slowly, distinctly, close to
her ear. I read her the *Commercial Appeal* ev'ry night, read her the classified ads in
it, even, she never missed a word of it. But was she a mean ole thing! Know what I   425
got when she died? Her unexpired subscriptions to five magazines and the Book-of-
the-Month Club and a LIBRARY full of ev'ry dull book ever written! All else went
to her hellcat of a sister . . . meaner than she was, even!

[BIG MAMA *has been straightening things up in the room during this speech.*]

BIG MAMA: [*closing closet door on discarded clothes*] Miss Sally sure is a case! Big Daddy says she's always got her hand out fo' something. He's not mistaken. That poor ole thing always has her hand out fo' somethin'. I don't think Big Daddy gives her as much as he should.   430

[*Somebody shouts for her downstairs and she shouts:*]

I'm comin'!

[*She starts out. At the hall door, turns and jerks a forefinger, first toward the bathroom door, then toward the liquor cabinet, meaning: "Has Brick been drinking?"* MARGARET *pretends not to understand, cocks her head and raises her brows as if the pantomimic performance was completely mystifying to her.*]

[BIG MAMA *rushes back to* MARGARET:]

Shoot! Stop playin' so dumb!—I mean has he been drinkin' that stuff much yet?
MARGARET: [*with a little laugh*] Oh! I think he had a highball after supper.   435
BIG MAMA: Don't laugh about it!—Some single men stop drinkin' when they git married and others start! Brick never touched liquor before he—!
MARGARET: [*crying out*] *THAT'S NOT FAIR!*
BIG MAMA: Fair or not fair I want to ask you a question, one question: D'you make Brick happy in bed?   440
MARGARET: Why don't you ask if he makes *me* happy in bed?
BIG MAMA: Because I know that—
MARGARET: It works both ways!
BIG MAMA: Something's not right! You're childless and my son drinks!

[*Someone has called her downstairs and she has rushed to the door on the line above. She turns at the door and points at the bed.*]

When a marriage goes on the rocks, the rocks are *there*, right *there*!   445
MARGARET: That's—

[BIG MAMA *has swept out of the room and slammed the door.*]

—not *fair* . . .

[MARGARET *is alone, completely alone, and she feels it. She draws in, hunches her shoulders, raises her arms with fists clenched, shuts her eyes tight as a child about to be stabbed with a vaccination needle. When she opens her eyes again, what she sees is the long oval mirror and she rushes straight to it, stares into it with a grimace and says: "Who are you?"—Then she crouches a little and answers herself in a different voice which is high, thin, mocking: "I am Maggie the Cat!"—Straightens quickly as bathroom door opens a little and* BRICK *calls out to her.*]

BRICK: Has Big Mama gone?
MARGARET: She's gone.

[*He opens the bathroom door and hobbles out, with his liquor glass now empty, straight to the liquor cabinet. He is whistling softly.* MARGARET*'s head pivots on her long, slender throat to watch him.*]

[*She raises a hand uncertainly to the base of her throat, as if it was difficult for her to swallow, before she speaks:*]

You know, our sex life didn't just peter out in the usual way, it was cut off short, long   450
before the natural time for it to, and it's going to revive again, just as sudden as that.
I'm confident of it. That's what I'm keeping myself attractive for. For the time when
you'll see me again like other men see me. Yes, like other men see me. They still see
me, Brick, and they like what they see. Uh-huh. Some of them would give their—
      Look, Brick!   455

[*She stands before the long oval mirror, touches her breast and then her hips with her two hands.*]

How high my body stays on me!—Nothing has fallen on me—not a fraction. . . .

[*Her voice is soft and trembling: a pleading child's. At this moment as he turns to glance at her—a look which is like a player passing a ball to another player, third down and goal to go—she has to capture the audience in a grip so tight that she can hold it till the first intermission without any lapse of attention.*]

Other men still want me. My face looks strained, sometimes, but I've kept my
figure as well as you've kept yours, and men admire it. I still turn heads on the
street. Why, last week in Memphis everywhere that I went men's eyes burned holes
in my clothes, at the country club and in restaurants and department stores, there   460
wasn't a man I met or walked by that didn't just eat me up with his eyes and turn
around when I passed him and look back at me. Why, at Alice's party for her New
York cousins, the best-lookin' man in the crowd—followed me upstairs and tried to
force his way in the powder room with me, followed me to the door and tried
to force his way in!   465
BRICK: Why didn't you let him, Maggie?
MARGARET: Because I'm not that common, for one thing. Not that I wasn't almost
      tempted to. You like to know who it was? It was Sonny Boy Maxwell, that's who!
BRICK: Oh, yeah, Sonny Boy Maxwell, he was a good end-runner but had a little injury
      to his back and had to quit.   470
MARGARET: He has no injury now and has no wife and still has a lech for me!
BRICK: I see no reason to lock him out of a powder room in that case.
MARGARET: And have someone catch me at it? I'm not that stupid. Oh, I might sometime
      cheat on you with someone, since you're so insultingly eager to have me do it!—But
      if I do, you can be damned sure it will be in a place and time where no one but me   475
      and the man could possibly know. Because I'm not going to give you any excuse to
      divorce me for being unfaithful or anything else. . . .
BRICK: Maggie, I wouldn't divorce you for being unfaithful or anything else. Don't you
      know that? Hell. I'd be relieved to know that you'd found yourself a lover.
MARGARET: Well, I'm taking no chances. No, I'd rather stay on this hot tin roof.   480
BRICK: A hot tin roof's 'n uncomfo'table place t' stay on. . . .

[*He starts to whistle softly.*]

MARGARET: [*through his whistle*] Yeah, but I can stay on it just as long as I have to.
BRICK: You could leave me, Maggie.

[*He resumes whistle. She wheels about to glare at him.*]

MARGARET: Don't want to and will not! Besides if I did, you don't have a cent to pay for
      it but what you get from Big Daddy and he's dying of cancer!   485

[*For the first time a realization of* **BIG DADDY**'s *doom seems to penetrate to* **BRICK**'s *consciousness, visibly, and he looks at* **MARGARET**.]

BRICK: Big Mama just said he *wasn't,* that the report was okay.

MARGARET: That's what she thinks because she got the same story that they gave Big Daddy. And was just as taken in by it as he was, poor ole things. . . .

But tonight they're going to tell her the truth about it. When Big Daddy goes to bed, they're going to tell her that he is dying of cancer. 490

[*She slams the dresser drawer.*]

—It's malignant and it's terminal.

BRICK: Does Big Daddy know it?

MARGARET: Hell, do they *ever* know it? Nobody says, "You're dying." You have to fool them. They have to fool *themselves.*

BRICK: Why? 495

MARGARET: Why? Because human beings dream of life everlasting, that's the reason! But most of them want it on earth and not in heaven.

[*He gives a short, hard laugh at her touch of humor.*]

Well. . . . [*She touches up her mascara.*] That's how it is, anyhow. . . . [*She looks about.*] Where did I put down my cigarette? Don't want to burn up the home place, at least not with Mae and Gooper and their five monsters in it! 500

[*She has found it and sucks at it greedily. Blows out smoke and continues:*]

So this is Big Daddy's last birthday. And Mae and Gooper, they know it, oh, *they* know it, all right. They got the first information from the Ochsner Clinic. That's why they rushed down here with their no-neck monsters. Because. Do you know something? Big Daddy's made no will? Big Daddy's never made out any will in his life, and so this campaign's afoot to impress him, forcibly as possible, with the fact 505 that you drink and I've borne no children!

[*He continues to stare at her a moment, then mutters something sharp but not audible and hobbles rather rapidly out onto the long gallery in the fading, much faded, gold light.*]

MARGARET: [*continuing her liturgical chant*] Y'know, I'm *fond* of Big Daddy, I am genu- inely fond of that old man, I really *am,* you know. . . .

BRICK: [*faintly, vaguely*] Yes, I know you are. . . .

MARGARET: I've always sort of admired him in spite of his coarseness, his four-letter 510 words, and so forth. Because Big Daddy *is* what he *is,* and he makes no bones about it. He hasn't turned gentleman farmer, he's still a Mississippi redneck, as much of a redneck as he must have been when he was just overseer here on the old Jack Straw and Peter Ochello place. But he got hold of it an' built it into th' biggest an' finest plantation in the Delta.—I've always *liked* Big Daddy. . . . 515

[*She crosses to the proscenium.*]

Well, this is Big Daddy's last birthday. I'm sorry about it. But I'm facing the facts. It takes money to take care of a drinker and that's the office that I've been elected to lately.

BRICK: You don't have to take care of me.

MARGARET: Yes, I do. Two people in the same boat have got to take care of each other. At 520 least you want money to buy more Echo Spring when this supply is exhausted, or will you be satisfied with a ten-cent beer?

Mae an' Gooper are plannin' to freeze us out of Big Daddy's estate because you drink and I'm childless. But we can defeat that plan. We're going to defeat that plan!

Brick, y'know, I've been so goddam disgustingly poor all my life!—That's the 525
truth, Brick!

BRICK: I'm not sayin' it isn't.

MARGARET: Always had to suck up to people I couldn't stand because they had money and I was poor as Job's turkey. You don't know what that's like. Well, I'll tell you, it's like you would feel a thousand miles away from Echo Spring!—And had to get back 530 to it on that broken ankle . . . without a crutch!

That's how it feels to be as poor as Job's turkey and have to suck up to relatives that you hated because they had money and all you had was a bunch of hand-me-down clothes and a few old moldly three-percent government bonds. My daddy loved his liquor, he fell in love with his liquor the way you've fallen in love with Echo 535 Spring!—And my poor Mama, having to maintain some semblance of social position, to keep appearances up, on an income of one hundred and fifty dollars a month on those old government bonds!

When I came out, the year that I made my debut, I had just two evening dresses! One Mother made me from a pattern in *Vogue*, the other a hand-me-down 540 from a snotty rich cousin I hated!

—The dress that I married you in was my grandmother's weddin' gown. . . . So that's why I'm like a cat on a hot tin roof!

[BRICK *is still on the gallery. Someone below calls up to him in a warm Negro voice, "Hiya, Mistuh Brick, how yuh feelin'?"* BRICK *raises his liquor glass as if that answered the question.*]

MARGARET: You can be young without money, but you can't be old without it. You've got to be old *with* money because to be old without it is just too awful, you've got to be 545 one or the other, either *young* or *with money,* you can't be old and *without* it.—That's the *truth,* Brick. . . .

[BRICK *whistles softly, vaguely.*]

Well, now I'm dressed, I'm all dressed, there's nothing else for me to do.

[*forlornly, almost fearfully*]

I'm dressed, all dressed, nothing else for me to do. . . .

[*She moves about restlessly, aimlessly, and speaks, as if to herself.*]

I know when I made my mistake.—What am I—? Oh!—my bracelets. . . . 550

[*She starts working a collection of bracelets over her hands onto her wrists, about six on each, as she talks.*]

I've thought a whole lot about it and now I know when I made my mistake. Yes, I made my mistake when I told you the truth about that thing with Skipper. Never should have confessed it, a fatal error, tellin' you about that thing with Skipper.

BRICK: Maggie, shut up about Skipper. I mean it, Maggie; you got to shut up about Skipper.

MARGARET: You ought to understand that Skipper and I— 555

BRICK: You don't think I'm serious, Maggie? You're fooled by the fact that I am saying this quiet? Look, Maggie. What you're doing is a dangerous thing to do. You're—you're—you're—

MARGARET: This time I'm going to finish what I have to say to you. Skipper and I made love, if love you could call it, because it made both of us feel a little bit closer to you. You see, you son of a bitch, you asked too much of people, of me, of him, of all the unlucky poor damned sons of bitches that happen to love you, and there was a whole pack of them, yes, there was a pack of them besides me and Skipper, you asked too goddam much of people that loved you, you—superior creature!—you godlike being!—And so we made love to each other to dream it was you, both of us! Yes, yes, yes! Truth, truth! What's so awful about it? I like it, I think the truth is—yeah! I shouldn't have told you. . . . 560

565

BRICK: [*holding his head unnaturally still and uptilted a bit*] It was Skipper that told me about it. Not you, Maggie.

MARGARET: I told you!

BRICK: After he told me!

570

MARGARET: What does it matter who?

[BRICK *turns suddenly out upon the gallery and calls:*]

BRICK: Little girl! Hey, little girl!

LITTLE GIRL: [*at a distance*] What, Uncle Brick?

BRICK: Tell the folks to come up!—Bring everybody upstairs!

575

MARGARET: I can't stop myself! I'd go on telling you this in front of them all, if I had to!

BRICK: Little girl! Go on, go on, will you? Do what I told you, call them!

MARGARET: Because it's got to be told and you, you!—you never let me!

[*She sobs, then controls herself, and continues almost calmly.*]

It was one of those beautiful, ideal things they tell about in the Greek legends, it couldn't be anything else, you being you, and that's what made it so sad, that's what made it so awful, because it was love that never could be carried through to anything satisfying or even talked about plainly. Brick, I tell you, you got to believe me, Brick, I *do* understand all about it! I—I think it was—*noble!* Can't you tell I'm sincere when I say I respect it? My only point, the only point that I'm making, is life has got to be allowed to continue even after the *dream* of life is—all—over. . . . 580

585

[BRICK *is without his crutch. Leaning on furniture, he crosses to pick it up as she continues as if possessed by a will outside herself:*]

Why, I remember when we double-dated at college, Gladys Fitzgerald and I and you and Skipper, it was more like a date between you and Skipper. Gladys and I were just sort of tagging along as if it was necessary to chaperone you!—to make a good public impression—

BRICK: [*turns to face her, half lifting his crutch*] Maggie, you want me to hit you with this crutch? Don't you know I could kill you with this crutch? 590

MARGARET: Good Lord, man, d' you think I'd care if you did?

BRICK: One man has one great good true thing in his life. One great good thing which is true!—I had friendship with Skipper.—You are naming it dirty!

MARGARET: I'm not naming it dirty! I am naming it clean. 595

BRICK: Not love with you, Maggie, but friendship with Skipper was that one great true thing, and you are naming it dirty!

MARGARET: Then you haven't been listenin', not understood what I'm saying! I'm naming it so damn clean that it killed poor Skipper!—You two had something that had to be kept on ice, yes, incorruptible, yes!—and death was the only icebox where you could keep it. . . . 600

BRICK: I married you, Maggie. Why would I marry you, Maggie, if I was—?

MARGARET: Brick, don't brain me yet, let me finish!—I know, believe me I know, that it was only Skipper that harbored even any *unconscious* desire for anything not perfectly pure between you two!—Now let me skip a little. You married me early that summer we graduated out of Ole Miss, and we were happy, weren't we, we were blissful, yes, hit heaven together ev'ry time that we loved! But that fall you an' Skipper turned down wonderful offers of jobs in order to keep on bein' football heroes—pro football heroes. You organized the Dixie Stars that fall, so you could keep on bein' teammates forever! But somethin' was not right with it!—*Me included!*—between you. Skipper began hittin' the bottle . . . you got a spinal injury—couldn't play the Thanksgivin' game in Chicago, watched it on TV from a traction bed in Toledo. I joined Skipper. The Dixie Stars lost because poor Skipper was drunk. We drank together that night all night in the bar of the Blackstone and when cold day was comin' up over the lake an' we were comin' out drunk to take a dizzy look at it, I said, "SKIPPER! STOP LOVIN' MY HUSBAND OR TELL HIM HE'S GOT TO LET YOU ADMIT IT TO HIM!"—one way or another!

HE SLAPPED ME HARD ON THE MOUTH!—then turned and ran without stopping once, I am sure, all the way back into his room at the Blackstone. . . .

—When I came to his room that night, with a little scratch like a shy little mouse at his door, he made that pitiful, ineffectual little attempt to prove that what I had said wasn't true. . . .

[BRICK *strikes at her with crutch, a blow that shatters the gemlike lamp on the table.*]

—In this way, I destroyed him, by telling him truth that he and his world which he was born and raised in, yours and his world, had told him could not be told?

—From then on Skipper was nothing at all but a receptacle for liquor and drugs. . . .

Who shot Cock Robin? I with my—

[*She throws back her head with tight shut eyes.*]

—*merciful arrow!*

[BRICK *strikes at her; misses.*]

Missed me!—Sorry—I'm not tryin' to whitewash my behavior, Christ, no! Brick, I'm not good. I don't know why people have to pretend to be good, nobody's good. The rich or the well-to-do can afford to respect moral patterns, conventional moral patterns, but I could never afford to, yeah, but—I'm honest! Give me credit for just that, will you *please?*—Born poor, raised poor, expect to die poor unless I manage to get us something out of what Big Daddy leaves when he dies of cancer! But Brick?!—*Skipper is dead! I'm alive!* Maggie the Cat is—

[BRICK *hops awkwardly forward and strikes at her again with his crutch.*]

—alive! I am alive, alive! I am . . .

[*He hurls the crutch at her, across the bed she took refuge behind, and pitches forward on the floor as she completes her speech.*]

—alive!

[*A little girl,* DIXIE, *bursts into the room, wearing an Indian war bonnet and firing a cap pistol at* MARGARET *and shouting: "Bang, bang, bang!"*]

[*Laughter downstairs floats through the open hall door.* MARGARET *had crouched gasping to bed at child's entrance. She now rises and says with cool fury:*]

Little girl, your mother or someone should teach you—[*gasping*]—to knock at a door before you come into a room. Otherwise people might think that you—lack—good breeding. . . .   640

DIXIE: Yanh, yanh, yanh, what is Uncle Brick doin' on th' floor?

BRICK: I tried to kill your Aunt Maggie, but I failed—and I fell. Little girl, give me my crutch so I can get up off th' floor.

MARGARET: Yes, give your uncle his crutch, he's a cripple, honey, he broke his ankle last night jumping hurdles on the high school athletic field!   645

DIXIE: What were you jumping hurdles for, Uncle Brick?

BRICK: Because I used to jump them, and people like to do what they used to do, even after they've stopped being able to do it. . . .

MARGARET: That's right, that's your answer, now go away, little girl.

[DIXIE *fires cap pistol at* MARGARET *three times.*]

Stop, you stop that, monster! You little no-neck monster!   650

[*She seizes the cap pistol and hurls it through gallery doors.*]

DIXIE: [*with a precocious instinct for the cruelest thing*] You're *jealous!*—You're just jealous because you can't have babies!

[*She sticks out her tongue at* MARGARET *as she sashays past her with her stomach stuck out, to the gallery.* MARGARET *slams the gallery doors and leans panting against them. There is a pause.* BRICK *has replaced his spilt drink and sits, faraway, on the great four-poster bed.*]

MARGARET: You see?—they gloat over us being childless, even in front of their five little no-neck monsters!

[*Pause. Voices approach on the stairs.*]

Brick?—I've been to a doctor in Memphis, a—a gynecologist. . . .   655
I've been completely examined, and there is no reason why we can't have a child whenever we want one. And this is my time by the calendar to conceive. Are you listening to me? Are you? Are you LISTENING TO ME!

BRICK: Yes. I hear you, Maggie.

[*His attention returns to her inflamed face.*]

—But how in hell on Earth do you imagine—that you're going to have a child by a   660
man that can't stand you?

MARGARET: That's a problem that I will have to work out.

[*She wheels about to face the hall door.*]

Here they come!

[*The lights dim.*]

CURTAIN

ACT II

There is no lapse of time. MARGARET *and* BRICK *are in the same positions they held at the end of Act I.*

MARGARET: [*at door*]: *Here they come!*

> [BIG DADDY *appears first, a tall man with a fierce, anxious look, moving carefully not to betray his weakness even, or especially, to himself.*]

BIG DADDY: Well, Brick.
BRICK: Hello, Big Daddy.—Congratulations!
BIG DADDY: —Crap. . . .

> [*Some of the people are approaching through the hall, others along the gallery: voices from both directions.* GOOPER *and* REVEREND TOOKER *become visible outside gallery doors, and their voices come in clearly.*]

> [*They pause outside as* GOOPER *lights a cigar.*]

REVEREND TOOKER: [*vivaciously*] Oh, but St. Paul's in Grenada has three memorial   5
windows, and the latest one is a Tiffany stained-glass window that cost twenty-five
hundred dollars, a picture of Christ the Good Shepherd with a Lamb in His arms.
GOOPER: Who give that window, Preach?
REVEREND TOOKER: Clyde Fletcher's widow. Also presented St. Paul's with a baptismal
font.   10
GOOPER: Y'know what somebody ought t' give your church is a *coolin'* system, Preach.
REVEREND TOOKER: Yes, siree, Bob! And y'know what Gus Hamma's family gave in his
memory to the church at Two Rivers? A complete new stone parish-house with a
basketball court in the basement and a—
BIG DADDY: [*uttering a loud barking laugh, which is far from truly mirthful*] Hey, Preach!   15
What's all this talk about memorials, Preach? Y' think somebody's about t' kick off
around here? 'S that it?

> [*Startled by this interjection,* REVEREND TOOKER *decides to laugh at the question almost as loud as he can.*]

> [*How he would answer the question we'll never know, as he's spared that embarrassment by the voice of* GOOPER'S *wife,* MAE, *rising high and clear as she appears with* "DOC" BAUGH, *the family doctor, through the hall door.*]

MAE: [*almost religiously*]—Let's see now, they've had their *tyyy*-phoid shots, and their teta-
nus shots, their diphtheria shots and their hepatitis shots and their polio shots, they
got *those* shots every month from May through September and—Gooper? Hey!   20
Gooper!—What all have the kiddies been shot faw?
MARGARET: [*overlapping a bit*] Turn on the hi-fi, Brick! Let's have some music t' start off
th' party with!

> [*The talk becomes so general that the room sounds like a great aviary of chattering birds. Only* BRICK *remains unengaged, leaning upon the liquor cabinet with his faraway smile, an ice cube in a paper napkin with which he now and then rubs his forehead. He doesn't respond to* MARGARET's *command. She bounds forward and stoops over the instrument panel of the console.*]

GOOPER: We gave 'em that thing for a third anniversary present, got three speakers in it.

[*The room is suddenly blasted by the climax of a Wagnerian opera or a Beethoven symphony.*]

BIG DADDY: Turn that dam thing off!   25

[*Almost instant silence, almost instantly broken by the shouting charge of* BIG MAMA, *entering through hall door like a charging rhino.*]

BIG MAMA: Wha's my Brick, wha's mah precious baby!!
BIG DADDY: Sorry! Turn it back on!

[*Everyone laughs very loud.* BIG DADDY *is famous for his jokes at* BIG MAMA'*s expense, and nobody laughs louder at these jokes than* BIG MAMA *herself, though sometimes they're pretty cruel and* BIG MAMA *has to pick up or fuss with something to cover the hurt that the loud laugh doesn't quite cover.*]

[*On this occasion, a happy occasion because the dread in her heart has also been lifted by the false report on* BIG DADDY'*s condition, she giggles, grotesquely, coyly, in* BIG DADDY'*s direction and bears down upon* BRICK, *all very quick and alive.*]

BIG MAMA: Here he is, here's my precious baby! What's that you've got in your hand? You put that liquor down, son, your hand was made fo' holdin' somethin' better than that!   30
GOOPER: Look at Brick put it down!

[BRICK *has obeyed* BIG MAMA *by draining the glass and handing it to her. Again everyone laughs, some high, some low.*]

BIG MAMA: Oh, you bad boy, you're my bad little boy. Give Big Mama a kiss, you bad boy, you!—Look at him shy away, will you? Brick never liked bein' kissed or made a fuss over, I guess because he's always had too much of it!
Son, you turn that thing off!   35

[BRICK *has switched on the TV set.*]

I can't stand TV, radio was bad enough but TV has gone it one better, I mean— [*plops wheezing in chair*]—one worse, ha ha! Now what'm I sittin' down here faw? I want t' sit next to my sweetheart on the sofa, hold hands with him and love him up a little!

[BIG MAMA *has on a black-and-white–figured chiffon. The large irregular patterns, like the markings of some massive animal, the luster of her great diamonds and many pearls, the brilliants set in the silver frames of her glasses, her riotous voice, booming laugh, have dominated the room since she entered.* BIG DADDY *has been regarding her with a steady grimace of chronic annoyance.*]

BIG MAMA: [*still louder*] Preacher, Preacher, hey, Preach! Give me you' hand an' help me   40
up from this chair!
REVEREND TOOKER: None of your tricks, Big Mama!
BIG MAMA: What tricks? You give me you' hand so I can get up an'—

[REVEREND TOOKER *extends her his hand. She grabs it and pulls him into her lap with a shrill laugh that spans an octave in two notes.*]

Ever seen a preacher in a fat lady's lap? Hey, hey, folks! Ever seen a preacher in a fat lady's lap?   45

[BIG MAMA *is notorious throughout the Delta for this sort of inelegant horseplay.* MARGARET *looks on with indulgent humor, sipping Dubonnet "on the rocks" and watching* BRICK, *but* MAE *and* GOOPER *exchange signs of humorless anxiety over these antics, the sort of behavior which* MAE *thinks may account for their failure to quite get in with the smartest young married set in Memphis, despite all. One of the negroes,* LACY *or* SOOKEY, *peeks in, cackling. They are waiting for a sign to bring in the cake and champagne. But* BIG DADDY'*s not amused. He doesn't understand why, in spite of the infinite mental relief he's received from the doctor's report, he still has these same old fox teeth in his guts. "This spastic thing sure is something," he says to himself, but aloud he roars at* BIG MAMA:]

BIG DADDY: BIG MAMA, WILL YOU QUIT HORSIN'?—You're too old an' too fat fo' that sort of crazy kid stuff an' besides a woman with your blood pressure—she had two hundred last spring!—is riskin' a stroke when you mess around like that. . . .

BIG MAMA: Here comes Big Daddy's birthday!   50

[*Negroes in white jackets enter with an enormous birthday cake ablaze with candles and carrying buckets of champagne with satin ribbons about the bottle necks.*]

[MAE *and* GOOPER *strike up song, and everybody, including the Negroes and* CHILDREN, *joins in. Only* BRICK *remains aloof.*]

EVERYONE:
Happy birthday to you.
Happy birthday to you.
Happy birthday, Big Daddy

[*Some sing:* "Dear, Big Daddy!"]

Happy birthday to you.

[*Some sing:* "How old are you?"]

[MAE *has come down center and is organizing her children like a chorus. She gives them a barely audible:* "One, two, three!" *and they are off in the new tune.*]

CHILDREN:
Skinamarinka—dinka—dink   55
Skinamarinka—do
We love you.
Skinamarinka—dinka—dink
Skinamarinka—do.

[*All together, they turn to* BIG DADDY.]

Big Daddy, you!   60

[*They turn back front, like a musical comedy chorus.*]

We love you in the morning;
We love you in the night.
We love you when we're with you,
And we love you out of sight.
Skinamarinka—dinka—dink   65
Skinamarinka—do.

[MAE *turns to* BIG MAMA.]

Big Mama, too!

[BIG MAMA *bursts into tears. The Negroes leave.*]

BIG DADDY: Now Ida, what the hell is the matter with you?
MAE: She's just so happy.
BIG MAMA: I'm just so happy, Big Daddy, I have to cry or something.   70

[*Sudden and loud in the hush:*]

Brick, do you know the wonderful news that Doc Baugh got from the clinic about
Big Daddy? Big Daddy's one hundred percent!
MARGARET: Isn't that wonderful?
BIG MAMA: He's just one hundred percent. Passed the examination with flying colors. Now
that we know there's nothing wrong with Big Daddy but a spastic colon, I can tell   75
you something. I was worried sick, half out of my mind, for fear that Big Daddy
might have a thing like—

[MARGARET *cuts through this speech, jumping up and exclaiming shrilly:*]

MARGARET: Brick, honey, aren't you going to give Big Daddy his birthday present?

[*Passing by him, she snatches his liquor glass from him.*]

[*She picks up a fancily wrapped package.*]

Here it is, Big Daddy, this is from Brick!
BIG MAMA: This is the biggest birthday Big Daddy's ever had, a hundred presents and   80
bushels of telegrams from—
MAE: [*at same time*] What is it, Brick?
GOOPER: I bet 500 to 50 that Brick don't know what it is.
BIG MAMA: The fun of presents is not knowing what they are till you open the package.
Open your present, Big Daddy.   85
BIG DADDY: Open it you'self. I want to ask Brick somethin! Come here, Brick.
MARGARET: Big Daddy's callin' you, Brick.

[*She is opening the package.*]

BRICK: Tell Big Daddy I'm crippled.
BIG DADDY: I see you're crippled. I want to know how you got crippled.
MARGARET: [*making diversionary tactics*] Oh, look, oh, look, why, it's a cashmere robe!   90

[*She holds the robe up for all to see.*]

MAE: You sound surprised, Maggie.
MARGARET: I never saw one before.
MAE: That's funny.—*Hah!*
MARGARET: [*turning on her fiercely, with a brilliant smile*] Why is it funny? All my family
ever had was family—and luxuries such as cashmere robes still surprise me!   95
BIG DADDY: [*ominously*] Quiet!
MAE: [*heedless in her fury*] I don't see how you could be so surprised when you bought it
yourself at Loewenstein's in Memphis last Saturday. You know how I know?
BIG DADDY: I said, "Quiet!"
MAE: —I know because the salesgirl that sold it to you waited on me and said, "Oh, Mrs.   100
Pollitt, your sister-in-law just bought a cashmere robe for your husband's father!"
MARGARET: Sister Woman! Your talents are wasted as a housewife and mother, you really
ought to be with the FBI or—

BIG DADDY: QUIET!

> [REVEREND TOOKER's *reflexes are slower than the others'. He finishes a sentence after the bellow.*]

REVEREND TOOKER: [*to* DOC BAUGH]—the Stork and the Reaper are running neck   105
and neck!

> [*He starts to laugh gaily when he notices the silence and* BIG DADDY's *glare. His laugh dies falsely.*]

BIG DADDY: Preacher, I hope I'm not butting in on more talk about memorial stained-glass windows, am I, Preacher?

> [REVEREND TOOKER *laughs feebly, then coughs dryly in the embarrassed silence.*]

Preacher?

BIG MAMA: Now, Big Daddy, don't you pick on Preacher!   110

BIG DADDY: [*raising his voice*] You ever hear that expression "all hawk and no spit"? You bring that expression to mind with that little dry cough of yours, all hawk an' no spit. . . .

> [*The pause is broken only by a short startled laugh from* MARGARET, *the only one there who is conscious of and amused by the grotesque.*]

MAE: [*raising her arms and jangling her bracelets*] I wonder if the mosquitoes are active tonight?

BIG DADDY: What's that, Little Mama? Did you make some remark?   115

MAE: Yes, I said I wondered if the mosquitoes would eat us alive if we went out on the gallery for a while.

BIG DADDY: Well, if they do, I'll have your bones pulverized for fertilizer!

BIG MAMA: [*quickly*] Last week we had an airplane spraying the place and I think it done some good, at least I haven't had a—   120

BIG DADDY: [*cutting her speech*] Brick, they tell me, if what they tell me is true, that you done some jumping last night on the high school athletic field?

BIG MAMA: Brick, Big Daddy is talking to you, son.

BRICK: [*smiling vaguely over his drink*] What was that, Big Daddy?

BIG DADDY: They said you done some jumping on the high school track field last night.   125

BRICK: That's what they told me, too.

BIG DADDY: Was it jumping or humping that you were doing out there? What were you doing out there at three A.M., layin' a woman on that cinder track?

BIG MAMA: Big Daddy, you are off the sick-list, now, and I'm not going to excuse you for talkin' so—   130

BIG DADDY: Quiet!

BIG MAMA: —*nasty* in front of Preacher and—

BIG DADDY: *QUIET!*—I ast you, Brick, if you was cuttin' you'self a piece o' poon-tang last night on that cinder track? I thought maybe you were chasin poon-tang on that track an' tripped over something in the heat of the chase—'sthat it?   135

> [GOOPER *laughs, loud and false, others nervously following suit.* BIG MAMA *stamps her foot, and purses her lips, crossing to* MAE *and whispering something to her as* BRICK *meets his father's hard, intent, grinning stare with a slow, vague smile that he offers all situations from behind the screen of his liquor.*]

BRICK: No, sir, I don't think so. . . .

MAE: [*at the same time, sweetly*] Reverend Tooker, let's you and I take a stroll on the widow's walk.

[*She and the preacher go out on the gallery as* BIG DADDY *says:*]

BIG DADDY: Then what the hell were you doing out there at three o'clock in the morning?

BRICK: Jumping the hurdles, Big Daddy, runnin' and jumpin' the hurdles, but those high   140
hurdles have gotten too high for me, now.

BIG DADDY: 'Cause you was drunk?

BRICK: [*his vague smile fading a little*] Sober I wouldn't have tried to jump the *low* ones. . . .

BIG MAMA: [*quickly*] Big Daddy, blow out the candles on your birthday cake!   145

MARGARET: [*at the same time*] I want to propose a toast to Big Daddy Pollitt on his sixty-fifth birthday, the biggest cotton planter in—

BIG DADDY: [*bellowing with fury and disgust*] *I told you to stop it, now stop it, quit this!*

BIG MAMA: [*coming in front of* BIG DADDY *with the cake*] Big Daddy, I will not allow you to talk that way, not even on your birthday, I—   150

BIG DADDY: I'll talk like I want to on my birthday, Ida, or any other goddam day of the year and anybody here that don't like it knows what they can do!

BIG MAMA: You don't mean that!

BIG DADDY: What makes you think I don't mean it?

[*Meanwhile various discreet signals have been exchanged and* GOOPER *has also gone out on the gallery.*]

BIG MAMA: I just know you don't mean it.   155

BIG DADDY: You don't know a goddam thing and you never did!

BIG MAMA: Big Daddy, you don't mean that.

BIG DADDY: Oh, yes, I do, oh, yes, I do, I mean it! I put up with a whole lot of crap around here because I thought I was dying. And you thought I was dying and you started taking over, well, you can stop taking over now, Ida, because I'm not gonna   160
die, you can just stop now this business of taking over because you're not taking over because I'm not dying, I went through the laboratory and the goddam exploratory operation and there's nothing wrong with me but a spastic colon. And I'm not dying of cancer which you thought I was dying of. Ain't that so? Didn't you think that I was dying of cancer, Ida?   165

[*Almost everybody is out on the gallery but the two old people glaring at each other across the blazing cake.*]

[BIG MAMA'*s chest heaves and she presses a fat fist to her mouth.*]

[BIG DADDY *continues, hoarsely:*]

Ain't that so, Ida? Didn't you have an idea I was dying of cancer and now you could take control of this place and everything on it? I got that impression, I seemed to get that impression. Your loud voice everywhere, your fat old body butting in here and there!

BIG MAMA: Hush! The preacher!   170

BIG DADDY: Rut the goddam preacher!

[BIG MAMA *gasps loudly and sits down on the sofa, which is almost too small for her.*]

Did you hear what I said? I said rut the goddam preacher!

[*Somebody closes the gallery doors from outside just as there is a burst of fireworks and excited cries from the children.*]

BIG MAMA: I never seen you act like this before and I can't think what's got in you!

BIG DADDY: I went through all that laboratory and operation and all just so I would know if you or me was boss here! Well, now it turns out that I am and you ain't—and that's my birthday present—and my cake and champagne!—because for three years now you been gradually taking over. Bossing. Talking. Sashaying your fat old body around the place I made! I made this place! I was overseer on it! I was the overseer on the old Straw and Ochello plantation. I quit school at ten! I quit school at ten years old and went to work like a nigger in the fields. And I rose to be overseer of the Straw and Ochello plantation. And old Straw died and I was Ochello's partner and the place got bigger and bigger and bigger and bigger and bigger! I did all that myself with no goddam help from you, and now you think you're just about to take over. Well, I am just about to tell you that you are not just about to take over, you are not just about to take over a goddam thing. Is that clear to you, Ida? Is that very plain to you, now? Is that understood completely? I been through the laboratory from A to Z. I've had the goddam exploratory operation, and nothing is wrong with me but a spastic colon—made spastic, I guess, by *disgust!* By all the goddam lies and liars that I have had to put up with, and all the goddam hypocrisy that I lived with all these forty years that we been livin' together!

Hey! Ida!! Blow out the candles on the birthday cake! Purse up your lips and draw a deep breath and blow out the goddam candles on the cake!

BIG MAMA: Oh, Big Daddy, oh, oh, oh, Big Daddy!

BIG DADDY: What's the matter with you?

BIG MAMA: In all these years you never believed that I loved you??

BIG DADDY: Huh?

BIG MAMA: And I did, I did so much, I did love you!—I even loved your hate and your hardness, Big Daddy!

[*She sobs and rushes awkwardly out onto the gallery.*]

BIG DADDY: [*to himself*] Wouldn't it be funny if that was true. . . .

[*A pause is followed by a burst of light in the sky from the fireworks.*]

BRICK! HEY, BRICK

[*He stands over his blazing birthday cake.*]

[*After some moments,* BRICK *hobbles in on his crutch, holding his glass.*]

[MARGARET *follows him with a bright, anxious smile.*]

I didn't call you, Maggie. I called Brick.

MARGARET: I'm just delivering him to you.

[*She kisses* BRICK *on the mouth, which he immediately wipes with the back of his hand. She flies girlishly back out.* BRICK *and his father are alone.*]

BIG DADDY: Why did you do that?

BRICK: Do what, Big Daddy?

BIG DADDY: Wipe her kiss off your mouth like she'd spit on you.

BRICK: I don't know. I wasn't conscious of it.

BIG DADDY: That woman of yours has a better shape on her than Gooper's but somehow or other they got the same look about them.

BRICK: What sort of look is that, Big Daddy?

BIG DADDY: I don't know how to describe it but it's the same look. 210

BRICK: They don't look peaceful, do they?

BIG DADDY: No, they sure in hell don't.

BRICK: They look nervous as cats?

BIG DADDY: That's right, they look nervous as cats.

BRICK: Nervous as a couple of cats on a hot tin roof? 215

BIG DADDY: That's right, boy, they look like a couple of cats on a hot tin roof. It's funny that you and Gooper being so different would pick out the same type of woman.

BRICK: Both of us married into society, Big Daddy.

BIG DADDY: Crap . . . I wonder what gives them both that look?

BRICK: Well. They're sittin' in the middle of a big piece of land, Big Daddy, twenty-eight 220 thousand acres is a pretty big piece of land and so they're squaring off on it, each determined to knock off a bigger piece of it than the other whenever you let it go.

BIG DADDY: I got a surprise for those women. I'm not gonna let it go for a long time yet if that's what they're waiting for.

BRICK: That's right, Big Daddy. You just sit tight and let them scratch each other's eyes 225 out. . . .

BIG DADDY: You bet your life I'm going to sit tight on it and let those sons of bitches scratch their eyes out, ha ha ha. . . .

But Gooper's wife's a good breeder, you got to admit she's fertile. Hell, at sup-per tonight she had them all at the table and they had to put a couple of extra leafs 230 in the table to make room for them, she's got five head of them, now, and another one's comin'.

BRICK: Yep, number six is comin'. . . .

BIG DADDY: Brick, you know, I swear to God, I don't know the way it happens?

BRICK: The way what happens, Big Daddy? 235

BIG DADDY: You git you a piece of land, by hook or crook, an' things start growin' on it, things accumulate on it, and the first thing you know it's completely out of hand, completely out of hand!

BRICK: Well, they say nature hates a vacuum, Big Daddy.

BIG DADDY: That's what they say, but sometimes I think that a vacuum is a hell of a lot 240 better than some of the stuff that nature replaces it with.

Is someone out there by that door?

BRICK: Yep.

BIG DADDY: Who?

[*He has lowered his voice.*]

BRICK: Someone int'rested in what we say to each other. 245

BIG DADDY: Gooper?—*GOOPER!*

[*After a discreet pause,* MAE *appears in the gallery door.*]

MAE: Did you call Gooper, Big Daddy?

BIG DADDY: Aw, it was you.

MAE: Do you want Gooper, Big Daddy?

BIG DADDY: No, and I don't want you. I want some privacy here, while I'm having a 250 confidential talk with my son Brick. Now it's too hot in here to close them doors, but if I have to close those rutten doors in order to have a private talk with my son Brick, just let me know and I'll close 'em. Because I hate eavesdroppers, I don't like any kind of sneakin' an' spyin'.

MAE: Why, Big Daddy— 255

BIG DADDY: You stood on the wrong side of the moon, it threw your shadow!

MAE: I was just—

BIG DADDY: You was just nothing but *spyin'* an' you *know* it!

MAE: [*begins to sniff and sob*] Oh, Big Daddy, you're so unkind for some reason to those that really love you! 260

BIG DADDY: Shut up, shut up, shut up! I'm going to move you and Gooper out of that room next to this! It's none of your goddam business what goes on in here at night between Brick an' Maggie. You listen at night like a couple of rutten peekhole spies and go and give a report on what you hear to Big Mama an' she comes to me and says they say such and such and so and so about what they heard goin' on between 265 Brick an' Maggie, and Jesus, it makes me sick. I'm goin' to move you an' Gooper out of that room, I can't stand sneakin' an' spyin', it makes me sick. . . .

[MAE *throws back her head and rolls her eyes heavenward and extends her arms as if invoking God's pity for this unjust martyrdom; then she presses a handkerchief to her nose and flies from the room with a loud swish of skirts.*]

BRICK: [*now at the liquor cabinet*] They listen, do they?

BIG DADDY: Yeah. They listen and give reports to Big Mama on what goes on in here between you and Maggie. They say that— 270

[*He stops as if embarrassed.*]

—You won't sleep with her, that you sleep on the sofa. Is that true or not true? If you don't like Maggie, get rid of Maggie!—What are you doin' there now?

BRICK: Fresh'nin' up my drink.

BIG DADDY: Son, you know you got a real liquor problem?

BRICK: Yes, sir, yes, I know. 275

BIG DADDY: Is that why you quit sports announcing, because of this liquor problem?

BRICK: Yes, sir, yes, sir, I guess so.

[*He smiles vaguely and amiably at his father across his replenished drink.*]

BIG DADDY: Son, don't guess about it, it's too important.

BRICK: [*vaguely*] Yes, sir.

BIG DADDY: And listen to me, don't look at the damn chandelier. . . . 280

[*Pause.* BIG DADDY*'s voice is husky.*]

—Somethin' else we picked up at th' big fire sale in Europe.

[*another pause*]

Life is important. There's nothing else to hold onto. A man that drinks is throwing his life away. Don't do it, hold onto your life. There's nothing else to hold onto. . . . Sit down over here so we don't have to raise our voices, the walls have ears in this place. 285

BRICK: [*hobbling over to sit on the sofa beside him*] All right, Big Daddy.

BIG DADDY: Quit!—how'd that come about? Some disappointment?

BRICK: I don't know. Do you?

BIG DADDY: I'm askin' you, goddam it! How in hell would I know if you don't?

BRICK: I just got out there and found that I had a mouth full of cotton. I was always two 290 or three beats behind what was goin' on on the field and so I—

BIG DADDY: Quit!

BRICK: [*amiably*] Yes, quit.

BIG DADDY: Son?

BRICK: Huh?   295

BIG DADDY: [*inhales loudly and deeply from his cigar; then bends suddenly a little forward, exhaling loudly and raising a hand to his forehead*]

—Whew!—ha ha!—I took in too much smoke, it made me a little light-headed. . . .

[*The mantel clock chimes.*]

Why is it so damn hard for people to talk?

BRICK: Yeah. . . .   300

[*The clock goes on sweetly chiming till it has completed the stroke of ten.*]

—Nice peaceful-soundin' clock, I like to hear it all night. . . .

[*He slides low and comfortable on the sofa;* BIG DADDY *sits up straight and rigid with some unspoken anxiety. All his gestures are tense and jerky as he talks. He wheezes and pants and sniffs through his nervous speech, glancing quickly, shyly, from time to time, at his son.*]

BIG DADDY: We got that clock the summer we wint to Europe, me an' Big Mama on that damn Cook's Tour, never had such an awful time in my life, I'm tellin' you, son, those gooks over there, they gouge your eyeballs out in their grand hotels. And Big Mama bought more stuff than you could haul in a couple of boxcars, that's no crap.   305 Everywhere she wint on this whirlwind tour, she bought, bought, bought. Why, half that stuff she bought is still crated up in the cellar, under water last spring!

[*He laughs.*]

That Europe is nothin' on earth but a great big auction, that's all it is, that bunch of worn-out places, it's just a big fire sale, the whole rutten thing, an' Big Mama wint wild in it, why, you couldn't hold that woman with a mule's harness! Bought, bought,   310 bought!—lucky I'm a rich man, yes, siree, Bob, an' half that stuff is mildewin' in th' basement. It's lucky I'm a rich man, it sure is lucky, well, I'm a rich man, Brick, yep, I'm a mighty rich man.

[*His eyes light up for a moment.*]

Y'know how much I'm worth? Guess, Brick! Guess how much I'm worth!

[BRICK *smiles vaguely over his drink.*]

Close on ten million in cash an' blue-chip stocks, outside, mind you, of twenty-eight   315 thousand acres of the richest land this side of the valley Nile!

[*A puff and crackle and the night sky blooms with an eerie greenish glow. Children shriek on the gallery.*]

But a man can't buy his life with it, he can't buy back his life with it when his life has been spent, that's one thing not offered in the Europe fire sale or in the American markets or any markets on earth, a man can't buy his life with it, he can't buy back his life when his life is finished. . . .   320

That's a sobering thought, a very sobering thought, and that's a thought that I was turning over in my head, over and over and over—until today. . . .

I'm wiser and sadder, Brick, for this experience which I just gone through. They's one thing else that I remember in Europe.

BRICK: What is that, Big Daddy?   325

BIG DADDY: The hills around Barcelona in the country of Spain and the children running over those bare hills in their bare skins beggin' like starvin' dogs with howls and screeches, and how fat the priests are on the streets of Barcelona, so many of them and so fat and so pleasant, ha ha!—Y'know I could feed that country? I got money enough to feed that goddam country, but the human animal is a selfish beast and I don't reckon the money I passed out there to those howling children in the hills around Barcelona would more than upholster one of the chairs in this room, I mean pay to put a new cover on this chair! 330

Hell, I threw them money like you'd scatter feed corn for chickens, I threw money at them just to get rid of them long enough to climb back into th' car and—drive away. . . . 335

And then in Morocco, them Arabs, why, prostitution begins at four or five, that's no exaggeration, why, I remember one day in Marrakech, that old walled Arab city, I set on a broken-down wall to have a cigar, it was fearful hot there and this Arab woman stood in the road and looked at me till I was embarrassed, she stood stock still in the dusty hot road and looked at me till I was embarrassed. But listen to this. She had a naked child with her, a little naked girl with her, barely able to toddle, and after a while she set this child on the ground and give her a push and whispered something to her. 340

This child come toward me, barely able t' walk, come toddling up to me and—Jesus, it makes you sick t' remember a thing like this! 345

It stuck out its hand and tried to unbutton my trousers!

That child was not yet five! Can you believe me? Or do you think that I am making this up? I wint back to the hotel and said to Big Mama, "Git packed! We're clearing out of this country." . . .

BRICK: Big Daddy, you're on a talkin' jag tonight. 350

BIG DADDY: [*ignoring this remark*] Yes, sir, that's how it is, the human animal is a beast that dies but the fact that he's dying don't give him pity for others, no, sir, it——Did you say something?

BRICK: Yes.

BIG DADDY: What? 355

BRICK: Hand me over that crutch so I can get up.

BIG DADDY: Where you goin'?

BRICK: I'm takin' a little short trip to Echo Spring.

BIG DADDY: To where?

BRICK: Liquor cabinet. . . . 360

BIG DADDY: Yes, sir, boy——

[*He hands* BRICK *the crutch.*]

—the human animal is a beast that dies and if he's got money he buys and buys and buys and I think the reason he buys everything he can buy is that in the back of his mind he has the crazy hope that one of his purchases will be life everlasting!—Which it never can be. . . . The human animal is a beast that—— 365

BRICK: [*at the liquor cabinet*] Big Daddy, you sure are shootin' th' breeze here tonight.

[*There is a pause and voices are heard outside.*]

BIG DADDY: I been quiet here lately, spoke not a word, just sat and stared into space. I had something heavy weighing on my mind but tonight that load was took off me. That's why I'm talking.—The sky looks diff'rent to me. . . .

BRICK: You know what I like to hear most? 370

BIG DADDY: What?

BRICK: Solid quiet. Perfect unbroken quiet.
BIG DADDY: Why?
BRICK: Because it's more peaceful.
BIG DADDY: Man, you'll hear a lot of that in the grave.   375

> [*He chuckles agreeably.*]

BRICK: Are you through talkin' to me?
BIG DADDY: Why are you so anxious to shut me up?
BRICK: Well, sir, ever so often you say to me, "Brick, I want to have a talk with you," but
    when we talk, it never materializes. Nothing is said. You sit in a chair and gas about
    this and that and I look like I listen. I try to look like I listen, but I don't listen, not   380
    much. Communication is—awful hard between people an'—somehow between you
    and me, it just don't—
BIG DADDY: Have you ever been scared? I mean have you ever felt downright terror of
    something?

> [*He gets up.*]

> Just one moment. I'm going to close these doors. . . .   385

> [*He closes doors on gallery as if he were going to tell an important secret.*]

BRICK: What?
BIG DADDY: Brick?
BRICK: Huh?
BIG DADDY: Son, I thought I had it!
BRICK: Had what? Had what, Big Daddy?   390
BIG DADDY: Cancer!
BRICK: Oh . . .
BIG DADDY: I thought the old man made out of bones had laid his cold and heavy hand
    on my shoulder!
BRICK: Well, Big Daddy, you kept a tight mouth about it.   395
BIG DADDY: A pig squeals. A man keeps a tight mouth about it, in spite of a man not
    having a pig's advantage.
BRICK: What advantage is that?
BIG DADDY: Ignorance—of mortality—is a comfort. A man don't have that comfort, he's
    the only living thing that conceives of death, that knows what it is. The others go   400
    without knowing, which is the way that anything living should go, go without
    knowing, without any knowledge of it, and yet a pig squeals, but a man sometimes,
    he can keep a tight mouth about it. Sometimes he—

> [*There is a deep, smoldering ferocity in the old man.*]

—can keep a tight mouth about it. I wonder if—
BRICK: What, Big Daddy?   405
BIG DADDY: A whiskey highball would injure this spastic condition?
BRICK: No, sir, it might do it good.
BIG DADDY: [*grins suddenly, wolfishly*] Jesus, I can't tell you! The sky is open! Christ it's
    open again! It's open, boy, it's open!

> [BRICK *looks down at his drink.*]

BRICK: You feel better, Big Daddy?   410

BIG DADDY: Better? Hell! I can breathe!—All of my life I been like a doubled-up fist. . . .

[*He pours a drink.*]

—Poundin', smashin', drivin'!—now I'm going to loosen these doubled-up hands and touch things easy with them. . . .

[*He spreads his hands as if caressing the air.*]

You know what I'm contemplating?   415
BRICK: [*vaguely*] No, sir. What are you contemplating?
BIG DADDY: Ha ha!—*Pleasure!*—pleasure with *women!*

[BRICK's *smile fades a little but lingers.*]

Brick, this stuff burns me!—
—Yes, boy. I'll tell you something that you might not guess. I still have desire for women and this is my sixty-fifth birthday.   420
BRICK: I think that's mighty remarkable, Big Daddy.
BIG DADDY: Remarkable?
BRICK: Admirable, Big Daddy.
BIG DADDY: You're damn right it is, remarkable and admirable both. I realize now that I never had me enough. I let many chances slip by because of scruples about it, scruples,   425 convention—crap. . . . All that stuff is bull, bull, bull!—It took the shadow of death to make me see it. Now that shadow's lifted, I'm going to cut loose and have, what is it they call it, have me a—ball!
BRICK: A ball, huh?
BIG DADDY: That's right, a ball, a ball! Hell!—I slept with Big Mama till, let's see, five years   430 ago, till I was sixty and she was fifty-eight, and never even liked her, never did!

[*The phone has been ringing down the hall.* BIG MAMA *enters, exclaiming.*]

BIG MAMA: Don't you men hear that phone ring? I heard it way out on the gall'ry.
BIG DADDY: There's five rooms off this front gall'ry that you could go through. Why do you go through this one?

[BIG MAMA *makes a playful face as she bustles out the hall door.*]

Hunh!—Why, when Big Mama goes out of a room, I can't remember what that   435 woman looks like, but when Big Mama comes back into the room, boy, then I see what she looks like, and I wish I didn't!

[*Bends over laughing at this joke till it hurts his guts and he straightens with a grimace. The laugh subsides to a chuckle as he puts the liquor glass a little distrustfully down on the table.*]

[BRICK *has risen and hobbled to the gallery doors.*]

Hey! Where you goin'?
BRICK: Out for a breather.
BIG DADDY: Not yet you ain't. Stay here till this talk is finished, young fellow.   440
BRICK: I thought it was finished, Big Daddy.
BIG DADDY: It ain't even begun.
BRICK: My mistake. Excuse me. I just wanted to feel that river breeze.
BIG DADDY: Turn on the ceiling fan and set back down in that chair.

[BIG MAMA's *voice rises, carrying down the hall.*]

BIG MAMA: Miss Sally, you're a case! You're a caution, Miss Sally. Why didn't you give me   445
a chance to explain it to you?

BIG DADDY: Jesus, she's talking to my old maid sister again.

BIG MAMA: Well, goodbye, now, Miss Sally. You come down real soon, Big Daddy's dying
to see you! Yaisss, goodbye, Miss Sally. . . .

[*She hangs up and bellows with mirth.* BIG DADDY *groans and covers his ears as
she approaches.*]

[*Bursting in:*]

Big Daddy, that was Miss Sally callin' from Memphis again! You know what she   450
done, Big Daddy? She called her doctor in Memphis to git him to tell her what
that spastic thing is! Ha-*HAAAA!*—And called back to tell me how relieved she was
that—Hey! Let me in!

[BIG DADDY *has been holding the door half closed against her.*]

BIG DADDY: Naw I ain't. I told you not to come and go through this room. You just back
out and go through those five other rooms.   455

BIG MAMA: Big Daddy? Big Daddy? Oh, Big Daddy!—You didn't mean those things you
said to me, did you?

[*He shuts door firmly against her but she still calls.*]

Sweetheart? Sweetheart? Big Daddy? You didn't mean those awful things you said to
me?—I know you didn't. I know you didn't mean those things in your heart. . . .

[*The childlike voice fades with a sob and her heavy footsteps retreat down the hall.*
BRICK *has risen once more on his crutches and starts for the gallery again.*]

BIG DADDY: All I ask of that woman is that she leave me alone. But she can't admit to   460
herself that she makes me sick. That comes of having slept with her too many years.
Should of quit much sooner but that old woman she never got enough of it—and
I was good in bed. . . . I never should of wasted so much of it on her. . . . They say
you got just so many and each one is numbered. Well, I got a few left in me, a few,
and I'm going to pick me a good one to spend 'em on! I'm going to pick me a choice   465
one, I don't care how much she costs, I'll smother her in—minks! Ha ha! I'll strip
her naked and smother her in minks and choke her with diamonds! Ha ha! I'll strip
her naked and choke her with diamonds and smother her with minks and hump her
from hell to breakfast. *Ha aha ha ha ha!*

MAE: [*gaily at door*] Who's that laughin' in there?   470

GOOPER: Is Big Daddy laughin' in there?

BIG DADDY: Crap!—them two—*drips.* . . .

[*He goes over and touches* BRICK's *shoulder.*]

Yes, son. Brick, boy.—I'm—*happy!* I'm happy, son, I'm happy!

[*He chokes a little and bites his under lip, pressing his head quickly, shyly against
his son's head and then, coughing with embarrassment, goes uncertainly back to
the table where he set down the glass. He drinks and makes a grimace as it burns
his guts.* BRICK *sighs and rises with effort.*]

What makes you so restless? Have you got ants in your britches?

BRICK: Yes, sir. . . .   475

BIG DADDY: Why?

BRICK: —Something—hasn't happened. . . .

BIG DADDY: Yeah? What is that!

BRICK: [*sadly*]—the click. . . .

BIG DADDY: Did you say "click"?   480

BRICK: Yes, click.

BIG DADDY: What click?

BRICK: A click that I get in my head that makes me peaceful.

BIG DADDY: I sure in hell don't know what you're talking about, but it disturbs me.

BRICK: It's just a mechanical thing.   485

BIG DADDY: What is a mechanical thing?

BRICK: This click that I get in my head that makes me peaceful. I got to drink till I get it. It's just a mechanical thing, something like a—like a—like a—

BIG DADDY: Like a—

BRICK: Switch clicking off in my head, turning the hot light off and the cool night on   490
and—

   [*He looks up, smiling sadly.*]

—all of a sudden there's—peace!

BIG DADDY: [*whistles long and soft with astonishment; he goes back to* BRICK *and clasps his son's two shoulders*] Jesus! I didn't know it had gotten that bad with you. Why, boy, you're—*alcoholic!*   495

BRICK: That's the truth, Big Daddy. I'm alcoholic.

BIG DADDY: This shows how I—let things go!

BRICK: I have to hear that little click in my head that makes me peaceful. Usually I hear it sooner than this, sometimes as early as—noon, but—
   —Today it's—dilatory. . . .   500
   —I just haven't got the right level of alcohol in my bloodstream yet!

   [*This last statement is made with energy as he freshens his drink.*]

BIG DADDY: Uh—huh. Expecting death made me blind. I didn't have no idea that a son of mine was turning into a drunkard under my nose.

BRICK: [*gently*] Well, now you do, Big Daddy, the news has penetrated.

BIG DADDY: Uh-huh, yes, now I do, the news has—penetrated. . . .   505

BRICK: And so if you'll excuse me—

BIG DADDY: No, I won't excuse you.

BRICK: —I'd better sit by myself till I hear that click in my head, it's just a mechanical thing but it don't happen except when I'm alone or talking to no one. . . .

BIG DADDY: You got a long, long time to sit still, boy, and talk to no one, but now you're   510
talkin' to me. At least I'm talking to you. And you set there and listen until I tell you the conversation is over!

BRICK: But this talk is like all the others we've ever had together in our lives! It's nowhere, nowhere!—it's—it's *painful*, Big Daddy. . . .

BIG DADDY: All right, then let it be painful, but don't you move from that chair!—I'm   515
going to remove that crutch. . . .

   [*He seizes the crutch and tosses it across room.*]

BRICK: I can hop on one foot, and if I fall, I can crawl!

BIG DADDY: If you ain't careful you're gonna crawl off this plantation and then, by Jesus, you'll have to hustle your drinks along Skid Row!

BRICK: That'll come, Big Daddy. 520

BIG DADDY: Naw, it won't. You're my son and I'm going to straighten you out; now that *I'm* straightened out, I'm going to straighten out you!

BRICK: Yeah?

BIG DADDY: Today the report come in from Ochsner Clinic. Y'know what they told me?

[*His face glows with triumph.*]

The only thing that they could detect with all the instruments of science in that 525 great hospital is a little spastic condition of the colon! And nerves torn to pieces by all that worry about it.

[*A little girl bursts into room with a sparkler clutched in each fist, hops and shrieks like a monkey gone mad and rushes back out again as* BIG DADDY *strikes at her.*]

[*Silence. The two men stare at each other. A woman laughs gaily outside.*]

I want you to know I breathed a sigh of relief almost as powerful as the Vicksburg tornado!

BRICK: You weren't ready to go? 530

BIG DADDY: GO WHERE?—crap. . . .

—When you are gone from here, boy, you are long gone and no where! The human machine is not no different from the animal machine or the fish machine or the bird machine or the reptile machine or the insect machine! It's just a whole goddam lot more complicated and consequently more trouble to keep together. Yep. 535 I thought I had it. The earth shook under my foot, the sky come down like the black lid of a kettle and I couldn't breathe!—Today!!—that lid was lifted, I drew my first free breath in—how many years?—*God!*—three. . . .

[*There is laughter outside, running footsteps, the soft, plushy sound and light of exploding rockets.*]

[BRICK *stares at him soberly for a long moment; then makes a sort of startled sound in his nostrils and springs up on one foot and hops across the room to grab his crutch, swinging on the furniture for support. He gets the crutch and flees as if in horror for the gallery. His father seizes him by the sleeve of his white silk pajamas.*]

Stay here, you son of a bitch!—till I say go!

BRICK: I can't. 540

BIG DADDY: You sure in hell will, goddamn it.

BRICK: No, I can't. We talk, you talk, in—circles! We get no where, no where! It's always the same, you say you want to talk to me and don't have a ruttin' thing to say to me!

BIG DADDY: Nothin' to say when I'm tellin' you I'm going to live when I thought I was dying?! 545

BRICK: Oh—*that!*—Is that what you have to say to me?

BIG DADDY: Why, you son of a bitch! Ain't that, ain't that—*important?!*

BRICK: Well, you said that, that's said, and now I—

BIG DADDY: Now you set back down.

BRICK: You're all balled up, you— 550

BIG DADDY: I ain't balled up!

BRICK: You are, you're all balled up!

BIG DADDY: Don't tell me what I am, you drunken whelp! I'm going to tear this coat sleeve off if you don't set down!

BRICK: Big Daddy— 555

BIG DADDY: Do what I tell you! I'm the boss here, now! I want you to know I'm back in the driver's seat now!

[BIG MAMA *rushes in, clutching her great heaving bosom.*]

What in hell do you want in here, Big Mama?

BIG MAMA: Oh, Big Daddy! Why are you shouting like that? I just cain't *stainnnnnnnd— it.* . . . 560

BIG DADDY: [*raising the back of his hand above his head*] GIT!—outa here.

[*She rushes back out, sobbing.*]

BRICK: [*softly, sadly*] Christ. . . .

BIG DADDY: [*fiercely*] Yeah! Christ!—is right. . . .

[BRICK *breaks loose and hobbles toward the gallery.*]

[BIG DADDY *jerks his crutch from under* BRICK *so he steps with the injured ankle. He utters a hissing cry of anguish, clutches a chair and pulls it over on top of him on the floor.*]

Son of a—tub of—hog fat. . . .

BRICK: Big Daddy! Give me my crutch. 565

[BIG DADDY *throws the crutch out of reach.*]

Give me that crutch, Big Daddy.

BIG DADDY: Why do you drink?

BRICK: Don't know, give me my crutch!

BIG DADDY: You better think why you drink or give up drinking!

BRICK: Will you please give me my crutch so I can get up off this floor? 570

BIG DADDY: First you answer my question. Why do you drink? Why are you throwing your life away, boy, like somethin' disgusting you picked up on the street?

BRICK: [*getting onto his knees*] Big Daddy, I'm in pain, I stepped on that foot.

BIG DADDY: Good! I'm glad you're not too numb with the liquor in you to feel some pain! 575

BRICK: You—spilled my—drink. . . .

BIG DADDY: I'll make a bargain with you. You tell me why you drink and I'll hand you one. I'll pour you the liquor myself and hand it to you.

BRICK: Why do I drink?

BIG DADDY: Yea! Why? 580

BRICK: Give me a drink and I'll tell you.

BIG DADDY: Tell me first!

BRICK: I'll tell you in one word.

BIG DADDY: What word?

BRICK: DISGUST! 585

[*The clock chimes softly, sweetly.* BIG DADDY *gives it a short, outraged glance.*]

Now how about that drink?

BIG DADDY: What are you disgusted with? You got to tell me that, first. Otherwise being disgusted don't make no sense!

BRICK: Give me my crutch.

BIG DADDY: You heard me, you got to tell me what I asked you first. 590

BRICK: I told you, I said to kill my disgust!

BIG DADDY: DISGUST WITH WHAT!
BRICK: You strike a hard bargain.
BIG DADDY: What are you disgusted with?—an' I'll pass you the liquor.
BRICK: I can hop on one foot, and if I fall, I can crawl. 595
BIG DADDY: You want liquor that bad?
BRICK: [*dragging himself up, clinging to bedstead*] Yeah, I want it that bad.
BIG DADDY: If I give you a drink, will you tell me what it is you're disgusted with, Brick?
BRICK: Yes, sir, I will try to.

[*The old man pours him a drink and solemnly passes it to him.*]

[*There is silence as* BRICK *drinks.*]

Have you ever heard the word "mendacity"? 600
BIG DADDY: Sure. Mendacity is one of them five-dollar words that cheap politicians throw
back and forth at each other.
BRICK: You know what it means?
BIG DADDY: Don't it mean lying and liars?
BRICK: Yes, sir, lying and liars. 605
BIG DADDY: Has someone been lying to you?
CHILDREN: [*chanting in chorus offstage*]
We want Big Dad-dee!
We want Big Dad-dee!

[GOOPER *appears in the gallery door.*]

GOOPER: Big Daddy, the kiddies are shouting for you out there. 610
BIG DADDY: [*fiercely*] Keep out, Gooper!
GOOPER: 'Scuse *me!*

[BIG DADDY *slams the doors after* GOOPER.]

BIG DADDY: Who's been lying to you, has Margaret been lying to you, has your wife been
lying to you about something, Brick?
BRICK: Not her. That wouldn't matter. 615
BIG DADDY: Then who's been lying to you, and what about?
BRICK: No one single person and no one lie. . . .
BIG DADDY: Then what, what then, for Christ's sake?
BRICK: The whole, the whole—thing. . . .
BIG DADDY: Why are you rubbing your head? You got a headache? 620
BRICK: No, I'm tryin' to—
BIG DADDY: —Concentrate, but you can't because your brain's all soaked with liquor, is
that the trouble? Wet brain!

[*He snatches the glass from* BRICK's *hand.*]

What do you know about this mendacity thing? Hell! I could write a book on it!
Don't you know that? I could write a book on it and still not cover the subject? Well, 625
I could, I could write a goddam book on it and still not cover the subject anywhere
near enough!!—Think of all the lies I got to put up with!—Pretenses! Ain't that
mendacity? Having to pretend stuff you don't think or feel or have any idea of?
Having for instance to act like I care for Big Mama!—I haven't been able to stand
the sight, sound, or smell of that woman for forty years now!—even when I *laid* 630
her!—regular as a piston. . . .

Pretend to love that son of a bitch of a Gooper and his wife Mae and those five same screechers out there like parrots in a jungle? Jesus! Can't stand to look at 'em!

Church!—it bores the bejesus out of me but I go!—I go an' sit there and listen to the fool preacher!

Clubs!—Elks! Masons! Rotary!—*crap!*

[*A spasm of pain makes him clutch his belly. He sinks into a chair and his voice is softer and hoarser.*]

You I *do* like for some reason, did always have some kind of real feeling for— affection—respect yes, always. . . .

You and being a success as a planter is all I ever had any devotion to in my whole life and that's the truth. . . .

I don't know why, but it is!

I've lived with mendacity!—Why can't *you* live with it? Hell, you *got* to live with it, there's nothing *else* to *live* with except mendacity, is there?

BRICK: Yes, sir. Yes, sir, there is something else that you can live with!

BIG DADDY: What?

BRICK: [*lifting his glass*] This!—Liquor. . . .

BIG DADDY: That's not living, that's dodging away from life.

BRICK: I want to dodge away from it.

BIG DADDY: Then why don't you kill yourself, man?

BRICK: I like to drink. . . .

BIG DADDY: Oh, God, I can't talk to you. . . .

BRICK: I'm sorry, Big Daddy.

BIG DADDY: Not as sorry as I am. I'll tell you something. A little while back when I thought my number was up—

[*This speech should have torrential pace and fury.*]

—before I found out it was just this—spastic—colon. I thought about you. Should I or should I not, if the jig was up, give you this place when I go—since I hate Gooper an' Mae an' know that they hate me, and since all five same monkeys are little Maes an' Goopers.—And I thought, No!—Then I thought, Yes!—I couldn't make up my mind. I hate Gooper and his five same monkeys and that bitch Mae! Why should I turn over twenty-eight thousand acres of the richest land this side of the valley Nile to not my kind?—But why in hell, on the other hand, Brick—should I subsidize a goddam fool on the bottle?—Liked or not liked, well, maybe even—*loved!*—Why should I do that?—Subsidize worthless behavior? Rot? Corruption?

BRICK: [*smiling*] I understand.

BIG DADDY: Well, if you do, you're smarter than I am, goddam it, because I don't understand. And this I will tell you frankly. I didn't make up my mind at all on that question and still to this day I ain't made out no will!—Well, now I don't have to. The pressure is gone. I can just wait and see if you pull yourself together or if you don't.

BRICK: That's right, Big Daddy.

BIG DADDY: You sound like you thought I was kidding.

BRICK: [*rising*] No, sir, I know you're not kidding.

BIG DADDY: But you don't care—?

BRICK: [*hobbling toward the gallery door*] No, sir, I don't care. . . .

Now how about taking a look at your birthday fireworks and getting some of that cool breeze off the river?

[*He stands in the gallery doorway as the night sky turns pink and green and gold with successive flashes of light.*]

BIG DADDY: WAIT!—Brick. . . .

> [*His voice drops. Suddenly there is something shy, almost tender, in his restraining gesture.*]

Don't let's—leave it like this, like them other talks we've had, we've always—talked around things, we've—just talked around things for some rutten reason, I don't know what, it's always like something was left not spoken, something avoided because neither of us was honest enough with the—other. . . .   680

BRICK: I never lied to you, Big Daddy.

BIG DADDY: Did I ever to *you?*

BRICK: No, sir. . . .

BIG DADDY: Then there is at least two people that never lied to each other.

BRICK: But we've never *talked* to each other.   685

BIG DADDY: We can *now.*

BRICK: Big Daddy, there don't seem to be anything much to say.

BIG DADDY: You say that you drink to kill your disgust with lying.

BRICK: You said to give you a reason.

BIG DADDY: Is liquor the only thing that'll kill this disgust?   690

BRICK: Now. Yes.

BIG DADDY: But not once, huh?

BRICK: Not when I was still young an' believing. A drinking man's someone who wants to forget he isn't still young an' believing.

BIG DADDY: Believing what?   695

BRICK: Believing. . . .

BIG DADDY: Believing *what?*

BRICK: [*stubbornly evasive*] Believing. . . .

BIG DADDY: I don't know what the hell you mean by "believing" and I don't think you know what you mean by "believing" but if you still got sports in your blood, go back   700
to sports announcing and—

BRICK: Sit in a glass box watching games I can't play? Describing what I can't do while players do it? Sweating out their disgust and confusion in contests I'm not fit for? Drinkin' a Coke, half bourbon, so I can stand it? That's no goddam good any more, no help—time just outran me, Big Daddy—got there first. . . .   705

BIG DADDY: I think you're passing the buck.

BRICK: You know many drinkin' men?

BIG DADDY: [*with a slight, charming smile*] I have known a fair number of that species.

BRICK: Could any of them tell you why he drank?

BIG DADDY: Yep, you're passin' the buck to things like time and disgust with "mendacity"   710
and—crap!—if you got to use that kind of language about a thing, it's ninety-proof bull, and I'm not buying any.

BRICK: I had to give you a reason to get a drink!

BIG DADDY: You started drinkin' when your friend Skipper died.

> [*Silence for five beats. Then* BRICK *makes a startled movement, reaching for his crutch.*]

BRICK: What are you suggesting?   715

BIG DADDY: I'm suggesting nothing.

> [*The shuffle and clop of* BRICK's *rapid hobble away from his father's steady, grave attention.*]

—But Gooper an' Mae suggested that there was something not right exactly in your—

BRICK: [*stopping short downstage as if backed to a wall*] "Not right"?

BIG DADDY: Not, well, exactly normal in your friendship with—   720

BRICK: They suggested that, too? I thought that was Maggie's suggestion.

[BRICK's *detachment is at last broken through. His heart is accelerated; his forehead sweat-beaded; his breath becomes more rapid and his voice hoarse. The thing they're discussing, timidly and painfully on the side of* BIG DADDY, *fiercely, violently on* BRICK's *side, is the inadmissible thing that Skipper died to disavow between them. The fact that if it existed it had to be disavowed to "keep face" in the world they lived in, may be at the heart of the "mendacity" that* BRICK *drinks to kill his disgust with. It may be the root of his collapse. Or maybe it is only a single manifestation of it, not even the most important. The bird that I hope to catch in the net of this play is not the solution of one man's psychological problem. I'm trying to catch the true quality of experience in a group of people, that cloudy, flickering, evanescent—fiercely charged!—interplay of live human beings in the thundercloud of a common crisis. Some mystery should be left in the revelation of character in a play, just as a great deal of mystery is always left in the revelation of character in life, even in one's own character to himself. This does not absolve the playwright of his duty to observe and probe as clearly and deeply as he legitimately can: but it should steer him away from "pat" conclusions, facile definitions which make a play just a play, not a snare for the truth of human experience.*]

[*The following scene should be played with great concentration, with most of the power leashed but palpable in what is left unspoken.*]

Who else's suggestion is it, is it yours? How many others thought that Skipper and I were—

BIG DADDY: [*gently*] Now, hold on, hold on a minute, son.—I knocked around in my time.

BRICK: What's that got to do with—   725

BIG DADDY: I said "Hold on!"—I bummed, I bummed this country till I was—

BRICK: Whose suggestion, who else's suggestion is it?

BIG DADDY: Slept in hobo jungles and railroad Y's and flophouses in all cities before I—

BRICK: Oh, *you* think so, too, you call me your son and a queer. Oh! Maybe that's why you put Maggie and me in this room that was Jack Straw's and Peter Ochello's, in which   730
that pair of old sisters slept in a double bed where both of 'em died!

BIG DADDY: Now just don't go throwing rocks at—

[*Suddenly* REVEREND TOOKER *appears in the gallery doors, his head slightly, playfully, fatuously cocked, with a practiced clergyman's smile, sincere as a bird call blown on a hunter's whistle, the living embodiment of the pious, conventional lie.*]

[BIG DADDY *gasps a little at this perfectly timed, but incongruous, apparition.*]

—What're you lookin' for, Preacher?

REVEREND TOOKER: The gentleman's lavatory, ha ha!—heh, heh . . .

BIG DADDY: [*with strained courtesy*]—Go back out and walk down to the other end of the   735
gallery, Reverend Tooker, and use the bathroom connected with my bedroom, and
if you can't find it, ask them where it is!

REVEREND TOOKER: Ah, thanks.

[*He goes out with a deprecatory chuckle.*]

BIG DADDY: It's hard to talk in this place. . . .

BRICK: Son of a—!   740

BIG DADDY: [*leaving a lot unspoken*]—I seen all things and understood a lot of them, till
　　1910. Christ, the year that—I had worn my shoes through, hocked my—I hopped
　　off a yellow dog freight car half a mile down the road, slept in a wagon of cotton
　　outside the gin—Jack Straw an' Peter Ochello took me in. Hired me to manage this
　　place which grew into this one. When Jack Straw died—why, old Peter Ochello quit　745
　　eatin' like a dog does when its master's dead, and died, too!
BRICK: Christ!
BIG DADDY: I'm just saying I understand such—
BRICK: [*violently*] Skipper is dead. I have not quit eating!
BIG DADDY: No, but you started drinking.　　　　　　　　　　　　　　　　　　　750

　　　　　[BRICK *wheels on his crutch and hurls his glass across the room shouting.*]

BRICK: YOU THINK SO, TOO?
BIG DADDY: Shhh!

　　　　　[*Footsteps run on the gallery. There are women's calls.*]

　　　　　[BIG DADDY *goes toward the door.*]

　　Go way!—Just broke a glass. . . .

　　　　　[BRICK *is transformed, as if a quiet mountain blew suddenly up in volcanic flame.*]

BRICK: You think so, too? You think so, too? You think me an' Skipper did, did, did!—
　　sodomy!—together?　　　　　　　　　　　　　　　　　　　　　　　　755
BIG DADDY: Hold—!
BRICK: That what you—
BIG DADDY: —*ON*—a minute!
BRICK: You think we did dirty things between us, Skipper an'—
BIG DADDY: Why are you shouting like that? Why are you—　　　　　　　　　760
BRICK: —Me, is that what you think of Skipper, is that—
BIG DADDY: —so excited? I don't think nothing. I don't know nothing. I'm simply telling
　　you what—
BRICK: You think that Skipper and me were a pair of dirty old men?
BIG DADDY: Now that's—　　　　　　　　　　　　　　　　　　　765
BRICK: Straw? Ochello? A couple of—
BIG DADDY: Now just—
BRICK: —ducking sissies? Queers? Is that what you—
BIG DADDY: Shhh.
BRICK: —think?　　　　　　　　　　　　　　　　　　　　　　770

　　　　　[*He loses his balance and pitches to his knees without noticing the pain. He grabs
　　　　　the bed and drags himself up.*]

BIG DADDY: Jesus!—Whew. . . . Grab my hand!
BRICK: Naw, I don't want your hand. . . .
BIG DADDY: Well, I want yours. Git up!

　　　　　[*He draws him up, keeps an arm about him with concern and affection.*]

　　You broken out in a sweat! You're panting like you'd run a race with—
BRICK: [*freeing himself from his father's hold*] Big Daddy, you shock me, Big Daddy, you,　775
　　you—shock me! Talkin' so—

　　　　　[*He turns away from his father.*]

—casually!—about a—thing like that. . . .

—Don't you know how people *feel* about things like that? How, how *disgusted* they are by things like that? Why, at Ole Miss when it was discovered a pledge to our fraternity, Skipper's and mine, did a, attempted to do a, unnatural thing with— 780
We not only dropped him like a hot rock!—We told him to git off the campus, and he did, he got!—All the way to—

[*He halts, breathless.*]

BIG DADDY: —Where?
BRICK: —North Africa, last I heard!
BIG DADDY: Well, I have come back from further away than that, I have just now returned 785
from the other side of the moon, death's country, son, and I'm not easy to shock by anything here.

[*He comes downstage and faces out.*]

Always, anyhow, lived with too much space around me to be infected by ideas of other people. One thing you can grow on a big place more important than cotton!—is *tolerance!*—I grown it. 790

[*He returns toward* BRICK.]

BRICK: Why can't exceptional friendship, *real, real, deep, deep friendship!* between two men be respected as something clean and decent without being thought of as—
BIG DADDY: It can, it is, for God's sake.
BRICK: —*Fairies.* . . .

[*In his utterance of this word, we gauge the wide and profound reach of the conventional mores he got from the world that crowned him with early laurel.*]

BIG DADDY: I told Mae an' Gooper— 795
BRICK: Frig Mae and Gooper, frig all dirty lies and liars!—Skipper and me had a clean, true thing between us!—had a clean friendship, practically all our lives, till Maggie got the idea you're talking about. Normal? No!—It was too rare to be normal, any true thing between two people is too rare to be normal. Oh, once in a while he put his hand on my shoulder or I'd put mine on his, oh, maybe even, when we were 800 touring the country in pro football an' shared hotel rooms we'd reach across the space between the two beds and shake hands to say goodnight, yeah, one or two times we—
BIG DADDY: Brick, nobody thinks that that's not normal!
BRICK: Well, they're mistaken, it was! It was a pure an' true thing an' that's not normal. 805

[*They both stare straight at each other for a long moment. The tension breaks and both turn away as if tired.*]

BIG DADDY: Yeah, it's—hard t'—talk. . . .
BRICK: All right, then, let's—let it go. . . .
BIG DADDY: Why did Skipper crack up? Why have you?

[BRICK *looks back at his father again. He has already decided, without knowing that he has made this decision, that he is going to tell his father that he is dying of cancer. Only this could even the score between them: one inadmissible thing in return for another.*]

BRICK: [*ominously*] All right. You're asking for it, Big Daddy. We're finally going to have that real true talk you wanted. It's too late to stop it, now, we got to carry it through 810 and cover every subject.

[*He hobbles back to the liquor cabinet.*]

Uh-huh.

[*He opens the ice bucket and picks up the silver tongs with slow admiration of their frosty brightness.*]

Maggie declares that Skipper and I went into pro football after we left Ole Miss because we were scared to grow up. . . .

[*He moves downstage with the shuffle and clop of a cripple on a crutch. As* MAR-GARET *did when her speech became "recitative," he looks out into the house, commanding its attention by his direct, concentrated gaze—a broken, "tragically elegant" figure telling simply as much as he knows of "the Truth":*]

—Wanted to—keep on tossing—those long, long!—high, high!—passes that— 815
couldn't be intercepted except by time, the aerial attack that made us famous! And so we did, we did, we kept it up for one season, that aerial attack, we held it high!—Yeah, but—

—that summer, Maggie, she laid the law down to me, said, Now or never, and so I married Maggie. . . . 820

BIG DADDY: How was Maggie in bed?

BRICK: [*wryly*] Great! the greatest!

[BIG DADDY *nods as if he thought so.*]

She went on the road that fall with the Dixie Stars. Oh, she made a great show of being the world's best sport. She wore a—wore a—tall bearskin cap! A "shako," they call it, a dyed moleskin coat, a moleskin coat dyed red!—Cut up crazy! Rented 825
hotel ballrooms for victory celebrations, wouldn't cancel them when it—turned out—defeat. . . .

MAGGIE THE CAT! Ha ha!

[BIG DADDY *nods.*]

—But Skipper, he had some fever which came back on him which doctors couldn't explain and I got that injury—turned out to be just a shadow on the X-ray plate— 830
and a touch of bursitis. . . .

I lay in a hospital bed, watched our games on TV, saw Maggie on the bench next to Skipper when he was hauled out of a game for stumbles, fumbles!—Burned me up the way she hung on his arm!—Y'know, I think that Maggie had always felt sort of left out because she and me never got any closer together than two people just 835
get in bed, which is not much closer than two cats on a—fence humping. . . .

So! She took this time to work on poor dumb Skipper. He was a less-than-average student at Ole Miss, you know that, don't you?!—Poured in his mind the dirty, false idea that what we were, him and me, was a frustrated case of that ole pair of sisters that lived in this room, Jack Straw and Peter Ochello!—He, poor Skipper, 840
went to bed with Maggie to prove it wasn't true, and when it didn't work out, he thought it was true!—Skipper broke in two like a rotten stick—nobody ever turned so fast to a lush—or died of it so quick. . . .

—Now are you satisfied?

[BIG DADDY *has listened to this story, dividing the grain from the chaff. Now he looks at his son.*]

BIG DADDY: Are *you* satisfied? 845

BRICK: With what?

BIG DADDY: That half-ass story!

BRICK: What's half-ass about it?

BIG DADDY: Something's left out of that story. What did you leave out?

> [*The phone has started ringing in the hall. As if it reminded him of something,* BRICK *glances suddenly toward the sound and says:*]

BRICK: Yes!—I left out a long-distance call which I had from Skipper, in which he made a   850
drunken confession to me and on which I hung up!—last time we spoke to each
other in our lives. . . .

> [*Muted ring stops as someone answers phone in a soft, indistinct voice in hall.*]

BIG DADDY: You hung up?

BRICK: Hung up. Jesus! Well—

BIG DADDY: Anyhow now!—we have tracked down the lie with which you're disgusted   855
and which you are drinking to kill your disgust with, Brick. You been passing the
buck. This disgust with mendacity is disgust with yourself.
     You!—dug the grave of your friend and kicked him in it!—before you'd face
truth with him!

BRICK: His truth, not *mine!*   860

BIG DADDY: His truth, okay! But you wouldn't face it with him!

BRICK: Who *can* face truth? Can *you?*

BIG DADDY: Now don't start passin' the rotten buck again, boy!

BRICK: How about these birthday congratulations, these many, many happy returns of the
day, when ev'rybody but you knows there won't be any!   865

> [*Whoever has answered the hall phone lets out a high, shrill laugh; the voice becomes audible saying: "No, no, you got it all wrong! Upside down! Are you crazy?"*]

> [BRICK *suddenly catches his breath as he realizes that he has made a shocking disclosure. He hobbles a few paces, then freezes, and without looking at his father's shocked face, says:*]

Let's let's—go out, now, and—

> [BIG DADDY *moves suddenly forward and grabs hold of the boy's crutch like it was a weapon for which they were fighting for possession.*]

BIG DADDY: Oh, no, no! No one's going out! What did you start to say?

BRICK: I don't remember.

BIG DADDY: "Many happy returns when they know there won't be any"?

BRICK: Aw, hell, Big Daddy, forget it. Come on out on the gallery and look at the fireworks   870
they're shooting off for your birthday. . . .

BIG DADDY: First you finish that remark you were makin' before you cut off. "Many happy
returns when they know there won't be any"?—Ain't that what you just said?

BRICK: Look, now. I can get around without that crutch if I have to but it would be a lot
easier on the furniture an' glassware if I didn' have to go swinging along like Tarzan   875
of th'—

BIG DADDY: FINISH! WHAT YOU WAS SAYIN'!

> [*An eerie green glow shows in sky behind him.*]

BRICK: [*sucking the ice in his glass, speech becoming thick*] Leave th' place to Gooper and
Mae an' their five little same little monkeys. All I want is—

BIG DADDY: "LEAVE TH' PLACE," did you say? 880

BRICK: [*vaguely*] All twenty-eight thousand acres of the richest land this side of the valley Nile.

BIG DADDY: Who said I was "leaving the place" to Gooper or anybody? This is my sixty-fifth birthday! I got fifteen years or twenty years left in me! I'll outlive *you!* I'll bury you an' have to pay for your coffin! 885

BRICK: Sure. Many happy returns. Now let's go watch the fireworks, come on, let's—

BIG DADDY: Lying, have they been lying? About the report from th'—clinic? did they, did they—find something?—*Cancer.* Maybe?

BRICK: Mendacity is a system that we live in. Liquor is one way out an' death's the other. . . .

[*He takes the crutch from* BIG DADDY's *loose grip and swings out on the gallery leaving the doors open.*]

[*A song, "Pick a Bale of Cotton," is heard.*]

MAE: [*appearing in door*] Oh, Big Daddy, the field hands are singin' fo' you! 890

BIG DADDY: [*shouting hoarsely*] BRICK! BRICK!

MAE: He's outside drinkin', Big Daddy.

BIG DADDY: BRICK!

[MAE *retreats, awed by the passion of his voice. Children call "Brick" in tones mocking* BIG DADDY. *His face crumbles like broken yellow plaster about to fall into dust.*]

[*There is a glow in the sky.* BRICK *swings back through the doors, slowly, gravely, quite soberly.*]

BRICK: I'm sorry, Big Daddy. My head don't work any more and it's hard for me to understand how anybody could care if he lived or died or was dying or cared about any thing but whether or not there was liquor left in the bottle and so I said what I said without thinking. In some ways I'm no better than the others, in some ways worse because I'm less alive. Maybe it's being alive that makes them lie, and being almost not alive makes me sort of accidentally truthful—I don't know but—anyway—we've been friends. . . . 895

—And being friends is telling each other the truth. . . . 900

[*There is a pause.*]

You told *me!* I told *you!*

[*A child rushes into the room and grabs a fistful of firecrackers and runs out again.*]

CHILD: [*screaming*] Bang, bang, bang, bang, bang, bang, bang, bang, bang!

BIG DADDY: [*slowly and passionately*] CHRIST—DAMN—ALL—LYING SONS OF—LYING BITCHES! 905

[*He straightens at last and crosses to the inside door. At the door he turns and looks back as if he had some desperate question he couldn't put into words. Then he nods reflectively and says in a hoarse voice:*]

Yes, all liars, all liars, all lying dying liars!

[*This is said slowly, slowly, with a fierce revulsion. He goes on out.*]

—Lying! Dying! Liars!

[*His voice dies out. There is a sound of a child being slapped. It rushes, hideously bawling, through room and out the hall door.*]

[BRICK *remains motionless as the lights dim out and the curtain falls.*]

CURTAIN

────────────────── **ACT III** ──────────────────

There is no lapse of time. MAE *enters with* REVEREND TOOKER.

MAE: Where is Big Daddy! Big Daddy?
BIG MAMA: [*entering*] Too much smell of burnt fireworks makes me feel a little bit sick at my stomach.—Where is Big Daddy?
MAE: That's what I want to know, where has Big Daddy gone?
BIG MAMA: He must have turned in, I reckon he went to baid. . . .   5

       [GOOPER *enters.*]

GOOPER: Where is Big Daddy?
MAE: We don't know where he is!
BIG MAMA: I reckon he's gone to baid.
GOOPER: Well, then, now we can talk.
BIG MAMA: What *is* this talk, *what* talk?   10

       [MARGARET *appears on gallery, talking to* DR. BAUGH.]

MARGARET: [*musically*] My family freed their slaves ten years before abolition, my great-great-grandfather gave his slaves their freedom five years before the War between the States started!
MAE: Oh, for God's sake! Maggie's climbed back up in her family tree!
MARGARET: [*sweetly*] What, Mae?—Oh, where's Big Daddy?!   15

       [*The pace must be very quick. Great Southern animation.*]

BIG MAMA: [*addressing them all*] I think Big Daddy was just worn out. He loves his family, he loves to have them around him, but it's a strain on his nerves. He wasn't himself tonight, Big Daddy wasn't himself, I could tell he was all worked up.
REVEREND TOOKER: I think he's remarkable.
BIG MAMA: Yaisss! Just remarkable. Did you all notice the food he ate at that table? Did   20
you all notice the supper he put away? Why, he ate like a hawss!
GOOPER: I hope he doesn't regret it.
BIG MAMA: Why, that man—ate a huge piece of cawn-bread with molasses on it! Helped himself twice to hoppin' john.
MARGARET: Big Daddy loves hoppin' john.—We had a real country dinner.   25
BIG MAMA: [*overlapping* MARGARET] Yais, he simply adores it! An' candied yams? That man put away enough food at that table to stuff a nigger *field* hand!

GOOPER: [*with grim relish*] I hope he don't have to pay for it later on. . . .

BIG MAMA: [*fiercely*] What's *that*, Gooper?

MAE: Gooper says he hopes Big Daddy doesn't suffer tonight.

BIG MAMA: Oh, shoot, Gooper says, Gooper says! Why should Big Daddy suffer for sat- isfying a normal appetite? There's nothin' wrong with that man but nerves, he's sound as a dollar! And now he knows he is an' that's why he ate such a supper. He had a big load off his mind, knowin' he wasn't doomed t'—what he thought he was doomed to. . . .

MARGARET: [*sadly and sweetly*] Bless his old sweet soul. . . .

BIG MAMA: [*vaguely*] Yais, bless his heart, where's Brick?

MAE: Outside.

GOOPER: —Drinkin' . . .

BIG MAMA: I know he's drinkin'. You all don't have to keep tellin' *me* Brick is drinkin'. Cain't I see he's drinkin' without you continually tellin' me that boy's drinkin'?

MARGARET: Good for you, Big Mama!

[*She applauds.*]

BIG MAMA: Other people *drink* and *have* drunk an' will *drink,* as long as they make that stuff an' put it in bottles.

MARGARET: That's the truth. I never trusted a man that didn't drink.

MAE: Gooper never drinks. Don't you trust Gooper?

MARGARET: Why, Gooper, don't you drink? If I'd known you didn't drink, I wouldn't of made that remark—

BIG MAMA: Brick?

MARGARET: —at least not in your presence.

[*She laughs sweetly.*]

BIG MAMA: Brick!

MARGARET: He's still on the gall'ry. I'll go bring him in so we can talk.

BIG MAMA: [*worriedly*] I don't know what this mysterious family conference is about.

[*Awkward silence.* BIG MAMA *looks from face to face, then belches slightly and mutters, "Excuse me. . . . " She opens an ornamental fan suspended about her throat, a black lace fan to go with her black lace gown, and fans her wilting cor- sage, sniffing nervously and looking from face to face in the uncomfortable silence as* MARGARET *calls* "Brick?" *and* BRICK *sings to the moon on the gallery.*]

I don't know what's wrong here, you all have such long faces! Open that door on the hall and let some air circulate through here, will you please, Gooper?

MAE: I think we'd better leave that door closed, Big Mama, till after the talk.

BIG MAMA: Reveren' Tooker, will *you* please open that door?!

REVEREND TOOKER: I sure will, Big Mama.

MAE: I just didn't think we ought t' take any chance of Big Daddy hearin' a word of this discussion.

BIG MAMA: I *swan!* Nothing's going to be said in Big Daddy's house that he cain't hear if he wants to!

GOOPER: Well, Big Mama, it's—

[MAE *gives him a quick, hard poke to shut him up. He glares at her fiercely as she circles before him like a burlesque ballerina, raising her skinny bare arms over her head, jangling her bracelets, exclaiming:*]

MAE: *A breeze! A breeze!*

REVEREND TOOKER: I think this house is the coolest house in the Delta.—Did you all   65
know that Halsey Banks' widow put air-conditioning units in the church and rectory
at Friar's Point in memory of Halsey?

[*General conversation has resumed; everybody is chatting so that the stage sounds
like a big bird cage.*]

GOOPER: Too bad nobody cools your church off for you. I bet you sweat in that pulpit
these hot Sundays, Reverend Tooker.

REVEREND TOOKER: Yes, my vestments are drenched.   70

MAE: [*at the same time to* DR. BAUGH] You think those vitamin B$_{12}$ injections are what
they're cracked up t' be, Doc Baugh?

DOCTOR BAUGH: Well, if you want to be stuck with something I guess they're as good to
be stuck with as anything else.

BIG MAMA: [*at gallery door*] *Maggie, Maggie, aren't you comin' with Brick?*   75

MAE: [*suddenly and loudly, creating a silence*] *I have a strange feeling, I have a peculiar
feeling!*

BIG MAMA: [*turning from gallery*] What feeling?

MAE: That Brick said somethin' he shouldn't of said t' Big Daddy.

BIG MAMA: Now what on earth could Brick of said t' Big Daddy that he shouldn't say?   80

GOOPER: Big Mama, there's somethin'—

MAE: NOW, WAIT!

[*She rushes up to* BIG MAMA *and gives her a quick hug and kiss.* BIG MAMA
pushes her impatiently off as the REVEREND TOOKER*'s voice rises serenely in a
little pocket of silence:*]

REVEREND TOOKER: Yes, last Sunday the gold in my chasuble faded into th' purple. . . .

GOOPER: Reveren', you must of been preachin' hell's fire last Sunday!

[*He guffaws at this witticism but the* REVEREND *is not sincerely amused. At the
same time* BIG MAMA *has crossed over to* DR. BAUGH *and is saying to him:*]

BIG MAMA: [*her breathless voice rising high-pitched above the others*]   85
In my day they had what they call the Keeley cure for heavy drinkers. But now I
understand they just take some kind of tablets, they call them "Annie Bust" tablets.
But *Brick* don't need to take *nothin'*.

[BRICK *appears in gallery doors with* MARGARET *behind him.*]

BIG MAMA: [*unaware of his presence behind her*] That boy is just broken up over Skipper's
death. You know how poor Skipper died. They gave him a big, big dose of that   90
sodium amytal stuff at his home and then they called the ambulance and give him
another big, big dose of it at the hospital and that and all of the alcohol in his system
fo' months an' months an' months just proved too much for his heart. . . . I'm scared
of needles! I'm more scared of a needle than the knife. . . . I think more people have
been needled out of this world than—   95

[*She stops short and wheels about.*]

OH!—here's Brick! My precious baby—

[*She turns upon* BRICK *with short, fat arms extended, at the same time uttering a
loud, short sob, which is both comic and touching.*]

[BRICK *smiles and bows slightly, making a burlesque gesture of gallantry for*
MARGARET *to pass before him into the room. Then he hobbles on his crutch*

*directly to the liquor cabinet and there is absolute silence, with everybody look-
ing at* BRICK *as everybody has always looked at* BRICK *when he spoke or moved
or appeared. One by one he drops ice cubes in his glass, then suddenly, but not
quickly, looks back over his shoulder with a wry, charming smile, and says:*]

BRICK: I'm sorry! Anyone else?

BIG MAMA: [*sadly*] No, son. I *wish* you wouldn't!

BRICK: I wish I didn't have to, Big Mama, but I'm still waiting for that click in my head
    which makes it all smooth out! 100

BIG MAMA: Aw, Brick, you—BREAK MY HEART!

MARGARET: [*at the same time*] Brick, go sit with Big Mama!

BIG MAMA: I just cain't *staiiiiiiii-nnnnnd*—it. . . .

[*She sobs.*]

MAE: Now that we're all assembled—

GOOPER: We kin talk. . . . 105

BIG MAMA: Breaks my heart. . . .

MARGARET: Sit with Big Mama, Brick, and hold her hand.

[BIG MAMA *sniffs very loudly three times, almost like three drum beats in the
pocket of silence.*]

BRICK: You do that, Maggie. I'm a restless cripple. I got to stay on my crutch.

[BRICK *hobbles to the gallery door; leans there as if waiting.* MAE *sits beside* BIG
MAMA, *while* GOOPER *moves in front and sits on the end of the couch, facing
her.* REVEREND TOOKER *moves nervously into the space between them; on the
other side,* DR. BAUGH *stands looking at nothing in particular and lights a cigar.*
MARGARET *turns away.*]

BIG MAMA: Why're you all *surroundin'* me—like this? Why're you all starin' at me like this
    an' makin' signs at each other? 110

[REVEREND TOOKER *steps back startled.*]

MAE: Calm yourself, Big Mama.

BIG MAMA: Calm you'self, *you'self*, Sister Woman. How could I calm myself with everyone
    starin' at me as if big drops of blood had broken out on m' face? What's this all about,
    annh! What?

[GOOPER *coughs and takes a center position.*]

GOOPER: Now, Doc Baugh. 115

MAE: Doc Baugh?

BRICK: [*suddenly*] SHHH!

[*Then he grins and chuckles and shakes his head regretfully.*]

    —Naw!—that wasn't th' click.

GOOPER: Brick, shut up or stay out there on the gallery with your liquor! We got to talk
    about a serious matter. Big Mama wants to know the complete truth about the 120
    report we got today from the Ochsner Clinic.

MAE: [*eagerly*]—on Big Daddy's condition!

GOOPER: Yais, on Big Daddy's condition, we got to face it.

DOCTOR BAUGH: Well. . . .

BIG MAMA: [*terrified, rising*] Is there? Something? Something that I? Don't—Know? 125

> [*In these few words, this startled, very soft, question,* BIG MAMA *reviews the history of her forty-five years with* BIG DADDY, *her great, almost embarrassingly true-hearted and simple-minded devotion to* BIG DADDY, *who must have had something* BRICK *has, who made himself loved so much by the "simple expedient" of not loving enough to disturb his charming detachment, also once coupled, like* BRICK's, *with virile beauty.*]

> [BIG MAMA *has a dignity at this moment: she almost stops being fat.*]

DOCTOR BAUGH: [*after a pause, uncomfortably*] Yes?—Well—

BIG MAMA: I!!!—want to—*knowwwwwwww.* . . .

> [*Immediately she thrusts her fist to her mouth as if to deny that statement.*]

> [*Then, for some curious reason, she snatches the withered corsage from her breast and hurls it on the floor and steps on it with her short, fat feet.*]

—*Somebody must be lyin'!*—*I want to know!*

MAE: Sit down, Big Mama, sit down on this sofa.

MARGARET: [*quickly*] Brick, go sit with Big Mama. 130

BIG MAMA: What is it, what is it?

DOCTOR BAUGH: I never have seen a more thorough examination than Big Daddy Pollitt was given in all my experience with the Ochsner Clinic.

GOOPER: It's one of the best in the country.

MAE: It's *THE* best in the country—bar *none!* 135

> [*For some reason she gives* GOOPER *a violent poke as she goes past him. He slaps at her hand without removing his eyes from his mother's face.*]

DOCTOR BAUGH: Of course, they were ninety-nine and nine-tenths percent sure before they even started.

BIG MAMA: Sure of what, sure of what, sure of—*what?*—*what!*

> [*She catches her breath in a startled sob.* MAE *kisses her quickly. She thrusts* MAE *fiercely away from her, staring at the doctor.*]

MAE: Mommy, be a brave girl!

BRICK: [*in the doorway, softly*] 140
> "*By the light, by the light,*
> *Of the sil-ve-ry mo-ooo-n* . . . "

GOOPER: Shut up!—Brick.

BRICK: —Sorry. . . .

> [*He wanders out on the gallery.*]

DOCTOR BAUGH: But now, you see, Big Mama, they cut a piece off this growth, a specimen 145
of the tissue and—

BIG MAMA: Growth? You told Big Daddy—

DOCTOR BAUGH: Now wait.

BIG MAMA: [*fiercely*] You told me and Big Daddy there wasn't a thing wrong with him but—

MAE: Big Mama, they always— 150

GOOPER: Let Doc Baugh talk, will yuh?

BIG MAMA: —little spastic condition of—

> [*Her breath gives out in a sob.*]

DOCTOR BAUGH: Yes, that's what we told Big Daddy. But we had this bit of tissue run through the laboratory and I'm sorry to say the test was positive on it. It's—well— malignant. . . . 155

[*Pause.*]

BIG MAMA: —Cancer?! Cancer?!

[DR. BAUGH *nods gravely.*]

[BIG MAMA *gives a long gasping cry.*]

MAE AND GOOPER: Now, now, now, Big Mama, you had to know. . . .
BIG MAMA: *WHY DIDN'T THEY CUT IT OUT OF HIM? HANH? HANH?*
DOCTOR BAUGH: Involved too much, Big Mama, too many organs affected.
MAE: Big Mama, the liver's affected and so's the kidneys, both! It's gone way past what they 160
   call a—
GOOPER: A Surgical risk.
MAE: —Uh-huh. . . .

[BIG MAMA *draws a breath like a dying gasp.*]

REVEREND TOOKER: Tch, tch, tch, tch, tch!
DOCTOR BAUGH: Yes, it's gone past the knife. 165
MAE: That's why he's turned yellow, Mommy!
BIG MAMA: Git away from me, git away from me, Mae!

[*She rises abruptly.*]

I want Brick! Where's Brick? Where is my only son?
MAE: Mama! Did she say "*only* son"?
GOOPER: What does that make *me*? 170
MAE: A sober responsible man with five precious children!—*Six!*
BIG MAMA: I want Brick to tell me! Brick! Brick!
MARGARET: [*rising from her reflections in a corner*] Brick was so upset he went back out.
BIG MAMA: Brick!
MARGARET: Mama, let *me* tell you!
BIG MAMA: No, no, leave me alone, you're not my blood! 175
GOOPER: Mama, I'm your son! Listen to *me!*
MAE: Gooper's your son, Mama, he's your first-born!
BIG MAMA: Gooper never liked Daddy.
MAE: [*as if terribly shocked*] That's not TRUE!

[*There is a pause. The minister coughs and rises.*]

REVEREND TOOKER: [*to* MAE] I think I'd better slip away at this point. 180
MAE: [*sweetly and sadly*] Yes, Doctor Tooker, you go.
REVEREND TOOKER: [*discreetly*] Goodnight, goodnight, everybody, and God bless you all
   . . . on this place. . . .

[*He slips out.*]

DOCTOR BAUGH: That man is a good man but lacking in tact. Talking about people giving memorial windows—if he mentioned one memorial window, he must have 185
   spoke of a dozen, and saying how awful it was when somebody died intestate, the
   legal wrangles, and so forth.

[MAE *coughs, and points at* BIG MAMA.]

DOCTOR BAUGH: Well, Big Mama. . . .

[*He sighs.*]

BIG MAMA: It's all a mistake, I know it's just a bad dream.

DOCTOR BAUGH: We're gonna keep Big Daddy as comfortable as we can.   190

BIG MAMA: Yes, it's just a bad dream, that's all it is, it's just an awful dream.

GOOPER: In my opinion Big Daddy is having some pain but won't admit that he has it.

BIG MAMA: Just a dream, a bad dream.

DOCTOR BAUGH: That's what lots of them do, they think if they don't admit they're
  having the pain they can sort of escape the fact of it.   195

GOOPER: [*with relish*] Yes, they get sly about it, they get real sly about it.

MAE: Gooper and I think—

GOOPER: Shut up, Mae!—Big Daddy ought to be started on morphine.

BIG MAMA: Nobody's going to give Big Daddy morphine.

DOCTOR BAUGH: Now, Big Mama, when that pain strikes it's going to strike mighty hard   200
  and Big Daddy's going to need the needle to bear it.

BIG MAMA: I tell you, nobody's going to give him morphine.

MAE: Big Mama, you don't want to see Big Daddy suffer, you know you—

  [GOOPER *standing beside her gives her a savage poke.*]

DOCTOR BAUGH: [*placing a package on the table*] I'm leaving this stuff here, so if there's a
  sudden attack you all won't have to send out for it.   205

MAE: I know how to give a hypo.

GOOPER: Mae took a course in nursing during the war.

MARGARET: Somehow I don't think Big Daddy would want Mae to give him a hypo.

MAE: You think he'd want *you* to do it?

  [DR. BAUGH *rises.*]

GOOPER: Doctor Baugh is goin'.   210

DOCTOR BAUGH: Yes, I got to be goin'. Well, keep your chin up, Big Mama.

GOOPER: [*with jocularity*] She's gonna keep *both* chins up, aren't you, Big Mama?

  [BIG MAMA *sobs.*]

  Now stop that, Big Mama.

MAE: Sit down with me, Big Mama.

GOOPER: [*at door with* DR. BAUGH] Well, Doc, we sure do appreciate all you done. I'm   215
  telling you, we're surely obligated to you for—

  [DR. BAUGH *has gone out without a glance at him.*]

GOOPER: I guess that doctor has got a lot on his mind but it wouldn't hurt him to act a
  little more human. . . .

  [BIG MAMA *sobs.*]

  Now be a brave girl, Mommy.

BIG MAMA: It's not true, I know that it's just not true!   220

GOOPER: Mama, those tests are infallible!

BIG MAMA: Why are you so determined to see your father daid?

MAE: Big Mama!

MARGARET: [*gently*] I know what Big Mama means.

MAE: [*fiercely*] Oh, do you?   225

MARGARET: [*quietly and very sadly*] Yes, I think I do.

MAE: For a newcomer in the family you sure do show a lot of understanding.

MARGARET: Understanding is needed on this place.

MAE: I guess you must have needed a lot of it in your family, Maggie, with your father's liquor problem and now you've got Brick with his!   230

MARGARET: Brick does not have a liquor problem at all. Brick is devoted to Big Daddy. This thing is a terrible strain on him.

BIG MAMA: Brick is Big Daddy's boy, but he drinks too much and it worries me and Big Daddy, and, Margaret, you've got to cooperate with us, you've got to cooperate with Big Daddy and me in getting Brick straightened out. Because it will break Big Daddy's   235
heart if Brick don't pull himself together and take hold of things.

MAE: Take hold of *what* things, Big Mama?

BIG MAMA: The place.

[*There is a quick violent look between* MAE *and* GOOPER.]

GOOPER: Big Mama, you've had a shock.

MAE: Yais, we've all had a shock, but . . .   240

GOOPER: Let's be realistic—

MAE: —Big Daddy would never, would never, be foolish enough to—

GOOPER: —put this place in irresponsible hands!

BIG MAMA: Big Daddy ain't going to leave the place in anybody's hands; Big Daddy is *not*
going to die. I want you to get that in your heads, all of you!   245

MAE: Mommy, Mommy, Big Mama, we're just as hopeful an' optimistic as you are about Big Daddy's prospects, we have faith in *prayer*—but nevertheless there are certain matters that have to be discussed an' dealt with, because otherwise—

GOOPER: Eventualities have to be considered and now's the time. . . . Mae, will you please
get my briefcase out of our room?   250

MAE: Yes, honey.

[*She rises and goes out through the hall door.*]

GOOPER: [*standing over* BIG MAMA] Now, Big Mom. What you said just now was not at all true and you know it. I've always loved Big Daddy in my own quiet way. I never made a show of it, and I know that Big Daddy has always been fond of me in a quiet
way, too, and he never made a show of it, neither.   255

[MAE *returns with* GOOPER's *briefcase.*]

MAE: Here's your briefcase, Gooper, honey.

GOOPER: [*handing the briefcase back to her*] Thank you. . . . Of ca'use, my relationship with Big Daddy is different from Brick's.

MAE: You're eight years older'n Brick an' always had t' carry a bigger load of th' responsibilities than Brick ever had t' carry. He never carried a thing in his life but a football or   260
a highball.

GOOPER: Mae, will y' let me talk, please?

MAE: Yes, honey.

GOOPER: Now, a twenty-eight-thousand-acre plantation's a mighty big thing t' run.

MAE: Almost singlehanded.   265

[MARGARET *has gone out onto the gallery, and can be heard calling softly* BRICK.]

BIG MAMA: You never had to run this place! What are you talking about? As if Big Daddy was dead and in his grave, you had to run it? Why, you just helped him out with a few business details and had your law practice at the same time in Memphis!

MAE: Oh, Mommy, Mommy, Big Mommy! Let's be fair! Why, Gooper has given himself body and soul to keeping this place up for the past five years since Big Daddy's health started failing. Gooper won't say it, Gooper never thought of it as a duty, he just did it. And what did Brick do? Brick kept living in his past glory at college! Still a football player at twenty-seven! 270

MARGARET: [*returning alone*] Who are you talking about, now? Brick? A football player? He isn't a football player and you know it. Brick is a sports announcer on TV and one of the best-known ones in the country! 275

MAE: I'm talking about what he was.

MARGARET: Well, I wish you would just stop talking about my husband.

GOOPER: I've got a right to discuss my brother with other members of MY OWN family which don't include *you*. Why don't you go out there and drink with Brick? 280

MARGARET: I've never seen such malice toward a brother.

GOOPER: How about his for me? Why, he can't stand to be in the same room with me!

MARGARET: This is a deliberate campaign of vilification for the most disgusting and sordid reason on earth, and I know what it is! It's *avarice, avarice, greed, greed!*

BIG MAMA: Oh, I'll scream! I will scream in a moment unless this stops! 285

> [GOOPER *has stalked up to* MARGARET *with clenched fists at his sides as if he would strike her.* MAE *distorts her face again into a hideous grimace behind* MARGARET's *back.*]

MARGARET: We only remain on the place because of Big Mom and Big Daddy. If it is true what they say about Big Daddy we are going to leave here just as soon as it's over. Not a moment later.

BIG MAMA: [*sobs*] Margaret. Child. Come here. Sit next to Big Mama.

MARGARET: Precious Mommy. I'm sorry, I'm so sorry, I—! 290

> [*She bends her long graceful neck to press her forehead to* BIG MAMA's *bulging shoulder under its black chiffon.*]

GOOPER: How beautiful, how touching, this display of devotion!

MAE: Do you know why she's childless? She's childless because that big beautiful athlete husband of hers won't go to bed with her!

GOOPER: You jest won't let me do this in a nice way, will yah? Aw right—Mae and I have five kids with another one coming! I don't give a goddam if Big Daddy likes me or 295 don't like me or did or never did or will or will never! I'm just appealing to a sense of common decency and fair play. I'll tell you the truth. I've resented Big Daddy's partiality to Brick ever since Brick was born, and the way I've been treated like I was just barely good enough to spit on and sometimes not even good enough for that. Big Daddy is dying of cancer, and it's spread all through him and it's attacked all his 300 vital organs including the kidneys and right now he is sinking into uremia, and you all know what uremia is, it's poisoning of the whole system due to the failure of the body to eliminate its poisons.

MARGARET: [*to herself, downstage, hissingly*] Poisons, poisons! Venomous thoughts and words! In hearts and minds!—That's poisons! 305

GOOPER: [*overlapping her*] I am asking for a square deal, and I expect to get one. But if I don't get one, if there's any peculiar shenanigans going on around here behind my back, or before me, well, I'm not a corporation lawyer for nothing, I know how to protect my own interests.—OH! A late arrival!

> [BRICK *enters from the gallery with a tranquil, blurred smile, carrying an empty glass with him.*]

MAE: Behold the conquering hero comes! 310

GOOPER: The fabulous Brick Pollitt! Remember him?—Who could forget him!

MAE: He looks like he's been injured in a game!

GOOPER: Yep, I'm afraid you'll have to warm the bench at the Sugar Bowl this year, Brick!

[MAE *laughs shrilly.*]

Or was it the Rose Bowl that he made that famous run in?

MAE: The punch bowl, honey. It was in the punch bowl, the cut-glass punch bowl! 315

GOOPER: Oh, that's right, I'm getting the bowls mixed up!

MARGARET: Why don't you stop venting your malice and envy on a sick boy?

BIG MAMA: *Now you two hush, I mean it, hush, all of you, hush!*

GOOPER: All right, Big Mama. A family crisis brings out the best and the worst in every
member of it. 320

MAE: *That's* the truth.

MARGARET: *Amen!*

BIG MAMA: I said, "hush!" I won't tolerate any more catty talk in my house.

[MAE *gives* GOOPER *a sign indicating briefcase.*]

[BRICK's *smile has grown both brighter and vaguer. As he prepares a drink, he
sings softly:*]

BRICK: *Show me the way to go home,*
                          I'm tired and I wanta go to bed, 325
                          I had a little drink about an hour ago—

GOOPER: [*at the same time*] Big Mama, you know it's necessary for me t' go back to Memphis in th' mornin' t' represent the Parker estate in a lawsuit.

[MAE *sits on the bed and arranges papers she has taken from the briefcase.*]

BRICK: [*continuing the song*]
                          Wherever I may roam, 330
                          On land or sea or foam.

BIG MAMA: Is it, Gooper?

MAE: Yaiss.

GOOPER: That's why I'm forced to—to bring up a problem that—

MAE: Somethin' that's too important t' be put off! 335

GOOPER: If Brick was sober, he ought to be in on this.

MARGARET: Brick is present; we're here.

GOOPER: Well, good. I will now give you this outline my partner, Tom Bullitt, an' me have
drawn up—a sort of dummy—trusteeship.

MARGARET: Oh, that's it! You'll be in charge an' dole out remittances, will you? 340

GOOPER: This we did as soon as we got the report on Big Daddy from th' Ochsner Labo-
ratories. We did this thing, I mean we drew up this dummy outline with the advice
and assistance of the Chairman of the Boa'd of Directors of th' Southern Plantahs
Bank and Trust Company in Memphis, C.C. Bellowes, a man who handles estates
for all th' prominent fam'lies in West Tennessee and th' Delta. 345

BIG MAMA: Gooper?

GOOPER: [*crouching in front of* BIG MAMA] Now this is not—not final, or anything like
it. This is just a preliminary outline. But it does provide a basis—a design—a—possible,
feasible—*plan!*

MARGARET: Yes, I'll bet. 350

MAE: It's a plan to protect the biggest estate in the Delta from irresponsibility an'—

BIG MAMA: Now you listen to me, all of you, you listen here! They's not goin' to be any more catty talk in my house! And Gooper, you put that away before I grab it out of your hand and tear it right up! I don't know what the hell's in it, and I don't want to know what the hell's in it. I'm talkin' in Big Daddy's language now; I'm his *wife,*   355
not his *widow,* I'm still his *wife!* And I'm talkin' to you in his language an'—

GOOPER: Big Mama, what I have here is—

MAE: Gooper explained that it's just a plan. . . .

BIG MAMA: I don't care what you got there. Just put it back where it came from, an' don't let me see it again, not even the outside of the envelope of it! Is that understood?   360
Basis! Plan! Preliminary! Design! I say—what is it Big Daddy always says when he's disgusted?

BRICK: [*from the bar*] Big Daddy says "crap" when he's disgusted.

BIG MAMA: [*rising*] That's right—*CRAP!* I say *CRAP,* too, like Big Daddy!

MAE: Coarse language doesn't seem called for in this—   365

GOOPER: Somethin' in me is *deeply outraged* by hearin' you talk like this.

BIG MAMA: *Nobody's goin' to take nothin'!*—till Big Daddy lets go of it, and maybe, just possibly, not—not even then! No, not even then!

BRICK: *You can always hear me singin' this song,*
                             Show me the way to go home.   370

BIG MAMA: Tonight Brick looks like he used to look when he was a little boy, just like he did when he played wild games and used to come home all sweaty and pink-cheeked and sleepy, with his—red curls shining. . . .

> [*She comes over to him and runs her fat shaky hand through his hair. He draws aside as he does from all physical contact and continues the song in a whisper, opening the ice bucket and dropping in the ice cubes one by one as if he were mixing some important chemical formula.*]

BIG MAMA: [*continuing*] Time goes by so fast. Nothin' can outrun it. Death commences too early—almost before you're half acquainted with life—you meet with the other. . . .   375
Oh, you know we just got to love each other an' stay together, all of us, just as close as we can, especially now that such a *black* thing has come and moved into this place without invitation.

> [*Awkwardly embracing* BRICK, *she presses her head to his shoulder.*]

> [GOOPER *has been returning papers to* MAE, *who has restored them to briefcase with an air of severely tried patience.*]

GOOPER: Big Mama? Big Mama?

> [*He stands behind her, tense with sibling envy.*]

BIG MAMA: [*oblivious of* GOOPER] Brick, you hear me, don't you?   380

MARGARET: Brick hears you, Big Mama, he understands what you're saying.

BIG MAMA: Oh, Brick, son of Big Daddy! Big Daddy does so love you! Y'know what would be his fondest dream come true? If before he passed on, if Big Daddy has to pass on, you gave him a child of yours, a grandson as much like his son as his son is like Big Daddy!   385

MAE: [*zipping briefcase shut: an incongruous sound*] Such a pity that Maggie an' Brick can't oblige!

MARGARET: [*suddenly and quietly but forcefully*] Everybody listen.

> [*She crosses to the center of the room, holding her hands rigidly together.*]

MAE: Listen to what, Maggie?

MARGARET: I have an announcement to make.

GOOPER: A sports announcement, Maggie?

MARGARET: Brick and I are going to—*have a child!* 390

[BIG MAMA *catches her breath in a loud gasp.*]

[*Pause.* BIG MAMA *rises.*]

BIG MAMA: Maggie! Brick! This is too good to believe!

MAE: That's right, too good to believe.

BIG MAMA: Oh, my, my! This is Big Daddy's dream, his dream come true! I'm going to tell him right now before he—

MARGARET: We'll tell him in the morning. Don't disturb him now. 395

BIG MAMA: I want to tell him before he goes to sleep, I'm going to tell him his dream's come true this minute! And Brick! A child will make you pull yourself together and quit this drinking!

[*She seizes the glass from his hand.*]

The responsibilities of a father will—

[*Her face contorts and she makes an excited gesture; bursting into sobs, she rushes out, crying.*]

I'm going to tell Big Daddy right this minute! 400

[*Her voice fades out down the hall.*]

[BRICK *shrugs slightly and drops an ice cube into another glass.* MARGARET *crosses quickly to his side, saying something under her breath, and she pours the liquor for him, staring up almost fiercely into his face.*]

BRICK: [*coolly*] Thank you, Maggie, that's a nice big shot.

[MAE *has joined* GOOPER *and she gives him a fierce poke, making a low hissing sound and a grimace of fury.*]

GOOPER: [*pushing her aside*] Brick, could you possibly spare me one small shot of that liquor?

BRICK: Why, help yourself, Gooper boy.

GOOPER: I will. 405

MAE: [*shrilly*] Of course we know that this is—

GOOPER: Be still, Mae!

MAE: I won't be still! I know she's made this up!

GOOPER: Goddam it, I said to shut up!

MARGARET: Gracious! I didn't know that my little announcement was going to provoke 410
such a storm!

MAE: *That* woman isn't *pregnant!*

GOOPER: Who said she was?

MAE: *She* did.

GOOPER: The doctor didn't. Doc Baugh didn't. 415

MARGARET: I haven't gone to Doc Baugh.

GOOPER: Then who'd you go to, Maggie?

MARGARET: One of the best gynecologists in the South.

GOOPER: Uh huh, uh huh!—I see. . . .

[*He takes out pencil and notebook.*]

—May we have his name, please? 420
MARGARET: No, you may not, Mister Prosecuting Attorney!
MAE: He doesn't have any name, he doesn't exist!
MARGARET: Oh, he exists all right, and so does my child, Brick's baby!
MAE: You can't conceive a child by a man that won't sleep with you unless you think
you're— 425

[BRICK *has turned on the phonograph. A scat song cuts* MAE's *speech.*]

GOOPER: *Turn that off!*
MAE: We know it's a lie because we hear you in here; he won't sleep with you, we hear you!
So don't imagine you're going to put a trick over on us, to fool a dying man with a—

[*A long drawn cry of agony and rage fills the house.* MARGARET *turns phonograph down to a whisper.*]

[*The cry is repeated.*]

MAE: [*awed*] Did you hear that, Gooper, did you hear that?
GOOPER: Sounds like the pain has struck. 430
MAE: Go see, Gooper!
GOOPER: Come along and leave these lovebirds together in their nest!

[*He goes out first.* MAE *follows but turns at the door, contorting her face and hissing at* MARGARET.]

MAE: Liar!

[*She slams the door.*]

[MARGARET *exhales with relief and moves a little unsteadily to catch hold of*
BRICK's *arm.*]

MARGARET: Thank you for—keeping still. . . .
BRICK: Okay, Maggie. 435
MARGARET: It was gallant of you to save my face!
BRICK: —It hasn't happened yet.
MARGARET: What?
BRICK: The click. . . .
MARGARET: —the click in your head that makes you peaceful, honey? 440
BRICK: Uh-huh. It hasn't happened. . . . I've got to make it happen before I can
sleep. . . .
MARGARET: —I—know what you—mean. . . .
BRICK: Give me that pillow in the big chair, Maggie.
MARGARET: I'll put it on the bed for you. 445
BRICK: No, put it on the sofa, where I sleep.
MARGARET: Not tonight, Brick.
BRICK: I want it on the sofa. That's where I sleep.

[*He has hobbled to the liquor cabinet. He now pours down three shots in quick
succession and stands waiting, silent. All at once he turns with a smile and says:*]

There!
MARGARET: What?
BRICK: The *click.* . . . 450

[*His gratitude seems almost infinite as he hobbles out on the gallery with a drink. We hear his crutch as he swings out of sight. Then, at some distance, he begins singing to himself a peaceful song.*]

[MARGARET *holds the big pillow forlornly as if it were her only companion, for a few moments, then throws it on the bed. She rushes to the liquor cabinet, gathers all the bottles in her arms, turns about undecidedly, then runs out of the room with them, leaving the door ajar on the dim yellow hall.* BRICK *is heard hobbling back along the gallery, singing his peaceful song. He comes back in, sees the pillow on the bed, laughs lightly, sadly, picks it up. He has it under his arm as* MARGARET *returns to the room.* MARGARET *softly shuts the door and leans against it, smiling softly at* BRICK.]

MARGARET: Brick, I used to think that you were stronger than me and I didn't want to be overpowered by you. But now, since you've taken to liquor—you know what?—I guess it's bad, but now I'm stronger than you and I can love you more truly! Don't move that pillow. I'll move it right back if you do!
      —Brick?   455

[*She turns out all the lamps but a single rose-silk-shaded one by the bed.*]

I really have been to a doctor and I know what to do and—Brick?—this is my time by the calendar to conceive!
BRICK: Yes, I understand, Maggie. But how are you going to conceive a child by a man in love with his liquor?
MARGARET: By locking his liquor up and making him satisfy my desire before I unlock it!   460
BRICK: Is that what you've done, Maggie?
MARGARET: Look and see. That cabinet's mighty empty compared to before!
BRICK: Well, I'll be a son of a—

[*He reaches for his crutch but she beats him to it and rushes out on the gallery, hurls the crutch over the rail and comes back in, panting.*]

[*There are running footsteps.* BIG MAMA *bursts into the room, her face all awry, gasping, stammering.*]

BIG MAMA: Oh, my God, oh, my God, oh, my God, where is it?
MARGARET: Is this what you want, Big Mama?   465

[MARGARET *hands her the package left by the doctor.*]

BIG MAMA: I can't bear it, oh, God! Oh, Brick! Brick, baby!

[*She rushes at him. He averts his face from her sobbing kisses.* MARGARET *watches with a tight smile.*]

My son, Big Daddy's boy! Little Father!

[*The groaning cry is heard again. She runs out, sobbing.*]

MARGARET: And so tonight we're going to make the lie true, and when that's done, I'll bring the liquor back here and we'll get drunk together, here, tonight, in this place that death has come into. . . .
      —What do you say?   470
BRICK: I don't say anything. I guess there's nothing to say.
MARGARET: Oh, you weak people, you weak, beautiful people!—who give up.—What you want is someone to—

[*She turns out the rose-silk lamp.*]

—take hold of you.—Gently, gently, with love! And—

475

[*The curtain begins to fall slowly.*]

I *do* love you, Brick, I *do!*
BRICK: [*smiling with charming sadness*] Wouldn't it be funny if that was true?

CURTAIN—THE END

The Strong Breed
(1964)

In *The Strong Breed*, the dramatic action focuses on a ritual that in one form or another is found in various societies—the selection and expulsion of a scapegoat. This theme exists in *Oedipus Rex*, as well as many other plays. In Soyinka's play, the protagonist Eman's mistake lies in thinking the ritual is observed everywhere as it was in his own community, where someone willingly allowed the troubles and cares of the village to be loaded into a symbolic vessel that a "carrier" then took away down the river, thereby cleansing the community in preparation for the new year. In Eman's village, the carrier was honored for his strength, courage, and wisdom. However, in the village to which Eman has recently come, the carrier himself becomes the object of loathing and is driven from the village permanently. In this village, outsiders are chosen as carriers and then are drugged, hypnotized, and subjected to beatings and curses as well as other forms of abuse. As one of only two outsiders present in the village, Eman quickly becomes an obvious candidate to serve as the carrier.

In the first part of the play, little is revealed about Eman's past or why he is here. But as the villagers begin to close in on him, Eman relives his past and his attempt to escape its unpleasantness. In a flashback, his father reminds him that he comes from a family of carriers (the strong breed) and that he cannot escape his fate. Eventually, the villagers track down Eman and kill him, but the act fills most of them with shame and makes them question following their leaders blindly.

The Strong Breed develops a number of themes common in Soyinka's plays: the need to balance the traditional and the modern; the habit of following custom and mistaken beliefs unquestioningly; and the special individual, who through dedication and vision awakens the people and leads them toward better ways, even though he may become a victim of the society he seeks to benefit.

In this and his other plays, Soyinka draws his material from native sources but reinterprets it, often showing the conflict between traditional customs and modern consciousness. Soyinka, a strong advocate for peace and reconciliation in postcolonial Africa, has sought a balance between appreciation for the culture of the past and the need to alter conditions to achieve a just society. In addition to being a playwright, Soyinka is also an acclaimed poet, novelist, and essay writer. His many accomplishments were acknowledged when he became the first African dramatist to win the Nobel Prize for Literature.

The Strong Breed
(1964)

Characters

EMAN, *a stranger*

SUNMA, *Jaguna's daughter*

IFADA, *an idiot*

GIRL

JAGUNA

ORAGE

THE VILLAGERS, *attendants stalwarts*

from EMAN'S *past*—

OLD MAN, *his father*

OMAE, *his betrothed*

TUTOR

PRIEST

THE VILLAGERS, *attendants*

The scenes are described briefly, but very often a darkened stage with lit areas will not only suffice but is necessary. Except for the one indicated place, there can be no break in the action. A distracting scene-change would be ruinous.

A mud house, with space in front of it. EMAN, *in light buba and trousers stands at the window, looking out. Inside,* SUNMA *is clearing the table of what looks like a modest clinic, putting the things away in the cupboard. Another rough table in the room is piled with exercise books, two or three worn text-books, etc.* SUNMA *appears agitated. Outside, just below the window crouches* IFADA. *He looks up with a shy smile from time to time, waiting for* EMAN *to notice him.*

SUNMA: [*hesitant*] You will have to make up your mind soon Eman. The lorry leaves very shortly.

> [As EMAN *does not answer,* SUNMA *continues her work, more nervously. Two villagers, obvious travellers, pass hurriedly in front of the house; the man has a small raffia sack, the woman a cloth-covered basket; the man enters first, turns and urges the woman who is just emerging to hurry.*]

SUNMA: [*Seeing them, her tone is more intense.*] Eman, are we going or aren't we? You will leave it till too late.

EMAN: [*quietly*] There is still time—if you want to go.

SUNMA: If I want to go . . . and you?

> [EMAN *makes no reply.*]

SUNMA: [*bitterly*] You don't really want to leave here. You never want to go away—even for a minute.

> [IFADA *continues his antics.* EMAN *eventually pats him on the head and the boy grins happily. Leaps up suddenly and returns with a basket of oranges which he offers to* EMAN.]

EMAN: My gift for today's festival enh?

5

[IFADA *nods, grinning.*]

EMAN: They look ripe—that's a change.

SUNMA: [*She has gone inside the room. Looks round the door.*] Did you call me?

EMAN: No. [*She goes back.*] And what will you do tonight Ifada? Will you take part in the dancing? Or perhaps you will mount your own masquerade?

[IFADA *shakes his head, regretfully.*]

EMAN: You won't? So you haven't any? But you would like to own one.

[IFADA *nods eagerly.*]

EMAN: Then why don't you make your own?

[IFADA *stares, puzzled by this idea.*]

EMAN: Sunma will let you have some cloth you know. And bits of wool . . .

SUNMA: [*coming out*] Who are you talking to Eman?

EMAN: Ifada. I am trying to persuade him to join the young maskers.

SUNMA: [*losing control*] What does he want here? Why is he hanging around us?

EMAN: [*amazed*] What . . . ? I said Ifada, Ifada.

SUNMA: Just tell him to go away. Let him go and play somewhere else!

EMAN: What is this? Hasn't he always played here?

SUNMA: I don't want him here. [*rushes to the window*] Get away idiot. Don't bring your foolish face here any more, do you hear? Go on, go away from here . . .

EMAN: [*restraining her*] Control yourself Sunma. What on earth has got into you?

[IFADA, *hurt and bewildered, backs slowly away.*]

SUNMA: He comes crawling around here like some horrible insect. I never want to lay my eyes on him again.

EMAN: I don't understand. It *is* Ifada you know. Ifada! The unfortunate one who runs errands for you and doesn't hurt a soul.

SUNMA: I cannot bear the sight of him.

EMAN: You can't do what? It can't be two days since he last fetched water for you.

SUNMA: What else can he do except that? He is useless. Just because we have been kind to him . . . Others would have put him in an asylum.

EMAN: You are not making sense. He is not a madman, he is just a little more unlucky than other children. [*looks keenly at her*] But what is the matter?

SUNMA: It's nothing. I only wish we had sent him off to one of those places for creatures like him.

EMAN: He is quite happy here. He doesn't bother anyone and he makes himself useful.

SUNMA: Useful! Is that one of any use to anybody? Boys of his age are already earning a living but all he can do is hang around and drool at the mouth.

EMAN: But he does work. You know he does a lot for you.

SUNMA: Does he? And what about the farm you started for him! Does he ever work on it? Or have you forgotten that it was really for Ifada you cleared that brush. Now you have to go and work it yourself. You spend all your time on it and you have no room for anything else.

EMAN: That wasn't his fault. I should first have asked him if he was fond of farming.

SUNMA: Oh, so he can choose? As if he shouldn't be thankful for being allowed to live.

EMAN: Sunma!

SUNMA: He does not like farming but he knows how to feast his dumb mouth on the fruits.

EMAN: But I want him to. I encourage him.

SUNMA: Well keep him. I don't want to see him any more.

EMAN: [*after some moments*] But why? You cannot be telling all the truth. What has he done?

SUNMA: The sight of him fills me with revulsion.

EMAN: [*goes to her and holds her*] What really is it? [SUNMA *avoids his eyes.*] It is almost as   55
if you are forcing yourself to hate him. Why?

SUNMA: That is not true. Why should I?

EMAN: Then what is the secret? You've even played with him before.

SUNMA: I have always merely tolerated him. But I cannot any more. Suddenly my disgust
won't take him any more. Perhaps . . . perhaps it is the new year. Yes, yes, it must   60
be the new year.

EMAN: I don't believe that.

SUNMA: It must be. I am a woman, and these things matter. I don't want a mis-shape near
me. Surely for one day in the year, I may demand some wholesomeness.

EMAN: I do not understand you.   65

[SUNMA *is silent.*]

It was cruel of you. And to Ifada who is helpless and alone. We are the only friends
he has.

SUNMA: No, just you. I have told you, with me it has always been only an act of kindness.
And now I haven't any pity left for him.

EMAN: No. He is not a wholesome being.   70

[*He turns back to looking through the window.*]

SUNMA: [*half-pleading*] Ifada can rouse your pity. And yet if anything, I need more kindness
from you. Every time my weakness betrays me, you close your mind against me . . .
Eman . . . Eman . . .

[*A* GIRL *comes in view, dragging an effigy by a rope attached to one of its legs.
She stands for a while gazing at* EMAN. IFADA, *who has crept back shyly to his
accustomed position, becomes somewhat excited when he sees the effigy. The* GIRL
*is unsmiling. She possesses in fact, a kind of inscrutability which does not make
her hard but is unsettling.*]

GIRL: Is the teacher in?

EMAN: [*smiling*] No.   75

GIRL: Where is he gone?

EMAN: I really don't know. Shall I ask?

GIRL: Yes, do.

EMAN: [*turning slightly*] Sunma, a girl outside wants to know . . .

[SUNMA *turns away, goes into the inside room.*]

EMAN: Oh. [*returns to the* GIRL, *but his slight gaiety is lost*] There is no one at home who   80
can tell me.

GIRL: Why are you not in?

EMAN: I don't really know. Maybe I went somewhere.

GIRL: All right. I will wait until you get back.

[*She pulls the effigy to her, sits down.*]

EMAN: [*slowly regaining his amusement*] So you are all ready for the new year.   85

GIRL: [*without turning around*] I am not going to the festival.

EMAN: Then why have you got that?

GIRL: Do you mean my carrier? I am unwell you know. My mother says it will take away
my sickness with the old year.

EMAN: Won't you share the carrier with your playmates?   90

GIRL: Oh, no. Don't you know I play alone? The other children won't come near me. Their
mothers would beat them.

EMAN: But I have never seen you here. Why don't you come to the clinic?

GIRL: My mother said No.

[*gets up, begins to move off*]

EMAN: You are not going away?   95

GIRL: I must not stay talking to you. If my mother caught me . . .

EMAN: All right, tell me what you want before you go.

GIRL: [*Stops. For some moments she remains silent.*] I must have some clothes for my carrier.

EMAN: Is that all? You wait a moment.

[SUNMA *comes out as he takes down a buba from the wall. She goes to the window
and glares almost with hatred at the* GIRL. *The* GIRL *retreats hastily, still impassive.*]

By the way Sunma, do you know who that girl is?   100

SUNMA: I hope you don't really mean to give her that.

EMAN: Why not? I hardly ever use it.

SUNMA: Just the same don't give it to her. She is not a child. She is as evil as the rest of them.

EMAN: What has got into you today?

SUNMA: All right, all right. Do what you wish.   105

[*She withdraws. Baffled,* EMAN *returns to the window.*]

EMAN: Here . . . will this do? Come and look at it.

GIRL: Throw it.

EMAN: What is the matter? I am not going to eat you.

GIRL: No one lets me come near them.

EMAN: But I am not afraid of catching your disease.   110

GIRL: Throw it.

[EMAN *shrugs and tosses the buba. She takes it without a word and slips it on
the effigy, completely absorbed in the task.* EMAN *watches for a while, then joins*
SUNMA *in the inner room.*]

GIRL: [*after a long, cool survey of* IFADA] You have a head like a spider's egg, and your mouth
dribbles like a roof. But there is no one else. Would you like to play?

[IFADA *nods eagerly, quite excited.*]

GIRL: You will have to get a stick.

[IFADA *rushes around, finds a big stick and whirls it aloft, bearing down on
the carrier.*]

GIRL: Wait. I don't want you to spoil it. If it gets torn I shall drive you away. Now, let me   115
see how you are going to beat it.

[IFADA *hits it gently.*]

GIRL: You may hit harder than that. As long as there is something left to hang at the end.

[*She appraises him up and down.*]

You are not very tall . . . will you be able to hang it from a tree?

[IFADA *nods, grinning happily.*]

GIRL: You will hang it up and I will set fire to it. [*then, with surprising venom*] But just because you are helping me, don't think it is going to cure you. I am the one who will get well at midnight, do you understand? It is my carrier and it is for me alone.   120

[*She pulls at the rope to make sure that it is well attached to the leg.*]

Well don't stand there drooling. Let's go.

[*She begins to walk off, dragging the effigy in the dust.* IFADA *remains where he is for some moments, seemingly puzzled. Then his face breaks into a large grin and he leaps after the procession, belabouring the effigy with all his strength. The stage remains empty for some moments. Then the horn of a lorry is sounded and* SUNMA *rushes out. The hooting continues for some time with a rhythmic pattern.* EMAN *comes out.*]

EMAN: I am going to the village . . . I shan't be back before nightfall.
SUNMA: [*blankly*] Yes.
EMAN: [*hesitates*] Well what do you want me to do?   125
SUNMA: The lorry was hooting just now.
EMAN: I didn't hear it.
SUNMA: It will leave in a few minutes. And you did promise we could go away.
EMAN: I promised nothing. Will you go home by yourself or shall I come back for you?
SUNMA: You don't even want me here?   130
EMAN: But you have to go home haven't you?
SUNMA: I had hoped we would watch the new year together—in some other place.
EMAN: Why do you continue to distress yourself?
SUNMA: Because you will not listen to me. Why do you continue to stay where nobody wants you?   135
EMAN: That is not true.
SUNMA: It is. You are wasting your life on people who really want you out of their way.
EMAN: You don't know what you are saying.
SUNMA: You think they love you? Do you think they care at all for what you—or I—do for them?   140
EMAN: *Them?* These are your own people. Sometimes you talk as if you were a stranger too.
SUNMA: I wonder if I really sprang from here. I know they are evil and I am not. From, the oldest to the smallest child, they are nourished in evil and unwholesomeness in which I have no part.
EMAN: You knew this when you returned?   145
SUNMA: You reproach me for trying at all?
EMAN: I reproach you with nothing? But you must leave me out of your plans. I can have no part in them.
SUNMA: [*nearly pleading*] Once I could have run away. I would have gone and never looked back.   150
EMAN: I cannot listen when you talk like that.
SUNMA: I swear to you, I do not mind what happens afterwards. But you must help me tear myself away from here. I can no longer do it myself . . . It is only a little thing. And we have worked so hard this past year . . . surely we can go away for a week . . . even a few days would be enough.   155
EMAN: I have told you Sunma . . .

SUNMA: [*desperately*] Two days Eman. Only two days.

EMAN: [*distressed*] But I tell you I have no wish to go.

SUNMA: [*suddenly angry*] Are you so afraid then?

EMAN: Me? Afraid of what?   160

SUNMA: You think you will not want to come back.

EMAN: [*pitying*] You cannot dare me that way.

SUNMA: Then why won't you leave here, even for an hour? If you are so sure that your life
is settled here, why are you afraid to do this thing for me? What is so wrong that you
will not go into the next town for a day or two?   165

EMAN: I don't want to. I do not have to persuade you, or myself about anything. I simply
have no desire to go away.

SUNMA: [*His quiet confidence appears to incense her.*] You are afraid. You accuse me of losing
my sense of mission, but you are afraid to put yours to the test.

EMAN: You are wrong Sunma. I have no sense of mission. But I have found peace here and   170
I am content with that.

SUNMA: I haven't. For a while I thought that too, but I found there could be no peace
in the midst of so much cruelty. Eman, tonight at least, the last night of the old
year . . .

EMAN: No Sunma. I find this too distressing; you should go home now.   175

SUNMA: It is the time for making changes in one's life Eman. Let's breathe in the new year
away from here.

EMAN: You are hurting yourself.

SUNMA: Tonight. Only tonight. We will come back tomorrow as early as you like. But let
us go away for this one night. Don't let another year break on me in this place . . .   180
you don't know how important it is to me, but I will tell you, I will tell you on the
way . . . but we must not be here today, Eman, do this one thing for me.

EMAN: [*sadly*] I cannot.

SUNMA: [*suddenly calm*] I was a fool to think it would be otherwise. The whole village may
use you as they will but for me there is nothing. Sometimes I think you believe that   185
doing anything for me makes you unfaithful to some part of your life. If it was a
woman then I pity her for what she must have suffered.

[EMAN *winces and hardens slowly.* SUNMA *notices nothing.*]

Keeping faith with so much is slowly making you inhuman.
[*seeing the change in* EMAN] Eman. Eman. What is it?

[*As she goes towards him,* EMAN *goes into the house.*]

SUNMA: [*apprehensive, follows him*] What did I say? Eman. Forgive me, forgive me please.   190

[EMAN *remains facing into the slow darkness of the room.* SUNMA, *distressed,
cannot decide what to do.*]

I swear I didn't know . . . I would not have said it for all the world.

[*A lorry is heard taking off somewhere nearby. The sound comes up and slowly
fades away into the distance.* SUNMA *starts visibly, goes slowly to the window.*]

SUNMA: [*as the sound dies off, to herself*] What happens now?

EMAN: [*joining her at the window*] What did you say?

SUNMA: Nothing.

EMAN: Was that not the lorry going off?   195

SUNMA: It was.

EMAN: I am sorry I couldn't help you.

[SUNMA, *about to speak, changes her mind.*]

EMAN: I think you ought to go home now.

SUNMA: No, don't send me away. It's the least you can do for me. Let me stay here until all the noise is over. 200

EMAN: But are you not needed at home? You have a part in the festival.

SUNMA: I have renounced it; I am Jaguna's eldest daughter only in name.

EMAN: Renouncing one's self is not so easy—surely you know that.

SUNMA: I don't want to talk about it. Will you at least let us be together tonight?

EMAN: But . . . 205

SUNMA: Unless you are afraid my father will accuse you of harbouring me.

EMAN: All right, we will go out together.

SUNMA: Go out? I want us to stay here?

EMAN: When there is so much going on outside?

SUNMA: Some day you will wish that you went away when I tried to make you. 210

EMAN: Are we going back to that?

SUNMA: No. I promise you I will not recall it again. But you must know that it was also for your sake that I tried to get us away.

EMAN: For me? How?

SUNMA: By yourself you can do nothing here. Have you not noticed how tightly we shut 215 out strangers? Even if you lived here for a lifetime, you would remain a stranger.

EMAN: Perhaps that is what I like. There is peace in being a stranger.

SUNMA: For a while perhaps. But they would reject you in the end. I tell you it is only I who stand between you and contempt. And because of this you have earned their hatred. I don't know why I say this now, except that somehow, I feel that it no longer 220 matters. It is only I who have stood between you and much humiliation.

EMAN: Think carefully before you say any more. I am incapable of feeling indebted to you. This will make no difference at all.

SUNMA: I ask for nothing. But you must know it all the same. It is true I hadn't the strength to go by myself. And I must confess this now, if you had come with me, I would have 225 done everything to keep you from returning.

EMAN: I know that.

SUNMA: You see, I bare myself to you. For days I had thought it over, this was to be a new beginning for us. And I placed my fate wholly in your hands. Now the thought will not leave me, I have a feeling which will not be shaken off, that in some way, you 230 have tonight totally destroyed my life.

EMAN: You are depressed, you don't know what you are saying.

SUNMA: Don't think I am accusing you. I say all this only because I cannot help it.

EMAN: We must not remain shut up here. Let us go and be part of the living.

SUNMA: No leave me alone. 235

EMAN: Surely you don't want to stay indoors when the whole town is alive with rejoicing.

SUNMA: Rejoicing! Is that what it seems to you? No, let us remain here. Whatever happens I must not go out until all this is over.

[*There is silence. It has grown much darker.*]

EMAN: I shall light the lamp.

SUNMA: [*eager to do something*] No, let me do it. 240

[*She goes into the inner room.* EMAN *paces the room, stops by a shelf and toys with the seed in an "ayo" board, takes down the whole board and places it on a table, playing by himself. The* GIRL *is now seen coming back, still dragging her "carrier."* IFADA *brings up the rear as before. As she comes round the corner of the house two men emerge from the shadows. A sack is thrown over* IFADA'*s head, the rope is pulled tight rendering him instantly helpless. The* GIRL *has reached the front of the house before she turns round at the sound of the scuffle. She is in time to see* IFADA *thrown over the shoulders and borne away. Her face betraying no emotion at all, the* GIRL *backs slowly away, turns and flees, leaving the "carrier" behind.* SUNMA *enters, carrying two kerosene lamps. She hangs one up from the wall.*]

EMAN: One is enough.
SUNMA: I want to leave one outside.

[*She goes out, hangs the lamp from a nail just above the door. As she turns she sees the effigy and gasps.* EMAN *rushes out.*]

EMAN: What is it? Oh, is that what frightened you?
SUNMA: I thought . . . I didn't really see it properly.

[EMAN *goes towards the object, stoops to pick it up.*]

EMAN: It must belong to that sick girl.   245
SUNMA: Don't touch it.
EMAN: Let's keep it for her.
SUNMA: Leave it alone. Don't touch it Eman.
EMAN: [*shrugs and goes back*] You are very nervous.
SUNMA: Let's go in.   250
EMAN: Wait. [*He detains her by the door, under the lamp.*] I know there is something more
    than you've told me. What are you afraid of tonight?
SUNMA: I was only scared by that thing. There is nothing else.
EMAN: I am not blind Sunma. It is true I would not run away when you wanted me to, but
    that doesn't mean I do not feel things. What does tonight really mean that it makes you 255
    so helpless?
SUNMA: It is only a mood. And your indifference to me . . . let's go in.

[EMAN *moves aside and she enters; he remains there for a moment and then follows. She fiddles with the lamp, looks vaguely round the room, then goes and shuts the door, bolting it. When she turns, it is to meet* EMAN'*s eyes, questioning.*]

SUNMA: There is a cold wind coming in.

[EMAN *keeps his gaze on her.*]

SUNMA: It was getting cold.

[*She moves guiltily to the table and stands by the "ayo" board, rearranging the seed.* EMAN *remains where he is a few moments, then brings a stool and sits opposite her. She sits down also and they begin to play in silence.*]

SUNMA: What brought you here at all, Eman? And what makes you stay?   260

[*There is another silence.*]

SUNMA: I am not trying to share your life. I know you too well by now. But at least we
    have worked together since you came. Is there nothing at all I deserve to know?
EMAN: Let me continue a stranger—especially to you. Those who have much to give fulfill
    themselves only in total loneliness.

SUNMA: Then there is no love in what you do.   265

EMAN: There is. Love comes to me more easily with strangers.

SUNMA: That is unnatural.

EMAN: Not for me. I know I find consummation only when I have spent myself for a total
    stranger.

SUNMA: It seems unnatural to me. But then I am a woman. I have a woman's longings and   270
    weaknesses. And the ties of blood are very strong in me.

EMAN: [*smiling*] You think I have cut loose from all these—ties of blood.

SUNMA: Sometimes you are so inhuman.

EMAN: I don't know what that means. But I am very much my father's son.

       [*They play in silence. Suddenly* EMAN *pauses listening.*]

EMAN: Did you hear that?   275

SUNMA: [*quickly*] I heard nothing . . . it's your turn.

EMAN: Perhaps some of the mummers are coming this way.

       [EMAN *about to play, leaps up suddenly.*]

SUNMA: What is it? Don't you want to play any more?

       [EMAN *moves to the door.*]

SUNMA: No. Don't go out Eman.

EMAN: If it's the dancers I want to ask them to stay. At least we won't have to miss everything.   280

SUNMA: No, no. Don't open the door. Let us keep out everyone tonight.

       [*A terrified and disordered figure bursts suddenly around the corner, past the
       window and begins hammering at the door. It is* IFADA. *Desperate with terror, he
       pounds madly at the door, dumb-moaning all the while.*]

EMAN: Isn't that Ifada?

SUNMA: They are only fooling about. Don't pay any attention.

EMAN: [*looks round the window*] That is Ifada. [*begins to unbolt the door*]

SUNMA: [*pulling at his hands*] It is only a trick they are playing on you. Don't take any   285
    notice Eman.

EMAN: What are you saying? The boy is out of his senses with fear.

SUNMA: No, no. Don't interfere Eman. For God's sake don't interfere.

EMAN: Do you know something of this then?

SUNMA: You are a stranger here Eman. Just leave us alone and go your own way. There is   290
    nothing you can do.

EMAN: [*He tries to push her out of the way but she clings fiercely to him.*] Have you gone mad?
    I tell you the boy must come in.

SUNMA: Why won't you listen to me Eman? I tell you it's none of your business. For your
    own sake do as I say.   295

       [EMAN *pushes her off, unbolts the door.* IFADA *rushes in, clasps* EMAN *round the
       knees, dumb-moaning against his legs.*]

EMAN: [*manages to re-bolt the door*] What is it Ifada? What is the matter?

       [*Shouts and voices are heard coming nearer the house.*]

SUNMA: Before it's too late, let him go. For once Eman, believe what I tell you. Don't
    harbour him or you will regret it all your life.

[EMAN *tries to calm* IFADA *who becomes more and more abject as the outside voices get nearer.*]

EMAN: What have they done to him? At least tell me that. What is going on Sunma?

SUNMA: [*with sudden venom*] Monster! Could you not take yourself somewhere else?   300

EMAN: Stop talking like that.

SUNMA: He could have run into the bush couldn't he? Toad! Why must he follow us with his own disasters!

VOICES OUTSIDE: It's here . . . Round the back . . . Spread, spread . . . this way . . . no, head him off . . . use the bush path and head him off . . . get some more lights . . .   305

[EMAN *listens. Lifts* IFADA *bodily and carries him into the inner room. Returns at once, shutting the door behind him.*]

SUNMA: [*slumps into a chair, resigned*] You always follow your own way.

JAGUNA: [*comes round the corner followed by* OROGE *and three men, one bearing a torch*] I knew he would come here.

OROGE: I hope our friend won't make trouble.

JAGUNA: He had better not. You, recall all the men and tell them to surround the house.   310

OROGE: But he may not be in the house after all.

JAGUNA: I know he is here . . . [*to the men*] . . . go on, do as I say.

[*He bangs on the door.*]

Teacher, open your door . . . you two stay by the door. If I need you I will call you.

[EMAN *opens the door.*]

JAGUNA: [*speaks as he enters*] We know he is here.

EMAN: Who?   315

JAGUNA: Don't let us waste time. We are grown men, teacher. You understand me and I understand you. But we must take back the boy.

EMAN: This is my house.

JAGUNA: Daughter, you'd better tell your friend. I don't think he quite knows our ways. Tell him why he must give up the boy.   320

SUNMA: Father, I . . .

JAGUNA: Are you going to tell him or aren't you?

SUNMA: Father, I beg you, leave us alone tonight . . .

JAGUNA: I thought you might be a hindrance. Go home then if you will not use your sense.

SUNMA: But there are other ways . . .   325

JAGUNA: [*turning to the men*] See that she gets home. I no longer trust her. If she gives trouble carry her. And see that the women stay with her until this is all over.

[SUNMA *departs, accompanied by one of the men.*]

JAGUNA: Now teacher . . .

OROGE: [*restrains him*] You see, Mister Eman, it is like this. Right now, nobody knows that Ifada has taken refuge here. No one except us and our men—and they know   330
how to keep their mouths shut. We don't want to have to burn down the house you see, but if the word gets around, we would have no choice.

JAGUNA: In fact, it may be too late already. A carrier should end up in the bush, not in a house. Anyone who doesn't guard his door when the carrier goes by has himself to blame. A contaminated house should be burnt down.   335

OROGE: But we are willing to let it pass. Only, you must bring him out quickly.

EMAN: All right. But at least you will let me ask you something.

JAGUNA: What is there to ask? Don't you understand what we have told you?

EMAN: Yes. But why did you pick on a helpless boy. Obviously he is not willing.

JAGUNA: What is the man talking about? Ifada is a godsend. Does he have to be willing?   340

EMAN: In my home we believe that a man should be willing.

OROGE: Mister Eman, I don't think you quite understand. This is not a simple matter at all. I don't know what you do, but here, it is not a cheap task for anybody. No one in his senses would do such a job. Why do you think we give refuge to idiots like him? We don't know where he came from. One morning, he is simply there, just like   345 that. From nowhere at all. You see, there is purpose in that.

JAGUNA: We only waste time.

OROGE: Jaguna, be patient. After all, the man has been with us for some time now and deserves to know. The evil of the old year is no light thing to load on any man's head.

EMAN: I know something about that.   350

OROGE: You do? [*turns to* JAGUNA *who snorts impatiently*] You see I told you so didn't I? From the moment you came I saw you were one of the knowing ones.

JAGUNA: Then let him behave like a man and give back the boy.

EMAN: It is you who are not behaving like men.

JAGUNA: [*advances aggressively*] That is a quick mouth you have . . .   355

OROGE: Patience Jaguna . . . if you want the new year to cushion the land there must be no deeds of anger. What did you mean my friend?

EMAN: It is a simple thing. A village which cannot produce its own carrier contains no men.

JAGUNA: Enough. Let there be no more talk or this business will be ruined by some rash-   360 ness. You . . . come inside. Bring the boy out, he must be in the room there.

EMAN: Wait.

[*The men hesitate.*]

JAGUNA: [*hitting the nearer one and propelling him forward*] Go on. Have you changed masters now that you listen to what he says?

OROGE: [*sadly*] I am sorry you would not understand Mister Eman. But you ought to know   365 that no carrier may return to the village. If he does, the people will stone him to death. It has happened before. Surely it is too much to ask a man to give up his own soil.

EMAN: I know others who have done more.

[IFADA *is brought out, abjectly dumb-moaning.*]

EMAN: You can see him with your own eyes. Does it really have meaning to use one as unwilling as that.   370

OROGE: [*smiling*] He shall be willing. Not only willing but actually joyous. I am the one who prepares them all, and I have seen worse. This one escaped before I began to prepare him for the event. But you will see him later tonight, the most joyous creature in the festival. Then perhaps you will understand.

EMAN: Then it is only a deceit. Do you believe the spirit of a new year is so easily fooled?   375

JAGUNA: Take him out. [*The men carry out* IFADA.] You see, it is so easy to talk. You say there are no men in this village because they cannot provide a willing carrier. And yet I heard Oroge tell you we only use strangers. There is only one other stranger in the village, but I have not heard him offer himself [*spits*] It is so easy to talk, is it not?

[*He turns his back on him. They go off, taking* IFADA *with them, limp and silent. The only sign of life is that he strains his neck to keep his eyes on* EMAN *till the very moment that he disappears from sight.* EMAN *remains where they left him, staring after the group.*]

[*A blackout lasting no more than a minute. The lights come up slowly and* IFADA *is seen returning to the house. He stops at the window and looks in. Seeing no one, he bangs on the sill. Appears surprised that there is no response. He slithers down on his favourite spot, then sees the effigy still lying where the* GIRL *had dropped it in her flight. After some hesitation, he goes towards it, begins to strip it of the clothing. Just then the* GIRL *comes in.*]

GIRL: Hey, Leave that alone. You know it's mine.   380

[IFADA *Pauses, then speeds up his action.*]

GIRL: I said it is mine. Leave it where you found it.

[*She rushes at him and begins to struggle for possession of the "carrier."*]

GIRL: Thief! Thief! Let it go, it is mine. Let it go. You animal, just because I let you play with it. Idiot! Idiot!

[*The struggle becomes quite violent. The* GIRL *is hanging onto the effigy and* IFADA *lifts her with it, flinging her all about. The* GIRL *hangs on grimly.*]

GIRL: You are spoiling it . . . why don't you get your own? Thief! Let it go you thief!

[SUNMA *comes in walking very fast, throwing apprehensive glances over her shoulder. Seeing the two children, she becomes immediately angry. Advances on them.*]

SUNMA: So you've made this place your playground. Get away you untrained pigs. Get out   385
of here.

[IFADA *flees at once, the* GIRL *retreats also, retaining possession of the "carrier."* SUNMA *goes to the door. She has her hand on the door when the significance of* IFADA's *presence strikes her for the first time. She stands rooted to the spot, then turns slowly around.*]

SUNMA: Ifada! What are you doing here?

[IFADA *is bewildered.* SUNMA *turns suddenly and rushes into the house, flying into the inner room and out again.*]

Eman! Eman! Eman!

[*She rushes outside.*]

Where did he go? Where did they take him?

[IFADA *distressed, points.* SUNMA *seizes him by the arm, drags him off.*]

Take me there at once. God help you if we are too late. You loathsome thing, if you   390
let him suffer . . .

[*Her voice fades into other shouts, running footsteps, banged tins, bells, dogs, etc., rising in volume.*]

[*It is a narrow passageway between two mud-houses. At the far end one man after another is seen running across the entry, the noise dying off gradually. About half-way down the passage,* EMAN *is crouching against the wall, tense with apprehension. As the noise dies off, he seems to relax, but the alert hunted look is still in his eyes, which are ringed in a reddish colour. The rest of his body has been whitened with a floury substance. He is naked down to the waist, wears a baggy pair of trousers, calf-length, and around both feet are bangles.*]

EMAN: I will simply stay here till dawn. I have done enough. [*A window is thrown open and a* WOMAN *empties some slop from a pail. With a startled cry* EMAN *leaps aside to avoid it and the* WOMAN *puts out her head.*]

WOMAN: Oh, my head. What have I done? Forgive me neighbour . . . Eh, it's the carrier!   395

[*Very rapidly she clears her throat and spits on him, flings the pail at him and runs off, shouting.*]

He's here. The carrier is hiding in the passage. Quickly, I have found the carrier!

[*The cry is taken up and* EMAN *flees down the passage. Shortly afterwards his pursuers come pouring down the passage in full cry. After the last of them come* JAGUNA *and* OROGE.]

OROGE: Wait, wait. I cannot go so fast.

JAGUNA: We will rest a little then. We can do nothing anyway.

OROGE: If only he had let me prepare him.

JAGUNA: They are the ones who break first, these fools who think they were born to carry   400
suffering like a hat. What are we to do now?

OROGE: When they catch him I must prepare him.

JAGUNA: He? It will be impossible now. There can be no joy left in that one.

OROGE: Still, it took him by surprise. He was not expecting what he met.

JAGUNA: Why then did he refuse to listen? Did he think he was coming to sit down to a   405
feast. He had not even gone through one compound before he bolted. Did he think
he was taken round the people to be blessed? A woman, that is all he is.

OROGE: No, no. He took the beating well enough. I think he is the kind who would let
himself be beaten from night till dawn and not utter a sound. He would let himself
be stoned until he dropped dead.   410

JAGUNA: Then what made him run like a coward?

OROGE: I don't know. I really don't know. It is a night of curses Jaguna. It is not many
unprepared minds will remain unhinged under the load.

JAGUNA: We must find him. It is a poor beginning for a year when our own curses remain
hovering over our homes because the carrier refused to take them.   415

[*They go. The scene changes.* EMAN *is crouching beside some shrubs, torn and bleeding.*]

EMAN: They are even guarding my house . . . as if I would go there, but I need water . . . they
could at least grant me that . . . I can be thirsty too . . . [*He pricks his ears.*] . . . there
must be a stream near by . . . [*As he looks round him, his eyes widen at a scene he encoun-
ters. An* OLD MAN, *short and vigorous looking is seated on a stool. He is also wearing calf-
length baggy trousers, white. On his head, a white cap. An* ATTENDANT *is engaged in   420
rubbing his body with oil. Round his eyes, two white rings have already been marked.*]

OLD MAN: Have they prepared the boat?

ATTENDANT: They are making the last sacrifice.

OLD MAN: Good. Did you send for my son?

ATTENDANT: He's on his way.   425

OLD MAN: I have never met the carrying of the boat with such a heavy heart. I hope nothing comes of it.

ATTENDANT: The gods will not desert us on that account.

OLD MAN: A man should be at his strongest when he takes the boat my friend. To be
weighed down inside and out is not a wise thing. I hope when the moment comes I   430
shall have found my strength.

[*Enter* EMAN, *a wrapper round his waist and a "danski" (a brief Yoruba attire) over it.*]

OLD MAN: I meant to wait until after my journey to the river, but my mind is so burdened with my own grief and yours I could not delay it. You know I must have all my strength. But I sit here, feeling it all eaten slowly away by my unspoken grief. It helps to say it out. It even helps to cry sometimes.   435

[*He signals to the* ATTENDANT *to leave them.*]

Come nearer . . . we will never meet again son. Not on this side of the flesh. What I do not know is whether you will return to take my place.

EMAN: I will never come back.

OLD MAN: Do you know what you are saying? Ours is a strong breed, my son. It is only a strong breed that can take this boat to the river year after year and wax stronger on it. I   440 have taken down each year's evils for over twenty years. I hoped you would follow me.

EMAN: My life here died with Omae.

OLD MAN: Omae died giving birth to your child and you think the world is ended. Eman, my pain did not begin when Omae died. Since you sent her to stay with me, son, I lived with the burden of knowing that this child would die bearing your son.   445

EMAN: Father . . .

OLD MAN: Don't you know it was the same with you? And me? No woman survives the bearing of the strong ones. Son, it is not the mouth of the boaster that says he belongs to the strong breed. It is the tongue that is red with pain and black with sorrow. Twelve years you were away my son, and for those twelve years I knew the love of an old man   450 for his daughter and the pain of a man helplessly awaiting his loss.

EMAN: I wish I had stayed away. I wish I never came back to meet her.

OLD MAN: It had to be. But you know now what slowly ate away my strength. I awaited your return with love and fear. Forgive me then if I say that your grief is light. It will pass. This grief may drive you now from home. But you must return.   455

EMAN: You do not understand. It is not grief alone.

OLD MAN: What is it then? Tell me I can still learn.

EMAN: I was away twelve years. I changed much in that time.

OLD MAN: I am listening.

EMAN: I am unfitted for your work, father. I wish to say no more. But I am totally unfitted   460 for your call.

OLD MAN: It is only time you need son. Stay longer and you will answer the urge of your blood.

EMAN: That I stayed at all was because of Omae. I did not expect to find her waiting. I would have taken her away, but hard as you claim to be, it would have killed you.   465 And I was a tired man. I needed peace. Because Omae was peace, I stayed. Now nothing holds me here.

OLD MAN: Other men would rot and die doing this task year after year. It is strong medicine which only we can take. Our blood is strong like no other. Anything you do in life must be less than this, son.   470

EMAN: That is not true father.

OLD MAN: I tell you it is true. Your own blood will betray you son, because you cannot hold it back. If you make it do less than this, it will rush to your head and burst it open. I say what I know my son.

EMAN: There are other tasks in life father. This one is not for me. There are even greater   475 things you know nothing of.

OLD MAN: I am very sad. You only go to give others what rightly belongs to us. You will use your strength among thieves. They are thieves because they take what is ours, they have no claim of blood to it. They will even lack the knowledge to use it wisely. Truth is my companion at this moment my son. I know everything I say will surely 480 bring the sadness of truth.

EMAN: I am going father.

OLD MAN: Call my attendant. And be with me in your strength for this last journey. A-ah, did you hear that? It came out without my knowing it; this is indeed my last journey. But I am not afraid. 485

[EMAN *goes out. A few moments later, the* ATTENDANT *enters.*]

ATTENDANT: The boat is ready.

OLD MAN: So am I.

[*He sits perfectly still for several moments. Drumming begins somewhere in the distance, and the* OLD MAN *sways his head almost imperceptibly. Two men come in bearing a miniature boat, containing an indefinable mound. They rush it in and set it briskly down near the* OLD MAN, *and stand well back. The* OLD MAN *gets up slowly, the* ATTENDANT *watching him keenly. He signs to the men, who lift the boat quickly onto the* OLD MAN's *head. As soon as it touches his head, he holds it down with both hands and runs off, the men give him a start, then follow at a trot.*

As the last man disappears OROGE *limps in and comes face to face with* EMAN—*as carrier—who is now seen still standing beside the shrubs, staring into the scene he has just witnessed.* OROGE, *struck by the look on* EMAN's *face, looks anxiously behind him to see what has engaged* EMAN's *attention.* EMAN *notices him then, and the pair stare at each other.* JAGUNA *enters, sees him and shouts, Here he is, rushes at* EMAN *who is whipped back to the immediate and flees,* JAGUNA *in pursuit. Three or four others enter and follow them.* OROGE *remains where he is, thoughtful.*]

JAGUNA: [*re-enters*] They have closed in on him now, we'll get him this time.

OROGE: It is nearly midnight.

JAGUNA: You were standing there looking at him as if he was some strange spirit. Why 490 didn't you shout?

OROGE: You shouted didn't you? Did that catch him?

JAGUNA: Don't worry. We have him now. But things have taken a bad turn. It is no longer enough to drive him past every house. There is too much contamination about already.

OROGE: [*not listening*] He saw something. Why may I not know what it was? 495

JAGUNA: What are you talking about?

OROGE: Hm. What is it?

JAGUNA: I said there is too much harm done already. The year will demand more from this carrier than we thought.

OROGE: What do you mean? 500

JAGUNA: Do we have to talk with the full mouth?

OROGE: S-sh . . . look!

[JAGUNA *turns just in time to see* SUNMA *fly at him, clawing at his face like a crazed tigress.*]

SUNMA: Murderer! What are you doing to him. Murderer! Murderer!

[JAGUNA *finds himself struggling really hard to keep off his daughter, he succeeds in pushing her off and striking her so hard on the face that she falls to her knees. He moves on her to hit her again.*]

OROGE: [*comes between*] Think what you are doing Jaguna, she is your daughter.

JAGUNA: My daughter! Does this one look like my daughter? Let me cripple the harlot   505
for life.

OROGE: That is a wicked thought Jaguna.

JAGUNA: Don't come between me and her.

OROGE: Nothing in anger—do you forget what tonight is?

JAGUNA: Can you blame me for forgetting?   510

[*Draws his hand across his cheek—it is covered with blood.*]

OROGE: This is an unhappy night for us all. I fear what is to come of it.

JAGUNA: Let's go. I cannot restrain myself in this creature's presence. My own daughter . . .
and for a stranger . . .

[*They go off.* IFADA, *who came in with* SUNMA *and had stood apart, horror-stricken, comes shyly forward. He helps* SUNMA *up. They go off, he holding* SUNMA *bent and sobbing.*]

[*Enter* EMAN—*as carrier. He is physically present in the bounds of this next scene, a side of a round thatched hut. A young girl, about fourteen, runs in, stops beside the hut. She looks carefully to see that she is not observed, puts her mouth to a little hole in the wall.*]

OMAE: Eman . . . Eman . . .

[EMAN—*as carrier—responds, as he does throughout the scene, but they are unaware of him.*]

EMAN: [*from inside*] Who is it?   515

OMAE: It is me, Omae.

EMAN: How dare you come here!

[*Two hands appear at the hole and, pushing outwards, create a much larger hole through which* EMAN *puts out his head. It is* EMAN *as a boy, the same age as the girl.*]

Go away at once. Are you trying to get me in trouble!

OMAE: What is the matter?

EMAN: You. Go away.

OMAE: But I came to see you.   520

EMAN: Are you deaf? I say I don't want to see you. Now go before my tutor catches you.

OMAE: All right. Come out.

EMAN: Do what!

OMAE: Come out.   525

EMAN: You must be mad.

OMAE: [*sits on the ground*] All right, if you don't come out I shall simply stay here until your
tutor arrives.

EMAN: [*about to explode, thinks better of it and the head disappears. A moment later he emerges
from behind the hut.*] What sort of evil has got into you?   530

OMAE: None. I just wanted to see you.

EMAN: [*His mimicry is nearly hysterical.*] None. I just wanted to see you. Do you think this
place is the stream where you can go and molest innocent people?

OMAE: [*coyly*] Aren't you glad to see me?

EMAN: I am not. 535

OMAE: Why?

EMAN: Why? Do you really ask me why? Because you are a woman and a most troublesome woman. Don't you know anything about this at all. We are not meant to see any woman. So go away before more harm is done.

OMAE: [*flirtatious*] What is so secret about it anyway? What do they teach you. 540

EMAN: Nothing any woman can understand.

OMAE: Ha ha. You think we don't know eh? You've all come to be circumcised.

EMAN: Shut up. You don't know anything.

OMAE: Just think, all this time you haven't been circumcised, and you dared make eyes at us women. 545

EMAN: Thank you—woman. Now go.

OMAE: Do they give you enough to eat?

EMAN: [*testily*] No. We are so hungry that when silly girls like you turn up, we eat them.

OMAE: [*feigning tears*] Oh, oh, oh, he's abusing me. He's abusing me.

EMAN: [*alarmed*] Don't try that here. Go quickly if you are going to cry. 550

OMAE: All right, I won't cry.

EMAN: Cry or no cry, go away and leave me alone. What do you think will happen if my tutor turns up now.

OMAE: He won't.

EMAN: [*mimicking*] He won't. I suppose you are his wife and he tells you where he goes. 555 In fact this is just the time he comes round to our huts. He could be at the next hut this very moment.

OMAE: Ha-ha. You're lying. I left him by the stream, pinching the girls' bottoms. Is that the sort of thing he teaches you?

EMAN: Don't say anything against him or I shall beat you. Isn't it you loose girls who tease 560 him, wiggling your bottoms under his nose?

OMAE: [*going tearful again*] A-ah, so I am one of those girls eh?

EMAN: Now don't you start accusing me of things I didn't say.

OMAE: But you said it. You said it.

EMAN: I didn't. Look Omae, someone will hear you and I'll be in disgrace. Why don't you 565 go before anything happens.

OMAE: It's all right. My friends have promised to hold your old rascal tutor till I get back.

EMAN: Then you go back right now. I have work to do. [*going in*]

OMAE: [*runs after and tries to hold him.* EMAN *leaps back, genuinely scared.*] What is the matter? I was not going to bite you. 570

EMAN: Do you know what you nearly did? You almost touched me!

OMAE: Well?

EMAN: Well! Isn't it enough that you let me set my eyes on you? Must you now totally pollute me with your touch? Don't you understand anything?

OMAE: Oh, that. 575

EMAN: [*nearly screaming*] It is not "oh that." Do you think this is only a joke or a little visit like spending the night with your grandmother? This is an important period of my life. Look, these huts, we built them with our own hands. Every boy builds his own. We learn things, do you understand? And we spend much time just thinking. At least, I do. It is the first time I have had nothing to do except think. Don't you see, I am 580 becoming a man. For the first time, I understand that I have a life to fulfil. Has that thought ever worried you?

OMAE: You are frightening me.

EMAN: There. That is all you can say. And what use will that be when a man finds himself alone—like that? [*points to the hut*] A man must go on his own, go where no one can help him, and test his strength. Because he may find himself one day sitting alone in a wall round as that. In there, my mind could hold no other thought. I may never have such moments again to myself. Don't dare come to steal any more of it. 585

OMAE: [*this time genuinely tearful*] Oh, I know you hate me. You only want to drive me away. 590

EMAN: [*impatiently*] Yes, yes, I know I hate you—but go.

OMAE: [*going, all tears. Wipes her eyes, suddenly all mischief.*] Eman.

EMAN: What now?

OMAE: I only want to ask one thing . . . do you promise to tell me?

EMAN: Well, what is it? 595

OMAE: [*gleefully*] Does it hurt?

[*She turns instantly and flees, landing straight into the arms of the returning tutor.*]

TUTOR: Te-he-he . . . what have we here? What little mouse leaps straight into the beak of the wise old owl eh?

[OMAE *struggles to free herself, flies to the opposite side, grimacing with distaste.*]

TUTOR: I suppose you merely came to pick some fruits eh? You did not sneak here to see any of my children. 600

OMAE: Yes, I came to steal your fruits.

TUTOR: Te-he-he . . . I thought so. And that dutiful son of mine over there. He saw you and came to chase you off my fruit trees didn't he? Te-he-he . . . I'm sure he did, isn't that so my young Eman?

EMAN: I was talking to her. 605

TUTOR: Indeed you were. Now be good enough to go into your hut until I decide your punishment. [EMAN *withdraws.*] Te-he-he . . . now my little daughter, you need not be afraid of me.

OMAE: [*spiritedly*] I am not.

TUTOR: Good. Very good. We ought to be friendly. [*His voice becomes leering.*] Now this is nothing to worry you my daughter . . . a very small thing indeed. Although of course if I were to let it slip that your young Eman had broken a strong taboo, it might go hard on him you know. I am sure you would not like that to happen, would you? 610

OMAE: No. 615

TUTOR: Good. You are sensible my girl. Can you wash clothes?

OMAE: Yes.

TUTOR: Good. If you will come with me now to my hut, I shall give you some clothes to wash, and then we will forget all about this matter eh? Well, come on.

OMAE: I shall wait here. You go and bring the clothes. 620

TUTOR: Eh? What is that? Now now, don't make me angry. You should know better than to talk back to your elders. Come now.

[*He takes her by the arm, and tries to drag her off.*]

OMAE: No no, I won't come to your hut. Leave me. Leave me alone you shameless old man.

TUTOR: If you don't come I shall disgrace the whole family of Eman, and yours too.

[EMAN *re-enters with a small bundle.*]

EMAN: Leave her alone. Let us go Omae. 625

TUTOR: And where do you think you are going?

EMAN: Home.

TUTOR: Te-he-he . . . As easy as that eh? You think you can leave here at any time you please? Get right back inside that hut!

[EMAN *takes* OMAE *by the arm and begins to walk off.*]

TUTOR: Come back at once.   630

[*He goes after him and raises his stick.* EMAN *catches it, wrenches it from him and throws it away.*]

OMAE: [*hopping delightedly*] Kill him. Beat him to death.

TUTOR: Help! Help! He is killing me! Help!

[*Alarmed,* EMAN *clamps his hand over his mouth.*]

EMAN: Old tutor, I don't mean you any harm, but you mustn't try to harm me either. [*He removes his hand.*]

TUTOR: You think you can get away with your crime. My report shall reach the elders   635
before you ever get into town.

EMAN: You are afraid of what I will say about you? Don't worry. Only if you try to shame me, then will I speak. I am not going back to the village anyway. Just tell them I have gone, no more. If you say one word more then I shall hear of it the same day and I shall come back.   640

TUTOR: You are telling me what to do? But don't think to come back here even ten years from now. And don't send your children.

[*Goes off with threatening gestures.*]

EMAN: I won't come back.

OMAE: Smoked vulture! But Eman, he says you cannot return next year. What will you do?

EMAN: It is a small thing one can do in the big towns.   645

OMAE: I thought you were going to beat him that time. Why didn't you crackle his dirty hide?

EMAN: Listen carefully Omae . . . I am going on a journey.

OMAE: Come on. Tell me about it on the way.

EMAN: No, I go that way. I cannot return to the village.   650

OMAE: Because of that wretched man? Anyway you will first talk to your father.

EMAN: Go and see him for me. Tell him I have gone away for some time. I think he will know.

OMAE: But Eman . . .

EMAN: I haven't finished. You will go and live with him till I get back. I have spoken to him   655
about you. Look after him!

OMAE: But what is this journey? When will you come back?

EMAN: I don't know. But this is a good moment to go. Nothing ties me down.

OMAE: But Eman, you want to leave me.

EMAN: Don't forget all I said. I don't know how long I will be. Stay in my father's house as   660
long as you remember me. When you become tired of waiting, you must do as you please. You understand? You must do as you please.

OMAE: I cannot understand anything Eman. I don't know where you are going or why. Suppose you never came back! Don't go, Eman. Don't leave me by myself.

EMAN: I must go. Now let me see you on your way.   665

OMAE: I shall come with you.

EMAN: Come with me! And who will look after you? Me? You will only be in my way, you know that! You will hold me back and I shall desert you in a strange place. Go home and do as I say. Take care of my father and let him take care of you.

[*He starts going but* OMAE *clings to him.*]

OMAE: But Eman, stay the night at least. You will only lose your way. Your father Eman, what will he say? I won't remember what you said . . . come back to the village . . . I cannot return alone Eman . . . come with me as far as the crossroads.   670

[*His face set,* EMAN *strides off and* OMAE *loses balance as he increases his pace. Falling, she quickly wraps her arms around his ankle, but* EMAN *continues unchecked, dragging her along.*]

OMAE: Don't go Eman . . . Eman, don't leave me, don't leave me . . . don't leave your Omae . . . don't go Eman . . . don't leave your Omae . . .

[EMAN—*as carrier*—*makes a nervous move as if he intends to go after the vanished pair. He stops but continues to stare at the point where he last saw them. There is stillness for a while. Then the* GIRL *enters from the same place and remains looking at* EMAN. *Startled,* EMAN *looks apprehensively round him. The* GIRL *goes nearer but keeps beyond arm's length.*]

GIRL: Are you the carrier?   675
EMAN: Yes. I am Eman.
GIRL: Why are you hiding?
EMAN: I really came for a drink of water . . . er . . . is there anyone in front of the house?
GIRL: No.
EMAN: But there might be people in the house. Did you hear voices?   680
GIRL: There is no one here.
EMAN: Good. Thank you. [*he is about to go, stops suddenly*] Er . . . would you . . . you will find a cup on the table. Could you bring me the water out here? The water-pot is in a corner. [*The* GIRL *goes. She enters the house, then, watching* EMAN *carefully, slips out and runs off.*]   685
EMAN: [*sitting*] Perhaps they have all gone home. It will be good to rest. [*He hears voices and listens hard.*] Too late. [*moves cautiously nearer the house*] Quickly girl, I can hear people coming. Hurry up. [*looks through the window*] Where are you? Where is she? [*The truth dawns on him suddenly and he moves off, sadly.*]

[*Enter* JAGUNA *and* OROGE, *led by the* GIRL.]

GIRL: [*pointing*]: He was there.   690
JAGUNA: Ay, he's gone now. He is a sly one is your friend. But it won't save him for ever.
OROGE: What was he doing when you saw him?
GIRL: He asked me for a drink of water.
JAGUNA, OROGE: Ah! [*They look at each other.*]
OROGE: We should have thought of that.   695
JAGUNA: He is surely finished now. If only we had thought of it earlier.
OROGE: It is not too late. There is still an hour before midnight.
JAGUNA: We must call back all the men. Now we need only wait for him—in the right place.
OROGE: Everyone must be told. We don't want anyone heading him off again.   700
JAGUNA: And it works so well. This is surely the help of the gods themselves Oroge. Don't you know at once what is on the path to the stream?

OROGE: The sacred trees.

JAGUNA: I tell you it is the very hand of the gods. Let us go.

> [*An overgrown part of the village.* EMAN *wanders in, aimlessly, seemingly uncaring of discovery. Beyond him, an area lights up, revealing a group of people clustered round a spot, all the heads are bowed. One figure stands away and separate from them. Even as* EMAN *looks, the group breaks up and the people disperse, coming down and past him. Only three people are left, a man (*EMAN*) whose back is turned, the village* PRIEST, *and the isolated one. They stand on opposite sides of the grave, the man on the mound of earth. The* PRIEST *walks round to the man's side and lays a hand on his shoulder.*]

PRIEST: Come.   705

EMAN: I will. Give me a few moments here alone.

PRIEST: Be comforted.

> [*They fall silent.*]

EMAN: I was gone twelve years but she waited. She whom I thought had too much of the laughing child in her. Twelve years I was a pilgrim, seeking the vain shrine of secret strength. And all the time, strange knowledge, this silent strength of my child-woman.   710

PRIEST: We all saw it. It was a lesson to us; we did not know that such goodness could be found among us.

EMAN: Then why? Why the wasted years if she had to perish giving birth to my child? [*They are both silent.*] I do not really know for what great meaning I searched. When I returned, I could not be certain I had found it. Until I reached my home and I 715 found her a full-grown woman, still a child at heart. When I grew to believe it, I thought this, after all, is what I sought. It was here all the time. And I threw away my new-gained knowledge. I buried the part of me that was formed in strange places. I made a home in my birthplace.

PRIEST: That was as it should be.   720

EMAN: Any truth of that was killed in the cruelty of her brief happiness.

PRIEST: [*looks up and sees the figure standing away from them, the child in his arms. He is totally still.*] Your father—he is over there.

EMAN: I knew he would come. Has he my son with him?

PRIEST: Yes.   725

EMAN: He will let no one take the child. Go and comfort him priest. He loved Omae like a daughter, and you all know how well she looked after him. You see how strong we really are. In his heart of hearts the old man's love really awaited a daughter. Go and comfort him. His grief is more than mine.

> [*The* PRIEST *goes. The* OLD MAN *has stood well away from the burial group. His face is hard and his gaze unswerving from the grave. The* PRIEST *goes to him, pauses, but sees that he can make no dent in the man's grief. Bowed, he goes on his way.*]

> [*EMAN, as carrier, walking towards the graveside, the other* EMAN *having gone. His feet sink into the mound and he breaks slowly onto his knees, scooping up the sand in his hands and pouring it on his head. The scene blacks out slowly.*]

> [*Enter* JAGUNA *and* OROGE.]

OROGE: We have only a little time.   730

JAGUNA: He will come. All the wells are guarded. There is only the stream left him. The animal must come to drink.

OROGE: You are sure it will not fail—the trap I mean.

JAGUNA: When Jaguna sets the trap, even elephants pay homage—their trunks downwards and one leg up in the sky. When the carrier steps on the fallen twigs, it is up in the sacred trees with him. 735

OROGE: I shall breathe again when this long night is over.

[*They go out.*]

[*Enter* EMAN—*as carrier—from the same direction as the last two entered. In front of him is still a figure, the* OLD MAN *as he was, carrying the dwarf boat.*]

EMAN: [*joyfully*] Father.

[*The figure does not turn round.*]

EMAN: It is your son. Eman. [*He moves nearer.*] Don't you want to look at me? It is I, Eman. [*He moves nearer still.*] 740

OLD MAN: You are coming too close. Don't you know what I carry on my head?

EMAN: But father, I am your son.

OLD MAN: Then go back. We cannot give the two of us.

EMAN: Tell me first where you are going.

OLD MAN: Do you ask that? Where else but to the river? 745

EMAN: [*visibly relieved*] I only wanted to be sure. My throat is burning. I have been looking for the stream all night.

OLD MAN: It is the other way.

EMAN: But you said . . .

OLD MAN: I take the longer way, you know how I must do this. It is quicker if you take the other way. Go now. 750

EMAN: No, I will only get lost again. I shall go with you.

OLD MAN: Go back my son. Go back.

EMAN: Why? Won't you even look at me?

OLD MAN: Listen to your father. Go back. 755

EMAN: But father!

[*He makes to hold him. Instantly the* OLD MAN *breaks into a rapid trot.* EMAN *hesitates, then follows, his strength nearly gone.*]

EMAN: Wait father. I am coming with you . . . wait . . . wait for me father . . .

[*There is a sound of twigs breaking, of a sudden trembling in the branches. Then silence.*]

[*The front of* EMAN'*s house. The effigy is hanging from the sheaves. Enter* SUNMA, *still supported by* IFADA, *she stands transfixed as she sees the hanging figure.* IFADA *appears to go mad, rushes at the object and tears it down.* SUNMA, *her last bit of will gone, crumbles against the wall. Some distance away from them, partly hidden, stands the* GIRL, *impassively watching.* IFADA *hugs the effigy to him, stands above* SUNMA. *The* GIRL *remains where she is, observing.*
Almost at once, the villagers begin to return, subdued and guilty. They walk across the front, skirting the house as widely as they can. No word is exchanged. JAGUNA, *who is leading, sees* SUNMA *as soon as he comes in view. He stops at once, retreating slightly.*]

OROGE: [*almost whispering*] What is it?

JAGUNA: The viper.

[OROGE *looks cautiously at the woman.*]

OROGE: I don't think she will even see you.   760

JAGUNA: Are you sure? I am in no frame of mind for another meeting with her.

OROGE: Let's go home.

JAGUNA: I am sick to the heart of the cowardice I have seen tonight.

OROGE: That is the nature of men.

JAGUNA: Then it is a sorry world to live in. We did it for them. It was all for their own   765
common good. What did it benefit me whether the man lived or died. But did you
see them? One and all they looked up at the man and words died in their throats.

OROGE: It was no common sight.

JAGUNA: Women could not have behaved so shamefully. One by one they crept off like
sick dogs. Not one could raise a curse.   770

OROGE: It was not only him they fled. Do you see how unattended we are?

JAGUNA: There are those who will pay for this night's work!

OROGE: Ay, let us go home.

[*They go off.* SUNMA, IFADA *and the* GIRL *remain as they are, the light fading
slowly on them.*]

THE END

Sam Shepard (1943–)

True West
(1980)

S AM SHEPARD has been among the most prolific and provocative of contemporary American playwrights. He began his writing career in 1964 in the Off-Off-Broadway theatre. From the mid-1970s to the mid-1980s, he wrote his most successful plays: *Curse of the Starving Class* (1977), *Buried Child* (1979, Pulitzer Prize), *True West* (1980), *Fool for Love* (1983), and *A Lie of the Mind* (1985). While there is variety in Shepard's work, a number of motifs recur: attempts to escape or deny the past, the cowboy and the West as basic American myths, the family as a battleground, and characters caught between empty dreams and an insubstantial reality.

True West is Shepard's most produced play. It is a tightly focused work, dominated by the intense interactions between two brothers. The younger brother, Austin, is an Ivy League–educated screenwriter while the older brother, Lee, is a petty thief and drifter. Over the course of the play, each brother finds himself wishing he were in the other's place. While the brothers are very different, the play suggests that their contrasting roles and identities may be found inside all of us. The desire to be our own boss may conflict with our desire for a comfortable income. The desire for freedom battles with the desire for security and safety. In one sense Lee and Austin are two sides of one personality as they embody impulses that tempt us and desires between which we must often choose.

The title *True West* evokes multiple images, suggesting the traditional terrain of cowboys, open spaces, freedom, self-made law, and the gunfights one might find in a Hollywood Western. (Some critics see the play's ambiguous ending as a pseudo-contemporary Western, with the characters facing off in a duel-like fashion.) In the play, the characters suggest that the mythic old West has died; Lee says, "Built up? Wiped out is more like it." Later, when a Hollywood producer says that Lee's screenplay shows "the real West," Austin retorts, "There's no such thing as the West anymore!" Instead of cowboys roaming the prairie, Austin suggests that the West is now freeways, smog, color TVs, and Safeway supermarkets. The West is also Hollywood, the place that can make you a star, with its call of the big screen that has become its own American Dream. In part, the play deals with the myth of the American West, an image that helped define the American character, but the play suggests that myth is no longer viable.

True West also engages with another central component of the American mythos—the family. As with the West, the image of family does not live up to its ideal. Instead of the desired supportive loving family, there is tension, rivalry, and violence as the brothers battle for dominance and control. Traditionally, the home and family are realms of safety and security, but in this play, dysfunction is carried to an extreme, and the neatly organized suburban home that opens the play is left in chaotic ruins at the play's end.

True West
(1980)

Characters

AUSTIN, *early thirties, light blue sports shirt, light tan cardigan sweater, clean blue jeans, white tennis shoes*

LEE, *his older brother, early forties, filthy white t-shirt, tattered brown overcoat covered with dust, dark blue baggy suit pants from the Salvation Army, pink suede belt, pointed black forties dress shoes scuffed up, holes in the soles, no socks, no hat, long pronounced sideburns, "Gene Vincent" hairdo, two days' growth of beard, bad teeth*

SAUL KIMMER, *late forties, Hollywood producer, pink and white flower print sports shirt, white sports coat with matching polyester slacks, black and white loafers*

MOM, *early sixties, mother of the brothers, small woman, conservative white skirt and matching jacket, red shoulder bag, two pieces of matching red luggage*

SCENE————*All nine scenes take place on the same set; a kitchen and adjoining alcove of an older home in a Southern California suburb, about 40 miles east of Los Angeles. The kitchen takes up most of the playing area to stage left. The kitchen consists of a sink, upstage center, surrounded by counter space, a wall telephone, cupboards, and a small window just above it bordered by neat yellow curtains. Stage left of sink is a stove. Stage right, a refrigerator. The alcove adjoins the kitchen to stage right. There is no wall division or door to the alcove. It is open and easily accessible from the kitchen and defined only by the objects in it: a small round glass breakfast table mounted on white iron legs, two matching white iron chairs set across from each other. The two exterior walls of the alcove which prescribe a corner in the upstage right are composed of many small windows, beginning from a solid wall about three feet high and extending to the ceiling. The windows look out to bushes and citrus trees. The alcove is filled with all sorts of house plants in various pots, mostly Boston ferns hanging in planters at different levels. The floor of the alcove is composed of green synthetic grass.*

All entrances and exits are made stage left from the kitchen. There is no door. The actors simply go off and come onto the playing area.

NOTE ON SET AND COSTUME————*The set should be constructed realistically with no attempt to distort its dimensions, shapes, objects, or colors. No objects should be introduced which might draw special attention to themselves other than the props demanded by the script. If a stylistic "concept" is grafted onto the set design it will only serve to confuse the evolution of the characters' situation, which is the most important focus of the play.*

Likewise, the costumes should be exactly representative of who the characters are and not added onto for the sake of making a point to the audience.

NOTE ON SOUND——*The Coyote of Southern California has a distinct yapping, dog-like bark, similar to a Hyena. This yapping grows more intense and maniacal as the pack grows in numbers, which is usually the case when they lure and kill pets from suburban yards. The sense of growing frenzy in the pack should be felt in the background, particularly in Scenes 7 and 8. In any case, these Coyotes never make the long, mournful, solitary howl of the Hollywood stereotype.*

The sound of Crickets can speak for itself.

These sounds should also be treated realistically even though they sometimes grow in volume and numbers.

ACT I

SCENE I

Night. Sound of crickets in dark. Candlelight appears in alcove, illuminating AUSTIN, *seated at glass table hunched over a writing notebook, pen in hand, cigarette burning in ashtray, cup of coffee, typewriter on table, stacks of paper, candle burning on table.*

Soft moonlight fills kitchen illuminating LEE, *beer in hand, six-pack on counter behind him. He's leaning against the sink, mildly drunk; takes a slug of beer.*

LEE: So, Mom took off for Alaska, huh?
AUSTIN: Yeah.
LEE: Sorta' left you in charge.
AUSTIN: Well, she knew I was coming down here so she offered me the place.
LEE: You keepin' the plants watered?   5
AUSTIN: Yeah.
LEE: Keepin' the sink clean? She don't like even a single tea leaf in the sink ya' know.
AUSTIN: (*Trying to concentrate on writing.*) Yeah, I know.

(*Pause.*)

LEE: She gonna' be up there a long time?
AUSTIN: I don't know.   10
LEE: Kinda' nice for you, huh? Whole place to yourself.
AUSTIN: Yeah, it's great.
LEE: Ya' got crickets anyway. Tons a' crickets out there. (*Looks around kitchen.*) Ya' got groceries? Coffee?
AUSTIN: (*Looking up from writing.*) What?   15
LEE: You got coffee?
AUSTIN: Yeah.
LEE: At's good. (*Short pause.*) Real coffee? From the bean?
AUSTIN: Yeah. You want some?
LEE: Naw. I brought some uh—(*Motions to beer.*)   20
AUSTIN: Help yourself to whatever's—(*Motions to refrigerator.*)

LEE: I will. Don't worry about me. I'm not the one to worry about. I mean I can uh— (*Pause.*) You always work by candlelight?

AUSTIN: No—uh—Not always.

LEE: Just sometimes? 25

AUSTIN: (*Puts pen down, rubs his eyes.*) Yeah. Sometimes it's soothing.

LEE: Isn't that what the old guys did?

AUSTIN: What old guys?

LEE: The Forefathers. You know.

AUSTIN: Forefathers? 30

LEE: Isn't that what they did? Candlelight burning into the night? Cabins in the wilderness.

AUSTIN: (*Rubs hand through his hair.*) I suppose.

LEE: I'm not botherin' you am I? I mean I don't wanna break into yer uh—concentration or nothin'.

AUSTIN: No, it's all right. 35

LEE: That's good. I mean I realize that yer line a' work demands a lota' concentration.

AUSTIN: It's okay.

LEE: You probably think that I'm not fully able to comprehend somethin' like that, huh?

AUSTIN: Like what?

LEE: That stuff yer doin'. That art. You know. Whatever you call it. 40

AUSTIN: It's just a little research.

LEE: You may not know it but I did a little art myself once.

AUSTIN: You did?

LEE: Yeah! I did some a' that. I fooled around with it. No future in it.

AUSTIN: What'd you do? 45

LEE: Never mind what I did! Just never mind about that. (*Pause.*) It was ahead of its time.

(*Pause.*)

AUSTIN: So, you went out to see the old man, huh?

LEE: Yeah, I seen him.

AUSTIN: How's he doing?

LEE: Same. He's doin' just about the same. 50

AUSTIN: I was down there too, you know.

LEE: What d'ya' want, an award? You want some kinda' medal? You were down there. He told me all about you.

AUSTIN: What'd he say?

LEE: He told me. Don't worry. 55

(*Pause.*)

AUSTIN: Well—

LEE: You don't have to say nothin'.

AUSTIN: I wasn't.

LEE: Yeah, you were gonna' make somethin' up. Somethin' brilliant.

(*Pause.*)

AUSTIN: You going to be down here very long, Lee? 60

LEE: Might be. Depends on a few things.

AUSTIN: You got some friends down here?

LEE: (*Laughs.*) I know a few people. Yeah.

AUSTIN: Well, you can stay here as long as I'm here.

LEE: I don't need your permission do I? 65

AUSTIN: No.
LEE: I mean she's my mother too, right?
AUSTIN: Right.
LEE: She might've just as easily asked me to take care of her place as you.
AUSTIN: That's right.   70
LEE: I mean I know how to water plants.

(*Long pause.*)

AUSTIN: So you don't know how long you'll be staying then?
LEE: Depends mostly on houses, ya' know.
AUSTIN: Houses?
LEE: Yeah. Houses. Electric devices. Stuff like that. I gotta' make a little tour first.   75

(*Short pause.*)

AUSTIN: Lee, why don't you just try another neighborhood, all right?
LEE: (*Laughs.*) What'sa' matter with this neighborhood? This is a great neighborhood. Lush. Good class a' people. Not many dogs.
AUSTIN: Well, our uh—Our mother just happens to live here. That's all.
LEE: Nobody's gonna' know. All they know is somethin's missing. That's all. She'll never   80
even hear about it. Nobody's gonna' know.
AUSTIN: You're going to get picked up if you start walking around here at night.
LEE: Me? I'm gonna' git picked up? What about you? You stick out like a sore thumb. Look at you. You think yer regular lookin'?
AUSTIN: I've got too much to deal with here to be worrying about—   85
LEE: Yer not gonna' have to worry about me! I've been doin' all right without you. I haven't been anywhere near you for five years! Now isn't that true?
AUSTIN: Yeah.
LEE: So you don't have to worry about me. I'm a free agent.
AUSTIN: All right.   90
LEE: Now all I wanna' do is borrow yer car.
AUSTIN: No!
LEE: Just fer a day. One day.
AUSTIN: No!
LEE: I won't take it outside a twenty mile radius. I promise ya'. You can check the   95
speedometer.
AUSTIN: You're not borrowing my car! That's all there is to it.

(*Pause.*)

LEE: Then I'll just take the damn thing.
AUSTIN: Lee, look—I don't want any trouble, all right?
LEE: That's a dumb line. That is a dumb fuckin' line. You git paid fer dreamin' up a line   100
like that?
AUSTIN: Look, I can give you some money if you need money.

(LEE *suddenly lunges at* AUSTIN, *grabs him violently by the shirt and shakes him with tremendous power.*)

LEE: Don't you say that to me! Don't you ever say that to me! (*Just as suddenly he turns him loose, pushes him away and backs off.*) You may be able to git away with that with the Old Man. Git him tanked up for a week! Buy him off with yer Hollywood   105
blood money, but not me! I can git my own money my own way. Big money!

AUSTIN: I was just making an offer.

LEE: Yeah, well keep it to yourself!

(*Long pause.*)

Those are the most monotonous fuckin' crickets I ever heard in my life.

AUSTIN: I kinda' like the sound. 110

LEE: Yeah. Supposed to be able to tell the temperature by the number a' pulses. You believe that?

AUSTIN: The temperature?

LEE: Yeah. The air. How hot it is.

AUSTIN: How do you do that? 115

LEE: I don't know. Some woman told me that. She was a Botanist. So I believed her.

AUSTIN: Where'd you meet her?

LEE: What?

AUSTIN: The woman Botanist?

LEE: I met her on the desert. I been spendin' a lota' time on the desert. 120

AUSTIN: What were you doing out there?

LEE: (*Pause, stares in space.*) I forgit. Had me a Pit Bull there for a while but I lost him.

AUSTIN: Pit Bull?

LEE: Fightin' dog. Damn I made some good money off that little dog. Real good money.

(*Pause.*)

AUSTIN: You could come up north with me, you know. 125

LEE: What's up there?

AUSTIN: My family.

LEE: Oh, that's right, you got the wife and kiddies now don't ya'. The house, the car, the whole slam. That's right.

AUSTIN: You could spend a couple days. See how you like it. I've got an extra room. 130

LEE: Too cold up there.

(*Pause.*)

AUSTIN: You want to sleep for a while?

LEE: (*Pause, stares at* AUSTIN.) I don't sleep.

(*Lights to black.*)

SCENE II

Morning. AUSTIN *is watering plants with a vaporizer,* LEE *sits at glass table in alcove drinking beer.*

LEE: I never realized the old lady was so security-minded.

AUSTIN: How do you mean? 135

LEE: Made a little tour this morning. She's got locks on everything. Locks and double-locks and chain locks and—What's she got that's so valuable?

AUSTIN: Antiques I guess. I don't know.

LEE: Antiques? Brought everything with her from the old place, huh. Just the same crap we always had around. Plates and spoons. 140

AUSTIN: I guess they have personal value to her.

LEE: Personal value. Yeah. Just a lota' junk. Most of it's phony anyway. Idaho decals. Now who in the hell wants to eat offa' plate with the State of Idaho starin' ya' in the face. Every time ya' take a bite ya' get to see a little bit more.

AUSTIN: Well it must mean something to her or she wouldn't save it.   145

LEE: Yeah, well personally I don't wann' be invaded by Idaho when I'm eatin'. When I'm eatin' I'm home. Ya' know what I'm sayin? I'm not driftin', I'm home. I don't need my thoughts swept off to Idaho. I don't need that!

(*Pause.*)

AUSTIN: Did you go out last night?

LEE: Why?   150

AUSTIN: I thought I heard you go out.

LEE: Yeah, I went out. What about it?

AUSTIN: Just wondered.

LEE: Damn coyotes kept me awake.

AUSTIN: Oh yeah, I heard them. They must've killed somebody's dog or something.   155

LEE: Yappin' their fool heads off. They don't yap like that on the desert. They howl. These are city coyotes here.

AUSTIN: Well, you don't sleep anyway do you?

(*Pause,* LEE *stares at him.*)

LEE: You're pretty smart aren't ya?

AUSTIN: How do you mean?   160

LEE: I mean you never had any more on the ball than I did. But here you are gettin' invited into prominent people's houses. Sittin' around talkin' like you know somethin'.

AUSTIN: They're not so prominent.

LEE: They're a helluva' lot more prominent than the houses I get invited into.

AUSTIN: Well you invite yourself.   165

LEE: That's right. I do. In fact I probably got a wider range a' choices than you do, come to think of it.

AUSTIN: I wouldn't doubt it.

LEE: In fact I been inside some pretty classy places in my time. And I never even went to an Ivy League school either.   170

AUSTIN: You want some breakfast or something?

LEE: Breakfast?

AUSTIN: Yeah. Don't you eat breakfast?

LEE: Look, don't worry about me pal. I can take care a' myself. You just go ahead as though I wasn't even here, all right?   175

(AUSTIN *goes into kitchen, makes coffee.*)

AUSTIN: Where'd you walk to last night?

(*Pause.*)

LEE: I went up in the foothills there. Up in the San Gabriels. Heat was drivin' me crazy.

AUSTIN: Well, wasn't it hot out on the desert?

LEE: Different kinda' heat. Out there it's clean. Cools off at night. There's a nice little breeze.

AUSTIN: Where were you, the Mojave?

LEE: Yeah. The Mojave. That's right.   180

AUSTIN: I haven't been out there in years.

LEE: Out past Needles there.

AUSTIN: Oh yeah.

LEE: Up here it's different. This country's real different.

AUSTIN: Well, it's been built up.   185

LEE: Built up? Wiped out is more like it. I don't even hardly recognize it.

AUSTIN: Yeah. Foothills are the same though, aren't they?

LEE: Pretty much. It's funny goin' up in there. The smells and everything. Used to catch snakes up there, remember?

AUSTIN: You caught snakes.   190

LEE: Yeah. And you'd pretend you were Geronimo or some damn thing. You used to go right out to lunch.

AUSTIN: I enjoyed my imagination.

LEE: That what you call it? Looks like yer still enjoyin' it.

AUSTIN: So you just wandered around up there, huh?   195

LEE: Yeah. With a purpose.

AUSTIN: See any houses?

(*Pause.*)

LEE: Couple. Couple a' real nice ones. One of 'em didn't even have a dog. Walked right up and stuck my head in the window. Not a peep. Just a sweet kinda' suburban silence.

AUSTIN: What kind of a place was it?   200

LEE: Like a paradise. Kinda' place that sorta' kills ya' inside. Warm yellow lights. Mexican tile all around. Copper pots hangin' over the stove. Ya' know like they got in the magazines. Blonde people movin' in and outa' the rooms, talkin' to each other. (*Pause.*) Kinda' place you wish you sorta' grew up in, ya' know.

AUSTIN: That's the kind of place you wish you'd grown up in?   205

LEE: Yeah, why not?

AUSTIN: I thought you hated that kind of stuff.

LEE: Yeah, well you never knew too much about me did ya'?

(*Pause.*)

AUSTIN: Why'd you go out to the desert in the first place?

LEE: I was on my way to see the old man.   210

AUSTIN: You mean you just passed through there?

LEE: Yeah. That's right. Three months of passin' through.

AUSTIN: Three months?

LEE: Somethin' like that. Maybe more. Why?

AUSTIN: You lived on the Mojave for three months?   215

LEE: Yeah. What'sa' matter with that?

AUSTIN: By yourself?

LEE: Mostly. Had a couple a' visitors. Had that dog for a while.

AUSTIN: Didn't you miss people?

LEE: (*Laughs.*) People?   220

AUSTIN: Yeah. I mean I go crazy if I have to spend three nights in a motel by myself.

LEE: Yer not in a motel now.

AUSTIN: No, I know. But sometimes I have to stay in motels.

LEE: Well, they got people in motels don't they?

AUSTIN: Strangers.   225

LEE: Yer friendly aren't ya'? Aren't you the friendly type?

(*Pause.*)

AUSTIN: I'm going to have somebody coming by here later, Lee.

LEE: Ah! Lady friend?
AUSTIN: No, a producer.
LEE: Aha! What's he produce?   230
AUSTIN: Film. Movies. You know.
LEE: Oh, movies. Motion Pictures! A Big Wig huh?
AUSTIN: Yeah.
LEE: What's he comin' by here for?
AUSTIN: We have to talk about a project.   235
LEE: Whadya' mean, "a project"? What's a "project"?
AUSTIN: A script.
LEE: Oh. That's what yer doin' with all these papers?
AUSTIN: Yeah.
LEE: Well, what's the project about?   240
AUSTIN: We're uh—it's a period piece.
LEE: What's "a period piece"?
AUSTIN: Look, it doesn't matter. The main thing is we need to discuss this alone. I mean—
LEE: Oh, I get it. You want me outa' the picture.
AUSTIN: Not exactly. I just need to be alone with him for a couple of hours. So we can talk.   245
LEE: Yer afraid I'll embarrass ya' huh?
AUSTIN: I'm not afraid you'll embarrass me!
LEE: Well, I tell ya' what—Why don't you just gimme the keys to yer car and I'll be back here around six o'clock or so. That give ya' enough time?
AUSTIN: I'm not loaning you my car, Lee.   250
LEE: You want me to just git lost huh? Take a hike? Is that it? Pound the pavement for a few hours while you bullshit yer way into a million bucks.
AUSTIN: Look, it's going to be hard enough for me to face this character on my own without—
LEE: You don't know this guy?   255
AUSTIN: No I don't know—He's a producer. I mean I've been meeting with him for months but you never get to know a producer.
LEE: Yer tryin' to hustle him? Is that it?
AUSTIN: I'm not trying to hustle him! I'm trying to work out a deal! It's not easy.
LEE: What kinda' deal?   260
AUSTIN: Convince him it's a worthwhile story.
LEE: He's not convinced? How come he's comin' over here if he's not convinced? I'll convince him for ya'.
AUSTIN: You don't understand the way things work down here.
LEE: How do things work down here?   265

(*Pause.*)

AUSTIN: Look, if I loan you my car will you have it back here by six?
LEE: On the button. With a full tank a' gas.
AUSTIN: (*Digging in his pocket for keys.*) Forget about the gas.
LEE: Hey, these days gas is gold, old buddy.

(AUSTIN *hands the keys to* LEE.)

You remember that car I used to loan you?
AUSTIN: Yeah.
LEE: Forty Ford. Flathead.   270
AUSTIN: Yeah.
LEE: Sucker hauled ass didn't it?

AUSTIN: Lee, it's not that I don't want to loan you my car—

LEE: You are loanin' me yer car.   275

> (LEE *gives* AUSTIN *a pat on the shoulder, pause.*)

AUSTIN: I know. I just wish—

LEE: What? You wish what?

AUSTIN: I don't know. I wish I wasn't—I wish I didn't have to be doing business down here. I'd like to just spend some time with you.

LEE: I thought it was "Art" you were doin'.   280

> (LEE *moves across kitchen toward exit, tosses keys in his hand.*)

AUSTIN: Try to get it back here by six, okay?

LEE: No sweat. Hey, ya' know, if that uh—story of yours doesn't go over with the guy—tell him I got a couple a' "projects" he might be interested in. Real commercial. Full a' suspense. True-to-life stuff.

> (LEE *exits,* AUSTIN *stares after* LEE *then turns, goes to papers at table, leafs through pages, lights fade to black.*)

SCENE III

Afternoon. Alcove, SAUL KIMMER *and* AUSTIN *seated across from each other at table.*

SAUL: Well, to tell you the truth Austin, I have never felt so confident about a project in   285
quite a long time.

AUSTIN: Well, that's good to hear, Saul.

SAUL: I am absolutely convinced we can get this thing off the ground. I mean we'll have to make a sale to television and that means getting a major star. Somebody bankable. But I think we can do it. I really do.   290

AUSTIN: Don't you think we need a first draft before we approach a star?

SAUL: No, no, not at all. I don't think it's necessary. Maybe a brief synopsis. I don't want you to touch the typewriter until we have some seed money.

AUSTIN: That's fine with me.

SAUL: I mean it's a great story. Just the story alone. You've really managed to capture   295
something this time.

AUSTIN: I'm glad you like it, Saul.

> (LEE *enters abruptly into kitchen carrying a stolen television set, short pause.*)

LEE: Aw shit, I'm sorry about that. I am really sorry Austin.

AUSTIN: (*Standing.*) That's all right.

LEE: (*Moving toward them.*) I mean I thought it was way past six already. You said to have   300
it back here by six.

AUSTIN: We were just finishing up. (*To* SAUL.) This is my, uh—brother, Lee.

SAUL: (*Standing.*) Oh, I'm very happy to meet you.

> (LEE *sets T.V. on sink counter, shakes hands with* SAUL.)

LEE: I can't tell ya' how happy I am to meet you sir.

SAUL: Saul Kimmer.   305

LEE: Mr. Kipper.

SAUL: Kimmer.

AUSTIN: Lee's been living out on the desert and he just uh—
SAUL: Oh, that's terrific! (*To* LEE.) Palm Springs?
LEE: Yeah. Yeah, right. Right around in that area. Near uh—Bob Hope Drive there.   310
SAUL: Oh I love it out there. I just love it. The air is wonderful.
LEE: Yeah. Sure is. Healthy.
SAUL: And the golf. I don't know if you play golf, but the golf is just about the best.
LEE: I play a lota' golf.
SAUL: Is that right?   315
LEE: Yeah. In fact I was hoping I'd run into somebody out here who played a little golf.
     I've been lookin' for a partner.
SAUL: Well, I uh—
AUSTIN: Lee's just down for a visit while our mother's in Alaska.
SAUL: Oh, your mother's in Alaska?   320
AUSTIN: Yes. She went up there on a little vacation. This is her place.
SAUL: I see. Well isn't that something. Alaska.
LEE: What kinda' handicap do ya' have, Mr. Kimmer?
SAUL: Oh I'm just a Sunday duffer really. You know.
LEE: That's good 'cause I haven't swung a club in months.   325
SAUL: Well we ought to get together sometime and have a little game. Austin, do you play?

(SAUL *mimes a Johnny Carson golf swing for* AUSTIN.)

AUSTIN: No. I don't uh—I've watched it on T.V.
LEE: (*To* SAUL.) How 'bout tomorrow morning? Bright and early. We could get out there
     and put in eighteen holes before breakfast.
SAUL: Well, I've got uh—I have several appointments—   330
LEE: No, I mean real early. Crack a' dawn. While the dew's still thick on the fairway.
SAUL: Sounds really great.
LEE: Austin could be our caddie.
SAUL: Now that's an idea. (*Laughs.*)
AUSTIN: I don't know the first thing about golf.   335
LEE: There's nothin' to it. Isn't that right, Saul? He'd pick it up in fifteen minutes.
SAUL: Sure. Doesn't take long. 'Course you have to play for years to find your true form.
     (*Chuckles.*)
LEE: (*To* AUSTIN.) We'll give ya' a quick run-down on the club faces. The irons, the woods.
     Show ya' a couple pointers on the basic swing. Might even let ya' hit the ball a couple   340
     times. Whadya' think, Saul?
SAUL: Why not. I think it'd be great. I haven't had any exercise in weeks.
LEE: At's the spirit! We'll have a little orange juice right afterwards.

(*Pause.*)

SAUL: Orange juice?
LEE: Yeah! Vitamin C! Nothin' like a shot a' orange juice after a round a' golf. Hot shower.   345
     Snappin' towels at each others' privates. Real sense a' fraternity.
SAUL: (*Smiles at* AUSTIN.) Well, you make it sound very inviting, I must say. It really does
     sound great.
LEE: Then it's a date.
SAUL: Well, I'll call the country club and see if I can arrange something.   350
LEE: Great! Boy, I sure am sorry that I busted in on ya' all in the middle of yer meeting.
SAUL: Oh that's quite all right. We were just about finished anyway.
LEE: I can wait out in the other room if you want.
SAUL: No really—

LEE: Just got Austin's color T.V. back from the shop. I can watch a little amateur boxing   355
now.

(LEE *and* AUSTIN *exchange looks.*)

SAUL: Oh—Yes.

LEE: You don't fool around in Television, do you Saul?

SAUL: Uh—I have in the past. Produced some T.V. Specials. Network stuff. But it's mainly features now.

LEE: That's where the big money is, huh?   360

SAUL: Yes. That's right.

AUSTIN: Why don't I call you tomorrow, Saul and we'll get together. We can have lunch or something.

SAUL: That'd be terrific.

LEE: Right after the golf.   365

(*Pause.*)

SAUL: What?

LEE: You can have lunch right after the golf.

SAUL: Oh, right.

LEE: Austin was tellin' me that yer interested in stories.

SAUL: Well, we develop certain projects that we feel have commercial potential.   370

LEE: What kinda' stuff do ya' go in for?

SAUL: Oh, the usual. You know. Good love interest. Lots of action. (*Chuckles at* AUSTIN.)

LEE: Westerns?

SAUL: Sometimes.

AUSTIN: I'll give you a ring, Saul.   375

(AUSTIN *tries to move* SAUL *across the kitchen but* LEE *blocks their way.*)

LEE: I got a Western that'd knock yer lights out.

SAUL: Oh really?

LEE: Yeah. Contemporary Western. Based on a true story. 'Course I'm not a writer like my brother here. I'm not a man of the pen.

SAUL: Well—   380

LEE: I mean I can tell ya' a story off the tongue but I can't put it down on paper. That don't make any difference though does it?

SAUL: No, not really.

LEE: I mean plenty a' guys have stories don't they? True-life stories. Musta' been a lota' movies made from real life.   385

SAUL: Yes. I suppose so.

LEE: I haven't seen a good Western since "Lonely Are the Brave." You remember that movie?

SAUL: No, I'm afraid I—

LEE: Kirk Douglas. Helluva' movie. You remember that movie, Austin?

AUSTIN: Yes.   390

LEE: (*To* SAUL.) The man dies for the love of a horse.

SAUL: Is that right?

LEE: Yeah. Ya' hear the horse screamin' at the end of it. Rain's comin' down. Horse is screamin'. Then there's a shot. BLAM! Just a single shot like that. Then nothin' but the sound of rain. And Kirk Douglas is ridin' in the ambulance. Ridin' away from   395
the scene of the accident. And when he hears that shot he knows that his horse has died. He knows. And you see his eyes. And his eyes die. Right inside his face. And then his eyes close. And you know that he's died too. You know that Kirk Douglas has died from the death of his horse.

SAUL: (*Eyes* AUSTIN *nervously.*) Well, it sounds like a great movie. I'm sorry I missed it.   400
LEE: Yeah, you shouldn't a' missed that one.
SAUL: I'll have to try to catch it some time. Arrange a screening or something. Well, Austin, I'll have to hit the freeway before rush hour.
AUSTIN: (*Ushers him toward exit.*) It's good seeing you, Saul.

   (AUSTIN *and* SAUL *shake hands.*)

LEE: So ya' think there's room for a real Western these days? A true-to-life Western?   405
SAUL: Well, I don't see why not. Why don't you uh—tell the story to Austin and have him write a little outline.
LEE: You'd take a look at it then?
SAUL: Yes. Sure. I'll give it a read-through. Always eager for new material. (*Smiles at* AUSTIN.)
LEE: That's great! You'd really read it then huh?   410
SAUL: It would just be my opinion of course.
LEE: That's all I want. Just an opinion. I happen to think it has a lota' possibilities.
SAUL: Well, it was great meeting you and I'll—

   (SAUL *and* LEE *shake.*)

LEE: I'll call you tomorrow about the golf.
SAUL: Oh. Yes, right.   415
LEE: Austin's got your number, right?
SAUL: Yes.
LEE: So long Saul. (*Gives* SAUL *a pat on the back.*)

   (SAUL *exits,* AUSTIN *turns to* LEE, *looks at T.V. then back to lee.*)

AUSTIN: Give me the keys.

   (AUSTIN *extends his hand toward* LEE, LEE *doesn't move, just stares at* AUSTIN, *smiles, lights to black.*)

SCENE IV

Night. Coyotes in distance, fade, sound of typewriter in dark, crickets, candlelight in alcove, dim light in kitchen, lights reveal AUSTIN *at glass table typing,* LEE *sits across from him, foot on table, drinking beer and whiskey, the T.V. is still on sink counter,* AUSTIN *types for a while, then stops.*

LEE: All right, now read it back to me.   420
AUSTIN: I'm not reading it back to you, Lee. You can read it when we're finished. I can't spend all night on this.
LEE: You got better things to do?
AUSTIN: Let's just go ahead. Now what happens when he leaves Texas?
LEE: Is he ready to leave Texas yet? I didn't know we were that far along. He's not ready to   425
leave Texas.
AUSTIN: He's right at the border.
LEE: (*Sitting up.*) No, see this is one a' the crucial parts. Right here. (*Taps paper with beer can.*) We can't rush through this. He's not right at the border. He's a good fifty miles from the border. A lot can happen in fifty miles.   430
AUSTIN: It's only an outline. We're not writing an entire script now.

LEE: Well ya' can't leave things out even if it is an outline. It's one a' the most important parts. Ya' can't go leavin' it out.
AUSTIN: Okay, okay. Let's just—get it done.
LEE: All right. Now. He's in the truck and he's got his horse trailer and his horse. 435
AUSTIN: We've already established that.
LEE: And he sees this other guy comin' up behind him in another truck. And that truck is pullin' a gooseneck.
AUSTIN: What's a gooseneck?
LEE: Cattle trailer. You know the kind with a gooseneck, goes right down in the bed a' the 440 pick-up.
AUSTIN: Oh. All right. (*Types.*)
LEE: It's important.
AUSTIN: Okay. I got it.
LEE: All these details are important. 445

(AUSTIN *types as they talk.*)

AUSTIN: I've got it.
LEE: And this other guy's got his horse all saddled up in the back a' the gooseneck.
AUSTIN: Right.
LEE: So both these guys have got their horses right along with 'em, see.
AUSTIN: I understand. 450
LEE: Then this first guy suddenly realizes two things.
AUSTIN: The guy in front?
LEE: Right. The guy in front realizes two things almost at the same time. Simultaneous.
AUSTIN: What were the two things?
LEE: Number one, he realizes that the guy behind him is the husband of the woman he's 455 been—

(LEE *makes gesture of screwing by pumping his arm.*)

AUSTIN: (*Sees* LEE's *gesture.*) Oh. Yeah.
LEE: And number two, he realizes he's in the middle of Tornado Country.
AUSTIN: What's "Tornado Country"?
LEE: Panhandle. 460
AUSTIN: Panhandle?
LEE: Sweetwater. Around in that area. Nothin'. Nowhere. And number three—
AUSTIN: I thought there was only two.
LEE: There's three. There's a third unforeseen realization.
AUSTIN: And what's that? 465
LEE: That he's runnin' outa' gas.
AUSTIN: (*Stops typing.*) Come on, Lee.

(AUSTIN *gets up, moves to kitchen, gets a glass of water.*)

LEE: Whadya' mean, "come on"? That's what it is. Write it down! He's runnin' outa' gas.
AUSTIN: It's too—
LEE: What? It's too what? It's too real! That's what ya' mean isn't it? It's too much like 470 real life!
AUSTIN: It's not like real life! It's not enough like real life. Things don't happen like that.
LEE: What! Men don't fuck other men's women?
AUSTIN: Yes. But they don't end up chasing each other across the Panhandle. Through "Tornado Country." 475
LEE: They do in this movie!

AUSTIN: And they don't have horses conveniently along with them when they run out of gas! And they don't run out of gas either!

LEE: These guys run outa' gas! This is my story and one a' these guys runs outa' gas!

AUSTIN: It's just a dumb excuse to get them into a chase scene. It's contrived.   480

LEE: It is a chase scene! It's already a chase scene. They been chasin' each other fer days.

AUSTIN: So now they're supposed to abandon their trucks, climb on their horses and chase each other into the mountains?

LEE: (*Standing suddenly.*) There aren't any mountains in the Panhandle! It's flat!

(LEE *turns violently toward windows in alcove and throws beer can at them.*)

LEE: Goddamn these crickets! (*Yells at crickets.*) Shut up out there! (*Pause, turns back*   485 *toward table.*) This place is like a fuckin' rest home here. How're you supposed to think!

AUSTIN: You wanna' take a break?

LEE: No, I don't wanna' take a break! I wanna' get this done! This is my last chance to get this done.   490

AUSTIN: (*Moves back into alcove.*) All right. Take it easy.

LEE: I'm gonna' be leavin' this area. I don't have time to mess around here.

AUSTIN: Where are you going?

LEE: Never mind where I'm goin'! That's got nothin' to do with you. I just gotta' get this done. I'm not like you. Hangin' around bein' a parasite offa' other fools. I gotta' do   495 this thing and get out.

(*Pause.*)

AUSTIN: A parasite? Me?

LEE: Yeah, you!

AUSTIN: After you break into people's houses and take their televisions?

LEE: They don't need their televisions! I'm doin' them a service.

AUSTIN: Give me back my keys, Lee.   500

LEE: Not until you write this thing! You're gonna' write this outline thing for me or that car's gonna' wind up in Arizona with a different paint job.

AUSTIN: You think you can force me to write this? I was doing you a favor.

LEE: Git off yer high horse will ya'! Favor! Big favor. Handin' down favors from the   505 mountain top.

AUSTIN: Let's just write it, okay? Let's sit down and not get upset and see if we can just get through this.

(AUSTIN *sits at typewriter.*)

(*Long pause.*)

LEE: Yer not gonna' even show it to him, are ya'?

AUSTIN: What?   510

LEE: This outline. You got no intention of showin' it to him. Yer just doin' this 'cause yer afraid a' me.

AUSTIN: You can show it to him yourself.

LEE: I will, boy! I'm gonna' read it to him on the golf course.

AUSTIN: And I'm not afraid of you either.   515

LEE: Then how come yer doin' it?

AUSTIN: (*Pause.*) So I can get my keys back.

(*Pause as* LEE *takes keys out of his pocket slowly and throws them on table, long pause,* AUSTIN *stares at keys.*)

LEE: There. Now you got yer keys back.

(AUSTIN *looks up at* LEE *but doesn't take keys.*)

LEE: Go ahead. There's yer keys.

(AUSTIN *slowly takes keys off table and puts them back in his own pocket.*)

Now what're you gonna' do? Kick me out?

AUSTIN: I'm not going to kick you out, Lee.   520

LEE: You couldn't kick me out, boy.

AUSTIN: I know.

LEE: So you can't even consider that one. (*Pause.*) You could call the police. That'd be the obvious thing.

AUSTIN: You're my brother.   525

LEE: That don't mean a thing. You go down to the L.A. Police Department there and ask them what kinda' people kill each other the most. What do you think they'd say?

AUSTIN: Who said anything about killing?

LEE: Family people. Brothers. Brothers-in-law. Cousins. Real American-type people. They kill each other in the heat mostly. In the Smog-Alerts. In the Brush Fire Season.   530
Right about this time a' year.

AUSTIN: This isn't the same.

LEE: Oh no? What makes it different?

AUSTIN: We're not insane. We're not driven to acts of violence like that. Not over a dumb movie script. Now sit down.   535

(*Long pause,* LEE *considers which way to go with it.*)

LEE: Maybe not. (*He sits back down at table across from* AUSTIN.) Maybe you're right. Maybe we're too intelligent, huh? (*Pause.*) We got our heads on our shoulders. One of us has even got a Ivy League diploma. Now that means somethin' don't it? Doesn't that mean somethin'?

AUSTIN: Look, I'll write this thing for you, Lee. I don't mind writing it. I just don't want   540
to get all worked up about it. It's not worth it. Now, come on. Let's just get through it, okay?

LEE: Nah. I think there's easier money. Lotsa' places I could pick up thousands. Maybe millions. I don't need this shit. I could go up to Sacramento Valley and steal me a diesel. Ten thousand a week dismantling one a' those suckers. Ten thousand a week!   545

(LEE *opens another beer, puts his foot back up on table.*)

AUSTIN: No, really, look, I'll write it out for you. I think it's a great idea.

LEE: Nah, you got yer own work to do. I don't wanna' interfere with yer life.

AUSTIN: I mean it'd be really fantastic if you could sell this. Turn it into a movie. I mean it.

(*Pause.*)

LEE: Ya' think so huh?   550

AUSTIN: Absolutely. You could really turn your life around, you know. Change things.

LEE: I could get me a house maybe.

AUSTIN: Sure you could get a house. You could get a whole ranch if you wanted to.

LEE: (*Laughs.*) A ranch? I could get a ranch?

AUSTIN: 'Course you could. You know what a screenplay sells for these days?   555

LEE: No. What's it sell for?

AUSTIN: A lot. A whole lot of money.

LEE: Thousands?

AUSTIN: Yeah. Thousands.

LEE: Millions?   560

AUSTIN: Well—

LEE: We could get the old man outa' hock then.

AUSTIN: Maybe.

LEE: Maybe? Whadya' mean, maybe?

AUSTIN: I mean it might take more than money.   565

LEE: You were just tellin' me it'd change my whole life around. Why wouldn't it change his?

AUSTIN: He's different.

LEE: Oh, he's of a different ilk huh?

AUSTIN: He's not gonna' change. Let's leave the old man out of it.   570

LEE: That's right. He's not gonna' change but I will. I'll just turn myself right inside out. I could be just like you then, huh? Sittin' around dreamin' stuff up. Gettin' paid to dream. Ridin' back and forth on the freeway just dreamin' my fool head off.

AUSTIN: It's not all that easy.

LEE: It's not, huh?

AUSTIN: No. There's a lot of work involved.   575

LEE: What's the toughest part? Deciding whether to jog or play tennis?

(*Long pause.*)

AUSTIN: Well, look. You can stay here—do whatever you want to. Borrow the car. Come in and out. Doesn't matter to me. It's not my house. I'll help you write this thing or—not. Just let me know what you want. You tell me.   580

LEE: Oh. So now suddenly you're at my service. Is that it?

AUSTIN: What do you want to do Lee?

(*Long pause,* LEE *stares at him then turns and dreams at windows.*)

LEE: I tell ya' what I'd do if I still had that dog. Ya' wanna' know what I'd do?

AUSTIN: What?

LEE: Head out to Ventura. Cook up a little match. God that little dog could bear down. 585
Lota' money in dog fightin'. Big money.

(*Pause.*)

AUSTIN: Why don't we try to see this through, Lee. Just for the hell of it. Maybe you've really got something here. What do you think?

(*Pause,* LEE *considers.*)

LEE: Maybe so. No harm in tryin' I guess. You think it's such a hot idea. Besides, I always wondered what'd be like to be you.   590

AUSTIN: You did?

LEE: Yeah, sure. I used to picture you walkin' around some campus with yer arms fulla' books. Blondes chasin' after ya'.

AUSTIN: Blondes? That's funny.

LEE: What's funny about it?

AUSTIN: Because I always used to picture you somewhere.   595

LEE: Where'd you picture me?

AUSTIN: Oh, I don't know. Different places. Adventures. You were always on some adventure.

LEE: Yeah.   600

AUSTIN: And I used to say to myself, "Lee's got the right idea. He's out there in the world and here I am. What am I doing?"

LEE: Well you were settin' yourself up for somethin'.

AUSTIN: I guess.

LEE: We better get started on this thing then.   605

AUSTIN: Okay.

(AUSTIN *sits up at typewriter, puts new paper in.*)

LEE: Oh. Can I get the keys back before I forget?

(AUSTIN *hesitates.*)

You said I could borrow the car if I wanted, right? Isn't that what you said?

AUSTIN: Yeah. Right.

(AUSTIN *takes keys out of his pocket, sets them on table, takes keys slowly, plays with them in his hand.*)

LEE: I could get a ranch, huh?

AUSTIN: Yeah. We have to write it first though.   610

LEE: Okay. Let's write it.

(*Lights start dimming slowly to end as* AUSTIN *types,* LEE *speaks.*)

So they take off after each other straight into an endless black prairie. The sun is just comin' down and they can feel the night on their backs. What they don't know is that each one of 'em is afraid, see. Each one separately thinks that he's the only one that's afraid. And they keep ridin' like that straight into the night. Not knowing. And the one who's chasin' doesn't know where the other one is taking him. And the one who's being chased doesn't know where he's going.

(*Lights to black, typing stops in the dark, crickets fade.*)

ACT II

SCENE V

Morning. LEE *at the table in alcove with a set of golf clubs in a fancy leather bag,* AUSTIN *at sink washing a few dishes.*

AUSTIN: He really liked it, huh?

LEE: He wouldn't a' gave me these clubs if he didn't like it.

AUSTIN: He gave you the clubs?

LEE: Yeah. I told ya' he gave me the clubs. The bag too.

AUSTIN: I thought he just loaned them to you.   5

LEE: He said it was part a' the advance. A little gift like. Gesture of his good faith.

AUSTIN: He's giving you an advance?

LEE: Now what's so amazing about that? I told ya' it was a good story. You even said it was a good story.

AUSTIN: Well that is really incredible Lee. You know how many guys spend their 10 whole lives down here trying to break into this business? Just trying to get in the door?

LEE: (*Pulling clubs out of bag, testing them.*) I got no idea. How many?

(*Pause.*)

AUSTIN: How much of an advance is he giving you?

LEE: Plenty. We were talkin' big money out there. Ninth hole is where I sealed the deal. 15

AUSTIN: He made a firm commitment?

LEE: Absolutely.

AUSTIN: Well, I know Saul and he doesn't fool around when he says he likes something.

LEE: I thought you said you didn't know him.

AUSTIN: Well, I'm familiar with his tastes. 20

LEE: I let him get two up on me goin' into the back nine. He was sure he had me cold. You shoulda' seen his face when I pulled out the old pitching wedge and plopped it pin-high, two feet from the cup. He 'bout shit his pants. "Where'd a guy like you ever learn how to play golf like that?" he says.

(LEE *laughs,* AUSTIN *stares at him.*)

AUSTIN: 'Course there's no contract yet. Nothing's final until it's on paper. 25

LEE: It's final, all right. There's no way he's gonna' back out of it now. We gambled for it.

AUSTIN: Saul, gambled?

LEE: Yeah, sure. I mean he liked the outline already so he wasn't risking that much. I just guaranteed it with my short game.

(*Pause.*)

AUSTIN: Well, we should celebrate or something. I think Mom left a bottle of champagne 30 in the refrigerator. We should have a little toast.

(AUSTIN *gets glasses from cupboard, goes to refrigerator, pulls out bottle of champagne.*)

LEE: You shouldn't oughta' take her champagne, Austin. She's gonna' miss that.

AUSTIN: Oh, she's not going to mind. She'd be glad we put it to good use. I'll get her another bottle. Besides, it's perfect for the occasion.

(*Pause.*)

LEE: Yer gonna' get a nice fee fer writin' the script a' course. Straight fee. 35

(AUSTIN *stops, stares at* LEE, *puts glasses and bottle on table, pause.*)

AUSTIN: I'm writing the script?

LEE: That's what he said. Said we couldn't hire a better screenwriter in the whole town.

AUSTIN: But I'm already working on a script. I've got my own project. I don't have time to write two scripts.

LEE: No, he said he was gonna' drop that other one. 40

(*Pause.*)

AUSTIN: What? You mean mine? He's going to drop mine and do yours instead?

LEE: (*Smiles.*) Now look, Austin, it's jest beginner's luck ya' know. I mean I sank a fifty foot putt for this deal. No hard feelings.

(AUSTIN *goes to phone on wall, grabs it, starts dialing.*)

He's not gonna' be in, Austin. Told me he wouldn't be in 'till late this afternoon.

AUSTIN: (*Stays on phone, dialing, listen.*) I can't believe this. I just can't believe it. Are you sure he said that? Why would he drop mine?   45

LEE: That's what he told me.

AUSTIN: He can't do that without telling me first. Without talking to me at least. He wouldn't just make a decision like that without talking to me!

LEE: Well I was kinda' surprised myself. But he was real enthusiastic about my story.

(AUSTIN *hangs up phone violently, paces.*)

AUSTIN: What'd he say! Tell me everything he said!   50

LEE: I been tellin' ya'! He said he liked the story a whole lot. It was the first authentic Western to come along in a decade.

AUSTIN: He liked that story! Your story?

LEE: Yeah! What's so surprisin' about that?

AUSTIN: It's stupid! It's the dumbest story I ever heard in my life.   55

LEE: Hey, hold on! That's my story yer talkin' about!

AUSTIN: It's a bullshit story! It's idiotic. Two lamebrains chasing each other across Texas! Are you kidding? Who do you think's going to go see a film like that?

LEE: It's not a film! It's a movie. There's a big difference. That's somethin' Saul told me.

AUSTIN: Oh he did, huh?   60

LEE: Yeah, he said, "In this business we make movies, American movies. Leave the films to the French."

AUSTIN: So you got real intimate with old Saul huh? He started pouring forth his vast knowledge of Cinema.

LEE: I think he liked me a lot, to tell ya' the truth. I think he felt I was somebody he could   65
confide in.

AUSTIN: What'd you do, beat him up or something?

LEE: (*Stands fast.*) Hey, I've about had it with the insults buddy! You think yer the only one in the brain department here? Yer the only one that can sit around and cook things up? There's other people got ideas too, ya' know!   70

AUSTIN: You must've done something. Threatened him or something. Now what'd you do Lee?

LEE: I convinced him!

(LEE *makes sudden menacing lunge toward* AUSTIN, *wielding golf club above his head, stops himself, frozen moment, long pause,* LEE *lowers club.*)

AUSTIN: Oh, Jesus. You didn't hurt him did you?

(*Long silence,* LEE *sits back down at table.*)

Lee! Did you hurt him?

LEE: I didn't do nothin' to him! He liked my story. Pure and simple. He said it was the   75
best story he's come across in a long, long time.

AUSTIN: That's what he told me about my story! That's the same thing he said to me.

LEE: Well, he musta' been lyin'. He musta' been lyin' to one of us anyway.

AUSTIN: You can't come into this town and start pushing people around. They're gonna'
put you away!   80

LEE: I never pushed anybody around! I beat him fair and square. (*Pause.*) They can't touch me anyway. They can't put a finger on me. I'm gone. I can come in through the window and go out through the door. They never knew what hit 'em. You, yer stuck. Yer the one that's stuck. Not me. So don't be warnin' me what to do in this town.

(*Pause,* AUSTIN *crosses to table, sits at typewriter, rests.*)

AUSTIN: Lee, come on, level with me will you? It doesn't make any sense that suddenly 85
    he'd throw my idea out the window. I've been talking to him for months. I've got
    too much at stake. Everything's riding on this project.

LEE: What's yer idea?

AUSTIN: It's just a simple love story.

LEE: What kinda' love story? 90

AUSTIN: (*Stands, cross into kitchen.*) I'm not telling you!

LEE: Ha! 'Fraid I'll steal it huh? Competition's gettin' kinda' close to home isn't it?

AUSTIN: Where did Saul say he was going?

LEE: He was gonna' take my story to a couple studios.

AUSTIN: That's *my* outline you know! I wrote that outline! You've got no right to be 95
    peddling it around.

LEE: You weren't ready to take credit for it last night.

AUSTIN: Give me my keys!

LEE: What?

AUSTIN: The keys! I want my keys back! 100

LEE: Where you goin'?

AUSTIN: Just give me my keys! I gotta' take a drive. I gotta' get out of here for a while.

LEE: Where you gonna' go, Austin?

AUSTIN: (*Pause.*) I might just drive out to the desert for a while. I gotta' think.

LEE: You can think here just as good. This is the perfect setup for thinkin'. We got some 105
    writin' to do here, boy. Now let's just have us a little toast. Relax. We're partners now.

(LEE *pops the cork of the champagne bottle, pours two drinks as the lights fade to black.*)

SCENE VI

Afternoon. LEE *and* SAUL *in kitchen,* AUSTIN *in alcove.*

LEE: Now you tell him. You tell him, Mr. Kipper.

SAUL: Kimmer.

LEE: Kimmer. You tell him what you told me. He don't believe me.

AUSTIN: I don't want to hear it. 110

SAUL: It's really not a big issue, Austin. I was simply amazed by your brother's story
    and—

AUSTIN: Amazed? You lost a bet! You gambled with my material!

SAUL: That's really beside the point, Austin. I'm ready to go all the way with your
    brother's story. I think it has a great deal of merit. 115

AUSTIN: I don't want to hear about it, okay? Go tell it to the executives! Tell it to
    somebody who's going to turn it into a package deal or something. A T.V. series.
    Don't tell it to me.

SAUL: But I want to continue with your project too, Austin. It's not as though we can't do
    both. We're big enough for that aren't we? 120

AUSTIN: "We"? *I* can't do both! I don't know about "we."

LEE: (*To* SAUL.) See, what'd I tell ya'. He's totally unsympathetic.

SAUL: Austin, there's no point in our going to another screenwriter for this. It just doesn't make sense. You're brothers. You know each other. There's a familiarity with the material that just wouldn't be possible otherwise. 125

AUSTIN: There's no familiarity with the material! None! I don't know what "Tornado Country" is. I don't know what a "gooseneck" is. And I don't want to know! (*Pointing to* LEE.) He's a hustler! He's a bigger hustler than you are! If you can't see that, then—

LEE: (*To* AUSTIN.) Hey, now hold on. I didn't have to bring this bone back to you, boy. I 130 persuaded Saul here that you were the right man for the job. You don't have to go throwin' up favors in my face.

AUSTIN: Favors! I'm the one who wrote the fuckin' outline! You can't even spell.

SAUL: (*To* AUSTIN.) Your brother told me about the situation with your father.

(*Pause.*)

AUSTIN: What? (*Looks at* LEE.) 135

SAUL: That's right. Now we have a clear-cut deal here, Austin. We have big studio money standing behind this thing. Just on the basis of your outline.

AUSTIN: (*To* SAUL.) What'd he tell you about my father?

SAUL: Well—that he's destitute. He needs money.

LEE: That's right. He does. 140

(AUSTIN *shakes his head, stares at them both.*)

AUSTIN: (*To* LEE.) And this little assignment is supposed to go toward the old man? A charity project? Is that what this is? Did you cook this up on the ninth green too?

SAUL: It's a big slice, Austin.

AUSTIN: (*To* LEE.) I gave him money! I already gave him money. You know that. He drank it all up! 145

LEE: This is a different deal here.

SAUL: We can set up a trust for your father. A large sum of money. It can be doled out to him in parcels so he can't misuse it.

AUSTIN: Yeah, and who's doing the doling?

SAUL: Your brother volunteered. 150

(AUSTIN *laughs.*)

LEE: That's right. I'll make sure he uses it for groceries.

AUSTIN: (*To* SAUL.) I'm not doing this script! I'm not writing this crap for you or anybody else. You can't blackmail me into it. You can't threaten me into it. There's no way I'm doing it. So just give it up. Both of you.

(*Long pause.*)

SAUL: Well, that's it then. I mean this is an easy three hundred grand. Just for a first draft. 155 It's incredible, Austin. We've got three different studios all trying to cut each other's throats to get this material. In one morning. That's how hot it is.

AUSTIN: Yeah, well you can afford to give me a percentage on the outline then. And you better get the genius here an agent before he gets burned.

LEE: Saul's gonna' be my agent. Isn't that right, Saul? 160

SAUL: That's right. (*To* AUSTIN.) Your brother has really got something, Austin. I've been around too long not to recognize it. Raw talent.

AUSTIN: He's got a lota' balls is what he's got. He's taking you right down the river.

SAUL: Three hundred thousand, Austin. Just for a first draft. Now you've never been offered that kind of money before. 165

AUSTIN: I'm not writing it.

(*Pause.*)

SAUL: I see. Well—

LEE: We'll just go to another writer then. Right, Saul? Just hire us somebody with some enthusiasm. Somebody who can recognize the value of a good story.

SAUL: I'm sorry about this, Austin.   170

AUSTIN: Yeah.

SAUL: I mean I was hoping we could continue both things but now I don't see how it's possible.

AUSTIN: So you're dropping my idea altogether. Is that it? Just trade horses in midstream? After all these months of meetings.   175

SAUL: I wish there was another way.

AUSTIN: I've got everything riding on this, Saul. You know that. It's my only shot. If this falls through—

SAUL: I have to go with what my instincts tell me—

AUSTIN: Your instincts!   180

SAUL: My gut reaction.

AUSTIN: You lost! That's your gut reaction. You lost a gamble. Now you're trying to tell me you like his story? How could you possibly fall for that story? It's as phony as Hopalong Cassidy. What do you see in it? I'm curious.

SAUL: It has the ring of truth, Austin.   185

AUSTIN: (*Laughs.*) Truth?

LEE: It is true.

SAUL: Something about the real West.

AUSTIN: Why? Because it's got horses? Because it's got grown men acting like little boys?

SAUL: Something about the land. Your brother is speaking from experience.   190

AUSTIN: So am I!

SAUL: But nobody's interested in love these days, Austin. Let's face it.

LEE: That's right.

AUSTIN: (*To* SAUL.) He's been camped out on the desert for three months. Talking to cactus. What's he know about what people wanna' see on the screen! I drive on the   195
freeway every day. I swallow the smog. I watch the news in color. I shop in the Safeway. I'm the one who's in touch! Not him!

SAUL: I have to go now, Austin.

(SAUL *starts to leave.*)

AUSTIN: There's no such thing as the West anymore! It's a dead issue! It's dried up, Saul, and so are you.   200

(SAUL *stops and turns to* AUSTIN.)

SAUL: Maybe you're right. But I have to take the gamble, don't I?

AUSTIN: You're a fool to do this, Saul.

SAUL: I've always gone on my hunches. Always. And I've never been wrong. (*To* LEE.) I'll talk to you tomorrow, Lee.

LEE: All right, Mr. Kimmer.   205

SAUL: Maybe we could have some lunch.

LEE: Fine with me. (*Smiles at* AUSTIN.)

SAUL: I'll give you a ring.

(SAUL *exits, lights to black as brothers look at each other from a distance.*)

SCENE VII

Night. Coyotes, crickets, sound of typewriter in dark, candlelight up on LEE *at typewriter strug-gling to type with one finger system,* AUSTIN *sits sprawled out on kitchen floor with whiskey bottle, drunk.*

AUSTIN: (*Singing, from floor.*)

> "Red sails in the sunset   210
> Way out on the blue
> Please carry my loved one
> Home safely to me
>
> Red sails in the sunset—"

LEE: (*Slams fist on table.*) Hey! Knock it off will ya'! I'm tryin' to concentrate here.   215
AUSTIN: (*Laughs.*) You're tryin' to concentrate?
LEE: Yeah. That's right.
AUSTIN: Now you're tryin' to concentrate.
LEE: Between you, the coyotes and the crickets a thought don't have much of a chance.
AUSTIN: "Between me, the coyotes and the crickets." What a great title.   220
LEE: I don't need a title! I need a thought.
AUSTIN: (*Laughs.*) A thought! Here's a thought for ya'—
LEE: I'm not askin' fer yer thoughts! I got my own. I can do this thing on my own.
AUSTIN: You're going to write an entire script on your own?
LEE: That's right.   225

(*Pause.*)

AUSTIN: Here's a thought. Saul Kimmer—
LEE: Shut up will ya'!
AUSTIN: He thinks we're the same person.
LEE: Don't get cute.
AUSTIN: He does! He's lost his mind. Poor old Saul. (*Giggles.*) Thinks we're one and the   230
   same.
LEE: Why don't you ease up on that champagne.
AUSTIN: (*Holding up bottle.*) This isn't champagne anymore. We went through the
   champagne a long time ago. This is serious stuff. The days of champagne are long
   gone.   235
LEE: Well, go outside and drink it.
AUSTIN: I'm enjoying your company, Lee. For the first time since your arrival I am finally
   enjoying your company. And now you want me to go outside and drink alone?
LEE: That's right.

(LEE *reads through paper in typewriter, makes an erasure.*)

AUSTIN: You think you'll make more progress if you're alone? You might drive yourself   240
   crazy.
LEE: I could have this thing done in a night if I had a little silence.
AUSTIN: Well you'd still have the crickets to contend with. The coyotes. The sounds of
   the Police Helicopters prowling above the neighborhood. Slashing their searchlights
   down through the streets. Hunting for the likes of you.   245
LEE: I'm a screenwriter now! I'm legitimate.
AUSTIN: (*Laughing.*) A screenwriter!

LEE: That's right. I'm on salary. That's more'n I can say for you. I got an advance coming.

AUSTIN: This is true. This is very true. An advance. (*Pause.*) Well, maybe I oughta' go
out and try my hand at your trade. Since you're doing so good at mine. 250

LEE: Ha!

> (LEE *attempts to type some more but gets the ribbon tangled up, starts trying to
> re-thread it as they continue talking.*)

AUSTIN: Well why not? You don't think I've got what it takes to sneak into people's
houses and steal their T.V.s?

LEE: You couldn't steal a toaster without losin' yer lunch.

> (AUSTIN *stands with a struggle, supports himself by the sink.*)

AUSTIN: You don't think I could sneak into somebody's house and steal a toaster?

LEE: Go take a shower or somethin' will ya! 255

> (LEE *gets more tangled up with the typewriter ribbon, pulling it out of the
> machine as though it was fishing line.*)

AUSTIN: You really don't think I could steal a crumby toaster? How much you wanna' bet
I can't steal a toaster! How much? Go ahead! You're a gambler aren't you? Tell me
how much yer willing to put on the line. Some part of your big advance? Oh, you
haven't got that yet have you. I forgot. 260

LEE: All right. I'll bet you your car that you can't steal a toaster without gettin' busted.

AUSTIN: You already got my car!

LEE: Okay, your house then.

AUSTIN: What're you gonna' give me! I'm not talkin' about my house and my car, I'm
talkin' about what are you gonna' give me. You don't have nothin' to give me. 265

LEE: I'll give you—shared screen credit. How 'bout that? I'll have it put in the contract that
this was written by the both of us.

AUSTIN: I don't want my name on that piece of shit! I want something of value. You got
anything of value? You got any tidbits from the desert? Any Rattlesnake bones? I'm
not a greedy man. Any little personal treasure will suffice. 270

LEE: I'm gonna' just kick yer ass out in a minute.

AUSTIN: Oh, so now you're gonna' kick me out! Now I'm the intruder. I'm the one who's
invading your precious privacy.

LEE: I'm trying to do some screenwriting here!!

> (LEE *stands, picks up typewriter, slams it down hard on table, pause, silence
> except for crickets.*)

AUSTIN: Well, you got everything you need. You got plenty a' coffee? Groceries. You got 275
a car. A contract. (*Pause.*) Might need a new typewriter ribbon but other than that
you're pretty well fixed. I'll just leave ya' alone for a while.

> (AUSTIN *tries to steady himself to leave,* LEE *makes a move toward him.*)

LEE: Where you goin'?

AUSTIN: Don't worry about me. I'm not the one to worry about.

> (AUSTIN *weaves toward exit, stops.*)

LEE: What're you gonna' do? Just go wander out into the night? 280

AUSTIN: I'm gonna' make a little tour.

LEE: Why don't ya' just go to bed for Christ's sake. Yer makin' me sick.

AUSTIN: I can take care a' myself. Don't worry about me.

(AUSTIN *weaves badly in another attempt to exit, he crashes to the floor,* LEE *goes to him but remains standing.*)

LEE: You want me to call your wife for ya' or something?

AUSTIN: (*From floor.*) My wife? 285

LEE: Yeah. I mean maybe she can help ya' out. Talk to ya' or somethin'.

AUSTIN: (*Struggles to stand again.*) She's five hundred miles away. North. North of here. Up in the North country where things are calm. I don't need any help. I'm gonna' go outside and I'm gonna' steal a toaster. I'm gonna' steal some other stuff too. I might even commit bigger crimes. Bigger than you ever dreamed of. Crimes beyond 290 the imagination!

(AUSTIN *manages to get himself vertical, tries to head for exit again.*)

LEE: Just hang on a minute, Austin.

AUSTIN: Why? What for? You don't need my help, right? You got a handle on the project. Besides, I'm lookin' forward to the smell of the night. The bushes. Orange blossoms. Dust in the driveways. Rain bird sprinklers. Lights in people's houses. You're right 295 about the lights, Lee. Everybody else is livin' the life. Indoors. Safe. This is a Paradise down here. You know that? We're livin' in a Paradise. We've forgotten about that.

LEE: You sound just like the old man now.

AUSTIN: Yeah, well we all sound alike when we're sloshed. We just sorta' echo each other.

LEE: Maybe if we could work on this together we could bring him back out here. Get him 300 settled down some place.

(AUSTIN *turns violently toward* LEE, *takes a swing at him, misses and crashes to the floor again,* LEE *stays standing.*)

AUSTIN: I don't want him out here! I've had it with him! I went all the way out there! I went out of my way. I gave him money and all he did was play Al Jolson records and spit at me! I gave him money!

(*Pause.*)

LEE: Just help me a little with the characters, all right? You know how to do it, Austin. 305

AUSTIN: (*On floor, laughs.*) The characters!

LEE: Yeah. You know. The way they talk and stuff. I can hear it in my head but I can't get it down on paper.

AUSTIN: What characters?

LEE: The guys. The guys in the story. 310

AUSTIN: Those aren't characters.

LEE: Whatever you call 'em then. I need to write somethin' out.

AUSTIN: Those are illusions of characters.

LEE: I don't give a damn what ya' call 'em! You know what I'm talkin' about!

AUSTIN: Those are fantasies of a long lost boyhood. 315

LEE: I gotta' write somethin' out on paper!!

(*Pause.*)

AUSTIN: What for? Saul's gonna' get you a fancy screenwriter isn't he?

LEE: I wanna' do it myself!

AUSTIN: Then do it! Yer on your own now, old buddy. You bulldogged yer way into contention. Now you gotta' carry it through. 320

LEE: I will but I need some advice. Just a couple a' things. Come on, Austin. Just help me get 'em talkin' right. It won't take much.

AUSTIN: Oh, now you're having a little doubt huh? What happened? The pressure's on, boy. This is it. You gotta' come up with it now. You don't come up with a winner on your first time out they just cut your head off. They don't give you a second chance ya' know.   325

LEE: I got a good story! I know it's a good story. I just need a little help is all.

AUSTIN: Not from me. Not from yer little old brother. I'm retired.

LEE: You could save this thing for me, Austin. I'd give ya' half the money. I would. I only need half anyway. With this kinda' money I could be a long time down the road. I'd never bother ya' again. I promise. You'd never even see me again.   330

AUSTIN: (*Still on floor.*) You'd disappear?

LEE: I would for sure.

AUSTIN: Where would you disappear to?

LEE: That don't matter. I got plenty a' places.   335

AUSTIN: Nobody can disappear. The old man tried that. Look where it got him. He lost his teeth.

LEE: He never had any money.

AUSTIN: I don't mean that. I mean his teeth! His real teeth. First he lost his real teeth, then he lost his false teeth. You never knew that did ya'? He never confided in you.   340

LEE: Nah, I never knew that.

AUSTIN: You wanna' drink?

(AUSTIN *offers bottle to* LEE, LEE *takes it, sits down on kitchen floor with* AUSTIN, *they share the bottle.*)

Yeah, he lost his real teeth one at a time. Woke up every morning with another tooth lying on the mattress. Finally, he decides he's gotta' get 'em all pulled out but he doesn't have any money. Middle of Arizona with no money and no insurance and every morning another tooth is lying on the mattress. (*Takes a drink.*) So what does he do?

LEE: I dunno'. I never knew about that.

AUSTIN: He begs the government. G.I. Bill or some damn thing. Some pension plan he remembers in the back of his head. And they send him out the money.   345

LEE: They did?

(*They keep trading the bottle between them, taking drinks.*)

AUSTIN: Yeah. They send him the money but it's not enough money. Costs a lot to have all yer teeth yanked. They charge by the individual tooth, ya' know. I mean one tooth isn't equal to another tooth. Some are more expensive. Like the big ones in the back—   350

LEE: So what happened?

AUSTIN: So he locates a Mexican dentist in Juarez who'll do the whole thing for a song. And he takes off hitchhiking to the border.

LEE: Hitchhiking?

AUSTIN: Yeah. So how long you think it takes him to get to the border? A man his age.   355

LEE: I dunno.

AUSTIN: Eight days it takes him. Eight days in the rain and the sun and every day he's droppin' teeth on the blacktop nobody'll pick him up 'cause his mouth's full a' blood.

(*Pause, they drink.*)

So finally he stumbles into the dentist. Dentist takes all his money and all his teeth. And there he is, in Mexico, with his gums sewed up and his pockets empty.

(*Long silence,* AUSTIN *drinks.*)

LEE: That's it?   360

AUSTIN: Then I go out to see him, see. I go out there and I take him out for a nice Chinese dinner. But he doesn't eat. All he wants to do is drink Martinis outa' plastic cups. And he takes his teeth out and lays 'em on the table 'cause he can't stand the feel of 'em. And we ask the waitress for one a' those doggie bags to take the Chop Suey home in. So he drops his teeth in the doggie bag along with the Chop Suey.   365 And then we go out to hit all the bars up and down the highway. Says he wants to introduce me to all his buddies. And in one a' those bars, in one a' those bars up and down the highway, he left that doggie bag with his teeth laying in the Chop Suey.

LEE: You never found it?   370

AUSTIN: We went back but we never did find it. (*Pause.*) Now that's a true story. True to life.

(*They drink as lights fade to black.*)

SCENE VIII

Very early morning, between night and day. No crickets, coyotes yapping feverishly in distance before light comes up, a small fire blazes up in the dark from alcove area, sound of LEE *smashing typewriter with a golf club, lights coming up,* LEE *seen smashing typewriter methodically then dropping pages of his script into a burning bowl set on the floor of alcove, flames leap up,* AUSTIN *has a whole bunch of stolen toasters lined up on the sink counter along with* LEE'*s stolen T.V., the toasters are of a wide variety of models, mostly chrome,* AUSTIN *goes up and down the line of toasters, breathing on them and polishing them with a dish towel, both men are drunk, empty whiskey bottles and beer cans litter floor of kitchen, they share a half empty bottle on one of the chairs in the alcove,* LEE *keeps periodically taking deliberate ax-chops at the typewriter using a nine-iron as* AUSTIN *speaks, all of their mother's house plants are dead and drooping.*

AUSTIN: (*Polishing toasters.*) There's gonna' be a general lack of toast in the neighborhood this morning. Many, many unhappy, bewildered breakfast faces. I guess it's best not to even think of the victims. Not to even entertain it. Is that the right psychology?   375

LEE: (*Pauses.*) What?

AUSTIN: Is that the correct criminal psychology? Not to think of the victims?

LEE: What victims?

(LEE *takes another swipe at typewriter with nine-iron, adds pages to the fire.*)

AUSTIN: The victims of crime. Of breaking and entering. I mean is it a prerequisite for a criminal not to have a conscience?   380

LEE: Ask a criminal.

(*Pause,* LEE *stares at* AUSTIN.)

What're you gonna' do with all those toasters? That's the dumbest thing I ever saw in my life.

AUSTIN: I've got hundreds of dollars worth of household appliances here. You may not realize that.

LEE: Yeah, and how many hundreds of dollars did you walk right past?

AUSTIN: It was toasters you challenged me to. Only toasters. I ignored every other temptation.   385

LEE: I never challenged you! That's no challenge. Anybody can steal a toaster.

(LEE *smashes typewriter again.*)

AUSTIN: You don't have to take it out on my typewriter ya' know. It's not the machine's fault that you can't write. It's a sin to do that to a good machine.

LEE: A sin?

AUSTIN: When you consider all the writers who never even had a machine. Who would   390
have given an eyeball for a good typewriter. Any typewriter.

(LEE *smashes typewriter again.*)

AUSTIN: (*Polishing toasters.*) All the ones who wrote on matchbook covers. Paper bags. Toilet paper. Who had their writing destroyed by their jailers. Who persisted beyond all odds. Those writers would find it hard to understand your actions.

(LEE *comes down on typewriter with one final crushing blow of the nine-iron then collapses in one of the chairs, takes a drink from bottle, pause.*)

AUSTIN: (*After pause.*) Not to mention demolishing a perfectly good golf club. What   395
about all the struggling golfers? What about Lee Trevino? What do you think he would've said when he was batting balls around with broomsticks at the age of nine. Impoverished.

(*Pause.*)

LEE: What time is it anyway?

AUSTIN: No idea. Time stands still when you're havin' fun.   400

LEE: Is it too late to call a woman? You know any women?

AUSTIN: I'm a married man.

LEE: I mean a local woman.

(AUSTIN *looks out at light through window above sink.*)

AUSTIN: It's either too late or too early. You're the nature enthusiast. Can't you tell the time by the light in the sky? Orient yourself around the North Star or something?   405

LEE: I can't tell anything.

AUSTIN: Maybe you need a little breakfast. Some toast! How 'bout some toast?

(AUSTIN *goes to cupboard, pulls out loaf of bread and starts dropping slices into every toaster,* LEE *stays sitting, drinks, watches* AUSTIN.)

LEE: I don't need toast. I need a woman.

AUSTIN: A woman isn't the answer. Never was.

LEE: I'm not talkin' about permanent. I'm talkin' about temporary.   410

AUSTIN: (*Putting toast in toasters.*) We'll just test the merits of these little demons. See which brands have a tendency to burn. See which one can produce a perfectly golden piece of fluffy toast.

LEE: How much gas you got in yer car?

AUSTIN: I haven't driven my car for days now. So I haven't had an opportunity to look   415
at the gas gauge.

LEE: Take a guess. You think there's enough to get me to Bakersfield?

AUSTIN: Bakersfield? What's in Bakersfield?

LEE: Just never mind what's in Bakersfield! You think there's enough goddamn gas in the car!   420

AUSTIN: Sure.

LEE: Sure. You could care less, right. Let me run outa' gas on the Grapevine. You could give a shit.

AUSTIN: I'd say there was enough gas to get you just about any-where, Lee. With your
    determination and guts.   425

LEE: What the hell time is it anyway?

        (LEE *pulls out his wallet, starts going through dozens of small pieces of paper with*
        phone numbers written on them, drops some on the floor, drops others in the fire.)

AUSTIN: Very early. This is the time of morning when the coyotes kill people's cocker
    spaniels. Did you hear them? That's what they were doing out there. Luring
    innocent pets away from their homes.

LEE: (*Searching through his papers.*) What's the area code for Bakersfield? You know?   430

AUSTIN: You could always call the operator.

LEE: I can't stand that voice they give ya'.

AUSTIN: What voice?

LEE: That voice that warns you that if you'd only tried harder to find the number in the
    phone book you wouldn't have to be calling the operator to begin with.   435

        (LEE *gets up, holding a slip of paper from his wallet, stumbles toward phone on*
        wall, yanks receiver, starts dialing.)

AUSTIN: Well I don't understand why you'd want to talk to anybody else anyway. I mean
    you can talk to me. I'm your brother.

LEE: (*Dialing.*) I wanna' talk to a woman. I haven't heard a woman's voice in a long time.

AUSTIN: Not since the Botanist?

LEE: What?   440

AUSTIN: Nothing. (*Starts singing as he tends toast.*)

        "Red sails in the sunset
        Way out on the blue
        Please carry my loved one
        Home safely to me"   445

LEE: Hey, knock it off will ya'! This is long distance here.

AUSTIN: Bakersfield?

LEE: Yeah, Bakersfield. It's Kern County.

AUSTIN: Well, what County are *we* in?

LEE: You better get yourself a 7-Up, boy.   450

AUSTIN: One County's as good as another.

      (AUSTIN *hums "Red Sails" softly as* LEE *talks on phone.*)

LEE: (*To phone.*) Yeah, operator look—first off I wanna' know the area code for
    Bakersfield. Right. Bakersfield! Okay. Good. Now I wanna' know if you can help
    me track somebody down. (*Pause.*) No, no I mean a phone number. Just a phone
    number. Okay. (*Holds a piece of paper up and reads it.*) Okay, the name is Melly   455
    Ferguson. Melly. (*Pause.*) I dunno'. Melly. Maybe. Yeah. Maybe Melanie. Yeah.
    Melanie Ferguson. Okay. (*Pause.*) What? I can't hear ya' so good. Sounds like yer
    under the ocean. (*Pause.*) You got ten Melanie Fergusons? How could that be? Ten
    Melanie Fergusons in Bakersfield? Well gimme all of 'em then. (*Pause.*) What d'ya
    mean? Gimme all ten Melanie Fergusons! That's right. Just a second. (*To* AUSTIN.)   460
    Gimme a pen.

AUSTIN: I don't have a pen.

LEE: Gimme a pencil then!

AUSTIN: I don't have a pencil.

LEE: (*To phone.*) Just a second, operator. (*To* AUSTIN.) Yer a writer and ya' don't have   465
    a pen or a pencil!
AUSTIN: I'm not a writer. You're a writer.
LEE: I'm on the phone here! Get me a pen or a pencil.
AUSTIN: I gotta' watch the toast.
LEE: (*To phone.*) Hang on a second, operator.   470

> (LEE *lets the phone drop then starts pulling all the drawers in the kitchen out on the floor and dumping the contents, searching for a pencil,* AUSTIN *watches him casually.*)

LEE: (*Crashing through drawers, throwing contents around kitchen.*) This is the last time I
try to live with people, boy! I can't believe it. Here I am! Here I am again in a
desperate situation! This would never happen out on the desert. I would never be in
this kinda' situation out on the desert. Isn't there a pen or a pencil in this house!
Who lives in this house anyway!   475
AUSTIN: Our mother.
LEE: How come she don't have a pen or a pencil! She's a social person isn't she? Doesn't
she have to make shopping lists? She's gotta' have a pencil. (*Finds a pencil.*) Aaha!
(*He rushes back to phone, picks up receiver.*) All right operator. Operator? Hey!
Operator! Goddamnit!   480

> (LEE *rips the phone off the wall and throws it down, goes back to chair and falls into it, drinks, long pause.*)

AUSTIN: She hung up?
LEE: Yeah, she hung up. I knew she was gonna' hang up. I could hear it in her voice.

> (LEE *starts going through his slips of paper again.*)

AUSTIN: Well, you're probably better off staying here with me anyway. I'll take care of you.
LEE: I don't need takin' care of! Not by you anyway.
AUSTIN: Toast is almost ready.   485

> (AUSTIN *starts buttering all the toast as it pops up.*)

LEE: I don't want any toast!

> (*Long pause.*)

AUSTIN: You gotta' eat something. Can't just drink. How long have we been drinking,
anyway?
LEE: (*Looking through slips of paper.*) Maybe it was Fresno. What's the area code for
Fresno? How could I have lost that number! She was beautiful.   490

> (*Pause.*)

AUSTIN: Why don't you just forget about that, Lee. Forget about the woman.
LEE: She had green eyes. You know what green eyes do to me?
AUSTIN: I know but you're not gonna' get it on with her now anyway. It's dawn already.
She's in Bakersfield for Christ's sake.

> (*Long pause,* LEE *considers the situation.*)

LEE: Yeah. (*Looks at windows.*) It's dawn?   495
AUSTIN: Let's just have some toast and—

LEE: What is this bullshit with the toast anyway! You make it sound like salvation or something. I don't want any goddamn toast! How many times I gotta' tell ya'! *(LEE gets up, crosses upstage to windows in alcove, looks out, AUSTIN butters toast.)*

AUSTIN: Well it is like salvation sort of. I mean the smell. I love the smell of toast. And   500
the sun's coming up. It makes me feel like anything's possible. Ya' know?

LEE: *(Back to AUSTIN, facing windows upstage.)* So go to church why don't ya'.

AUSTIN: Like a beginning. I love beginnings.

LEE: Oh yeah. I've always been kinda' partial to endings myself.

AUSTIN: What if I come with you, Lee?   505

LEE: *(Pause as LEE turns toward AUSTIN.)* What?

AUSTIN: What if I come with you out to the desert?

LEE: Are you kiddin'?

AUSTIN: No. I'd just like to see what it's like.

LEE: You wouldn't last a day out there pal.   510

AUSTIN: That's what you said about the toasters. You said I couldn't steal a toaster either.

LEE: A toaster's got nothin' to do with the desert.

AUSTIN: I could make it, Lee. I'm not that helpless. I can cook.

LEE: Cook?   515

AUSTIN: I can.

LEE: So what! You can cook. Toast.

AUSTIN: I can make fires. I know how to get fresh water from condensation.

(AUSTIN *stacks buttered toast up in a tall stack on plate.*)

(LEE *slams table.*)

LEE: It's not somethin' you learn out of a Boy Scout handbook!

AUSTIN: Well how do you learn it then! How're you supposed to learn it!   520

(Pause.)

LEE: Ya' just learn it, that's all. Ya' learn it 'cause ya' have to learn it. You don't *have* to learn it.

AUSTIN: You could teach me.

LEE: *(Stands.)* What're you, crazy or somethin'? You went to college. Here, you are down here, rollin' in bucks. Floatin' up and down in elevators. And you wanna' learn how   525
to live on the desert!

AUSTIN: I do, Lee. I really do. There's nothin' down here for me. There never was. When we were kids here it was different. There was a life here then. But now—I keep comin' down here thinkin' it's the fifties or somethin'. I keep finding myself getting off the freeway at familiar landmarks that turn out to be unfamiliar. On the way to   530
appointments. Wandering down streets I thought I recognized that turn out to be replicas of streets I remember. Streets I misremember. Streets I can't tell if I lived on or saw in a postcard. Fields that don't even exist anymore.

LEE: There's no point cryin' about that now.

AUSTIN: There's nothin' real down here, Lee! Least of all me!   535

LEE: Well I can't save you from that!

AUSTIN: You can let me come with you.

LEE: No dice, pal.

AUSTIN: You could let me come with you, Lee!

LEE: Hey, do you actually think I chose to live out in the middle a' nowhere? Do ya'? Ya'   540
think it's some kinda' philosophical decision I took or somethin'? I'm livin' out
there 'cause I can't make it here! And yer bitchin' to me about all yer success!

AUSTIN: I'd cash it all in in a second. That's the truth.

LEE: (*Pause, shakes his head.*) I can't believe this.

AUSTIN: Let me go with you.   545

LEE: Stop sayin' that will ya'! Yer worse than a dog.

    (AUSTIN *offers out the plate of neatly stacked toast to* LEE.)

AUSTIN: You want some toast?

    (LEE *suddenly explodes and knocks the plate out of* AUSTIN's *hand, toast goes fly-
ing, long frozen moment where it appears* LEE *might go all the way this time when*
AUSTIN *breaks it by slowly lowering himself to his knees and begins gathering the
scattered toast from the floor and stacking it back on the plate,* LEE *begins to circle*
AUSTIN *in a slow, predatory way, crushing pieces of toast in his wake, no words for
a while,* AUSTIN *keeps gathering toast, even the crushed pieces.*)

LEE: Tell ya' what I'll do, little brother. I might just consider makin' you a deal. Little trade.
(AUSTIN *continues gathering toast as lee circles him through this.*) You write me up
this screenplay thing just like I tell ya'. I mean you can use all yer usual tricks and   550
stuff. Yer fancy language. Yer artistic hocus pocus. But ya' gotta' write everything
like I say. Every move. Every time they run outa' gas, they run outa' gas. Every time
they wanna' jump on a horse, they do just that. If they wanna' stay in Texas, by God
they'll stay in Texas! (*Keeps circling.*) And you finish the whole thing up for me. Top
to bottom. And you put my name on it. And I own all the rights. And every dime   555
goes in my pocket. You do that and I'll sure enough take ya' with me to the desert.
(LEE *stops, pause, looks down at* AUSTIN.) How's that sound?

    (*Pause as* AUSTIN *stands slowly holding plate of demolished toast, their faces are
very close, pause.*)

AUSTIN: It's a deal.

    (LEE *stares straight into* AUSTIN's *eyes, then he slowly takes a piece of toast off the
plate, raises it to his mouth and takes a huge crushing bite never taking his eyes off*
AUSTIN's *as* LEE *crunches into the toast the lights black out.*)

SCENE IX

*Mid-day. No sound, blazing heat, the stage is ravaged; bottles, toasters, smashed typewriter,
ripped out telephone, etc. All the debris from previous scene is now starkly visible in intense yellow light, the effect should be like a desert junkyard at high noon, the coolness of the preceding
scenes is totally obliterated.* AUSTIN *is seated at table in alcove, shirt open, pouring with sweat,
hunched over a writing notebook, scribbling notes desperately with a ballpoint pen.* LEE *with
no shirt, beer in hand, sweat pouring down his chest, is walking a slow circle around the table,
picking his way through the objects, sometimes kicking them aside.*

LEE: (*As he walks.*) All right, read it back to me. Read it back to me!

AUSTIN: (*Scribbling at top speed.*) Just a second.   560

LEE: Come on, come on! Just read what ya' got.

AUSTIN: I can't keep up! It's not the same as if I had a typewriter.

LEE: Just read what we got so far. Forget about the rest.

AUSTIN: All right. Let's see—okay—(*Wipes sweat from his face, reads as lee circles.*) Luke   565
says uh—

LEE: Luke?

AUSTIN: Yeah.

LEE: His name's Luke? All right, all right—we can change the names later. What's he say?
Come on, come on.

AUSTIN: He says uh—(*Reading.*) "I told ya' you were a fool to follow me in here. I know   570
this prairie like the back a' my hand."

LEE: No, no, no! That's not what I said. I never said that.

AUSTIN: That's what I wrote.

LEE: It's not what I said. I never said "like the back a' my hand." That's stupid. That's
one a' those—whadya' call it? Whadya' call that?   575

AUSTIN: What?

LEE: Whadya' call it when somethin's been said a thousand times before. Whadya' call that?

AUSTIN: Um—a cliché?

LEE: Yeah. That's right. Cliché. That's what that is. A cliché. "The back a' my hand."
That's stupid.   580

AUSTIN: That's what you said.

LEE: I never said that! And even if I did, that's where yer supposed to come in. That's
where yer supposed to change it to somethin' better.

AUSTIN: Well how am I supposed to do that and write down what you say at the same
time?   585

LEE: Ya' just do, that's all! You hear a stupid line you change it. That's yer job.

AUSTIN: All right. (*Makes more notes.*)

LEE: What're you changin' it to?

AUSTIN: I'm not changing it. I'm just trying to catch up.

LEE: Well change it! We gotta' change that, we can't leave that in there like that. ". . . the   590
back a' my hand." That's dumb.

AUSTIN: (*Stops writing, sits back.*) All right.

LEE: (*Pacing.*) So what'll we change it to?

AUSTIN: Um—How 'bout—"I'm on intimate terms with this prairie."

LEE: (*To himself considering line as he walks.*) "I'm on intimate terms with this prairie."   595
Intimate terms, intimate terms. Intimate—that means like uh—sexual right?

AUSTIN: Well—yeah—or—

LEE: He's on sexual terms with the prairie? How dya' figure that?

AUSTIN: Well it doesn't necessarily have to mean sexual.

LEE: What's it mean then?   600

AUSTIN: It means uh—close—personal—

LEE: All right. How's it sound? Put it into the uh—the line there. Read it back. Let's see
how it sounds. (*To himself.*) "Intimate terms."

AUSTIN: (*Scribbles in notebook.*) Okay. It'd go something like this: (*Reads.*) "I told ya'
you were a fool to follow me in here. I'm on intimate terms with this prairie."   605

LEE: That's good. I like that. That's real good.

AUSTIN: You do?

LEE: Yeah. Don't you?

AUSTIN: Sure.

LEE: Sounds original now. "Intimate terms." That's good. Okay. Now we're cookin! That   610
has a real ring to it.

(AUSTIN *makes more notes,* LEE *walks around, pours beer on his arms and rubs it over his chest feeling good about the new progress, as he does this* MOM *enters unobtrusively down left with her luggage, she stops and stares at the scene still holding luggage as the two men continue, unaware of her presence,* AUSTIN *absorbed in his writing,* LEE *cooling himself off with beer.*)

LEE: (*Continues.*) "He's on intimate terms with this prairie." Sounds real mysterious and kinda' threatening at the same time.

AUSTIN: (*Writing rapidly.*) Good.

LEE: Now—(LEE *turns and suddenly sees mom, he stares at her for a while, she stares back,*   615
AUSTIN *keeps writing feverishly, not noticing,* LEE *walks slowly over to* MOM *and takes a closer look, long pause.*)

LEE: Mom?

(AUSTIN *looks up suddenly from his writing, sees* MOM, *stands quickly, long pause,* MOM *surveys the damage.*)

AUSTIN: Mom. What're you doing back?

MOM: I'm back.   620

LEE: Here, lemme take those for ya.

(LEE *sets beer on counter then takes both her bags but doesn't know where to set them down in the sea of junk so he just keeps holding them.*)

AUSTIN: I wasn't expecting you back so soon. I thought uh—How was Alaska?

MOM: Fine.

LEE: See any igloos?

MOM: No. Just glaciers.   625

AUSTIN: Cold huh?

MOM: What?

AUSTIN: It must've been cold up there?

MOM: Not really.

LEE: Musta' been colder than this here. I mean we're havin' a real scorcher here.   630

MOM: Oh? (*She looks at damage.*)

LEE: Yeah. Must be in the hundreds.

AUSTIN: You wanna' take your coat off, Mom?

MOM: No. (*Pause, she surveys space.*) What happened in here?

AUSTIN: Oh um—Me and Lee were just sort of celebrating and uh—   635

MOM: Celebrating?

AUSTIN: Yeah. Uh—Lee sold a screenplay. A story, I mean.

MOM: Lee did?

AUSTIN: Yeah.

MOM: Not you?   640

AUSTIN: No. Him.

MOM: (*To* LEE.) You sold a screenplay?

LEE: Yeah. That's right. We're just sorta' finishing it up right now. That's what we're doing here.

AUSTIN: Me and Lee are going out to the desert to live.   645

MOM: You and Lee?

AUSTIN: Yeah. I'm taking off with Lee.

MOM: (*She looks back and forth at each of them, pause.*) You gonna go live with your father?

AUSTIN: No. We're going to a different desert Mom.   650

MOM: I see. Well, you'll probably wind up on the same desert sooner or later. What're all these toasters doing here?

AUSTIN: Well—we had kind of a contest.

MOM: Contest?

LEE: Yeah.   655

AUSTIN: Lee won.

MOM: Did you win a lot of money, Lee?

LEE: Well not yet. It's comin' in any day now.

MOM: (*To* LEE.) What happened to your shirt?

LEE: Oh. I was sweatin' like a pig and I took it off.   660

> (AUSTIN *grabs* LEE's *shirt off the table and tosses it to him,* LEE *sets down suitcases and puts his shirt on.*)

MOM: Well it's one hell of a mess in here isn't it?

AUSTIN: Yeah, I'll clean it up for you, Mom. I just didn't know you were coming back so soon.

MOM: I didn't either.

AUSTIN: What happened?   665

MOM: Nothing. I just started missing all my plants.

> (*She notices dead plants.*)

AUSTIN: Oh.

MOM: Oh, they're all dead aren't they. (*She crosses toward them, examines them closely.*) You didn't get a chance to water I guess.

AUSTIN: I was doing it and then Lee came and—   670

LEE: Yeah I just distracted him a whole lot here, Mom. It's not his fault.

> (*Pause, as* MOM *stares at plants.*)

MOM: Oh well, one less thing to take care of I guess. (*Turns toward brothers.*) Oh, that reminds me—You boys will probably never guess who's in town. Try and guess.

> (*Long pause, brothers stare at her.*)

AUSTIN: Whadya' mean, Mom?

MOM: Take a guess. Somebody very important has come to town. I read it, coming down   675
on the Greyhound.

LEE: Somebody very important?

MOM: See if you can guess. You'll never guess.

AUSTIN: Mom—we're trying to uh—(*Points to writing pad.*)

MOM: Picasso. (*Pause.*) Picasso's in town. Isn't that incredible? Right now.   680

> (*Pause.*)

AUSTIN: Picasso's dead, Mom.

MOM: No, he's not dead. He's visiting the museum. I read it on the bus. We have to go down there
AND SEE HIM.

AUSTIN: Mom—   685

MOM: This is the chance of a lifetime. Can you imagine? We could all go down and meet him. All
THREE OF US.

LEE: Uh—I don't think I'm really up fer meetin' anybody right now. I'm uh—What's his name?   690

MOM: Picasso! Picasso! You've never heard of Picasso? Austin, you've heard of Picasso.

AUSTIN: Mom, we're not going to have time.

MOM: It won't take long. We'll just hop in the car and go down there. An opportunity like this doesn't come along every day.

AUSTIN: We're gonna' be leavin' here, Mom! 695

(*Pause.*)

MOM: Oh.

LEE: Yeah.

(*Pause.*)

MOM: You're both leaving?

LEE: (*Looks at* AUSTIN.) Well we were thinkin' about that before but now I—

AUSTIN: No, we are! We're both leaving. We've got it all planned. 700

MOM: (*To* AUSTIN.) Well you can't leave. You have a family.

AUSTIN: I'm leaving. I'm getting out of here.

LEE: (*To* MOM.) I don't really think Austin's cut out for the desert do you?

MOM: No. He's not.

AUSTIN: I'm going with you, Lee! 705

MOM: He's too thin.

LEE: Yeah, he'd just burn up out there.

AUSTIN: (*To* LEE.) We just gotta' finish this screenplay and then we're gonna' take off. That's the plan. That's what you said. Come on, let's get back to work, Lee.

LEE: I can't work under these conditions here. It's too hot. 710

AUSTIN: Then we'll do it on the desert.

LEE: Don't be tellin' me what we're gonna do!

MOM: Don't shout in the house.

LEE: We're just gonna' have to postpone the whole deal.

AUSTIN: I can't postpone it! It's gone past postponing! I'm doing everything you said. 715
I'm writing down exactly what you tell me.

LEE: Yeah, but you were right all along see. It is a dumb story. "Two lamebrains chasin' each other across Texas." That's what you said, right?

AUSTIN: I never said that.

(LEE *sneers in* AUSTIN's *face then turns to* MOM.)

LEE: I'm gonna' just borrow some a' your antiques, Mom. You don't mind do ya'? Just a 720
few plates and things. Silverware.

(LEE *starts going through all the cupboards in kitchen pulling out plates and stacking them on counter as* MOM *and* AUSTIN *watch.*)

MOM: You don't have any utensils on the desert?

LEE: Nah, I'm fresh out.

AUSTIN: (*To* LEE.) What're you doing?

MOM: Well some of those are very old. Bone China. 725

LEE: I'm tired of eatin' outa' my bare hands, ya' know. It's not civilized.

AUSTIN: (*To* LEE.) What're you doing? We made a deal!

MOM: Couldn't you borrow the plastic ones instead? I have plenty of plastic ones.

LEE: (*As he stacks plates.*) It's not the same. Plastic's not the same at all. What I need is somethin' authentic. Somethin' to keep me in touch. It's easy to get outa' touch 730
out there. Don't worry I'll get 'em back to ya'.

(AUSTIN *rushes up to* LEE, *grabs him by shoulders.*)

AUSTIN: You can't just drop the whole thing, Lee!

> (LEE *turns, pushes* AUSTIN *in the chest knocking him backwards into the alcove,* MOM *watches numbly,* LEE *returns to collecting the plates, silverware, etc.*)

MOM: You boys shouldn't fight in the house. Go outside and fight.
LEE: I'm not fightin'. I'm leavin'.
MOM: There's been enough damage done already. 735
LEE: (*His back to* AUSTIN *and* MOM, *stacking dishes on counter.*) I'm clearin' outa' here once and for all. All this town does is drive a man insane. Look what it's done to Austin there. I'm not lettin' that happen to me. Sell myself down the river. No sir. I'd rather be a hundred miles from nowhere than let that happen to me.

> (*During this* AUSTIN *has picked up the ripped-out phone from the floor and wrapped the cord tightly around both his hands, he lunges at* LEE *whose back is still to him, wraps the cord around* LEE's *neck, plants a foot in* LEE's *back and pulls back on the cord, tightening it,* LEE *chokes desperately, can't speak and can't reach* AUSTIN *with his arms,* AUSTIN *keeps applying pressure on* LEE's *back with his foot, bending him into the sink,* MOM *watches.*)

AUSTIN: (*Tightening cord.*) You're not goin' anywhere! You're not takin' anything with 740 you. You're not takin' my car! You're not takin' the dishes! You're not takin' anything! You're stayin' right here!
MOM: You'll have to stop fighting in the house. There's plenty of room outside to fight. You've got the whole outdoors to fight in.

> (LEE *tries to tear himself away, he crashes across the stage like an enraged bull dragging* AUSTIN *with him, he snorts and bellows but* AUSTIN *hangs on and manages to keep clear of* LEE's *attempts to grab him, they crash into the table, to the floor,* LEE *is face down thrashing wildly and choking,* AUSTIN *pulls cord tighter, stands with one foot planted on* LEE's *back and the cord stretched taut.*)

AUSTIN: (*Holding cord.*) Gimme back my keys, Lee! Take the keys out! Take 'em out! 745

> (LEE *desperately tries to dig in his pockets, searching for the car keys,* MOM *moves closer.*)

MOM: (*Calmly to* AUSTIN.) You're not killing him are you?
AUSTIN: I don't know. I don't know if I'm killing him. I'm stopping him. That's all. I'm just stopping him.

> (LEE *thrashes but* AUSTIN *is relentless.*)

MOM: You oughta' let him breathe a little bit.
AUSTIN: Throw the keys out, Lee! 750

> (LEE *finally gets keys out and throws them on floor but out of* AUSTIN's *reach,* AUSTIN *keeps pressure on cord, pulling* LEE's *neck back,* LEE *gets one hand to the cord but can't relieve the pressure.*)

Reach me those keys would ya', Mom.
MOM: (*Not moving.*) Why are you doing this to him?
AUSTIN: Reach me the keys!
MOM: Not until you stop choking him.

AUSTIN: I can't stop choking him! He'll kill me if I stop choking him!

MOM: He won't kill you. He's your brother.   755

AUSTIN: Just get me the keys would ya'!

(*Pause.* MOM *picks keys up off floor, hands them to* AUSTIN.)

AUSTIN: (*To* MOM.) Thanks.

MOM: Will you let him go now?

AUSTIN: I don't know. He's not gonna' let me get outa' here.

MOM: Well you can't kill him.   760

AUSTIN: I can kill him! I can easily kill him. Right now. Right here. All I gotta' do is just tighten up. See? (*He tightens cord, lee thrashes wildly.* AUSTIN *releases pressure a little, maintaining control.*) Ya' see that?

MOM: That's a savage thing to do.

AUSTIN: Yeah well don't tell me I can't kill him because I can. I can just twist. I can just   765
keep twisting. (AUSTIN *twists the cord tighter,* LEE *weakens, his breathing changes to a short rasp.*)

MOM: Austin!

(AUSTIN *relieves pressure,* LEE *breathes easier but* AUSTIN *keeps him under control.*)

AUSTIN: (*Eyes on* LEE, *holding cord.*) I'm goin' to the desert. There's nothing stopping me. I'm going by myself to the desert.   770

(MOM *moving toward her luggage.*)

MOM: Well, I'm going to go check into a motel. I can't stand this anymore.

AUSTIN: Don't go yet!

(MOM *pauses.*)

MOM: I can't stay here. This is worse than being homeless.

AUSTIN: I'll get everything fixed up for you, Mom. I promise. Just stay for a while.

MOM: (*Picking up luggage.*) You're going to the desert.   775

AUSTIN: Just wait!

(LEE *thrashes,* AUSTIN *subdues him,* MOM *watches holding luggage, pause.*)

MOM: It was the worst feeling being up there. In Alaska. Staring out a window. I never felt so desperate before. That's why when I saw that article on Picasso I thought—

AUSTIN: Stay here, Mom. This is where you live.

(*She looks around the stage.*)

MOM: I don't recognize it at all.   780

(*She exits with luggage,* AUSTIN *makes a move toward her but* LEE *starts to struggle and* AUSTIN *subdues him again with cord, pause.*)

AUSTIN: (*Holding cord.*) Lee? I'll make ya' a deal. You let me get outa' here. Just let me get to my car. All right, Lee? Gimme a little headstart and I'll turn you loose. Just gimme a little headstart. All right?

(LEE *makes no response,* AUSTIN *slowly releases tension cord, still nothing from* LEE.)

AUSTIN: Lee?

(LEE *is motionless,* AUSTIN *very slowly begins to stand, still keeping a tenuous hold on the cord and his eyes riveted to* LEE *for any sign of movement,* AUSTIN *slowly drops the cord and stands, he stares down at* LEE *who appears to be dead.*)

AUSTIN: (*Whispers.*) Lee?

(*Pause,* AUSTIN *considers, looks toward exit, back to* LEE, *then makes a small movement as if to leave. Instantly* LEE *is on his feet and moves toward exit, blocking* AUSTIN's *escape. They square off to each other, keeping a distance between them. Pause, a single coyote heard in distance, lights fade softly into moonlight, the figures of the brothers now appear to be caught in a vast desert-like landscape, they are very still but watchful for the next move, lights go slowly to black as the after-image of the brothers pulses in the dark, coyote fades.*)

August Wilson (1945–2005)

Fences
(1985)

FENCES is part of August Wilson's ten-play cycle that examines the black experience in twentieth-century America—one play for each decade. All of the plays, except *Ma Rainey's Black Bottom,* are set in Pittsburgh, where Wilson was raised. Wilson's project stemmed from his belief that you must know your past, so you can understand the present, in order to build a better future. Set in 1957, *Fences* occurs on the brink of the Civil Rights Movement. The protagonist, Troy Maxson, is a 53-year-old family man who struggles with the psychological wounds of his past. Throughout the play, Troy harbors deep resentment over having been denied the opportunity to play Major League Baseball, as racial integration did not occur until 1947.

Fences shares similarities with Arthur Miller's *Death of a Salesman,* as both examine a hardworking family man who struggles to find his place in society. In *Fences,* Troy lives on the underside of the American Dream, and as much as anything he is a survivor. He takes pride and refuge in his family; it has been his salvation, but it has also left him stagnant. He believes his chief duty is to provide for his family. While his sense of responsibility is admirable, Troy does not provide his son Cory the kind of love and approval that he seeks. Troy also seeks escape in an extramarital affair that results in a child. As in *Death of a Salesman,* the father's affair causes the son to lose respect for his father.

The final scene of the play leaps forward seven years to the day of Troy's funeral (another echo of *Salesman*). Cory has returned home for the first time since their fight. Still resenting his father, Cory initially refuses to attend the funeral; however, Troy's wife Rose urges forgiveness: "Your daddy wanted you to be everything he wasn't . . . and at the same time he tried to make you into everything he was. I don't know if he was right or wrong . . . but I do know he meant to do more good than he meant to do harm." Through the sum of his strengths and his weaknesses, his success and failures, Troy is a man who commands our attention.

In some of his other works, Wilson incorporates elements of the supernatural, but the Pulitzer Prize–winning *Fences* is rooted firmly in the realist tradition and its focus on family issues—husband-wife dynamics, father-son relationships, infidelity, and parental responsibilities—marks it as his most mainstream. The original 1987 Broadway production, starring James Earl Jones, won four Tony Awards; the 2010 revival, starring Denzel Washington, received 10 Tony nominations, tying the record for the most nominations for a non-musical.

Ultimately Wilson's work shows us both our similarities and our differences. Likewise, his career shows an artist who is specifically African American while also mainstream. By the time of his death in 2005, Wilson had secured his place as one of the five best American playwrights of all time.

Fences
(1985)

Characters

TROY MAXSON

IM BONO, *Troy's friend*

ROSE, *Troy's wife*

LYONS, *Troy's oldest son by previous marriage*

GABRIEL, *Troy's brother*

CORY, *Troy and Rose's son*

RAYNELL, *Troy's daughter*

> When the sins of our fathers visit us
> We do not have to play host.
> We can banish them with forgiveness
> As God, in His Largeness and Laws.
>
> —AUGUST WILSON

SETTING——*The setting is the yard which fronts the only entrance to the Maxson household, an ancient two-story brick house set back off a small alley in a big-city neighborhood. The entrance to the house is gained by two or three steps leading to a wooden porch badly in need of paint.*

A relatively recent addition to the house and running its full width, the porch lacks congruence. It is a sturdy porch with a flat roof. One or two chairs of dubious value sit at one end where the kitchen window opens onto the porch. An old-fashioned icebox stands silent guard at the opposite end.

The yard is a small dirt yard, partially fenced, except for the last scene, with a wooden sawhorse, a pile of lumber, and other fence-building equipment set off to the side. Opposite is a tree from which hangs a ball made of rags. A baseball bat leans against the tree. Two oil drums serve as garbage receptacles and sit near the house at right to complete the setting.

THE PLAY—— *Near the turn of the century, the destitute of Europe sprang on the city with tenacious claws and an honest and solid dream. The city devoured them. They swelled its belly until it burst into a thousand furnaces and sewing machines, a thousand butcher shops and bakers' ovens, a thousand churches and hospitals and funeral parlors and moneylenders. The city grew. It nourished itself and offered each man a partnership limited only by his talent, his guile, and his willingness and capacity for hard work. For the immigrants of Europe, a dream dared and won true.*

The descendants of African slaves were offered no such welcome or participation. They came from places called the Carolinas and the Virginias, Georgia, Alabama, Mississippi, and

Tennessee. They came strong, eager, searching. The city rejected them and they fled and settled along the riverbanks and under bridges in shallow, ramshackle houses made of sticks and tarpaper. They collected rags and wood. They sold the use of their muscles and their bodies. They cleaned houses and washed clothes, they shined shoes, and in quiet desperation and vengeful pride, they stole, and lived in pursuit of their own dream. That they could breathe free, finally, and stand to meet life with the force of dignity and whatever eloquence the heart could call upon.

By 1957, the hard-won victories of the European immigrants had solidified the industrial might of America. War had been confronted and won with new energies that used loyalty and patriotism as its fuel. Life was rich, full, and flourishing. The Milwaukee Braves won the World Series, and the hot winds of change that would make the sixties a turbulent, racing, dangerous, and provocative decade had not yet begun to blow full.

ACT I

SCENE I

It is 1957. TROY *and* BONO *enter the yard, engaged in conversation.* TROY *is fifty-three years old, a large man with thick, heavy hands; it is this largeness that he strives to fill out and make an accommodation with. Together with his blackness, his largeness informs his sensibilities and the choices he has made in his life.*

Of the two men, BONO *is obviously the follower. His commitment to their friendship of thirty-odd years is rooted in his admiration of* TROY'S *honesty, capacity for hard work, and his strength, which* BONO *seeks to emulate.*

It is Friday night, payday, and the one night of the week the two men engage in a ritual of talk and drink. TROY *is usually the most talkative and at times he can be crude and almost vulgar, though he is capable of rising to profound heights of expression. The men carry lunch buckets and wear or carry burlap aprons and are dressed in clothes suitable to their jobs as garbage collectors.*

BONO: Troy, you ought to stop that lying!

TROY: I ain't lying! The nigger had a watermelon this big.

(*He indicates with his hands.*)

Talking about . . . "What watermelon, Mr. Rand?" I liked to fell out! "What watermelon, Mr. Rand?" . . . And it sitting there big as life.

BONO: What did Mr. Rand say?   5

TROY: Ain't said nothing. Figure if the nigger too dumb to know he carrying a watermelon, he wasn't gonna get much sense out of him. Trying to hide that great big old watermelon under his coat. Afraid to let the white man see him carry it home.

BONO: I'm like you . . . I ain't got no time for them kind of people.

TROY: Now what he look like getting mad cause he see the man from the union talking to Mr. Rand?   10

BONO: He come to me talking about . . . "Maxson gonna get us fired." I told him to get away from me with that. He walked away from me calling you a troublemaker. What Mr. Rand say?

TROY: Ain't said nothing. He told me to go down the Commissioner's office next Friday.   15
They called me down there to see them.

BONO: Well, as long as you got your complaint filed, they can't fire you. That's what one
of them white fellows tell me.

TROY: I ain't worried about them firing me. They gonna fire me cause I asked a question?
That's all I did. I went to Mr. Rand and asked him, "Why? Why you got the white   20
mens driving and the colored lifting?" Told him, "what's the matter, don't I count?
You think only white fellows got sense enough to drive a truck. That ain't no paper
job! Hell, anybody can drive a truck. How come you got all whites driving and the
colored lifting?" He told me "take it to the union." Well, hell, that's what I done!
Now they wanna come up with this pack of lies.   25

BONO: I told Brownie if the man come and ask him any questions . . . just tell the truth!
It ain't nothing but something they done trumped up on you cause you filed a
complaint on them.

TROY: Brownie don't understand nothing. All I want them to do is change the job
description. Give everybody a chance to drive the truck. Brownie can't see that. He   30
ain't got that much sense.

BONO: How you figure he be making out with that gal be up at Taylors' all the time . . .
that Alberta gal?

TROY: Same as you and me. Getting just as much as we is. Which is to say nothing.

BONO: It is, huh? I figure you doing a little better than me . . . and I ain't saying what   35
I'm doing.

TROY: Aw, nigger, look here . . . I know you. If you had got anywhere near that gal, twenty
minutes later you be looking to tell somebody. And the first one you gonna tell . . .
that you gonna want to brag to . . . is gonna be me.

BONO: I ain't saying that. I see where you be eyeing her.   40

TROY: I eye all the women. I don't miss nothing. Don't never let nobody tell you Troy
Maxson don't eye the women.

BONO: You been doing more than eyeing her. You done bought her a drink or two.

TROY: Hell yeah, I bought her a drink! What that mean? I bought you one, too. What that
mean cause I buy her a drink? I'm just being polite.   45

BONO: It's alright to buy her one drink. That's what you call being polite. But when you
wanna be buying two or three . . . that's what you call eyeing her.

TROY: Look here, as long as you known me . . . you ever known me to chase after women?

BONO: Hell yeah! Long as I done known you. You forgetting I knew you when.

TROY: Naw, I'm talking about since I been married to Rose?   50

BONO: Oh, not since you been married to Rose. Now, that's the truth, there. I can say that.

TROY: Alright then! Case closed.

BONO: I see you be walking up around Alberta's house. You supposed to be at Taylors'
and you be walking up around there.

TROY: What you watching where I'm walking for? I ain't watching after you.   55

BONO: I seen you walking around there more than once.

TROY: Hell, you liable to see me walking anywhere! That don't mean nothing cause you
see me walking around there.

BONO: Where she come from anyway? She just kinda showed up one day.

TROY: Tallahassee. You can look at her and tell she one of them Florida gals. They got   60
some big healthy women down there. Grow them right up out the ground. Got a
little bit of Indian in her. Most of them niggers down in Florida got some Indian
in them.

BONO: I don't know about that Indian part. But she damn sure big and healthy. Woman wear
some big stockings. Got them great big old legs and hips as wide as the Mississippi   65
River.

TROY: Legs don't mean nothing. You don't do nothing but push them out of the way. But them hips cushion the ride!

BONO: Troy, you ain't got no sense.

TROY: It's the truth! Like you riding on Goodyears!   70

(ROSE *enters from the house. She is ten years younger than* TROY, *her devotion to him stems from her recognition of the possibilities of her life without him: a succession of abusive men and their babies, a life of partying and running the streets, the Church, or aloneness with its attendant pain and frustration. She recognizes* TROY'S *spirit as a fine and illuminating one and she either ignores or forgives his faults, only some of which she recognizes. Though she doesn't drink, her presence is an integral part of the Friday night rituals. She alternates between the porch and the kitchen, where supper preparations are under way.*)

ROSE: What you all out here getting into?

TROY: What you worried about what we getting into for? This is men talk, woman.

ROSE: What I care what you all talking about? Bono, you gonna stay for supper?

BONO: No, I thank you, Rose. But Lucille say she cooking up a pot of pigfeet.

TROY: Pigfeet! Hell, I'm going home with you! Might even stay the night if you got some   75
pigfeet. You got something in there to top them pigfeet, Rose?

ROSE: I'm cooking up some chicken. I got some chicken and collard greens.

TROY: Well, go on back in the house and let me and Bono finish what we was talking about. This is men talk. I got some talk for you later. You know what kind of talk I mean. You go on and powder it up.   80

ROSE: Troy Maxson, don't you start that now!

TROY: (*Puts his arm around her.*) Aw, woman . . . come here. Look here, Bono . . . when I met this woman . . . I got out that place, say, "Hitch up my pony, saddle up my mare . . . there's a woman out there for me somewhere. I looked here. Looked there. Saw Rose and latched on to her." I latched on to her and told her—I'm gonna tell   85
you the truth—I told her, "Baby, I don't wanna marry, I just wanna be your man." Rose told me . . . tell him what you told me, Rose.

ROSE: I told him if he wasn't the marrying kind, then move out the way so the marrying kind could find me.

TROY: That's what she told me. "Nigger, you in my way. You blocking the view! Move   90
out the way so I can find me a husband." I thought it over two or three days. Come back—

ROSE: Ain't no two or three days nothing. You was back the same night.

TROY: Come back, told her . . . "Okay, baby . . . but I'm gonna buy me a banty rooster and put him out there in the backyard . . . and when he sees a stranger come, he'll flap his   95
wings and crow . . ." Look here, Bono, I could watch the front door by myself . . . it was that back door I was worried about.

ROSE: Troy, you ought not talk like that. Troy ain't doing nothing but telling a lie.

TROY: Only thing is . . . when we first got married . . . forget the rooster . . . we ain't had no yard!   100

BONO: I hear you tell it. Me and Lucille was staying down there on Logan Street. Had two rooms with the outhouse in the back. I ain't mind the outhouse none. But when that goddamn wind blow through there in the winter . . . that's what I'm talking about! To this day I wonder why in the hell I ever stayed down there for six long years. But see, I didn't know I could do no better. I thought only white folks   105
had inside toilets and things.

ROSE: There's a lot of people don't know they can do no better than they doing now. That's just something you got to learn. A lot of folks still shop at Bella's.

TROY: Ain't nothing wrong with shopping at Bella's. She got fresh food.

ROSE: I ain't said nothing about if she got fresh food. I'm talking about what she charge. 110
She charge ten cents more than the A&P.

TROY: The A&P ain't never done nothing for me. I spends my money where I'm treated right. I go down to Bella, say, "I need a loaf of bread, I'll pay you Friday." She give it to me. What sense that make when I got money to go and spend it somewhere else and ignore the person who done right by me? That ain't in the Bible. 115

ROSE: We ain't talking about what's in the Bible. What sense it make to shop there when she overcharge?

TROY: You shop where you want to. I'll do my shopping where the people been good to me.

ROSE: Well, I don't think it's right for her to overcharge. That's all I was saying.

BONO: Look here . . . I got to get on. Lucille going be raising all kind of hell. 120

TROY: Where you going, nigger? We ain't finished this pint. Come here, finish this pint.

BONO: Well, hell, I am . . . if you ever turn the bottle loose.

TROY: (*Hands him the bottle.*) The only thing I say about the A&P is I'm glad Cory got that job down there. Help him take care of his school clothes and things. Gabe done moved out and things getting tight around here. He got that job . . . He can start to 125 look out for himself.

ROSE: Cory done went and got recruited by a college football team.

TROY: I told that boy about that football stuff. The white man ain't gonna let him get nowhere with that football. I told him when he first come to me with it. Now you come telling me he done went and got more tied up in it. He ought to go and get 130 recruited in how to fix cars or something where he can make a living.

ROSE: He ain't talking about making no living playing foot-ball. It's just something the boys in school do. They gonna send a recruiter by to talk to you. He'll tell you he ain't talking about making no living playing football. It's a honor to be recruited.

TROY: It ain't gonna get him nowhere. Bono'll tell you that. 135

BONO: If he be like you in the sports . . . he's gonna be alright. Ain't but two men ever played baseball as good as you. That's Babe Ruth and Josh Gibson. Them's the only two men ever hit more home runs than you.

TROY: What it ever get me? Ain't got a pot to piss in or a window to throw it out of.

ROSE: Times have changed since you was playing baseball, Troy. That was before the war. 140
Times have changed a lot since then.

TROY: How in hell they done changed?

ROSE: They got lots of colored boys playing ball now. Baseball and football.

BONO: You right about that, Rose. Times have changed, Troy. You just come along too early. 145

TROY: There ought not never have been no time called too early! Now you take that fellow . . . what's that fellow they had playing right field for the Yankees back then? You know who I'm talking about, Bono. Used to play right field for the Yankees.

ROSE: Selkirk?

TROY: Selkirk! That's it! Man batting .269, understand? .269. What kind of sense that 150
make? I was hitting .432 with thirty-seven home runs! Man batting .269 and playing right field for the Yankees! I saw Josh Gibson's daughter yesterday. She walking around with raggedy shoes on her feet. Now I bet you Selkirk's daughter ain't walking around with raggedy shoes on her feet! I bet you that!

ROSE: They got a lot of colored baseball players now. Jackie Robinson was the first. Folks 155
had to wait for Jackie Robinson.

TROY: I done seen a hundred niggers play baseball better than Jackie Robinson. Hell, I know some teams Jackie Robinson couldn't even make! What you talking about

Jackie Robinson. Jackie Robinson wasn't nobody. I'm talking about if you could play
ball then they ought to have let you play. Don't care what color you were. Come   160
telling me I come along too early. If you could play . . . then they ought to have let
you play.

(TROY *takes a long drink from the bottle.*)

ROSE: You gonna drink yourself to death. You don't need to be drinking like that.
TROY: Death ain't nothing. I done seen him. Done wrassled with him. You can't tell me
nothing about death. Death ain't nothing but a fastball on the outside corner. And   165
you know what I'll do to that! Lookee here, Bono . . . am I lying? You get one of
them fastballs, about waist high, over the outside corner of the plate where you can
get the meat of the bat on it . . . and good god! You can kiss it goodbye. Now, am I
lying?
BONO: Naw, you telling the truth there. I seen you do it.   170
TROY: If I'm lying . . . that 450 feet worth of lying!

(*Pause.*)

That's all death is to me. A fastball on the outside corner.
ROSE: I don't know why you want to get on talking about death.
TROY: Ain't nothing wrong with talking about death. That's part of life. Everybody gonna
die. You gonna die, I'm gonna die. Bono's gonna die. Hell, we all gonna die.   175
ROSE: But you ain't got to talk about it. I don't like to talk about it.
TROY: You the one brought it up. Me and Bono was talking about baseball . . . you tell
me I'm gonna drink myself to death. Ain't that right, Bono? You know I don't drink
this but one night out of the week. That's Friday night. I'm gonna drink just enough
to where I can handle it. Then I cuts it loose. I leave it alone. So don't you worry   180
about me drinking myself to death. 'Cause I ain't worried about Death. I done seen
him. I done wrestled with him.
    Look here, Bono . . . I looked up one day and Death was marching straight at
me. Like Soldiers on Parade! The Army of Death was marching straight at me.
The middle of July, 1941. It got real cold just like it be winter. It seem like Death   185
himself reached out and touched me on the shoulder. He touch me just like I
touch you. I got cold as ice and Death standing there grinning at me.
ROSE: Troy, why don't you hush that talk.
TROY: I say . . . What you want, Mr. Death? You be wanting me? You done brought your
army to be getting me? I looked him dead in the eye. I wasn't fearing nothing. I was   190
ready to tangle. Just like I'm ready to tangle now. The Bible say be ever vigilant.
That's why I don't get but so drunk. I got to keep watch.
ROSE: Troy was right down there in Mercy Hospital. You remember he had pneumonia?
Laying there with a fever talking plumb out of his head.
TROY: Death standing there staring at me . . . carrying that sickle in his hand. Finally he   195
say, "You want bound over for another year?" See, just like that . . . "You want bound
over for another year?" I told him, "Bound over hell! Let's settle this now!"
    It seem like he kinda fell back when I said that, and all the cold went out of me.
I reached down and grabbed that sickle and threw it just as far as I could throw
it . . . and me and him commenced to wrestling.   200
    We wrestled for three days and three nights. I can't say where I found the
strength from. Every time it seemed like he was gonna get the best of me, I'd reach
way down deep inside myself and find the strength to do him one better.
ROSE: Every time Troy tell that story he find different ways to tell it. Different things to
make up about it.   205

TROY: I ain't making up nothing. I'm telling you the facts of what happened. I wrestled with Death for three days and three nights and I'm standing here to tell you about it.

(*Pause.*)

Alright. At the end of the third night we done weakened each other to where we can't hardly move. Death stood up, throwed on his robe . . . had him a white robe with a hood on it. He throwed on that robe and went off to look for his sickle. Say, "I'll be back." Just like that. "I'll be back." I told him, say, "Yeah, but . . . you gonna have to find me!" I wasn't no fool. I wasn't going looking for him. Death ain't nothing to play with. And I know he's gonna get me. I know I got to join his army . . . his camp followers. But as long as I keep my strength and see him coming . . . as long as I keep up my vigilance . . . he's gonna have to fight to get me. I ain't going easy. — 210 — 215
BONO: Well, look here, since you got to keep up your vigilance . . . let me have the bottle.
TROY: Aw hell, I shouldn't have told you that part. I should have left out that part.
ROSE: Troy be talking that stuff and half the time don't even know what he be talking about. — 220
TROY: Bono know me better than that.
BONO: That's right. I know you. I know you got some Uncle Remus in your blood. You got more stories than the devil got sinners.
TROY: Aw hell, I done seen him too! Done talked with the devil.
ROSE: Troy, don't nobody wanna be hearing all that stuff. — 225

(LYONS *enters the yard from the street. Thirty-four years old,* TROY'S *son by a previous marriage, he sports a neatly trimmed goatee, sport coat, white shirt, tie-less and buttoned at the collar. Though he fancies himself a musician, he is more caught up in the rituals and "idea" of being a musician than in the actual practice of the music. He has come to borrow money from* TROY, *and while he knows he will be successful, he is uncertain as to what extent his lifestyle will be held up to scrutiny and ridicule.*)

LYONS: Hey, Pop.
TROY: What you come "Hey, Popping" me for?
LYONS: How you doing, Rose?

(*He kisses her.*)

Mr. Bono. How you doing?
BONO: Hey, Lyons . . . how you been? — 230
TROY: He must have been doing alright. I ain't seen him around here last week.
ROSE: Troy, leave your boy alone. He come by to see you and you wanna start all that nonsense.
TROY: I ain't bothering Lyons.

(*Offers him the bottle.*)

Here . . . get you a drink. We got an understanding. I know why he come by to see me and he know I know. — 235
LYONS: Come on, Pop . . . I just stopped by to say hi . . . see how you was doing.
TROY: You ain't stopped by yesterday.
ROSE: You gonna stay for supper, Lyons? I got some chicken cooking in the oven.
LYONS: No, Rose . . . thanks. I was just in the neighborhood and thought I'd stop by for a minute. — 240

TROY: You was in the neighborhood alright, nigger. You telling the truth there. You was in the neighborhood cause it's my payday.

LYONS: Well, hell, since you mentioned it . . . let me have ten dollars.

TROY: I'll be damned! I'll die and go to hell and play blackjack with the devil before I give   245
you ten dollars.

BONO: That's what I wanna know about . . . that devil you done seen.

LYONS: What . . . Pop done seen the devil? You too much, Pops.

TROY: Yeah, I done seen him. Talked to him too!

ROSE: You ain't seen no devil. I done told you that man ain't had nothing to do with the   250
devil. Anything you can't understand, you want to call it the devil.

TROY: Look here, Bono . . . I went down to see Hertzberger about some furniture. Got
three rooms for two-ninety-eight. That what it say on the radio. "Three rooms . . .
two-ninety-eight." Even made up a little song about it. Go down there . . . man tell
me I can't get no credit. I'm wor-king every day and can't get no credit. What to do?   255
I got an empty house with some raggedy furniture in it. Cory ain't got no bed. He's
sleeping on a pile of rags on the floor. Working every day and can't get no credit.
Come back here—Rose'll tell you—madder than hell. Sit down . . . try to figure what
I'm gonna do. Come a knock on the door. Ain't been living here but three days.
Who know I'm here? Open the door . . . devil standing there bigger than life. White   260
fellow . . . got on good clothes and everything. Standing there with a clipboard in his
hand. I ain't had to say nothing. First words come out of his mouth was . . . "I understand you need some furniture and can't get no credit." I liked to fell over. He say
"I'll give you all the credit you want, but you got to pay the interest on it." I told him,
"Give me three rooms worth and charge whatever you want." Next day a truck pulled   265
up here and two men unloaded them three rooms. Man what drove the truck give me
a book. Say send ten dollars, first of every month to the address in the book and everything will be alright. Say if I miss a payment the devil was coming back and it'll be
hell to pay. That was fifteen years ago. To this day . . . the first of the month I send
my ten dollars, Rose'll tell you.   270

ROSE: Troy lying.

TROY: I ain't never seen that man since. Now you tell me who else that could have been
but the devil? I ain't sold my soul or nothing like that, you understand. Naw, I
wouldn't have truck with the devil about nothing like that. I got my furniture and
pays my ten dollars the first of the month just like clockwork.   275

BONO: How long you say you been paying this ten dollars a month?

TROY: Fifteen years!

BONO: Hell, ain't you finished paying for it yet? How much the man done charged you.

TROY: Aw hell, I done paid for it. I done paid for it ten times over! The fact is I'm scared
to stop paying it.   280

ROSE: Troy lying. We got that furniture from Mr. Glickman. He ain't paying no ten
dollars a month to nobody.

TROY: Aw hell, woman. Bono know I ain't that big a fool.

LYONS: I was just getting ready to say . . . I know where there's a bridge for sale.

TROY: Look here, I'll tell you this . . . it don't matter to me if he was the devil. It don't   285
matter if the devil give credit. Somebody has got to give it.

ROSE: It ought to matter. You going around talking about having truck with the devil . . .
God's the one you gonna have to answer to. He's the one gonna be at the Judgment.

LYONS: Yeah, well, look here, Pop . . . let me have that ten dollars. I'll give it back to you.
Bonnie got a job working at the hospital.   290

TROY: What I tell you, Bono? The only time I see this nigger is when he wants something.
That's the only time I see him.

LYONS: Come on, Pop, Mr. Bono don't want to hear all that. Let me have the ten dollars. I told you Bonnie working.

TROY: What that mean to me? "Bonnie working." I don't care if she working. Go ask her   295
for the ten dollars if she working. Talking about "Bonnie working." Why ain't you working?

LYONS: Aw, Pop, you know I can't find no decent job. Where am I gonna get a job at? You know I can't get no job.

TROY: I told you I know some people down there. I can get you on the rubbish if you want   300
to work. I told you that the last time you came by here asking me for something.

LYONS: Naw, Pop . . . thanks. That ain't for me. I don't wanna be carrying nobody's rubbish. I don't wanna be punching nobody's time clock.

TROY: What's the matter, you too good to carry people's rub-bish? Where you think that
ten dollars you talking about come from? I'm just supposed to haul people's rubbish   305
and give my money to you cause you too lazy to work. You too lazy to work and wanna know why you ain't got what I got.

ROSE: What hospital Bonnie working at? Mercy?

LYONS: She's down at Passavant working in the laundry.

TROY: I ain't got nothing as it is. I give you that ten dollars and I got to eat beans the rest   310
of the week. Naw . . . you ain't getting no ten dollars here.

LYONS: You ain't got to be eating no beans. I don't know why you wanna say that.

TROY: I ain't got no extra money. Gabe done moved over to Miss Pearl's paying her the
rent and things done got tight around here. I can't afford to be giving you every
payday.   315

LYONS: I ain't asked you to give me nothing. I asked you to loan me ten dollars. I know you got ten dollars.

TROY: Yeah, I got it. You know why I got it? Cause I don't throw my money away out
there in the streets. You living the fast life . . . wanna be a musician . . . running
around in them clubs and things . . . then, you learn to take care of yourself. You   320
ain't gonna find me going and asking nobody for nothing. I done spent too many years without.

LYONS: You and me is two different people, Pop.

TROY: I done learned my mistake and learned to do what's right by it. You still trying to
get something for nothing. Life don't owe you nothing. You owe it to yourself. Ask   325
Bono. He'll tell you I'm right.

LYONS: You got your way of dealing with the world . . . I got mine. The only thing that matters to me is the music.

TROY: Yeah, I can see that! It don't matter how you gonna eat . . . where your next dollar
is coming from. You telling the truth there.   330

LYONS: I know I got to eat. But I got to live too. I need some-thing that gonna help me to
get out of the bed in the morning. Make me feel like I belong in the world. I don't
bother nobody. I just stay with my music cause that's the only way I can find to live
in the world. Otherwise there ain't no telling what I might do. Now I don't come
criti-cizing you and how you live. I just come by to ask you for ten dollars. I don't   335
wanna hear all that about how I live.

TROY: Boy, your mama did a hell of a job raising you.

LYONS: You can't change me, Pop. I'm thirty-four years old. If you wanted to change me,
you should have been there when I was growing up. I come by to see you . . . ask for
ten dollars and you want to talk about how I was raised. You don't know nothing   340
about how I was raised.

ROSE: Let the boy have ten dollars, Troy.

TROY: (*To* LYONS.) What the hell you looking at me for? I ain't got no ten dollars. You know what I do with my money.

(*To* ROSE.)

Give him ten dollars if you want him to have it.   345
ROSE: I will. Just as soon as you turn it loose.
TROY: (*Handing rose the money.*) There it is. Seventy-six dollars and forty-two cents. You see this, Bono? Now, I ain't gonna get but six of that back.
ROSE: You ought to stop telling that lie. Here, Lyons.

(*She hands him the money.*)

LYONS: Thanks, Rose. Look . . . I got to run . . . I'll see you later.   350
TROY: Wait a minute. You gonna say, "thanks, Rose" and ain't gonna look to see where she got that ten dollars from? See how they do me, Bono?
LYONS: I know she got it from you, Pop. Thanks. I'll give it back to you.
TROY: There he go telling another lie. Time I see that ten dollars . . . he'll be owing me thirty more.   355
LYONS: See you, Mr. Bono.
BONO: Take care, Lyons!
LYONS: Thanks, Pop. I'll see you again.

(LYONS *exits the yard.*)

TROY: I don't know why he don't go and get him a decent job and take care of that woman he got.   360
BONO: He'll be alright, Troy. The boy is still young.
TROY: The *boy* is thirty-four years old.
ROSE: Let's not get off into all that.
BONO: Look here . . . I got to be going. I got to be getting on. Lucille gonna be waiting.
TROY: (*Puts his arm around* ROSE.) See this woman, Bono? I love this woman. I love this   365
woman so much it hurts. I love her so much . . . I done run out of ways of loving her. So I got to go back to basics. Don't you come by my house Monday morning talking about time to go to work . . . 'cause I'm still gonna be stroking!
ROSE: Troy! Stop it now!
BONO: I ain't paying him no mind, Rose. That ain't nothing but gin-talk. Go on, Troy.   370
I'll see you Monday.
TROY: Don't you come by my house, nigger! I done told you what I'm gonna be doing.

(*The lights go down to black.*)

SCENE II

The lights come up on ROSE *hanging up clothes. She hums and sings softly to herself. It is the following morning.*

ROSE: (*Sings.*)
　　Jesus, be a fence all around me every day.
　　Jesus, I want you to protect me as I travel on my way.   375
　　Jesus, be a fence all around me every day.

(TROY *enters from the house.*)

ROSE: (*Continues.*)
Jesus, I want you to protect me
As I travel on my way.

(*To* TROY.)

'Morning. You ready for breakfast? I can fix it soon as I finish hanging up these   380
clothes?

TROY: I got the coffee on. That'll be alright. I'll just drink some of that this morning.

ROSE: That 651 hit yesterday. That's the second time this month. Miss Pearl hit for a
dollar . . . seem like those that need the least always get lucky. Poor folks can't get
nothing.   385

TROY: Them numbers don't know nobody. I don't know why you fool with them. You
and Lyons both.

ROSE: It's something to do.

TROY: You ain't doing nothing but throwing your money away.

ROSE: Troy, you know I don't play foolishly. I just play a nickel here and a nickel there.   390

TROY: That's two nickels you done thrown away.

ROSE: Now I hit sometimes . . . that makes up for it. It always comes in handy when I do
hit. I don't hear you complaining then.

TROY: I ain't complaining now. I just say it's foolish. Trying to guess out of six hundred
ways which way the number gonna come. If I had all the money niggers, these   395
Negroes, throw away on numbers for one week—just one week—I'd be a rich man.

ROSE: Well, you wishing and calling it foolish ain't gonna stop folks from playing
numbers. That's one thing for sure. Besides . . . some good things come from
playing numbers. Look where Pope done bought him that restaurant off of
numbers.   400

TROY: I can't stand niggers like that. Man ain't had two dimes to rub together. He
walking around with his shoes all run over bumming money for cigarettes. Alright.
Got lucky there and hit the numbers . . .

ROSE: Troy, I know all about it.

TROY: Had good sense, I'll say that for him. He ain't throwed his money away. I seen   405
niggers hit the numbers and go through two thousand dollars in four days. Man
bought him that restaurant down there . . . fixed it up real nice . . . and then didn't
want nobody to come in it! A Negro go in there and can't get no kind of service.
I seen a white fellow come in there and order a bowl of stew. Pope picked all the meat
out the pot for him. Man ain't had nothing but a bowl of meat! Negro come behind   410
him and ain't got nothing but the potatoes and carrots. Talking about what numbers
do for people, you picked a wrong example. Ain't done nothing but make a worser
fool out of him than he was before.

ROSE: Troy, you ought to stop worrying about what happened at work yesterday.

TROY: I ain't worried. Just told me to be down there at the Commissioner's office on   415
Friday. Everybody think they gonna fire me. I ain't worried about them firing me.
You ain't got to worry about that.

(*Pause.*)

Where's Cory? Cory in the house? (*Calls.*) Cory?

ROSE: He gone out.

TROY: Out, huh? He gone out 'cause he know I want him to help me with this fence.   420
I know how he is. That boy scared of work.

(GABRIEL *enters. He comes halfway down the alley and, hearing* TROY'S *voice, stops.*)

TROY: (*Continues.*) He ain't done a lick of work in his life.

ROSE: He had to go to football practice. Coach wanted them to get in a little extra practice before the season start.

TROY: I got his practice . . . running out of here before he get his chores done.   425

ROSE: Troy, what is wrong with you this morning? Don't nothing set right with you. Go on back in there and go to bed . . . get up on the other side.

TROY: Why something got to be wrong with me? I ain't said nothing wrong with me.

ROSE: You got something to say about everything. First it's the numbers . . . then it's the way the man runs his restaurant . . . then you done got on Cory. What's it gonna be   430 next? Take a look up there and see if the weather suits you . . . or is it gonna be how you gonna put up the fence with the clothes hanging in the yard.

TROY: You hit the nail on the head then.

ROSE: I know you like I know the back of my hand. Go on in there and get you some coffee . . . see if that straighten you up. 'Cause you ain't right this morning.   435

(TROY *starts into the house and sees* GABRIEL. GABRIEL *starts singing.* TROY'S *brother, he is seven years younger than* TROY. *Injured in World War II, he has a metal plate in his head. He carries an old trumpet tied around his waist and believes with every fiber of his being that he is the Archangel Gabriel. He carries a chipped basket with an assortment of discarded fruits and vegetables he has picked up in the strip district and which he attempts to sell.*)

GABRIEL: (*Singing.*)
Yes, ma'am, I got plums
You ask me how I sell them
Oh ten cents apiece
Three for a quarter   440
Come and buy now
'Cause I'm here today
And tomorrow I'll be gone

(GABRIEL *enters.*)

Hey, Rose!

ROSE: How you doing, Gabe?   445

GABRIEL: There's Troy . . . Hey, Troy!

TROY: Hey, Gabe.

(*Exit into kitchen.*)

ROSE: (*To* GABRIEL.) What you got there?

GABRIEL: You know what I got, Rose. I got fruits and vegetables.

ROSE: (*Looking in basket.*) Where's all these plums you talking about?   450

GABRIEL: I ain't got no plums today, Rose. I was just singing that. Have some tomorrow. Put me in a big order for plums. Have enough plums tomorrow for St. Peter and everybody.

(TROY *re-enters from kitchen, crosses to steps.*)

(*To* ROSE.)

Troy's mad at me.

TROY: I ain't mad at you. What I got to be mad at you about? You ain't done nothing   455
    to me.
GABRIEL: I just moved over to Miss Pearl's to keep out from in your way. I ain't mean no
    harm by it.
TROY: Who said anything about that? I ain't said anything about that.
GABRIEL: You ain't mad at me, is you?   460
TROY: Naw . . . I ain't mad at you, Gabe. If I was mad at you I'd tell you about it.
GABRIEL: Got me two rooms. In the basement. Got my own door too. Wanna see
    my key?

(*He holds up a key.*)

That's my own key! Ain't nobody else got a key like that. That's my key! My two
rooms!   465
TROY: Well, that's good, Gabe. You got your own key . . . that's good.
ROSE: You hungry, Gabe? I was just fixing to cook Troy his breakfast.
GABRIEL: I'll take some biscuits. You got some biscuits? Did you know when I was in
    heaven . . . every morning me and St. Peter would sit down by the gate and eat some
    big fat biscuits? Oh, yeah! We had us a good time. We'd sit there and eat us them   470
    biscuits and then St. Peter would go off to sleep and tell me to wake him up when
    it's time to open the gates for the judgment.
ROSE: Well, come on . . . I'll make up a batch of biscuits.

(ROSE *exits into the house.*)

GABRIEL: Troy . . . St. Peter got your name in the book. I seen it. It say . . . Troy Maxson.
    I say . . . I know him! He got the same name like what I got. That's my brother!   475
TROY: How many times you gonna tell me that, Gabe?
GABRIEL: Ain't got my name in the book. Don't have to have my name. I done died and
    went to heaven. He got your name though. One morning St. Peter was looking at
    his book . . . marking it for the judgment . . . and he let me see your name. Got it in
    there under M. Got Rose's name . . . I ain't seen it like I seen yours . . . but I know   480
    it's in there. He got a great big book. Got everybody's name what was ever been
    born. That's what he told me. But I seen your name. Seen it with my own eyes.
TROY: Go on in the house there. Rose going to fix you something to eat.
GABRIEL: Oh, I ain't hungry. I done had breakfast with Aunt Jemimah. She come by and
cooked me up a whole mess of flapjacks. Remember how we used to eat them flapjacks.   485
TROY: Go on in the house and get you something to eat now.
GABRIEL: I got to go sell my plums. I done sold some tomatoes. Got me two quarters.
    Wanna see?

(*He shows* TROY *his quarters.*)

I'm gonna save them and buy me a new horn so St. Peter can hear me when it's
time to open the gates.   490

(GABRIEL *stops suddenly. Listens.*)

Hear that? That's the hellhounds. I got to chase them out of here. Go on get out of
here! Get out!

(GABRIEL *exits singing.*)

    Better get ready for the judgment
    Better get ready for the judgment
    My Lord is coming down   495

(ROSE *enters from the house.*)

TROY: He gone off somewhere.
GABRIEL: (*Offstage.*)

> Better get ready for the judgment
> Better get ready for the judgment morning
> Better get ready for the judgment
> My God is coming down

500

ROSE: He ain't eating right. Miss Pearl say she can't get him to eat nothing.
TROY: What you want me to do about it, Rose? I done did everything I can for the man. I can't make him get well. Man got half his head blown away . . . what you expect?
ROSE: Seem like something ought to be done to help him.

505

TROY: Man don't bother nobody. He just mixed up from that metal plate he got in his head. Ain't no sense for him to go back into the hospital.
ROSE: Least he be eating right. They can help him take care of himself.
TROY: Don't nobody wanna be locked up, Rose. What you wanna lock him up for? Man go over there and fight the war . . . messin' around with them Japs, get half his head blown off . . . and they give him a lousy three thousand dollars. And I had to swoop down on that.

510

ROSE: Is you fixing to go into that again?
TROY: That's the only way I got a roof over my head . . . cause of that metal plate.
ROSE: Ain't no sense you blaming yourself for nothing. Gabe wasn't in no condition to manage that money. You done what was right by him. Can't nobody say you ain't done what was right by him. Look how long you took care of him . . . till he wanted to have his own place and moved over there with Miss Pearl.

515

TROY: That ain't what I'm saying, woman! I'm just stating the facts. If my brother didn't have that metal plate in his head . . . I wouldn't have a pot to piss in or a window to throw it out of. And I'm fifty-three years old. Now see if you can understand that!

520

(TROY *gets up from the porch and starts to exit the yard.*)

ROSE: Where you going off to? You been running out of here every Saturday for weeks. I thought you was gonna work on this fence?
TROY: I'm gonna walk down to Taylors'. Listen to the ball game. I'll be back in a bit. I'll work on it when I get back.

525

(*He exits the yard. The lights go to black.*)

SCENE III

The lights come up on the yard. It is four hours later. ROSE *is taking down the clothes from the line.* CORY *enters carrying his football equipment.*

ROSE: Your daddy like to had a fit with you running out of here this morning without doing your chores.
CORY: I told you I had to go to practice.
ROSE: He say you were supposed to help him with this fence.
CORY: He been saying that the last four or five Saturdays, and then he don't never do nothing, but go down to Taylors'. Did you tell him about the recruiter?

530

ROSE: Yeah, I told him.

CORY: What he say?

ROSE: He ain't said nothing too much. You get in there and get started on your chores before he gets back. Go on and scrub down them steps before he gets back here 535 hollering and carrying on.

CORY: I'm hungry. What you got to eat, Mama?

ROSE: Go on and get started on your chores. I got some meat loaf in there. Go on and make you a sandwich . . . and don't leave no mess in there.

(CORY *exits into the house.* ROSE *continues to take down the clothes.* TROY *enters the yard and sneaks up and grabs her from behind.*)

Troy! Go on, now. You liked to scared me to death. What was the score of the 540 game? Lucille had me on the phone and I couldn't keep up with it.

TROY: What I care about the game? Come here, woman.

(*He tries to kiss her.*)

ROSE: I thought you went down Taylors' to listen to the game. Go on, Troy! You supposed to be putting up this fence.

TROY: (*Attempting to kiss her again.*) I'll put it up when I finish with what is at hand. 545

ROSE: Go on, Troy. I ain't studying you.

TROY: (*Chasing after her.*) I'm studying you . . . fixing to do my homework!

ROSE: Troy, you better leave me alone.

TROY: Where's Cory? That boy brought his butt home yet?

ROSE: He's in the house doing his chores. 550

TROY: (*Calling.*) Cory! Get your butt out here, boy!

(ROSE *exits into the house with the laundry.* TROY *goes over to the pile of wood, picks up a board, and starts sawing.* CORY *enters from the house.*)

TROY: You just now coming in here from leaving this morning?

CORY: Yeah, I had to go to football practice.

TROY: Yeah, what?

CORY: Yessir. 555

TROY: I ain't but two seconds off you noway. The garbage sitting in there overflowing . . . you ain't done none of your chores . . . and you come in here talking about "Yeah."

CORY: I was just getting ready to do my chores now, Pop . . .

TROY: Your first chore is to help me with this fence on Saturday. Everything else come after that. Now get that saw and cut them boards. 560

(CORY *takes the saw and begins cutting the boards.* TROY *continues working. There is a long pause.*)

CORY: Hey, Pop . . . why don't you buy a TV?

TROY: What I want with a TV? What I want one of them for?

CORY: Everybody got one. Earl, Ba Bra . . . Jesse!

TROY: I ain't asked you who had one. I say what I want with one?

CORY: So you can watch it. They got lots of things on TV. Baseball games and everything. 565 We could watch the World Series.

TROY: Yeah . . . and how much this TV cost?

CORY: I don't know. They got them on sale for around two hundred dollars.

TROY: Two hundred dollars, huh?

CORY: That ain't that much, Pop. 570

TROY: Naw, it's just two hundred dollars. See that roof you got over your head at night? Let me tell you something about that roof. It's been over ten years since that roof was last tarred. See now . . . the snow come this winter and sit up there on that roof like it is . . . and it's gonna seep inside. It's just gonna be a little bit . . . ain't gonna hardly notice it. Then the next thing you know, it's gonna be leaking all over the   575
house. Then the wood rot from all that water and you gonna need a whole new roof. Now, how much you think it cost to get that roof tarred?

CORY: I don't know.

TROY: Two hundred and sixty-four dollars . . . cash money. While you thinking about a TV, I got to be thinking about the roof . . . and whatever else go wrong around here.   580
Now if you had two hundred dollars, what would you do . . . fix the roof or buy a TV?

CORY: I'd buy a TV. Then when the roof started to leak . . . when it needed fixing . . . I'd fix it.

TROY: Where you gonna get the money from? You done spent it for a TV. You gonna sit   585
up and watch the water run all over your brand new TV.

CORY: Aw, Pop. You got money. I know you do.

TROY: Where I got it at, Huh?

CORY: You got it in the bank.

TROY: You wanna see my bankbook? You wanna see that seventy-three dollars and   590
twenty-two cents I got sitting up in there.

CORY: You ain't got to pay for it all at one time. You can put a down payment on it and carry it on home with you.

TROY: Not me. I ain't gonna owe nobody nothing if I can help it. Miss a payment and they come and snatch it right out your house. Then what you got? Now, soon as   595
I get two hundred dollars clear, then I'll buy a TV. Right now, as soon as I get two hundred and sixty-four dollars, I'm gonna have this roof tarred.

CORY: Aw . . . Pop!

TROY: You go on and get you two hundred dollars and buy one if ya want it. I got better things to do with my money.   600

CORY: I can't get no two hundred dollars. I ain't never seen two hundred dollars.

TROY: I'll tell you what . . . you get you a hundred dollars and I'll put the other hundred with it.

CORY: Alright, I'm gonna show you.

TROY: You gonna show me how you can cut them boards right now.   605

(CORY *begins to cut the boards. There is a long pause.*)

CORY: The Pirates won today. That makes five in a row.

TROY: I ain't thinking about the Pirates. Got an all-white team. Got that boy . . . that Puerto Rican boy . . . Clemente. Don't even half-play him. That boy could be something if they give him a chance. Play him one day and sit him on the bench the next.   610

CORY: He gets a lot of chances to play.

TROY: I'm talking about playing regular. Playing every day so you can get your timing. That's what I'm talking about.

CORY: They got some white guys on the team that don't play every day. You can't play everybody at the same time.   615

TROY: If they got a white fellow sitting on the bench . . . you can bet your last dollar he can't play! The colored guy got to be twice as good before he get on the team. That's why I don't want you to get all tied up in them sports. Man on the team and what it get him? They got colored on the team and don't use them. Same as not having them. All them teams the same.   620

CORY: The Braves got Hank Aaron and Wes Covington. Hank Aaron hit two home runs today. That makes forty-three.

TROY: Hank Aaron ain't nobody. That's what you supposed to do. That's how you supposed to play the game. Ain't nothing to it. It's just a matter of timing . . . getting the right follow-through. Hell, I can hit forty-three home runs right now!   625

CORY: Not off no major-league pitching, you couldn't.

TROY: We had better pitching in the Negro leagues. I hit seven home runs off of Satchel Paige. You can't get no better than that!

CORY: Sandy Koufax. He's leading the league in strikeouts.

TROY: I ain't thinking of no Sandy Koufax.   630

CORY: You got Warren Spahn and Lew Burdette. I bet you couldn't hit no home runs off of Warren Spahn.

TROY: I'm through with it now. You go on and cut them boards.

(*Pause.*)

Your mama tell me you done got recruited by a college football team? Is that right?

CORY: Yeah. Coach Zellman say the recruiter gonna be coming by to talk to you. Get you   635
to sign the permission papers.

TROY: I thought you supposed to be working down there at the A&P. Ain't you suppose to be working down there after school?

CORY: Mr. Stawicki say he gonna hold my job for me until after the football season. Say starting next week I can work weekends.   640

TROY: I thought we had an understanding about this football stuff? You suppose to keep up with your chores and hold that job down at the A&P. Ain't been around here all day on a Saturday. Ain't none of your chores done . . . and now you telling me you done quit your job.

CORY: I'm gonna be working weekends.   645

TROY: You damn right you are! And ain't no need for nobody coming around here to talk to me about signing nothing.

CORY: Hey, Pop . . . you can't do that. He's coming all the way from North Carolina.

TROY: I don't care where he coming from. The white man ain't gonna let you get nowhere with that football noway. You go on and get your book-learning so you   650
can work yourself up in that A&P or learn how to fix cars or build houses or something, get you a trade. That way you have something can't nobody take away from you. You go on and learn how to put your hands to some good use. Besides hauling people's garbage.

CORY: I get good grades, Pop. That's why the recruiter wants to talk with you. You got to   655
keep up your grades to get recruited. This way I'll be going to college. I'll get a chance . . .

TROY: First you gonna get your butt down there to the A&P and get your job back.

CORY: Mr. Stawicki done already hired somebody else 'cause I told him I was playing football.   660

TROY: You a bigger fool than I thought . . . to let somebody take away your job so you can play some football. Where you gonna get your money to take out your girlfriend and whatnot? What kind of foolishness is that to let somebody take away your job?

CORY: I'm still gonna be working weekends.

TROY: Naw . . . naw. You getting your butt out of here and finding you another job.   665

CORY: Come on, Pop! I got to practice. I can't work after school and play football too. The team needs me. That's what Coach Zellman say . . .

TROY: I don't care what nobody else say. I'm the boss . . . you understand? I'm the boss around here. I do the only saying what counts.

CORY: Come on, Pop!   670

TROY: I asked you . . . did you understand?

CORY: Yeah . . .

TROY: What?!

CORY: Yessir.

TROY: You go on down there to that A&P and see if you can get your job back. If you   675
can't do both . . . then you quit the football team. You've got to take the crookeds
with the straights.

CORY: Yessir.

(*Pause.*)

Can I ask you a question?

TROY: What the hell you wanna ask me? Mr. Stawicki the one you got the questions for.   680

CORY: How come you ain't never liked me?

TROY: Liked you? Who the hell say I got to like you? What law is there say I got to like
you? Wanna stand up in my face and ask a damn fool-ass question like that. Talking
about liking somebody. Come here boy, when I talk to you.

(CORY *comes over to where* TROY *is working. He stands slouched over and*
TROY *shoves him on his shoulder.*)

Straighten up, goddammit! I asked you a question . . . what law is there say I got to   685
like you?

CORY: None.

TROY: Well, alright then! Don't you eat every day?

(*Pause.*)

Answer me when I talk to you! Don't you eat every day?

CORY: Yeah.   690

TROY: Nigger, as long as you in my house, you put that sir on the end of it when you
talk to me!

CORY: Yes . . . sir.

TROY: You eat every day.

CORY: Yessir!   695

TROY: Got a roof over your head.

CORY: Yessir!

TROY: Got clothes on your back.

CORY: Yessir.

TROY: Why you think that is?   700

CORY: Cause of you.

TROY: Aw, hell I know it's 'cause of me . . . but why do you think that is?

CORY: (*Hesitant.*) Cause you like me.

TROY: Like you? I go out of here every morning . . . bust my butt . . . putting up with them
crackers every day . . . cause I like you? You about the biggest fool I ever saw.   705

(*Pause.*)

It's my job. It's my responsibility! You understand that? A man got to take care of his family. You live in my house . . . sleep you behind on my bedclothes . . . fill you belly up with my food . . . cause you my son. You my flesh and blood. Not 'cause I like you! Cause it's my duty to take care of you. I owe a responsibility to you! Let's get this straight right here . . . before it go along any further . . . I ain't got to 710 like you. Mr. Rand don't give me my money come payday cause he likes me. He gives me cause he owe me. I done give you everything I had to give you. I gave you your life! Me and your mama worked that out between us. And liking your black ass wasn't part of the bargain. Don't you try and go through life worrying about if somebody like you or not. You best be making sure they doing right by you. You 715 understand what I'm saying, boy?

CORY: Yessir.

TROY: Then get the hell out of my face, and get on down to that A&P.

> (ROSE *has been standing behind the screen door for much of the scene. She enters as* CORY *exits.*)

ROSE: Why don't you let the boy go ahead and play football, Troy? Ain't no harm in that. He's just trying to be like you with the sports. 720

TROY: I don't want him to be like me! I want him to move as far away from my life as he can get. You the only decent thing that ever happened to me. I wish him that. But I don't wish him a thing else from my life. I decided seventeen years ago that boy wasn't getting involved in no sports. Not after what they did to me in the sports.

ROSE: Troy, why don't you admit you was too old to play in the major leagues? For 725 once . . . why don't you admit that?

TROY: What do you mean too old? Don't come telling me I was too old. I just wasn't the right color. Hell, I'm fifty-three years old and can do better than Selkirk's .269 right now!

ROSE: How's was you gonna play ball when you were over forty? Sometimes I can't get 730 no sense out of you.

TROY: I got good sense, woman. I got sense enough not to let my boy get hurt over playing no sports. You been mothering that boy too much. Worried about if people like him.

ROSE: Everything that boy do . . . he do for you. He wants you to say "Good job, son." 735 That's all.

TROY: Rose, I ain't got time for that. He's alive. He's healthy. He's got to make his own way. I made mine. Ain't nobody gonna hold his hand when he get out there in that world.

ROSE: Times have changed from when you was young, Troy. People change. The world's 740 changing around you and you can't even see it.

TROY: (*Slow, methodical.*) Woman . . . I do the best I can do. I come in here every Friday. I carry a sack of potatoes and a bucket of lard. You all line up at the door with your hands out. I give you the lint from my pockets. I give you my sweat and my blood. I ain't got no tears. I done spent them. We go upstairs in that room at night . . . and 745 I fall down on you and try to blast a hole into forever. I get up Monday morning . . . find my lunch on the table. I go out. Make my way. Find my strength to carry me through to the next Friday.

> (*Pause.*)

That's all I got, Rose. That's all I got to give. I can't give nothing else.

> (TROY *exits into the house. The lights go down to black.*)

SCENE IV

It is Friday. Two weeks later. CORY *starts out of the house with his football equipment. The phone rings.*

CORY: (*Calling.*) I got it!   750

       (*He answers the phone and stands in the screen door talking.*)

    Hello? Hey, Jesse. Naw . . . I was just getting ready to leave now.
ROSE: (*Calling.*) Cory!
CORY: I told you, man, them spikes is all tore up. You can use them if you want, but they
    ain't no good. Earl got some spikes.
ROSE: (*Calling.*) Cory!   755
CORY: (*Calling to* ROSE.) Mam? I'm talking to Jesse.

      (*Into phone.*)

    When she say that. (*Pause.*) Aw, you lying, man. I'm gonna tell her you said that.
ROSE: (*Calling.*) Cory, don't you go nowhere!
CORY: I got to go to the game, Ma!

      (*Into the phone.*)

    Yeah, hey, look, I'll talk to you later. Yeah, I'll meet you over Earl's house. Later.   760
    Bye, Ma.

      (CORY *exits the house and starts out the yard.*)

ROSE: Cory, where you going off to? You got that stuff all pulled out and thrown all over
    your room.
CORY: (*In the yard.*) I was looking for my spikes. Jesse wanted to borrow my spikes.
ROSE: Get up there and get that cleaned up before your daddy get back in here.   765
CORY: I got to go to the game! I'll clean it up when I get back.

      (CORY *exits.*)

ROSE: That's all he need to do is see that room all messed up.

      (ROSE *exits into the house.* TROY *and* BONO *enter the yard.* TROY *is dressed in
      clothes other than his work clothes.*)

BONO: He told him the same thing he told you. Take it to the union.
TROY: Brownie ain't got that much sense. Man wasn't thinking about nothing. He wait
    until I confront them on it . . . then he wanna come crying seniority.   770

    (*Calls.*)

    Hey, Rose!
BONO: I wish I could have seen Mr. Rand's face when he told you.
TROY: He couldn't get it out of his mouth! Liked to bit his tongue! When they called me
    down there to the Com-missioner's office . . . he thought they was gonna fire me.
    Like everybody else.   775
BONO: I didn't think they was gonna fire you. I thought they was gonna put you on the
    warning paper.
TROY: Hey, Rose!

(*To* BONO.)

Yeah, Mr. Rand like to bit his tongue.

(TROY *breaks the seal on the bottle, takes a drink, and hands it to* BONO.)

BONO: I see you run right down to Taylors' and told that Alberta gal.   780

TROY: (*Calling.*) Hey Rose! (*To* BONO.) I told everybody. Hey, Rose! I went down there
to cash my check.

ROSE: (*Entering from the house.*) Hush all that hollering, man! I know you out here. What
they say down there at the Commissioner's office?

TROY: You supposed to come when I call you, woman. Bono'll tell you that.   785

(*To* BONO.)

Don't Lucille come when you call her?

ROSE: Man, hush your mouth. I ain't no dog . . . talk about "come when you call me."

TROY: (*Puts his arm around* ROSE.) You hear this, Bono? I had me an old dog used to get
uppity like that. You say, "C'mere, Blue!" . . . and he just lay there and look at you.
End up getting a stick and chasing him away trying to make him come.   790

ROSE: I ain't studying you and your dog. I remember you used to sing that old song.

TROY: (*He sings.*) Hear it ring! Hear it ring! I had a dog his name was Blue.

ROSE: Don't nobody wanna hear you sing that old song.

TROY: (*Sings.*) You know Blue was mighty true.

ROSE: Used to have Cory running around here singing that song.   795

BONO: Hell, I remember that song myself.

TROY: (*Sings.*)

     You know Blue was a good old dog.
     Blue treed a possum in a hollow log.

That was my daddy's song. My daddy made up that song.   800

ROSE: I don't care who made it up. Don't nobody wanna hear you sing it.

TROY: (*Makes a song like calling a dog.*) Come here, woman.

ROSE: You come in here carrying on, I reckon they ain't fired you. What they say down
there at the Commissioner's office?

TROY: Look here, Rose . . . Mr. Rand called me into his office today when I got back   805
from talking to them people down there . . . it come from up top . . . he called me
in and told me they was making me a driver.

ROSE: Troy, you kidding!

TROY: No I ain't. Ask Bono.

ROSE: Well, that's great, Troy. Now you don't have to hassle them people no more.   810

(LYONS *enters from the street.*)

TROY: Aw hell, I wasn't looking to see you today. I thought you was in jail. Got it all over
the front page of the *Courier* about them raiding Sefus' place . . . where you be
hanging out with all them thugs?

LYONS: Hey, Pop . . . that ain't got nothing to do with me. I don't go down there
gambling. I go down there to sit in with the band. I ain't got nothing to do with   815
the gambling part. They got some good music down there.

TROY: They got some rogues . . . is what they got.

LYONS: How you been, Mr. Bono? Hi, Rose.

BONO: I see where you playing down at the Crawford Grill tonight.

ROSE: How come you ain't brought Bonnie like I told you. You should have brought   820
    Bonnie with you, she ain't been over in a month of Sundays.

LYONS: I was just in the neighborhood . . . thought I'd stop by.

TROY: Here he come . . .

BONO: Your daddy got a promotion on the rubbish. He's gonna be the first colored driver.
    Ain't got to do nothing but sit up there and read the paper like them white fellows.   825

LYONS: Hey, Pop . . . if you knew how to read you'd be alright.

BONO: Naw . . . naw . . . you mean if the nigger knew how to drive he'd be all right. Been
    fighting with them people about driving and ain't even got a license. Mr. Rand
    know you ain't got no driver's license?

TROY: Driving ain't nothing. All you do is point the truck where you want it to go.   830
    Driving ain't nothing.

BONO: Do Mr. Rand know you ain't got no driver's license? That's what I'm talking about.
    I ain't asked if driving was easy. I asked if Mr. Rand know you ain't got no driver's
    license.

TROY: He ain't got to know. The man ain't got to know my business. Time he find out,   835
    I have two or three driver's licenses.

LYONS: (*Going into his pocket.*) Say, look here, Pop . . .

TROY: I knew it was coming. Didn't I tell you, Bono? I know what kind of "Look here,
    Pop" that was. The nigger fixing to ask me for some money. It's Friday night. It's
    my payday. All them rogues down there on the avenue . . . the ones that ain't in   840
    jail . . . and Lyons is hopping in his shoes to get down there with them.

LYONS: See, Pop . . . if you give somebody else a chance to talk sometime, you'd see that
    I was fixing to pay you back your ten dollars like I told you. Here . . . I told you I'd
    pay you when Bonnie got paid.

TROY: Naw . . . you go ahead and keep that ten dollars. Put it in the bank. The next time   845
    you feel like you wanna come by here and ask me for something . . . you go on down
    there and get that.

LYONS: Here's your ten dollars, Pop. I told you I don't want you to give me nothing.
    I just wanted to borrow ten dollars.

TROY: Naw . . . you go on and keep that for the next time you want to ask me.   850

LYONS: Come on, Pop . . . here go your ten dollars.

ROSE: Why don't you go on and let the boy pay you back, Troy?

LYONS: Here you go, Rose. If you don't take it I'm gonna have to hear about it for the
    next six months.

(*He hands her the money.*)

ROSE: You can hand yours over here too, Troy.   855

TROY: You see this, Bono. You see how they do me.

BONO: Yeah, Lucille do me the same way.

(**GABRIEL** *is heard singing offstage. He enters.*)

GABRIEL: Better get ready for the Judgment! Better get ready for . . . Hey! . . . Hey! . . .
    There's Troy's boy!

LYONS: How you doing, Uncle Gabe?   860

GABRIEL: Lyons . . . The King of the Jungle! Rose . . . hey, Rose. Got a flower for you.

(*He takes a rose from his pocket.*)

Picked it myself. That's the same rose like you is!

ROSE: That's right nice of you, Gabe.

LYONS: What you been doing, Uncle Gabe?

GABRIEL: Oh, I been chasing hellhounds and waiting on the time to tell St. Peter to open   865
the gates.

LYONS: You been chasing hellhounds, huh? Well . . . you doing the right thing, Uncle
Gabe. Somebody got to chase them.

GABRIEL: Oh, yeah . . . I know it. The devil's strong. The devil ain't no pushover.
Hellhounds snipping at everybody's heels. But I got my trumpet waiting on the   870
judgment time.

LYONS: Waiting on the Battle of Armageddon, huh?

GABRIEL: Ain't gonna be too much of a battle when God get to waving that Judgment
sword. But the people's gonna have a hell of a time trying to get into heaven if them
gates ain't open.   875

LYONS: (*Putting his arm around* GABRIEL.) You hear this, Pop. Uncle Gabe, you alright!

GABRIEL: (*Laughing with* LYONS.) Lyons! King of the Jungle.

ROSE: You gonna stay for supper, Gabe. Want me to fix you a plate?

GABRIEL: I'll take a sandwich, Rose. Don't want no plate. Just wanna eat with my hands.
I'll take a sandwich.   880

ROSE: How about you, Lyons? You staying? Got some short ribs cooking.

LYONS: Naw, I won't eat nothing till after we finished playing.

(*Pause.*)

You ought to come down and listen to me play, Pop.

TROY: I don't like that Chinese music. All that noise.

ROSE: Go on in the house and wash up, Gabe . . . I'll fix you a sandwich.   885

GABRIEL: (*To* LYONS, *as he exits.*) Troy's mad at me.

LYONS: What you mad at Uncle Gabe for, Pop.

ROSE: He thinks Troy's mad at him cause he moved over to Miss Pearl's.

TROY: I ain't mad at the man. He can live where he want to live at.

LYONS: What he move over there for? Miss Pearl don't like nobody.   890

ROSE: She don't mind him none. She treats him real nice. She just don't allow all that
singing.

TROY: She don't mind that rent he be paying . . . that's what she don't mind.

ROSE: Troy, I ain't going through that with you no more. He's over there cause he want
to have his own place. He can come and go as he please.   895

TROY: Hell, he could come and go as he please here. I wasn't stopping him. I ain't put no
rules on him.

ROSE: It ain't the same thing, Troy. And you know it.

(GABRIEL *comes to the door.*)

Now, that's the last I wanna hear about that. I don't wanna hear nothing else about
Gabe and Miss Pearl. And next week . . .   900

GABRIEL: I'm ready for my sandwich, Rose.

ROSE: And next week . . . when that recruiter come from that school . . . I want you to
sign that paper and go on and let Cory play football. Then that'll be the last I have
to hear about that.

TROY: (*To* ROSE *as she exits into the house.*) I ain't thinking about Cory nothing.   905

LYONS: What . . . Cory got recruited? What school he going to?

TROY: That boy walking around here smelling his piss . . . thinking he's grown. Thinking
he's gonna do what he want, irrespective of what I say. Look here, Bono . . . I left
the Commissioner's office and went down to the A&P . . . that boy ain't working
down there. He lying to me. Telling me he got his job back . . . telling me he working   910

weekends . . . telling me he working after school . . . Mr. Stawicki tell me he ain't working down there at all!

LYONS: Cory just growing up. He's just busting at the seams trying to fill out your shoes.

TROY: I don't care what he's doing. When he get to the point where he wanna disobey me . . . then it's time for him to move on. Bono'll tell you that. I bet he ain't never disobeyed his daddy without paying the consequences. 915

BONO: I ain't never had a chance. My daddy came on through . . . but I ain't never knew him to see him . . . or what he had on his mind or where he went. Just moving on through. Searching out the New Land. That's what the old folks used to call it. See a fellow moving around from place to place . . . woman to woman . . . called it 920 searching out the New Land. I can't say if he ever found it. I come along, didn't want no kids. Didn't know if I was gonna be in one place long enough to fix on them right as their daddy. I figured I was going searching too. As it turned out I been hooked up with Lucille near about as long as your daddy been with Rose. Going on sixteen years. 925

TROY: Sometimes I wish I hadn't known my daddy. He ain't cared nothing about no kids. A kid to him wasn't nothing. All he wanted was for you to learn how to walk so he could start you to working. When it come time for eating . . . he ate first. If there was anything left over, that's what you got. Man would sit down and eat two chickens and give you the wing. 930

LYONS: You ought to stop that, Pop. Everybody feed their kids. No matter how hard times is . . . everybody care about their kids. Make sure they have something to eat.

TROY: The only thing my daddy cared about was getting them bales of cotton into Mr. Lubin. That's the only thing that mattered to him. Sometimes I used to wonder why he was living. Wonder why the devil hadn't come and got him. "Get them bales 935 of cotton in to Mr. Lubin" and find out he owe him money . . .

LYONS: He should have just went on and left when he saw he couldn't get nowhere. That's what I would have done.

TROY: How he gonna leave with eleven kids? And where he gonna go? He ain't knew how to do nothing but farm. No, he was trapped and I think he knew it. But I'll say this 940 for him . . . he felt a responsibility toward us. Maybe he ain't treated us the way I felt he should have . . . but without that responsibility he could have walked off and left us . . . made his own way.

BONO: A lot of them did. Back in those days what you talking about . . . they walk out their front door and just take on down one road or another and keep on walking. 945

LYONS: There you go! That's what I'm talking about.

BONO: Just keep on walking till you come to something else. Ain't you never heard of nobody having the walking blues? Well, that's what you call it when you just take off like that.

TROY: My daddy ain't had them walking blues! What you talking about? He stayed right 950 there with his family. But he was just as evil as he could be. My mama couldn't stand him. Couldn't stand that evilness. She run off when I was about eight. She sneaked off one night after he had gone to sleep. Told me she was coming back for me. I ain't never seen her no more. All his women run off and left him. He wasn't good for nobody. 955

When my turn come to head out, I was fourteen and got to sniffing around Joe Canewell's daughter. Had us an old mule we called Greyboy. My daddy sent me out to do some plowing and I tied up Greyboy and went to fooling around with Joe Canewell's daughter. We done found us a nice little spot, got real cozy with each other. She about thirteen and we done figured we was grown anyway . . . 960

so we down there enjoying ourselves . . . ain't thinking about nothing. We didn't know Greyboy had got loose and wandered back to the house and my daddy was looking for me. We down there by the creek enjoying ourselves when my daddy come up on us. Surprised us. He had them leather straps off the mule and commenced to whupping me like there was no tomorrow. I jumped up, mad and 965
embarrassed. I was scared of my daddy. When he commenced to whupping on me . . . quite naturally I run to get out of the way.

(*Pause.*)

Now I thought he was mad cause I ain't done my work. But I see where he was chasing me off so he could have the gal for himself. When I see what the matter of it was, I lost all fear of my daddy. Right there is where I become a man . . . at 970
fourteen years of age.

(*Pause.*)

Now it was my turn to run him off. I picked up them same reins that he had used on me. I picked up them reins and commenced to whupping on him. The gal jumped up and run off . . . and when my daddy turned to face me, I could see why the devil had never come to get him . . . cause he was the devil himself. 975
I don't know what happened. When I woke up, I was laying right there by the creek, and Blue . . . this old dog we had . . . was licking my face. I thought I was blind. I couldn't see nothing. Both my eyes were swollen shut. I layed there and cried. I didn't know what I was gonna do. The only thing I knew was the time had come for me to leave my daddy's house. And right there the world suddenly got big. And 980
it was a long time before I could cut it down to where I could handle it.

Part of that cutting down was when I got to the place where I could feel him kicking in my blood and knew that the only thing that separated us was the matter of a few years.

(**GABRIEL** *enters from the house with a sandwich.*)

LYONS: What you got there, Uncle Gabe? 985
GABRIEL: Got me a ham sandwich. Rose gave me a ham sandwich.
TROY: I don't know what happened to him. I done lost touch with everybody except Gabriel. But I hope he's dead. I hope he found some peace.
LYONS: That's a heavy story, Pop. I didn't know you left home when you was fourteen.
TROY: And didn't know nothing. The only part of the world I knew was the forty-two 990
acres of Mr. Lubin's land. That's all I knew about life.
LYONS: Fourteen's kinda young to be out on your own. (*Phone rings.*) I don't even think I was ready to be out on my own at fourteen. I don't know what I would have done.
TROY: I got up from the creek and walked on down to Mobile. I was through with farm- 995
ing. Figured I could do better in the city. So I walked the two hundred miles to Mobile.
LYONS: Wait a minute . . . you ain't walked no two hundred miles, Pop. Ain't nobody gonna walk no two hundred miles. You talking about some walking there.
BONO: That's the only way you got anywhere back in them days. 1000
LYONS: Shhh. Damn if I wouldn't have hitched a ride with somebody!
TROY: Who you gonna hitch it with? They ain't had no cars and things like they got now. We talking about 1918.
ROSE: (*Entering.*) What you all out here getting into?

TROY: (*To* ROSE.) I'm telling Lyons how good he got it. He don't know nothing about   1005
this I'm talking.

ROSE: Lyons, that was Bonnie on the phone. She say you supposed to pick her up.

LYONS: Yeah, okay, Rose.

TROY: I walked on down to Mobile and hitched up with some of them fellows that was
heading this way. Got up here and found out . . . not only couldn't you get a job . . .   1010
you couldn't find no place to live. I thought I was in free-dom. Shhh. Colored folks
living down there on the river-banks in whatever kind of shelter they could find for
themselves. Right down there under the Brady Street Bridge. Living in shacks made
of sticks and tarpaper. Messed around there and went from bad to worse. Started
stealing. First it was food. Then I figured, hell, if I steal money I can buy me some   1015
food. Buy me some shoes too! One thing led to another. Met your mama. I was
young and anxious to be a man. Met your mama and had you. What I do that for?
Now I got to worry about feeding you and her. Got to steal three times as much.
Went out one day looking for somebody to rob . . . that's what I was, a robber. I'll
tell you the truth. I'm ashamed of it today. But it's the truth. Went to rob this   1020
fellow . . . pulled out my knife . . . and he pulled out a gun. Shot me in the chest. It
felt just like somebody had taken a hot branding iron and laid it on me. When he
shot me I jumped at him with my knife. They told me I killed him and they put me
in the penitentiary and locked me up for fifteen years. That's where I met Bono.
That's where I learned how to play baseball. Got out that place and your mama had   1025
taken you and went on to make life without me. Fifteen years was a long time for her
to wait. But that fifteen years cured me of that robbing stuff. Rose'll tell you. She asked
me when I met her if I had gotten all that foolishness out of my system. And I told
her, "Baby, it's you and baseball all what count with me." You hear me, Bono?
I meant it too. She say, "Which one comes first?" I told her, "Baby, ain't no doubt it's   1030
baseball . . . but you stick and get old with me and we'll both outlive this baseball."
Am I right, Rose? And it's true.

ROSE: Man, hush your mouth. You ain't said no such thing. Talking about, "Baby, you
know you'll always be number one with me." That's what you was talking.

TROY: You hear that, Bono. That's why I love her.   1035

BONO: Rose'll keep you straight. You get off the track, she'll straighten you up.

ROSE: Lyons, you better get on up and get Bonnie. She waiting on you.

LYONS: (*Gets up to go.*) Hey, Pop, why don't you come on down to the Grill and hear
me play?

TROY: I ain't going down there. I'm too old to be sitting around in them clubs.   1040

BONO: You got to be good to play down at the Grill.

LYONS: Come on, Pop . . .

TROY: I got to get up in the morning.

LYONS: You ain't got to stay long.

TROY: Naw, I'm gonna get my supper and go on to bed.   1045

LYONS: Well, I got to go. I'll see you again.

TROY: Don't you come around my house on my payday.

ROSE: Pick up the phone and let somebody know you coming. And bring Bonnie with
you. You know I'm always glad to see her.

LYONS: Yeah, I'll do that, Rose. You take care now. See you, Pop. See you, Mr. Bono. See   1050
you, Uncle Gabe.

GABRIEL: Lyons! King of the Jungle!

(**LYONS** *exits.*)

TROY: Is supper ready, woman? Me and you got some business to take care of. I'm gonna
tear it up too.

ROSE: Troy, I done told you now!   1055

TROY: (*Puts his arm around* BONO.) Aw hell, woman . . . this is Bono. Bono like family.
I done known this nigger since . . . how long I done know you?

BONO: It's been a long time.

TROY: I done known this nigger since Skippy was a pup. Me and him done been through
some times.   1060

BONO: You sure right about that.

TROY: Hell, I done know him longer than I known you. And we still standing shoulder to
shoulder. Hey, look here, Bono . . . a man can't ask for no more than that.

> (*Drinks to him.*)

I love you, nigger.

BONO: Hell, I love you too . . . but I got to get home see my woman. You got yours in   1065
hand. I got to go get mine.

> (BONO *starts to exit as* CORY *enters the yard, dressed in his football uniform.*
> *He gives* TROY *a hard, uncompromising look.*)

CORY: What you do that for, Pop?

> (*He throws his helmet down in the direction of* TROY.)

ROSE: What's the matter? Cory . . . what's the matter?

CORY: Papa done went up to the school and told Coach Zellman I can't play football
no more. Wouldn't even let me play the game. Told him to tell the recruiter not   1070
to come.

ROSE: Troy . . .

TROY: What you Troying me for? Yeah, I did it. And the boy know why I did it.

CORY: Why you wanna do that to me? That was the one chance I had.

ROSE: Ain't nothing wrong with Cory playing football, Troy.   1075

TROY: The boy lied to me. I told the nigger if he wanna play football . . . to keep his
chores and hold down that job at the A&P. That was the conditions. Stopped down
there to see Mr. Stawicki . . .

CORY: I can't work after school during the football season, Pop! I tried to tell you that
Mr. Stawicki's holding my job for me. You don't never want to listen to nobody.   1080
And then you wanna go and do this to me!

TROY: I ain't done nothing to you. You done it to yourself.

CORY: Just cause you didn't have a chance! You just scared I'm gonna be better than you,
that's all.

TROY: Come here.   1085

ROSE: Troy . . .

> (CORY *reluctantly crosses over to* TROY.)

TROY: Alright! See. You done made a mistake.

CORY: I didn't even do nothing!

TROY: I'm gonna tell you what your mistake was. See . . . you swung at the ball and didn't
hit it. That's strike one. See, you in the batter's box now. You swung and you missed.   1095
That's strike one. Don't you strike out!

> (*Lights fade to black.*)

ACT II

SCENE I

The following morning. CORY *is at the tree hitting the ball with the bat. He tries to mimic* TROY, *but his swing is awkward, less sure.* rose *enters from the house.*

ROSE: Cory, I want you to help me with this cupboard.

CORY: I ain't quitting the team. I don't care what Poppa say.

ROSE: I'll talk to him when he gets back. He had to go see about your Uncle Gabe. The police done arrested him. Say he was disturbing the peace. He'll be back directly. Come on in here and help me clean out the top of this cupboard.   5

      (CORY *exits into the house.* ROSE *sees* TROY *and* BONO *coming down the alley.*)

      Troy . . . what they say down there?

TROY: Ain't said nothing. I give them fifty dollars and they let him go. I'll talk to you about it. Where's Cory?

ROSE: He's in there helping me clean out these cupboards.

TROY: Tell him to get his butt out here.   10

      (TROY *and* BONO *go over to the pile of wood.* BONO *picks up the saw and begins sawing.*)

TROY: (*To* BONO.) All they want is the money. That makes six or seven times I done went down there and got him. See me coming they stick out their hands.

BONO: Yeah. I know what you mean. That's all they care about . . . that money. They don't care about what's right.

      (*Pause.*)

      Nigger, why you got to go and get some hard wood? You ain't doing nothing but   15
building a little old fence. Get you some soft pine wood. That's all you need.

TROY: I know what I'm doing. This is outside wood. You put pine wood inside the house. Pine wood is inside wood. This here is outside wood. Now you tell me where the fence is gonna be?

BONO: You don't need this wood. You can put it up with pine wood and it's stand as long   20
as you gonna be here looking at it.

TROY: How you know how long I'm gonna be here, nigger? Hell, I might just live forever. Live longer than old man Horsely.

BONO: That's what Magee used to say.

TROY: Magee's a damn fool. Now you tell me who you ever heard of gonna pull their own   25
teeth with a pair of rusty pliers.

BONO: The old folks . . . my granddaddy used to pull his teeth with pliers. They ain't had no dentists for the colored folks back then.

TROY: Get clean pliers! You understand? Clean pliers! Sterilize them! Besides we ain't living back then. All Magee had to do was walk over to Doc Goldblums.   30

BONO: I see where you and that Tallahassee gal . . . that Alberta . . . I see where you all done got tight.

TROY: What you mean "got tight"?

BONO: I see where you be laughing and joking with her all the time.

TROY: I laughs and jokes with all of them, Bono. You know me. 35

BONO: That ain't the kind of laughing and joking I'm talking about.

(CORY *enters from the house.*)

CORY: How you doing, Mr. Bono?

TROY: Cory? Get that saw from Bono and cut some wood. He talking about the wood's too hard to cut. Stand back there, Jim, and let that young boy show you how it's done. 40

BONO: He's sure welcome to it.

(CORY *takes the saw and begins to cut the wood.*)

Whew-e-e! Look at that. Big old strong boy. Look like Joe Louis. Hell, must be getting old the way I'm watching that boy whip through that wood.

CORY: I don't see why Mama want a fence around the yard noways.

TROY: Damn if I know either. What the hell she keeping out with it? She ain't got nothing 45
nobody want.

BONO: Some people build fences to keep people out . . . and other people build fences to keep people in. Rose wants to hold on to you all. She loves you.

TROY: Hell, nigger, I don't need nobody to tell me my wife loves me, Cory . . . go on in the house and see if you can find that other saw. 50

CORY: Where's it at?

TROY: I said find it! Look for it till you find it!

(CORY *exits into the house.*)

What's that supposed to mean? Wanna keep us in?

BONO: Troy . . . I done known you seem like damn near my whole life. You and Rose both. I done know both of you all for a long time. I remember when you met Rose. 55
When you was hitting them baseball out the park. A lot of them old gals was after you then. You had the pick of the litter. When you picked Rose, I was happy for you. That was the first time I knew you had any sense. I said . . . My man Troy knows what he's doing . . . I'm gonna follow this nigger . . . he might take me somewhere. I been following you too. I done learned a whole heap of things about life watching 60
you. I done learned how to tell where the shit lies. How to tell it from the alfalfa. You done learned me a lot of things. You showed me how to not make the same mistakes . . . to take life as it comes along and keep putting one foot in front of the other.

(*Pause.*)

Rose a good woman, Troy. 65

TROY: Hell, nigger, I know she a good woman. I been married to her for eighteen years. What you got on your mind, Bono?

BONO: I just say she a good woman. Just like I say anything. I ain't got to have nothing on my mind.

TROY: You just gonna say she a good woman and leave it hanging out there like that? 70
Why you telling me she a good woman?

BONO: She loves you, Troy. Rose loves you.

TROY: You saying I don't measure up. That's what you trying to say. I don't measure up cause I'm seeing this other gal. I know what you trying to say.

BONO: I know what Rose means to you, Troy. I'm just trying to say I don't want to see 75
you mess up.

TROY: Yeah, I appreciate that, Bono. If you was messing around on Lucille I'd be telling you the same thing.

BONO: Well, that's all I got to say. I just say that because I love you both.

TROY: Hell, you know me . . . I wasn't out there looking for nothing. You can't find a better woman than Rose. I know that. But seems like this woman just stuck onto me where I can't shake her loose. I done wrestled with it, tried to throw her off me . . . but she just stuck on tighter. Now she's stuck on for good. 80

BONO: You's in control . . . that's what you tell me all the time. You responsible for what you do. 85

TROY: I ain't ducking the responsibility of it. As long as it sets right in my heart . . . then I'm okay. Cause that's all I listen to. It'll tell me right from wrong every time. And I ain't talking about doing Rose no bad turn. I love Rose. She done carried me a long ways and I love and respect her for that.

BONO: I know you do. That's why I don't want to see you hurt her. But what you gonna do when she find out? What you got then? If you try and juggle both of them . . . sooner or later you gonna drop one of them. That's common sense. 90

TROY: Yeah, I hear what you saying, Bono. I been trying to figure a way to work it out.

BONO: Work it out right, Troy. I don't want to be getting all up between you and Rose's business . . . but work it so it come out right. 95

TROY: Aw hell, I get all up between you and Lucille's business. When you gonna get that woman that refrigerator she been wanting? Don't tell me you ain't got no money now. I know who your banker is. Mellon don't need that money bad as Lucille want that refrigerator. I'll tell you that.

BONO: Tell you what I'll do . . . when you finish building this fence for Rose . . . I'll buy Lucille that refrigerator. 100

TROY: You done stuck your foot in your mouth now!

(TROY *grabs up a board and begins to saw.* BONO *starts to walk out the yard.*)

Hey, nigger . . . where you going?

BONO: I'm going home. I know you don't expect me to help you now. I'm protecting my money. I wanna see you put that fence up by yourself. That's what I want to see. You'll be here another six month without me. 105

TROY: Nigger, you ain't right.

BONO: When it comes to my money . . . I'm right as fireworks on the Fourth of July.

TROY: Alright, we gonna see now. You better get out your bankbook.

(BONO *exits, and* TROY *continues to work.* ROSE *enters from the house.*)

ROSE: What they say down there? What's happening with Gabe? 110

TROY: I went down there and got him out. Cost me fifty dollars. Say he was disturbing the peace. Judge set up a hearing for him in three weeks. Say to show cause why he shouldn't be re-committed.

ROSE: What was he doing that cause them to arrest him?

TROY: Some kids was teasing him and he run them off home. Say he was howling and carrying on. Some folks seen him and called the police. That's all it was. 115

ROSE: Well, what's you say? What'd you tell the judge?

TROY: Told him I'd look after him. It didn't make no sense to recommit the man. He stuck out his big greasy palm and told me to give him fifty dollars and take him on home. 120

ROSE: Where's he at now? Where'd he go off to?

TROY: He's gone on about his business. He don't need nobody to hold his hand.

ROSE: Well, I don't know. Seem like that would be the best place for him if they did put him into the hospital. I know what you're gonna say. But that's what I think would be best. 125

TROY: The man done had his life ruined fighting for what? And they wanna take and lock him up. Let him be free. He don't bother nobody.

ROSE: Well, everybody got their own way of looking at it I guess. Come on and get your lunch. I got a bowl of lima beans and some cornbread in the oven. Come on get something to eat. Ain't no sense you fretting over Gabe. 130

(ROSE *turns to go into the house.*)

TROY: Rose . . . got something to tell you.

ROSE: Well, come on . . . wait till I get this food on the table.

TROY: Rose!

(*She stops and turns around.*)

I don't know how to say this.

(*Pause.*)

I can't explain it none. It just sort of grows on you till it gets out of hand. It starts out like a little bush . . . and the next thing you know it's a whole forest. 135

ROSE: Troy . . . what is you talking about?

TROY: I'm talking, woman, let me talk. I'm trying to find a way to tell you . . . I'm gonna be a daddy. I'm gonna be somebody's daddy.

ROSE: Troy . . . you're not telling me this? You're gonna be . . . what? 140

TROY: Rose . . . now . . . see . . .

ROSE: You telling me you gonna be somebody's daddy? You telling your wife this?

(GABRIEL *enters from the street. He carries a rose in his hand.*)

GABRIEL: Hey, Troy! Hey, Rose!

ROSE: I have to wait eighteen years to hear something like this.

GABRIEL: Hey, Rose . . . I got a flower for you. 145

(*He hands it to her.*)

That's a rose. Same rose like you is.

ROSE: Thanks, Gabe.

GABRIEL: Troy, you ain't mad at me is you? Them bad mens come and put me away. You ain't mad at me is you?

TROY: Naw, Gabe, I ain't mad at you. 150

ROSE: Eighteen years and you wanna come with this.

GABRIEL: (*Takes a quarter out of his pocket.*) See what I got? Got a brand new quarter.

TROY: Rose . . . it's just . . .

ROSE: Ain't nothing you can say, Troy. Ain't no way of explaining that.

GABRIEL: Fellow that give me this quarter had a whole mess of them. I'm gonna keep this quarter till it stop shining. 155

ROSE: Gabe, go on in the house there. I got some watermelon in the frigidaire. Go on and get you a piece.

GABRIEL: Say, Rose . . . you know I was chasing hellhounds and them bad mens come and get me and take me away. Troy helped me. He come down there and told them they better let me go before he beat them up. Yeah, he did! 160

ROSE: You go on and get you a piece of watermelon, Gabe. Them bad mens is gone now.

GABRIEL: Okay, Rose . . . gonna get me some watermelon. The kind with the stripes on it.

(GABRIEL *exits into the house.*)

ROSE: Why, Troy? Why? After all these years to come dragging this in to me now. It don't   165
make no sense at your age. I could have expected this ten or fifteen years ago, but
not now.

TROY: Age ain't got nothing to do with it, Rose.

ROSE: I done tried to be everything a wife should be. Every-thing a wife could be. Been
married eighteen years and I got to live to see the day you tell me you been seeing   170
another woman and done fathered a child by her. And you know I ain't never
wanted no half nothing in my family. My whole family is half. Everybody got
different fathers and mothers . . . my two sisters and my brother. Can't hardly tell
who's who. Can't never sit down and talk about Papa and Mama. It's your papa
and your mama and my papa and my mama . . .   175

TROY: Rose . . . stop it now.

ROSE: I ain't never wanted that for none of my children. And now you wanna drag your
behind in here and tell me something like this.

TROY: You ought to know. It's time for you to know.

ROSE: Well, I don't want to know, goddamn it!   180

TROY: I can't just make it go away. It's done now. I can't wish the circumstance of the
thing away.

ROSE: And you don't want to either. Maybe you want to wish me and my boy away.
Maybe that's what you want? Well, you can't wish us away. I've got eighteen years
of my life invested in you. You ought to have stayed upstairs in my bed where you   185
belong.

TROY: Rose . . . now listen to me . . . we can get a handle on this thing. We can talk this
out . . . come to an understanding.

ROSE: All of a sudden it's "we." Where was "we" at when you was down there rolling
around with some godforsaken woman? "We" should have come to an understand-   190
ing before you started making a damn fool of yourself. You're a day late and a dollar
short when it comes to an understanding with me.

TROY: It's just . . . She gives me a different idea . . . a different understanding about myself.
I can step out of this house and get away from the pressures and problems . . . be a
different man. I ain't got to wonder how I'm gonna pay the bills or get the roof fixed.   195
I can just be a part of myself that I ain't never been.

ROSE: What I want to know . . . is do you plan to continue seeing her. That's all you can
say to me.

TROY: I can sit up in her house and laugh. Do you understand what I'm saying. I can
laugh out loud . . . and it feels good. It reaches all the way down to the bottom of   200
my shoes.

(*Pause.*)

Rose, I can't give that up.

ROSE: Maybe you ought to go on and stay down there with her . . . if she a better woman
than me.

TROY: It ain't about nobody being a better woman or nothing. Rose, you ain't the blame.   205
A man couldn't ask for no woman to be a better wife than you've been. I'm respon-
sible for it. I done locked myself into a pattern trying to take care of you all that
I forgot about myself.

ROSE: What the hell was I there for? That was my job, not somebody else's.

TROY: Rose, I done tried all my life to live decent . . . to live a clean . . . hard . . . useful 210
life. I tried to be a good husband to you. In every way I knew how. Maybe I come
into the world backwards, I don't know. But . . . you born with two strikes on you
before you come to the plate. You got to guard it closely . . . always looking for the
curve-ball on the inside corner. You can't afford to let none get past you. You can't
afford a call strike. If you going down . . . you going down swinging. Everything 215
lined up against you. What you gonna do. I fooled them, Rose. I bunted. When I
found you and Cory and a halfway decent job . . . I was safe. Couldn't nothing
touch me. I wasn't gonna strike out no more. I wasn't going back to the penitentiary.
I wasn't gonna lay in the streets with a bottle of wine. I was safe. I had me a family.
A job. I wasn't gonna get that last strike. I was on first looking for one of them boys 220
to knock me in. To get me home.

ROSE: You should have stayed in my bed, Troy.

TROY: Then when I saw that gal . . . she firmed up my backbone. And I got to thinking
that if I tried . . . I just might be able to steal second. Do you understand after
eighteen years I wanted to steal second. 225

ROSE: You should have held me tight. You should have grabbed me and held on.

TROY: I stood on first base for eighteen years and I thought . . . well, goddamn it . . . go
on for it!

ROSE: We're not talking about baseball! We're talking about you going off to lay in bed
with another woman . . . and then bring it home to me. That's what we're talking 230
about. We ain't talking about no baseball.

TROY: Rose, you're not listening to me. I'm trying the best I can to explain it to you. It's
not easy for me to admit that I been standing in the same place for eighteen years.

ROSE: I been standing with you! I been right here with you, Troy. I got a life too. I gave
eighteen years of my life to stand in the same spot with you. Don't you think I ever 235
wanted other things? Don't you think I had dreams and hopes? What about my life?
What about me? Don't you think it ever crossed my mind to want to know other
men? That I wanted to lay up somewhere and forget about my responsibilities? That
I wanted someone to make me laugh so I could feel good? You not the only one
who's got wants and needs. But I held on to you, Troy. I took all my feelings, my 240
wants and needs, my dreams . . . and I buried them inside you. I planted a seed and
watched and prayed over it. I planted myself inside you and waited to bloom. And
it didn't take me no eighteen years to find out the soil was hard and rocky and it
wasn't never gonna bloom.

But I held on to you, Troy. I held you tighter. You was my husband. I owed you 245
everything I had. Every part of me I could find to give you. And upstairs in that
room . . . with the darkness falling in on me . . . I gave everything I had to try and
erase the doubt that you wasn't the finest man in the world. And wherever you was
going . . . I wanted to be there with you. Cause you was my husband. Cause that's
the only way I was gonna survive as your wife. You always talking about what you 250
give . . . and what you don't have to give. But you take too. You take . . . and don't
even know nobody's giving!

(ROSE *turns to exit into the house;* TROY *grabs her arm.*)

TROY: You say I take and don't give!

ROSE: Troy! You're hurting me!

TROY: You say I take and don't give. 255

ROSE: Troy . . . you're hurting my arm! Let go!

TROY: I done give you everything I got. Don't you tell that lie on me.

ROSE: Troy!

TROY: Don't you tell that lie on me!

(CORY *enters from the house.*)

CORY: Mama!   260
ROSE: Troy. You're hurting me.
TROY: Don't you tell me about no taking and giving.

> (CORY *comes up behind* TROY *and grabs him.* TROY, *surprised, is thrown off
> balance just as* CORY *throws a glancing blow that catches him on the chest and
> knocks him down.* TROY *is stunned, as is* CORY.)

ROSE: Troy. Troy. No!

(TROY *gets to his feet and starts at* CORY.)

Troy . . . no. Please! Troy!

(ROSE *pulls on* TROY *to hold him back.* TROY *stops himself.*)

TROY: (*To* CORY.) Alright. That's strike two. You stay away from around me, boy. Don't   265
you strike out. You living with a full count. Don't you strike out.

(TROY *exits out the yard as the lights go down.*)

SCENE II

It is six months later, early afternoon. TROY *enters from the house and starts to exit the yard.*
ROSE *enters from the house.*

ROSE: Troy, I want to talk to you.
TROY: All of a sudden, after all this time, you want to talk to me, huh? You ain't wanted
to talk to me for months. You ain't wanted to talk to me last night. You ain't wanted
no part of me then. What you wanna talk to me about now?   270
ROSE: Tomorrow's Friday.
TROY: I know what day tomorrow is. You think I don't know tomorrow's Friday? My
whole life I ain't done nothing but look to see Friday coming and you got to tell me
it's Friday.
ROSE: I want to know if you're coming home.   275
TROY: I always come home, Rose. You know that. There ain't never been a night I ain't
come home.
ROSE: That ain't what I mean . . . and you know it. I want to know if you're coming
straight home after work.
TROY: I figure I'd cash my check . . . hang out at Taylors' with the boys . . . maybe play a 280
game of checkers . . .
ROSE: Troy, I can't live like this. I won't live like this. You livin' on borrowed time with
me. It's been going on six months now you ain't been coming home.
TROY: I be here every night. Every night of the year. That's 365 days.
ROSE: I want you to come home tomorrow after work.   285
TROY: Rose . . . I don't mess up my pay. You know that now. I take my pay and I give it
to you. I don't have no money but what you give me back. I just want to have a little
time to myself . . . a little time to enjoy life.
ROSE: What about me? When's my time to enjoy life?

TROY: I don't know what to tell you, Rose. I'm doing the best I can.   290

ROSE: You ain't been home from work but time enough to change your clothes and run out . . . and you wanna call that the best you can do?

TROY: I'm going over to the hospital to see Alberta. She went into the hospital this afternoon. Look like she might have the baby early. I won't be gone long.

ROSE: Well, you ought to know. They went over to Miss Pearl's and got Gabe today. She   295 said you told them to go ahead and lock him up.

TROY: I ain't said no such thing. Whoever told you that is telling a lie. Pearl ain't doing nothing but telling a big fat lie.

ROSE: She ain't had to tell me. I read it on the papers.

TROY: I ain't told them nothing of the kind.   300

ROSE: I saw it right there on the papers.

TROY: What it say, huh?

ROSE: It said you told them to take him.

TROY: Then they screwed that up, just the way they screw up everything. I ain't worried about what they got on the paper.   305

ROSE: Say the government send part of his check to the hospital and the other part to you.

TROY: I ain't got nothing to do with that if that's the way it works. I ain't made up the rules about how it work.

ROSE: You did Gabe just like you did Cory. You wouldn't sign the paper for Cory . . . but   310 you signed for Gabe. You signed that paper.

(The telephone is heard ringing inside the house.)

TROY: I told you I ain't signed nothing, woman! The only thing I signed was the release form. Hell, I can't read, I don't know what they had on that paper! I ain't signed nothing about sending Gabe away.

ROSE: I said send him to the hospital . . . you said let him be free . . . now you done went   315 down there and signed him to the hospital for half his money. You went back on yourself, Troy. You gonna have to answer for that.

TROY: See now . . . you been over there talking to Miss Pearl. She done got mad cause she ain't getting Gabe's rent money. That's all it is. She's liable to say anything.

ROSE: Troy, I seen where you signed the paper.   320

TROY: You ain't seen nothing I signed. What she doing got papers on my brother anyway? Miss Pearl telling a big fat lie. And I'm gonna tell her about it too! You ain't seen nothing I signed. Say . . . you ain't seen nothing I signed.

(ROSE exits into the house to answer the telephone. Presently she returns.)

ROSE: Troy . . . that was the hospital. Alberta had the baby.

TROY: What she have? What is it?   325

ROSE: It's a girl.

TROY: I better get on down to the hospital to see her.

ROSE: Troy . . .

TROY: Rose . . . I got to go see her now. That's only right . . . what's the matter . . . the baby's alright, ain't it?   330

ROSE: Alberta died having the baby.

TROY: Died . . . you say she's dead? Alberta's dead?

ROSE: They said they done all they could. They couldn't do nothing for her.

TROY: The baby? How's the baby?

ROSE: They say it's healthy. I wonder who's gonna bury her.   335

TROY: She had family, Rose. She wasn't living in the world by herself.

ROSE: I know she wasn't living in the world by herself.

TROY: Next thing you gonna want to know if she had any insurance.

ROSE: Troy, you ain't got to talk like that.

TROY: That's the first thing that jumped out your mouth. "Who's gonna bury her?" Like   340
    I'm fixing to take on that task for myself.

ROSE: I am your wife. Don't push me away.

TROY: I ain't pushing nobody away. Just give me some space. That's all. Just give me
    some room to breathe.

(ROSE *exits into the house.* TROY *walks about the yard.*)

TROY: (*With a quiet rage that threatens to consume him.*) Alright . . . Mr. Death. See   345
    now . . . I'm gonna tell you what I'm gonna do. I'm gonna take and build me a
    fence around this yard. See? I'm gonna build me a fence around what belongs to me.
    And then I want you to stay on the other side. See? You stay over there until you're
    ready for me. Then you come on. Bring your army. Bring your sickle. Bring your
    wrestling clothes. I ain't gonna fall down on my vigilance this time. You ain't gonna   350
    sneak up on me no more. When you ready for me . . . when the top of your list say
    Troy Maxson . . . that's when you come around here. You come up and knock on
    the front door. Ain't nobody else got nothing to do with this. This is between you
    and me. Man to man. You stay on the other side of that fence until you ready for me.
    Then you come up and knock on the front door. Anytime you want. I'll be ready   355
    for you.

(*The lights go down to black.*)

SCENE III

The lights come up on the porch. It is late evening three days later. ROSE *sits listening to the ball game waiting for* TROY. *The final out of the game is made and* ROSE *switches off the radio.* TROY *enters the yard carrying an infant wrapped in blankets. He stands back from the house and calls.*

    ROSE *enters and stands on the porch. There is a long, awkward silence, the weight of which grows heavier with each passing second.*

TROY: Rose . . . I'm standing here with my daughter in my arms. She ain't but a wee
    bittie little old thing. She don't know nothing about grownups' business. She
    innocent . . . and she ain't got no mama.

ROSE: What you telling me for, Troy?   360

(*She turns and exits into the house.*)

TROY: Well . . . I guess we'll just sit out here on the porch.

(*He sits down on the porch. There is an awkward indelicateness about the way he handles the baby. His largeness engulfs and seems to swallow it. He speaks loud enough for* ROSE *to hear.*)

A man's got to do what's right for him. I ain't sorry for nothing I done. It felt right
in my heart.

(*To the baby.*)

What you smiling at? Your daddy's a big man. Got these great big old hands. But sometimes he's scared. And right now your daddy's scared cause we sitting out here and ain't got no home. Oh, I been homeless before. I ain't had no little baby with me. But I been homeless. You just be out on the road by your lonesome and you see one of them trains coming and you just kinda go like this . . .   365

(*He sings as a lullaby.*)

> Please, Mr. Engineer let a man ride the line
> Please, Mr. Engineer let a man ride the line   370
> I ain't got no ticket please let me ride the blinds

(**ROSE** *enters from the house.* **TROY** *hearing her steps behind him, stands and faces her.*)

She's my daughter, Rose. My own flesh and blood. I can't deny her no more than I can deny them boys.

(*Pause.*)

You and them boys is my family. You and them and this child is all I got in the world. So I guess what I'm saying is . . . I'd appreciate it if you'd help take care   375
of her.

ROSE: Okay, Troy . . . you're right. I'll take care of your baby for you . . . cause . . . like you say . . . she's innocent . . . and you can't visit the sins of the father upon the child. A motherless child has got a hard time.

(*She takes the baby from him.*)

From right now . . . this child got a mother. But you a womanless man.   380

(**ROSE** *turns and exits into the house with the baby. Lights go down to black.*)

SCENE IV

It is two months later. LYONS *enters from the street. He knocks on the door and calls.*

LYONS: Hey, Rose! (*Pause.*) Rose!
ROSE: (*From inside the house.*) Stop that yelling. You gonna wake up Raynell. I just got her to sleep.
LYONS: I just stopped by to pay Papa this twenty dollars I owe him. Where's Papa at?
ROSE: He should be here in a minute. I'm getting ready to go down to the church. Sit   385
down and wait on him.
LYONS: I got to go pick up Bonnie over her mother's house.
ROSE: Well, sit it down there on the table. He'll get it.
LYONS: (*Enters the house and sets the money on the table.*) Tell Papa I said thanks. I'll see
you again.   390
ROSE: Alright, Lyons. We'll see you.

(**LYONS** *starts to exit as* **CORY** *enters.*)

CORY: Hey, Lyons.
LYONS: What's happening, Cory. Say man, I'm sorry I missed your graduation. You know I had a gig and couldn't get away. Otherwise, I would have been there, man. So what you doing?   395

CORY: I'm trying to find a job.

LYONS: Yeah I know how that go, man. It's rough out here. Jobs are scarce.

CORY: Yeah, I know.

LYONS: Look here, I got to run. Talk to Papa . . . he know some people. He'll be able to help get you a job. Talk to him . . . see what he say.   400

CORY: Yeah . . . alright, Lyons.

LYONS: You take care. I'll talk to you soon. We'll find some time to talk.

> (LYONS *exits the yard.* CORY *wanders over to the tree, picks up the bat and assumes a batting stance. He studies an imaginary pitcher and swings. Dissatisfied with the result, he tries again.* TROY *enters. They eye each other for a beat.* CORY *puts the bat down and exits the yard.* TROY *starts into the house as* ROSE *exits with* RAYNELL. *She is carrying a cake.*)

TROY: I'm coming in and everybody's going out.

ROSE: I'm taking this cake down to the church for the bake-sale. Lyons was by to see. you He stopped by to pay you your twenty dollars. It's laying in there on the table.   405

TROY: (*Going into his pocket.*) Well . . . here go this money.

ROSE: Put it in there on the table, Troy. I'll get it.

TROY: What time you coming back?

ROSE: Ain't no use in you studying me. It don't matter what time I come back.   410

TROY: I just asked you a question, woman. What's the matter . . . can't I ask you a question?

ROSE: Troy, I don't want to go into it. Your dinner's in there on the stove. All you got to do is heat it up. And don't you be eating the rest of them cakes in there. I'm coming back for them. We having a bakesale at the church tomorrow.   415

> (ROSE *exits the yard.* TROY *sits down on the steps, takes a pint bottle from his pocket, opens it and drinks. He begins to sing.*)

TROY: Hear it ring! Hear it ring!
    Had an old dog his name was Blue
    You know Blue was mighty true
    You know Blue as a good old dog
    Blue trees a possum in a hollow log   420
    You know from that he was a good old dog.

> (BONO *enters the yard.*)

BONO: Hey, Troy.

TROY: Hey, what's happening, Bono?

BONO: I just thought I'd stop by to see you.

TROY: What you stop by and see me for? You ain't stopped by in a month of Sundays.   425
Hell, I must owe you money or something.

BONO: Since you got your promotion I can't keep up with you. Used to see you everyday.
Now I don't even know what route you working.

TROY: They keep switching me around. Got me out in Green-tree now . . . hauling white folks' garbage.   430

BONO: Greentree, huh? You lucky, at least you ain't got to be lifting them barrels. Damn if they ain't getting heavier. I'm gonna put in my two years and call it quits.

TROY: I'm thinking about retiring myself.

BONO: You got it easy. You can drive for another five years.

TROY: It ain't the same, Bono. It ain't like working the back of the truck. Ain't got nobody   435
to talk to . . . feel like you working by yourself. Naw, I'm thinking about retiring.
How's Lucille?
BONO: She alright. Her arthritis get to acting up on her sometime. Saw Rose on my way
in. She going down to the church, huh?
TROY: Yeah, she took up going down there. All them preachers looking for somebody to   440
fatten their pockets.

(*Pause.*)

Got some gin here.
BONO: Naw, thanks. I just stopped by to say hello.
TROY: Hell, nigger . . . you can take a drink. I ain't never known you to say no to a drink.
You ain't got to work tomorrow.   445
BONO: I just stopped by. I'm fixing to go over to Skinner's. We got us a domino game
going over his house every Friday.
TROY: Nigger, you can't play no dominoes. I used to whup you four games out of five.
BONO: Well, that learned me. I'm getting better.
TROY: Yeah? Well, that's alright.   450
BONO: Look here . . . I got to be getting on. Stop by sometime, huh?
TROY: Yeah, I'll do that, Bono. Lucille told Rose you bought her a new refrigerator.
BONO: Yeah, Rose told Lucille you had finally built your fence . . . so I figured we'd call
it even.
TROY: I knew you would.   455
BONO: Yeah . . . okay. I'll be talking to you.
TROY: Yeah, take care, Bono. Good to see you. I'm gonna stop over.
BONO: Yeah. Okay, Troy.

(**BONO** *exits.* **TROY** *drinks from the bottle.*)

TROY: Old Blue died and I dig his grave
Let him down with a golden chain   460
Every night when I hear old Blue bark
I know Blue treed a possum in Noah's Ark.
Hear it ring! Hear it ring!

(**CORY** *enters the yard. They eye each other for a beat.* **TROY** *is sitting in the
middle of the steps.* **CORY** *walks over.*)

CORY: I got to get by.
TROY: Say what? What's you say?   465
CORY: You in my way. I got to get by.
TROY: You got to get by where? This is my house. Bought and paid for. In full. Took me
fifteen years. And if you wanna go in my house and I'm sitting on the steps . . . you
say excuse me. Like your mama taught you.
CORY: Come on, Pop . . . I got to get by.   470

(**CORY** *starts to maneuver his way past* **TROY**. **TROY** *grabs his leg and shoves
him back.*)

TROY: You just gonna walk over top of me?
CORY: I live here too!
TROY: (*Advancing toward him.*) You just gonna walk over top of me in my own house?
CORY: I ain't scared of you.
TROY: I ain't asked if you was scared of me. I asked you if you was fixing to walk over top   475
of me in my own house? That's the question. You ain't gonna say excuse me? You
just gonna walk over top of me?

CORY: If you wanna put it like that.

TROY: How else am I gonna put it?

CORY: I was walking by you to go into the house cause you sitting on the steps drunk, 480
singing to yourself. You can put it like that.

TROY: Without saying excuse me???

(CORY *doesn't respond.*)

I asked you a question. Without saying excuse me???

CORY: I ain't got to say excuse me to you. You don't count around here no more.

TROY: Oh, I see . . . I don't count around here no more. You ain't got to say excuse me to 485
your daddy. All of a sudden you done got so grown that your daddy don't count
around here no more . . . Around here in his own house and yard that he done paid
for with the sweat of his brow. You done got so grown to where you gonna take over.
You gonna take over my house. Is that right? You gonna wear my pants. You gonna
go in there and stretch out on my bed. You ain't got to say excuse me cause I don't 490
count around here no more. Is that right?

CORY: That's right. You always talking this dumb stuff. Now, why don't you just get out
my way.

TROY: I guess you got someplace to sleep and something to put in your belly. You got that,
huh? You got that? That's what you need. You got that, huh? 495

CORY: You don't know what I got. You ain't got to worry about what I got.

TROY: You right! You one hundred percent right! I done spent the last seventeen years
worrying about what you got. Now it's your turn, see? I'll tell you what to do. You
grown . . . we done established that. You a man. Now, let's see you act like one.
Turn your behind around and walk out this yard. And when you get out there in 500
the alley . . . you can forget about this house. See? Cause this is my house. You go
on and be a man and get your own house. You can forget about this. Cause this is
mine. You go on and get yours cause I'm through with doing for you.

CORY: You talking about what you did for me . . . what'd you ever give me?

TROY: Them feet and bones! That pumping heart, nigger! I give you more than anybody 505
else is ever gonna give you.

CORY: You ain't never gave me nothing! You ain't never done nothing but hold me back.
Afraid I was gonna be better than you. All you ever did was try and make me scared
of you. I used to tremble every time you called my name. Every time I heard your
footsteps in the house. Wonder-ing all the time . . . what's Papa gonna say if I do 510
this? . . . What's he gonna say if I do that? . . . What's Papa gonna say if I turn on
the radio? And Mama, too . . . she tries . . . but she's scared of you.

TROY: You leave your mama out of this. She ain't got nothing to do with this.

CORY: I don't know how she stand you . . . after what you did to her.

TROY: I told you to leave your mama out of this! 515

(*He advances toward* CORY.)

CORY: What you gonna do . . . give me a whupping? You can't whup me no more. You're
too old. You just an old man.

TROY: (*Shoves him on his shoulder.*) Nigger! That's what you are. You just another nigger
on the street to me!

CORY: You crazy! You know that? 520

TROY: Go on now! You got the devil in you. Get on away from me!

CORY: You just a crazy old man . . . talking about I got the devil in me.

TROY: Yeah, I'm crazy! If you don't get on the other side of that yard . . . I'm gonna show
you how crazy I am! Go on . . . get the hell out of my yard.

CORY: It ain't your yard. You took Uncle Gabe's money he got from the army to buy this   525
house and then you put him out.
TROY: (TROY *advances on* CORY.) Get your black ass out of my yard!

(TROY'S *advance backs* CORY *up against the tree.* CORY *grabs up the bat.*)

CORY: I ain't going nowhere! Come on . . . put me out! I ain't scared of you.
TROY: That's my bat!
CORY: Come on!   530
TROY: Put my bat down!
CORY: Come on, put me out.

(CORY *swings at* TROY, *who backs across the yard.*)

What's the matter? You so bad . . . put me out!

(TROY *advances toward* CORY.)

CORY: (*Backing up.*) Come on! Come on!
TROY: You're gonna have to use it! You wanna draw that bat back on me . . . you're gonna   535
have to use it.
CORY: Come on! . . . Come on!

(CORY *swings the bat at* TROY *a second time. He misses.* TROY *continues to
advance toward him.*)

TROY: You're gonna have to kill me! You wanna draw that bat back on me. You're gonna
have to kill me.

(CORY, *backed up against the tree, can go no farther.* TROY *taunts him. He
sticks out his head and offers him a target.*)

Come on! Come on!   540

(CORY *is unable to swing the bat.* TROY *grabs it.*)

TROY: Then I'll show you.

(CORY *and* TROY *struggle over the bat. The struggle is fierce and fully engaged.*
TROY *ultimately is the stronger, and takes the bat from* CORY *and stands over
him ready to swing. He stops himself.*)

Go on and get away from around my house.

(CORY, *stung by his defeat, picks himself up, walks slowly out of the yard and up
the alley.*)

CORY: Tell Mama I'll be back for my things.
TROY: They'll be on the other side of that fence.

(CORY *exits.*)

TROY: I can't taste nothing. Helluljah! I can't taste nothing no more. (TROY *assumes a*   545
batting posture and begins to taunt Death, the fastball in the outside corner.) Come on!
It's between you and me now! Come on! Anytime you want! Come on! I be ready for
you . . . but I ain't gonna be easy.

(*The lights go down on the scene.*)

SCENE V

The time is 1965. The lights come up in the yard. It is the morning of TROY'S *funeral. A funeral plaque with a light hangs beside the door. There is a small garden plot off to the side. There is noise and activity in the house as* ROSE, LYONS *and* BONO *have gathered. The door opens and* RAYNELL, *seven years old, enters dressed in a flannel nightgown. She crosses to the garden and pokes around with a stick.* ROSE *calls from the house.*

ROSE: Raynell!
RAYNELL: Mam?   550
ROSE: What you doing out there?
RAYNELL: Nothing.

> (ROSE *comes to the door.*)

ROSE: Girl, get in here and get dressed. What you doing?
RAYNELL: Seeing if my garden growed.
ROSE: I told you it ain't gonna grow overnight. You got to wait.   555
RAYNELL: It don't look like it never gonna grow. Dag!
ROSE: I told you a watched pot never boils. Get in here and get dressed.
RAYNELL: This ain't even no pot, Mama.
ROSE: You just have to give it a chance. It'll grow. Now you come on and do what I told
    you. We got to be getting ready. This ain't no morning to be playing around. You   560
    hear me?
RAYNELL: Yes, mam.

> (ROSE *exits into the house.* RAYNELL *continues to poke at her garden with
> a stick.* CORY *enters. He is dressed in a Marine corporal's uniform, and carries
> a duffel bag. His posture is that of a military man, and his speech has a clipped
> sternness.*)

CORY: (*To* RAYNELL.) Hi.

> (*Pause.*)

    I bet your name is Raynell.
RAYNELL: Uh huh.   565
CORY: Is your mama home?

> (RAYNELL *runs up on the porch and calls through the screen door.*)

RAYNELL: Mama . . . there's some man out here. Mama?

> (ROSE *comes to the door.*)

ROSE: Cory? Lord have mercy! Look here, you all!

> (ROSE *and* CORY *embrace in a tearful reunion as* BONO *and* LYONS *enter
> from the house dressed in funeral clothes.*)

BONO: Aw, looka here . . .
ROSE: Done got all grown up!   570
CORY: Don't cry, Mama. What you crying about?
ROSE: I'm just so glad you made it.
CORY: Hey Lyons. How you doing, Mr. Bono.

(LYONS *goes to embrace* CORY.)

LYONS: Look at you, man. Look at you. Don't he look good, Rose. Got them Corporal stripes.   575

ROSE: What took you so long.

CORY: You know how the Marines are, Mama. They got to get all their paperwork straight before they let you do anything.

ROSE: Well, I'm sure glad you made it. They let Lyons come. Your Uncle Gabe's still in the hospital. They don't know if they gonna let him out or not. I just talked to them   580
a little while ago.

LYONS: A Corporal in the United States Marines.

BONO: Your daddy knew you had it in you. He used to tell me all the time.

LYONS: Don't he look good, Mr. Bono?

BONO: Yeah, he remind me of Troy when I first met him.   585

(*Pause.*)

Say, Rose, Lucille's down at the church with the choir. I'm gonna go down and get the pallbearers lined up. I'll be back to get you all.

ROSE: Thanks, Jim.

CORY: See you, Mr. Bono.

LYONS: (*With his arm around* RAYNELL.) Cory . . . look at Raynell. Ain't she precious?   590
She gonna break a whole lot of hearts.

ROSE: Raynell, come and say hello to your brother. This is your brother, Cory. You remember Cory.

RAYNELL: No, Mam.

CORY: She don't remember me, Mama.   595

ROSE: Well, we talk about you. She heard us talk about you. (*To* RAYNELL.) This is your brother, Cory. Come on and say hello.

RAYNELL: Hi.

CORY: Hi. So you're Raynell. Mama told me a lot about you.

ROSE: You all come on into the house and let me fix you some breakfast. Keep up your   600
strength.

CORY: I ain't hungry, Mama.

LYONS: You can fix me something, Rose. I'll be in there in a minute.

ROSE: Cory, you sure you don't want nothing. I know they ain't feeding you right.

CORY: No, Mama . . . thanks. I don't feel like eating. I'll get something later.   605

ROSE: Raynell . . . get on upstairs and get that dress on like I told you.

(ROSE *and* RAYNELL *exit into the house.*)

LYONS: So . . . I hear you thinking about getting married.

CORY: Yeah, I done found the right one, Lyons. It's about time.

LYONS: Me and Bonnie been split up about four years now. About the time Papa retired.   610
I guess she just got tired of all them changes I was putting her through.

(*Pause.*)

I always knew you was gonna make something out your-self. Your head was always in the right direction. So . . . you gonna stay in . . . make it a career . . . put in your twenty years?

CORY: I don't know. I got six already, I think that's enough.

LYONS: Stick with Uncle Sam and retire early. Ain't nothing out here. I guess Rose told   615
you what happened with me. They got me down the workhouse. I thought I was being slick cashing other people's checks.

CORY: How much time you doing?

LYONS: They give me three years. I got that beat now. I ain't got but nine more months. It ain't so bad. You learn to deal with it like anything else. You got to take the crookeds with the straights. That's what Papa used to say. He used to say that when he struck out. I seen him strike out three times in a row . . . and the next time up he hit the ball over the grandstand. Right out there in Home-stead Field. He wasn't satisfied hitting in the seats . . . he want to hit it over everything! After the game he had two hundred people standing around waiting to shake his hand. You got to take the crookeds with the straights. Yeah, papa was something else.

CORY: You still playing?

LYONS: Cory . . . you know I'm gonna do that. There's some fellows down there we got us a band . . . we gonna try and stay together when we get out . . . but yeah, I'm still playing. It still helps me to get out of bed in the morning. As long as it do that I'm gonna be right there playing and trying to make some sense out of it.

ROSE: (*Calling.*) Lyons, I got these eggs in the pan.

LYONS: Let me go on and get these eggs, man. Get ready to go bury Papa.

(*Pause.*)

How you doing? You doing alright?

(CORY *nods.* LYONS *touches him on the shoulder and they share a moment of silent grief.* LYONS *exits into the house.* CORY *wanders about the yard.* RAYNELL *enters.*)

RAYNELL: Hi.

CORY: Hi.

RAYNELL: Did you used to sleep in my room?

CORY: Yeah . . . that used to be my room.

RAYNELL: That's what Papa call it. "Cory's room." It got your football in the closet.

(ROSE *comes to the door.*)

ROSE: Raynell, get in there and get them good shoes on.

RAYNELL: Mama, can't I wear these. Them other ones hurt my feet.

ROSE: Well, they just gonna have to hurt your feet for a while. You ain't said they hurt your feet when you went down to the store and got them.

RAYNELL: They didn't hurt then. My feet done got bigger.

ROSE: Don't you give me no backtalk now. You get in there and get them shoes on.

(RAYNELL *exits into the house.*)

Ain't too much changed. He still got that piece of rag tied to that tree. He was out here swinging that bat. I was just ready to go back in the house. He swung that bat and then he just fell over. Seem like he swung it and stood there with this grin on his face . . . and then he just fell over. They carried him on down to the hospital, but I knew there wasn't no need . . . why don't you come on in the house?

CORY: Mama . . . I got something to tell you. I don't know how to tell you this . . . but I've got to tell you . . . I'm not going to Papa's funeral.

ROSE: Boy, hush your mouth. That's your daddy you talking about. I don't want hear that kind of talk this morning. I done raised you to come to this? You standing there all healthy and grown talking about you ain't going to your daddy's funeral.

CORY: Mama . . . listen . . .

ROSE: I don't want to hear it, Cory. You just get that thought out of your head.

CORY: I can't drag Papa with me everywhere I go. I've got to say no to him. One time in my life I've got to say no.

ROSE: Don't nobody have to listen to nothing like that. I know you and your daddy ain't 660 seen eye to eye, but I ain't got to listen to that kind of talk this morning. Whatever was between you and your daddy . . . the time has come to put it aside. Just take it and set it over there on the shelf and forget about it. Disrespecting your daddy ain't gonna make you a man, Cory. You got to find a way to come to that on your own. Not going to your daddy's funeral ain't gonna make you a man. 665

CORY: The whole time I was growing up . . . living in his house . . . Papa was like a shadow that followed you every-where. It weighed on you and sunk into your flesh. It would wrap around you and lay there until you couldn't tell which one was you anymore. That shadow digging in your flesh. Trying to crawl in. Trying to live through you. Everywhere I looked, Troy Maxson was staring back at me . . . hiding 670 under the bed . . . in the closet. I'm just saying I've got to find a way to get rid of that shadow, Mama.

ROSE: You just like him. You got him in you good.

CORY: Don't tell me that, Mama.

ROSE: You Troy Maxson all over again. 675

CORY: I don't want to be Troy Maxson. I want to be me.

ROSE: You can't be nobody but who you are, Cory. That shadow wasn't nothing but you growing into yourself. You either got to grow into it or cut it down to fit you. But that's all you got to make life with. That's all you got to measure yourself against that world out there. Your daddy wanted you to be everything he wasn't . . . and at 680 the same time he tried to make you into everything he was. I don't know if he was right or wrong . . . but I do know he meant to do more good than he meant to do harm. He wasn't always right. Sometimes when he touched he bruised. And sometimes when he took me in his arms he cut.

When I first met your daddy I thought . . . Here is a man I can lay down with 685 and make a baby. That's the first thing I thought when I seen him. I was thirty years old and had done seen my share of men. But when he walked up to me and said, "I can dance a waltz that'll make you dizzy," I thought, Rose Lee, here is a man that you can open yourself up to and be filled to bursting. Here is a man that can fill all them empty spaces you been tipping around the edges of. One of them 690 empty spaces was being somebody's mother.

I married your daddy and settled down to cooking his supper and keeping clean sheets on the bed. When your daddy walked through the house he was so big he filled it up. That was my first mistake. Not to make him leave some room for me. For my part in the matter. But at that time I wanted that. 695 I wanted a house that I could sing in. And that's what your daddy gave me. I didn't know to keep up his strength I had to give up little pieces of mine. I did that. I took on his life as mine and mixed up the pieces so that you couldn't hardly tell which was which anymore. It was my choice. It was my life and I didn't have to live it like that. But that's what life offered me in the 700 way of being a woman and I took it. I grabbed hold of it with both hands.

By the time Raynell came into the house, me and your daddy had done lost touch with one another. I didn't want to make my blessing off of nobody's misfortune . . . but I took on to Raynell like she was all them babies I had wanted and never had. 705

(*The phone rings.*)

Like I'd been blessed to relive a part of my life. And if the Lord see fit to keep up my strength . . . I'm gonna do her just like your daddy did you . . . I'm gonna give her the best of what's in me.

RAYNELL: (*Entering, still with her old shoes.*) Mama . . . Reverend Tollivier on the phone.

(ROSE *exits into the house.*)

RAYNELL: Hi.   710
CORY: Hi.
RAYNELL: You in the Army or the Marines?
CORY: Marines.
RAYNELL: Papa said it was the Army. Did you know Blue?
CORY: Blue? Who's Blue?   715
RAYNELL: Papa's dog what he sing about all the time.
CORY: (*Singing.*)
    Hear it ring! Hear it ring!
    I had a dog his name was Blue
    You know Blue was mighty true   720
    You know Blue was a good old dog
    Blue treed a possum in a hollow log
    You know from that he was a good old dog.
    Hear it ring! Hear it ring!

(RAYNELL *joins in singing.*)

CORY and RAYNELL: Blue treed a possum out on a limb   725
    Blue looked at me and I looked at him
    Grabbed that possum and put him in a sack
    Blue stayed there till I came back
    Old Blue's feets was big and round
    Never allowed a possum to touch the ground.   730
    Old Blue died and I dug his grave
    I dug his grave with a silver spade
    Let him down with a golden chain
    And every night I call his name
    Go on Blue, you good dog you   735
    Go on Blue, you good dog you
RAYNELL: Blue laid down and died like a man
    Blue laid down and died . . .
BOTH: Blue laid down and died like a man
    Now he's treeing possums in the Promised Land   740
    I'm gonna tell you this to let you know
    Blue's gone where the good dogs go
    When I hear old Blue bark
    When I hear old Blue bark
    Blue treed a possum in Noah's Ark   745
    Blue treed a possum in Noah's Ark.

(ROSE *comes to the screen door.*)

ROSE: Cory, we gonna be ready to go in a minute.
CORY: (*To* RAYNELL.) You go on in the house and change them shoes like Mama told you so we can go to Papa's funeral.

RAYNELL: Okay, I'll be back. 750

> (RAYNELL *exits into the house.* CORY *gets up and crosses over to the tree.* ROSE *stands in the screen door watching him.* GABRIEL *enters from the alley.*)

GABRIEL: (*Calling.*) Hey, Rose!
ROSE: Gabe?
GABRIEL: I'm here, Rose. Hey Rose, I'm here!

> (ROSE *enters from the house.*)

ROSE: Lord . . . Look here, Lyons!
LYONS: See, I told you, Rose . . . I told you they'd let him come. 755
CORY: How you doing, Uncle Gabe?
LYONS: How you doing, Uncle Gabe?
GABRIEL: Hey, Rose. It's time. It's time to tell St. Peter to open the gates. Troy, you ready? You ready, Troy. I'm gonna tell St. Peter to open the gates. You get ready now.

> (GABRIEL, *with great fanfare, braces himself to blow. The trumpet is without a mouthpiece. He puts the end of it into his mouth and blows with great force, like a man who has been waiting some twenty-odd years for this single moment. No sound comes out of the trumpet. He braces himself and blows again with the same result. A third time he blows. There is a weight of impossible description that falls away and leaves him bare and exposed to a frightful realization. It is a trauma that a sane and normal mind would be unable to withstand. He begins to dance. A slow, strange dance, eerie and lifegiving. A dance of atavistic signature and ritual.* LYONS *attempts to embrace him.* GABRIEL *pushes* LYONS *away. He begins to howl in what is an attempt at song, or perhaps a song turning back into itself in an attempt at speech. He finishes his dance and the gates of heaven stand open as wide as God's closet.*)

That's the way that go! 760

> (*Blackout.*)

Tony Kushner (1956–)

Angels in America, Part I: Millennium Approaches
(1992)

In his program note for the production of *Angels in America* at the Royal National Theatre in London, Tony Kushner wrote that his initial idea for the play had several seemingly disconnected elements: "I wanted to write about three things: Roy Cohn, who had just died; AIDS; and Mormons. I had no idea what Mormons might have to do with Roy Cohn or AIDS, but I wanted to find out. I had a title: *Angels in America.*" The play that resulted from this idea, *Angels in America: A Gay Fantasia on National Themes*, weaves these threads together in a sweeping epic of American life in 1980s New York. In *Angels*, Kushner realistically depicts the horrors and human costs of the AIDS epidemic while using characters such as Roy Cohn to metaphorically call attention to the larger sickness infecting American values. Originally intended as a single play, Kushner expanded the story into two parts: *Millennium Approaches* and *Perestroika*. Both received Tony Awards for Best Play, and *Millennium Approaches* was also recognized for the Pulitzer Prize.

Angels is difficult to classify as a particular genre because it contains both realistic and non-realistic elements. The scenes between the characters Joe and Harper, for instance, are intimately drawn through realistic dialogue that depicts their struggles to reconcile their Mormon faith with their repressed psychological yearnings. Harper's interactions with "Mr. Lies," by contrast, take place in a drug-induced hallucinatory world of conscious theatricality. A student of the work of Bertolt Brecht, Kushner uses non-realistic storytelling devices in the play to call attention to theatrical artifice. In his notes to the play, Kushner invites theatre artists to embrace this technique: "it's OK if the wires show and maybe it's good that they do." The play is thus both intimately real and intentionally theatrical.

Though *Angels* is rightly regarded as a landmark in queer theatre for its nuanced depiction of same-sex relationships, it is not a play whose meaning is easily reduced to a social issue. In his review of the original production, *New York Times* critic Frank Rich argued that the play had a "wrenching grasp on such timeless dramatic matters as life, death, and faith." Indeed, the play endures not only because of its still-topical political explorations but also because of the accessible humanity of its flawed characters.

In the twenty years since the play's first performance at the Eureka Theatre in San Francisco in 1991, *Angels* has become one of the most studied and produced plays of the twentieth century. It was revived in New York as recently as 2010 and continues to be performed in regional, community, and university theatres across the country.

Tony Kushner

Angels in America, Part I: Millennium Approaches
(1992)

Characters

ROY M. COHN, *a successful New York lawyer and unofficial power broker*

JOSEPH (JOE) PORTER PITT, *chief clerk for Justice Theodore Wilson of the Federal Court of Appeals, Second Circuit*

HARPER AMATY PITT, *Joe's wife, an agoraphobic with a mild Valium addiction*

LOUIS IRONSON, *a word processor working for the Second Circuit Court of Appeals*

PRIOR WALTER, *Louis's boyfriend. Occasionally works as a club designer or caterer, otherwise lives very modestly but with great style off a small trust fund*

HANNAH PORTER PITT, *Joe's mother, currently residing in Salt Lake City, living off her deceased husband's army pension*

BELIZE, *a former drag queen and former lover of Prior's: A registered nurse. Belize's name was originally Norman Arriaga; Belize is a drag name that stuck*

THE ANGEL, *four divine emanations, Fluor, Phosphor, Lumen and Candle; manifest in One: the Continental Principality of America. She has magnificent steel-gray wings*

RABBI ISIDOR CHEMELWITZ, *an orthodox Jewish rabbi, played by the actor playing Hannah*

MR. LIES, *Harper's imaginary friend, a travel agent, who in style of dress and speech suggests a jazz musician; he always wears a large lapel badge emblazoned "IOTA" (The International Order of Travel Agents). He is played by the actor playing Belize*

THE MAN IN THE PARK, *played by the actor playing Prior*

THE VOICE, *the voice of The Angel*

HENRY, *Roy's doctor, played by the actor playing Hannah*

EMILY, *a nurse, played by the actor playing The Angel*

MARTIN HELLER, *a Reagan Administration Justice Department flackman, played by the actor playing Harper*

SISTER ELLA CHAPTER, *a Salt Lake City real-estate saleswoman, played by the actor playing The Angel*

PRIOR 1, *the ghost of a dead Prior Walter from the 13th century, played by the actor playing Joe. He is a blunt, gloomy medieval farmer with a gutteral Yorkshire accent*

PRIOR 2, *the ghost of a dead Prior Walter from the 17th century, played by the actor playing Roy. He is a Londoner, sophisticated, with a High British accent*

THE ESKIMO, *played by the actor playing Joe*

THE WOMAN IN THE SOUTH BRONX, *played by the actor playing The Angel*

ETHEL ROSENBERG, *played by the actor playing Hannah*

PLAYWRIGHT'S NOTES

A DISCLAIMER:——*Roy M. Cohn, the character, is based on the late Roy M. Cohn (1927–1986), who was all too real; for the most part the acts attributed to the character Roy, such as his illegal conferences with Judge Kaufmann during the trial of Ethel Rosenberg, are to be found in the historical record. But this Roy is a work of dramatic fiction; his words are my invention, and liberties have been taken.*

A NOTE ABOUT THE STAGING:——*The play benefits from a pared-down style of presentation, with minimal scenery and scene shifts done rapidly (no blackouts!), employing the cast as well as stagehands—which makes for an actor-driven event, as this must be. The moments of magic—the appearance and disappearance of Mr. Lies and the ghosts, the Book hallucination, and the ending—are to be fully realized, as bits of wonderful theatrical illusion—which means it's OK if the wires show, and maybe it's good that they do, but the magic should at the same time be thoroughly amazing.*

> . . . In a murderous time
> the heart breaks and breaks
> and lives by breaking.
>
> —STANLEY KUNITZ
> "THE TESTING-TREE"

ACT I

Bad News October–November 1985

SCENE I

The last days of October. RABBI ISIDOR CHEMELWITZ *alone onstage with a small coffin. It is a rough pine box with two wooden pegs, one at the foot and one at the head, holding the lid in place. A prayer shawl embroidered with a Star of David is draped over the lid, and by the head a yarzheit candle is burning.*

RABBI ISIDOR CHEMELWITZ: (*He speaks sonorously, with a heavy Eastern European accent, unapologetically consulting a sheet of notes for the family names.*) Hello and good morning. I am Rabbi Isidor Chemelwitz of the Bronx Home for Aged Hebrews. We are here this morning to pay respects at the passing of Sarah Ironson, devoted wife of Benjamin Ironson, also deceased, loving and caring mother of her sons Morris, Abraham, and Samuel, and her daughters Esther and Rachel; beloved grandmother of Max, Mark, Louis, Lisa, Maria . . . uh . . . Lesley, Angela, Doris, Luke and Eric. (*Looks more closely at paper.*) Eric? This is a Jewish name? (*Shrugs.*) Eric. A large and loving family. We assemble that we may mourn collectively this good and righteous woman.

(*He looks at the coffin.*)

This woman. I did not know this woman. I cannot accurately describe her attributes, nor do justice to her dimensions. She was. . . . Well, in the Bronx Home of Aged Hebrews are many like this, the old, and to many I speak but not to be frank with this one. She preferred silence. So I do not know her and yet I know her. She was . . .   15

(*He touches the coffin.*)

. . . not a person but a whole kind of person, the ones who crossed the ocean, who brought with us to America the villages of Russia and Lithuania—and how we struggled, and how we fought, for the family, for the Jewish home, so that you would not grow up *here,* in this strange place, in the melting pot where nothing melted. Descendants of this immigrant woman, you do not grow up in America,   20
you and your children and their children with the goyische names. You do not live in America. No such place exists. Your clay is the clay of some Litvak shtetl, your air the air of the steppes—because she carried the old world on her back across the ocean, in a boat, and she put it down on Grand Concourse Avenue, or in Flatbush, and she worked that earth into your bones, and you pass it to your children, this   25
ancient, ancient culture and home.

(*Little pause.*)

You can never make that crossing that she made, for such Great Voyages in this world do not any more exist. But every day of your lives the miles that voyage between that place and this one you cross. Every day. You understand me? In you that journey is.   30
So . . .
     She was the last of the Mohicans, this one was. Pretty soon . . . all the old will be dead.

SCENE II

Same day. ROY *and* JOE *in* ROY'S *office.* ROY *at an impressive desk, bare except for a very elaborate phone system, rows and rows of flashing buttons which bleep and beep and whistle incessantly, making chaotic music underneath* ROY'S *conversations.* JOE *is sitting, waiting.* ROY *conducts business with great energy, impatience and sensual abandon: gesticulating, shouting, cajoling, crooning, playing the phone, receiver and hold button with virtuosity and love.*

ROY: (*Hitting a button.*) Hold. (*To* JOE.) I wish I was an octopus, a fucking octopus. Eight loving arms and all those suckers. Know what I mean?   35
JOE: No, I . . .
ROY: (*Gesturing to a deli platter of little sandwiches on his desk.*) You want lunch?
JOE: No, that's OK really I just . . .
ROY: (*Hitting a button.*) Ailene? Roy Cohn. Now what kind of a greeting is. . . . I thought we were friends, Ai. . . . Look Mrs. Soffer you don't have to get. . . . You're upset.   40
You're yelling. You'll aggravate your condition, you shouldn't yell, you'll pop little blood vessels in your face if you yell. . . . No that was a joke, Mrs. Soffer, I was joking. . . . I already apologized sixteen times for that, Mrs. Soffer, you . . . (*While she's fulminating,* ROY *covers the mouthpiece with his hand and talks to* JOE.) This'll

take a minute, eat already, what is this tasty sandwich here it's—(*He takes a bite of*   45
a sandwich.) Mmmmm, liver or some. . . . Here.

(*He pitches the sandwich to* JOE, *who catches it and returns it to the platter.*)

ROY: (*Back to Mrs. Soffer.*) Uh huh, uh huh. . . . No, I already told you, it wasn't a
vacation, it was business. Mrs. Soffer, I have clients in Haiti, Mrs. Soffer, I. . . .
Listen, Ailene, YOU THINK I'M THE ONLY GODDAM LAWYER IN
HISTORY EVER MISSED A COURT DATE? Don't make such a big fucking. . . .   50
Hold. (*He hits the hold button.*) You HAG!

JOE: If this is a bad time . . .

ROY: Bad time? This is a good time! (*Button.*) Baby doll, get me. . . . Oh fuck, wait . . .
(*Button, button.*) Hello? Yah. Sorry to keep you holding, Judge Hollins, I. . . . Oh
Mrs. Hollins, sorry dear deep voice you got. Enjoying your visit? (*Hand over mouth-*   55
piece, to JOE.) She sounds like a truckdriver and he sounds like Kate Smith, very
confusing. Nixon appointed him, all the geeks are Nixon appointees . . . (*To
Mrs. Hollins.*) Yeah yeah right good so how many tickets dear? Seven. For what,
Cats, 42nd Street, what? No you wouldn't like La Cage, trust me, I know. Oh for
godsake. . . . Hold. (*Button, button.*) Baby doll, seven for Cats or something, any-   60
thing hard to get, I don't give a fuck what and neither will they. (*Button; to* JOE.)
You see *La Cage?*

JOE: No, I . . .

ROY: Fabulous. Best thing on Broadway. Maybe ever. (*Button.*) Who? Aw, Jesus H. Christ,
Harry, no, Harry, Judge John Francis Grimes, Manhattan Family Court. Do I have   65
to do every goddam thing myself? *Touch* the bastard, Harry, and don't call me on
this line again, I told you not to . . .

JOE: (*Starting to get up.*) Roy, uh, should I wait outside or . . .

ROY: (*To* JOE.) Oh sit. (*To* HARRY.) You hold. I pay you to hold fuck you Harry you
jerk. (*Button.*) Half-wit dick-brain. (*Instantly philosophical.*) I see the universe, Joe,   70
as a kind of sandstorm in outer space with winds of mega-hurricane velocity, but
instead of grains of sand it's shards and splinters of glass. You ever feel that way?
Ever have one of those days?

JOE: I'm not sure I . . .

ROY: So how's life in Appeals? How's the Judge?   75

JOE: He sends his best.

ROY: He's a good man. Loyal. Not the brightest man on the bench, but he has manners.
And a nice head of silver hair.

JOE: He gives me a lot of responsibility.

ROY: Yeah, like writing his decisions and signing his name.   80

JOE: Well . . .

ROY: He's a nice guy. And you cover admirably.

JOE: Well, thanks, Roy, I . . .

ROY: (*Button.*) Who is *this?* Well who the fuck are *you?* Hold—(*Button.*) Harry? Eighty-
seven grand, something like that. Fuck him. Eat me. New Jersey, chain of porno film   85
stores in, uh, Weehawken. That's—Harry, that's the beauty of the law. (*Button.*) So,
baby doll, what? *Cats?* Bleah. (*Button.*) Cats! It's about cats. Singing cats, you'll love
it. Eight o'clock, the theatre's always at eight. (*Button.*) Fucking tourists. (*Button,
then to* JOE.) Oh live a little, Joe, *eat* something for Christ sake—

JOE: Um, Roy, could you . . .   90

ROY: What? (*To* HARRY.) Hold a minute. (*Button.*) Mrs. Soffer? Mrs. . . . (*Button.*)
God-fucking-dammit to hell, where is . . .

JOE: (*Overlapping.*) Roy, I'd really appreciate it if . . .
ROY: (*Overlapping.*) Well she was here a minute ago, baby doll, see if . . .

(*The phone starts making three different beeping sounds, all at once.*)

ROY: (*Smashing buttons.*) Jesus fuck this goddam thing . . .   95
JOE: (*Overlapping.*) I really wish you wouldn't . . .
ROY: (*Overlapping.*) Baby doll? Ring the Post get me Suzy see if . . .

(*The phone starts whistling loudly.*)

ROY: CHRIST!
JOE: Roy.
ROY: (*Into receiver.*) Hold. (*Button; to* JOE.) What?   100
JOE: Could you please not take the Lord's name in vain?

(*Pause.*)

I'm sorry. But please. At least while I'm . . .
ROY: (*Laughs, then.*) Right. Sorry. Fuck.
    Only in America. (*Punches a button.*) Baby doll, tell 'em all to fuck off. Tell 'em I   105
    died. You handle Mrs. Soffer. Tell her it's on the way. Tell her I'm schtupping the
    judge. I'll call her back. I *will* call her. I *know* how much I borrowed. She's got four
    hundred times that stuffed up her. . . . Yeah, tell her I said that. (*Button. The phone
    is silent.*)
    So, Joe.
JOE: I'm sorry Roy, I just . . .   110
ROY: No no no no, principles count, I respect principles, I'm not religious but I like
    God and God likes me. Baptist, Catholic?
JOE: Mormon.
ROY: Mormon. Delectable. Absolutely. Only in America. So, Joe. Whattya think?
JOE: It's . . . well . . .   115
ROY: Crazy life.
JOE: Chaotic.
ROY: Well but God bless chaos. Right?
JOE: Ummm . . .
ROY: Huh. Mormons. I knew Mormons, in, um, Nevada.   120
JOE: Utah, mostly.
ROY: No, these Mormons were in Vegas.
    So. So, how'd you like to go to Washington and work for the Justice Department?
JOE: Sorry?
ROY: How'd you like to go to Washington and work for the Justice Department? All I gotta   125
    do is pick up the phone, talk to Ed, and you're in.
JOE: In . . . what, exactly?
ROY: Associate Assistant Something Big. Internal Affairs, heart of the woods, something
    nice with clout.
JOE: Ed . . . ?   130
ROY: Meese. The Attorney General.
JOE: Oh.
ROY: I just have to pick up the phone . . .
JOE: I have to think.
                                                                                                135
ROY: Of course.

(*Pause.*)

It's a great time to be in Washington, Joe.

JOE: Roy, it's incredibly exciting . . .

ROY: And it would mean something to me. You understand?

> (*Little pause.*)

JOE: I . . . can't say how much I appreciate this Roy, I'm sort of . . . well, stunned, I
mean. . . . Thanks, Roy. But I have to give it some thought. I have to ask my wife.   140

ROY: Your wife. Of course.

JOE: But I really appreciate . . .

ROY: Of course. Talk to your wife.

SCENE III

Later that day. HARPER *at home, alone. She is listening to the radio and talking to herself, as
she often does. She speaks to the audience.*

HARPER: People who are lonely, people left alone, sit talking nonsense to the air, imagining . . . beautiful systems dying, old fixed orders spiraling apart . . .   145
When you look at the ozone layer, from outside, from a spaceship, it looks like a
pale blue halo, a gentle, shimmering aureole encircling the atmosphere encircling
the earth. Thirty miles above our heads, a thin layer of three-atom oxygen mol-
ecules, product of photosynthesis, which explains the fussy vegetable preference for
visible light, its rejection of darker rays and emanations. Danger from without. It's   150
a kind of gift, from God, the crowning touch to the creation of the world: guardian angels, hands linked, make a spherical net, a blue-green nesting orb, a shell of
safety for life itself. But everywhere, things are collapsing, lies surfacing, systems of
defense giving way. . . . This is why, Joe, this is why I shouldn't be left alone.

> (*Little pause.*)

I'd like to go traveling. Leave you behind to worry. I'll send postcards with strange   155
stamps and tantalizing messages on the back. "Later maybe." "Nevermore . . . "

> (MR. LIES, *a travel agent, appears.*)

HARPER: Oh! You startled me!

MR. LIES: Cash, check or credit card?

HARPER: I remember you. You're from Salt Lake. You sold us the plane tickets when we
flew here. What are you doing in Brooklyn?   160

MR. LIES: You said you wanted to travel . . .

HARPER: And here you are. How thoughtful.

MR. LIES: Mr. Lies. Of the International Order of Travel Agents. We mobilize the globe,
we set people adrift, we stir the populace and send nomads eddying across the planet.
We are adepts of motion, acolytes of the flux. Cash, check or credit card. Name your   165
destination.

HARPER: Antarctica, maybe. I want to see the hole in the ozone. I heard on the radio . . .

MR. LIES: (*He has a computer terminal in his briefcase.*) I can arrange a guided tour. Now?

HARPER: Soon. Maybe soon. I'm not safe here you see. Things aren't right with me.
Weird stuff happens . . .   170

MR. LIES: Like?

HARPER: Well, like you, for instance. Just appearing. Or last week . . . well never mind. People are like planets, you need a thick skin. Things get to me, Joe stays away and now. . . . Well look. My dreams are talking back to me.

MR. LIES: It's the price of rootlessness. Motion sickness. The only cure: to keep moving. 175

HARPER: I'm undecided. I feel . . . that something's going to give. It's 1985. Fifteen years till the third millennium. Maybe Christ will come again. Maybe seeds will be planted, maybe there'll be harvests then, maybe early figs to eat, maybe new life, maybe fresh blood, maybe companionship and love and protection, safety from what's outside, maybe the door will hold, or maybe . . . maybe the troubles will come, and the end 180 will come, and the sky will collapse and there will be terrible rains and showers of poison light, or maybe my life is really fine, maybe Joe loves me and I'm only crazy thinking otherwise, or maybe not, maybe it's even worse than I know, maybe . . . I want to know, maybe I don't. The suspense, Mr. Lies, it's killing me.

MR. LIES: I suggest a vacation. 185

HARPER: (*Hearing something.*) That was the elevator. Oh God, I should fix myself up, I. . . . You have to go, you shouldn't be here . . . you aren't even real.

MR. LIES: Call me when you decide . . .

HARPER: Go!

(*The travel agent* [MR. LIES] *vanishes as* JOE *enters.*)

JOE: Buddy? 190
Buddy? Sorry I'm late. I was just . . . out. Walking. Are you mad?

HARPER: I got a little anxious.

JOE: Buddy kiss.

(*They kiss.*)

Nothing to get anxious about.
So. So how'd you like to move to Washington? 195

SCENE IV

Same day. LOUIS *and* PRIOR *outside the funeral home, sitting on a bench, both dressed in funereal finery, talking. The funeral service for Sarah Ironson has just concluded and* LOUIS *is about to leave for the cemetery.*

LOUIS: My grandmother actually saw Emma Goldman speak. In Yiddish. But all Grandma could remember was that she spoke well and wore a hat.
What a weird service. That rabbi . . .

PRIOR: A definite find. Get his number when you go to the graveyard. I want him to bury me. 200

LOUIS: Better head out there. Everyone gets to put dirt on the coffin once it's lowered in.

PRIOR: Oooh. Cemetery fun. Don't want to miss that.

LOUIS: It's an old Jewish custom to express love. Here, Grandma, have a shovelful. Latecomers run the risk of finding the grave completely filled.
She was pretty crazy. She was up there in that home for ten years, talking to 205 herself. I never visited. She looked too much like my mother.

PRIOR: (*Hugs him.*) Poor Louis. I'm sorry your grandma is dead.

LOUIS: Tiny little coffin, huh?

Sorry I didn't introduce you to. . . . I always get so closety at these family things.

PRIOR: Butch. You get butch. (*Imitating.*) "Hi Cousin Doris, you don't remember me I'm   210
Lou, Rachel's boy." Lou, not Louis, because if you say Louis they'll hear the sibilant S.

LOUIS: I don't have a . . .

PRIOR: I don't blame you, hiding. Bloodlines. Jewish curses are the worst. I personally
would dissolve if anyone ever looked me in the eye and said "Feh." Fortunately WASPs
don't say "Feh." Oh and by the way, darling, cousin Doris is a dyke.   215

LOUIS: No.

Really?'

PRIOR: You don't notice anything. If I hadn't spent the last four years fellating you I'd
swear you were straight.

LOUIS: You're in a pissy mood. Cat still missing?   220

(*Little pause.*)

PRIOR: Not a furball in sight. It's your fault.

LOUIS: It is?

PRIOR: I warned you, Louis. Names are important. Call an animal "Little Sheba" and you
can't expect it to stick around. Besides, it's a dog's name.

LOUIS: I wanted a dog in the first place, not a cat. He sprayed my books.   225

PRIOR: He was a female cat.

LOUIS: Cats are stupid, high-strung predators. Babylonians sealed them up in bricks. Dogs
have brains.

PRIOR: Cats have intuition.

LOUIS: A sharp dog is as smart as a really dull two-year-old child.   230

PRIOR: Cats know when something's wrong.

LOUIS: Only if you stop feeding them.

PRIOR: They know. That's why Sheba left, because she knew.

LOUIS: Knew what?

(*Pause.*)

PRIOR: I did my best Shirley Booth this morning, floppy slippers, housecoat, curlers, can   235
of Little Friskies; "Come back, little Sheba, come back. . . ." To no avail. Le chat, elle
ne reviendra jamais, jamais . . .

(*He removes his jacket, rolls up his sleeve, shows* LOUIS *a dark purple spot on the
underside of his arm near the shoulder.*)

See.

LOUIS: That's just a burst blood vessel.

PRIOR: Not according to the best medical authorities.   240

LOUIS: What?

(*Pause.*)

Tell me.

PRIOR: K.S., baby. Lesion number one. Lookit. The wine-dark kiss of the angel of death.

LOUIS: (*Very softly, holding* PRIOR'S *arm.*) Oh please . . .

PRIOR: I'm a lesionnaire. The Foreign Lesion. The American Lesion. Lesionnaire's disease.   245

LOUIS: Stop.

PRIOR: My troubles are lesion.
LOUIS: Will you *stop*.
PRIOR: Don't you think I'm handling this well? I'm going to die.
LOUIS: Bullshit.   250
PRIOR: Let go of my arm.
LOUIS: No.
PRIOR: Let go.
LOUIS: (*Grabbing* PRIOR, *embracing him ferociously.*) No.
PRIOR: I can't find a way to spare you baby. No wall like the wall of hard scientific fact.   255
    K.S. Wham. Bang your head on that.
LOUIS: Fuck you. (*Letting go.*) Fuck you fuck you fuck you.
PRIOR: Now that's what I like to hear. A mature reaction.
    Let's go see if the cat's come home.
    Louis?   260
LOUIS: When did you find this?
PRIOR: I couldn't tell you.
LOUIS: Why?
PRIOR: I was scared, Lou.
LOUIS: Of what?   265
PRIOR: That you'll leave me.
LOUIS: Oh.

    (*Little pause.*)

PRIOR: Bad timing, funeral and all, but I figured as long as we're on the subject of death . . .
LOUIS: I have to go bury my grandma.
PRIOR: Lou?   270

    (*Pause.*)

    Then you'll come home?
LOUIS: Then I'll come home.

SCENE V

Same day, later on. Split scene: JOE *and* HARPER *at home;* LOUIS *at the cemetery with* RABBI
ISIDOR CHEMELWITZ *and the little coffin.*

HARPER: Washington?
JOE: It's an incredible honor, buddy, and . . .
HARPER: I have to think.   275
JOE: Of course.
HARPER: Say no.
JOE: You said you were going to think about it.
HARPER: I don't want to move to Washington.
JOE: Well I do.   280
HARPER: It's a giant cemetery, huge white graves and mausoleums everywhere.
JOE: We could live in Maryland. Or Georgetown.

HARPER: We're happy here.

JOE: That's not really true, buddy, we . . .

HARPER: Well happy enough! Pretend-happy. That's better than nothing.   285

JOE: It's time to make some changes, Harper.

HARPER: No changes. Why?

JOE: I've been chief clerk for four years. I make twenty-nine thousand dollars a year. That's ridiculous. I graduated fourth in my class and I make less than anyone I know. And I'm . . . I'm tired of being a clerk, I want to go where something good is happening.   290

HARPER: Nothing good happens in Washington. We'll forget church teachings and buy furniture at . . . at *Conran's* and become yuppies. I have too much to do here.

JOE: Like what?

HARPER: I *do* have things . . .

JOE: What things?   295

HARPER: I have to finish painting the bedroom.

JOE: You've been painting in there for over a year.

HARPER: I know, I. . . . It just isn't done because I never get time to finish it.

JOE: Oh that's . . . that doesn't make sense. You have all the time in the world. You could finish it when I'm at work.   300

HARPER: I'm afraid to go in there alone.

JOE: Afraid of what?

HARPER: I heard someone in there. Metal scraping on the wall. A man with a knife, maybe.

JOE: There's no one in the bedroom, Harper.

HARPER: Not now.   305

JOE: Not this morning either.

HARPER: How do you know? You were at work this morning. There's something creepy about this place. Remember *Rosemary's Baby?*

JOE: *Rosemary's Baby?*

HARPER: Our apartment looks like that one. Wasn't that apartment in Brooklyn?   310

JOE: No, it was . . .

HARPER: Well, it looked like this. It did.

JOE: Then let's move.

HARPER: Georgetown's worse. *The Exorcist* was in Georgetown.

JOE: The devil, everywhere you turn, huh, buddy.   315

HARPER: Yeah. Everywhere.

JOE: How many pills today, buddy?

HARPER: None. One. Three. Only three.

LOUIS: (*Pointing at the coffin.*) Why are there just two little wooden pegs holding the lid down?   320

RABBI ISIDOR CHEMELWITZ: So she can get out easier if she wants to.

LOUIS: I hope she stays put.
    I pretended for years that she was already dead. When they called to say she had died it was a surprise. I abandoned her.

RABBI ISIDOR CHEMELWITZ: "Sharfer vi di tson fun a shlang iz an umdankbar kind!"   325

LOUIS: I don't speak Yiddish.

RABBI ISIDOR CHEMELWITZ: Sharper than the serpent's tooth is the ingratitude of children. Shakespeare. *Kenig Lear.*

LOUIS: Rabbi, what does the Holy Writ say about someone who abandons someone he loves at a time of great need?   330

RABBI ISIDOR CHEMELWITZ: Why would a person do such a thing?

LOUIS: Because he has to.

Maybe because this person's sense of the world, that it will change for the better with struggle, maybe a person who has this neo-Hegelian positivist sense of constant historical progress towards happiness or perfection or something, who feels very powerful because he feels connected to these forces, moving uphill all the time . . . maybe that person can't, um, incorporate sickness into this sense of how things are supposed to go. Maybe vomit . . . and sores and disease . . . really frighten him, maybe . . . he isn't so good with death. 335

RABBI ISIDOR CHEMELWITZ: The Holy Scriptures have nothing to say about such a person. 340

LOUIS: Rabbi, I'm afraid of the crimes I may commit.

RABBI ISIDOR CHEMELWITZ: Please, mister. I'm a sick old rabbi facing a long drive home to the Bronx. You want to confess, better you should find a priest.

LOUIS: But I'm not a Catholic, I'm a Jew. 345

RABBI ISIDOR CHEMELWITZ: Worse luck for you, bubbulah. Catholics believe in forgiveness. Jews believe in Guilt. (*He pats the coffin tenderly.*)

LOUIS: You just make sure those pegs are in good and tight.

RABBI ISIDOR CHEMELWITZ: Don't worry, mister. The life she had, she'll stay put. She's better off. 350

JOE: Look, I know this is scary for you. But try to understand what it means to me. Will you try?

HARPER: Yes.

JOE: Good. Really try.

I think things are starting to change in the world. 355

HARPER: But I don't want . . .

JOE: Wait. For the good. Change for the good. America has rediscovered itself. Its sacred position among nations. And people aren't ashamed of that like they used to be. This is a great thing. The truth restored. Law restored. That's what President Reagan's done, Harper. He says "Truth exists and can be spoken proudly." And the country 360 responds to him. We become better. More good. I need to be a part of that, I need something big to lift me up. I mean, six years ago the world seemed in decline, horrible, hopeless, full of unsolvable problems and crime and confusion and hunger and . . .

HARPER: But it still seems that way. More now than before. They say the ozone layer 365 is . . .

JOE: Harper . . .

HARPER: And today out the window on Atlantic Avenue there was a schizophrenic traffic cop who was making these . . .

JOE: Stop it! I'm trying to make a point. 370

HARPER: So am I.

JOE: You aren't even making sense, you . . .

HARPER: My point is the world seems just as . . .

JOE: It only seems that way to you because you never go out in the world, Harper, and you have emotional problems. 375

HARPER: I do so get out in the world.

JOE: You don't. You stay in all day, fretting about imaginary . . .

HARPER: I get out. I do. You don't know what I do.

JOE: You don't stay in all day.

HARPER: No. 380

JOE: Well. . . . Yes you do.

HARPER: That's what you think.

JOE: Where do you go?

HARPER: Where do *you* go? When you walk.

(*Pause, then angrily.*) And I DO NOT have emotional problems.

JOE: I'm sorry.   385

HARPER: And if I do have emotional problems it's from living with you. Or . . .

JOE: I'm sorry buddy, I didn't mean to . . .

HARPER: Or if you do think I do then you should never have married me. You have all these secrets and lies.

JOE: I want to be married to you, Harper.   390

HARPER: You shouldn't. You never should.

(*Pause.*)

Hey buddy. Hey buddy.

JOE: Buddy kiss . . .

(*They kiss.*)

HARPER: I heard on the radio how to give a blowjob.

JOE: What?   395

HARPER: You want to try?

JOE: You really shouldn't listen to stuff like that.

HARPER: Mormons can give blowjobs.

JOE: *Harper.*

HARPER: (*Imitating his tone.*) *Joe.*   400

It was a little Jewish lady with a German accent. This is a good time. For me to make a baby.

(*Little pause.* JOE *turns away.*)

HARPER: Then they went on to a program about holes in the ozone layer. Over Antarctica. Skin burns, birds go blind, icebergs melt. The world's coming to an end.

SCENE VI

First week of November. In the men's room of the offices of the Brooklyn Federal Court of Appeals; LOUIS *is crying over the sink;* JOE *enters.*

JOE: Oh, um. . . . Morning.   405

LOUIS: Good morning, counselor.

JOE: (*He watches* LOUIS *cry.*) Sorry, I . . . I don't know your name.

LOUIS: Don't bother. Word processor. The lowest of the low.

JOE: (*Holding out hand.*) Joe Pitt. I'm with Justice Wilson . . .

LOUIS: Oh, I know that. Counselor Pitt. Chief Clerk.   410

JOE: Were you . . . are you OK?

LOUIS: Oh, yeah. Thanks. What a nice man.

JOE: Not so nice.

LOUIS: What?

JOE: Not so nice. Nothing. You sure you're . . .   415

LOUIS: Life sucks shit. Life . . . just sucks shit.

JOE: What's wrong?

LOUIS: Run in my nylons.

JOE: Sorry . . . ?

LOUIS: Forget it. Look, thanks for asking.   420

JOE: Well . . .

LOUIS: I mean it really is nice of you.

      (*He starts crying again.*)

    Sorry, sorry, sick friend . . .

JOE: Oh, I'm sorry.

LOUIS: Yeah, yeah, well, that's sweet.   425

    Three of your colleagues have preceded you to this baleful sight and you're the first one to ask. The others just opened the door, saw me, and fled. I hope they had to pee real bad.

JOE: (*Handing him a wad of toilet paper.*) They just didn't want to intrude.

LOUIS: Hah. Reaganite heartless macho asshole lawyers.   430

JOE: Oh, that's unfair.

LOUIS: What is? Heartless? Macho? Reaganite? Lawyer?

JOE: I voted for Reagan.

LOUIS: You did?

JOE: Twice.   435

LOUIS: Twice? Well, oh boy. A Gay Republican.

JOE: Excuse me?

LOUIS: Nothing.

JOE: I'm not . . .

    Forget it.   440

LOUIS: Republican? Not Republican? Or . . .

JOE: What?

LOUIS: What?

JOE: Not gay. I'm not gay.

LOUIS: Oh. Sorry. (*Blows his nose loudly.*) It's just . . .   445

JOE: Yes?

LOUIS: Well, sometimes you can tell from the way a person sounds that . . . I mean you *sound* like a . . .

JOE: No I don't. Like what?

LOUIS: Like a Republican.   450

    (*Little pause.* JOE *knows he's being teased;* LOUIS *knows he knows.* JOE *decides to be a little brave.*)

JOE: (*Making sure no one else is around.*) Do I? Sound like a . . . ?

LOUIS: What? Like a . . . ? Republican, or . . . ? Do *I*?

JOE: Do you what?

LOUIS: Sound like a . . . ?

JOE: Like a . . . ?   455

    I'm confused.

LOUIS: Yes.

    My name is Louis. But all my friends call me Louise. I work in Word Processing. Thanks for the toilet paper.

    (LOUIS *offers* JOE *his hand,* JOE *reaches,* LOUIS *feints and pecks* JOE *on the cheek, then exits.*)

SCENE VII

A week later. Mutual dream scene. PRIOR *is at a fantastic makeup table, having a dream, applying the face.* HARPER *is having a pill-induced hallucination. She has these from time to time. For some reason,* PRIOR *has appeared in this one. Or* HARPER *has appeared in* PRIOR's *dream. It is bewildering.*

PRIOR: (*Alone, putting on makeup, then examining the results in the mirror; to the audience.*)   460
"I'm ready for my closeup, Mr. DeMille."
    One wants to move through life with elegance and grace, blossoming infrequently but with exquisite taste, and perfect timing, like a rare bloom, a zebra orchid. . . . One wants. . . . But one so seldom gets what one wants, does one? No. One does not. One gets fucked. Over. One . . . dies at thirty, robbed of . . .   465
decades of majesty.
    Fuck this shit. Fuck this shit.

> (*He almost crumbles; he pulls himself together; he studies his handiwork in the mirror.*)

I look like a corpse. A corpsette. Oh my queen; you know you've hit rock-bottom when even drag is a drag.

> (HARPER *appears.*)

HARPER: Are you. . . . Who are you?   470
PRIOR: Who are you?
HARPER: What are you doing in my hallucination?
PRIOR: I'm not in your hallucination. You're in my dream.
HARPER: You're wearing makeup.
PRIOR: So are you.   475
HARPER: But you're a man.
PRIOR: (*Feigning dismay, shock, he mimes slashing his throat with his lipstick and dies, fabulously tragic. Then.*) The hands and feet give it away.
HARPER: There must be some mistake here. I don't recognize you. You're not. . . . Are you my . . . some sort of imaginary friend?   480
PRIOR: No. Aren't you too old to have imaginary friends?
HARPER: I have emotional problems. I took too many pills. Why are you wearing makeup?
PRIOR: I was in the process of applying the face, trying to make myself feel better—I swiped the new fall colors at the Clinique counter at Macy's. (*Showing her.*)
HARPER: You stole these?   485
PRIOR: I was out of cash; it was an emotional emergency!
HARPER: Joe will be so angry. I promised him. No more pills.
PRIOR: These pills you keep alluding to?
HARPER: Valium. I take Valium. Lots of Valium.
PRIOR: And you're dancing as fast as you can.   490
HARPER: I'm not *addicted*. I don't believe in addiction, and I never . . . well, I *never* drink. And I *never* take drugs.
PRIOR: Well, smell *you*, Nancy Drew.
HARPER: Except Valium.
PRIOR: Except Valium; in wee fistfuls.   495
HARPER: It's terrible. Mormons are not supposed to be addicted to anything. I'm a Mormon.

PRIOR: I'm a homosexual.

HARPER: Oh! In my church we don't believe in homosexuals.

PRIOR: In my church we don't believe in Mormons.

HARPER: What church do . . . oh! (*She laughs.*) I get it.

    I don't understand this. If I didn't ever see you before and I don't think I did then I don't think you should be here, in this hallucination, because in my experience the mind, which is where hallucinations come from, shouldn't be able to make up anything that wasn't there to start with, that didn't enter it from experience, from the real world. Imagination can't create anything new, can it? It only recycles bits and pieces from the world and reassembles them into visions. . . . Am I making sense right now?

PRIOR: Given the circumstances, yes.

HARPER: So when we think we've escaped the unbearable ordinariness and, well, untruthfulness of our lives, it's really only the same old ordinariness and falseness rearranged into the appearance of novelty and truth. Nothing unknown is knowable. Don't you think it's depressing?

PRIOR: The limitations of the imagination?

HARPER: Yes.

PRIOR: It's something you learn after your second theme party: It's All Been Done Before.

HARPER: The world. Finite. Terribly, terribly. . . . Well . . . This is the most depressing hallucination I've ever had.

PRIOR: Apologies. I do try to be amusing.

HARPER: Oh, well, don't apologize, you. . . . I can't expect someone who's really sick to entertain me.

PRIOR: How on earth did you know . . .

HARPER: Oh that happens. This is the very threshold of revelation sometimes. You can see things . . . how sick you are. Do you see anything about me?

PRIOR: Yes.

HARPER: What?

PRIOR: You are amazingly unhappy.

HARPER: Oh big deal. You meet a Valium addict and you figure out she's unhappy. That doesn't count. Of course I. . . . Something else. Something surprising.

PRIOR: Something surprising.

HARPER: Yes.

PRIOR: Your husband's a homo.

    (*Pause.*)

HARPER: Oh, ridiculous.

    (*Pause, then very quietly.*)

    Really?

PRIOR: (*Shrugs.*) Threshold of revelation.

HARPER: Well I don't like your revelations. I don't think you intuit well at all. Joe's a very normal man, he . . .

    Oh God. Oh God. He. . . . Do homos take, like, lots of long walks?

PRIOR: Yes. We do. In stretch pants with lavender coifs. I just looked at you, and there was . . .

HARPER: A sort of blue streak of recognition.

PRIOR: Yes.

HARPER: Like you knew me incredibly well.

PRIOR: Yes.

HARPER: Yes.   545
    I have to go now, get back, something just . . . fell apart. Oh God, I feel so sad . . .
PRIOR: I . . . I'm sorry. I usually say, "Fuck the truth," but mostly, the truth fucks you.
HARPER: I see something else about you . . .
PRIOR: Oh?
HARPER: Deep inside you, there's a part of you, the most inner part, entirely free of disease.   550
    I can see that.
PRIOR: Is that. . . . That isn't true.
HARPER: Threshold of revelation.
    Home . . .

       (*She vanishes.*)

PRIOR: People come and go so quickly here . . .   555
    (*To himself in the mirror.*) I don't think there's any uninfected part of me. My
heart is pumping polluted blood. I feel dirty.

       (*He begins to wipe makeup off with his hands, smearing it around. A large gray
       feather falls from up above.* PRIOR *stops smearing the makeup and looks at the
       feather. He goes to it and picks it up.*)

THE VOICE: (*It is an incredibly beautiful voice.*) Look up!
PRIOR: (*Looking up, not seeing anyone.*) Hello?
THE VOICE: Look up!   560
PRIOR: Who is that?
THE VOICE: Prepare the way!
PRIOR: I don't see any . . .

       (*There is a dramatic change in lighting, from above.*)

A VOICE: Look up, look up,
    prepare the way   565
    the infinite descent
    A breath in air
    floating down
    Glory to . . .

       (*Silence.*)

PRIOR: Hello? Is that it? Helloooo!   570
    What the fuck . . . ? (*He holds himself.*)
    Poor me. Poor poor me. Why me? Why poor poor me?
Oh I don't feel good right now. I really don't.

SCENE VIII

That night. Split scene: HARPER *and* JOE *at home;* PRIOR *and* LOUIS *in bed.*

HARPER: Where were you?
JOE: Out.   575
HARPER: Where?

JOE: Just out. Thinking.

HARPER: It's late.

JOE: I had a lot to think about.

HARPER: I burned dinner. 580

JOE: Sorry.

HARPER: Not my dinner. My dinner was fine. Your dinner. I put it back in the oven and turned everything up as high as it could go and I watched till it burned black. It's still hot. Very hot. Want it?

JOE: You didn't have to do that. 585

HARPER: I know. It just seemed like the kind of thing a mentally deranged sex-starved pill-popping housewife would do.

JOE: Uh huh.

HARPER: So I did it. Who knows anymore what I have to do?

JOE: How many pills? 590

HARPER: A bunch. Don't change the subject.

JOE: I won't talk to you when you . . .

HARPER: No. No. Don't do that! I'm . . . fine, pills are not the problem, not our problem, I WANT TO KNOW WHERE YOU'VE BEEN! I WANT TO KNOW WHAT'S GOING ON! 595

JOE: Going on with what? The job?

HARPER: Not the job.

JOE: I said I need more time.

HARPER: Not the job!

JOE: Mr. Cohn, I talked to him on the phone, he said I had to hurry . . . 600

HARPER: Not the . . .

JOE: But I can't get you to talk sensibly about anything so . . .

HARPER: SHUT UP!

JOE: Then what?

HARPER: Stick to the subject. 605

JOE: I don't know what that is. You have something you want to ask me? Ask me. Go.

HARPER: I . . . can't. I'm scared of you.

JOE: I'm tired, I'm going to bed.

HARPER: Tell me without making me ask. Please.

JOE: This is crazy, I'm not . . . 610

HARPER: When you come through the door at night your face is never exactly the way I remembered it. I get surprised by something . . . mean and hard about the way you look. Even the weight of you in the bed at night, the way you breathe in your sleep seems unfamiliar.
You terrify me. 615

JOE: (*Cold.*) I know who you are.

HARPER: Yes. I'm the enemy. That's easy. That doesn't change. You think you're the only one who hates sex; I do; I hate it with you; I do. I dream that you batter away at me till all my joints come apart, like wax, and I fall into pieces. It's like a punishment. It was wrong of me to marry you. I knew you . . . (*She stops herself.*) It's a sin, and it's 620 killing us both.

JOE: I can always tell when you've taken pills because it makes you red-faced and sweaty and frankly that's very often why I don't want to . . .

HARPER: Because . . .

JOE: Well, you aren't pretty. Not like this. 625

HARPER: I have something to ask you.

JOE: Then ASK! ASK! What in hell are you . . .

HARPER: Are you a homo?

> (*Pause.*)

Are you? If you try to walk out right now I'll put your dinner back in the oven and turn it up so high the whole building will fill with smoke and everyone in it will asphyxiate. So help me God I will.
> Now answer the question.   630

JOE: What if I . . .

> (*Small pause.*)

HARPER: Then tell me, please. And we'll see.
JOE: No. I'm not.   635
> I don't see what difference it makes.

LOUIS: Jews don't have any clear textual guide to the afterlife; even that it exists. I don't think much about it. I see it as a perpetual rainy Thursday afternoon in March. Dead leaves.
PRIOR: Eeeugh. Very Greco-Roman.   640
LOUIS: Well for us it's not the verdict that counts, it's the act of judgment. That's why I could never be a lawyer. In court all that matters is the verdict.
PRIOR: You could never be a lawyer because you are oversexed. You're too distracted.
LOUIS: Not distracted, *ab*stracted. I'm trying to make a point:
PRIOR: Namely: 645
LOUIS: It's the judge in his or her chambers, weighing, books open, pondering the evidence, ranging freely over categories: good, evil, innocent, guilty; the judge in the chamber of circumspection, not the judge on the bench with the gavel. The shaping of the law, not its execution.
PRIOR: The point, dear, the point . . .   650
LOUIS: That it should be the questions and shape of a life, its total complexity gathered, arranged and considered, which matters in the end, not some stamp of salvation or damnation which disperses all the complexity in some unsatisfying little decision— the balancing of the scales . . .
PRIOR: I like this; very zen; it's . . . reassuringly incomprehensible and useless. We who are   655
about to die thank you.
LOUIS: You are not about to die.
PRIOR: It's not going well, really . . . two new lesions. My leg hurts. There's protein in my urine, the doctor says, but who knows what the fuck that portends. Anyway it shouldn't be there, the protein. My butt is chapped from diarrhea and yesterday I   660
shat blood.
LOUIS: I really hate this. You don't tell me . . .
PRIOR: You get too upset, I wind up comforting you. It's easier . . .
LOUIS: Oh thanks.
PRIOR: If it's bad I'll tell you.   665
LOUIS: Shitting blood sounds bad to me.
PRIOR: And I'm telling you.
LOUIS: And I'm handling it.
PRIOR: Tell me some more about justice.
LOUIS: I *am* not handling it.   670
PRIOR: Well Louis you win Trooper of the Month.

> (**LOUIS** *starts to cry.*)

PRIOR: I take it back. You aren't Trooper of the Month.
    This isn't working . . .
    Tell me some more about justice.
LOUIS: You are not about to die.   675
PRIOR: Justice . . .
LOUIS: is an immensity, a confusing vastness. Justice is God. Prior?
PRIOR: Hmmm?
LOUIS: You love me.
PRIOR: Yes.   680
LOUIS: What if I walked out on this?
    Would you hate me forever?

(PRIOR *kisses* LOUIS *on the forehead.*)

PRIOR: Yes.

JOE: I think we ought to pray. Ask God for help. Ask him together . . .
HARPER: God won't talk to me. I have to make up people to talk to me.   685
JOE: You have to keep asking.
HARPER: I forgot the question.
    Oh yeah. God, is my husband a . . .
JOE: (*Scary.*) Stop it. Stop it. I'm warning you.
    Does it make any difference? That I might be one thing deep within, no matter   690
    how wrong or ugly that thing is, so long as I have fought, with everything I have,
    to kill it. What do you want from me? What do you want from me, Harper?
    More than that? For God's sake, there's nothing left, I'm a shell. There's nothing left
    to kill.
    As long as my behavior is what I know it has to be. Decent. Correct. That alone   695
    in the eyes of God.
HARPER: No, no, not that, that's Utah talk, Mormon talk, I hate it, Joe, tell me, say it . . .
JOE: All I will say is that I am a very good man who has worked very hard to become good
    and you want to destroy that. You want to destroy me, but I am not going to let you
    do that.   700

    (*Pause.*)

HARPER: I'm going to have a baby.
JOE: Liar.
HARPER: You liar.
    A baby born addicted to pills. A baby who does not dream but who hallucinates,
    who stares up at us with big mirror eyes and who does not know who we are.   705

    (*Pause.*)

JOE: Are you really . . .
HARPER: No. Yes. No. Yes. Get away from me.
    Now we both have a secret.
PRIOR: One of my ancestors was a ship's captain who made money bringing whale oil to
    Europe and returning with immigrants—Irish mostly, packed in tight, so many   710
    dollars per head. The last ship he captained foundered off the coast of Nova Scotia
    in a winter tempest and sank to the bottom. He went down with the ship—la
    Grande Geste—but his crew took seventy women and kids in the ship's only longboat,
    this big, open rowboat, and when the weather got too rough, and they thought the
    boat was overcrowded, the crew started lifting people up and hurling them into the   715

sea. Until they got the ballast right. They walked up and down the longboat, eyes to the waterline, and when the boat rode low in the water they'd grab the nearest passenger and throw them into the sea. The boat was leaky, see; seventy people; they arrived in Halifax with nine people on board.

LOUIS: Jesus.

PRIOR: I think about that story a lot now. People in a boat, waiting, terrified, while implacable, unsmiling men, irresistibly strong, seize . . . maybe the person next to you, maybe you, and with no warning at all, with time only for a quick intake of air you are pitched into freezing, turbulent water and salt and darkness to drown.

    I like your cosmology, baby. While time is running out I find myself drawn to anything that's suspended, that lacks an ending—but it seems to me that it lets you off scot-free.

LOUIS: What do you mean?

PRIOR: No judgment, no guilt or responsibility.

LOUIS: For me.

PRIOR: For anyone. It was an editorial "you."

LOUIS: Please get better. Please.

    Please don't get any sicker.

SCENE IX

Third week in November. ROY *and* HENRY, *his doctor, in* HENRY's *office.*

HENRY: Nobody knows what causes it. And nobody knows how to cure it. The best theory is that we blame a retrovirus, the Human Immunodeficiency Virus. Its presence is made known to us by the useless antibodies which appear in reaction to its entrance into the bloodstream through a cut, or an orifice. The antibodies are powerless to protect the body against it. Why, we don't know. The body's immune system ceases to function. Sometimes the body even attacks itself. At any rate it's left open to a whole horror house of infections from microbes which it usually defends against.
    Like Kaposi's sarcomas. These lesions. Or your throat problem. Or the glands.
    We think it may also be able to slip past the blood-brain barrier into the brain. Which is of course very bad news. And it's fatal in we don't know what percent of people with suppressed immune responses.

    (*Pause.*)

ROY: This is very interesting, Mr. Wizard, but why the fuck are you telling me this?

    (*Pause.*)

HENRY: Well, I have just removed one of three lesions which biopsy results will probably tell us is a Kaposi's sarcoma lesion. And you have a pronounced swelling of glands in your neck, groin, and armpits—lymphadenopathy is another sign. And you have oral candidiasis and maybe a little more fungus under the fingernails of two digits on your right hand. So that's why . . .

ROY: This disease . . .

HENRY: Syndrome.

ROY: Whatever. It afflicts mostly homosexuals and drug addicts.

HENRY: Mostly. Hemophiliacs are also at risk.

ROY: Homosexuals and drug addicts. So why are you implying that I . . .

720

725

730

735

740

745

750

755

(*Pause.*)

What are you implying, Henry?

HENRY: I don't . . .

ROY: I'm not a drug addict.

HENRY: Oh come on Roy.

ROY: What, what, come on Roy what? Do you think I'm a junkie, Henry, do you see   760
tracks?

HENRY: This is absurd.

ROY: Say it.

HENRY: Say what?

ROY: Say, "Roy Cohn, you are a . . ."   765

HENRY: Roy.

ROY: "You are a . . . ." Go on. Not "Roy Cohn you are a drug fiend." "Roy Marcus Cohn,
you are a . . . "
Go on, Henry, it starts with an "H."

HENRY: Oh I'm not going to . . .   770

ROY: *With an "H,"* Henry, and it isn't "Hemophiliac." Come on . . .

HENRY: What are you doing, Roy?

ROY: No, say it. I mean it. Say: "Roy Cohn, you are a homosexual."

(*Pause.*)

And I will proceed, systemically, to destroy your reputation and your practice and
your career in New York State, Henry. Which you know I can do.   775

(*Pause.*)

HENRY: Roy, you have been seeing me since 1958. Apart from the facelifts I have treated
you for everything from syphilis . . .

ROY: From a whore in Dallas.

HENRY: From syphilis to venereal warts. In your rectum. Which you may have gotten
from a whore in Dallas, but it wasn't a female whore.   780

(*Pause.*)

ROY: So say it.

HENRY: Roy Cohn, you are . . .
You have had sex with men, many many times, Roy, and one of them, or any
number of them, has made you very sick. You have AIDS.

ROY: AIDS.   785
Your problem, Henry, is that you are hung up on words, on labels, that you believe
they mean what they seem to mean. AIDS. Homosexual. Gay. Lesbian. You think
these are names that tell you who someone sleeps with, but they don't tell you that.

HENRY: No?

ROY: No. Like all labels they tell you one thing and one thing only: where does an indi-   790
vidual so identified fit in the food chain, in the pecking order? Not ideology, or
sexual taste, but something much simpler: clout. Not who I fuck or who fucks me,
but who will pick up the phone when I call, who owes me favors. This is what a label
refers to. Now to someone who does not understand this, homosexual is what I am
because I have sex with men. But really this is wrong. Homosexuals are not men who   795
sleep with other men. Homosexuals are men who in fifteen years of trying cannot
get a pissant antidiscrimination bill through City Council. Homosexuals are men
who know nobody and who nobody knows. Who have zero clout. Does this sound
like me, Henry?

HENRY: No.

ROY: No. I have clout. A lot. I can pick up this phone, punch fifteen numbers, and you know who will be on the other end in under five minutes, Henry?

HENRY: The President.

ROY: Even better, Henry. His wife.

HENRY: I'm impressed.

ROY: I don't want you to be impressed. I want you to understand. This is not sophistry. And this is not hypocrisy. This is reality. I have sex with men. But unlike nearly every other man of whom this is true, I bring the guy I'm screwing to the White House and President Reagan smiles at us and shakes his hand. Because *what* I am is defined entirely by *who* I am. Roy Cohn is not a homosexual. Roy Cohn is a heterosexual man, Henry, who fucks around with guys.

HENRY: OK, Roy.

ROY: And what is my diagnosis, Henry?

HENRY: You have AIDS, Roy.

ROY: No, Henry, no. AIDS is what homosexuals have. I have liver cancer.

> (*Pause.*)

HENRY: Well, whatever the fuck you have, Roy, it's very serious, and I haven't got a damn thing for you. The NIH in Bethesda has a new drug called AZT with a two-year waiting list that not even I can get you onto. So get on the phone, Roy, and dial the fifteen numbers, and tell the First Lady you need in on an experimental treatment for liver cancer, because you can call it any damn thing you want, Roy, but what it boils down to is very bad news.

ACT II

In Vitro December 1985–January 1986

SCENE I

Night, the third week in December. PRIOR *alone on the floor of his bedroom; he is much worse.*

PRIOR: Louis, Louis, please wake up, oh God.

> (LOUIS *runs in.*)

PRIOR: I think something horrible is wrong with me I can't breathe . . .

LOUIS: (*Starting to exit.*) I'm calling the ambulance.

PRIOR: No, wait, I . . .

LOUIS: *Wait?* Are you fucking crazy? Oh God you're on fire, your head is on fire.

PRIOR: It hurts, it hurts . . .

LOUIS: I'm calling the ambulance.

PRIOR: I don't want to go to the hospital, I don't want to go to the hospital please let me lie here, just . . .

LOUIS: No, no, God, Prior, stand up . . .

PRIOR: DON'T TOUCH MY LEG!

LOUIS: We have to . . . oh God this is so crazy.

PRIOR: I'll be OK if I just lie here Lou, really, if I can only sleep a little . . .

    (LOUIS *exits.*)

PRIOR: Louis?

    NO! NO! Don't call, you'll send me there and I won't come back, please, please   15
    Louis I'm begging, baby, please . . . (*Screams.*) LOUIS!!

LOUIS: (*From off; hysterical.*) WILL YOU SHUT THE FUCK UP!

PRIOR: (*Trying to stand.*) Aaaah. I have . . . to go to the bathroom. Wait. Wait, just . . .
    oh. Oh God. (*He shits himself.*)

LOUIS: (*Entering.*) Prior? They'll be here in . . . Oh my God.   20

PRIOR: I'm sorry, I'm sorry.

LOUIS: What did . . . ? What?

PRIOR: I had an accident.

    (LOUIS *goes to him.*)

LOUIS: This is blood.

PRIOR: Maybe you shouldn't touch it . . . me. . . . I . . . (*He faints.*)   25

LOUIS: (*Quietly.*) Oh help. Oh help. Oh God oh God oh God help me I can't I can't
    I can't.

SCENE II

Same night. HARPER *is sitting at home, all alone, with no lights on. We can barely see her.* JOE *enters, but he doesn't turn on the lights.*

JOE: Why are you sitting in the dark? Turn on the light.

HARPER: *No.* I heard the sounds in the bedroom again. I know someone was in there.

JOE: No one was.   30

HARPER: Maybe actually in the bed, under the covers with a knife.
    Oh, boy. Joe. I, um, I'm thinking of going away. By which I mean: I think I'm
    going off again. You . . . you know what I mean?

JOE: Please don't. Stay. We can fix it. I pray for that. This is my fault, but I can correct it.
    You have to try too . . .   35

    (*He turns on the light. She turns it off again.*)

HARPER: When you pray, what do you pray for?

JOE: I pray for God to crush me, break me up into little pieces and start all over again.

HARPER: Oh. Please. Don't pray for that.

JOE: I had a book of Bible stories when I was a kid. There was a picture I'd look at twenty
    times every day: Jacob wrestles with the angel. I don't really remember the story, or   40
    why the wrestling—just the picture. Jacob is young and very strong. The angel is . . .
    a beautiful man, with golden hair and wings, of course. I still dream about it. Many
    nights. I'm. . . . It's me. In that struggle. Fierce, and unfair. The angel is not human,
    and it holds nothing back, so how could anyone human win, what kind of a fight is
    that? It's not just. Losing means your soul thrown down in the dust, your heart torn   45
    out from God's. But you can't not lose.

HARPER: In the whole entire world, you are the only person, the only person I love or have ever loved. And I love you terribly. Terribly. That's what's so awfully, irreducibly real. I can make up anything but I can't dream that away.

JOE: Are you . . . are you really going to have a baby? 50

HARPER: It's my time and there's no blood. I don't really know. I suppose it wouldn't be a great thing. Maybe I'm just not bleeding because I take too many pills. Maybe I'll give birth to a pill. That would give a new meaning to pill-popping, huh?

I think you should go to Washington. Alone. Change, like you said.

JOE: I'm not going to leave you, Harper. 55

HARPER: Well maybe not. But I'm going to leave you.

SCENE III

One A.M., *the next morning.* LOUIS *and a nurse,* EMILY, *are sitting in* PRIOR'*s room in the hospital.*

EMILY: He'll be all right now.

LOUIS: No he won't.

EMILY: No. I guess not. I gave him something that makes him sleep.

LOUIS: Deep asleep?

EMILY: Orbiting the moons of Jupiter. 60

LOUIS: A good place to be.

EMILY: Anyplace better than here. You his . . . uh?

LOUIS: Yes. I'm his uh.

EMILY: This must be hell for you. 65

LOUIS: It is. Hell. The After Life. Which is not at all like a rainy afternoon in March, by the way, Prior. A lot more vivid than I'd expected. Dead leaves, but the crunchy kind. Sharp, dry air. The kind of long, luxurious dying feeling that breaks your heart.

EMILY: Yeah, well we all get to break our hearts on this one. He seems like a nice guy. 70 Cute.

LOUIS: Not like this.

Yes, he is. Was. Whatever.

EMILY: Weird name. Prior Walter. Like, "The Walter before this one."

LOUIS: Lots of Walters before this one. Prior is an old old family name in an old old 75 family. The Walters go back to the Mayflower and beyond. Back to the Norman Conquest. He says there's a Prior Walter stitched into the Bayeux tapestry.

EMILY: Is that impressive?

LOUIS: Well, it's old. Very old. Which in some circles equals impressive.

EMILY: Not in my circle. What's the name of the tapestry? 80

LOUIS: The Bayeux tapestry. Embroidered by La Reine Mathilde.

EMILY: I'll tell my mother. She embroiders. Drives me nuts.

LOUIS: Manual therapy for anxious hands.

EMILY: Maybe you should try it.

LOUIS: Mathilde stitched while William the Conqueror was off to war. She was capable 85 of . . . more than loyalty. Devotion. She waited for him, she stitched for years. And if he had come back broken and defeated from war, she would have loved him even more. And if he had returned mutilated, ugly, full of infection and horror, she would still have loved him; fed by pity, by a sharing of pain, she would love him even more,

and even more, and she would never, never have prayed to God, please let him die 90
if he can't return to me whole and healthy and able to live a normal life. . . . If he
had died, she would have buried her heart with him.

    So what the fuck is the matter with me?

    (*Little pause.*)

    Will he sleep through the night?
EMILY: At least. 95
LOUIS: I'm going.
EMILY: It's one A.M. Where do you have to go at . . .
LOUIS: I know what time it is. A walk. Night air, good for the. . . . The park.
EMILY: Be careful.
LOUIS: Yeah. Danger. 100
    Tell him, if he wakes up and you're still on, tell him goodbye, tell him I had
to go.

SCENE IV

An hour later. Split scene: JOE *and* ROY *in a fancy (straight) bar;* LOUIS *and a* MAN *in the Rambles in Central Park.* JOE *and* ROY *are sitting at the bar; the place is brightly lit.* JOE *has a plate of food in front of him but he isn't eating.* ROY *occasionally reaches over the table and forks small bites off* JOE's *plate.* ROY *is drinking heavily,* JOE *not at all.* LOUIS *and the* MAN *are eyeing each other, each alternating interest and indifference.*

JOE: The pills were something she started when she miscarried or . . . no, she took some
before that. She had a really bad time at home, when she was a kid, her home was
really bad. I think a lot of drinking and physical stuff. She doesn't talk about that, 105
instead she talks about . . . the sky falling down, people with knives hiding under
sofas. Monsters. Mormons. Everyone thinks Mormons don't come from homes like
that, we aren't supposed to behave that way, but we do. It's not lying, or being two-
faced. Everyone tries very hard to live up to God's strictures, which are very . . .
um . . . 110
ROY: Strict.
JOE: I shouldn't be bothering you with this.
ROY: No, please. Heart to heart. Want another. . . . What is that, seltzer?
JOE: The failure to measure up hits people very hard. From such a strong desire to be good
they feel very far from goodness when they fail. 115
    What scares me is that maybe what I really love in her is the part of her that's
farthest from the light, from God's love; maybe I was drawn to that in the first
place. And I'm keeping it alive because I need it.
ROY: Why would you need it?
JOE: There are things. . . . I don't know how well we know ourselves. I mean, what if? I 120
know I married her because she . . . because I loved it that she was always wrong,
always doing something wrong, like one step out of step. In Salt Lake City that
stands out. I never stood out, on the outside, but inside, it was hard for me. To
pass.
ROY: Pass? 125
JOE: Yeah.
ROY: Pass as what?

JOE: Oh. Well. . . . As someone cheerful and strong. Those who love God with an open heart unclouded by secrets and struggles are cheerful; God's easy simple love for them shows in how strong and happy they are. The saints. 130

ROY: But you had secrets? Secret struggles . . .

JOE: I wanted to be one of the elect, one of the Blessed. You feel you ought to be, that the blemishes are yours by choice, which of course they aren't. Harper's sorrow, that really deep sorrow, she didn't choose that. But it's there.

ROY: You didn't put it there. 135

JOE: No.

ROY: You sound like you think you did.

JOE: I am responsible for her.

ROY: Because she's your wife.

JOE: That. And I do love her. 140

ROY: Whatever. She's your wife. And so there are obligations. To her. But also to yourself.

JOE: She'd fall apart in Washington.

ROY: Then let her stay here.

JOE: She'll fall apart if I leave her.

ROY: Then bring her to Washington. 145

JOE: I just can't, Roy. She needs me.

ROY: Listen, Joe. I'm the best divorce lawyer in the business.

(*Little pause.*)

JOE: Can't Washington wait?

ROY: You do what you need to do, Joe. What you need. You. Let her life go where it wants to go. You'll both be better for that. *Somebody* should get what they want. 150

MAN: What do you want?

LOUIS: I want you to fuck me, hurt me, make me bleed.

MAN: I want to.

LOUIS: Yeah?

MAN: I want to hurt you. 155

LOUIS: Fuck me.

MAN: Yeah?

LOUIS: Hard.

MAN: Yeah? You been a bad boy?

(*Pause.* LOUIS *laughs, softly.*)

LOUIS: Very bad. Very bad. 160

MAN: You need to be punished, boy?

LOUIS: Yes. I do.

MAN: Yes what?

(*Little pause.*)

LOUIS: Um, I . . .

MAN: Yes *what,* boy?

LOUIS: Oh. Yes sir. 165

MAN: I want you to take me to your place, boy.

LOUIS: No, I can't do that.

MAN: No *what?*

LOUIS: No sir, I can't, I . . .
    I don't live alone, sir. 170

MAN: Your lover know you're out with a man tonight, boy?

LOUIS: No sir, he . . .

My lover doesn't know.

MAN: Your lover know you . . .   175

LOUIS: Let's change the subject, OK? Can we go to your place?

MAN: I live with my parents.

LOUIS: Oh.

ROY: Everyone who makes it in this world makes it because somebody older and more
powerful takes an interest. The most precious asset in life, I think, is the ability to be   180
a good son. You have that, Joe. Somebody who can be a good son to a father who
pushes them farther than they would otherwise go. I've had many fathers, I owe my
life to them, powerful, powerful men. Walter Winchell, Edgar Hoover. Joe McCarthy
most of all. He valued me because I am a good lawyer, but he loved me because I was
and am a good son. He was a very difficult man, very guarded and cagey; I brought   185
out something tender in him. He would have died for me. And me for him. Does
this embarrass you?

JOE: I had a hard time with my father.

ROY: Well sometimes that's the way. Then you have to find other fathers, substitutes, I
don't know. The father-son relationship is central to life. Women are for birth, begin-   190
ning, but the father is continuance. The son offers the father his life as a vessel for
carrying forth his father's dream. Your father's living?

JOE: Um, dead.

ROY: He was . . . what? A difficult man?

JOE: He was in the military. He could be very unfair. And cold.   195

ROY: But he loved you.

JOE: I don't know.

ROY: No, no, Joe, he did, I know this. Sometimes a father's love has to be very, very hard,
unfair even, cold to make his son grow strong in a world like this. This isn't a good
world.   200

MAN: Here, then.

LOUIS: I. . . . Do you have a rubber?

MAN: I don't use rubbers.

LOUIS: You should. (*He takes one from his coat pocket.*) Here.

MAN: I don't use them.   205

LOUIS: Forget it, then. (*He starts to leave.*)

MAN: No, wait.

Put it on me. Boy.

LOUIS: Forget it, I have to get back. Home. I must be going crazy.

MAN: Oh come on please he won't find out.   210

LOUIS: It's cold. Too cold.

MAN: It's never too cold, let me warm you up. Please?

(*They begin to fuck.*)

MAN: Relax.

LOUIS: (*A small laugh.*) Not a chance.

MAN: It . . .   215

LOUIS: What?

MAN: I think it broke. The rubber. You want me to keep going? (*Little pause.*) Pull out?
Should I . . .

LOUIS: Keep going.
>Infect me.
>I don't care. I don't care.

(*Pause. The* MAN *pulls out.*)

MAN: I . . . um, look, I'm sorry, but I think I want to go.
LOUIS: Yeah.
>Give my best to mom and dad.

(*The* MAN *slaps him.*)

LOUIS: Ow!

(*They stare at each other.*)

LOUIS: It was a joke.

(*The* MAN *leaves.*)

ROY: How long have we known each other?
JOE: Since 1980.
ROY: Right. A long time. I feel close to you, Joe. Do I advise you well?
JOE: You've been an incredible friend, Roy, I . . .
ROY: I want to be family. Familia, as my Italian friends call it. La Familia. A lovely word.
>It's important for me to help you, like I was helped.
JOE: I owe practically everything to you, Roy.
ROY: I'm dying, Joe. Cancer.
JOE: Oh my God.
ROY: Please. Let me finish.
>Few people know this and I'm telling you this only because. . . . I'm not afraid
>of death. What can death bring that I haven't faced? I've lived; life is the worst.
>(*Gently mocking himself.*) Listen to me, I'm a philosopher.
>   Joe. You must do this. You must must must. Love; that's a trap. Responsibility;
>that's a trap too. Like a father to a son I tell you this: Life is full of horror; nobody
>escapes, nobody; save yourself. Whatever pulls on you, whatever needs from you,
>threatens you. Don't be afraid; people are so afraid; don't be afraid to live in the
>raw wind, naked, alone. . . . Learn at least this: What you are capable of. Let
>nothing stand in your way.

SCENE V

Three days later. PRIOR *and* BELIZE *in* PRIOR's *hospital room.* PRIOR *is very sick but improving.* BELIZE *has just arrived.*

PRIOR: Miss Thing.
BELIZE: Ma cherie bichette.
PRIOR: Stella.
BELIZE: Stella for star. Let me see. (*Scrutinizing* PRIOR.) You look like shit, why yes indeed
>you do, comme la merde!
PRIOR: Merci.

BELIZE: (*Taking little plastic bottles from his bag, handing them to* PRIOR.) Not to despair, Belle Reeve. Lookie! Magic goop!

PRIOR: (*Opening a bottle, sniffing.*) Pooh! What kinda crap is that?

BELIZE: Beats me. Let's rub it on your poor blistered body and see what it does. 255

PRIOR: This is not Western medicine, these bottles . . .

BELIZE: Voodoo cream. From the botanica 'round the block.

PRIOR: And you a registered nurse.

BELIZE: (*Sniffing it.*) Beeswax and cheap perfume. Cut with Jergen's Lotion. Full of good vibes and love from some little black Cubana witch in Miami. 260

PRIOR: Get that trash away from me. I am immune-suppressed.

BELIZE: I *am* a health professional. I *know* what I'm doing.

PRIOR: It stinks. Any word from Louis?

(*Pause.* BELIZE *starts giving* PRIOR *a gentle massage.*)

PRIOR: Gone.

BELIZE: He'll be back. I know the type. Likes to keep a girl on edge. 265

PRIOR: It's been . . .

(*Pause*)

BELIZE: (*Trying to jog his memory.*) How long?

PRIOR: I don't remember.

BELIZE: How long have you been here?

PRIOR: (*Getting suddenly upset.*) I don't remember, I don't give a fuck. I want Louis. I want 270 my fucking boyfriend, where the fuck is he? I'm dying, I'm dying, where's Louis?

BELIZE: Shhhh, shhh . . .

PRIOR: This is a very strange drug, this drug. Emotional lability, for starters.

BELIZE: Save a tab or two for me.

PRIOR: Oh no, not this drug, ce n'est pas pour la joyeux noël et la bonne année, this drug 275 she is serious poisonous chemistry, ma pauvre bichette.
And not just disorienting. I hear things. Voices.

BELIZE: Voices.

PRIOR: A voice.

BELIZE: Saying what? 280

(*Pause.*)

PRIOR: I'm not supposed to tell.

BELIZE: You better tell the doctor. Or I will.

PRIOR: No no don't. Please. I want the voice; it's wonderful. It's all that's keeping me alive. I don't want to talk to some intern about it.
You know what happens? When I hear it, I get hard. 285

BELIZE: Oh my.

PRIOR: Comme ça. (*He uses his arm to demonstrate.*) And you know I am slow to rise.

BELIZE: My jaw aches at the memory.

PRIOR: And would you deny me this little solace—betray my concupiscence to Florence Nightingale's storm troopers? 290

BELIZE: Perish the thought, ma bébé.

PRIOR: They'd change the drug just to spoil the fun.

BELIZE: You and your boner can depend on me.

PRIOR: Je t'adore, ma belle nègre.

BELIZE: All this girl-talk shit is politically incorrect, you know. We should have dropped it back when we gave up drag.

PRIOR: I'm sick, I get to be politically incorrect if it makes me feel better. You sound like Lou.

(*Little pause.*)

Well, at least I have the satisfaction of knowing he's in anguish somewhere. I loved his anguish. Watching him stick his head up his asshole and eat his guts out over some relatively minor moral conundrum—it was the best show in town. But Mother warned me; if they get overwhelmed by the little things . . .

BELIZE: They'll be belly-up bustville when something big comes along.

PRIOR: Mother warned me.

BELIZE: And they do come along.

PRIOR: But I didn't listen.

BELIZE: No. (*Doing Hepburn.*) Men are beasts.

PRIOR: (*Also Hepburn.*) The absolute lowest.

BELIZE: I have to go. If I want to spend my whole lonely life looking after white people I can get underpaid to do it.

PRIOR: You're just a Christian martyr.

BELIZE: Whatever happens, baby, I will be here for you.

PRIOR: Je t'aime.

BELIZE: Je t'aime. Don't go crazy on me, girlfriend, I already got enough crazy queens for one lifetime. For two. I can't be bothering with dementia.

PRIOR: I promise.

BELIZE: (*Touching him; softly.*) Ouch.

PRIOR: Ouch. Indeed.

BELIZE: Why'd they have to pick on you?
And eat more, girlfriend, you really do look like shit.

(BELIZE *leaves.*)

PRIOR: (*After waiting a beat.*) He's gone.
Are you still . . .

VOICE: I can't stay. I will return.

PRIOR: Are you one of those "Follow me to the other side" voices?

VOICE: No. I am no nightbird. I am a messenger . . .

PRIOR: You have a beautiful voice, it sounds . . . like a viola, like a perfectly tuned, tight string, balanced, the truth. . . . Stay with me.

THE VOICE: Not now. Soon I will return, I will reveal myself to you; I am glorious, glorious; my heart, my countenance and my message. You must prepare.

PRIOR: For what? I don't want to . . .

THE VOICE: No death, no:
A marvelous work and a wonder we undertake, an edifice awry we sink plumb and straighten, a great Lie we abolish, a great error correct, with the rule, sword and broom of Truth!

PRIOR: What are you talking about, I . . .

THE VOICE: I am on my way; when I am manifest, our Work begins;
Prepare for the parting of the air,
The breath, the ascent,
Glory to . . .

SCENE VI

The second week of January. MARTIN, ROY *and* JOE *in a fancy Manhattan restaurant.*

MARTIN: It's a revolution in Washington, Joe. We have a new agenda and finally a real   340
    leader. They got back the Senate but we have the courts. By the nineties the Supreme
    Court will be block-solid Republican appointees, and the Federal bench—Republican
    judges like land mines, everywhere, everywhere they turn. Affirmative action? Take
    it to court. Boom! Land mine. And we'll get our way on just about everything:
    abortion, defense, Central America, family values, a live investment climate. We   345
    have the White House locked till the year 2000. And beyond. A permanent fix on
    the Oval Office? It's possible. By '92 we'll get the Senate back, and in ten years the
    South is going to give us the House. It's really the end of Liberalism. The end of
    New Deal Socialism. The end of ipso facto secular humanism. The dawning of a
    genuinely American political personality. Modeled on Ronald Wilson Reagan.   350
JOE: It sounds great, Mr. Heller.
MARTIN: Martin. And Justice is the hub. Especially since Ed Meese took over. He doesn't
    specialize in Fine Points of the Law. He's a flatfoot, a cop. He reminds me of Teddy
    Roosevelt.
JOE: I can't wait to meet him.   355
MARTIN: Too bad, Joe, he's been dead for sixty years!

    (*There is a little awkwardness.* JOE *doesn't respond.*)

MARTIN: Teddy Roosevelt. You said you wanted to. . . . Little joke. It reminds me of the
    story about the . . .
ROY: (*Smiling, but nasty.*) Aw shut the fuck up Martin.
    (*To* JOE.) You see that? Mr. Heller here is one of the mighty, Joseph, in D.C. he   360
    sitteth on the right hand of the man who sitteth on the right hand of The Man.
    And yet I can say "shut the fuck up" and he will take no offense. Loyalty. He . . .
    Martin?
MARTIN: Yes, Roy?
ROY: Rub my back.   365
MARTIN: Roy . . .
ROY: No no really, a sore spot, I get them all the time now, these. . . . Rub it for me
    darling, would you do that for me?

    (MARTIN *rubs* ROY'*s back. They both look at* JOE.)

ROY: (*To* JOE.) How do you think a handful of Bolsheviks turned St. Petersburg into
    Leningrad in one afternoon? *Comrades.* Who do for each other. Marx and Engels.   370
    Lenin and Trotsky. Josef Stalin and Franklin Delano Roosevelt.

    (MARTIN *laughs.*)

ROY: *Comrades,* right Martin?
MARTIN: This man, Joe, is a Saint of the Right.
JOE: I know, Mr. Heller, I . . .
ROY: And you see what I mean, Martin? He's special, right?   375
MARTIN: Don't embarrass him, Roy.
ROY: Gravity, decency, smarts! His strength is as the strength of ten because his heart is
    pure! *And* he's a Royboy, one hundred percent.
MARTIN: We're on the move, Joe. On the move.

JOE: Mr. Heller, I . . .   380
MARTIN: (*Ending backrub.*) We can't wait any longer for an answer.

      (*Little pause.*)

JOE: Oh. Um, I . . .
ROY: Joe's a married man, Martin.
MARTIN: Aha.
ROY: With a wife. She doesn't care to go to D.C., and so Joe cannot go. And keeps us   385
    dangling. We've seen that kind of thing before, haven't we? These men and their
    wives.
MARTIN: Oh yes. Beware.
JOE: I really can't discuss this under . . .
MARTIN: Then *don't* discuss. Say yes, Joe.   390
ROY: Now.
MARTIN: Say yes I will.
ROY: Now.
    Now. I'll hold my breath till you do, I'm turning blue waiting. . . . *Now,*
    goddammit!   395
MARTIN: Roy, calm down, it's not . . .
ROY: Aw, fuck it. (*He takes a letter from his jacket pocket, hands it to* JOE.)
    Read. Came today.

      (JOE *reads the first paragraph, then looks up.*)

JOE: Roy. This is . . . Roy, this is terrible.
ROY: You're telling me.   400
    A letter from the New York State Bar Association, Martin. They're gonna try
    and disbar me.
MARTIN: Oh my.
JOE: Why?
ROY: Why, Martin?   405
MARTIN: Revenge.
ROY: The whole Establishment. Their little rules. Because I know no rules. Because
    I don't see the Law as a dead and arbitrary collection of antiquated dictums, thou
    shall, thou shalt not, because, because I know the Law's a pliable, breathing,
    sweating . . . *organ,* because, because . . .   410
MARTIN: Because he borrowed half a million from one of his clients.
ROY: Yeah, well, there's that.
MARTIN: *And* he forgot to *return* it.
JOE: Roy, that's. . . . You borrowed money from a client?
ROY: I'm deeply ashamed.   415

    (*Little pause.*)

JOE: (*Very sympathetic.*) Roy, you know how much I admire you. Well I mean I know you
    have unorthodox ways, but I'm sure you only did what you thought at the time you
    needed to do. And I have faith that . . .
ROY: Not so damp, please. I'll deny it was a loan. She's got no paperwork. Can't prove a
    fucking thing.   420

    (*Little pause.* MARTIN *studies the menu.*)

JOE: (*Handing back the letter, more official in tone.*) Roy I really appreciate your telling me
    this, and I'll do whatever I can to help.

ROY: (*Holding up a hand, then, carefully.*) I'll tell you what you can do.

    I'm about to be tried, Joe, by a jury that is not a jury of my peers. The disbar-   425
ment committee: genteel gentleman Brahmin lawyers, country-club men. I offend
them, to these men . . . I'm what, Martin, some sort of filthy little Jewish troll?

MARTIN: Oh well, I wouldn't go so far as . . .

ROY: Oh well I would.

    Very fancy lawyers, these disbarment committee lawyers, fancy lawyers with
fancy corporate clients and complicated cases. Antitrust suits. Deregulation. Envi-   430
ronmental control. Complex cases like these need Justice Department cooperation
like flowers need the sun. Wouldn't you say that's an accurate assessment, Martin?

MARTIN: I'm not here, Roy. I'm not hearing any of this.

ROY: No. Of course not.

    Without the light of the sun, Joe, these cases, and the fancy lawyers who   435
represent them, will wither and die.

    A well-placed friend, someone in the Justice Department, say, can turn off the
sun. Cast a deep shadow on my behalf. Make them shiver in the cold. If they over-
step. They would fear that.

    (*Pause.*)

JOE: Roy. I don't understand.   440

ROY: You do.

    (*Pause.*)

JOE: You're not asking me to . . .

ROY: Ssshhhh. Careful.

JOE: (*A beat, then.*) Even if I said yes to the job, it would be illegal to interfere. With
the hearings. It's unethical. No. I can't.   445

ROY: Un-ethical.

    Would you excuse us, Martin?

MARTIN: Excuse you?

ROY: Take a walk, Martin. For real.

    (MARTIN *leaves.*)

ROY: Un-ethical. Are you trying to embarrass me in front of my friend?   450

JOE: Well it is unethical, I can't . . .

ROY: Boy, you are really something. What the fuck do you think this is, Sunday School?

JOE: No, but Roy this is . . .

ROY: This is . . . this is gastric juices churning, this is enzymes and acids, this is intestinal
is what this is, bowel movement and blood-red meat—this stinks, this is *politics*, Joe,   455
the game of being alive. And you think you're. . . . What? Above that? Above alive is
what? Dead! In the clouds! You're on earth, goddammit! Plant a foot, stay a while.

    I'm sick. They smell I'm weak. They want blood this time. I must have eyes in
Justice. In Justice you will protect me.

JOE: Why can't Mr. Heller . . .   460

ROY: Grow up, Joe. The administration can't get involved.

JOE: But I'd be part of the administration. The same as him.

ROY: Not the same. Martin's Ed's man. And Ed's Reagan's man. So Martin's Reagan's man.
And you're mine.

    (*Little pause. He holds up the letter.*)

This will never be. Understand me?   465

(*He tears the letter up.*)

I'm gonna be a lawyer, Joe, I'm gonna be a lawyer, Joe, I'm gonna be a goddam motherfucking legally licensed member of the bar lawyer, just like my daddy was, till my last bitter day on earth, Joseph, until the day I die.

(MARTIN *returns.*)

ROY: Ah, Martin's back.
MARTIN: So are we agreed? 470
ROY: Joe?

(*Little pause.*)

JOE: I will think about it.
    (*To* ROY.) I will.
ROY: Huh.
MARTIN: It's the fear of what comes after the doing that makes the doing hard to do. 475
ROY: Amen.
MARTIN: But you can almost always live with the consequences.

SCENE VII

That afternoon. On the granite steps outside the Hall of Justice, Brooklyn. It is cold and sunny. A Sabrett wagon is selling hot dogs. LOUIS, *in a shabby overcoat, is sitting on the steps contemplatively eating one.* JOE *enters with three hot dogs and a can of Coke.*

JOE: Can I . . . ?
LOUIS: Oh sure. Sure. Crazy cold sun.
JOE: (*Sitting.*) Have to make the best of it. How's your friend? 480
LOUIS: My . . . ? Oh. He's worse. My friend is worse.
JOE: I'm sorry.
LOUIS: Yeah, well. Thanks for asking. It's nice. You're nice. I can't believe you voted for
    Reagan.
JOE: I hope he gets better. 485
LOUIS: Reagan?
JOE: Your friend.
LOUIS: He won't. Neither will Reagan.
JOE: Let's not talk politics, OK?
LOUIS: (*Pointing to* JOE'*s lunch.*) You're eating three of those? 490
JOE: Well . . . I'm . . . hungry.
LOUIS: They're really terrible for you. Full of rat-poo and beetle legs and wood shavings
    'n' shit.
JOE: Huh.
LOUIS: And . . . um . . . irridium, I think. Something toxic.
JOE: You're eating one. 495
LOUIS: Yeah, well, the shape, I can't help myself, plus I'm trying to commit suicide,
    what's your excuse?
JOE: I don't have an excuse. I just have Pepto-Bismol.

(JOE *takes a bottle of Pepto-Bismol and chugs it.* LOUIS *shudders audibly.*)

JOE: Yeah I know but then I wash it down with Coke.   500

> (*He does this.* LOUIS *mimes barfing in* JOE's *lap.* JOE *pushes* LOUIS's *head away.*)

JOE: Are you always like this?

LOUIS: I've been worrying a lot about his kids.

JOE: Whose?

LOUIS: Reagan's. Maureen and Mike and little orphan Patti and Miss Ron Reagan Jr., the
you-should-pardon-the-expression heterosexual.   505

JOE: Ron Reagan Jr. is *not* . . . You shouldn't just make these assumptions about people.
How do you know? About him? What he is? You don't know.

LOUIS: (*Doing Tallulah.*) Well darling he never sucked *my* cock but . . .

JOE: Look, if you're going to get vulgar . . .

LOUIS: No no really I mean. . . . What's it like to be the child of the Zeitgeist? To have   510
the American Animus as your dad? It's not really a *family*, the Reagans, I read *People*,
there aren't any connections there, no love, they don't ever even speak to each other
except through their agents. So what's it like to be Reagan's kid? Enquiring minds
want to know.

JOE: You can't believe everything you . . .   515

LOUIS: (*Looking away.*) But . . . I think we all know what that's like. Nowadays. No connections. No responsibilities. All of us . . . falling through the cracks that separate what
we owe to our selves and . . . and what we owe to love.

JOE: You just. . . . Whatever you feel like saying or doing, you don't care, you just . . .
do it.   520

LOUIS: Do what?

JOE: It. Whatever. Whatever it is you want to do.

LOUIS: Are you trying to tell me something?

> (*Little pause, sexual. They stare at each other.* JOE *looks away.*)

JOE: No, I'm just observing that you . . .

LOUIS: Impulsive.   525

JOE: Yes, I mean it must be scary, you . . .

LOUIS: (*Shrugs.*) Land of the free. Home of the brave. Call me irresponsible.

JOE: It's kind of terrifying.

LOUIS: Yeah, well, freedom is. Heartless, too.

JOE: Oh you're not heartless.   530

LOUIS: You don't know.
    Finish your weenie.

> (*He pats* JOE *on the knee, starts to leave.*)

JOE: Um . . .

> (LOUIS *turns, looks at him.* JOE *searches for something to say.*)

JOE: Yesterday was Sunday but I've been a little unfocused recently and I thought it
was Monday. So I came here like I was going to work. And the whole place was   535
empty. And at first I couldn't figure out why, and I had this moment of incredible . . .
fear and also. . . . It just flashed through my mind: The whole Hall of Justice, it's
empty, it's deserted, it's gone out of business. Forever. The people that make it run
have up and abandoned it.

LOUIS: (*Looking at the building.*) Creepy.   540

JOE: Well yes but. I felt that I was going to scream. Not because it was creepy, but because
the emptiness felt so *fast*. And . . . well, good. A . . . happy scream.

I just wondered what a thing it would be . . . if overnight everything you owe anything to, justice, or love, had really gone away. Free.

It would be . . . heartless terror. Yes. Terrible, and . . .   545

Very great. To shed your skin, every old skin, one by one and then walk away, unencumbered, into the morning.

(*Little pause. He looks at the building.*)

I can't go in there today.

LOUIS: Then don't.

JOE: (*Not really hearing* LOUIS.) I can't go in, I need . . .   550

(*He looks for what he needs. He takes a swig of Pepto-Bismol.*)

I can't *be* this anymore. I need . . . a change, I should just . . .

LOUIS: (*Not a come-on, necessarily; he doesn't want to be alone.*) Want some company? For whatever?

(*Pause.* JOE *looks at* LOUIS *and looks away, afraid.* LOUIS *shrugs.*)

LOUIS: Sometimes, even if it scares you to death, you have to be willing to break the law. Know what I mean?   555

(*Another little pause.*)

JOE: Yes.

(*Another little pause.*)

LOUIS: I moved out. I moved out on my . . .

I haven't been sleeping well.

JOE: Me neither.

(LOUIS *goes up to* JOE, *licks his napkin and dabs at* JOE*'s mouth.*)

LOUIS: Antacid moustache.   560

(*Points to the building.*) Maybe the court won't convene.

Ever again. Maybe we are free. To do whatever.

Children of the new morning, criminal minds. Selfish and greedy and loveless and blind. Reagan's children.

You're scared. So am I. Everybody is in the land of the free.   565

God help us all.

SCENE VIII

Late that night. JOE *at a payphone phoning* HANNAH *at home in Salt Lake City.*

JOE: Mom?

HANNAH: Joe?

JOE: Hi.

HANNAH: You're calling from the street. It's . . . it must be four in the morning. What's   570

happened?

JOE: Nothing, nothing, I . . .

HANNAH: It's Harper. Is Harper. . . . Joe? Joe?

JOE: Yeah, hi. No, Harper's fine. Well, no, she's . . . not fine. How are you, Mom?

HANNAH: What's happened? 575

JOE: I just wanted to talk to you. I, uh, wanted to try something out on you.

HANNAH: Joe, you haven't . . . have you been drinking, Joe?

JOE: Yes ma'am. I'm drunk.

HANNAH: That isn't like you.

JOE: No. I mean, who's to say? 580

HANNAH: Why are you out on the street at four A.M.? *In that crazy city. It's dangerous.*

JOE: Actually, Mom, I'm not on the street. I'm near the boathouse in the park.

HANNAH: What park?

JOE: Central Park.

HANNAH: CENTRAL PARK! Oh my Lord. What on earth are you doing in Central 585
Park at this time of night? Are you . . . Joe, I think you ought to go home right now.
Call me from home.

(*Little pause.*)

Joe?

JOE: I come here to watch, Mom. Sometimes. Just to watch.

HANNAH: Watch what? What's there to watch at four in the . . . 590

JOE: Mom, did Dad love me?

HANNAH: What?

JOE: Did he?

HANNAH: You ought to go home and call from there.

JOE: Answer. 595

HANNAH: Oh now really. This is maudlin. I don't like this conversation.

JOE: Yeah, well, it gets worse from here on.

(*Pause.*)

HANNAH: Joe?

JOE: Mom. Momma. I'm a homosexual, Momma.
Boy, did that come out awkward. 600

(*Pause.*)

Hello? Hello?
I'm a homosexual.

(*Pause.*)

Please, Momma, Say something.

HANNAH: You're old enough to understand that your father didn't love you without
being ridiculous about it. 605

JOE: What?

HANNAH: You're ridiculous. You're being ridiculous.

JOE: I'm . . .
What?

HANNAH: You really ought to go home now to your wife. I need to go to bed. This 610
phone call. . . . We will just forget this phone call.

JOE: Mom.

HANNAH: No more talk. Tonight. This . . .

(*Suddenly very angry.*) *Drinking is a sin! A sin! I raised you better than that.*
(*She hangs up.*)

SCENE IX

The following morning, early. Split scene: HARPER *and* JOE *at home;* LOUIS *and* PRIOR *in* PRIOR's *hospital room.* JOE *and* LOUIS *have just entered. This should be fast and obviously furious; overlapping is fine; the proceedings may be a little confusing but not the final results.*

HARPER: Oh God. Home. The moment of truth has arrived.

JOE: Harper.   615

LOUIS: I'm going to move out.

PRIOR: The fuck you are.

JOE: Harper. Please listen. I still love you very much. You're still my best buddy; I'm not going to leave you.

HARPER: No, I don't like the sound of this. I'm leaving.   620

LOUIS: I'm leaving.
   I already have.

JOE: Please listen. Stay. This is really hard. We have to talk.

HARPER: We are talking. Aren't we. Now please shut up. OK?

PRIOR: Bastard. Sneaking off while I'm flat out here, that's low. If I could get up now I'd   625
   beat the holy shit out of you.

JOE: Did you take pills? How many?

HARPER: No pills. Bad for the . . . (*Pats stomach.*)

JOE: You aren't pregnant. I called your gynecologist.

HARPER: I'm seeing a new gynecologist.   630

PRIOR: You have no right to do this.

LOUIS: Oh, that's ridiculous.

PRIOR: No right. It's criminal.

JOE: Forget about that. Just listen. You want the truth. This is the truth.
   I knew this when I married you. I've known this I guess for as long as I've   635
   known anything, but . . . I don't know, I thought maybe that with enough effort
   and will I could change myself . . . but I can't . . .

PRIOR: Criminal.

LOUIS: There oughta be a law.

PRIOR: There is a law. You'll see.   640

JOE: I'm losing ground here, I go walking, you want to know where I walk, I . . . go to the
   park, or up and down 53rd Street, or places where. . . . And I keep swearing I won't
   go walking again, but I just can't.

LOUIS: I need some privacy.

PRIOR: That's new.   645

LOUIS: Everything's new, Prior.

JOE: I try to tighten my heart into a knot, a snarl, I try to learn to live dead, just numb,
   but then I see someone I want, and it's like a nail, like a hot spike right through my
   chest, and I know I'm losing.

PRIOR: Apartment too small for three? Louis and Prior comfy but not Louis and Prior and   650
   Prior's disease?

LOUIS: Something like that.
   I won't be judged by you. This isn't a crime, just—the inevitable consequence of
   people who run out of—whose limitations . . .

PRIOR: Bang bang bang. The court will come to order.   655

LOUIS: I mean let's talk practicalities, schedules; I'll come over if you want, spend nights
   with you when I can, I can . . .

PRIOR: Has the jury reached a verdict?

LOUIS: I'm doing the best I can.

PRIOR: Pathetic. Who cares?   660

JOE: My whole life has conspired to bring me to this place, and I can't despise my whole life. I think I believed when I met you I could save you, you at least if not myself, but . . . I don't have any sexual feelings for you, Harper. And I don't think I ever did.

> (*Little pause.*)

HARPER: I think you should go.

JOE: Where?   665

HARPER: Washington. Doesn't matter.

JOE: What are you talking about?

HARPER: Without me.
Without me, Joe. Isn't that what you want to hear?

> (*Little pause.*)

JOE: Yes.   670

LOUIS: You can love someone and fail them. You can love someone and not be able to . . .

PRIOR: You *can*, theoretically, yes. A person can, maybe an editorial "you" can love, Louis, but not *you*, specifically you, I don't know, I think you are excluded from that general category.

HARPER: You were going to save me, but the whole time you were spinning a lie. I just   675
don't understand that.

PRIOR: A person could theoretically love and maybe many do but we both know now you can't.

LOUIS: I do.

PRIOR: You can't even say it.   680

LOUIS: I love you, Prior.

PRIOR: I repeat. Who cares?

HARPER: This is so scary, I want this to stop, to go back . . .

PRIOR: We have reached a verdict, your honor. This man's heart is deficient. He loves, but   685
his love is worth nothing.

JOE: Harper . . .

HARPER: Mr. Lies, I want to get away from here. Far away. Right now. Before he starts talking again. Please, please . . .

JOE: As long as I've known you Harper you've been afraid of . . . of men hiding under the   690
bed, men hiding under the sofa, men with knives.

PRIOR: (*Shattered; almost pleading; trying to reach him.*) I'm dying! You stupid fuck! Do you know what that is! Love! Do you know what love means? We lived together four-and-a-half years, you animal, you idiot.

LOUIS: I have to find some way to save myself.

JOE: Who are these men? I never understood it. Now I know.   695

HARPER: What?

JOE: It's me.

HARPER: It is?

PRIOR: GET OUT OF MY ROOM!

JOE: I'm the man with the knives.   700

HARPER: You are?

PRIOR: If I could get up now I'd kill you. I would. Go away. Go away or I'll scream.

HARPER: Oh God . . .

JOE: I'm sorry . . .   705

HARPER: It is you.

LOUIS: Please don't scream.
PRIOR: Go.
HARPER: I recognize you now.
LOUIS: Please . . .
JOE: Oh. Wait, I. . . . Oh!   710

>   (*He covers his mouth with his hand, gags, and removes his hand, red with blood.*)

I'm bleeding.

>   (PRIOR *screams.*)

HARPER: Mr. Lies.
MR. LIES: (*Appearing, dressed in antarctic explorer's apparel.*) Right here.
HARPER: I want to go away. I can't see him anymore.
MR. LIES: Where?   715
HARPER: Anywhere. Far away.
MR. LIES: Absolutamento.

>   (HARPER *and* MR. LIES *vanish.* JOE *looks up, sees that she's gone.*)

PRIOR: (*Closing his eyes.*) When I open my eyes you'll be gone.

>   (LOUIS *leaves.*)

JOE: Harper?
PRIOR: (*Opening his eyes.*) Huh. It worked.   720
JOE: (*Calling.*) Harper?
PRIOR: I hurt all over. I wish I was dead.

SCENE X

The same day, sunset. HANNAH *and* SISTER ELLA CHAPTER, *a real-estate saleswoman,*
HANNAH PITT*'s closest friend, in front of* HANNAH*'s house in Salt Lake City.*

SISTER ELLA CHAPTER: Look at that view! A view of heaven. Like the living city of heaven,
    isn't it, it just fairly glimmers in the sun.
HANNAH: Glimmers.   725
SISTER ELLA CHAPTER: Even the stone and brick it just glimmers and glitters like heaven
    in the sunshine. Such a nice view you get, perched up on a canyon rim. Some kind
    of beautiful place.
HANNAH: It's just Salt Lake, and you're selling the house *for* me, not *to* me.
SISTER ELLA CHAPTER: I like to work up an enthusiasm for my properties.   730
HANNAH: Just get me a good price.
SISTER ELLA CHAPTER: Well, the market's off.
HANNAH: At least fifty.
SISTER ELLA CHAPTER: Forty'd be more like it.
HANNAH: Fifty.   735
SISTER ELLA CHAPTER: Wish you'd wait a bit.
HANNAH: Well I can't.
SISTER ELLA CHAPTER: Wish you would. You're about the only friend I got.
HANNAH: Oh well now.

SISTER ELLA CHAPTER: Know why I decided to like you? I decided to like you 'cause   740
you're the only unfriendly Mormon I ever met.

HANNAH: Your wig is crooked.

SISTER ELLA CHAPTER: Fix it.

    (HANNAH *straightens* SISTER ELLA'*s wig.*)

SISTER ELLA CHAPTER: New York City. All they got there is tiny rooms.
    I always thought: People ought to stay put. That's why I got my license to   745
sell real estate. It's a way of saying: Have a house! Stay put! It's a way of saying
traveling's no good. Plus I needed the cash. (*She takes a pack of cigarettes out of her
purse, lights one, offers pack to* HANNAH.)

HANNAH: Not out here, anyone could come by.
    There's been days I've stood at this ledge and thought about stepping over.   750
    It's a hard place, Salt Lake: baked dry. Abundant energy; not much
intelligence. That's a combination that can wear a body out. No harm looking
someplace else. I don't need much room.
    My sister-in-law Libby thinks there's radon gas in the basement.

SISTER ELLA CHAPTER: Is there gas in the . . .   755

HANNAH: Of course not. Libby's a fool.

SISTER ELLA CHAPTER: 'Cause I'd have to include that in the description.

HANNAH: There's no gas, Ella. (*Little pause.*) Give a puff. (*She takes a furtive drag of* ELLA'*s
cigarette.*) Put it away now.

SISTER ELLA CHAPTER: So I guess it's goodbye.   760

HANNAH: You'll be all right, Ella, I wasn't ever much of a friend.

SISTER ELLA CHAPTER: I'll say something but don't laugh, OK? This is the home of
saints, the godliest place on earth, they say, and I think they're right. That means
there's no evil here? No. Evil's everywhere. Sin's everywhere. But this . . . is the
spring of sweet water in the desert, the desert flower. Every step a Believer takes away   765
from here is a step fraught with peril. I fear for you, Hannah Pitt, because you are my
friend. Stay put. This is the right home of saints.

HANNAH: Latter-day saints.

SISTER ELLA CHAPTER: Only kind left.

HANNAH: But still. Late in the day . . . for saints and everyone. That's all. That's all.   770
    Fifty thousand dollars for the house, Sister Ella Chapter; don't undersell. It's an
impressive view.

ACT III

Not-Yet-Conscious, Forward Dawning
January 1986

SCENE I

Late night, three days after the end of Act Two. The stage is completely dark. PRIOR *is in bed in
his apartment, having a nightmare. He wakes up, sits up and switches on a nightlight. He looks
at his clock. Seated by the table near the bed is a man dressed in the clothing of a 13th-century
British squire.*

PRIOR: (*Terrified.*) Who are you?
PRIOR 1: My name is Prior Walter.

(*Pause.*)

PRIOR: My name is Prior Walter.
PRIOR 1: I know that.
PRIOR: Explain.
PRIOR 1: You're alive. I'm not. We have the same name. What do you want me to explain?
PRIOR: A ghost?
PRIOR 1: An ancestor.
PRIOR: Not *the* Prior Walter? The Bayeux tapestry Prior Walter?
PRIOR 1: His great-great grandson. The fifth of the name.
PRIOR: I'm the thirty-fourth, I think.
PRIOR 1: Actually the thirty-second.
PRIOR: Not according to Mother.
PRIOR 1: She's including the two bastards, then; I say leave them out. I say no room for bastards. The little things you swallow . . .
PRIOR: Pills.
PRIOR 1: Pills. For the pestilence. I too . . .
PRIOR: Pestilence. . . . You too what?
PRIOR 1: The pestilence in my time was much worse than now. Whole villages of empty houses. You could look outdoors and see Death walking in the morning, dew dampening the ragged hem of his black robe. Plain as I see you now.
PRIOR: You died of the plague.
PRIOR 1: The spotty monster. Like you, alone.
PRIOR: I'm not alone.
PRIOR 1: You have no wife, no children.
PRIOR: I'm gay.
PRIOR 1: So? Be gay, dance in your altogether for all I care, what's that to do with not having children?
PRIOR: Gay homosexual, not bonny, blithe and . . . never mind.
PRIOR 1: I had twelve. When I died.

(*The second ghost appears, this one dressed in the clothing of an elegant 17th-century Londoner.*)

PRIOR 1: (*Pointing to* PRIOR 2.) And I was three years younger than him.

(PRIOR *sees the new ghost, screams.*)

PRIOR: Oh God another one.
PRIOR 2: Prior Walter. Prior to you by some seventeen others.
PRIOR 1: He's counting the bastards.
PRIOR: Are we having a convention?
PRIOR 2: We've been sent to declare her fabulous incipience. They love a well-paved entrance with lots of heralds, and . . .
PRIOR 1: The messenger come. Prepare the way. The infinite descent, a breath in air . . .
PRIOR 2: They chose us, I suspect, because of the mortal affinities. In a family as long-descended as the Walters there are bound to be a few carried off by plague.
PRIOR 1: The spotty monster.
PRIOR 2: Black Jack. Came from a water pump, half the city of London, can you imagine? His came from fleas. Yours, I understand, is the lamentable consequence of venery . . .
PRIOR 1: Fleas on rats, but who knew that?

PRIOR: Am I going to die? 45
PRIOR 2: We aren't allowed to discuss . . .
PRIOR 1: When you do, you don't get ancestors to help you through it. You may be surrounded by children but you die alone.
PRIOR: I'm afraid.
PRIOR 1: You should be. There aren't even torches, and the path's rocky, dark and steep. 50
PRIOR 2: Don't alarm him. There's good news before there's bad.
    We two come to strew rose petal and palm leaf before the triumphal procession. Prophet. Seer. Revelator. It's a great honor for the family.
PRIOR 1: He hasn't got a family.
PRIOR 2: I meant for the Walters, for the family in the larger sense. 55
PRIOR: (*Singing.*)
        All I want is a room somewhere,
        Far away from the cold night air . . .
PRIOR 2: (*Putting a hand on* PRIOR's *forehead.*) Calm, calm, this is no brain fever . . .

    (PRIOR *calms down, but keeps his eyes closed. The lights begin to change. Distant Glorious Music.*)

PRIOR 1: (*Low chant.*) Adonai, Adonai, 60
    Olam ha-yichud,
    Zefirot, Zazahot,
    Ha-adam, ha-gadol
    Daughter of Light,
    Daughter of Splendors, 65
    Fluor! Phosphor!
    Lumen! Candle!
PRIOR 2: (*Simultaneously.*) Even now,
    From the mirror-bright halls of heaven,
    Across the cold and lifeless infinity of space, 70
    The Messenger comes
    Trailing orbs of light,
    Fabulous, incipient,
    Oh Prophet,
    To you . . . 75
PRIOR 1 AND PRIOR 2: Prepare, prepare,
    The Infinite Descent,
    A breath, a feather,
    Glory to . . .

    (*They vanish.*)

SCENE II

The next day. Split scene: LOUIS *and* BELIZE *in a coffee shop.* PRIOR *is at the outpatient clinic at the hospital with* EMILY, *the nurse; she has him on a pentamidine IV drip.*

LOUIS: Why has democracy succeeded in America? Of course by succeeded I mean 80
    comparatively, not literally, not in the present, but what makes for the prospect of
    some sort of radical democracy spreading outward and growing up? Why does the

power that was once so carefully preserved at the top of the pyramid by the original framers of the Constitution seem drawn inexorably downward and outward in spite of the best effort of the Right to stop this? I mean it's the really hard thing about being Left in this country, the American Left can't help but trip over all these petrified little fetishes: freedom, that's the worst; you know, *Jeane Kirkpatrick* for God's sake will go on and on about freedom and so what does that mean, the word freedom, when she talks about it, or human rights; you have Bush talking about human rights, and so what are these people talking about, they might as well be talking about the mating habits of Venusians, these people don't begin to know what, ontologically, freedom is or human rights, like they see these bourgeois property-based Rights-of-Man-type rights but that's not enfranchisement, not democracy, not what's implicit, what's potential within the idea, not the idea with blood in it. That's just liberalism, the worst kind of liberalism, really, bourgeois tolerance, and what I think is that what AIDS shows us is the limits of tolerance, that it's not enough to be tolerated, because when the shit hits the fan you find out how much tolerance is worth. Nothing. And underneath all the tolerance is intense, passionate hatred. 85 90 95

BELIZE: Uh huh.

LOUIS: Well don't you think that's true? 100

BELIZE: Uh huh. It is.

LOUIS: *Power* is the object, not being tolerated. Fuck assimilation. But I mean in spite of all this the thing about America, I think, is that ultimately we're different from every other nation on earth, in that, with people here of every race, we can't. . . . Ultimately what defines us isn't race, but politics. Not like any European country where there's an insurmountable fact of a kind of racial, or ethnic, monopoly, or monolith, like all Dutchmen, I mean Dutch people, are well, Dutch, and the Jews of Europe were never Europeans, just a small problem. Facing the monolith. But here there are so many small problems, it's really just a collection of small problems, the monolith is missing. Oh, I mean, of course I suppose there's the monolith of White America. White Straight Male America. 105 110

BELIZE: Which is not unimpressive, even among monoliths.

LOUIS: Well, no, but when the race thing gets taken care of, and I don't mean to minimalize how major it is, I mean I know it is, this is a really, really incredibly racist country but it's like, well, the British. I mean, all these blue-eyed pink people. And it's just weird, you know, I mean I'm not all that Jewish-looking, or . . . well, maybe I am but, you know, in New York, everyone is . . . well, not everyone, but so many are but so but in England, in London I walk into bars and I feel like Sid the Yid, you know I mean like Woody Allen in *Annie Hall,* with the payess and the gabardine coat, like never, never anywhere so much—I mean, not actively despised, not like they're Germans, who I think are still terribly anti-Semitic, and racist too, I mean black-racist, they pretend otherwise but, anyway, in London, there's just . . . and at one point I met this black gay guy from Jamaica who talked with a lilt but he said his family'd been living in London since before the Civil War—the American one—and how the English never let him forget for a minute that he wasn't blue-eyed and pink and I said yeah, me too, these people are anti-Semites and he said yeah but the British Jews have the clothing business all sewed up and blacks there can't get a foothold. And it was an incredibly awkward moment of just. . . . I mean here we were, in this bar that was gay but it was a *pub,* you know, the beams and the plaster and those horrible little, like, two-day-old fish and egg sandwiches—and just so British, so *old,* and I felt, well, there's no way out of this because both of us are, right now, too much immersed in this history, hope is dissolved in the sheer age of this place, where race is what counts and there's no real hope of change—it's the racial destiny of the Brits that matters to them, not their political destiny, whereas in America . . . 115 120 125 130

BELIZE: Here in America race doesn't count. 135

LOUIS: No, no, that's not. . . . I mean you *can't* be hearing that . . .

BELIZE: I . . .

LOUIS: It's—look, race, yes, but ultimately race here is a political question, right? Racists just try to use race here as a tool in a political struggle. It's not really about race. Like the spiritualists try to use that stuff, are you enlightened, are you centered, 140 channeled, whatever, this reaching out for a spiritual past in a country where no indigenous spirits exist—only the Indians, I mean Native American spirits and we killed them off so now, there are no gods here, no ghosts and spirits in America, there are no angels in America, no spiritual past, no racial past, there's only the political, and the decoys and the ploys to maneuver around the inescapable battle of 145 politics, the shifting downwards and outwards of political power to the people . . .

BELIZE: POWER to the People! AMEN! (*Looking at his watch.*) *OH MY GOODNESS!* Will you look at the time, I gotta . . .

LOUIS: Do you. . . . You think this is, what, racist or naive or something?

BELIZE: Well it's certainly *something*. Look, I just remembered I have an appointment . . . 150

LOUIS: What? I mean I really don't want to, like, speak from some position of privilege and . . .

BELIZE: I'm sitting here, thinking, eventually he's *got* to run out of steam, so I let you rattle on and on saying about maybe seven or eight things I find really offensive.

LOUIS: What? 155

BELIZE: But I know you, Louis, and I know the guilt fueling this peculiar tirade is obviously already swollen bigger than your hemorrhoids.

LOUIS: I don't have hemorrhoids.

BELIZE: I hear different. May I finish?

LOUIS: Yes, but I don't have hemorrhoids. 160

BELIZE: So finally, when I . . .

LOUIS: Prior told you, he's an asshole, he shouldn't have . . .

BELIZE: You promised, Louis. Prior is not a subject.

LOUIS: You brought him up.

BELIZE: I brought up hemorrhoids. 165

LOUIS: So it's indirect. Passive-aggressive.

BELIZE: Unlike, I suppose, banging me over the head with your theory that America doesn't have a race problem.

LOUIS: Oh be fair I never said that.

BELIZE: Not exactly, but . . . 170

LOUIS: I said . . .

BELIZE: but it was close enough, because if it'd been that blunt I'd've just walked out and . . .

LOUIS: You deliberately misinterpreted! I . . .

BELIZE: Stop interrupting! I haven't been able to . . . 175

LOUIS: Just let me . . .

BELIZE: NO! What, *talk*? You've been running your mouth nonstop since I got here, yaddadda yaddadda blah blah blah, up the hill, down the hill, playing with your MONOLITH . . .

LOUIS: (*Overlapping*) Well, you could have joined in at any time instead of . . . 180

BELIZE: (*Continuing over* LOUIS.) . . . and girlfriend it is truly an awesome spectacle but I got better things to do with my time than sit here listening to this racist bullshit just because I feel sorry for you that . . .

LOUIS: I am not a racist!

BELIZE: Oh come on . . . 185

LOUIS: So maybe I am a racist but . . .

BELIZE: Oh I really hate that! It's no fun picking on you Louis; you're so guilty, it's like throwing darts at a glob of jello, there's no satisfying hits, just quivering, the darts just blop in and vanish.

LOUIS: I just think when you are discussing lines of oppression it gets very complicated and . . .   190

BELIZE: Oh is that a fact? You know, we black drag queens have a rather intimate knowledge of the complexity of the lines of . . .

LOUIS: *Ex*-black drag queen.

BELIZE: Actually ex-ex.   195

LOUIS: You're doing drag again?

BELIZE: I don't. . . . Maybe. I don't have to tell you. Maybe.

LOUIS: I think it's sexist.

BELIZE: I didn't ask you.

LOUIS: Well it is. The gay community, I think, has to adopt the same attitude towards   200
drag as black women have to take towards black women blues singers.

BELIZE: Oh my we *are* walking dangerous tonight.

LOUIS: Well, it's all internalized oppression, right, I mean the masochism, the stereotypes, the . . .

BELIZE: Louis, are you deliberately trying to make me hate you?   205

LOUIS: No, I . . .

BELIZE: I mean, are you deliberately transforming yourself into an arrogant, sexual-political Stalinist-slash-racist flag-waving thug for my benefit?

(*Pause.*)

LOUIS: You know what I think?

BELIZE: What?   210

LOUIS: You hate me because I'm a Jew.

BELIZE: I'm leaving.

LOUIS: It's true.

BELIZE: You have no basis except your . . .
    Louis, it's good to know you haven't changed; you are still an honorary citizen   215
    of the Twilight Zone, and after your pale, pale white polemics on behalf of racial
    insensitivity you have a flaming *fuck* of a lot of nerve calling me an anti-Semite.
    Now I really gotta go.

LOUIS: You called me Lou the Jew.

BELIZE: That was a joke.   220

LOUIS: I didn't think it was funny. It was hostile.

BELIZE: It was three years ago.

LOUIS: So?

BELIZE: You just called yourself Sid the Yid.

LOUIS: That's not the same thing.   225

BELIZE: Sid the Yid is different from Lou the Jew.

LOUIS: Yes.

BELIZE: Someday you'll have to explain that to me, but right now . . .
    You hate me because you hate black people.

LOUIS: I do not. But I do think most black people are anti-Semitic.   230

BELIZE: "Most black people." *That's* racist, Louis, and *I* think most Jews . . .

LOUIS: Louis Farrakhan.

BELIZE: Ed Koch.

LOUIS: Jesse Jackson.

BELIZE: Jackson. Oh really, Louis, this is . . .   235

LOUIS: Hymietown! Hymietown!

BELIZE: Louis, you voted for Jesse Jackson. You send checks to the Rainbow Coalition.

LOUIS: I'm ambivalent. The checks bounced.

BELIZE: All your checks bounce, Louis; you're ambivalent about everything.

LOUIS: What's that supposed to mean?   240

BELIZE: You may be dumber than shit but I refuse to believe you can't figure it out. Try.

LOUIS: I was never ambivalent about Prior. I love him. I do. I really do.

BELIZE: Nobody said different.

LOUIS: Love and ambivalence are. . . . Real love isn't ambivalent.

BELIZE: "Real love isn't ambivalent." I'd swear that's a line from my favorite bestselling   245
paperback novel, *In Love with the Night Mysterious,* except I don't think you ever
read it.

> (*Pause.*)

LOUIS: I never read it, no.

BELIZE: You ought to. Instead of spending the rest of your life trying to get through
Democracy in America. It's about this white woman whose Daddy owns a plantation   250
in the Deep South in the years before the Civil War—the American one—and her
name is Margaret, and she's in love with her Daddy's number-one slave, and his
name is Thaddeus, and she's married but her white slave-owner husband has AIDS:
Antebellum Insufficiently Developed Sexorgans. And there's a lot of hot stuff going
down when Margaret and Thaddeus can catch a spare torrid ten under the cotton-   255
picking moon, and then of course the Yankees come, and they set the slaves free, and
the slaves string up old Daddy, and so on. Historical fiction. Somewhere in there I
recall Margaret and Thaddeus find the time to discuss the nature of love; her face is
reflecting the flames of the burning plantation—you know, the way white people
do—and his black face is dark in the night and she says to him, "Thaddeus, real love   260
isn't ever ambivalent."

> (*Little pause.* EMILY *enters and turns off IV drip.*)

BELIZE: Thaddeus looks at her; he's contemplating her thesis; and he isn't sure he agrees.

EMILY: (*Removing IV drip from* PRIOR*'s arm.*) Treatment number . . . (*Consulting chart.*)
four.

PRIOR: Pharmaceutical miracle. Lazarus breathes again.   265

LOUIS: Is he. . . . How bad is he?

BELIZE: You want the laundry list?

EMILY: Shirt off, let's check the . . .

> (PRIOR *takes his shirt off. She examines his lesions.*)

BELIZE: There's the weight problem and the shit problem and the morale problem.

EMILY: Only six. That's good. Pants.   270

> (*He drops his pants. He's naked. She examines.*)

BELIZE: And. He thinks he's going crazy.

EMILY: Looking good. What else?

PRIOR: Ankles sore and swollen, but the leg's better. The nausea's mostly gone with
the little orange pills. BM's pure liquid but not bloody anymore, for now, my eye
doctor says everything's OK, for now, my dentist says "Yuck!" when he sees my   275
fuzzy tongue, and now he wears little condoms on his thumb and forefinger. And

a mask. So what? My dermatologist is in Hawaii and my mother . . . well leave my mother out of it. Which is usually where my mother is, out of it. My glands are like walnuts, my weight's holding steady for week two, and a friend died two days ago of bird tuberculosis; bird tuberculosis; that scared me and I didn't go to the funeral today because he was an Irish Catholic and it's probably open casket and I'm afraid of . . . something, the bird TB or seeing him or. . . . So I guess I'm doing OK. Except for of course I'm going nuts.   280

EMILY: We ran the toxoplasmosis series and there's no indication . . .

PRIOR: I know, I know, but I feel like something terrifying is on its way, you know, like a missile from outer space, and it's plummeting down towards the earth, and I'm ground zero, and . . . I am generally known where I am known as one cool, collected queen. And I am ruffled.   285

EMILY: There's really nothing to worry about. I think that shochen bamromim hamtzeh menucho nechono al kanfey haschino.   290

PRIOR: What?

EMILY: Everything's fine. Bemaalos k'doshim ut'horim kezohar horokeea mazhirim . . .

PRIOR: Oh I don't understand what you're . . .

EMILY: Es nishmas Prior sheholoch leolomoh, baavur shenodvoo z'dokoh b'ad hazkoras nishmosoh.   295

PRIOR: Why are you doing that?! Stop it! Stop it!

EMILY: Stop what?

PRIOR: You were just . . . weren't you just speaking in Hebrew or something.

EMILY: *Hebrew?* (*Laughs.*) I'm basically Italian-American. No. I didn't speak in Hebrew.

PRIOR: Oh no, oh God please I really think I . . .   300

EMILY: Look, I'm sorry, I have a waiting room full of. . . . I think you're one of the lucky ones, you'll live for years, probably—you're pretty healthy for someone with no immune system. Are you seeing someone? Loneliness is a danger. A therapist?

PRIOR: No, I don't need to see anyone, I just . . .

EMILY: Well think about it. You aren't going crazy. You're just under a lot of stress.   305
No wonder . . . (*She starts to write in his chart.*)

> (*Suddenly there is an astonishing blaze of light, a huge chord sounded by a gigantic choir, and a great book with steel pages mounted atop a molten-red pillar pops up from the stage floor. The book opens; there is a large Aleph inscribed on its pages, which bursts into flames. Immediately the book slams shut and disappears instantly under the floor as the lights become normal again.* EMILY *notices none of this, writing.* PRIOR *is agog.*)

EMILY: (*Laughing, exiting.*) Hebrew . . .

> (PRIOR *flees.*)

LOUIS: Help me.

BELIZE: I beg your pardon?

LOUIS: You're a nurse, give me something, I . . . don't know what to do anymore,   310
I. . . . Last week at work I screwed up the Xerox machine like permanently and so I . . . then I tripped on the subway steps and my glasses broke and I cut my forehead, here, see, and now I can't see much and my forehead . . . it's like the Mark of Cain, stupid, right, but it won't heal and every morning I see it and I think, Biblical things, Mark of Cain, Judas Iscariot and his silver and his noose, people who . . . in betraying   315
what they love betray what's truest in themselves, I feel . . . nothing but cold for myself, just cold, and every night I miss him, I miss him so much but then . . . those

sores, and the smell and . . . where I thought it was going. . . . I could be . . . I could be sick too, maybe I'm sick too. I don't know.

Belize. Tell him I love him. Can you do that?   320

BELIZE: I've thought about it for a very long time, and I still don't understand what love is. Justice is simple. Democracy is simple. Those things are unambivalent. But love is very hard. And it goes bad for you if you violate the hard law of love.

LOUIS: I'm dying.

BELIZE: He's dying. You just wish you were. Oh cheer up, Louis. Look at that heavy sky   325
out there.

LOUIS: Purple.

BELIZE: *Purple?* Boy, what kind of a homosexual are you, anyway? That's not purple, Mary, that color up there is (*Very grand.*) mauve.

All day today it's felt like Thanksgiving. Soon, this . . . ruination will be   330
blanketed white. You can smell it—can you smell it?

LOUIS: Smell what?

BELIZE: Softness, compliance, forgiveness, grace.

LOUIS: No . . .

BELIZE: I can't help you learn that. I can't help you, Louis. You're not my business. (*He exits.*)   335

(LOUIS *puts his head in his hands, inadvertently touching his cut forehead.*)

LOUIS: Ow FUCK! (*He stands slowly, looks towards where* BELIZE *exited.*) Smell what? (*He looks both ways to be sure no one is watching, then inhales deeply, and is surprised.*) Huh. Snow.

SCENE III

Same day. HARPER *in a very white, cold place, with a brilliant blue sky above; a delicate snowfall. She is dressed in a beautiful snowsuit. The sound of the sea, faint.*

HARPER: Snow! Ice! Mountains of ice! Where am I? I . . . feel better, I do, I . . . feel better. There are ice crystals in my lungs, wonderful and sharp. And the snow smells like   340
cold, crushed peaches. And there's something . . . some current of blood in the wind, how strange, it has that iron taste.

MR. LIES: Ozone.

HARPER: Ozone! Wow! Where am I?

MR. LIES: The Kingdom of Ice, the bottommost part of the world.   345

HARPER: (*Looking around, then realizing.*) Antarctica. This is Antarctica!

MR. LIES: Cold shelter for the shattered. No sorrow here, tears freeze.

HARPER: Antarctica, Antarctica, oh boy oh boy, LOOK at this, I. . . . Wow, I must've really snapped the tether, huh?

MR. LIES: Apparently . . .   350

HARPER: That's great. I want to stay here forever. Set up camp. Build things. Build a city, an enormous city made up of frontier forts, dark wood and green roofs and high gates made of pointed logs and bonfires burning on every street corner. I should build by a river. Where are the forests?

MR. LIES: No timber here. Too cold. Ice, no trees.   355

HARPER: Oh details! I'm sick of details! I'll plant them and grow them. I'll live off caribou fat, I'll melt it over the bon-fires and drink it from long, curved goat-horn cups. It'll be great. I want to make a new world here. So that I never have to go home again.

MR. LIES: As long as it lasts. Ice has a way of melting . . .

HARPER: No. Forever. I can have anything I want here—maybe even companionship,   360
someone who has . . . desire for me. You, maybe.

MR. LIES: It's against the by-laws of the International Order of Travel Agents to get involved
with clients. Rules are rules. Anyway, I'm not the one you really want.

HARPER: There isn't anyone . . . maybe an Eskimo. Who could ice-fish for food. And help
me build a nest for when the baby comes.   365

MR. LIES: There are no Eskimo in Antarctica. And you're not really pregnant. You made
that up.

HARPER: Well all of this is made up. So if the snow feels cold I'm pregnant. Right? Here,
I can be pregnant. And I can have any kind of a baby I want.

MR. LIES: This is a retreat, a vacuum, its virtue is that it lacks everything; deep-freeze for   370
feelings. You can be numb and safe here, that's what you came for. Respect the
delicate ecology of your delusions.

HARPER: You mean like no Eskimo in Antarctica.

MR. LIES: Correcto. Ice and snow, no Eskimo. Even hallucinations have laws.

HARPER: Well then who's that?   375

(The ESKIMO *appears.*)

MR. LIES: An Eskimo.

HARPER: An antarctic Eskimo. A fisher of the polar deep.

MR. LIES: There's something wrong with this picture.

(The ESKIMO *beckons.*)

HARPER: I'm going to like this place. It's my own National Geo-graphic Special! Oh! Oh!
(*She holds her stomach.*) I think . . . I think I felt her kicking. Maybe I'll give birth to   380
a baby covered with thick white fur, and that way she won't be cold. My breasts will
be full of hot cocoa so she doesn't get chilly. And if it gets really cold, she'll have a
pouch I can crawl into. Like a marsupial. We'll mend together. That's what we'll do;
we'll mend.

SCENE IV

Same day. An abandoned lot in the South Bronx. A homeless WOMAN *is standing near an oil
drum in which a fire is burning. Snowfall. Trash around.* HANNAH *enters dragging two heavy
suitcases.*

HANNAH: Excuse me? I said excuse me? Can you tell me where I am? Is this Brooklyn?   385
Do you know a Pineapple Street? Is there some sort of bus or train or . . . ?

I'm lost, I just arrived from Salt Lake. City. Utah? I took the bus that I was
told to take and I got off—well it was the very last stop, so I had to get off, and I
asked the driver was this Brooklyn, and he nodded yes but he was from one of those
foreign countries where they think it's good manners to nod at everything even   390
if you have no idea what it is you're nodding at, and in truth I think he spoke no
English at all, which I think would make him ineligible for employment on public
transportation. The public being English-speaking, mostly. Do you speak English?

(*The* WOMAN *nods.*)

HANNAH: I was supposed to be met at the airport by my son. He didn't show and I don't wait more than three and three-quarters hours for *anyone*. I should have been patient, I guess, I. . . . Is this . . . 395

WOMAN: Bronx.

HANNAH: Is that. . . . The *Bronx?* Well how in the name of Heaven did I get to the Bronx when the bus driver said . . .

WOMAN: (*Talking to herself.*) Slurp slurp slurp will you STOP that disgusting slurping! 400 YOU DISGUSTING SLURPING FEEDING ANIMAL! Feeding yourself, just feeding yourself, what would it matter, to you or to ANYONE, if you just stopped. Feeding. And DIED?

(*Pause.*)

HANNAH: Can you just tell me where I . . .

WOMAN: Why was the Kosciusko Bridge named after a Polack? 405

HANNAH: I don't know what you're . . .

WOMAN: That was a joke.

HANNAH: Well what's the punchline?

WOMAN: I don't know.

HANNAH: (*Looking around desperately.*) Oh for pete's sake, is there anyone else who . . . 410

WOMAN: (*Again, to herself.*) Stand further off you fat loathsome whore, you can't have any more of this soup, slurp slurp slurp you animal, and the—I know you'll just go pee it all away and where will you do that? Behind what bush? It's FUCKING COLD out here and I . . .
    Oh that's right, because it was supposed to have been a tunnel! 415
    That's not very funny.
    Have you read the prophecies of Nostradamus?

HANNAH: Who?

WOMAN: Some guy I went out with once somewhere, Nostradamus. Prophet, outcast, eyes like. . . . Scary shit, he . . . 420

HANNAH: Shut up. Please. Now I want you to stop jabbering for a minute and pull your wits together and tell me how to get to Brooklyn. Because you know! And you are going to tell me! Because there is no one else around to tell me and I am wet and cold and I am very angry! So I am sorry you're psychotic but just make the effort— take a deep breath—DO IT! 425

(HANNAH *and* WOMAN *breathe together.*)

HANNAH: That's good. Now exhale.

(*They do.*)

HANNAH: Good. Now how do I get to Brooklyn?

WOMAN: Don't know. Never been. Sorry. Want some soup?

HANNAH: Manhattan? Maybe you know . . . I don't suppose you know the location of the Mormon Visitor's . . . 430

WOMAN: 65th and Broadway.

HANNAH: How do you . . .

WOMAN: Go there all the time. Free movies. Boring, but you can stay all day.

HANNAH: Well. . . . So how do I . . .

WOMAN: Take the D Train. Next block make a right. 435

HANNAH: Thank you.

WOMAN: Oh yeah. In the new century I think we will all be insane.

SCENE V

Same day. JOE *and* ROY *in the study of* ROY's *brownstone.* ROY *is wearing an elegant bathrobe. He has made a considerable effort to look well. He isn't well, and he hasn't succeeded much in looking it.*

JOE: I can't. The answer's no. I'm sorry.
ROY: Oh, well, apologies . . .
    I can't see that there's anyone asking for apologies.   440

    (*Pause.*)

JOE: I'm sorry, Roy.
ROY: Oh, well, apologies.
JOE: My wife is missing, Roy. My mother's coming from Salt Lake to . . . to help look, I guess. I'm supposed to be at the airport now, picking her up but. . . . I just spent two days in a hospital, Roy, with a bleeding ulcer, I was spitting up blood.   445
ROY: Blood, huh? Look, I'm very busy here and . . .
JOE: It's just a job.
ROY: A *job*? A *job*? *Washington!* Dumb Utah Mormon hick shit!
JOE: Roy . . .
ROY: *WASHINGTON!* When Washington called me I was younger than you, you   450
    think I said "Aw fuck no I can't go I got two fingers up my asshole and a little moral nosebleed to boot!" When Washington calls you my pretty young punk friend you go or you can go fuck yourself sideways 'cause the train has pulled out of the station, and you are *out,* nowhere, out in the cold. Fuck you, Mary Jane, get outta here.
JOE: Just let me . . .   455
ROY: Explain? Ephemera. You broke my heart. Explain that. Explain that.
JOE: I love you. Roy.
    There's so much that I want, to be . . . what you see in me, I want to be
a participant in the world, in your world, Roy, I want to be capable of that,
I've tried, really I have but . . . I can't do this. Not because I don't believe in   460
you, but because I believe in you so much, in what you stand for, at heart, the
order, the decency. I would give anything to protect you, but. . . . There are
laws I can't break. It's too ingrained. It's not me. There's enough damage I've
already done.
    Maybe you were right, maybe I'm dead.   465
ROY: You're not dead, boy, you're a sissy.
    You love me; that's moving, I'm moved. It's nice to be loved. I warned you about
her, didn't I, Joe? But you don't listen to me, why, because you say Roy is smart
and Roy's a friend but Roy . . . well, he isn't nice, and you wanna be nice. Right?
A nice, nice man!   470

    (*Little pause.*)

You know what my greatest accomplishment was, Joe, in my life, what I am able to
look back on and be proudest of? And I have helped make Presidents and unmake
them and mayors and more goddam judges than anyone in NYC ever—AND
several million dollars, tax-free—and what do you think means the most to me?
    You ever hear of Ethel Rosenberg? Huh, Joe, huh?   475
JOE: Well, yeah, I guess I. . . . Yes.

ROY: Yes. Yes. You have heard of Ethel Rosenberg. Yes. Maybe you even read about her in the history books.

    If it wasn't for me, Joe, Ethel Rosenberg would be alive today, writing some personal-advice column for *Ms.* magazine. She isn't. Because during the trial, Joe, I was on the phone every day, talking with the judge . . .   480

JOE: Roy . . .

ROY: Every day, doing what I do best, talking on the telephone, making sure that timid Yid nebbish on the bench did his duty to America, to history. That sweet unprepossessing woman, two kids, boo-hoo-hoo, reminded us all of our little Jewish   485
mamas—she came this close to getting life; I pleaded till I wept to put her in the chair. Me. I did that. I would have fucking pulled the switch if they'd have let me. Why? Because I fucking hate traitors. Because I fucking hate communists. Was it legal? Fuck legal. Am I a nice man? Fuck nice. They say terrible things about me in the *Nation.* Fuck the *Nation.* You want to be Nice, or you want to be Effective? Make   490
the law, or subject to it. Choose. Your wife chose. A week from today, she'll be back. SHE knows how to get what SHE wants. Maybe I ought to send *her* to Washington.

JOE: I don't believe you.

ROY: Gospel.

JOE: You can't possibly mean what you're saying.   495

    Roy, you were the Assistant United States Attorney on the Rosenberg case, ex-parte communication with the judge during the trial would be . . . censurable, at least, probably conspiracy and . . . in a case that resulted in execution, it's . . .

ROY: What? Murder?

JOE: You're not well is all.   500

ROY: What do you mean, not well? Who's not well?

    (*Pause.*)

JOE: You said . . .

ROY: No I didn't. I said what?

JOE: Roy, you have cancer.

ROY: No I don't.   505

    (*Pause.*)

JOE: You told me you were dying.

ROY: What the fuck are you talking about, Joe? I never said that. I'm in perfect health. There's not a goddam thing wrong with me.

    (*He smiles.*)

Shake?

    (JOE *hesitates. He holds out his hand to* ROY. ROY *pulls* JOE *into a close, strong clinch.*)

ROY: (*More to himself than to* JOE.) It's OK that you hurt me because I love you, baby Joe.   510
That's why I'm so rough on you.

    (ROY *releases* JOE. JOE *backs away a step or two.*)

ROY: Prodigal son. The world will wipe its dirty hands all over you.

JOE: It already has, Roy.

ROY: Now go.

    (ROY *shoves* JOE *hard.* JOE *turns to leave.* ROY *stops him, turns him around.*)

ROY: (*Smoothing* JOE's *lapels, tenderly.*) I'll always be here, waiting for you . . .   515

  (*Then again, with sudden violence, he pulls* JOE *close, violently.*)

What did you want from me, what was all this, what do you want, treacherous ungrateful little . . .

  (JOE, *very close to belting* ROY, *grabs him by the front of his robe, and propels him across the length of the room. He holds* ROY *at arm's length, the other arm ready to hit.*)

ROY: (*Laughing softly, almost pleading to be hit.*) Transgress a little, Joseph.

  (JOE *releases* ROY.)

ROY: There are so many laws; find one you can break.

  (JOE *hesitates, then leaves, backing out. When* JOE *has gone,* ROY *doubles over in great pain, which he's been hiding throughout the scene with* JOE.)

ROY: Ah, Christ . . .   520
Andy! Andy! Get in here! Andy!

  (*The door opens, but it isn't* ANDY. *A small Jewish Woman dressed modestly in a fifties hat and coat stands in the doorway. The room darkens.*)

ROY: Who the fuck are you? The new nurse?

  (*The figure in the doorway says nothing. She stares at* ROY. *A pause.* ROY *looks at her carefully, gets up, crosses to her. He crosses back to the chair, sits heavily.*)

ROY: Aw, fuck. Ethel.
ETHEL ROSENBERG: (*Her manner is friendly, her voice is ice-cold.*) You don't look good, Roy.   525
ROY: Well, Ethel. I don't feel good.
ETHEL ROSENBERG: But you lost a lot of weight. That suits you. You were heavy back then. Zaftig, mit hips.
ROY: I haven't been that heavy since 1960. We were all heavier back then, before the body thing started. Now I look like a skeleton. They stare.   530
ETHEL ROSENBERG: The shit's really hit the fan, huh, Roy?

  (*Little pause.* ROY *nods.*)

ETHEL ROSENBERG: Well the fun's just started.
ROY: What is this, Ethel, Halloween? You trying to scare me?

  (ETHEL *says nothing.*)

ROY: Well you're wasting your time! I'm scarier than you any day of the week! So beat it, Ethel! BOOO! BETTER DEAD THAN RED! Somebody trying to shake me up?   535
HAH HAH! From the throne of God in heaven to the belly of hell, you can all fuck yourselves and then go jump in the lake because I'M NOT AFRAID OF YOU OR DEATH OR HELL OR ANYTHING!
ETHEL ROSENBERG: Be seeing you soon, Roy. Julius sends his regards.
ROY: Yeah, well send this to Julius!   540

  (*He flips the bird in her direction, stands and moves towards her. Half-way across the room he slumps to the floor, breathing laboriously, in pain.*)

ETHEL ROSENBERG: You're a very sick man, Roy.

ROY: Oh God . . . ANDY!

ETHEL ROSENBERG: Hmmm. He doesn't hear you, I guess. We should call the ambulance.

(*She goes to the phone.*)

Hah! Buttons! Such things they got now.
  What do I dial, Roy?   545

(*Pause.* ROY *looks at her, then:*)

ROY: 911.

ETHEL ROSENBERG: (*Dials the phone.*) It sings!
  (*Imitating dial tones.*) La la la . . .
  Huh.
  Yes, you should please send an ambulance to the home of Mister Roy Cohn, the   550
famous lawyer.
  What's the address, Roy?

ROY: (*A beat, then.*) 244 East 87th.

ETHEL ROSENBERG: 244 East 87th Street. No apartment number, he's got the whole
  building.   555
  My name? (*A beat.*) Ethel Greenglass Rosenberg.
  (*Small smile.*) Me? No I'm not related to Mr. Cohn. An old friend.

(*She hangs up.*)

They said a minute.

ROY: I have all the time in the world.

ETHEL ROSENBERG: You're immortal.   560

ROY: I'm immortal. Ethel. (*He forces himself to stand.*)
  I have *forced* my way into history. I ain't never gonna die.

ETHEL ROSENBERG: (*A little laugh, then.*) History is about to crack wide open.
  Millennium approaches.

SCENE VI

Late that night. PRIOR*'s bedroom.* PRIOR 1 *watching* PRIOR *in bed, who is staring back at him, terrified. Tonight* PRIOR 1 *is dressed in weird alchemical robes and hat over his historical clothing and he carries a long palm-leaf bundle.*

PRIOR 1: Tonight's the night! Aren't you excited? Tonight she arrives! Right through the   565
  roof! Ha-adam, Ha-gadol . . .

PRIOR 2: (*Appearing, similarly attired.*) Lumen! Phosphor! Fluor! Candle! An unending
  billowing of scarlet and . . .

PRIOR: Look. Garlic. A mirror. Holy water. A crucifix. FUCK OFF! Get the fuck out of
  my room! GO!   570

PRIOR 1: (*To* PRIOR 2.) Hard as a hickory knob, I'll bet.

PRIOR 2: We all tumesce when they approach. We wax full, like moons.

PRIOR 1: Dance.

PRIOR: Dance?

PRIOR 1: Stand up, dammit, give us your hands, dance!   575

PRIOR 2: Listen . . .

(*A lone oboe begins to play a little dance tune.*)

PRIOR 2: Delightful sound. Care to dance?

PRIOR: Please leave me alone, please just let me sleep . . .

PRIOR 2: Ah, he wants someone familiar. A partner who knows his steps. (*To* PRIOR.)
Close your eyes. Imagine . . .   580

PRIOR: I don't . . .

PRIOR 2: Hush. Close your eyes.

> (PRIOR *does.*)

PRIOR 2: Now open them.

> (PRIOR *does.* LOUIS *appears. He looks gorgeous. The music builds gradually into a full-blooded, romantic dance tune.*)

PRIOR: Lou.

LOUIS: Dance with me.   585

PRIOR: I can't, my leg, it hurts at night . . .
Are you . . . a ghost, Lou?

LOUIS: No. Just spectral. Lost to myself. Sitting all day on cold park benches. Wishing I
could be with you. Dance with me, babe . . .

> (PRIOR *stands up. The leg stops hurting. They begin to dance. The music is beautiful.*)

PRIOR 1: (*To* PRIOR 2.) Hah. Now I see why he's got no children. He's a sodomite.   590

PRIOR 2: Oh be quiet, you medieval gnome, and let them dance.

PRIOR 1: I'm not interfering, I've done my bit. Hooray, hooray, the messenger's come,
now I'm blowing off. I don't like it here.

> (PRIOR 1 *vanishes.*)

PRIOR 2: The twentieth century. Oh dear, the world has gotten so terribly, terribly old.

> (PRIOR 2 *vanishes.* LOUIS *and* PRIOR *waltz happily. Lights fade back to normal.* LOUIS *vanishes.*)

> (PRIOR *dances alone.*)

> (*Then suddenly, the sound of wings fills the room.*)

SCENE VII

Split scene: PRIOR *alone in his apartment;* LOUIS *alone in the park.*
Again, a sound of beating wings.

PRIOR: Oh don't come in here don't come in . . . LOUIS!! No. My name is Prior Walter,   595
I am . . . the scion of an ancient line, I am . . . abandoned I . . . no, my name is . . .
is . . . Prior and I live . . . *here and now,* and . . . in the dark, in the dark, the Recording Angel opens its hundred eyes and snaps the spine of the Book of Life and . . .
hush! Hush!

I'm talking nonsense, I . . . 600
No more mad scene, hush, hush . . .

(LOUIS *in the park on a bench.* JOE *approaches, stands at a distance. They stare at each other, then* LOUIS *turns away.*)

LOUIS: Do you know the story of Lazarus?
JOE: Lazarus?
LOUIS: Lazarus. I can't remember what happens, exactly.
JOE: I don't. . . . Well, he was dead, Lazarus, and Jesus breathed life into him. He brought 605
him back from death.
LOUIS: Come here often?
JOE: No. Yes. Yes.
LOUIS: Back from the dead. You believe that really happened?
JOE: I don't know anymore what I believe. 610
LOUIS: This is quite a coincidence. Us meeting.
JOE: I followed you.
From work. I . . . followed you here.

(*Pause.*)

LOUIS: You followed me.
You probably saw me that day in the washroom and thought: there's a sweet guy, 615
sensitive, cries for friends in trouble.
JOE: Yes.
LOUIS: You thought maybe I'll cry for you.
JOE: Yes.
LOUIS: Well I fooled you. Crocodile tears. Nothing . . . (*He touches his heart, shrugs.*) 620

(JOE *reaches tentatively to touch* LOUIS's *face.*)

LOUIS: (*Pulling back.*) What are you doing? Don't do that.
JOE: (*Withdrawing his hand.*) Sorry. I'm sorry.
LOUIS: I'm . . . just not . . . I think, if you touch me, your hand might fall off or something.
Worse things have happened to people who have touched me.
JOE: Please. 625
Oh, boy . . .
Can I . . .
I . . . want . . . to touch you. Can I please just touch you . . . um, here?

(*He puts his hand on one side of* LOUIS's *face. He holds it there.*)

I'm going to hell for doing this.
LOUIS: Big deal. You think it could be any worse than New York City? 630

(*He puts his hand on* JOE's *hand. He takes* JOE's *hand away from his face, holds it for a moment, then.*) Come on.

JOE: Where?
LOUIS: Home. With me.
JOE: This makes no sense. I mean I don't know you.
LOUIS: Likewise.
JOE: And what you do know about me you don't like. 635
LOUIS: The Republican stuff?
JOE: Yeah, well for starters.

LOUIS: I don't not like that. I hate that.
JOE: So why on earth should we . . .

(LOUIS *goes to* JOE *and kisses him.*)

LOUIS: Strange bedfellows. I don't know. I never made it with one of the damned before.   640
I would really rather not have to spend tonight alone.
JOE: I'm a pretty terrible person, Louis.
LOUIS: Lou.
JOE: No, I really really am. I don't think I deserve being loved.
LOUIS: There? See? We already have a lot in common.   645

(LOUIS *stands, begins to walk away. He turns, looks back at* JOE. JOE *follows. They exit.*)

(PRIOR *listens. At first no sound, then once again, the sound of beating wings, frighteningly near.*)

PRIOR: That sound, that sound, it. . . . What is that, like birds or something, like a *really*
big bird, I'm frightened, I . . . no, no fear, find the anger, find the . . . anger, my
blood is clean, my brain is fine, I can handle pressure, I am a gay man and I am used
to pressure, to trouble, I am tough and strong and. . . . Oh. Oh my goodness. I . . .
(*He is washed over by an intense sexual feeling.*) Ooohhhh. . . . I'm hot, I'm . . . so . . .   650
aw Jeez what is going on here I . . . must have a fever I . . .

(*The bedside lamp flickers wildly as the bed begins to roll forward and back.
There is a deep bass creaking and groaning from the bedroom ceiling, like the tim-
bers of a ship under immense stress, and from above a fine rain of plaster dust.*)

PRIOR: OH!
PLEASE, OH PLEASE! Something's coming in here, I'm scared, I don't like this
at all, something's approaching and
I. . . . OH!   655

(*There is a great blaze of triumphal music, heralding. The light turns an extraordinary harsh, cold, pale blue, then a rich, brilliant warm golden color, then a hot,
bilious green, and then finally a spectacular royal purple. Then silence.*)

PRIOR: (*An awestruck whisper.*) God almighty . . .
Very Steven Spielberg.

(*A sound, like a plummeting meteor, tears down from very, very far above the
earth, hurtling at an incredible velocity towards the bedroom; the light seems
to be sucked out of the room as the projectile approaches; as the room reaches
darkness, we hear a terrifying CRASH as something immense strikes earth; the
whole building shudders and a part of the bedroom ceiling, lots of plaster and
lathe and wiring, crashes to the floor. And then in a shower of unearthly white
light, spreading great opalescent gray-silver wings, the* ANGEL *descends into the
room and floats above the bed.*)

ANGEL: Greetings, Prophet;
The Great Work begins:
The Messenger has arrived.   660

(*Blackout.*)

Paula Vogel (1951–)

How I Learned to Drive
(1997)

HOW I LEARNED TO DRIVE draws a parallel between learning to drive a car and learning to make one's way through the difficulties of growing up. This parallel is particularly meaningful to the play's central character, Li'l Bit, who was taught to drive by her uncle—a pedophile who used her driving lessons as an opportunity to seduce her. The situation is made especially complex because the would-be seducer, Uncle Peck, is treated somewhat sympathetically. Uncle Peck seems to love his niece, Li'l Bit, and has far more concern for her than do members of her family, who constantly tease her and make her miserable with comments about the size of her breasts. The play strongly suggests that Uncle Peck himself has been a victim of pedophilia and that he honestly sees in Li'l Bit some hope for emotional fulfillment.

How I Learned to Drive is basically a memory play. It moves easily back and forth through time as Li'l Bit recalls her adolescent years and her relationship with Uncle Peck. The playwright frames the scenes through the use of captions, which Vogel suggests should be spoken in the type of voice heard in driver education films. Most of these captions are related to driving lessons such as "Idling in the Neutral Gear," "Shifting Forward from First to Second Gear," "You and the Reverse Gear," and "Driving in Today's World." Li'l Bit and Uncle Peck are the only clearly developed characters. All of the other roles in the play are performed by what the script labels the "Greek Chorus"—one male and two female actors who change identities quickly to become family members, students, waiters, and others needed to make the script function effectively. This choice by the playwright focuses our attention and sympathies on Uncle Peck and Li'l Bit.

Li'l Bit and Uncle Peck share a deep emotional relationship that is always more painful than fulfilling, one that can never be forgotten. As Li'l Bit says of her first understanding of what was happening between them: "That day was the last day I lived in my body. I retreated above the neck, and I've lived inside the 'fire' in my head ever since. . . . The nearest sensation I feel—of flight in the body—I guess I feel when I'm driving." And at the end of the play as she prepares to drive, she recalls and obeys all the rules that Uncle Peck taught her. At this point she seems near acceptance of what happened in the past and as close to reconciliation as is possible.

How I Learned to Drive won the Pulitzer Prize for Drama in 1998, and over the next decade was one of the most produced plays across the country. Typifying the complexity Vogel seeks, in an interview for the 2012 New York revival, she stated: "It's about the gifts we receive from the people who harm us."

How I Learned to Drive by Paula Vogel. From *The Mammary Plays* by Paula Vogel. © 1998 by Paula Vogel. Published by Theatre Communications Group.

How I Learned to Drive
(1997)

Characters

LI'L BIT—*A woman who ages forty-something to eleven years old. (See Notes on the New York Production.)*

PECK—*Attractive man in his forties. Despite a few problems, he should be played by an actor one might cast in the role of Atticus in* To Kill a Mockingbird.

THE GREEK CHORUS—*If possible, these three members should be able to sing three-part harmony.*

MALE GREEK CHORUS—*Plays Grandfather, Waiter, High School Boys. Thirties–Forties. (See Notes on the New York Production.)*

FEMALE GREEK CHORUS—*Plays Mother, Aunt Mary, High School Girls. Thirty–Fifty. (See Notes on the New York Production.)*

TEENAGE GREEK CHORUS—*Plays Grandmother, High School Girls, and the voice of eleven-year-old Li'l Bit. Note on the casting of this actor: I would strongly recommend casting a young woman who is of "legal age;" that is, twenty-one to twenty-five years old who can look as close to eleven as possible. The contrast with the other cast members will help. If the actor is too young, the audience may feel uncomfortable. (See Notes on the New York Production.)*

PRODUCTION NOTES

I urge directors to use the Greek Chorus in staging as environment and, well, part of the family—with the exception of the Teenage Greek Chorus member who, after the last time she appears onstage, should perhaps disappear.

As for music: Please have fun. I wrote sections of the play listening to music like Roy Orbison's "Dream Baby" and The Mamas and the Papas' "Dedicated to the One I Love." The vaudeville sections go well to the Tijuana Brass or any music that sounds like a Laugh-In soundtrack. Other sixties music is rife with pedophilish (?) reference: the "You're Sixteen" genre hits; The Beach Boys' "Little Surfer Girl"; Gary Puckett and the Union Gap's "This Girl Is a Woman Now"; "Come Back When You Grow Up," etc.

And whenever possible, please feel free to punctuate the action with traffic signs: "No Passing," "Slow Children," "Dangerous Curves," "One Way," and the visual signs for children, deer crossings, hills, school buses, etc. (See Notes on the New York Production.)

This script uses the notion of slides and projections, which were not used in the New York production of the play.

On titles: Throughout the script there are boldfaced titles. In production these should be spoken in a neutral voice (the type of voice that driver education films employ). In the New York production these titles were assigned to various members of the Greek Chorus and were done live.

NOTES ON THE NEW YORK PRODUCTION

The role of Li'l Bit was originally written as a character who is forty-something. When we cast Mary-Louise Parker in the role of Li'l Bit, we cast the Greek Chorus members with younger actors as the Female Greek and the Male Greek, and cast the Teenage Greek with an older (that is, mid-twenties) actor as well. There is a great deal of flexibility in age. Directors should change the age in the last monologue for Li'l Bit ("And before you know it, I'll be thirty-five . . .") to reflect the actor's age who is playing Li'l Bit.

  As the house lights dim, a **VOICE** *announces:*

Safety first—You and Driver Education.

  [*Then the sound of a key turning the ignition of a car.* LI'L BIT *steps into a spot-light on the stage; "well-endowed," she is a softer-looking woman in the present time than she was at seventeen.*]

LI'L BIT: Sometimes to tell a secret, you first have to teach a lesson. We're going to start our lesson tonight on an early, warm summer evening.

  In a parking lot overlooking the Beltsville Agricultural Farms in suburban Maryland.   5

Less than a mile away, the crumbling concrete of U.S. One wends its way past one-room revival churches, the porno drive-in, and boarded up motels with For Sale signs tumbling down.

  Like I said, it's a warm summer evening.

Here on the land the Department of Agriculture owns, the smell of sleeping farm 10 animal is thick in the air. The smells of clover and hay mix in with the smells of the leather dashboard. You can still imagine how Maryland used to be, before the malls took over. This countryside was once dotted with farmhouses—from their porches you could have witnessed the Civil War raging in the front fields.

  Oh yes. There's a moon over Maryland tonight, that spills into the car where I 15 sit beside a man old enough to be—did I mention how still the night is? Damp soil and tranquil air. It's the kind of night that makes a middle-aged man with a mort-gage feel like a country boy again.

  It's 1969. And I am very old, very cynical of the world, and I know it all. In short, I am seventeen years old, parking off a dark lane with a married man on an 20 early summer night.

  [*Lights up on two chairs facing front—or a Buick Riviera, if you will. Wait-ing patiently, with a smile on his face,* PECK *sits sniffing the night air.* LI'L BIT *climbs in beside him, seventeen years old and tense. Throughout the following, the two sit facing directly front. They do not touch. Their bodies remain passive. Only their facial expressions emote.*]

PECK: Ummm. I love the smell of your hair.
LI'L BIT: Uh-huh.
PECK: Oh, Lord. Ummmm. [*beat*] A man could die happy like this.
LI'L BIT: Well, *don't.*   25
PECK: What shampoo is this?
LI'L BIT: Herbal Essence.
PECK: Herbal Essence. I'm gonna buy me some. Herbal Essence. And when I'm all alone in the house, I'm going to get into the bathtub, and uncap the bottle and—
LI'L BIT: —Be good.   30
PECK: What?
LI'L BIT: Stop being . . . bad.
PECK: What did you think I was going to say? What do you think I'm going to do with the shampoo?
LI'L BIT: I don't want to know. I don't want to hear it.   35

PECK: I'm going to wash my hair. That's all.

LI'L BIT: Oh.

PECK: What did you think I was going to do?

LI'L BIT: Nothing . . . I don't know. Something . . . nasty.

PECK: With shampoo? Lord, gal—your mind! 40

LI'L BIT: And whose fault is it?

PECK: Not mine. I've got the mind of a boy scout.

LI'L BIT: Right. A horny boy scout.

PECK: Boy scouts are always horny. What do you think the first Merit Badge is for?

LI'L BIT: There. You're going to be nasty again. 45

PECK: Oh, no. I'm good. Very good.

LI'L BIT: It's getting late.

PECK: Don't change the subject. I was talking about how good I am. [beat] Are you ever gonna let me show you how good I am?

LI'L BIT: Don't go over the line now. 50

PECK: I won't. I'm not gonna do anything you don't want me to do.

LI'L BIT: That's right.

PECK: And I've been good all week.

LI'L BIT: You have?

PECK: Yes. All week. Not a single drink. 55

LI'L BIT: Good boy.

PECK: Do I get a reward? For not drinking?

LI'L BIT: A small one. It's getting late.

PECK: Just let me undo you. I'll do you back up.

LI'L BIT: All right. But be quick about it. [PECK *pantomimes undoing* LI'L BIT*'s brassiere* 60 *with one hand.*] You know, that's amazing. The way you can undo the hooks through my blouse with one hand.

PECK: Years of practice.

LI'L BIT: You would make an incredible brain surgeon with that dexterity.

PECK: I'll bet Clyde—what's the name of the boy taking you to the prom? 65

LI'L BIT: Claude Souders.

PECK: Claude Souders. I'll bet it takes him two hands, lights on, and you helping him on to get to first base.

LI'L BIT: Maybe.

[*beat*]

PECK: Can I . . . kiss them? Please? 70

LI'L BIT: I don't know.

PECK: Don't make a grown man beg.

LI'L BIT: Just one kiss.

PECK: I'm going to lift your blouse.

LI'L BIT: It's a little cold. 75

[PECK *laughs gently.*]

PECK: That's not why you're shivering. [*They sit, perfectly still, for a long moment of silence.* PECK *makes gentle, concentric circles with his thumbs in the air in front of him.*] How does that feel?

[LI'L BIT *closes her eyes, carefully keeps her voice calm:*]

LI'L BIT: It's . . . okay.

[*Sacred music, organ music, or a boy's choir swells beneath the following.*]

PECK: I tell you, you can keep all the cathedrals of Europe. Just give me a second with 80
these—these celestial orbs—

[PECK *bows his head as if praying. But he is kissing her nipple.* LI'L BIT, *eyes still closed, rears back her head on the leather Buick car seat.*]

LI'L BIT: Uncle Peck—we've got to go. I've got graduation rehearsal at school tomorrow
morning. And you should get on home to Aunt Mary—
PECK: —All right, Li'l Bit.
LI'L BIT: —*Don't* call me that no more. [*calmer*] Any more. I'm a big girl now, Uncle Peck. 85
As you know.

[LI'L BIT *pantomimes refastening her bra behind her back.*]

PECK: That you are. Going on eighteen. Kittens will turn into cats.
[*sighs*] I live all week long for these few minutes with you—you know that?
LI'L BIT: I'll drive.

[A VOICE *cuts in with:*]

Idling in the Neutral Gear. 90

[*Sound of a car revving cuts off the sacred music;* LI'L BIT, *now an adult, rises out of the car and comes to us.*]

LI'L BIT: In most families, relatives get names like "Junior," or "Brother," or "Bubba." In
my family, if we call someone "Big Papa," it's not because he's tall. In my family, folks
tend to get nicknamed for their genitalia. Uncle Peck, for example. My mama's adage
was "the titless wonder," and my cousin Bobby got branded for life as "B.B."

[*In unison with Greek Chorus:*]

LI'L BIT: For blue balls. 95
GREEK CHORUS: For blue balls.
FEMALE GREEK CHORUS: [*as Mother*] And of course, we were so excited to have a baby
girl that when the nurse brought you in and said, "It's a girl! It's a baby girl!" I just
had to see for myself. So we whipped your diapers down and parted your chubby
little legs—and right between your legs there was— 100

[PECK *has come over during the above and chimes along:*]

PECK: Just a little bit.
GREEK CHORUS: Just a little bit.
FEMALE GREEK CHORUS: [*as Mother*] And when you were born, you were so tiny that
you fit in Uncle Peck's outstretched hand.

[PECK *stretches his hand out.*]

PECK: Now that's a fact. I held you, one day old, right in this hand. 105

[*A traffic signal is projected of a bicycle in a circle with a diagonal red slash.*]

LI'L BIT: Even with my family background, I was sixteen or so before I realized that pedophilia did not mean people who loved to bicycle . . .

[A VOICE *intrudes:*]

Driving in First Gear.

LI'L BIT: 1969. A typical family dinner.

FEMALE GREEK CHORUS: [*as Mother*] Look, Grandma. Li'l Bit's getting to be as big in   110
the bust as you are.

LI'L BIT: Mother! Could we please change the subject?

TEENAGE GREEK CHORUS: [*as Grandmother*] Well, I hope you are buying her some
decent bras. I never had a decent bra, growing up in the Depression, and now my
shoulders are just crippled—crippled from the weight hanging on my shoulders—   115
the dents from my bra straps are big enough to put your finger in.—Here, let me
show you—

[*as Grandmother starts to open her blouse:*]

LI'L BIT: Grandma! Please don't undress at the dinner table.

PECK: I thought the entertainment came *after* the dinner.

LI'L BIT: [*to the audience*] This is how it always starts. My grandfather, Big Papa, will chime   120
in next with—

MALE GREEK CHORUS: [*as Grandfather*] Yup. If Li'l Bit gets any bigger, we're gonna
haveta buy her a wheelbarrow to carry in front of her—

LI'L BIT: —Damn it—

PECK: —How about those Redskins on Sunday, Big Papa?   125

LI'L BIT: [*to the audience*] The only sports Big Papa followed was chasing Grandma around
the house—

MALE GREEK CHORUS: [*as Grandfather*]—Or we could write to Kate Smith. Ask her for
somma her used brassieres she don't want anymore—she could maybe give to Li'l Bit
here—   130

LI'L BIT: —I can't stand it. I can't.

PECK: Now, honey, that's just their way—

FEMALE GREEK CHORUS: [*as Mother*] I tell you, Grandma, Li'l Bit's at that age. She's so
sensitive, you can't say boo—

LI'L BIT: I'd like some privacy, that's all. Okay? Some goddamn privacy—   135

PECK: —Well, at least she didn't use the savior's name—

LI'L BIT: [*to the audience*] And Big Papa wouldn't let a dead dog lie. No sirree.

MALE GREEK CHORUS: [*as Grandfather*] Well, she'd better stop being so sensitive. 'Cause
five minutes before Li'l Bit turns the corner, her tits turn first—

LI'L BIT: [*starting to rise from the table*]—That's it. That's it.   140

PECK: Li'l Bit, you can't let him get to you. Then he wins.

LI'L BIT: I hate him. *Hate* him.

PECK: That's fine. But hate him and eat a good dinner at the same time.

[LI'L BIT *calms down and sits with perfect dignity.*]

LI'L BIT: The gumbo is really good, Grandma.

MALE GREEK CHORUS: [*as Grandfather*] A'course, Li'l Bit's got a big surprise coming for   145
her when she goes to that fancy college this fall—

PECK: Big Papa—let it go.

MALE GREEK CHORUS: [*as Grandfather*] What does she need a college degree for? She's
got all the credentials she'll need on her chest—

LI'L BIT: —Maybe I want to learn things. Read. Rise above my cracker background—   150

PECK: —Whoa, now, Li'l Bit—

MALE GREEK CHORUS: [*as Grandfather*] What kind of things do you want to read?

LI'L BIT: There's a whole semester course, for example, on Shakespeare—

[*Greek Chorus, as Grandfather, laughs until he weeps.*]

MALE GREEK CHORUS: [*as Grandfather*] Shakespeare. That's a good one. Shakespeare is really going to help you in life. 155

PECK: I think it's wonderful. And on scholarship!

MALE GREEK CHORUS: [*as Grandfather*] How is Shakespeare going to help her lie on her back in the dark?

[LI'L BIT *is on her feet.*]

LI'L BIT: You're getting old, Big Papa. You are going to die—very, very soon. Maybe even *tonight*. And when you get to heaven, God's going to be a beautiful black woman in 160 a long white robe. She's gonna look at your chart and say: Uh-oh. Fornication. Dog-ugly mean with blood relatives. Oh. Uh-oh. Voted for George Wallace. Well, one last chance: If you can name the play, all will be forgiven. And then she'll quote: "The quality of mercy is not strained." Your answer? Oh, too bad—*Merchant of Venice:* Act IV, Scene iii. And then she'll send your ass to fry in hell with all the other 165 crackers. Excuse me, please.

[*to the audience*] And as I left the house, I would always hear Big Papa say:

MALE GREEK CHORUS: [*as Grandfather*] Lucy, your daughter's got a mouth on her. Well, no sense in wasting good gumbo. Pass me her plate, Mama.

LI'L BIT: And Aunt Mary would come up to Uncle Peck: 170

FEMALE GREEK CHORUS: [*as Aunt Mary*] Peck, go after her, will you? You're the only one she'll listen to when she gets like this.

PECK: She just needs to cool off.

FEMALE GREEK CHORUS: [*as Aunt Mary*] Please, honey—Grandma's been on her feet cooking all day. 175

PECK: All right.

LI'L BIT: And as he left the room, Aunt Mary would say:

FEMALE GREEK CHORUS: [*as Aunt Mary*] Peck's so good with them when they get to be this age.

[LI'L BIT *has stormed to another part of the stage, her back turned, weeping with a teenage fury.* PECK, *cautiously, as if stalking a deer, comes to her. She turns away even more. He waits a bit.*]

PECK: I don't suppose you're talking to family. [*no response*] Does it help that I'm in-law? 180

LI'L BIT: Don't you dare make fun of this.

PECK: I'm not. There's nothing funny about this. [*beat*] Although I'll bet when Big Papa is about to meet his maker, he'll remember *The Merchant of Venice*.

LI'L BIT: I've got to get away from here.

PECK: You're going away. Soon. Here, take this. 185

[PECK *hands her his folded handkerchief.* LI'L BIT *uses it, noisily. Hands it back. Without her seeing, he reverently puts it back.*]

LI'L BIT: I hate this family.

PECK: Your grandfather's ignorant. And you're right—he's going to die soon. But he's family. Family is . . . family.

LI'L BIT: Grown-ups are always saying that. Family.

PECK: Well, when you get a little older, you'll see what we're saying. 190

LI'L BIT: Uh-huh. So family is another acquired taste, like French kissing?

PECK: Come again?

LI'L BIT: You know, at first it really grosses you out, but in time you grow to like it?

PECK: Girl, you are . . . a handful.
LI'L BIT: Uncle Peck—you have the keys to your car?   195
PECK: Where do you want to go?
LI'L BIT: Just up the road.
PECK: I'll come with you.
LI'L BIT: No—please? I just need to . . . to drive for a little bit. Alone.

> [PECK *tosses her the keys.*]

PECK: When can I see you alone again?   200
LI'L BIT: Tonight.

> [LI'L BIT *crosses to center stage while the lights dim around her.* A VOICE *directs:*]

Shifting Forward from First to Second Gear.

LI'L BIT: There were a lot of rumors about why I got kicked out of that fancy school in
   1970. Some say I got caught with a man in my room. Some say as a kid on scholarship I fooled around with a rich man's daughter.   205
   [LI'L BIT *smiles innocently at the audience*.] I'm not talking.
       But the real truth was I had a constant companion in my dorm room—who was
   less than discrete. Canadian V.O. A fifth a day.
   1970. A Nixon recession. I slept on the floors of friends who were out of work themselves. Took factory work when I could find it. A string of dead-end day jobs that   210
   didn't last very long.
       What I did, most nights, was cruise the Beltway and the back roads of Mary-
   land, where there was still country, past the battlefields and farm houses. Racing in
   a 1965 Mustang—and as long as I had gasoline for my car and whiskey for me, the
   nights would pass. Fully tanked, I would speed past the churches and the trees on the   215
   bend, thinking just one notch of the steering wheel would be all it would take, and
   yet some . . . reflex took over. My hands on the wheel in the nine and three o'clock
   position—I never so much as got a ticket. He taught me well.

> [A VOICE *announces:*]

You and the Reverse Gear.

LI'L BIT: Back up. 1968. On the Eastern Shore. A celebration dinner.   220

> [LI'L BIT *joins* PECK *at a table in a restaurant.*]

PECK: Feeling better, missy?
LI'L BIT: The bathroom's really amazing here, Uncle Peck! They have these little soaps—
   instead of borax or something—and they're in the shape of shells.
PECK: I'll have to take a trip to the gentlemen's room just to see.
LI'L BIT: How did you know about this place?   225
PECK: This inn is famous on the Eastern Shore—it's been open since the seventeenth
   century. And I know how you like history . . .

> [LI'L BIT *is shy and pleased.*]

LI'L BIT: It's great.
PECK: And you've just done your first, legal, long-distance drive. You must be hungry.
LI'L BIT: I'm starved.   230

PECK: I would suggest a dozen oysters to start, and the crab imperial . . . [LI'L BIT *is genuinely agog.*] You might be interested to know the town history. When the British sailed up this very river in the dead of night—see outside where I'm pointing?—They were going to bombard the heck out of this town. But the town fathers were ready for them. They crept up all the trees with lanterns so that the British would think they saw the town lights and   235
they aimed their cannons too high. And that's why the inn is still here for business today.

LI'L BIT: That's a great story.

PECK: [*casually*] Would you like to start with a cocktail?

LI'L BIT: You're not . . . you're not going to start drinking, are you, Uncle Peck?

PECK: Not me. I told you, as long as you're with me, I'll never drink. I asked you if *you'd*   240
like a cocktail before dinner. It's nice to have a little something with the oysters.

LI'L BIT: But . . . I'm not . . . legal. We could get arrested. Uncle Peck, they'll never believe I'm twenty-one!

PECK: So? Today we celebrate your driver's license—on the first try. This establishment reminds me a lot of places back home.   245

LI'L BIT: What does that mean?

PECK: In South Carolina, like here on the Eastern Shore, they're . . . [*searches for the right euphemism*] . . . "European." Not so puritanical. And very understanding if gentle-men wish to escort very attractive young ladies who might want a before-dinner cocktail. If you want one, I'll order one.   250

LI'L BIT: Well—sure. Just . . . one.

[*The Female Greek Chorus appears in a spot.*]

FEMALE GREEK CHORUS: [*as Mother*] A Mother's Guide to Social Drinking:
     A lady never gets sloppy—she may, however, get tipsy and a little gay.
     Never drink on an empty stomach. Avail yourself of the bread basket and gener-ous portions of butter. Slather the butter on your bread.   255
Sip your drink, slowly, let the beverage linger in your mouth—interspersed with interesting, fascinating conversation. Sip, never . . . slurp or gulp. Your glass should always be three-quarters full when his glass is empty.
     Stay away from ladies' drinks: drinks like pink ladies, slow gin fizzes, daiquiris, gold cadillacs, Long Island iced teas, margaritas, pina colada, mai tais, planters   260
punch, white Russians, black Russians, red Russians, melon balls, blue balls, hum-mingbirds, hemorrhages, and hurricanes. In short, avoid anything with sugar, or anything with an umbrella. Get your vitamin C from fruit. Don't order anything with Voodoo or Vixen in the title or sexual positions in the name like Dead Man Screw or the Missionary. [*She sort of titters.*]   265
Believe me, they are lethal . . . I think you were conceived after one of those.
Drink, instead, like a man: straight up or on the rocks, with plenty of water in between.
     Oh, yes. And never mix your drinks. Stay with one all night long, like the man you came in with: bourbon, gin, or tequila till dawn, damn the torpedoes, full   270
speed ahead!

[*As the* FEMALE GREEK CHORUS *retreats, the* MALE GREEK CHORUS *approaches the table as a Waiter.*]

MALE GREEK CHORUS: [*as Waiter*] I hope you all are having a pleasant evening. Is there something I can bring you, sir, before you order?

[LI'L BIT *waits in anxious fear. Carefully, Uncle* PECK *says with command:*]

PECK: I'll have a plain iced tea. The lady would like a drink, I believe.

> [*The* MALE GREEK CHORUS *does a double take; there is a moment when Uncle* PECK *and he are in silent communication.*]

MALE GREEK CHORUS: [*as Waiter*] Very good. What would the . . . lady like?   275

LI'L BIT: [*a bit flushed*] Is there . . . is there any sugar in a martini?

PECK: None that I know of.

LI'L BIT: That's what I'd like then—a dry martini. And could we maybe have some bread?

PECK: A drink fit for a woman of the world.—Please bring the lady a dry martini, be gen-   280
erous with the olives, straight up.

> [*The* MALE GREEK CHORUS *anticipates a large tip.*]

MALE GREEK CHORUS: [*as Waiter*] Right away. Very good, sir.

> [*The* MALE GREEK CHORUS *returns with an empty martini glass which he puts in front of* LI'L BIT.]

PECK: Your glass is empty. Another martini, madam?

LI'L BIT: Yes, thank you.
> [PECK *signals the* MALE GREEK CHORUS, *who nods.*] So why did you leave South   285
Carolina, Uncle Peck?

PECK: I was stationed in D.C. after the war, and decided to stay. Go North, Young Man, someone might have said.

LI'L BIT: What did you do in the service anyway?

PECK: [*suddenly taciturn*] I . . . I did just this and that. Nothing heroic or spectacular.   290

LI'L BIT: But did you see fighting? Or go to Europe?

PECK: I served in the Pacific Theater. It's really nothing interesting to talk about.

LI'L BIT: It is to me. [*The Waiter has brought another empty glass.*] Oh, goody. I love the color of the swizzle sticks. What were we talking about?

PECK: Swizzle sticks.   295

LI'L BIT: Do you ever think of going back?

PECK: To the Marines?

LI'L BIT: No—to South Carolina.

PECK: Well, we do go back. To visit.

LI'L BIT: No, I mean to live.   300

PECK: Not very likely. I think it's better if my mother doesn't have a daily reminder of her disappointment.

LI'L BIT: Are these floorboards slanted?

PECK: Yes, the floor is very slanted. I think this is the original floor.

LI'L BIT: Oh, good.   305

> [*The* FEMALE GREEK CHORUS *as Mother enters swaying a little, a little past tipsy.*]

FEMALE GREEK CHORUS: [*as Mother*] Don't leave your drink unattended when you visit the ladies' room. There is such a thing as white slavery; the modus operandi is to spike an unsuspecting young girl's drink with a "mickey" when she's left the room to powder her nose.

> But if you feel you have had more than your sufficiency in liquor, do go to the   310
ladies' room—often. Pop your head out of doors for a refreshing breath of the night air. If you must, wet your face and head with tap water. Don't be afraid to dunk your head if necessary. A wet woman is still less conspicuous than a drunk woman.

[*The* FEMALE GREEK CHORUS *stumbles a little; conspiratorially.*] When in the
course of human events it becomes necessary, go to a corner stall and insert the index   315
and middle finger down the throat almost to the epiglottis. Divulge your stomach
contents by such persuasion, and then wait a few moments before rejoining your
beau waiting for you at your table.

   Oh, no. Don't be shy or embarrassed. In the very best of establishments, there's
always one or two debutantes crouched in the corner stalls, their beaded purses tossed   320
willy-nilly, sounding like cats in heat, heaving up the contents of their stomachs.

   [*The* FEMALE GREEK CHORUS *begins to wander off.*] I wonder what it is they
do in the men's rooms . . .

LI'L BIT: So why is your mother disappointed in you, Uncle Peck?

PECK: Every mother in Horry County has Great Expectations.   325

LI'L BIT: —Could I have another mar-ti-ni, please?

PECK: I think this is your last one.

   [PECK *signals the Waiter. The Waiter looks at* LI'L BIT *and shakes his head no.*
   PECK *raises his eyebrow, raises his finger to indicate one more, and then rubs his*
   fingers together. It looks like a secret code. The Waiter sighs, shakes his head sadly,
   and brings over another empty martini glass. He glares at PECK.]

LI'L BIT: The name of the county where you grew up is "Horry?" [LI'L BIT, *plastered, begins*
   to laugh. Then she stops.] I think your mother should be proud of you.

   [PECK *signals for the check.*]

PECK: Well, missy, she wanted me to do—to *be* everything my father was not. She wanted   330
   me to amount to something.

LI'L BIT: But you have! You've amounted a lot. . . .

PECK: I'm just a very ordinary man.

   [*The Waiter has brought the check and waits.* PECK *draws out a large bill and*
   hands it to the Waiter. LI'L BIT *is in the soppy stage.*]

LI'L BIT: I'll bet your mother loves you, Uncle Peck.

   [PECK *freezes a bit. To* MALE GREEK CHORUS *as Waiter:*]

PECK: Thank you. The service was exceptional. Please keep the change.   335

MALE GREEK CHORUS: [*as Waiter, in a tone that could freeze*] Thank you, sir. Will you be
   needing any help?

PECK: I think we can manage, thank you.

   [*Just then, the* FEMALE GREEK CHORUS *as Mother lurches on stage; the* MALE
   GREEK CHORUS *as Waiter escorts her off as she delivers:*]

FEMALE GREEK CHORUS: [*as Mother*] Thanks to judicious planning and several trips to
   the ladies' loo, your mother once out-drank an entire regiment of British officers on   340
   a goodwill visit to Washington! Every last man of them! Milquetoasts! How'd they
   ever kick Hitler's cahones, huh? No match for an American lady—I could drink
   every man in here under the table.

   [*She delivers one last crucial hint before she is gently "bounced."*] As a last resort,
   when going out for an evening on the town, be sure to wear a skintight girdle—so   345
   tight that only a surgical knife or acetylene torch can get it off you—so that if you
   do pass out in the arms of your escort, he'll end up with rubber burns on his fingers
   before he can steal your virtue—

[A VOICE *punctures the interlude with:*]

Vehicle Failure.

Even with careful maintenance and preventive operation of your automobile, it is 350
all too common for us to experience an unexpected breakdown. If you are driving
at any speed when a breakdown occurs, you must slow down and guide the automobile to the side of the road.

[PECK *is slowly propping up* LI'L BIT *as they work their way to his car in the
parking lot of the inn.*]

PECK: How are you doing, missy?
LI'L BIT: It's so far to the car, Uncle Peck. Like the lanterns in the trees the British fired 355
on . . .

[LI'L BIT *stumbles.* PECK *swoops her up in his arms.*]

PECK: Okay. I think we're going to take a more direct route.
[LI'L BIT *closes her eyes.*] Dizzy? [*She nods her head.*] Don't look at the ground.
Almost there—do you feel sick to your stomach? [LI'L BIT *nods. They reach the "car."*
PECK *gently deposits her on the front seat.*] Just settle here a little while until things 360
stop spinning. [LI'L BIT *opens her eyes.*]
LI'L BIT: What are we doing?
PECK: We're just going to sit here until your tummy settles down.
LI'L BIT: It's such nice upholst'ry—
PECK: Think you can go for a ride, now? 365
LI'L BIT: Where are you taking me?
PECK: Home.
LI'L BIT: You're not taking me—upstairs? There's no room at the inn?

[LI'L BIT *giggles.*]

PECK: Do you want to go upstairs? [LI'L BIT *doesn't answer.*] Or home?
LI'L BIT: —This isn't right, Uncle Peck. 370
PECK: What isn't right?
LI'L BIT: What we're doing. It's wrong. It's very wrong.
PECK: What are we doing? [LI'L BIT *doesn't answer.*] We're just going out to dinner.
LI'L BIT: You know. It's not nice to Aunt Mary.
PECK: You let me be the judge of what's nice and not nice to my wife. 375

[*beat*]

LI'L BIT: Now, you're mad.
PECK: I'm not mad. It's just that I thought you . . . understood me, Li'l Bit. I think you're
the only one who does.
LI'L BIT: Someone will get hurt.
PECK: Have I forced you to do anything? 380

[*There is a long pause as* LI'L BIT *tries to get sober enough to think this through.*]

LI'L BIT: . . . I guess not.
PECK: We're just enjoying each other's company. I've told you, nothing is going to happen
between us until you want it to. Do you know that?
LI'L BIT: Yes.

PECK: Nothing is going to happen until you want it to. [*A second more, with* PECK *staring* ⁣ 385
ahead at the river while seated at the wheel of his car. Then, softly:] Do you want
something to happen?

> [PECK *reaches over and strokes her face, very gently.* LI'L BIT *softens, reaches for*
> *him, and buries her head in his neck. Then she kisses him. Then she moves away,*
> *dizzy again.*]

LI'L BIT: . . . I don't know.

> [PECK *smiles; this has been good news for him—it hasn't been a "no."*]

PECK: Then I'll wait. I'm a very patient man. I've been waiting for a long time. I don't
mind waiting. ⁣ 390
LI'L BIT: Someone is going to get hurt.
PECK: No one is going to get hurt. [LI'L BIT *closes her eyes.*] Are you feeling sick?
LI'L BIT: Sleepy.

> [*Carefully,* PECK *props* LI'L BIT *up on the seat.*]

PECK: Stay here a second.
LI'L BIT: Where're you going? ⁣ 395
PECK: I'm getting something from the back seat.
LI'L BIT: [*scared; too loud*] What? What are you going to do?

> [PECK *reappears in the front seat with a lap rug.*]

PECK: Shhhh. [PECK *covers* LI'L BIT. *She calms down.*] There. Think you can sleep?

> [LI'L BIT *nods. She slides over to rest on his shoulder. With a look of happiness,*
> PECK *turns the ignition key. Beat.* PECK *leaves* LI'L BIT *sleeping in the car and*
> *strolls down to the audience. Wagner's Flying Dutchman comes up faintly.*]

[A VOICE *interjects:*]

Idling in the Neutral Gear.

TEENAGE GREEK CHORUS: Uncle Peck Teaches Cousin Bobby How to Fish. ⁣ 400
PECK: I get back once or twice a year—supposedly to visit Mama and the family, but the
real truth is to fish. I miss this the most of all. There's a smell in the Low Country—
where the swamp and fresh inlet join the saltwater—a scent of sand and cypress, that
I haven't found anywhere yet.

> I don't say this very often up North because it will just play into the stereotype ⁣ 405
> everyone has, but I will tell you: I didn't wear shoes in the summertime until I was
> sixteen. It's unnatural down here to pen up your feet in leather. Go ahead—take 'em
> off. Let yourself breathe—it really will make you feel better.

We're going to aim for some pompano today—and I have to tell you, they're a very
shy, mercurial fish. Takes patience, and psychology. You have to believe it doesn't ⁣ 410
matter if you catch one or not.

> Sky's pretty spectacular—there's some beer in the cooler next to the crab salad
> I packed, so help yourself if you get hungry. Are you hungry? Thirsty? Holler if
> you are.

> Okay. You don't want to lean over the bridge like that—pompano feed in shal- ⁣ 415
> low water, and you don't want to get too close—they're frisky and shy little things—
> wait, check your line. Yep, something's been munching while we were talking.

Okay, look: We take the sand flea and you take the hook like this—right through his little sand flea rump. Sand fleas should always keep their backs to the wall. Okay. Cast it in, like I showed you. That's great! I can taste that pompano now, sautéed   420
with some pecans and butter, a little bourbon—now—let it lie on the bottom—now, reel, jerk, reel, jerk—

Look—look at your line. There's something calling, all right. Okay, tip the rod up—not too sharp—hook it—all right, now easy, reel and then rest—let it play. And reel—play it out, that's right—really good! I can't believe it! It's a pompano.—Good   425
work! Way to go! You are an official fisherman now. Pompano are hard to catch. We are going to have a delicious little—

What? Well, I don't know how much pain a fish feels—you can't think of that. Oh, no, don't cry, come on now, it's just a fish—the other guys are going to see you.—No, no you're just real sensitive, and I think that's wonderful at your age—   430
look, do you want me to cut it free? You do?

Okay, hand me those pliers—look—I'm cutting the hook—okay? And we're just going to drop it in—no I'm not mad. It's just for fun, okay? There—it's going to swim back to its lady friend and tell her what a terrible day it had and she's going to stroke him with her fins until he feels better, and then they'll do something alone   435
together that will make them both feel good and sleepy . . .

[PECK *bends down, very earnest.*] I don't want you to feel ashamed about crying. I'm not going to tell anyone, okay? I can keep secrets. You know, men cry all the time. They just don't tell anybody, and they don't let anybody catch them. There's nothing you could do that would make me feel ashamed of you. Do you know that?   440
Okay. [PECK *straightens up, smiles.*]

Do you want to pack up and call it a day? I tell you what—I think I can still remember—there's a really neat tree house where I used to stay for days. I think it's still here—it was the last time I looked. But it's a secret place—you can't tell anybody we've gone there—least of all your mom or your sisters.—This is something   445
special just between you and me. Sound good? We'll climb up there and have a beer and some crab salad—okay, B.B.? Bobby? Robert . . .

[LI'L BIT *sits at a kitchen table with the two* FEMALE GREEK CHORUS *members.*]

LI'L BIT: [*to the audience*] Three women, three generations, sit at the kitchen table.

On Men, Sex, and Women: Part I:

FEMALE GREEK CHORUS: [*as Mother*] Men only want one thing.   450
LI'L BIT: [*wide-eyed*] But what? What is it they want?
FEMALE GREEK CHORUS: [*as Mother*] And once they have it, they lose all interest. So Don't Give It to Them.
TEENAGE GREEK CHORUS: [*as Grandmother*] I never had the luxury of the rhythm method. Your grandfather is just a big bull. A big bull. Every morning, every evening.   455
FEMALE GREEK CHORUS: [*as Mother, whispers to* LI'L BIT] And he used to come home for lunch every day.
LI'L BIT: My god, Grandma!
TEENAGE GREEK CHORUS: [*as Grandmother*] Your grandfather only cares that I do two things: have the table set and the bed turned down.   460
FEMALE GREEK CHORUS: [*as Mother*] And in all that time, Mother, you never have experienced—?

LI'L BIT: [*to the audience*]—Now my grandmother believed in all the sacraments of the church, to the day she died. She believed in Santa Claus and the Easter Bunny until she was fifteen. But she didn't believe in—   465

TEENAGE GREEK CHORUS: [*as Grandmother*]—Orgasm! That's just something you and Mary have made up! I don't believe you.

FEMALE GREEK CHORUS: [*as Mother*] Mother, it happens to women all the time—

TEENAGE GREEK CHORUS: [*as Grandmother*]—Oh, now you're going to tell me about the G force!   470

LI'L BIT: No, Grandma, I think that's astronauts—

FEMALE GREEK CHORUS: [*as Mother*] Well, Mama, after all, you were a child bride when Big Papa came and got you—you were a married woman and you still believed in Santa Claus.

TEENAGE GREEK CHORUS: [*as Grandmother*] It was legal, what Daddy and I did! I was   475
fourteen and in those days, fourteen was a grown-up woman—

[*Big Papa shuffles in the kitchen for a cookie.*]

MALE GREEK CHORUS: [*as Grandfather*]—Oh, now we're off on Grandma and the Rape of the Sa-bean Women!

TEENAGE GREEK CHORUS: [*as Grandmother*] Well, you were the one in such a big hurry—

MALE GREEK CHORUS: [*as Grandfather to* LI'L BIT]—I picked your grandmother out of   480
that herd of sisters just like a lion chooses the gazelle—the plump, slow, flaky gazelle dawdling at the edge of the herd—your sisters were too smart and too fast and too scrawny—

LI'L BIT: [*to the audience*]—The family story is that when Big Papa came for Grandma, my Aunt Lily was waiting for him with a broom—and she beat him over the head all the   485
way down the stairs as he was carrying out Grandma's hope chest—

MALE GREEK CHORUS: [*as Grandfather*]—And they were *mean.* 'Specially Lily.

FEMALE GREEK CHORUS: [*as Mother*] Well, you were robbing the baby of the family!

TEENAGE GREEK CHORUS: [*as Grandmother*] I still keep a broom handy in the kitchen! And I know how to use it! So get your hand out of the cookie jar and don't you spoil   490
your appetite for dinner—out of the kitchen!

[MALE GREEK CHORUS *as Grandfather leaves chuckling with a cookie.*]

FEMALE GREEK CHORUS: [*as Mother*] Just one thing a married woman needs to know how to use—the rolling pin or the broom. I prefer a heavy cast-iron fry pan—they're great on a man's head, no matter how thick the skull is.

TEENAGE GREEK CHORUS: [*as Grandmother*] Yes, sir, your father is ruled by only two   495
bosses! Mr. Gut and Mr. Peter! And sometimes, first thing in the morning, Mr. Sphincter Muscle!

FEMALE GREEK CHORUS: [*as Mother*] It's true. Men are like children. Just like little boys.

TEENAGE GREEK CHORUS: [*as Grandmother*] Men are bulls! Big bulls!   500

[*The* GREEK CHORUS *is getting aroused.*]

FEMALE GREEK CHORUS: [*as Mother*] They'd still be crouched on their haunches over a fire in a cave if we hadn't cleaned them up!

TEENAGE GREEK CHORUS: [*as Grandmother, flushed*] Coming in smelling of sweat—

FEMALE GREEK CHORUS: [*as Mother*]—Looking at those naughty pictures like boys in a dime store with a dollar in their pockets!   505

TEENAGE GREEK CHORUS: [*as Grandmother; raucous*] No matter to them what they smell like! They've got to have it, right then, on the spot, right there! Nasty!—

FEMALE GREEK CHORUS: [*as Mother*]—Vulgar!—
TEENAGE GREEK CHORUS: [*as Grandmother*] Primitive!—
FEMALE GREEK CHORUS: [*as Mother*]—Hot!— 510
LI'L BIT: And just about then, Big Papa would shuffle in with—
MALE GREEK CHORUS: [*as Grandfather*]—What are you all cackling about in here?
TEENAGE GREEK CHORUS: [*as Grandmother*] Stay out of the kitchen! This is just for girls!

[*as Grandfather leaves:*]

MALE GREEK CHORUS: [*as Grandfather*] Lucy, you'd better not be filling Mama's head with sex! Every time you and Mary come over and start in about sex, when I ask a simple 515 question like, "What time is dinner going to be ready?," Mama snaps my head off!
TEENAGE GREEK CHORUS: [*as Grandmother*] Dinner will be ready when I'm good and ready! Stay out of this kitchen!

[LI'L BIT *steps out.*]

[A VOICE *directs:*]

When Making a Left Turn, You Must Downshift While Going Forward.

LI'L BIT: 1979. A long bus trip to Upstate New York. I settled in to read, when a young man 520 sat beside me.
MALE GREEK CHORUS: [*as Young Man; voice cracking*] "What are you reading?"
LI'L BIT: He asked. His voice broke into that miserable equivalent of vocal acne, not quite falsetto and not tenor, either. I glanced a side view. He was appealing in an odd way, huge ears at a defiant angle springing forward at ninety degrees. He must have been 525 shaving, because his face, with a peach sheen, was speckled with nicks and styptic. "I have a class tomorrow," I told him.
MALE GREEK CHORUS: [*as Young Man*] "You're taking a class?"
LI'L BIT: "I'm teaching a class." He concentrated on lowering his voice.
MALE GREEK CHORUS: [*as Young Man*] "I'm a senior. Walt Whitman High." 530
LI'L BIT: The light was fading outside, so perhaps he was—with a very high voice. I felt his "interest" quicken. Five steps ahead of the hopes in his head, I slowed down, waited, pretended surprise, acted at listening, all the while knowing we would get off the bus, he would just then seem to think to ask me to dinner, he would chivalrously insist on walking me home, he would continue to converse in the street until I would 535 casually invite him up to my room—and—I was only into the second moment of conversation and I could see the whole evening before me.
  And dramaturgically speaking, after the faltering and slightly comical "first act," there was the very briefest of intermissions, and an extremely capable and forceful sustained second act. And after the second act climax and a gentle denouement— 540 before the post-play discussion—I lay on my back in the dark and I thought about you, Uncle Peck. Oh. Oh—this is the allure. Being older. Being the first. Being the translator, the teacher, the epicure, the already jaded. This is how the giver gets taken. [LI'L BIT *changes her tone.*] On Men, Sex, and Women: Part II:

[LI'L BIT *steps back into the scene as a fifteen year old, gawky and quiet, as the gazelle at the edge of the herd.*]

TEENAGE GREEK CHORUS: [*as Grandmother; to* LI'L BIT] You're being mighty quiet, missy. 545 Cat Got Your Tongue?
LI'L BIT: I'm just listening. Just thinking.
TEENAGE GREEK CHORUS: [*as Grandmother*] Oh, yes, Little Miss Radar Ears? Soaking it all in? Little Miss Sponge? Penny for your thoughts?

[LI'L BIT *hesitates to ask but she really wants to know.*]

LI'L BIT: Does it—when you do it—you know, theoretically when I do it and I haven't   550
done it before—I mean—does it hurt?

FEMALE GREEK CHORUS: [*as Mother*] Does what hurt, honey?

LI'L BIT: When a . . . when a girl does it for the first time—with a man—does it hurt?

TEENAGE GREEK CHORUS: [*as Grandmother; horrified*] That's what you're thinking
about?   555

FEMALE GREEK CHORUS: [*as Mother; calm*] Well, just a little bit. Like a pinch. And there's
a little blood.

TEENAGE GREEK CHORUS: [*as Grandmother*] Don't tell her that! She's too young to be
thinking those things!

FEMALE GREEK CHORUS: [*as Mother*] Well, if she doesn't find out from me, where is she   560
going to find out? In the street?

TEENAGE GREEK CHORUS: [*as Grandmother*] Tell her it hurts! It's agony! You think you're
going to die! Especially if you do it before marriage!

FEMALE GREEK CHORUS: [*as Mother*] Mama! I'm going to tell her the truth! Unlike you,
you left me and Mary completely in the dark with fairy tales and told us to go to the   565
priest! What does an eighty-year-old priest know about love-making with girls!

LI'L BIT: [*getting upset*] It's not fair!

FEMALE GREEK CHORUS: [*as Mother*] Now, see, she's getting upset—you're scaring her.

TEENAGE GREEK CHORUS: [*as Grandmother*] Good! Let her be good and scared! It hurts!
You bleed like a stuck pig! And you lay there and say, "Why, O Lord, have you for-   570
saken me?!"

LI'L BIT: It's not fair! Why does everything have to hurt for girls? Why is there always blood?

FEMALE GREEK CHORUS: [*as Mother*] It's not a lot of blood—and it feels wonderful after
the pain subsides . . .

TEENAGE GREEK CHORUS: [*as Grandmother*] You're encouraging her to just go out and   575
find out with the first drugstore joe who buys her a milk shake!

FEMALE GREEK CHORUS: [*as Mother*] Don't be scared. It won't hurt you—if the man you
go to bed with really loves you. It's important that he loves you.

TEENAGE GREEK CHORUS: [*as Grandmother*]—Why don't you just go out and rent a
motel room for her, Lucy?   580

FEMALE GREEK CHORUS: [*as Mother*] I believe in telling my daughter the truth! We have
a very close relationship! I want her to be able to ask me anything—I'm not scaring
her with stories about Eve's sin and snakes crawling on their bellies for eternity and
women's bearing children in mortal pain—

TEENAGE GREEK CHORUS: [*as Grandmother*]—If she stops and thinks before she takes   585
her knickers off, maybe someone in this family will finish high school!

[LI'L BIT *knows what is about to happen and starts to retreat from the scene at
this point.*]

FEMALE GREEK CHORUS: [*as Mother*] Mother! If you and Daddy had helped me—I
wouldn't have had to marry that—that no-good-son-of-a—

TEENAGE GREEK CHORUS: [*as Grandmother*]—He was good enough for you on a full
moon! I hold you responsible!   590

FEMALE GREEK CHORUS: [*as Mother*]—You could have helped me! You could have told
me something about the facts of life!

TEENAGE GREEK CHORUS: [*as Grandmother*]—I told you what my mother told me! A
girl with her skirt up can outrun a man with his pants down!

[*The* MALE GREEK CHORUS *enters the fray;* LI'L BIT *edges further downstage.*]

FEMALE GREEK CHORUS: [*as Mother*] And when I turned to you for a little help, all I got   595
   afterwards was—
MALE GREEK CHORUS: [*as Grandfather*] You Made Your Bed; Now Lie On It!

   [*The* GREEK CHORUS *freezes, mouths open, argumentatively.*]

LI'L BIT: [*to the audience*] Oh, please! I still can't bear to listen to it, after all these years—

   [*The* MALE GREEK CHORUS *"unfreezes," but out of his open mouth, as if to his
   surprise, comes a base refrain from a Motown song.*]

MALE GREEK CHORUS: "Do-Bee-Do-Wah!"

   [*The* FEMALE GREEK CHORUS *member is also surprised; but she, too,
   unfreezes.*]

FEMALE GREEK CHORUS: "Shoo-doo-be-doo-be-doo; shoo-doo-be-doo-be-doo."   600

   [*The* MALE *and* FEMALE GREEK CHORUS *members continue with their harmony, until the* TEENAGE *member of the* CHORUS *starts in with Motown
   lyrics such as "Dedicated to the One I Love," or "In the Still of the Night," or
   "Hold Me"—any Sam Cooke will do. The three modulate down into three-part
   harmony, softly, until they are submerged by the actual recording playing over the
   radio in the car in which Uncle* PECK *sits in the driver's seat, waiting.* LI'L BIT
   sits in the passenger seat.]

LI'L BIT: Ahh. That's better.

   [*Uncle* PECK *reaches over and turns the volume down; to* LI'L BIT:]

PECK: How can you hear yourself think?

   [LI'L BIT *does not answer.*]

   [*A* VOICE *insinuates itself in the pause:*]

Before You Drive.

**Always check under your car for obstructions—broken bottles, fallen tree branches,
and the bodies of small children. Each year hundreds of children are crushed   605
beneath the wheels of unwary drivers in their own driveways. Children depend on
you to watch them.**

   [*Pause. The* VOICE *continues:*]

You and the Reverse Gear.

   [*In the following section, it would be nice to have slides of erotic photographs
   of women and cars: women posed over the hood; women draped along the side-
   boards; women with water hoses spraying the car; and the actress playing* LI'L BIT
   with a Bel Air or any 1950s car one can find for the finale.]

LI'L BIT: 1967. In a parking lot of the Beltsville Agricultural Farms. The Initiation into a
   Boy's First Love.   610
PECK: [*with a soft look on his face*] Of course, my favorite car will always be the '56 Bel Air
   Sports Coupe. Chevy sold more '55s, but the '56!—a V-8 with Corvette option, 225
   horsepower, went from zero to sixty miles per hour in 8.9 seconds.

LI'L BIT: [*to the audience*] Long after a mother's tits, but before a woman's breasts:

PECK: Super-Turbo-Fire! What a Power Pack—mechanical lifters, twin four-barrel carbs, lightweight valves, dual exhausts—   615

LI'L BIT: [*to the audience*] After the milk but before the beer:

PECK: A specific intake manifold, higher-lift camshaft, and the tightest squeeze Chevy had ever made—

LI'L BIT: [*to the audience*] Long after he's squeezed down the birth canal but before he's pushed   620 his way back in: The boy falls in love with the thing that bears his weight with speed.

PECK: I want you to know your automobile inside and out.—Are you there? Li'l Bit?

[*Slides end here.*]

LI'L BIT: —What?

PECK: You're drifting. I need you to concentrate.

LI'L BIT: Sorry.   625

PECK: Okay. Get into the driver's seat. [LI'L BIT *does.*] Okay. Now. Show me what you're going to do before you start the car.

[LI'L BIT *sits, with her hands in her lap. She starts to giggle.*]

LI'L BIT: I don't know, Uncle Peck.

PECK: Now, come on. What's the first thing you're going to adjust?

LI'L BIT: My bra strap?—   630

PECK: —Li'l Bit. What's the most important thing to have control of on the inside of the car?

LI'L BIT: That's easy. The radio. I tune the radio from Mama's old fart tunes to—

[LI'L BIT *turns the radio up so we can hear a 1960s tune. With surprising firmness,* PECK *commands:*]

PECK: —Radio off. Right now. [LI'L BIT *turns the radio off.*] When you are driving your car, with your license, you can fiddle with the stations all you want. But when you are driving with a learner's permit in my car, I want all your attention to be on the road.   635

LI'L BIT: Yes, sir.

PECK: Okay. Now the seat—forward and up. [LI'L BIT *pushes it forward.*] Do you want a cushion?

LI'L BIT: No—I'm good.

PECK: You should be able to reach all the switches and controls. Your feet should be able   640 to push the accelerator, brake, and clutch all the way down. Can you do that?

LI'L BIT: Yes.

PECK: Okay, the side mirrors. You want to be able to see just a bit of the right side of the car in the right mirror—can you?

LI'L BIT: Turn it out more.   645

PECK: Okay. How's that?

LI'L BIT: A little more . . . Okay, that's good.

PECK: Now the left—again, you want to be able to see behind you—but the left lane— adjust it until you feel comfortable. [LI'L BIT *does so.*] Next. I want you to check the rearview mirror. Angle it so you have a clear vision of the back. [LI'L BIT *does so.*]   650 Okay. Lock your door. Make sure all the doors are locked.

LI'L BIT: [*making a joke of it*] But then I'm locked in with you.

PECK: Don't fool.

LI'L BIT: All right. We're locked in.

PECK: We'll deal with the air vents and defroster later. I'm teaching you on a manual—once   655 you learn manual, you can drive anything. I want you to be able to drive any car, any machine. Manual gives you *control*. In ice, if your brakes fail, if you need more power—okay? It's a little harder at first, but then it becomes like breathing. Now. Put your hands on the wheel. I never want to see you driving with one hand. Always two hands. [LI'L BIT *hesitates.*] What? What is it now?   660

LI'L BIT: If I put my hands on the wheel—how do I defend myself?

PECK: [*softly*] Now listen. Listen up close. We're not going to fool around with this. This is a serious business. I will never touch you when you are driving a car. Understand?

LI'L BIT: Okay.

PECK: Hands on the nine o'clock and three o'clock position gives you maximum control   665
and turn.

> [PECK *goes silent for a while.* LI'L BIT *waits for more instruction.*]

Okay. Just relax and listen to me, Li'l Bit, okay? I want you to lift your hands for a second and look at them. [LI'L BIT *feels a bit silly, but does it.*]

Those are your two hands. When you are driving, your life is in your own two hands. Understand? [LI'L BIT *nods.*]   670

I don't have any sons. You're the nearest to a son I'll ever have—and I want to give you something. Something that really matters to me.

There's something about driving—when you're in control of the car, just you and the machine and the road—that nobody can take from you. A power. I feel more myself in my car than anywhere else. And that's what I want to give to you.   675

There's a lot of assholes out there. Crazy men, arrogant idiots, drunks, angry kids, geezers who are blind—and you have to be ready for them. I want to teach you to drive like a man.

LI'L BIT: What does that mean?

PECK: Men are taught to drive with confidence—with aggression. The road belongs to   680
them. They drive defensively—always looking out for the other guy. Women tend to be polite—to hesitate. And that can be fatal.

You're going to learn to think what the other guy is going to do before he does it. If there's an accident, and ten cars pile up, and people get killed, you're the one who's gonna steer through it, put your foot on the gas if you have to, and be the   685
only one to walk away. I don't know how long you or I are going to live, but we're for damned sure not going to die in a car.

So if you're going to drive with me, I want you to take this very seriously.

LI'L BIT: I will, Uncle Peck. I want you to teach me to drive.

PECK: Good. You're going to pass your test on the first try. Perfect score. Before the next four   690
weeks are over, you're going to know this baby inside and out. Treat her with respect.

LI'L BIT: Why is it a "she"?

PECK: Good question. It doesn't have to be a "she"—but when you close your eyes and think of someone who responds to your touch—someone who performs just for you and gives you what you ask for—I guess I always see a "she." You can call her what   695
you like.

LI'L BIT: [*to the audience*] I closed my eyes—and decided not to change the gender.

> [*A* VOICE:]

**Defensive driving involves defending yourself from hazardous and sudden changes in your automotive environment. By thinking ahead, the defensive driver can adjust to weather, road conditions and road kill. Good defensive driving involves   700
mental and physical preparation. Are you prepared?**

> [*Another* VOICE *chimes in:*]

You and the Reverse Gear.

LI'L BIT: 1966. The Anthropology of the Female Body in Ninth Grade—Or A Walk Down Mammary Lane.

> [*Throughout the following, there is occasional rhythmic beeping, like a transmitter signaling.* LI'L BIT *is aware of it, but can't figure out where it is coming from. No one else seems to hear it.*]

MALE GREEK CHORUS: In the hallway of Francis Scott Key Middle School.   705

> [*A bell rings; the* GREEK CHORUS *is changing classes and meets in the hall, conspiratorially.*]

TEENAGE GREEK CHORUS: She's coming!

> [LI'L BIT *enters the scene; the* MALE GREEK CHORUS *member has a sudden, violent sneezing and lethal allergy attack.*]

FEMALE GREEK CHORUS: Jerome? Jerome? Are you all right?
MALE GREEK CHORUS: I—don't—know. I can't breathe—get Li'l Bit—
TEENAGE GREEK CHORUS: —He needs oxygen!—
FEMALE GREEK CHORUS: —Can you help us here?   710
LI'L BIT: What's wrong? Do you want me to get the school nurse—

> [*The* MALE GREEK CHORUS *member wheezes, grabs his throat, and sniffs at* LI'L BIT *'s chest, which is beeping away.*]

MALE GREEK CHORUS: No—it's okay—I only get this way when I'm around an allergy trigger—
LI'L BIT: Golly. What are you allergic to?
MALE GREEK CHORUS: [*with a sudden grab of her breast*] Foam rubber.   715

> [*The* GREEK CHORUS *members break up with hilarity; Jerome leaps away from* LI'L BIT *'s kicking rage with agility; as he retreats:*]

LI'L BIT: Jerome! Creep! Cretin! Cro-Magnon!
TEENAGE GREEK CHORUS: Rage is not attractive in a girl.
FEMALE GREEK CHORUS: Really. Get a Sense of Humor.

> [A VOICE *echoes:*]

**Good defensive driving involves mental and physical preparation.
Were You Prepared?**   720

FEMALE GREEK CHORUS: Gym Class: In the showers.

> [*The sudden sound of water; the* FEMALE GREEK CHORUS *members and* LI'L BIT, *while fully clothed, drape towels across their fronts, miming nudity. They stand, hesitate, at an imaginary shower's edge.*]

LI'L BIT: Water looks hot.
FEMALE GREEK CHORUS: Yesss . . . .

> [FEMALE GREEK CHORUS *members are not going to make the first move. One dips a tentative toe under the water, clutching the towel around her.*]

LI'L BIT: Well, I guess we'd better shower and get out of here.
FEMALE GREEK CHORUS: Yep. You go ahead. I'm still cooling off.   725
LI'L BIT: Okay.—Sally? Are you gonna shower?
TEENAGE GREEK CHORUS: After you—

> [LI'L BIT *takes a deep breath for courage, drops the towel and plunges in: The two* FEMALE GREEK CHORUS *members look at* LI'L BIT *in the all together, laugh, gasp, and high-five each other.*]

TEENAGE GREEK CHORUS: Oh my god! Can you believe—
FEMALE GREEK CHORUS: Told you! It's not foam rubber! I win! Jerome owes me fifty cents!

> [A VOICE *editorializes:*]

Were You Prepared?   730

> [LI'L BIT *tries to cover up; she is exposed, as suddenly 1960s Motown fills the room and we segue into:*]

FEMALE GREEK CHORUS: The Sock Hop.

> [LI'L BIT *stands up against the wall with her female classmates.* TEENAGE GREEK CHORUS *is mesmerized by the music and just sways alone, lip-synching the lyrics.*]

LI'L BIT: I don't know. Maybe it's just me—but—do you ever feel like you're just a walking Mary Jane joke?
FEMALE GREEK CHORUS: I don't know what you mean.
LI'L BIT: You haven't heard the Mary Jane jokes? [FEMALE GREEK CHORUS *member* 735 *shakes her head no.*] Okay. "Little Mary Jane is walking through the woods, when all of a sudden this man who was hiding behind a tree *jumps* out, *rips* open Mary Jane's blouse, and *plunges* his hands on her breasts. And Little Mary Jane just laughed and laughed because she knew her money was in her shoes."

> [LI'L BIT *laughs; the* FEMALE GREEK CHORUS *does not.*]

FEMALE GREEK CHORUS: You're weird.   740

> [*In another space, in a strange light, Uncle* PECK *stands and stares at* LI'L BIT*'s body. He is setting up a tripod, but he just stands, appreciative, watching her.*]

LI'L BIT: Well, don't you ever feel . . . self-conscious? Like you're being looked at all the time?
FEMALE GREEK CHORUS: That's not a problem for me.—Oh—look—Greg's coming over to ask you to dance.

> [TEENAGE GREEK CHORUS *becomes attentive, flustered.* MALE GREEK CHORUS *member, as Greg, bends slightly as a very short young man, whose head is at* LI'L BIT*'s chest level. Ardent, sincere, and socially inept, Greg will become a successful gynecologist.*]

TEENAGE GREEK CHORUS: [*softly*] Hi, Greg.

> [*Greg does not hear. He is intent on only one thing.*]

MALE GREEK CHORUS: [*as Greg, to* LI'L BIT] Good Evening. Would you care to dance?   745
LI'L BIT: [*gently*] Thank you very much, Greg—but I'm going to sit this one out.
MALE GREEK CHORUS: [*as Greg*] Oh. Okay. I'll try my luck later.

> [*He disappears.*]

TEENAGE GREEK CHORUS: Oohhh.

[LI'L BIT *relaxes. Then she tenses, aware of* PECK's *gaze.*]

FEMALE GREEK CHORUS: Take pity on him. Someone should.
LI'L BIT: But he's so short.   750
TEENAGE GREEK CHORUS: He can't help it.
LI'L BIT: But his head comes up to [LI'L BIT *gestures*] here. And I think he asks me on the
    fast dances so he can watch me—you know—jiggle.
FEMALE GREEK CHORUS: I wish I had your problems.

[*The tune changes; Greg is across the room in a flash.*]

MALE GREEK CHORUS: [*as Greg*] Evening again. May I ask you for the honor of a spin on   755
    the floor?
LI'L BIT: I'm . . . very complimented, Greg. But I . . . I just don't do fast dances.
MALE GREEK CHORUS: [*as Greg*] Oh. No problem. That's okay.

[*He disappears.* TEENAGE GREEK CHORUS *watches him go.*]

TEENAGE GREEK CHORUS: That is just so—*sad.*

[LI'L BIT *becomes aware of* PECK *waiting.*]

FEMALE GREEK CHORUS: You know, you should take it as a compliment that the guys   760
    want to watch you jiggle. They're guys. That's what they're supposed to do.
LI'L BIT: I guess you're right. But sometimes I feel like these alien life forces, these two
    mounds of flesh have grafted themselves onto my chest, and they're using me until
    they can "propagate" and take over the world and they'll just keep growing, with a
    mind of their own until I collapse under their weight and they suck all the nourish-   765
    ment out of my body and I finally just waste away while they get bigger and bigger
    and—[LI'L BIT's *classmates are just staring at her in disbelief.*]
FEMALE GREEK CHORUS: —You are the strangest girl I have ever met.

[LI'L BIT's *trying to joke but feels on the verge of tears.*]

LI'L BIT: Or maybe someone's implanted radio transmitters in my chest at a frequency I
    can't hear, that girls can't detect, but they're sending out these signals to men who get   770
    mesmerized, like sirens, calling them to dash themselves on these "rocks"—

[*Just then, the music segues into a slow dance, perhaps a Beach Boys tune like*
Little Surfer, but over the music there's a rhythmic, hypnotic beeping transmit-
ted, which both Greg and PECK *hear.* LI'L BIT *hears it too, and in horror she*
stares at her chest. She, too, is almost hypnotized. In a trance, Greg responds to the
signals and is called to her side—actually, her front. Like a zombie, he stands in
front of her, his eyes planted on her two orbs.]

MALE GREEK CHORUS: [*as Greg*] This one's a slow dance. I hope your dance card isn't . . .
    filled?

[LI'L BIT *is aware of* PECK; *but the signals are calling her to him. The signals are*
no longer transmitters, but an electromagnetic force, pulling LI'L BIT *to his side,*
where he again waits for her to join him. She must get away from the dance floor.]

LI'L BIT: Greg—you really are a nice boy. But I don't like to dance.
MALE GREEK CHORUS: [*as Greg*] That's okay. We don't have to move or anything. I could   775
    just hold you and we could just *sway* a little—

LI'L BIT: —No! I'm sorry—but I think I have to leave; I hear someone calling me—

[LI'L BIT *starts across the dance floor, leaving Greg behind. The beeping stops. The lights change, although the music does not. As* LI'L BIT *talks to the audience, she continues to change and prepare for the coming session. She should be wearing a tight tank top or a sheer blouse and very tight pants. To the audience:*]

In every man's home some small room, some zone in his house, is set aside. It might be the attic, or the study, or a den. And there's an invisible sign as if from the old treehouse: Girls Keep Out.   780

Here, away from female eyes, lace doilies and crochet, he keeps his manly toys: the Vargas pinups, the tackle. A scent of tobacco and WD-40. [*She inhales deeply.*] A dash of his Bay Rum. Ahhh . . . [LI'L BIT *savors it for just a moment more.*]

Here he keeps his secrets: a violin or saxophone, drum set or darkroom, and the stacks of Playboy. [*in a whisper*] Here, in my aunt's home, it was the basement.   785 Uncle Peck's turf.

[A VOICE *commands:*]

You and the Reverse Gear.

LI'L BIT: 1965. The Photo Shoot.

[LI'L BIT *steps into the scene as a nervous but curious thirteen year old. Music, from the previous scene, continues to play, changing into something like Roy Orbison later—something seductive with a beat.* PECK *fiddles, all business, with his camera. As in the driving lesson, he is all competency and concentration.* LI'L BIT *stands awkwardly. He looks through the Leica camera on the tripod, adjusts the back lighting, etc.*]

PECK: Are you cold? The lights should heat up some in a few minutes—
LI'L BIT: —Aunt Mary is?   790
PECK: At the National Theatre matinee. With your mother. We have time.
LI'L BIT: But—what if—
PECK: —And so what if they return? I told them you and I were going to be working with my camera. They won't come down. [LI'L BIT *is quiet, apprehensive.*]—Look, are you sure you want to do this?   795
LI'L BIT: I said I'd do it. But—
PECK: —I know. You've drawn the line.
LI'L BIT: [*reassured*] That's right. No frontal nudity.
PECK: Good heavens, girl, where did you pick that up?
LI'L BIT: [*defensive*] I read.   800

[PECK *tries not to laugh.*]

PECK: And I read *Playboy* for the interviews. Okay. Let's try some different music.

[PECK *goes to an expensive reel-to-reel and forwards. Something like "Sweet Dreams" begins to play.*]

LI'L BIT: I didn't know you listened to this.
PECK: I'm not dead, you know. I try to keep up. Do you like this song? [LI'L BIT *nods with pleasure.*] Good. Now listen—at professional photo shoots, they always play music for the models. Okay? I want you to just enjoy the music. Listen to it with your body,   805 and just—respond.
LI'L BIT: Respond to the music with my . . . body?

PECK: Right. Almost like dancing. Here—let's get you on the stool, first. [PECK *comes over and helps her up.*]

LI'L BIT: But nothing showing— 810

> [PECK *firmly, with his large capable hands, brushes back her hair, angles her face.* LI'L BIT *turns to him like a plant to the sun.*]

PECK: Nothing showing. Just a peek.

> [*He holds her by the shoulder, looking at her critically. Then he unbuttons her blouse to the midpoint, and runs his hands over the flesh of her exposed sternum, arranging the fabric, just touching her. Deliberately, calmly. Asexually,* LI'L BIT *quiets, sits perfectly still, and closes her eyes.*]

Okay?

LI'L BIT: Yes.

> [PECK *goes back to his camera.*]

PECK: I'm going to keep talking to you. Listen without responding to what I'm saying; you want to *listen* to the music. Sway, move just your torso or your head—I've got to 815 check the light meter.

LI'L BIT: But—you'll be watching.

PECK: No—I'm not here—just my voice. Pretend you're in your room all alone on a Friday night with your mirror—and the music feels good—just move for me, Li'l Bit—

> [LI'L BIT *closes her eyes. At first self-conscious; then she gets more into the music and begins to sway. We hear the camera start to whir. Throughout the shoot, there can be a slide montage of actual shots of the actor playing* LI'L BIT— *interspersed with other models à la Playboy, Calvin Klein, and Victoriana/Lewis Carroll's Alice Liddell.*]

That's it. That looks great. Okay. Just keep doing that. Lift your head up a bit more, 820 good, good, just keep moving, that a girl—you're a very beautiful young woman. Do you know that? [LI'L BIT *looks up, blushes.* PECK *shoots the camera. The audience should see this shot on the screen.*]

LI'L BIT: No. I don't know that.

PECK: Listen to the music. [LI'L BIT *closes her eyes again.*] Well you are. For a thirteen year 825 old, you have a body a twenty-year-old woman would die for.

LI'L BIT: The boys in school don't think so.

PECK: The boys in school are little Neanderthals in short pants. You're ten years ahead of them in maturity; it's gonna take a while for them to catch up.

> [PECK *clicks another shot; we see a faint smile on* LI'L BIT *on the screen.*]

Girls turn into women long before boys turn into men. 830

LI'L BIT: Why is that?

PECK: I don't know, Li'l Bit. But it's a blessing for men.
[LI'L BIT *turns silent.*] Keep moving. Try arching your back on the stool, hands behind you, and throw your head back. [*The slide shows a* Playboy *model in this pose.*] Oohh, great. That one was great. Turn your head away, same position. [*whir*] 835 Beautiful.

> [LI'L BIT *looks at him a bit defiantly.*]

LI'L BIT: I think Aunt Mary is beautiful.

[PECK *stands still.*]

PECK: My wife is a very beautiful woman. Her beauty doesn't cancel yours out. [*More casually; he returns to the camera.*] All the women in your family are beautiful. In fact, I think all women are. You're not listening to the music. [PECK *shoots some more film*   840
in silence.] All right, turn your head to the left. Good. Now take the back of your right hand and put it on your right cheek—your elbow angled up—now slowly, slowly, stroke your cheek, draw back your hair with the back of your hand. [*another classic* Playboy *or Vargas*] Good. One hand above and behind your head; stretch your body; smile. [*another pose*]   845
Li'l Bit. I want you to think of something that makes you laugh—

LI'L BIT: I can't think of anything.

PECK: Okay. Think of Big Papa chasing Grandma around the living room. [LI'L BIT *lifts her head and laughs. Click. We should see this shot.*] Good. Both hands behind your head. Great! Hold that! [*from behind his camera*] You're doing great work. If we keep   850
this up, in five years we'll have a really professional portfolio.

[LI'L BIT *stops.*]

LI'L BIT: What do you mean in five years?

PECK: You can't submit work to *Playboy* until you're eighteen—

[PECK *continues to shoot; he knows he's made a mistake.*]

LI'L BIT: —Wait a minute. You're joking, aren't you, Uncle Peck?

PECK: Heck, no. You can't get into *Playboy* unless you're the very best. And you are the   855
very best.

LI'L BIT: I would never do that!

[PECK *stops shooting. He turns off the music.*]

PECK: Why? There's nothing wrong with *Playboy*—it's a very classy maga—

LI'L BIT: [*more upset*] But I thought you said I should go to college!

PECK: Wait—Li'l Bit—it's nothing like that. Very respectable women model for *Playboy*—   860
actresses with major careers—women in college—there's an Ivy League issue every—

LI'L BIT: —I'm never doing anything like that! You'd show other people these—other *men*—these—what I'm doing.—Why would you do that?! Any *boy* around here could just pick up, just go into The Stop & Go and *buy*—Why would you ever want   865
to—to share—

PECK: —Whoa, whoa. Just stop a second and listen to me. Li'l Bit. Listen. There's nothing wrong in what we're doing. I'm very proud of you. I think you have a wonderful body and an even more wonderful mind. And of course I want other people to *appreciate* it. It's not anything shameful.   870

LI'L BIT: [*hurt*] But this is something—that I'm only doing for you. This is something—that you said was just between us.

PECK: It is. And if that's how you feel, five years from now, it will remain that way. Okay? I know you're not going to do anything you don't feel like doing.

[*He walks back to the camera.*]

Do you want to stop now? I've got just a few more shots on this roll—   875

LI'L BIT: I don't want anyone seeing this.

PECK: I swear to you. No one will. I'll treasure this—that you're doing this only for me.

[LI'L BIT, *still shaken, sits on the stool. She closes her eyes.*]

Li'l Bit? Open your eyes and look at me. [LI'L BIT *shakes her head no.*] Come on. Just open your eyes, honey.

LI'L BIT: If I look at you—if I look at the camera: You're gonna know what I'm thinking. You'll see right through me—   880

PECK: —No, I won't. I want you to look at me. All right, then. I just want you to listen. Li'l Bit. [*She waits.*] I love you. [LI'L BIT *opens her eyes; she is startled.* PECK *captures the shot. On the screen we see right through her.* PECK *says softly.*] Do you know that? [LI'L BIT *nods her head yes.*] I have loved you every day since the day you were born.   885

LI'L BIT: Yes.

[LI'L BIT *and* PECK *just look at each other. Beat. Beneath the shot of herself on screen,* LI'L BIT, *still looking at her uncle, begins to unbutton her blouse.*]

[*A neutral* VOICE *cuts off the above scene with:*]

Implied Consent.

As an individual operating a motor vehicle in the state of Maryland, you must abide by "Implied Consent." If you do not consent to take the blood alcohol content test, there may be severe penalties: a suspension of license, a fine, community service, and a possible jail sentence.   890

[*The* VOICE *shifts tone:*]

Idling in the Neutral Gear.

MALE GREEK CHORUS: [*announcing*] Aunt Mary on behalf of her husband.

[FEMALE GREEK CHORUS *checks her appearance, and with dignity comes to the front of the stage and sits down to talk to the audience.*]

FEMALE GREEK CHORUS: [*as Aunt Mary*] My husband was such a good man—is. Is such a good man. Every night, he does the dishes. The second he comes home, he's taking out the garbage, or doing yard work, lifting heavy things I can't. Everyone in the neighborhood borrows Peck—it's true—women with husbands of their own, men who just don't have Peck's abilities—there's always a knock on our door for a jump start on cold mornings, when anyone needs a ride, or help shoveling the sidewalk—I look out, and there Peck is, without a coat, pitching in. I know I'm lucky. The man works from dawn to dusk. And the overtime he does every year—my poor sister. She sits every Christmas when I come to dinner with a new stole, or diamonds, or with tickets to Bermuda.   895 900

I know he has troubles. And we don't talk about them. I wonder, sometimes, what happened to him during the war. The men who fought World War II didn't have "rap sessions" to talk about their feelings. Men in his generation were expected to be quiet about it and get on with their lives. And sometimes I can feel him just fighting the trouble—whatever has burrowed deeper than the scar tissue—and we don't talk about it. I know he's having a bad spell because he comes looking for me in the house, and just hangs around me until it passes. And I keep my banter light—I discuss a new recipe, or sales, or gossip—because I think domesticity can be a balm for men when they're lost. We sit in the house and listen to the peace of the clocks ticking in his well-ordered living room, until it passes.   905 910

[*sharply*] I'm not a fool. I know what's going on. I wish you could feel how hard Peck fights against it—he's swimming against the tide, and what he needs is   915 to see me on the shore, believing in him, knowing he won't go under, he won't give up—

And I want to say this about my niece. She's a sly one, that one is. She knows exactly what she's doing; she's twisted Peck around her little finger and thinks it's all a big secret. Yet another one who's borrowing my husband until it doesn't suit   920
her anymore.

Well. I'm counting the days until she goes away to school. And she manipulates someone else. And then he'll come back again, and sit in the kitchen while I bake, or beside me on the sofa when I sew in the evenings. I'm a very patient woman. But   925
I'd like my husband back.

I am counting the days.

[A VOICE *repeats:*]

You and the Reverse Gear.

MALE GREEK CHORUS: Li'l Bit's Thirteenth Christmas. Uncle Peck Does the Dishes. Christmas 1964.

[PECK *stands in a dress shirt and tie, nice pants, with an apron. He is washing dishes. He's in a mood we haven't seen. Quiet, brooding.* LI'L BIT *watches him a moment before seeking him out.*]

LI'L BIT: Uncle Peck? [*He does not answer. He continues to work on the pots.*] I didn't know   930
where you'd gone to. [*He nods. She takes this as a sign to come in.*] Don't you want to sit with us for a while?
PECK: No. I'd rather do the dishes.

[*Pause.* LI'L BIT *watches him.*]

LI'L BIT: You're the only man I know who does the dishes. [PECK *says nothing.*] I think it's really nice.   935
PECK: My wife has been on her feet all day. So's your grandmother and your mother.
LI'L BIT: I know. [*beat*] Do you want some help?
PECK: No. [*He softens a bit towards her.*] You can help just by talking to me.
LI'L BIT: Big Papa never does the dishes. I think it's nice.
PECK: I think men should be nice to women. Women are always working for us. There's   940
nothing particularly manly in wolfing down food and then sitting around in a stupor while the women clean up.
LI'L BIT: That looks like a really neat camera that Aunt Mary got you.
PECK: It is. It's a very nice one.

[*Pause, as* PECK *works on the dishes and some demon that* LI'L BIT *intuits.*]

LI'L BIT: Did Big Papa hurt your feelings?   945
PECK: [*tired*] What? Oh, no—it doesn't hurt me. Family is family. I'd rather have him picking on me than—I don't pay him any mind, Li'l Bit.
LI'L BIT: Are you angry with us?
PECK: No, Li'l Bit. I'm not angry.

[*Another pause.*]

LI'L BIT: We missed you at Thanksgiving. . . . I did. I missed you.   950
PECK: Well, there were . . . "things" going on. I didn't want to spoil anyone's Thanksgiving.
LI'L BIT: Uncle Peck? [*very carefully*] Please don't drink anymore tonight.

PECK: I'm not . . . overdoing it.

LI'L BIT: I know. [*beat*] Why do you drink so much?

[PECK *stops and thinks, carefully.*]

PECK: Well, Li'l Bit—let me explain it this way. There are some people who have a . . . a   955
  "fire" in the belly. I think they go to work on Wall Street or they run for office. And
  then there are people who have a "fire" in their heads—and they become writers or
  scientists or historians. [*He smiles a little at her.*] You. You've got a "fire" in the head.
  And then there are people like me.

LI'L BIT: Where do you have . . . a fire?   960

PECK: I have a fire in my heart. And sometimes the drinking helps.

LI'L BIT: There's got to be other things that can help.

PECK: I suppose there are.

LI'L BIT: Does it help—to talk to me?

PECK: Yes. It does. [*quiet*] I don't get to see you very much.   965

LI'L BIT: I know. [LI'L BIT *thinks.*] You could talk to me more.

PECK: Oh?

LI'L BIT: I could make a deal with you, Uncle Peck.

PECK: I'm listening.

LI'L BIT: We could meet and talk—once a week. You could just store up whatever's bother-   970
  ing you during the week—and then we could talk.

PECK: Would you like that?

LI'L BIT: As long as you don't drink. I'd meet you somewhere for lunch or for a walk—on
  the weekends—as long as you stop drinking. And we could talk about whatever you
  want.   975

PECK: You would do that for me?

LI'L BIT: I don't think I'd want Mom to know. Or Aunt Mary. I wouldn't want them to
  think—

PECK: —No. It would just be us talking.

LI'L BIT: I'll tell Mom I'm going to a girlfriend's. To study. Mom doesn't get home until   980
  six, so you can call me after school and tell me where to meet you.

PECK: You get home at four?

LI'L BIT: We can meet once a week. But only in public. You've got to let me—draw the
  line. And once it's drawn, you mustn't cross it.

PECK: Understood.   985

LI'L BIT: Would that help?

[PECK *is very moved.*]

PECK: Yes. Very much.

LI'L BIT: I'm going to join the others in the living room now. [LI'L BIT *turns to go.*]

PECK: Merry Christmas, Li'l Bit.

[LI'L BIT *bestows a very warm smile on him.*]

LI'L BIT: Merry Christmas, Uncle Peck.   990

[A VOICE *dictates:*]

Shifting Forward from Second to Third Gear.

[*The* MALE *and* FEMALE GREEK CHORUS *members come forward.*]

MALE GREEK CHORUS: 1969. Days and Gifts: A Countdown:

FEMALE GREEK CHORUS: A note. "September 3, 1969. Li'l Bit: You've only been away two days and it feels like months. Hope your dorm room is cozy. I'm sending you this tape cassette—it's a new model—so you'll have some music in your room. Also that music you're reading about for class—*Carmina Burana.* Hope you enjoy. Only ninety days to go!—Peck." 995

MALE GREEK CHORUS: September 22. A bouquet of roses. A note: "Miss you like crazy. Sixty-nine days . . ."

TEENAGE GREEK CHORUS: September 25. A box of chocolates. A card: "Don't worry 1000 about the weight gain. You still look great. Got a post office box—write to me there. Sixty-six days.—Love, your candy man."

MALE GREEK CHORUS: October 16. A note: "Am trying to get through the Jane Austen you're reading—*Emma*—here's a book in return: *Liaisons Dangereuses.* Hope you're saving time for me." Scrawled in the margin the number: "47." 1005

FEMALE GREEK CHORUS: November 16. "Sixteen days to go!—Hope you like the perfume.— Having a hard time reaching you on the dorm phone. You must be in the library a lot. Won't you think about me getting you your own phone so we can talk?"

TEENAGE GREEK CHORUS: November 18. "Li'l Bit—got a package returned to the P.O. Box. Have you changed dorms? Call me at work or write to the P.O. Am still on the 1010 wagon. Waiting to see you. Only two weeks more!"

MALE GREEK CHORUS: November 23. A letter. "Li'l Bit. So disappointed you couldn't come home for the turkey. Sending you some money for a nice dinner out—nine days and counting!"

GREEK CHORUS: [*in unison*] November 25th. A letter: 1015

LI'L BIT: "Dear Uncle Peck: I am sending this to you at work. Don't come up next weekend for my birthday. I will not be here—"

[A VOICE *directs:*]

Shifting Forward from Third to Fourth Gear.

MALE GREEK CHORUS: December 10, 1969. A hotel room. Philadelphia. There is no moon tonight. 1020

[PECK *sits on the side of the bed while* LI'L BIT *paces. He can't believe she's in his room, but there's a desperate edge to his happiness.* LI'L BIT *is furious, edgy. There is a bottle of champagne in an ice bucket in a very nice hotel room.*]

PECK: Why don't you sit?

LI'L BIT: I don't want to.—What's the champagne for?

PECK: I thought we might toast your birthday—

LI'L BIT: —I am so pissed off at you, Uncle Peck.

PECK: Why? 1025

LI'L BIT: I mean, are you crazy?

PECK: What did I do?

LI'L BIT: You scared the holy crap out of me—sending me that stuff in the mail—

PECK: —They were gifts! I just wanted to give you some little perks your first semester—

LI'L BIT: —Well, what the hell were those numbers all about! Forty-four days to go—only 1030 two more weeks.—And then just numbers—69—68—67—like some serial killer!

PECK: Li'l Bit! Whoa! This is me you're talking to—I was just trying to pick up your spirits, trying to celebrate your birthday.

LI'L BIT: My *eighteenth* birthday. I'm not a child, Uncle Peck. You were counting down to my eighteenth birthday. 1035

PECK: So?

LI'L BIT: So? So statutory rape is not in effect when a young woman turns eighteen. And you and I both know it.

[PECK *is walking on ice.*]

PECK: I think you misunderstand.

LI'L BIT: I think I understand all too well. I know what you want to do five steps ahead of   1040
you doing it. Defensive Driving 101.

PECK: Then why did you suggest we meet here instead of the restaurant?

LI'L BIT: I don't want to have this conversation in public.

PECK: Fine. Fine. We have a lot to talk about.

LI'L BIT: Yeah. We do.   1045
[LI'L BIT *doesn't want to do what she has to do.*] Could I . . . have some of that
champagne?

PECK: Of course, madam! [PECK *makes a big show of it.*] Let me do the honors. I wasn't
sure which you might prefer—Taittingers or Veuve Clicquot—so I thought we'd start
out with an old standard—Perrier Jouet. [*The bottle is popped.*]   1050
Quick—Li'l Bit—your glass! [UNCLE PECK *fills* LI'L BIT's *glass. He puts the
bottle back in the ice and goes for a can of ginger ale.*] Let me get some of this ginger
ale—my bubbly—and toast you.

[*He turns and sees that* LI'L BIT *has not waited for him.*]

LI'L BIT: Oh—sorry, Uncle Peck. Let me have another. [PECK *fills her glass and reaches for his
ginger ale; she stops him.*] Uncle Peck—maybe you should join me in the champagne.   1055

PECK: You want me to—drink?

LI'L BIT: It's not polite to let a lady drink alone.

PECK: Well, missy, if you insist . . . [PECK *hesitates.*]—Just one. It's been a while. [PECK
fills another flute for himself.] There. I'd like to propose a toast to you and your birthday! [PECK *sips it tentatively.*] I'm not used to this anymore.   1060

LI'L BIT: You don't have anywhere to go tonight, do you?

[PECK *hopes this is a good sign.*]

PECK: I'm all yours.—God, it's good to see you! I've gotten so used to . . . to . . . talking to
you in my head. I'm used to seeing you every week—there's so much—I don't quite
know where to begin. How's school, Li'l Bit?

LI'L BIT: I—it's hard. Uncle Peck. Harder than I thought it would be. I'm in the middle of   1065
exams and papers and—I don't know.

PECK: You'll pull through. You always do.

LI'L BIT: Maybe. I . . . might be flunking out.

PECK: You always think the worse, Li'l Bit, but when the going gets tough—[LI'L BIT
shrugs and pours herself another glass.]—Hey, honey, go easy on that stuff, okay?   1070

LI'L BIT: Is it very expensive?

PECK: Only the best for you. But the cost doesn't matter—champagne should be "sipped."
[LI'L BIT *is quiet.*] Look—if you're in trouble in school—you can always come back
home for a while.

LI'L BIT: No—[LI'L BIT *tries not to be so harsh.*]—Thanks, Uncle Peck, but I'll figure some   1075
way out of this.

PECK: You're supposed to get in scrapes, your first year away from home.

LI'L BIT: Right. How's Aunt Mary?

PECK: She's fine. [*pause*] Well—how about the new car?

LI'L BIT: It's real nice. What is it, again? 1080

PECK: It's a Cadillac El Dorado.

LI'L BIT: Oh. Well, I'm real happy for you, Uncle Peck.

PECK: I got it for you.

LI'L BIT: What?

PECK: I always wanted to get a Cadillac—but I thought, Peck, wait until Li'l Bit's old 1085
enough—and thought maybe you'd like to drive it, too.

LI'L BIT: [*confused*] Why would I want to drive your car?

PECK: Just because it's the best—I want you to have the best.

[*They are running out of "gas"; small talk.*]

LI'L BIT: Listen, Uncle Peck, I don't know   PECK: I have been thinking of how to say
how to begin this, but—   this in my head, over and over— 1090

PECK: Sorry.

LI'L BIT: You first.

PECK: Well, your going away—has just made me realize how much I miss you. Talking to
you and being alone with you. I've really come to depend on you, Li'l Bit. And it's
been so hard to get in touch with you lately—the distance and—and you're never in 1095
when I call—I guess you've been living in the library—

LI'L BIT: —No—the problem is, I haven't been in the library—

PECK: —Well, it doesn't matter—I hope you've been missing me as much.

LI'L BIT: Uncle Peck—I've been thinking a lot about this—and I came here tonight to tell
you that—I'm not doing very well. I'm getting very confused—I can't concentrate 1100
on my work—and now that I'm away—I've been going over and over it in my
mind—and I don't want us to "see" each other anymore. Other than with the rest
of the family.

PECK: [*quiet*] Are you seeing other men?

LI'L BIT: [*getting agitated*] I—no, that's not the reason—I—well, yes I am seeing other— 1105
listen, it's not really anybody's business!

PECK: Are you in love with anyone else?

LI'L BIT: That's not what this is about.

PECK: Li'l Bit—you're scared. Your mother and your grandparents have filled your head
with all kinds of nonsense about men—I hear them working on you all the time— 1110
and you're scared. It won't hurt you—if the man you go to bed with really loves you.
[LI'L BIT *is scared. She starts to tremble.*] And I have loved you since the day I held
you in my hand. And I think everyone's just gotten you frightened to death about
something that is just like breathing—

LI'L BIT: Oh, my god—[*She takes a breath.*] I can't see you anymore, Uncle Peck. 1115

[PECK *downs the rest of his champagne.*]

PECK: Li'l Bit. Listen. Open your eyes and look at me. Come on. Just open your eyes,
honey. [LI'L BIT, *eyes squeezed shut, refuses.*] All right then. I just want you to listen.
Li'l Bit—I'm going to ask you just this once. Of your own free will. Just lie down on
the bed with me—our clothes on—just lie down with me, a man and a woman . . .
and let's . . . hold one another. Nothing else. Before you say anything else. I want 1120
the chance to . . . hold you. Because sometimes the body knows things that the
mind isn't listening to . . . and after I've held you, then I want you to tell me what
you feel.

LI'L BIT: You'll just . . . hold me?

PECK: Yes. And then you can tell me what you're feeling. 1130

[LI'L BIT—*half wanting to run, half wanting to get it over with, half wanting to be held by him:*]

LI'L BIT: Yes. All right. Just hold. Nothing else.

[PECK *lies down on the bed and holds his arms out to her.* LI'L BIT *lies beside him, putting her head on his chest. He looks as if he's trying to soak her into his pores by osmosis. He strokes her hair, and she lies very still. The* MALE GREEK CHORUS *member and the* FEMALE GREEK CHORUS *member as Aunt Mary come into the room.*]

MALE GREEK CHORUS: Recipe for a Southern boy:
FEMALE GREEK CHORUS: [*as Aunt Mary*] A drawl of molasses in the way he speaks.
MALE GREEK CHORUS: A gumbo of red and brown mixed in the cream of his skin.

[*While* PECK *lies, his eyes closed,* LI'L BIT *rises in the bed and responds to her aunt.*]

LI'L BIT: Warm brown eyes—   1135
FEMALE GREEK CHORUS: [*as Aunt Mary*] Bedroom eyes—
MALE GREEK CHORUS: A dash of Southern Baptist Fire and Brimstone—
LI'L BIT: A curl of Elvis on his forehead—
FEMALE GREEK CHORUS: [*as Aunt Mary*] A splash of Bay Rum—
MALE GREEK CHORUS: A closely shaven beard that he razors just for you—   1140
FEMALE GREEK CHORUS: [*as Aunt Mary*] Large hands—rough hands—
LI'L BIT: Warm hands—
MALE GREEK CHORUS: The steel of the military in his walk—
LI'L BIT: The slouch of the fishing skiff in his walk—
MALE GREEK CHORUS: Neatly pressed khakis—   1145
FEMALE GREEK CHORUS: [*as Aunt Mary*] And under the wide leather of the belt—
LI'L BIT: Sweat of cypress and sand—
MALE GREEK CHORUS: Neatly pressed khakis—
LI'L BIT: His heart beating Dixie—
FEMALE GREEK CHORUS: [*as Aunt Mary*] The whisper of the zipper—you could reach 1150
    out with your hand and—
LI'L BIT: His mouth—
FEMALE GREEK CHORUS: [*as Aunt Mary*] You could just reach out and—
LI'L BIT: Hold him in your hand—
FEMALE GREEK CHORUS: [*as Aunt Mary*] And his mouth—   1155

[LI'L BIT *rises above her uncle and looks at his mouth; she starts to lower herself to kiss him—and wrenches herself free. She gets up from the bed.*]

LI'L BIT: —I've got to get back.
PECK: Wait—Li'l Bit. Did you . . . feel nothing?
LI'L BIT: [*lying*] No. Nothing.
PECK: Do you—do you think of me?

[*The* GREEK CHORUS *whispers:*]

FEMALE GREEK CHORUS: Khakis—   1160
MALE GREEK CHORUS: Bay Rum—
FEMALE GREEK CHORUS: The whisper of the—
LI'L BIT: —No.

[PECK, *in a rush, trembling, gets something out of his pocket.*]

PECK: I'm forty-five. That's not old for a man. And I haven't been able to do anything else but think of you. I can't concentrate on my work—Li'l Bit. You've got to—I want 1165 you to think about what I am about to ask you.

LI'L BIT: I'm listening.

[PECK *opens a small ring box.*]

PECK: I want you to be my wife.

LI'L BIT: This isn't happening

PECK: I'll tell Mary I want a divorce. We're not blood-related. It would be legal— 1170

LI'L BIT: —What have you been thinking! You are married to my aunt, Uncle Peck. She's my family. You have—you have gone way over the line. Family is family.

[*Quickly,* LI'L BIT *flies through the room, gets her coat.*]

I'm leaving. Now. I am not seeing you. Again.

[PECK *lies down on the bed for a moment, trying to absorb the terrible news. For a moment, he almost curls into a fetal position.*]

I'm not coming home for Christmas. You should go home to Aunt Mary. Go home now, Uncle Peck. 1175

[PECK *gets control, and sits, rigid.*]

Uncle Peck?—I'm sorry but I have to go.

[*pause*]

Are you all right.

[*With a discipline that comes from being told that boys don't cry,* PECK *stands upright.*]

PECK: I'm fine. I just think—I need a real drink.

[*The* MALE GREEK CHORUS *has become a bartender. At a small counter, he is lining up shots for* PECK. *As* LI'L BIT *narrates, we see* PECK *sitting, carefully and calmly downing shot glasses.*]

LI'L BIT: [*to the audience*] I never saw him again. I stayed away from Christmas and Thanksgiving for years after. 1180

It took my uncle seven years to drink himself to death. First he lost his job, then his wife, and finally his driver's license. He retreated to his house, and had his bottles delivered.

[PECK *stands, and puts his hands in front of him—almost like Superman flying.*]

One night he tried to go downstairs to the basement—and he flew down the steep basement stairs. My aunt came by weekly to put food on the porch, and she 1185 noticed the mail and the papers stacked up, uncollected.

They found him at the bottom of the stairs. Just steps away from his dark room.

Now that I'm old enough, there are some questions I would have liked to have asked him. Who did it to you, Uncle Peck? How old were you? Were you eleven? 1190

[PECK *moves to the driver's seat of the car and waits.*]

Sometimes I think of my uncle as a kind of Flying Dutchman. In the opera, the Dutchman is doomed to wander the sea; but every seven years he can come ashore, and if he finds a maiden who will love him of her own free will—he will be released.

And I see Uncle Peck in my mind, in his Chevy '56, a spirit driving up and down the back roads of Carolina—looking for a young girl who, of her own free will, will love him. Release him. 1195

[A VOICE *states:*]

You and the Reverse Gear.

LI'L BIT: The summer of 1962. On Men, Sex, and Women: Part III

[LI'L BIT *steps, as an eleven year old, into:*]

FEMALE GREEK CHORUS: [*as Mother*] It is out of the question. End of Discussion.
LI'L BIT: But why? 1200
FEMALE GREEK CHORUS: [*as Mother*] Li'l Bit—we are not discussing this. I said no.
LI'L BIT: But I could spend an extra week at the beach! You're not telling me why!
FEMALE GREEK CHORUS: [*as Mother*] Your uncle pays entirely too much attention to you.
LI'L BIT: He listens to me when I talk. And—and he talks to me. He teaches me about things. Mama—he knows an awful lot. 1205
FEMALE GREEK CHORUS: [*as Mother*] He's a small town hick who's learned how to mix drinks from Hugh Hefner.
LI'L BIT: Who's Hugh Hefner?

[*beat*]

FEMALE GREEK CHORUS: [*as Mother*] I am not letting an eleven-year-old girl spend seven hours alone in the car with a man. . . . I don't like the way your uncle looks at you. 1210
LI'L BIT: For god's sake, mother! Just because you've gone through a bad time with my father—you think every man is evil!
FEMALE GREEK CHORUS: [*as Mother*] Oh no, Li'l Bit—not all men . . . We . . . we just haven't been very lucky with the men in our family.
LI'L BIT: Just because you lost your husband—I still deserve a chance at having a father! 1215 Someone! A man who will look out for me! Don't I get a chance?
FEMALE GREEK CHORUS: [*as Mother*] I will feel terrible if something happens.
LI'L BIT: Mother! It's in your head! Nothing will happen! I can take care of myself. And I can certainly handle Uncle Peck.
FEMALE GREEK CHORUS: [*as Mother*] All right. But I'm warning you—if anything happens, 1220 I hold you responsible.

[LI'L BIT *moves out of this scene and toward the car.*]

LI'L BIT: 1962. On the Back Roads of Carolina: The First Driving Lesson.

[*The* TEENAGE GREEK CHORUS *member stands apart on stage. She will speak all of* LI'L BIT*'s lines.* LI'L BIT *sits beside* PECK *in the front seat. She looks at him closely, remembering.*]

PECK: Li'l Bit? Are you getting tired?
TEENAGE GREEK CHORUS: A little.
PECK: It's a long drive. But we're making really good time. We can take the back road from 1225 here and see . . . a little scenery. Say—I've got an idea—[PECK *checks his rearview mirror.*]

TEENAGE GREEK CHORUS: Are we stopping, Uncle Peck?

PECK: There's no traffic here. Do you want to drive?

TEENAGE GREEK CHORUS: I can't drive. 1230

PECK: It's easy. I'll show you how. I started driving when I was your age. Don't you want to?—

TEENAGE GREEK CHORUS: —But it's against the law at my age!

PECK: And that's why you can't tell anyone I'm letting you do this—

TEENAGE GREEK CHORUS: —But—I can't reach the pedals. 1235

PECK: You can sit in my lap and steer. I'll push the pedals for you. Did your father ever let you drive his car?

TEENAGE GREEK CHORUS: No way.

PECK: Want to try?

TEENAGE GREEK CHORUS: Okay. 1240

[LI'L BIT *moves into* PECK'*s lap. She leans against him, closing her eyes.*]

PECK: You're just a little thing, aren't you? Okay—now think of the wheel as a big clock—I want you to put your right hand on the clock where three o'clock would be; and your left hand on the nine—

[LI'L BIT *puts one hand to* PECK'*s face, to stroke him. Then, she takes the wheel.*]

TEENAGE GREEK CHORUS: Am I doing it right?

PECK: That's right. Now, whatever you do, don't let go of the wheel. You tell me whether 1245 to go faster or slower—

TEENAGE GREEK CHORUS: Not so fast, Uncle Peck!

PECK: Li'l Bit—I need you to watch the road—

[PECK *puts his hands on* LI'L BIT'*s breasts. She relaxes against him, silent, accepting his touch.*]

TEENAGE GREEK CHORUS: Uncle Peck—what are you doing?

PECK: Keep driving. [*He slips his hands under her blouse.*] 1250

TEENAGE GREEK CHORUS: Uncle Peck—please don't do this—

PECK: —Just a moment longer . . . [PECK *tenses against* LI'L BIT.]

TEENAGE GREEK CHORUS: [*trying not to cry*] This isn't happening.

[PECK *tenses more, sharply. He buries his face in* LI'L BIT'*s neck, and moans softly. The* TEENAGE GREEK CHORUS *exits, and* LI'L BIT *steps out of the car.* PECK, *too, disappears.*]

[A VOICE *reflects:*]

Driving in Today's World.

LI'L BIT: That day was the last day I lived in my body. I retreated above the neck, and I've 1255 lived inside the "fire" in my head ever since.

And now that seems like a long, long time ago. When we were both very young. And before you know it, I'll be thirty-five. That's getting up there for a woman. And I find myself believing in things that a younger self vowed never to believe in. Things like family and forgiveness. 1260

I know I'm lucky. Although I still have never known what it feels like to jog or dance. Any thing that . . . "jiggles." I do like to watch people on the dance floor, or out on the running paths, just jiggling away. And I say—good for them. [LI'L BIT *moves to the car with pleasure.*]

The nearest sensation I feel—of flight in the body—I guess I feel when I'm 1270 driving. On a day like today. It's five a.m. The radio says it's going to be clear and crisp. I've got five miles of highway ahead of me—and some back roads too. I filled the tank last night, and had the oil checked. Checked the tires, too. You've got to treat her . . . with respect.

First thing I do is: Check under the car. To see if any two year olds or household 1275 cats have crawled beneath, and strategically placed their skulls behind my back tires. [LI'L BIT *crouches.*]

Nope. Then I get in the car. [LI'L BIT *does so.*]

I lock the doors. And turn the key. Then I adjust the most important control on the dashboard—the radio—[LI'L BIT *turns the radio on: We hear all of the* GREEK 1280 CHORUS *overlapping, and static:*]

FEMALE GREEK CHORUS: [*overlapping*]—"You were so tiny you fit in his hand—"

MALE GREEK CHORUS: [*overlapping*]—"How is Shakespeare gonna help her lie on her back in the—"

TEENAGE GREEK CHORUS: [*overlapping*]—"Am I doing it right?" 1285

[LI'L BIT *fine-tunes the radio station. A song like "Dedicated to the One I Love" or Orbison's "Sweet Dreams" comes on, and cuts off the* GREEK CHORUS.]

LI'L BIT: Ahh . . . [*beat*] I adjust my seat. Fasten my seat belt. Then I check the right side mirror—check the left side. [*She does.*] Finally, I adjust the rearview mirror. [*As* LI'L BIT *adjusts the rearview mirror, a faint light strikes the spirit of Uncle* PECK *who is sitting in the back seat of the car. She sees him in the mirror. She smiles at him, and he nods at her. They are happy to be going for a long drive together.* LI'L BIT *slips the car into first gear; to* 1290 *the audience:*] And then—I floor it. [*Sound of a car taking off. Blackout.*]

END OF PLAY

Lydia
(2008)

American drama has become increasingly diverse over the past few decades as its voices have become more varied and the production of new works has decentralized. Octavio Solis has written more than a dozen plays and although his plays are not limited to characters and issues particular to Latino-Americans, they resonate deeply within that community. Solis wrote *Lydia* when commissioned to write a play by The Denver Center Theatre. The play's popularity has resulted in professional productions throughout the country, and *Lydia* was a finalist nominee for the American Theatre Critics Association prize for the best new play originally produced outside of New York City.

Lydia is set in El Paso, Texas, during the early 1970s. Solis has chosen to set many of his plays in El Paso, where he was born and raised. As an American city bordering Mexico, Solis has called El Paso "a crucible of cultures." This border-city setting is especially appropriate for the characters in *Lydia*, because, as Solis has put it, they are caught "between two ways of being, two ways of life." Similarly, his characters speak in English and Spanish as well as in regional mixtures of the two.

Lydia is the story of a family shattered by an accident that left Ceci—three days before her *quinceañera* (her fifteenth birthday)—brain damaged. That accident happened two years before the play's action begins, and we witness its effects upon the family. Lydia, the play's title character, is an illegal immigrant from Mexico whom the family has taken in to help with Ceci. It is difficult not to compare the two young women and see in Lydia the young woman Ceci might have become if not for the accident. Lydia serves as the catalyst to the play's action, bringing passion back into the house and with it all the joys and harm that passion can cause. Lydia bonds with Ceci and acts as a kind of *curandera* (a healer) who seemingly reads Ceci's thoughts and eventually reveals long-kept secrets about the accident.

The play is realistic in its approach to language, violence, and sexuality. However, there is also magic in the otherwise real world that Solis has created. Ceci speaks directly to the audience, conjuring images both poetic and accosting, and makes us aware that Ceci retains a vibrant spirit locked inside her uncommunicative body. Critics have written about the play's frank, and what some may find shocking, approach to sexuality. Still, no aspect of the play has raised more controversy than its ending, which readers and audiences may best judge for themselves.

Lydia
(2008)

(COMMISSIONED AND FIRST PRODUCED BY THE DENVER CENTER FOR
THE PERFORMING ARTS, KENT THOMPSON, ARTISTIC DIRECTOR)

Characters

CECI, *the sister, 17*
MISHA, *the younger brother, 16*
RENE, *the older brother, 19*
ROSA, *the mother*
CLAUDIO, *the father*
ALVARO, *the cousin, 22*
LYDIA, *the maid*

TIME————*The early '70s, in winter.*
PLACE————*The living room of the Flores home in El Paso, Texas. Early '70s furnishings.
A sofa with a coffee table, its surface scratched and stained. And old La-Z-Boy facing
the TV. A stereo console with a set of headphones attached. A door to the front porch.
A darkened hallway to the bedrooms. An entry to the kitchen. In the foreground by the
TV, a small mattress with pillows and stuffed animals.*
CECI'S CONDITION————*For most of the play, Ceci lies on her mattress locked in her
body in a semi-vegetative state. Her body's muscles rigid, her hands curled and fingers
knuckled, she undergoes degrees of spasticity which come and go in ways that score the
play. Her voice is fallen back into her throat and unfocused, her powers of expression are
utterly buried in a neurological prison.*

---------- ACT I ----------

[*AT RISE: The living room of the Flores home.* CLAUDIO *slumps on the La-Z-
Boy watching TV. Ironing his white shirts and pants is his wife* ROSA. *In her
mattress lies* CECI *in her pajama, a long thin scar rising from her eyebrow and
disappearing into her hairline.* CECI *lies very still, her eyes on the flickering light
of the TV. After a moment, an awareness dawns on her and she starts.*]

CECI: She touched me and I flew. Touched my fault-line. And I flew. With her hand
laid holy water on my scar. And I flew on wings of glass. My body *como una* bird
racing with the moon on a breath of air.[1] Flying out of range of pain, purpose,

---
[1] *Como una* bird–"like a bird"

this thing we call *Vida*,[2] soaring into *them*. I wake to this. Life inside my life. No
wings, no glass, no moon. Only *Loteria* which means Bingo, which means chance,   5
which means play. So I play the cards into view.

[*She looks down at her arms and legs curling under her as a light falls on her
mattress.*]

A card with me printed, *La Vida Cecilia*, a rag doll thumbing the stitching in her
head, forming the words in her vegetable tongue, what happened to me, *porque no
puedo* remember, I must remember.[3]

[*The light bears down on* CLAUDIO.]

There. A card called El Short-Order Cook. Broken man drowning in old *rancheras*   10
and TV.[4] I hear *voces antiguas* calling his name,[5] Claudio, my poor *Papi* Claudio in
your personal winter, drowning out the will of *Mami* saying come with me across
the *rio*,[6] give up that lie you thought was you and live mine, live American with me.
So the dish ran away with the greasy spoon and a girl jumped over the moon but
you don't spikka the English, only the word No, which in Spanish means No, No   15
at work, in bed, in your dreams, in your *cantos perdidos*.[7]

[*The light shifts to* ROSA, *ironing clothes and muttering silent prayers to herself.*]

Aqui,[8] the Mami Rosa card, dressmaker of flying girls, sewing up unfinished seams; a
beautiful woman losing beauty by the day, see it gathering at her feet like old panty
hose, *ay Ama!*[9] You were Rosei Flores, clerk for the County, making your life here,
Anglo words like lazy moths tumbling out your mouth, you were *toda* proud,[10] but   20
now. You're Rosa Reborn holy-rolling me to sleep with the prayers of your new
church. Your prayers for us to be family which hasn't really been family since they
stopped putting cork in soda bottle caps.

[RENE *comes in from down the hall. He goes to the front door and retrieves the
day's mail. He goes over it carefully.*]

Ayy. My wild card, *El Carnal Mayor*,[11] Rene, my elder volcano, bustin' noses just by
looking at 'em, both hands fulla middle fingers for the whole world, checking every   25
day for hate mail, but always *nada*. Cars go by and honk *Puto-Puto-Rene-Puto*! but
cowards, my brother is invincible.[12]

[*He throws the mail on the coffee table and stares at* CECI.]

---

[2] *Vida*–"Life"
[3] *porque no puedo* remember–"why can't I remember"
[4] *rancheras*–"ranch songs; Mexican country music"
[5] *voces antiguas*–"ancient voices"
[6] *Papi . . . Mami*–"daddy . . . mommy"
[7] *cantos perdidos*–"lost songs"
[8] *Aqui*–"Here"
[9] *Ay, Ama!*–"Oh, Ma!"
[10] *toda*–"all"
[11] *El Carnal Mayor*–slang for "older brother"
[12] *Puto-Puto-Rene-Puto!*–"faggot, faggot, Rene faggot!"

The army recruiter don't want you, huh, not like those other flag-draped *Chicanos* on our block, even those that come back alive look like they gave up the ghost, that's kinda what you want, that damned ghost taken out of you. 'Cause you're all messed up with some hard-core macho shit nobody gets.   30

[*He finally looks at* CECI *and slowly comes to her.*]

Andale,[13] plant a kiss on my head like that saint in church with the chipped nose—

[*He kisses her and leaves out the front door.*]

—dry-kiss and move away. *Simon, carnal*,[14] before the disgust starts to show.

[MISHA *enters with his books. Flops down on the couch.*]

Misha? *¿Eres tu?*[15] Card with the inscription Little Shit. *Carnalito* Misha bringing to my *nariz* fragrances of the street the school his body,[16] yes, the musk of you coming   35
of age, coming into yourself, coming all *over* yourself. I hear your little secrets like crystals of salt in the pockets of your eyes, sad-boy Misha, sad for me, for us, the things that darken the day, King and Kennedy, the killings of students, the killings of Nam—

[*Beat*]

Mi familia.[17] All sad and wounded cause of somethin'. Somethin' that broke. I gotta   40
read my scar for the story, it's in there, I know it! *¡Aguas!*[18] I see her. The girl that touched me . . . her face in a mirror looking back . . . showing me her own sccc—ggghn mmm her—own—ssccrrmmgfmhm. . .

MISHA: Mom, what's wrong with Ceci?
ROSA: *Alomejor* she went poo-poo.[19]   45
MISHA: She doesn't smell like it.
ROSA: Maybe she wants her therapy. Could you do it, Misha? I'm pressing your father's shirts for work.

[MISHA *sits by* CECI *and runs her through a repertoire of delicate physical exercises, shifting her position from time to time.*]

MISHA: *Orale, carnala.*[20] Let's get the blood pumping.
ROSA: *Con cariño*,[21] okay?   50
MISHA: Always gentle, *Ama*.[22] Hey Dad.
ROSA: He can't hear you.
MISHA: Dad!
ROSA: *¿Que te dije?*[23] What are you doing home so early? Don't you have practice?

---

[13] *andale*–"go on"
[14] *Simon, carnal*–"yeah, bro"
[15] *¿Eres tu?*–"Is that you?"
[16] *Carnalito*–"little brother"/*nariz*–"nose"
[17] *Mi familia*–"my family"
[18] *¡Aguas!*–literally, "Waters!" But commonly used slang for "Watch out!" or "Beware!"
[19] *Alomejor*–"maybe"
[20] *Orale, carnala*–"alright, sis"
[21] *Con cariño*–"with tenderness"
[22] *Ama*–"ma"
[23] *¿Que te dije?*–"What did I tell you?"

MISHA: [*as he rubs* CECI's *arms and hands*] I dropped out of the squad. Football ain't my 55
game. You hear that, Dad? I'm a wuss and I don't understand what all those little
circles and arrows mean. I can't hear the quarterback in the huddle. He grunts uhh
twenty-uhhh on huuu—uuhh! But I do on huuu and Coach yells at me. At the scrim-
mage today, a touchdown got called back on account of I was off-sides. I told them
it wasn't my fault. I told them we need enunciation in the huddle. In the showers 60
they all towel-whipped my bare *ass*.

ROSA: Watch your language.

MISHA: So you know what, Dad, I quit. I turned in my equipment and walked. I'm sorry,
Mom. I just feel I'm needed here.

ROSA: It's okay, *mijo*.[24] I never liked you playing with those *brutos*.[25] You're my special 65
boy. That's why I named you Misha.

MISHA: You named me Miguel.

ROSA: But after I saw that Baryshnikov on TV, I started calling you Misha.

MISHA: I don't even like ballet.

ROSA: The point is a brown boy named Misha in El Paso is special. I got my hopes pinned 70
all over you like dollars.

MISHA: Is there anything to eat?

ROSA: There's *albondigas* on the stove.

MISHA: Meatballs? From last night?

ROSA: They're a little dried out, but still good. You want some? 75

MISHA: ¿*Jefita?*[26] [ROSA *looks. He opens* CECI's *arms wide.*] I *wuv* you this much.

ROSA: *Sangron.*[27]

[*She laughs and goes into the kitchen.*]

CECI: Huuh onhuu-uuh.

MISHA: You sound like my quarterback.

CECI: Shhghgm. 80

MISHA: The truth is when I'm on the field, I don't pay attention. I watch the yellowing
grass and the zip-zip-zip of the sprinklers and the clouds making ponytails in the
sky.

CECI: Uhh. Ghhh. Gngngm.

MISHA: Mom. There's something different about her. 85

ROSA: What?

MISHA: I dunno. Something. Are you still giving her her meds?

ROSA: [*returning with a bowl of meatballs*] Of course!

MISHA: 'Cause I know you don't sometimes, Mom. I know how you "forget" sometimes.

ROSA: I don't forget, never! 90

MISHA: Where are they? Where're the pills? How much did you give her today? How
much, Mom!

---

[24] *mijo*—a contraction of *mi hijo,* "my son"

[25] *brutos*—brutes

[26] ¿*Jefita?*—literally, "little boss lady;" the terms "jefe" and "jefa" are sometimes used for parents, meaning male
and female boss, respectively

[27] *Sangron*—in this context the term seems to mean "joker" or "dummy"

ROSA: *Oye,*[28] it's not drugs she needs but faith! Faith! *Mijo*, the doctors said it was over, remember, she's a vegetable *para siempre,*[29] they said. What are these pills supposed to do then? 95

MISHA: Give me the pills. Or I'm telling him.

ROSA: Tell him. *Andale. Dile todo.*[30]

[MISHA *turns to his father.* CLAUDIO *takes off his headphones and stands.*]

CLAUDIO: *Que paso, Miguel.*[31] *¿Como te va en el* football?[32]

MISHA: Good.

ROSA: I'm almost done here. Just a few more shirts. 100

CLAUDIO: *¿Como?*[33]

ROSA: *Nomas estas camisas, Viejo.*[34]

CLAUDIO: *Miguel, una cerveza.*[35]

[MISHA *nods gravely as* CLAUDIO *goes down the hall to the bathroom.*]

ROSA: Praise God.

MISHA: I wish you'd keep your religion to yourself. It's not doing Ceci any good. 105

ROSA: *Oyeme*, Misha.[36] When your sister got hurt, I prayed to the *Virgen Santa, la Patronesa de todos los Mexicanos. La Virgen de Guadalupe* herself.[37] And she failed me. That's when I know. Us *Católicos,*[38] we worship the wrong things. Idols can't make miracles. Only God. So I go to a church with no other gods but God.

MISHA: Has that done her any good? Has it? 110

ROSA: Today. While your father was sleeping. You know what I did? I took her to Our Church of the Nazarene.

MISHA: What? You took her to those holy rollers? Are you kidding me?

ROSA: Misha, she loved it. All the peoples adored her. And Pastor Lujan himself baptized her. 115

MISHA: What?

ROSA: He put her in this big glass tub and laid his hand on her, *mijo*. Right here where her precious brains came out, and he prayed to God for her soul. He dipped her backward in the water and her face came alive! Eyes bright as nickels and her mouth wide open, taking in the light of heaven! Pastor Lujan said very clearly: Cecilia, prepare 120 you! Your redemption is knocking on you head. And he took her pills and poured them all into the same tub.

MISHA: Oh no. . . .

---

[28] *Oye*–"listen" or "hey"

[29] *para siempre*–"forever"

[30] *Dile todo*–"tell him everything"

[31] *Que paso, Miguel.*–"What happened, Miguel"

[32] *¿Como te va en el football?*–"How's it going in football?"

[33] *¿Como?*–literally, "how"; used idiomatically as, "what was that?" "how was that?" or "excuse me?"

[34] *Nomas estas camisas, Viejo*–"Just these shirts, old man." *Viejo* and *Vieja* may be used as terms of endearment just as "old man" or "old lady" may endearingly be used between husband and wife in English

[35] *una cerveza*–"a beer"

[36] *Oyeme*–"Listen to me"

[37] *Virgen . . . de Guadalupe*–"Holy Virgin, the Patroness of all Mexicans. The Virgin of Guadalupe" (Mary)

[38] *Catolicos*–Catholics

ROSA: He said we don't need them anymore! He said it's evil in our hearts that makes her sick.

125

MISHA: No more saving her soul. I mean it. Leave her soul alone.

ROSA: Don't you lecture me on how I care for *mija!*[39] Who stays home with her day and night, changing her when she needs to go, making her special food, rubbing her joints *y todo?*[40] Who?

MISHA: I help.

130

ROSA: *Por favor,*[41] Misha. You're in school all day.

MISHA: I know.

ROSA: Well, I know *more.* Nothing happens without me in this house. I see to our needs. That's how come we're getting a maid.

MISHA: A maid? Like, to clean the house?

135

ROSA: To clean the house, to cook the food, to watch your sister. I asked your Tia Mirna, and she said her maid knows this *chavala* from *Jalisco* who just came over and she needs work and she's cheap.[42]

MISHA: What about you?

ROSA: They called from the county office and told me my old position is available if I want it. Well, I want it. I'm tired of staying in this house all day. Plus we need the money.

140

MISHA: Is she legal?

ROSA: I don't ask about such things. I just ask her to come tomorrow.

MISHA: Tomorrow? Dammit, why didn't you tell me?

145

ROSA: I did. Watch your tongue. Last week. I mentioned it at dinner. But you never listen. You and your brother only hear what you want to hear.

[CLAUDIO *returns from the bathroom.*]

CLAUDIO: *¿Y mi cerveza?*[43]

MISHA: Mom *dice que* we're gonna have a maid, *una criada.*[44]

CLAUDIO: *Asi lo quiere.*[45]

150

MISHA: *¿Y tu, que quieres?*[46]

CLAUDIO: *Mi pinche cerveza.*[47]

[*He sits and puts his headphones on again.* MISHA *watches him.*]

ROSA: You heard him.

MISHA: What am I, his *mesero?*[48]

[*She glares at him.* MISHA *goes off to the kitchen and reenters with a can of beer.*]

---

[39] *Mija*–"daughter"

[40] *y todo*–"and everything"

[41] *Por favor*–"please"

[42] *chavala from Jalisco*–"chick from Jalisco" (a state in Mexico)

[43] *¿Y mi cerveza?*–"And my beer?"

[44] *dice que . . . una criada*–"says that . . . a maid"

[45] *Asi lo quiere*–"That's how she wants it"

[46] *¿Y tu, que quieres?*–"And you, what do you want?"

[47] *Mi pinche cerveza*–"My fucking beer"

[48] *mesero*–"waiter"

MISHA: Ask yourself, Mom. Do we really want this? Do we really want a stranger coming into our house?   155

ROSA: What's wrong with our house? What don't you want her to see? What are you ashamed of, Misha? Your sister?

MISHA: Not her.

ROSA: I promise you. When she comes here, she will find a close, caring Mexican *familia*   160
trying to make it in this blessed country.

CLAUDIO: [*impatiently waiting for his beer*] Miguel. . . .

ROSA: Get over your *verguenza* and give your father his beer.[49]

MISHA: Mom. . . .

ROSA: Do it, Miguel.   165

> [CLAUDIO *suddenly gets up, takes the beer and slaps* MISHA *across the face.*]

CLAUDIO: *Tres veces te lo pedí, cabrón. Tres veces.*[50]

> [*He sits, rips off the pull-tab and drops it on the floor by* CECI. *He watches TV as* MISHA's *eyes well with tears.*]

ROSA: *¿Que te dije?*[51] Pick up that thing before your sister cuts herself with it.

> [CECI *turns to speak to* MISHA *as he picks up the pull-tab, his cheek reddening with the heat of the blow, and goes to his room.*]

CECI: It's okay, *carnalito*. I hear your face clapping against the way things are, and I know it hurts, 'cause I feel my face smashing against the mad will of God. I remember that, Misha, like I remember we can't let the swelling block us off, we gotta believe that it   170
passes, bro, it passes. Sure as day passes into night.

> [*Suddenly, night.* CECI *lying on her mattress. Headlights swivel across the window drapes as* RENE *comes in the front door. He stands and waits in the dark until his breath is even. He watches* CECI *with a mix of fear and contempt.* MISHA *enters.*]

RENE: Any mail?

MISHA: No. [*notices* RENE's *bloody knuckles*] *Vato.*[52]

RENE: It's nothing.

MISHA: Nothing. You're bleeding.   175

RENE: What's a little *molé.*[53] You should see them.

MISHA: Are you drunk too?

RENE: It helps, don't you think? So you and me and some Buds?

MISHA: We're out. And it's too late to hit the Circle K.

RENE: I don't need no shit Circle fucking K, goddammit. I need me some *pisto. Watcha.*[54]   180

> [*He reaches under the cushions of the La-Z-Boy. A fifth of Southern Comfort.*]

---

[49] *verguenza*–literally, "shame"; seemingly used here as "embarrassment"
[50] *Tres . . . veces*–"Three times I asked you for it, you little shit. Three times."
[51] *¿Que te dije?*–"What did I tell you?"
[52] *Vato*–slang for "Man" or "Dude"
[53] *molé*–traditional Mexican paste of chocolate and chile; used here as slang for "blood"
[54] *Pisto*–"booze"

MISHA: Whoa.

RENE: Papa's gotta brand new bag.

MISHA: How'd you know it was there?

RENE: *Ese*,[55] he sits in that chair all *pinchi* day like he's incubating a fucking *huevo. Andale, tragito!*[56] [*They slug some down.*] Nothing like a little *pisto* to smooth out the rough   185
edges of a bad night.[57]

MISHA: Was it a bad night?

RENE: Hell no, it was a good night. We kicked some ass.

MISHA: What did you do?

RENE: We kicked some ass.   190

MISHA: How about a little more detail, *ese*?

RENE: We kicked some fucking ass.

MISHA: Rene.

RENE: You're too young. You don't get the vibe. This is me, Joey, and Sergio taking on the
pinchi world.   195

MISHA: Joey and Sergio? Those pussies?

RENE: *No mames, guey!*[58] These are my *camaradas*! Besides, we need Joey's van for the
ceremony.

MISHA: What ceremony?

RENE: *Pos*,[59] first we chug back some brew for a couple hours, listen to some Sabbath, toke   200
a little *mota* for courage.[60] Then we think of cheerleaders and whack off a little till
we're nice and hard and then we hit the road.

MISHA: And kick some ass.

RENE: Fuckin' A.

MISHA: I heard it was some *cholos*[61] last night.   205

RENE: Tough little fuckers in training for prison, gang tats *y toda la madre*.[62] We kicked their
ass. *Dame*.[63] [*He drinks. Some red and white lights flash by the window.*] *¡Trucha!*[64] Get
down! Down!

MISHA: Shit, Rene! Is that the cops?

RENE: Just be quiet and keep your head down.   210

[RENE *peeks through the drapes till the lights pass.*]

MISHA: What the fuck happened? You better tell me or I'm gonna wake up Mom and tell
her the cops are after you.

[55] *Ese*—literally, "that one." Often used in slang as "man" or "dude"

[56] *pinchi . . . huevo. Andale tragito!*—"fuckin' . . . egg. Go on, [take a] little drink/sip!"

[57] *pisto*—"booze"

[58] *No mames, guey!*—"no mames" slang term meaning, "don't mess around now," "*guey*" is a corruption of "buey,"
meaning "ass or donkey" and used in slang as a derogatory term

[59] *Pos*—corruption of *pues*, meaning "well" in this context

[60] *mota*—"weed" (marijuana)

[61] *cholos*—originally the term designated persons of mixed European and indigenous blood. Now used in slang
as "thugs"

[62] *y toda la madre*—literally, "and the whole mother," used in slang as "and all that shit"

[63] *Dame*—"gimme"

[64] *¡Trucha!*—slang for "Watch out!"

RENE: *Calamantes montes,* narc.[65] I'll tell you, but only as a cautionary tale for you not to put your ass where it's likely to be kicked, *me entiendes?*[66]

[MISHA *nods.*]

RENE: We took on some GI's.   215
MISHA: Shit. Oh shit.
RENE: Fresh outa Ft. Bliss. We went up a mountain on Scenic Drive and pulled over by these cars. And there they were, a *gringo salado* and a couple *negros.*[67] We just approached them like some tourists up to see the sights, you know? They offered us some beers and were really nice to us. But these *fags,* Meesh, you gotta watch out for them.   220
MISHA: How come?
RENE: Just 'cause I say so. Anyway, the *gringo* puts his hand on my knee so I gotta cut him with a right hook that snaps his head back. Joey and Serge lay into the others and man, it's on, We lay into these jive-turkey motherfuckers with basic-training biceps. Serge is swinging this bat on their heads and Joey's got nunchucks and blood is   225
shootin' volcanic all over the place.
MISHA: You hit 'em with bats? What if you put 'em in the hospital with like brain damage or something?
RENE: Hey, don't talk brain damage. Not in front of her. Pay your penance, fuck.

[RENE *offers the bottle and* MISHA *drinks.*]

MISHA: I don't get it, man. Why are you doing this shit? When are you gonna go to college   230
or get a real job?
RENE: I gotta job.
MISHA: Car detailing at Earl Scheib? You're smarter than that.
RENE: What's the *pinche* point, bro? I'm gonna get drafted anyway.
MISHA: Is that what you're looking for in the mail? Your draft notice? *Ese,* your birthdate's   235
not due in the lottery till next year.
RENE: *No mames, guey.*
MISHA: If you're so anxious about it, if you wanna kill someone, go enlist like Alvaro.
RENE: I ain't that stupid.
MISHA: Neither is he. He came back with a bronze star. Gung-ho guys like him always   240
seem to make out okay.
RENE: Varo's too hot-shit for us now. Back three months and he still hasn't come to our *chante.*[68]
MISHA: Mom says he's been focusing on getting some steady work.
CECI: Varo. Varo Varo Varo.   245
MISHA: I know this much. War keeps going like it is, I'm gonna have to go to Canada.
RENE: Canada? Why truck all the way up there, Mexico's right there, you dope!
MISHA: Well, on TV, that's where they all say they're going! Canada!
RENE: 'Cause they're white, stupid! Canada! You're a trip. What are you doing up?

---

[65] *Calamantes montes*–playful slang meaning in this context, "Take a chill pill"
[66] *me entiendes?*–"you understand me?"
[67] *gringo salado . . . negros*–"a salty white guy and a couple of blacks"
[68] *chante*–Mexican slang for house, similar to slang usage of "crib" for house in English

MISHA: I couldn't sleep. I had this dream. Hey, you know Mom's hiring some chick to   250
take care of Ceci?

RENE: Old news, bro.

MISHA: She's coming tomorrow to cook and do the wash. Tell you one thing, she ain't
touching my clothes.

RENE: You got some stains in your *chones* you don't want her to see?[69]   255

MISHA: Shut up.

RENE: Haha! Is that what you had? A wet dream?

MISHA: Cut it out. It was scary as shit. We were kids, you, me, Alvaro, and Ceci, all alone
in this house.

RENE: What happened?   260

MISHA: We were playing like we used to. We put chairs all over the living room, down the
hall, covered them up with sheets and we crawled under pretending we were ants in
our tunnels. We scurried from chamber to chamber, touching heads lightly, making
those little tee-tee sounds in ant-language. Ceci's eyes full of joy. She had those pearl
earrings she got for her *Quinceañera*.[70] We saw her go off with this shiny key in her   265
mouth. I think it was a key. It looked like a key. Her shadow against the sheet one
second, and the next, gone. We went through the tunnels looking for her, but
we couldn't find her. I wanted to call out "Ceci," but you said use ant-language.
I couldn't think of the words for please come back, and I went all through the tunnel,
looking for her. I woke up absolutely freaked. I came out here and saw the invisible   270
lines of the tunnels all over the floor.

RENE: I'm sackin' out before the old man comes home. You shouldn't be dreaming shit
like that, Misha.

[*He returns the bottle to the cushion seam and goes.*]

CECI: Gghn.

[*MISHA goes to CECI and looks into her eyes. He gently pries her mouth open. He
looks inside. He lets her go and then walks off to bed.*]

CECI: You won't find nothing down there but spit and the words to *Cielito Lindo*.[71] I feel   275
it coming around again like a Mexican yo-yo, little ball up on its string and plop
right into the bowl of my heart.

[*CLAUDIO enters from the shadows in white shirt and trousers with his paper hat.*]

CECI: It's the night of my race with the moon. He comes in his fry-cook whites to my
room, wearing that white paper hat like a general. I'm at the threshold of my *senorita*-
hood, pretending to sleep, feeling his raw breath in my ear singing for the last   280
time. . . .

[*He sings softly as he opens his hands and reveals a pair of pearl earrings.*]

CLAUDIO: *De la sierra morena*   [From the tanned sierra
            Cielito lindo viene bajando   Cielito lindo, comes down

---

[69] *chones*—slang for "underwear"

[70] *Quinceañera*—a girl's fifteenth birthday party which functions as a passage to womanhood ceremony in Latin
cultures

[71] *Cielito Lindo*—a traditional and popular Mexican song. The title means, "Lovely Sky" but *cielito* is also used as
a term of endearment

Un par de ojitos negros	A pair of little black eyes
Cielito lindo de contrabando	Cielito lindo, of contraband	285
Ese lunar que tienes	That beauty mark you have,
Cielito lindo junto a la boca	Cielito lindo, next to your mouth
No se lo des a nadie	Give it to no one,
Cielito lindo que a mi me toca	Cielito lindo, for it is mine.
Ay ay ay ay	ay, ay, ay, ay	290
Canta y no llores	Sing and don't weep
Porque cantando se alegran	Because it's by singing,
Cielito lindo los corazones	Cielito lindo, that hearts cheer up.]

[*He gets up and slowly walks off into the darkness.*]

CECI: A tear from each eye turned to pearl and laid on my pillow to make the moon jealous. Oh what is this yearning inside? What does it mean? 295

[*The next day.* ROSA *comes in dressed for work, fussing about, straightening up the house with a minimum of noise.*]

ROSA: *¡Ay Diosito diosito!* Where is this girl? *¡Ya son las ocho y media! ¡Ay, que nervio!*[72]
CECI: Ghghnn.
ROSA: Okay, okay, I'm coming! *Ya ya.* I know, I know. This house smells like a *cantina!*[73] What were these *barbaros* up to last night, Ceci?[74]
CECI: Gghhn. 300

[ROSA *goes to the kitchen and quickly returns with a bowl of oatmeal. She sits and stirs the oatmeal around with a spoon.*]

ROSA: *Ta bien, mija.*[75] I know everything in this house. I know they were drinking. I know Rene was fighting again. But what can I do? He does what he does. *¿Tienes apetito por* some oatmeal? *Ven.*[76] [*She holds* CECI *as she raises a spoonful of oatmeal.*] Oh, *espera.*[77] We forgot grace. [*She holds* CECI's *hands and closes her eyes.*] Dear Lord Jesus Holy Father, we submit this meal today for your blessing that we may not want and 305 pray for your mercy, for You made us in order to love us and as we take this meal please forgive our sins and heal us first in our *corazones* so that the body may follow. In your most precious and holy name, Amen. [*She guides the spoon into her mouth.*] Not too hot? Good. [*She continues to talk as she feeds her.*] My pretty girl. Even the accident couldn't keep this body from growing. It's my body, Ceci, the body I used 310 to have. The hip-huggers and halter tops I would have bought you! *¡Lastima de tu quinceañera!*[78] I made with my own Singer the whitest most beautiful dress with lace running all the way down the sleeve to the wrist. Like a Disney *Chicana* you would look! Regal and sexy, but definitely chaste. You would save that *cosita* for after your wedding. *Pero ahora, pobre mija.*[79] It's just a dead flower on you now. 315

---

[72] *¡Ay Diosito . . . que nervio!*–"Oh Lordy, Lordy! Where is this girl? It's already eight thirty! Oh, how nerve-wracking!"
[73] *cantina*–"saloon"
[74] *barbaros*–"barbarians"
[75] *Ta bien, mija*–"It's alright, honey"
[76] *¿Tienes apetito por . . . ? Ven*–"Are you hungry for . . . ?/Come."
[77] *espera*–"wait"
[78] *¡Lastima de tu quinceañera!*–"Shame about your quinceañera!"
[79] *cosita*–"little thing"/*Pero ahora, pobre mija.*–"But now, my poor daughter."

[CECI *jerks and thrusts the bowl of oatmeal all over herself and her mother.*]

CECI: GGGhhhmmm!

ROSA: *¡AY! ¡Cecilia Rosario! ¡Que has hecho!* Look at my dress! *¡Inutil!*[80]

[CECI *flails madly about.* LYDIA *appears at the door, bag in hand.*]

LYDIA: *¿Señora?*

ROSA: Oh. *Si, si, si. ¿Eres la muchacha de Jalisco?*[81]

LYDIA: Yes.   320

ROSA: *¿Hablas ingles?*[82]

LYDIA: *Si, Señora—o sea . . .*[83] Yes, I would prefer. I am learning.

ROSA: *Entonces,*[84] come in. Come in, please.

[LYDIA *enters.* CECI *is still angrily flailing her arms.*]

CECI: Ggnnhf!

LYDIA: *Perdón, pero me perdi.*[85] I . . . I . . . got lost. . . .   325

CECI: GGGhn!

ROSA: It's okay, okay, I understand.

LYDIA: Let me. I help. You go wash.

[LYDIA *puts down her bag and goes to* CECI. *She cleans her with her napkin.*]

ROSA: No, no, please, she's very hard to—

LYDIA: It's okay, I can do, she's strong, your—*como se dice*—your daughter?[86]   330

ROSA: Yes. Daughter. *Mija.*

LYDIA: You go change, I take care here. *Hola-hola chica.*[87] What is her name?

ROSA: Ceci.

LYDIA: *Hola, Ceci. Hola.* I am Lydia. How are you fine? I am fine too. *Que bonita te ves con la avena en la cara.*[88] Oatmeal is very good for the skin. Here.   335

[LYDIA *rubs more into her face.* CECI *freezes at the feel of the warm oatmeal.* ROSA *is taken aback.*]

Soon you be Miss *Tejas, que no?*[89] Soon you be Miss *Universo.*

[MISHA *enters as* CECI *coos softly throughout the next passage.*]

MISHA: What's going on?

CECI: Nnnnn . . . nnnnn . . .

ROSA: This is our maid—

LYDIA: Lydia.   340

ROSA: Lydia from Jalisco.

---

[80] *¡AY! ¡Cecilia Rosario! ¡Que has hecho!*–"Oh! Cecilia Rosario! What have you done!"/*¡Inutil!*–"Useless"

[81] *Oh. Si, . . . Jalisco?*–"Oh. Yes, yes, yes. Are you the girl from Jalisco?"

[82] *¿Hablas ingles?*–"Do you speak English?" or "You speak English?"

[83] *Si, Señora—o sea . . .*–"Yes, ma'am, I mean . . ."

[84] *Entonces*–"Then"

[85] *Perdón, pero me perdi*–"I'm sorry, but I got lost"

[86] *como se dice*–"how do you say"

[87] *Hola-hola chica*–"Hello-hello, girl"

[88] *Que bonita . . . la cara*–"How pretty you look with the oatmeal on your face"

[89] *. . . Miss Tejas, que no?*–". . . Miss Texas, won't you?"

MISHA: What's she doing to her?

ROSA: She spilled the oatmeal on me and—

LYDIA: Making her skin soft. If she won't eat, then she can be beautiful. *¿Verdad, Ceci?*[90]

CECI: Ooooh.   345

ROSA: I have to go change. I'm going to be late. I'm late already. [ROSA *goes.*]

LYDIA: *Asi, asi.*[91] Feels good, no? Feels like chocolate.

CECI: Gggnnh.

MISHA: Are you sure this works?

LYDIA: It worked on me, *que no?*[92] [*She looks up at* MISHA *for the first time.*] What is your   350
    name?

MISHA: Miguel. But they call me Misha.

LYDIA: Misha?

MISHA: My mother's called me that since I was little.

LYDIA: It's Russian.   355

MISHA: I know.

LYDIA: Is there Russian in your blood?

MISHA: No. Listen, I think you really should get her cleaned up before my old man sees
    her like this. He's not into beauty tips n' shit—

LYDIA: Speak slower. Or speak Spanish.   360

MISHA: I'm not that fluent in Spanish.

LYDIA: Then speak slower, Misha.

MISHA: My. Father. Will be pissed. When he sees this. Pissed as in pissed off.

LYDIA: Ceci, are you calm now? You want to clean up and eat?

CECI: Ggnnh. Ggnnhr.   365

MISHA: That means yes.

LYDIA: No, it means let me wear it for another minute. Are we sharing a room?

MISHA: What?

LYDIA: Me and Ceci, are we sharing a room?

MISHA: Yeah.   370

LYDIA: *Bueno. Asi va ser.*[93]

MISHA: How old are you?

LYDIA: How old are you?

MISHA: No, this is a relevant question. You can't take care of my sister if you're as young
    as you look.   375

LYDIA: Speak slower.

MISHA: I said, You, Can't, Take, Care—

LYDIA: I am as young as I look.

MISHA: Mom!

ROSA: [*enters wearing a new dress*] Shhht! *¡Tranquilo!* Don't you know your father's still   380
    sleeping! That's another thing. My husband, *mi marido*, he works night till 6 in the
    morning, then sleeps most of the day. You have to be very quiet.

---

[90] *¿Verdad, Ceci?*–"Right, Ceci?"
[91] *Asi, asi*–"Like this, like this"
[92] *Que no?*–"Didn't it?"
[93] *Bueno. Asi va ser*–"Good. That's how it'll be"

MISHA: You can't be serious.

ROSA: I'm going to work. *Toma,*[94] keys to the house. And here's my number at work. She eats only food that I've marked with her name in the fridge, *con su nombre,* okay?[95] And she wears diapers, *pero* still she has to be changed. *Si tienes tiempo.*[96] If you don't, I'll do it when I get home.

LYDIA: I do it.

MISHA: You're gonna leave her with her.

ROSA: My husband's name is Claudio and he keeps mostly to himself. Don't bother him. Stay away from Rene too, my oldest. This is Misha here, the only one who's not trouble.

LYDIA: I understand.

ROSA: The pay is thirty dollars a week and you'll be staying in Ceci's room at the end of the hall. *¿Que mas, que mas?*[97] Oh, dinner is at six. I should be home right around that time. Okay?

LYDIA: Okay.

ROSA: *Gracias,* Lydia. Go to school and do your homework.

MISHA: Mom—

ROSA: *¡Que Dios te cuide, mijo!*[98] [*She goes.*]

CECI: Gghght.

LYDIA: Okay, now, she says.

MISHA: What?

LYDIA: Get the bath ready with some hot water.

MISHA: I have to go to school.

LYDIA: *Pues,* go. No problem, I'll do it.

MISHA: Besides, she had a bath yesterday.

LYDIA: She needs one today.

MISHA: Plus it might wake up my dad. You don't want to wake him when he's in a mood.

LYDIA: Speak slow—

MISHA: You don't want to wake my dad.

CECI: Ggngh, Gghn. Mmmgh.

LYDIA: *Bueno.* Bring to me a towel and some water. [MISHA *goes.*]

CECI: Gghghnnnm.

LYDIA: It's not so good when it gets cold, ah? *Ay,* Ceci, you hold my hand so tight. *¿Que te pasa?*[99] What do you want to tell me?

[CECI *guides her hand into her drawers.* LYDIA *discovers blood.*]

Ah. *Sangrita.*[100] It's your time, eh? Good. I will wash you very clean, *vas a ver.*[101] [MISHA *returns with a towel and a bowl of water.*] Thank you.

[LYDIA *begins washing the oatmeal off* CECI's *face.*]

---

[94] *Toma*—"take" used in this instance as "here, take"

[95] *con su nombre*—"with her name"

[96] *pero* . . . changed. *Si tienes tiempo*—"but . . . changed. If you have time."

[97] *¿Que mas, que mas?*—"What else, what else?"

[98] *¡Que Dios te cuide, mijo!*—"May God take care of you, my son!"

[99] *¿Que te pasa?*—"What's going on with you?"

[100] *Sangrita*—"blood" (diminutive)

[101] *vas a ver*—"you'll see"

MISHA: Why are you trying to speak English?

LYDIA: It's a beautiful *idioma*.[102]

MISHA: But why do you want to learn it? You live in Jalisco. 420

LYDIA: I never say that. My friend, she is from Jalisco. I come from a *pueblo* outside of that. *En los montes*.[103]

MISHA: We don't know anything about you.

LYDIA: You know my name. Are you going to school?

MISHA: What's it to you? 425

LYDIA: Because if no, help me with her. Hold her while I take off the wet clothes.

MISHA: What?

LYDIA: Help.

[*He kneels by her as she pulls off* CECI's *pajamas*.]

MISHA: What do you want me to do?

LYDIA: Keep her not moving. [*She unbuttons her pajama top*.] 430

MISHA: Wait.

LYDIA: *Andale*, Ceci.

MISHA: Wait.

CECI: Gggngnh.

[LYDIA *pulls off her top exposing* CECI's *breasts*. MISHA *turns away*.]

MISHA: What are you doing! What the hell! I can't see her naked! 435

LYDIA: Why not?

MISHA: She's my sister! Jeez! Cover her. Please.

LYDIA: *¿Que onda?*[104] You have not ever seen *chichis*?

[CECI *begins to laugh*.]

CECI: Gggngng-ghgnh-hhhah-hhgnhah.

LYDIA: Your brother. 440

MISHA: It's not right. I can't see her like this.

LYDIA: Then don't look.

[LYDIA *washes her quietly*. MISHA *slowly turns his gaze toward her*.]

Your sister has beautiful tits. But no one to see them. Too bad.

[MISHA *is transfixed. Then his gaze meets* CECI's.]

MISHA: When we were kids, at the church bazaar, she loved to play *Loteria*. There was this card called *La Sirena*, the Mermaid, and in the picture, her bare breasts rose above 445 the water. It was her favorite card.

LYDIA: *¿Ves?*[105] English is a pretty *idioma*. Write those pretty words down.

MISHA: I have to go.

---

[102] *idioma*–"language"
[103] a *pueblo* . . . *En los montes*–"a village . . . in the hill/mountain country"
[104] *¿Que onda?*–"What's up?"
[105] *¿Ves?*–"See?"

[MISHA *gathers his books and rushes out.* LYDIA *fishes for a blouse from her own bag and puts it on* CECI.]

LYDIA: *Aver.*[106] You will like this. *Mi abuelita* made it for me.[107] The last time I wear, I was another girl. I sat before the *espejo* brushing my hair.[108] Wondering: who is that looking back? Hm? Now let me see your room, *palomita.*[109]   450

    [LYDIA *takes up her bag and goes down the hall.* CECI *feels the fabric of this new blouse.*]

CECI: Now I remember. I'm horny! I'm just horny! I want to be wanted. I want to be touched. Not just touched, groped! I want to be fondled and strummed and tickled and . . . I want to be fucked. I want someone to plunge their hands into my body and grab that ball of fire burning my insides and hold it super tight till the *picante*   455 bursts through my eyes![110] Ohhh! It feels so good but so BAD! How could you miss this, God? How could you take so much of my brain and still miss the part that craves the hokey pokey? Oh, who is this girl? What is she doing to me?

    [LYDIA *returns in a plain dress and slippers. She has been cleaning the house. Broom and dust mop. She starts straightening up the living room.*]

CECI: Hours pass like seconds. She's as fast as a bird's wing. Lydia the blur. She brings me soup but I don't remember slurping nothing but blur.   460

    [CLAUDIO *enters, gruff and disoriented after a long daylight sleep. He stands in the middle of the room and stares at* LYDIA, *who stops and stares back.*]

LYDIA: Lydia. I am your maid. [*No reply*] *¿Cuantos años tiene su hija?*[111]
CLAUDIO: *¿Hay café?*[112]
LYDIA: In the kitchen. What happen to her? [*No reply*] It's okay. She'll tell me.

    [*He glares at her then goes to the kitchen.*]

LYDIA: Your father, he reminds me of someone. One of my *novios.*[113] Always mad at something.   465

    [*He returns with a cup and turns on the stereo, puts on his headphones and sits to watch TV.*]

I don't comprehend your coffee machine. If it's not good, I make again some more.
CECI: GGGhhnj.
LYDIA: If it's too strong, tell me. I like it strong, but for some peoples, coffee is not good that way.   470
CECI: Ggnnrhg.
LYDIA: He can't hear? Why not? I'm right here, he's right there.
CECI: Ggnhnh.

---

[106] *Aver* [*A ver*]—"Let's see"
[107] *Mi abuelita*—"My granny"
[108] *espejo*—"mirror"
[109] *palomita*—"little dove" (a term of endearment)
[110] *picante*—"spiciness"
[111] *¿Cuantos años tiene su hija?*—"How old is your daughter?"
[112] *¿Hay café?*—"Is there coffee?"
[113] *novios*—"boyfriends"

LYDIA: I see. [LYDIA *dusts the TV, blocking his view. Then she dusts the stereo console. She finds* 475
the sleeve of the record album.] *¡Ay, mira! Pedro Infante!*[114] My mother's favorite!

> [*She raises the volume to full.* CLAUDIO *rips off the headphones and jumps to his feet, his eyes glaring with rage.*]

CLAUDIO: *¡HIJO DE LA CHINGADA!*[115]
LYDIA: How come she is like this?
CLAUDIO: *Un accidente. Chocó mi Pontiac.*[116]
LYDIA: How long ago?
CLAUDIO: *Hace dos años.*[117] 480
LYDIA: *¿Hace dos años?* Was it your fault?
CLAUDIO: *¿Que que?*[118]
LYDIA: You walk around like it's your fault. Did you crash the car with her inside?
CLAUDIO: *No.*
LYDIA: But you blame yourself. 485
CLAUDIO: *¿Que quieres de mi?*[119]
LYDIA: Only this one thing: you like the coffee or not?

> [*He downs the cup in one gulp and throws it violently into the kitchen, shattering it.*]

CLAUDIO: *No. No me gusta.*[120] [*He goes back to his bedroom.*]
LYDIA: *Pues* . . . I'll have to do better.
CECI: I . . . I see a new card, *El Pontiac Caliente*! The Pontiac in heat! Ceci in the Pontiac 490
mad-crazy for some loco. Si. That ball of fire inside! Daddy's little girl in hip-hugger
jeans, Red Keds, Carole King hair racing toward her miracle boy!

> [LYDIA *is cleaning up the mess as* RENE *comes in, sleepy.*]

RENE: What the hell was that?
LYDIA: I broke a cup.
RENE: Are you the maid? 495
LYDIA: Lydia. You are the other son.
RENE: Yeah. *¿Como the fuck esta?*[121]
LYDIA: I . . . what?
RENE: Is she giving you any trouble?
LYDIA: Who, Ceci? No. 500
RENE: Slap her upside the head if she gets out of line. Kidding! Is there *café, por favor?*
LYDIA: *Si, pero* it's not good.
RENE: What do you mean it's not good? Get me a cup.

> [LYDIA *goes.*]

CECI: Ggghnn.

---

[114] *¡Ay, mira! Pedro Infante!*–"Oh, look! Pedro Infante!" (a famous singer/actor during the 1940s and '50s)
[115] *¡HIJO DE LA CHINGADA!*–"Son of a bitch!"
[116] *Un accidente. Chocó mi Pontiac*–"An accident. Crashed my Pontiac"
[117] *Hace dos años*–"Two years ago"
[118] *¿Que que?*–idiomatic expression meaning, "what, now?"
[119] *¿Que quieres de mi?*–"What do you want from me?"
[120] *No. No me gusta.*–"No, I don't like it"
[121] *¿Como the fuck esta?*–"How the fuck is she?"

RENE: I said I was kidding. Jesus Christ. [*He stops and looks at* CECI.] Look. Every breath, 505
everybeat of my heart, every drop of my blood, is yours. You own me. So quit giving
me that look or die.

LYDIA: [*Returning with a new cup of coffee.*] Here for you.

RENE: Okay, if you're talking English on account of us trans-border Mexicans, spare me
the condescension. Talk Spanish in this house if you want. 510

LYDIA: *Bueno, si quiere que hable en mi idioma materno, asi lo prefiero también, pero prim-
eramente, me gustaria explicare un poco de mis deseos en este pais—*[122]

RENE: Look, if you want to speak English here, I'm not going to stop you. Spanish sounds
kinda uppity coming from you, anyway.

LYDIA: Uppit—uppit . . . ? 515

RENE: It means gimme the damn coffee. [*He takes it and sips as she watches him.*]

LYDIA: You don't like?

RENE: Not bad.

LYDIA: You don't go to school?

RENE: I'm done with that shit. You know, the more I look at you, the better this coffee 520
tastes.

LYDIA: I'm glad.

RENE: What do you think of us? You find us disgusting? I know how much you Mexicans
hold us in contempt.

LYDIA: Contempt . . . 525

RENE: You hate us. You hate us for coming here, for deserting the homeland for a chunk
of that goddamn American dream, whatever the fuck that is. We're you watered-
down and a little more well-off. So, do you like what you see?

LYDIA: I always like what I see.

RENE: So you think you're going to hold out long? 530

LYDIA: In this job or this country?

RENE: Both.

LYDIA: I hope yes.

RENE: I hope so too. You're easy on the eyes and hard somewhere else.

LYDIA: Your mama said you were trouble. 535

RENE: Better keep your door locked at night.

LYDIA: But I don't think you're trouble.

RENE: Righteous.

LYDIA: Is your coffee good now?

RENE: Best I ever tasted. 540

[*He finishes it up and throws the empty cup into the kitchen. He goes back to his
room.*]

LYDIA: *Mano* . . . what happen to the men in this house?[123]

CECI: Ghgngg, gghn. Ggn . . . teeee.

---

[122] *Bueno . . . en este pais*–"Alright, if you want me to speak in my mother tongue, I prefer that too, but first, I'd
like to explain to you a little about what I want in this country—"
[123] *Mano*–A shortening of *Hermano,* meaning "Brother," used in slang as English speakers might use "Oh,
Brother!"

[LYDIA *goes to her. She touches her scar.*]

LYDIA: *De acuerdo.*[124] [*She touches* CECI's *scar with tenderness.*] Love is a big hurt. Even for fathers and brothers.

> [CECI *touches her chest.* LYDIA *is caught in a pang she hadn't acknowledged before.*]

Have we met before, *muñeca?*[125]   545

> [LYDIA *goes. Lights change around* CECI.]

CECI: Maybe. Maybe we fell in each other's wounds one night. Into each other's mirrors. Crossed paths in our *vuelos,*[126] said wassup with you, and then took a nap in the after-life. Spooning in the afterlife, you and me. Or maybe we just wish we were sisters.

> [*The TV audio plays a mélange of everything that was on during the early '70s: news, variety shows, sitcoms, etc.* CLAUDIO, ROSA, RENE, *and* MISHA *slowly enter with their TV trays of food and sit to watch TV.* CLAUDIO *has his headphones on.* CECI *lies on her mattress.*]

RENE: This *pollo* ain't bad.
ROSA: It's good.   550
MISHA: Real good.
RENE: Come to think of it, we're all eating a little better lately.
ROSA: *Que,* you don't like my cooking, *sinverguenza?*[127]
MISHA: Mom, she makes chicken *molé* from scratch. She uses spices and stuff we don't even know how to pronounce. She's got recipes the Aztecs used on the damn pyramids.   555
ROSA: *Entonces* I won't cook for you no more. *Ingratos.*[128]
RENE: Hey, a-hole, speaking of Aztecs, where's my Abraxas album?
MISHA: Oh. I was gonna ask you. I borrowed it for inspiration. I'm writing some poems for English based on the songs from Santana's album.
RENE: *¡No mames, guey!* You took my album to school?   560
MISHA: What's wrong with that?
RENE: *Baboso.*[129] I had something special in the sleeve of that album.
MISHA: What?
RENE: Something very, very, imported.
ROSA: *¿De que estas hablando, mijo?*[130]   565
RENE: Just some special papers, Mom. I appreciate your interest in poetry and art, bro, but you get that effin' album back. And stay out of my effin' room, while you're at it.
MISHA: It's my effin' room too.
RENE: Then stay out of my TOP half of it.
MISHA: Okay, then anything that falls out of the top half of your room is MINE.   570
RENE: And anything I step on in the bottom half is BROKE.

---

[124] *De acuerdo*–"Agreed"
[125] *muñeca*–"doll"
[126] *vuelos*–"flights"
[127] *sinverguenza*–"shameless"
[128] *Entonces . . . Ingratos*–"then . . . Ingrates"
[129] *Baboso*–literally, "slobbery" but in this context a vulgar epithet for imbecile such as "dumbass"
[130] *¿De que estas hablando, mijo?*–"What are you talking about, son?"

ROSA: *¡YA! Ay*, Praise God, sometimes I wish I had my own headphones too.
RENE: *Oye. Mira.* The *jefe* hasn't touched his supper.[131]
MISHA: Maybe it's too spicy.
ROSA: *Oye, Viejo. ¿No tienes hambre?*[132]   575

[CLAUDIO *looks at her. He takes off the headphones.*]

CLAUDIO: *No. Tengo que ir temprano esta noche.*[133] [*He shrugs and goes.*]
ROSA: That's four nights in a row he's going to work early.
MISHA: I think the maid makes him nervous.
ROSA: So what do you think of her?
RENE: Besides her cooking and her perky little breasts?   580
ROSA: Which reminds me. I don't like the way you're looking at her. *Portate bien.*[134]
    Misha? What do you think of her?
MISHA: She does all right with Ceci. She likes her, too.
ROSA: She does, doesn't she?
CECI: Gggghhhn. Ggnhnn.   585
ROSA: Lydia!

[LYDIA *enters from down the hall. She notices* CLAUDIO *has not eaten his food.*]

LYDIA: *Señora.*
ROSA: Ceci needs her diaper changed.
LYDIA: *Si, señora.* [*She goes to* CECI *and slowly brings her to her feet.*]
ROSA: So what are these *poemas* you're writing, *mijo*?   590
MISHA: Ah, they're nothing special. Just some verses.
RENE: What about, bro? Oppression and *la raza unida* and our Indian roots?[135]
MISHA: No, not like that. My first one's called Ode to a *Chanate.*
ROSA: A grackle? You wrote a poem about those nasty black birds who mess on my car
    every morning??   595

[LYDIA *goes off with* CECI]

MISHA: They're beautiful. They got these oil-slick wings and yellow eyes and their song is
    so complex.

[*There is a light knock on the door.*]

ROSA: *¡Chale!*[136] More like a squeaky garage door, *mijo*! Don't write no poems about them
    chanates!

[ROSA *opens the door and* ALVARO *comes in, dressed in a large overcoat.*]

ALVARO: *Tia!*   600
ROSA: Oh my god! Alvaro!
ALVARO: I know, huh? I hope I'm not bothering you at this hour.

---

[131] *Oye. Mira. . . . jefe*–"Hey. Look. The boss hasn't touched his supper"
[132] *Oye, Viejo. ¿No tienes hambre?*–"Hey, old man. Aren't you hungry?"
[133] *No. Tengo que ir temprano esta noche.*–"No. I have to go early tonight."
[134] *Portate bien*–"Behave well" or simply "behave"
[135] *la raza unida*–"the united race" referring to the United Pro-Latino Movement consisting of Chicano advocates
[136] *¡Chale!*–slang term meaning roughly, "enough" or "you must be joking," depending on context

ROSA: No, no, we just finished eating. Come on, you, say hello to your cousin!

MISHA: Hey Varo. What's up?

ALVARO: You're growing tall, kid. 605

MISHA: About effin' time, dude.

ALVARO: I know. It's just, *sabes*,[137] I've been a little busy.

MISHA: Little busy being a damn hero! I saw your picture in the paper!

ALVARO: *Ay*, that was nothin'. Hey Rene.

ROSA: Varo, we're so proud of you! [*kisses him*] *Que lindo te ves!*[138] Take off your coat, make 610
   yourself at home! *¡Andale!*

ALVARO: Thank you, *Tia*.

   [ALVARO *takes off his coat and reveals his Border Patrol uniform underneath.*]

MISHA: *¡Vato!* You joined the Border Patrol?

ROSA: *¡Ay, dios mio, que barbaridad!*[139]

ALVARO: I thought you should be the first to know, being family and all. I signed up about 615
   a month ago and they fast-tracked me right into service. What do you think?

ROSA: I don't know what to say, *sobrino*![140]

MISHA: Are you nuts? You can't join *la Migra*![141]

ALVARO: Relax, cuz, I had to do it. Money, *sabes*. It was this or temp work at Manpower.

MISHA: It still doesn't make sense, Varo. You're better than this, *ese*. 620

ALVARO: You guys don't know what I been through. I learned some deep lessons
   in-country about—

   [LYDIA *enters.*]

LYDIA: *Cielos . . .*[142]

ROSA: Lydia! *¡Ven, ven!* Lydia's taking care of Ceci.

ALVARO: Oh, *mucho gusto*.[143] 625

ROSA: She has her papers and everything. We made sure of that.

ALVARO: *Placer*.[144]

LYDIA: You're the cousin. She told me about you.

ROSA: What? Oh, *Ceci* can't talk, silly! Alvaro, want to sit down and eat? Here, have this.

LYDIA: That's Don Claudio's. 630

ROSA: *No te apures*. He'll have a cheeseburger at work. *¡Andale, provecho!*[145]

ALVARO: It sure looks good, *Tia*.

ROSA: Just don't mess your uniform. It's so starched and clean, praise God! [*to* LYDIA] Go
   bring her. . . .

   [ALVARO *digs into* CLAUDIO's *plate with relish as* LYDIA *goes.*]

---

[137] *sabes*–"you know"

[138] *¡Que lindo te ves!*–"How handsome you look!"

[139] *¡Ay, dios mio, que barbaridad!*–"Oh, my lord, what a shock!"

[140] *sobrino*–"nephew"

[141] *la Migra*–"the immigration police"

[142] *Cielos . . .*–"Wow . . ."

[143] *mucho gusto*–"nice to meet you"

[144] *Placer*–"a pleasure"

[145] *No te apures. . . . ¡Andale, provecho!*–"Don't worry about it. . . . Go on, enjoy!"

RENE: Lessons like what?   635

ALVARO: Lessons about what matters. Lessons about the sacrifices our mothers and fathers made for us. We fight for that every day, *primo*.[146] Every day we protect the blessings of this life.

MISHA: And that's why you took the job?

ALVARO: We got our own DMZ right here.   640

MISHA: You mean the border?

ALVARO: As soon as I get back, what happens? Some *mojado* steals my mother's car.[147] I look at the neighborhood kids and they're all *marijuanos* now.[148] Everywhere I turn, there's some out-of-work alien taking up space. It doesn't matter what all I've done over there, I still have to wait in line for a job with these illegals.   645

MISHA: Dude, our dad was an illegal alien.

ALVARO: But he got his papers. He became a naturalized citizen using the proper channels, didn't he, *Tia*?

ROSA: Oh yes. Yes. *Claro que si*.[149]

MISHA: So you don't have any second thoughts about doing this to *raza*?   650

ALVARO: Who would you rather, the *gringos*? We take care of our own *mierda*,[150] excuse the language, *señora*.

RENE: Is that really why you came, Varo? To show us your new uniform?

ALVARO: There was a time, cuz, when I thought I knew who I was, and what I wanted, but I just needed to grow up.   655

RENE: Grow up?

ALVARO: I mean wake up to the real-real. Remember when we used to play like ants in this room? That was a child's dream, Rene. We think the dream carries us all the way, but I got different expectations now.

RENE: What do you expect?   660

ALVARO: To come back and start my life right. This war was the best thing that happened to me. It pulled me out of the dream.

RENE: It was more than a dream to some people.

ALVARO: Then some people better wake up.

CLAUDIO: [*calling from off*] ¡Rosa! ¡Papel del baño!*[151]   665

ROSA: ¡Ay! ¡Este señor! ¡Que verguenza! ¡Espera! . . .[152] [ROSA *gets a roll of toilet paper from the cabinets and goes off.*]

ALVARO: How you doing, little cuz?

MISHA: Not sure. It's hard to see that uniform in this house. But at the same time, you're family.   670

ALVARO: That's right.

RENE: Not one letter. Not one damn letter.

---

[146] *primo*–"cousin"

[147] *mojado*–"wetback"

[148] *marijuanos*–"pot-heads"

[149] *Claro que si*–"of course"

[150] *mierda*–"shit"

[151] *¡Papel del baño!*–"Toilet paper!"

[152] *¡Ay! ¡Este señor! ¡Que verguenza! ¡Espera!*–"Oh! This man! How embarrassing! Wait!"

ALVARO: I was short on stamps.

[MISHA *senses something between them.*]

MISHA: I'm gonna help . . . uh . . . I'm gonna . . .

[*He takes the plates from the trays and goes into the kitchen.*]

ALVARO: *Pos,* you're lookin' good. I heard you been in some fights.   675
RENE: What the hell do you think you're doing here?
ALVARO: What do you think? I came to see Ceci.
RENE: Bullshit.
ALVARO: Is that bed for her? Is that where she's sleeping now?
RENE: You got some nerve. In that uniform, too.   680
ALVARO: Never in my dreams did I see myself in this. But it suits me, Rene. It really does.
     I'm gonna be good at this.
RENE: I bet you will.
ALVARO: How is she?
RENE: Now you ask. Now it occurs to you.   685
ALVARO: Look, man, what do you want from me? I'm here.
RENE: I wanna know where we stand.
ALVARO: We stand by family, Rene. We stand by Ceci.
RENE: Why didn't you come sooner?
ALVARO: I couldn't.   690
RENE: But why? I'm talking to you!
ALVARO: 'Cause when I come near you, everything gets so confused. Things happen way
     too fast for me. You move at this crazy speed 'cause you're a blaze, *ese*, you don't give
     a shit. But I can't be selfish now. Look what happened.
RENE: She loved you, *ese*. She believed in you.   695
ALVARO: That's the problem. Everyone fucking believes in me.
RENE: Is that why you ran? Is that why you didn't even stay long enough to see how
     she was?
ALVARO: You eat shit. Don't forget where I been for the last two years. What I went
     through trumps anything you throw in my face. I've moved on. So don't lay your   700
     guilt at my feet.
RENE: She was crazy for you—
ALVARO: —Yeah?—
RENE: She waited years for some word from you. A card. Anything.
ALVARO: How do you know? How the fuck do you know? If she can't talk, how do you   705
     know she missed me?
RENE: 'Cause I stayed, fucker! I stayed and took the heat for you!
ALVARO: Poor cuz. Still picking glass off your face. . . .

[ALVARO *touches* RENE's *lip.* MISHA *enters and* RENE *moves away.*]

MISHA: What's going on.
ALVARO: *Nada,* Meesh.   710

[ROSA *enters with a photo album.*]

ROSA: *Oye, sobrino. Mira.*[153] She made a scrapbook of you. She glued all your pictures on
     it, Polaroids of you and her. See, your ribbons from track and wrestling.

---

[153] *Oye, sobrino, Mira.*–"Hey, nephew. Look."

ALVARO: Wow. I never realized.

ROSA: And the newspaper articles. When you were Homecoming King. And Student Council *y todo*. And look all your notes to her. And the songs she copied from the Hit Parade. 715

ALVARO: All of this for me.

ROSA: She has a big crush on you, *sobrino*. She woulda been so proud of your service.

MISHA: Mom, she ain't dead.

[CLAUDIO *enters dressed in his whites. He sizes* ALVARO *up with a scowl.*]

ALVARO: *Buenas, Tio.*[154] 720

CLAUDIO: *Sobrino. ¿Y tu Abuela Doña Yolie?*[155]

ALVARO: *Bien, gracias. Tio*, I'm in the *Migración.*[156]

CLAUDIO: Good. Keep them all out. [*He grabs his coat and walks out past them.*]

ROSA: Well. That was easy.

ALVARO: *Pues*, I better get going too. 725

ROSA: But you haven't seen Cecilia!—

ALVARO: Another day, *Tia*. I go on duty in fifteen minutes. I'm on the levee just up the road. Look, if you guys decide to hate me for this, I'll understand.

ROSA: [*kissing him on the cheek*] I'm going to pray for you. I'm going to ask Jesus to make these *mojaditos* lay their souls before your badge and give up without a struggle so 730 no one gets hurt.

ALVARO: *Gracias, Tia Rosa.*

CECI: Ggghfnaaaalgg.

[MISHA *is the first to see* LYDIA *ushering* CECI *into the room in her quinceañera dress and shoes and her hair pinned up. Everyone is stunned.*]

MISHA: Oh my god.

ALVARO: Ceci. 735

RENE: What do you think you're doing?

LYDIA: She wanted to wear this. She said Alvaro would have the first dance. In her *quinceañera*. First her dad, then you. Because you know her better than anyone.

ALVARO: Jesus.

ROSA: Lydia, *por favor*— 740

LYDIA: *A bailar, caballero.*[157]

[ALVARO *goes to* CECI *and takes her hands. He carefully lifts her up and dances gently around the room with her. Everyone watches except* RENE *who looks away.* "Sabor a Mi"[158] *plays in* CECI's *mind.*]

CECI: Lydia, in your world the things that never happen always happen. With him. All my urges saved for him. Catching moonlight on the folds of my gown. A big corsage aflame on my heart. My pearl earrings on, dancing super-slow with Varo in the

---

[154] *Buenas, Tio*—"Evening, Uncle"

[155] *Sobrino. ¿Y tu Abuela Doña Yolie?*—"Nephew. And your Grandmother, Mrs. Yolie?"

[156] *Bien, gracias. Tio . . . Migración*—"Fine, thank you. Uncle . . . immigration"

[157] *A bailar, caballero*—"Dance, gentleman"

[158] *"Sabor a Mi"*—A romantic ballad usually translated as "A Taste of Me" (referring to the retaining a trace of a beloved's essence long after the beloved has left)

middle of the *sálon* to *Sabor a Mi*, body to body, cheek to cheek, his breath in my   745
ear saying over and over—

ALVARO: Ceci . . . Ceci . . . Ceci—

[*She grasps* ALVARO *around the neck as if to hold him forever.*]

RENE: Ceci, let him go.
MISHA: Leave them alone.
LYDIA: Let her dance.   750
RENE: Ceci! I mean it!

[*A small wet spot gathers around* CECI *as she pees herself.*]

CECI: Gghgngg.
ROSA: *¡Ay dios mio! ¡Que desastre! ¡Mira nomas!*[159] She's doing number one!
ALVARO: Ceci . . . please . . . my uniform . . .
RENE: CECI, GODDAMMIT STUPID BITCH!   755
ROSA: RENE! NO!!

[RENE *tears her away from* ALVARO *and she collapses in a heap crying aloud.*]

MISHA: See what you done? Look at her! Are you happy? Is this what you wanted? You
asshole!

[LYDIA *rushes to* CECI]

ALVARO: I have to go.
ROSA: *¡Perdon, sobrino!*[160] We're so sorry about this! I wish you didn't—   760
ALVARO: No, I'm sorry! Thank you for the good food. I have to go!

[ALVARO *rushes out.* MISHA *and* LYDIA *console* CECI *as she cries.*]

MISHA: It's okay, sis. It's over now. [*to* RENE] You didn't have to be so rough with her.
RENE: I didn't put her in that dress.
MISHA: Still, you didn't have to push her away like that, fuckhead! What's your problem!
RENE: My problem is this maid doesn't realize what that fucking dress means in this house!   765
LYDIA: But she does.
RENE: Who asked you to talk?
LYDIA: She knows everyone's pain. All the time. Even yours.
RENE: Did she really ask you to put her in this dress?
LYDIA: How else would I know where to look?   770
ROSA: She told you?
RENE: Did she also tell you how she got her head stitched up like a baseball? Did she say
who did that to her?
LYDIA: Not everything she says comes out her mouth.
RENE: What's that supposed to mean? What are these riddles? Who the fuck are you?   775
ROSA: *¡No hables asi, Rene!*[161]

---

[159] *¡Ay dios mio! ¡Que desastre! ¡Mira nomas!*–"Oh my God! What a disaster! Just look!"
[160] *¡Perdon, sobrino!*–"Sorry, nephew"
[161] *¡No hables asi, Rene!*–"Don't talk like that, Rene!"

RENE: No! Explain to me! How do you know what she wants? As far as we can tell, the best she can do is nod when she needs to take a shit!

LYDIA: She loves you, Rene. She thinks you should be what you are, and not be sorry for it.

RENE: What?? 780

[*The sound of a car pulling up.*]

MISHA: Dad.

ROSA: [*eyes landing on his wallet*] *¡Dios mio!* He's coming back. Take her to the bathroom! Get the dress off *de volada!*[162]

LYDIA: Why?

RENE: You screwed yourself this time, maid. 785

MISHA: He's coming!

ROSA: *¡Andale!* [*seeing his wallet*] *¡Ay, la cartera!* His wallet!

[CLAUDIO *enters. He takes his wallet. He sees* CECI *in her dress.*]

CLAUDIO: *¿Quien hiso esto?*[163]

ROSA: *Mira,* Claudio, it's not a big—

CLAUDIO: *¿Quien le puso esta chingadera a mija?*[164] 790

CECI: Ggghgh.

CLAUDIO: *¿QUE QUIEN LO HISO?*[165]

[MISHA *steps forward.*]

MISHA: Me. I did it.

[CLAUDIO *looks at* CECI *and shakes his head.*]

I just thought it was time, Dad. She looks so . . . divine. *¿No se te parece divina, Apa?*[166]

[CLAUDIO *charges with flying fists at* MISHA *who collapses under the thrust.*]

CLAUDIO: *¡Cabron! ¡Te voy a matar, maldito!*[167] 795

ROSA: *¡Ay, Viejo!* NO! NO!

[*He pommels* MISHA. LYDIA *screams as* ROSA *tries to intercede.* RENE *turns his back to them.*]

ROSA: *¡Dejalo! ¡No le peges!*[168]

[CLAUDIO *blindly socks* ROSA *as he throws* MISHA *down the hall and follows him out, taking off his belt. The door slams. Everyone hears the lashes and* MISHA's *cries in the house.*]

ROSA: *Ya no le peges, Viejo,* please *Diosito Santo,*[169] make him stop, please not Misha, ayyy . . . ayyy . . .

---

[162] *de volada!*–"quickly!"

[163] *¿Quien hiso* [*hizo*] *esto?*–"Who did this?"

[164] *¿Quien le puso esta chingadera a mija?*–"Who put this damn thing on my daughter?"

[165] *¿QUE QUIEN LO HISO* [*HIZO*]?–"I asked who did this?"

[166] *¿No se te parece divina, Apa?*–"Doesn't she look divine to you, Dad?"

[167] *¡Cabron! ¡Te voy a matar, maldito!*–"Little shit! I'm going to kill you, you damned shit!"

[168] *¡Dejalo! ¡No le peges!*–"Leave him alone! Don't hit him!"

[169] *Ya no le peges, Viejo . . . Diosito Santo*–"Don't hit him anymore, old man . . . Holy Lord . . ."

[LYDIA *glares at* RENE, *who watches helplessly then runs out of the house. The lashes continue as the lights change.*]

CECI: New card. *La Mierda.* The Shit. This thing lashing me, this burning need to hurt, *carnal mayor*, you tore me away from him, my bronze star, how come! How come! And what's this thing that blackens my *corazón* when it's Varo my body craves?   800

[ROSA *enters, a shiner developing on her eye. She puts on her coat and gets her keys.*]

LYDIA: Are you sure you should be going, *señora*?
ROSA: I have to go look for him. Rene is very sensitive. He acts tough, but inside he's scared.
LYDIA: Of what?   805
ROSA: His father. Himself. Everything. He won't even drive a car since Ceci's accident. Lord, take care of my boy!
LYDIA: Where are you going to look?
ROSA: I'll drive around till I see him. He can't be far. Misha's sleeping now. He just needs some rest.   810
LYDIA: We should take him to the hospital.
ROSA: No, no, they ask too many questions. He'll be okay in the morning.
LYDIA: *Lo dudo, Señora. Se me parece muy malo.*[170] And your eye too.
ROSA: Please, Lydia. It's happened before. He'll be all right. Stay here with Ceci.

[ROSA *goes.* LYDIA *sits by the sofa and places her hand on her chest.*]

CECI: In your world, Lydia, people die and come back but not all the way. Not all the way.   815

[MISHA *comes back into the living room. Swollen and blue with pounding. A cut above his eye.*]

MISHA: Mom? Mom?

[CECI *sees him and whines in alarm for him.*]

CECI: Eeeeeey. Eeeeey.
MISHA: Shh. It's okay, girl. I'm all right. See? Just a little puffy.
LYDIA: You should be lying down. Go lie down.
MISHA: Where's Mom? Is she okay?   820
LYDIA: She's looking for Rene. Sit. I'll get some more ice.

[MISHA *sits while* LYDIA *goes to the kitchen.*]

MISHA: You know what, Ceci? He's getting old. He can't keep pace anymore. Still, when he's mad, he can land some real-life hurt.

[LYDIA *returns with some ice in a dishcloth.*]

LYDIA: He was an animal. Only an animal does this.
MISHA: Didn't you earn your whippings growing up?   825
LYDIA: *Nunca.*[171]
MISHA: In this town, it's a rite of passage.
LYDIA: Why did you do that? Why did you take blame for the *vestido*?[172]

---

[170] *Lo dudo, Señora. Se me parece muy malo*—"I doubt it, ma'am. It looks very bad to me."
[171] *Nunca*—"never"
[172] *vestido*—"dress"

MISHA: I wasn't gonna let him work you over.

LYDIA: He would not. 830

MISHA: You don't know my dad.

LYDIA: You don't know me.

MISHA: Besides, you made her beautiful. I didn't believe she could be like that and still look so beautiful.

LYDIA: She is. 835

MISHA: You can't leave now. Ceci needs you. [LYDIA *pops him with the ice on his face.*] Ow.

LYDIA: Sorry.

MISHA: So what do *you* do for kicks in your hometown?

LYDIA: Town? More like *campo santo.*[173] Barren fields and empty houses. A lot of people gone to *El Norte.* We go to school. In the afternoons, we help our *mamas* with the 840 chores. I'm an orphan so mostly I took care of my *abuela.*

MISHA: Did you have a . . . a *novio?*[174]

LYDIA: Once. But he was too possessive. Then my grandmother died. I needed something to do.

MISHA: What do you want to do? 845

LYDIA: Learn English. Work in a hospital. I could be a good nurse.

MISHA: Yeah, but you need skills for that. Owww! My back's on fire.

LYDIA: Take off your shirt. [*He gives her a look.*] *¡Ay, por favor!* Let me see your back!

[*He takes off his shirt. His back is covered with raised welts, some of them bleeding.*]

LYDIA: *O Señor.* Wait here.

[*She runs down the hall to her room.*]

CECI: Ggghgngn. 850

MISHA: Hey, it's only fair. I saw *you* topless.

CECI: Ggnn. Llglnh.

MISHA: You loved him, didn't you?

CECI: What sucks is that I still do. His thorns are all around my heart.

[LYDIA *returns with a small vial and a lit candle.*]

LYDIA: *Aver.* 855

MISHA: What's that?

LYDIA: I have skills. I learned them from my grandmother.

MISHA: Ahh. What is that stuff?

LYDIA: It's some liniment made from the *agave.* We use it to heal open wounds.

MISHA: Well, it's not working. 860

LYDIA: Of course not. You need to seal it with this.

[*She drips hot wax on his back.*]

MISHA: OOOWW! OWWW! What are you doing to me! That burns!

LYDIA: You'll start to feel better now.

---

[173] *campo santo*—"holy field" perhaps "grave yard"

[174] *novio*—"boyfriend"

MISHA: What is this, some kinda witchcraft?

LYDIA: *Mi abuela* was a *curandera*.[175] I learned the science of herbs growing up with her in her *botica*. 865

MISHA: Well, your science burns like shit.

LYDIA: Get your mind off it. Tell me this poem of the grackle.

MISHA: What?

LYDIA: You said you had a poem. How does it go? 870

MISHA: Well . . .

LYDIA: You don't know it from memory?

MISHA: I do.

LYDIA: *¿Entonces?* Don't be shy. What's it called?

MISHA: Ode to a *Chanate*. Ode means— 875

LYDIA: *Oda,* I know. *Dale.*[176]

MISHA: O bird
          You black bird
          You look like you flew through the darkest night and it stuck on you,
          Except you closed your eyes and they stayed yellow 880
          As the wasps that dance around the lawn.
          I see you sitting on the wire
          Making that song, that grackle, crackle, wheeze, and chirp
          That makes me wonder if you're trying to learn
          the language of manual transmissions 885
          Or maybe you're trying to say something in our broken tongue.
          O bird dressed in mourning but always so lively,
          Like death is just another occasion to find a she-grackle,
          You remind me of things I should be doing,
          Flights I should be taking, night I should be soaking my wings in. 890
          Except with eyes opened 'cause mine are already black.
      Well?

LYDIA: The transmission part. I didn't get that.

MISHA: It's a draft. I'm still working on it. Hey, I don't feel it anymore.

LYDIA: Put your shirt on. Your poem is good. But to know words, you have to know people. Not grackles. 895

[ROSA *enters and finds* MISHA *without his shirt on.*]

ROSA: *¿Que es esto?*[177]

MISHA: I was . . . I'm tired. I have to go to bed. [*He goes.*]

LYDIA: *Señora*—

ROSA: I found him. 900

[RENE *enters, morose and withdrawn. He looks like a child.*]

---

[175] *Mi abuela . . . curandera*–"My grandmother was a healer"/A "curendera" is a Mexican woman skilled in healing techniques, both spiritual and physical, using botanicals. This healing tradition seems to have been passed on from the Mayans.
[176] *Dale*–Literally, "give it"
[177] *¿Que es esto?*–"What is this?"

LYDIA: Rene?

ROSA: Don't talk to him. Go to bed, *mijo*.

[ROSA *kisses him and he starts to go, eyes to the floor. He stops and falls before* CECI.]

RENE: Sorrysorrysorrysorrysorrysorrysorryi'msorryi'msorrycecii'msorry.

[*He gets up and goes down the hall to his room.*]

ROSA: You too. Go sleep. I'm tired. I have to work tomorrow. [*feeling her puffy eye*] How will I explain this? 905

LYDIA: She wanted to wear the dress. She told me so.

ROSA: I understand. But leave the miracles to God.

[LYDIA *goes.* ROSA *casts a glance toward* CECI.]

You know where I found him, don't you?

[ROSA *goes.*]

CECI: Where hearts and Pontiacs break. It's all love, *Ama.* All a desperate *abrazo.*[178] All of us holding tight to each other so we don't fall so hard. So we can open our eyes again 910 and see the new sun dripping in through the blinds.

[*The following dawn.* CLAUDIO *comes in. His whites stained with grease and ketchup. He finds* CECI *sleeping, still wearing the dress.*]

CLAUDIO: *Mi pajarita. Como te quiero.*[179] 'Cause of you I given up.

[LYDIA *enters in her clothes with her bag.*]

LYDIA: *Ya me voy.*[180]

CLAUDIO: *¿A donde?*[181]

LYDIA: *¿Que te importa?*[182] You beat him very badly. Your own son. 915

CLAUDIO: *¡Pero mira como la vistio!*[183]

LYDIA: It was me, stupid. I dressed her in it. You going to beat me too?

CLAUDIO: *Espera.* [*She stops.* CLAUDIO *struggles to frame his words.*] *Era mi pajarita . . .*[184]

LYDIA: In English. You want me to listen, tell me in English.

CLAUDIO: Cecilia . . . my bird. Why you put the dress? 920

LYDIA: It's her dress. She wanted to look nice for . . . for you.

CLAUDIO: It's good you go back. The country rob your soul.

LYDIA: *Hombre,* you have a life here.

CLAUDIO: I had a life *aya*! *Pero* the way you want things and way things go: different. Rosa want her babies *que sean Americanos.*[185] So here I am, not one, not the other, but a, 925 *como se dice,* a stone. A stone for them to make their own great *pinche* dreams.

CECI: Ggngnnh.

---

[178] *abrazo*—"hug"

[179] *Mi pajarita. Como te quiero.*—"My little bird. How I love you."

[180] *Ya me voy*—"I'm leaving now"

[181] *¿A donde?*—"Where to?"

[182] *¿Que te importa?*—"What do you care?"

[183] *¡Pero mira como la vistio!*—"But look how he dressed her!"

[184] *Era mi pajarita*—"She was my little bird . . ."

[185] *que sean Americanos*—"to be Americans"

LYDIA: Except Cecilia.

CLAUDIO: You want to know *que paso*,[186] for real?

LYDIA: No.   930

CECI: Yes.

CLAUDIO: Three days till la *quinceañera*. Three days. Dinner set, salon reserve, the *comadres* all prepare.[187] But *en medio de la noche*,[188] everyone's sleeping and me at work, Ceci *y* Rene out the window, and nobody hears *nada*. Why?

CECI: 'Cause this is the night: the night of secrets: of dark streets and Pontiacs and fires in   935
my body.

CLAUDIO: Why push it the car in neutral down the street and then start it up? Why?

CECI: 'Cause a fierce voice in our hearts is hissing *Vamonos*!

CLAUDIO: *Con las alas del diablo* they tear down to the border *en el* West Side![189] Why!

CECI: There is no why! Fuck all the whys! Only me and Rene and the roar of the car!   940

CLAUDIO: Three nights till the *quinceañera y se van*, they go somewhere too fast, *los pendejos*—[190]

CECI: To Alvaro! Alvaro my love! I'm coming!

CLAUDIO: Too fast down *ese* dirt road by the Border fence, and the tires are bald *en ese* Pontiac, you can't drive too fast in that car! Then something happen—   945

CECI: This ugliness. This hot ugly bile inside rolling up my throat!

CLAUDIO: Rene's good, he drive good. But something make him miss the big curve, you have to slow down to turn, but Rene, he don't slow, he don't turn and—!

CECI: NO!

CLAUDIO: The car hit a pole *y ya*.   950

CECI: *El Pontiac* wrapped around a pole like a lover and me flying in a sky full of confetti glass.

CLAUDIO: *Mi* Cecilia, who is born on a full moon and dance the twist for me at six, who always understand me no matter what demon possess me, Cecilia Rosario Flores, her name on the cake of her fifteen year, fly through the windshield of the car into the   955
cold hard ground fifty feet *en frente*.

CECI: I see little bits of brain and blood on the road, and you trying to scoop up all the memories, my first words, my first dreams, you try to scoop them up in your hands, *Apa*.

LYDIA: And Rene.   960

CLAUDIO: *Nada*. I ask him why. I ask him where the *chingados* they go. A million whys I ask him. He sit in the dirt and cry. He never answer, never.

LYDIA: You still blame him, don't you?

CLAUDIO: Blame is not the word. I wish you peace of mind wherever you go.

[*He puts on his headphones and stares at the blank TV.*]

LYDIA: Peace of mind. What is that?   965

[*About to leave,* LYDIA *catches* CECI's *gaze. A kind of plea in her look.*]

---

[186] *que paso*–"what happened"

[187] *comadres*–literally, "godmothers"; perhaps "godparents" in this context

[188] *en medio de la noche*–"in the middle of the night"

[189] *Con las alas del diablo*–"With the wings of the Devil"

[190] *los pendejos*–"stupid, useless people" or, colloquially, "dumbasses"

CECI: I had a dream the night before you came. That you stand at the door and stop breathing. And a part of you falls away. . . .

> [LYDIA *sets her bag down and peels off her underwear. She approaches* CLAUDIO *who stares straight at the TV.*]

That you come like a ghost into our house and stand over my daddy, who's a ghost himself, and you take his crown and hear the voices in his heart crying for love. . . .

> [LYDIA *takes off his headphones. She places them over her head and listens for a moment.*]

And then you blind him. . . .

> [LYDIA *turns off the TV. He remains still with his eyes fixed ahead.*]

And land on his lap and take his breath away.

> [LYDIA *straddles him in his chair and kisses him. He enfolds her in his arms and begins to cry.*]

Each breathless *beso*[191] reaches into his heart and lays grout over the crumbling walls of his pride, you touch him who can't remember *touch* any more than I can. It was a dream more real than this maid on my father making sex like the last act of God, I see your eyes, Lydia, dreaming the same thing, burning their grief into me, their want, their reckless need for darkness—[*She turns and meets* LYDIA'*s gaze.*] I see— you! With the inscription *La Muerte, La Muerte, La Muerrr . . .*[192]

> [*They continue to make love as* CECI *goes into convulsions.*]

gngghgnghg. gfhghgngng.

> [*Out of the shadows,* RENE *watches them making love as music from the head- phones plays.*]

970

975

END OF ACT I

ACT II

> [*The living room in* CECI'*s dream. Bedsheets stretched everywhere over chairs and tables, creating a network of glowing tunnels amid the darkness.* CECI *wearing the quinceañera dress crawls on all fours like a toddler through the tunnels.*]

CECI: Teeteetee. Teeteetee. Teetee means home. Teeteetee. Queen ant Ceci looks for a nest for her *huevitos.*[193] Teeteetee in ant-language means SOON!

> [MISHA'*s shawdow appears crawling along a bedsheet.*]

---

[191] *beso*–"kiss"
[192] *La Muerte*–"Death"
[193] *huevitos*–"little eggs"

MISHA: Teeteeteeteeeeeee!
CECI: Teetee! That's Ant for over here, Misha! Teeteetee!

[MISHA *appears with a naked GI Joe in his mouth.*]

MISHA/CECI: Teeteeteeteeteetee!   5
CECI: What's this, worker ant?
MISHA: I bring you food, Queen.
CECI: This is not the stuffed mouse.
CECI: Well, this doll doesn't cut it.
MISHA: It's not a doll!   10
CECI: Ugh. It's got spit all over.
MISHA: Can we play?
CECI: Teeteeteeeee! That means how do you like my egg-laying chamber?
MISHA: Teeteetee means bitchin'. How many eggs?
CECI: I am a shy queen, so I can't tell you. But antenna to antenna you can read my mind.   15

[*They place their fingers on their heads and touch "antennae."*]

CECI/MISHA: Teee-teeeeeee-teeeeee.

[*More shadows appear on the suspended sheets.* RENE *and* ALVARO *crawl through a portal.*]

RENE: Tee-tee-teeee.
ALVARO: Tee-tee-teeee.
ALL: Tee-teee-teeeee.
CECI: Soldier ants! Defenders of the colony! Teetee means welcome!   20
RENE: *Mi reina*,[194] we got great news. We defeated the evil anteater and stripped the flesh from his *huesos*.[195]
ALVARO: And we attacked the boy who stepped on our anthill. We stung him right on the teetees!
CECI: Then let the ant-revels begin.   25

[*They crawl in frantic circles shaking their heads at each other.*]

ALL: TEE-TEE-TEE-TEE-TEE-TEEE!

[MISHA, RENE, *and* ALVARO *slip into the maelstrom of sheets, casting shadows on the walls.*]

CECI: Tee-tee means I love my ants. I love all my little ants crawling through *La Vida Cecilia*, memories of innocence, tee-tee, *ormigas* forever,[196] in ant-language there's no word for die. Teeee.

[*The shadows of* ALVARO *and* RENE *first touch antennae and then kiss, long and gently.*]

I see behind the sheets secret ant-affection in the tunnels of our *corazones*, cousins   30
and *carnales*, finding their hearts in each others' mouths.

---

[194] *Mi reina*–"My queen"
[195] *huesos*–"bones"
[196] *ormigas*–"ants"

[*The shadows vanish and* LYDIA *appears gathering the sheets into her laundry basket.* LYDIA *looks smart in* CECI'*s jeans and blouse.*]

In ant-language, there *is* a word for live and it's Lydia. I saw the love going dark in your eyes and it means we ain't lived enough yet, we ain't died enough yet . . . we ain't . . . Lydhghghg . . .

[*Lights up on the house. It's cleaner.* CECI *is in* CLAUDIO'*s chair, staring at the TV.* ROSA, RENE *and* LYDIA *work at the coffee table on stamp books, with the laundry basket beside* LYDIA. MISHA *sits by* CECI *writing on a legal pad.*]

ROSA: She's quiet.   35
MISHA: Saturdays. Space Ghost and Scooby Doo.
ROSA: *O si. Los monitos.*[197]
LYDIA: Tell me again, *Señora*, how does this work? I don't get it.
ROSA: *Primero,* you get these stamps from the Piggly-Wiggly when you shop and you put them away in the kitchen cabinet till you get a *monton* of them. Then you stick them   40
on these S&H saver books.[198] All of these pages you fill, *ves*? Then when you get enough *libritos* filled,[199] you go to the catalogue and pick out the things you want, go to the S&H store and trade the books for them.
LYDIA: *¿Gratis?*
ROSA: *Free*!   45
RENE: It's al crap, though.
ROSA: Oh *si*, Mr. Smarty-*calzones*? What about that umbrella stand I got last time?
RENE: We don't have any umbrellas.
MISHA: Plus it never rains here.
ROSA: And that casserole dish? That was nice, *verdad*!   50
RENE: You've never made a casserole in your life. You use it for the *chile*.
ROSA: And that little shelf for the family pictures? That cost me 10 books!
RENE: I saw that at the Winn's Five and Dime for three dollars!
ROSA: *¡Ay, si tu!*[200] Quit talking and keep licking!

[CLAUDIO *emerges from his room and walks through on his way to the kitchen, upstage.*]

Did we wake you? We were trying to be quiet.   55
CLAUDIO: I couldn't sleep. *¿Hay café?*
LYDIA: Fresh pot the way you like.
CLAUDIO: [*realizing that* LYDIA *is in* CECI'*s clothes*] *¿Que es eso?* [201]
LYDIA: Oh, some clothes *Señora* gave me.
ROSA: Just some old things *de* Ceci's. She fits into them perfect, *que no*?   60
LYDIA: *¿Le gusta, señor?*[202]

---

[197] *O si. Los monitos*–"Oh, yes, the cartoons"
[198] *monton*–a "stack," "pile," or "heap"
[199] *libritos*–"little books"
[200] *¡Ay, si tu!*–"Oh, yeah, you!"
[201] *¿Que es eso?*–"What's that?"
[202] *¿Le gusta, señor?*–"Do you like it, Sir?"

[*He regards her with a mixture of scorn and misgiving. Then goes into the kitchen.*]

        Maybe I should change.

ROSA: No, no, Lydia, he likes it! You look more like us, more American.

MISHA: More like Ceci.

RENE: That must trip the old man out.   65

LYDIA: I have to do the wash now.

ROSA: Misha, come take her place and help us lick the stamps.

MISHA: I'm busy.

ROSA: Busy-*ni-que*-busy! What are you doing!

RENE: Writin' poems, what else.   70

ROSA: Not about those *chanates*, I hope!

RENE: No, he's writing love poems for—

MISHA: Shuttup.

    [MISHA *puts his pad aside and goes to the stamp books as* CLAUDIO *calls for* LYDIA, *who glowers at* RENE.]

CLAUDIO: [*in the kitchen*] Lydia!

LYDIA: You're a bad one.   75

RENE: What?

    [LYDIA *goes into the kitchen.*]

ROSA: *¿De que hablan?*[203] What's going on here?

MISHA: Nothin', Mom.

ROSA: *Mira*, nothing gets past me. I see everything in this house.

RENE: Right.   80

ROSA: And what I don't see, the Lord does.

RENE: I bet he's enjoying the show. Right, bro?

    [*He licks stamps in a lewd way when* MISHA *looks.*]

CECI: I smell it. My dad and Lydia's combustion. Lydia sprayed some Glade, but I catch that whiff of sweat and bygone dreams. Like an invisible *piñata* full of stale candies.

    [*In the kitchen,* LYDIA *and* CLAUDIO *hover uneasily over the coffee.*]

CLAUDIO: *¿Que estas pensando con esta*—?[204]   85

LYDIA: English.

CECI: Nobody but me hears what they're saying in the kitchen.

CLAUDIO: Will you come to me again?

CECI: The longing in their voices. . . .

LYDIA: No.   90

CECI: Not for each other, but for other things out of their conception. Things that require light and mindless hurt. . . .

MISHA: What are you redeeming this time, Mom?

---

[203] *¿De que hablan?*–"What are you talking about?"
[204] *¿Que estas pensando con esta*—?–"What are you thinking with this—?"

ROSA: This set of knives, *mira*. These are special Cheff's knives, very high quality, five of them, *imaginate*. I always wanted a set.   95

MISHA: It's pronounced Shef, Mom. The French way.

ROSA: *Pues*, when I go to France, *asi lo digo*.[205] Here I say Cheff. How are you feeling?

MISHA: Mom, it's been a week. I'm fine.

[LYDIA *passes through with the wash.*]

ROSA: He didn't mean to hit you like that, you know. He was expecting me to stop him. I just didn't know how. It was my fault.   100

MISHA: It was nobody's fault, okay?

[CLAUDIO *walks through on his way to the bedroom. Silence.*]

ROSA: [*going through her purse*] Anyways. After work I stopped at Mr. Dickey's Jewelry Store and . . . [*She gives him a small case.*]

MISHA: Mom . . . [*He opens it.*]

ROSA: It's a Cross. A gold Cross pen.   105

RENE: *Vato.* Cool.

MISHA: [*taking the gold pen out.*] Mom, are you sure about this? These pens are expensive.

ROSA: I'm working, Misha. We're quasi-middle class as of today, which means we live a little *mas* better. Besides, it was on clearance, half off. I always wait for the half-off sales.

MISHA: Thanks, Mom. Feel this, Rene. Feel how heavy it is.   110

RENE: That's heavy.

MISHA: Words. Full of words, *carnal*.

ROSA: Just no bad words, okay? I hate when you write bad words.

MISHA: If I use them, Mom, I promise you won't know what they mean.

ROSA: Misha, you're going to be somebody. Even if you won't have God, God's grace is   115
on you.

[*She goes, wiping her eyes.*]

MISHA: What's with her? She's all goofy lately.

RENE: Leave her alone. She's doing her best.

MISHA: Her best to what?

RENE: Dude, you're so damned naïve. You got no idea how fucked up we are.   120

MISHA: I'm not as naïve as you think I am.

RENE: [*grabbing his pad*] Oh yeah? What's this, fuckhead?

MISHA: Don't touch that. Put it down.

RENE: "Black eyes drenched in the waters of the Rio."

MISHA: Give it!   125

RENE: "Black hair like a mantilla draped on me."

MISHA: I told you—

RENE: "Your brown hands rolling over the open plain of my back."

MISHA: Asshole.

RENE: I gotta say, Misha, I never seen you like this. It seems our little housekeeper from   130
Mexico-way has sparked your plumed serpent to life, *carnal*. [*tossing his pad back*]
Too bad it's wasted.

---

[205] *asi lo digo*—"I say it like this"

MISHA: What do you know? . . . Has she told you anything?

RENE: *¡No mames!* Seriously, in the interest of family pride and the welfare of my little
    brother who truly understands shit about the affairs of the *pinchi* heart, I gotta say   135
    this: get over this fucking bitch as quick as you can.

MISHA: What?

RENE: She's a whore, Miguel. You're writing love poems to a low-class Mexican whore.
    Come on, *ese*, she's the maid. Don't you know it's a taboo? Haven't you been watching
    the *novelas*?   140

MISHA: Fuck you. I'm not listening to this.

RENE: I'm just watching out for you, *ese*.

MISHA: Like you watched me get creamed by Dad last week? Like you came to my
    defense then?

RENE: That's different.   145

MISHA: How is that different?

RENE: I wanted to help.

MISHA: Then why didn't you?

RENE: It wasn't possible.

MISHA: What kind of fucked-up answer is that?   150

RENE: It wasn't possible, okay? I got my own ways of getting back at the old man.

MISHA: What good does that do me? Finally you're big enough to take him on. You can
    make it stop any time. Either you're a goddamn coward or you want him to kill me.

RENE: I'd drop this if I were you.

MISHA: Listen, do me a favor and go back to beating up defenseless homos like you actually   155
    do. We prefer reality here.

RENE: You're out of line, Miguel.

MISHA: C'mon, who are you fooling? It's not *gangas*[206] and Ft. Bliss GIs you've been
    jumpin'. Everyone knows it's just the local homos.

RENE: Where do you get this crap?   160

MISHA: Serge told his kid brother and he came and told me. You go to all the same places
    they go, the same strips, the same cruising spots, the word's out, man.

RENE: What are you saying?

MISHA: You're a fag-basher, you and your buddies. It's sick, it's pathetic, bro. And it's only
    a matter of time before this shit catches up with you.   165

RENE: What shit! Tell me, what shit is catching up with me!

MISHA: Lemme ask you: whose fuckin' ass do you really wanna kick! Ask yourself. Who
    do you really wanna hurt!

RENE: *¡No mames, guey!* You don't know Thing One about this.

MISHA: It's been two years, *carnal*. When are you gonna get over it? When are you gonna   170
    stop making everyone pay for that crash?

RENE: Keep your maid away from me. If you want her, fine, let her be your damned—

MISHA: Don't say it. Don't say that word to my face.

RENE: Whore.

[LYDIA *comes in with a pair of scissors. They all stand looking at each other.*]

---

[206] *gangas*–"gangs"

CECI: These cartoons, amazin' how they go through so much hell, but nobody ever gets   175
hurt. Just little bronze *estrellitas* over their heads and these magic bandages that vanish in the next frame.[207] That's why they don't have private parts. They'll be safe as
long as they don't screw each other blind.

> [RENE *falters under* LYDIA's *stare and stalks off to his room.* MISHA *gathers the
> saver books and puts them all in a bag.* LYDIA *starts cutting the plastic covers off
> the lampshades.* ROSA *enters.*]

ROSA: What are you doing?
LYDIA: *Señora*, I saw the pictures in that catalogue. Lampshades like yours.   180
ROSA: Yes?
LYDIA: Except they don't have *plastico* on them. It's just how they were . . . *como se dice* . . .
MISHA: Packaged.
ROSA: But it keeps the dust off them.
MISHA: Mom, she's right. You're supposed to take them off when you put them up.   185
ROSA: But we've had them like this forever.
LYDIA: Well, it's all wrong. That's why the light is so bad in this house.
ROSA: Then why didn't you say something? Why didn't none of you say something?
MISHA: We didn't want to embarrass you.
LYDIA: See? Don't they look *mas* better?   190
ROSA: *Pues* . . .
LYDIA: Now you can see things.
ROSA: Next time, ask me, Lydia.
LYDIA: I thought I—
ROSA: [*snapping at her angrily*] You didn't. Ask me before you start redoing my house!   195
LYDIA: *Mi culpa, Señora.*[208] I didn't mean to be so *presumida.*[209]

> [ROSA *glowers at her for a moment.*]

CECI: Mggn. Nggnh.
MISHA: Look, Mom, Ceci likes it too.

> [ROSA *looks uneasily at* CECI, *then at* LYDIA, *then at the lights in the room.*]

ROSA: *Ay, como soy tonta.*[210] You're right. It does look brighter. [*laughing nervously*] I can be
so dumb sometimes! Such a *ranchera!*[211]   200
LYDIA: *Señora Rosa*, don't talk like that. You're good people. You been nicer than my own
mother to me. I'm sorry.
ROSA: Thank you, *mija.* . . . [*touches her face*] You know what? Let me take you shopping.
¡*Andale, vamanos* shopping!
LYDIA: ¿*Que qué?*   205
ROSA: Come with me! I hate going to the stores alone! *Además,*[212] I'm going to need help
with the bags.

---

[207] *estrellitas*—"little stars"
[208] *Mi culpa, Señora*—"My fault, ma'am"
[209] *presumida*—"presumptuous" or "arrogant"
[210] *Ay, como soy tonta*—"Oh, how stupid of me"
[211] *ranchera*—"country girl;" the connotation being close to "country bumpkin" in English
[212] *Además*—"Besides"

LYDIA: O *señora*, there's work to do. . . .

ROSA: *Chale*,[213] the work can wait. Besides, you made Ceci happy. *Ven conmigo, mija.*[214] Help me pick out some things for the house. *Pronto*, get your *chaqueta* and let's go!²¹⁵ 210

LYDIA: *Señora*, you are too nice! [LYDIA *runs off for her jacket.*]

ROSA: Misha, stay with your sister. We'll be back. [*darkening in a flash*] And next time, you let me know about things like this, *me oyes?*²¹⁶

MISHA: Okay.

ROSA: *Vamos, mija.* 215

> [*She takes her keys and goes out.* LYDIA *enters with her jacket and starts to go out the door, but stops when she sees* MISHA *writing in his pad.*]

LYDIA: Read me *unas de tus* poems,[217] Misha.

MISHA: Uh . . . sure.

LYDIA: Tonight.

> [*She goes.* MISHA *exults.*]

CECI: Ghggng. Ghgng.

MISHA: You hear that, *carnala*? She wants my poems! [*He shuts off the TV and goes to her.*] 220

CECI: Gh. Ghgngn. [*She points to the pen in his pocket.*]

MISHA: Oh! You wanna poem. Okay. Ode to Ceci.

> [*He tries to write a poem in her palm, but he can't.*]

> Sorry, sis. All my poems come out for her. One for the way she laughs. One for the way she irons my pants. *Ayy*. Ten for the hurt that presses on me when she's near.

CECI: Where does it hurt? 225

MISHA: Mainly here. Pumping through my veins one single word. Lydia . . . Lydia . . . Lydia . . . I can't think, I can't sleep, I curl up in bed and cry.

CECI: I hear you.

MISHA: Sis, have you ever felt this? I don't mean puppy crushes or shit like that. I mean, blind dumb love. 230

CECI: Blinder, dumber.

MISHA: Is it legal to want her this much? 'Cause I want her.

CECI: Worker ant, do it.

MISHA: What if she doesn't like me? What if she just doesn't feel the same way I do?

CECI: Then hope to God she tells you, Meesh. 235

MISHA: Shit. You're lucky you don't have to deal with this anymore. Way too much hurt for the risk.

CECI: Lucky? I'm the opposite of lucky. If wanting to love and be loved back is lucky. I'm the opposite of luck, the opposite of possibility and love and Cecilia Rosario Florhhhggghn. 240

MISHA: I take it by your look you're saying I should go for it.

---

²¹³ *Chale*–a slang term that conveys disagreement or dismissal with something; equivalent to "forget about it"

²¹⁴ *Ven conmigo, mija*–"Come with me, honey"

²¹⁵ *chaqueta*–"jacket"

²¹⁶ *me oyes?*–"You hear me?"

²¹⁷ *unas* [*unos*] *de tus* poems–"some of your poems"

CECI: Ggggnh.

[CLAUDIO *enters again from his bedroom, a troubled look on his face.* MISHA *leaps up to take* CECI *off his La-Z-Boy and back to her mattress.*]

CLAUDIO: ¿Donde está Lydia?[218]
MISHA: Out with Mom.
CLAUDIO: ¿Cuando regresan?[219]   245
MISHA: No idea.

[*He reaches into the cushions of his chair for his bottle. He takes a swig. He spits it out.*]

CLAUDIO: ¡Que la Chingada Madre! ¡Cabrones![220]
MISHA: ¿Que onda, Dad?[221] What's wrong?
CLAUDIO: ¿Quien puso Wesson en mi botella?[222]
MISHA: What?   250
CLAUDIO: Who put cooking oil *en mi botella!*
MISHA: It wasn't me! I swear!
CLAUDIO: *Hijo de la chingada—!*
MISHA: I swear! I had nothing to do with that, Dad!

[CLAUDIO *raises his fist to strike him and* MISHA *cowers. He sees his son's terror.* MISHA *looks up at him and sees the same fear in his father's eyes.* CLAUDIO *turns away.*]

CLAUDIO: Get up. I know who did this.   255
MISHA: Who.
CLAUDIO: ¿Quien mas?[223] Rene. I don't lay my hand on him not since before *mija*, and see how he hates me.

[MISHA *disappears into the kitchen.*]

Nadie me escucha.[224] Nobody listen to me. I'm nothing *en esta casa.*[225] I work like a *negro* and still I nothing.   260

[MISHA *returns with a beer and offers it to* CLAUDIO.]

MISHA: It'll wash that greasy taste down.

[CLAUDIO *takes it and sips.*]

Is there anything else I can do?
CLAUDIO: No.
MISHA: Want me to take that for you?

[CLAUDIO *gives him the liquor bottle. Notices the pen in his breast pocket.*]

---

[218] *¿Donde está Lydia?*–"Where is Lydia?"
[219] *¿Cuando regresan?*–"When do they return?"
[220] *¡Que la Chingada Madre! ¡Cabrones!*–"What the fucking hell?! Bastards!"
[221] *¿Que onda, Dad?*–"What's up, Dad?"
[222] *¿Quien puso Wesson en mi botella?*–"Who put Wesson [a popular brand of cooking oil] in my bottle?"
[223] *¿Quien mas?*–"Who else?"
[224] *Nadie me escucha*–"Nobody listens to me"
[225] *en esta casa*–"in this house"

CLAUDIO: *¿Y eso, de donde chingaos viene?*[226] 265
MISHA: Mom bought it. Half-price.

> [CLAUDIO *nods. He sits in his chair.* MISHA *clicks on the TV and brings him his headphones.*]

CLAUDIO: *Eres un buen muchacho.*[227] You are a decent boy. *Tu mama,*[228] she raise you well.

> [CLAUDIO *puts on the headphones and stares at the TV.* MISHA *takes the bottle and starts to go back to his room. He stops.*]

MISHA: Dad? . . . *Jefe?*

> [*No response.*]

For what it's worth, it wasn't just Mom who raised me. It was you, too, asshole. You're half to blame. You're the idiot who knocked her up, right? Your last name is 270 mine, too, right? Everything about me you resent is half of you too, motherfucker. So take some credit, Dad. I'm your son. I'm your decent well-raised second son. You bred me with fists and belts and shoes and whatever else you could throw at me. You raised me to jump at the sound of your voice and the stamp of your foot. You taught me to cower and shake and cover my ears in bed at so I wouldn't hear Mom 275 screaming while you slapped her. You taught me shame. I should grow up to be a spiteful little fucker just like you, hating the world for the crap I bring on myself, piling some real hurt on the people who care for me most. Except you know what, I won't. No sir, I won't be you. I don't know what the hell I'm gonna be and God knows I may turn out worse than I think, but I won't be you. Someday, not today, 280 against my better sense, I'm gonna forgive you. You'll see.

> [*He turns and goes. A pause.* CLAUDIO *stands and goes to his stereo.*]

CLAUDIO: Next time put the needle on the record.

> [*He sits and watches TV. The glow from the TV intensifies, casting long shadows across the room. Then the lights brighten over* CECI.]

CECI: How come, Daddy? How come you don't unload on him now? Is it 'cause he's right? Is it 'cause like Rene you crave to be punished? Or is it 'cause of Lydia? Does it take a stranger to make you quit your *pendejadas?*[229] I see you, the man inside the man 285 who coulda been. All afternoon still as a lawn Mexican, you wait for the changes inside. You fall into a sleep that permits no dreaming, no dreaming on this side for you *Apa.* . .

> [CLAUDIO *sleeps. A knock.* ALVARO *in his street clothes steps in. A bag draped over his arm.*]

ALVARO: *Tio? Tio* Claudio? Hello? Hey Ceci. Your dad hibernates like a bear. *Oye.* About last week. I haven't been the same since . . . well, since. 290

> [*He comes toward her. Touches her dress.*]

---

[226] *¿Y eso, de donde chingaos viene?*–"And that, where the hell did that thing come from?"
[227] *Eres un buen muchacho*–"You're a good boy"
[228] *Tu mama*–"Your mama"
[229] *pendejadas*–"stupid crap"

That day I came over. You were wearing this.

CECI: I wanted to see what fifteen looked like.

ALVARO: But it wasn't finished yet. None of us were.

[*Some scratchy AM radio tune plays from somewhere down the hall.* ALVARO
hears it and then starts in its direction. Lights change. CECI *stirs and calls.*]

CECI: VARO!

ALVARO: Hey Ceci! I heard the radio and—whoa! Lookit you! 295

CECI: What do you think? You like it?

ALVARO: Turn around. *Prima*,[230] you look *fine*! Is it finished?

CECI: Almost. Just some hemming to do. Why are you looking at me like that?

ALVARO: I had no idea my cuz was such a fox. You're turning into a real beauty.

CECI: Hey, you better come to my *quinceañera*. 300

ALVARO: I'm there. I just can't get too messed up 'cause you know I'm shipping out the
next morning.

CECI: I wish you didn't have to go. Can't you get some exemption or something?

ALVARO: Actually, Ceci, I want to go.

CECI: But why? Don't you watch the body counts on the news? 305

ALVARO: Sure I do. That's why I need to be there. My mom and dad, when they came
over, they had nothing. Being American means a lot to them. C'mon, you know this.
We got a flag on our porch.

CECI: But you're the brain of the family! You should be in college!

ALVARO: *Mira*, Ceci, the truth is, since graduation, I've felt like some discipline's gone 310
AWOL in my life, and what better way to get it back than to do my duty *por Tio
Sam?*[231]

CECI: God, you are something. Varo, will you, like, be my first dance? At my *quinceañera*?

ALVARO: That's reserved for your father.

CECI: But after him, the next dance. Will you ask me, I mean, never mind, what am I 315
thinking, huh?

ALVARO: Cecilia Rosario, may I have the honor of throwing some *chancla* with you?

[*She smiles and offers her hand. They dance to some Temptations song on the radio.*]

CECI: I hope they play this song.

ALVARO: I'll see that they do. Anyways, is Rene home?

CECI: No, he's running some errands for Mom. What's up? 320

ALVARO: I gotta talk to that dude. There's something I gotta tell him.

CECI: Tell me. I'll tell him.

ALVARO: No, this is personal guy stuff, Ceci—

CECI: Is it drugs?

ALVARO: What? No! 325

CECI: Are you guys toking up or something?

ALVARO: God, you been watching too much Mod Squad, *esa*. Just tell him I came by. Tell
him I had to put my car in the shop.

CECI: Your car?

---

[230] *prima*—"cousin"

[231] *por Tio Sam*—"for Uncle Sam" (his duty to the United States government)

ALVARO: Tell him tonight's my only night. That's all. I gotta split. You're gonna kill 'em   330
in this.

[*He turns to leave.*]

CECI: Alvaro. Wait.

[*She kisses him hard on the mouth. He is startled.*]

ALVARO: Oh my god, Ceci—

[*He kisses her back.*]

CECI: I knew it. I knew you liked me. The first time at the Bronco Drive-in with you in
the backseat with my brothers. I let my hand slip into yours under the blanket and   335
you held it tight on your lap which was so warm. That's when I knew! *Te quiero,
Alvaro. Te quiero mucho.*[232] Oh my god, I can't believe what I'm saying!

ALVARO: Me neither—

CECI: I've come of age. I don't need no party to prove it. I know what I feel.

ALVARO: Ceci. You're my cousin.   340

CECI: Do you want me? That's all you have to say. Do you?

ALVARO: Tee-tee-tee. In ant language, that means you're the queen.

CECI: [*leaping into his arms*] I knew it! I knew it! Take me with you.

ALVARO: Take you . . . ?

CECI: You and Rene taking dad's car and partying tonight, aren't you?   345

ALVARO: Oh shit. Rene.

CECI: Can I come? I won't be any trouble. It'll be fun, like the three of us at the drive-in.

ALVARO: No, Ceci, and you can't tell anybody this. It's guys night out, that's all.

CECI: Please let me come. If you want me, you'll let me come.

[*He kisses her long and deep. The lights change back. The radio fades. When*
ALVARO *pulls away,* CECI *is restored to her brain-damaged state.*]

CECI: Uhhhh uuh.   350

ALVARO: You shouldn't've come. You should've stayed home. It wasn't you. It was
never you.

CLAUDIO: *Sobrino.*

[CLAUDIO, *awake for some time, takes off his headphones.*]

ALVARO: *Buenas noches. Disculpe si lo desperti, Tio.*[233]

CLAUDIO: *¿Como si te parece? ¿Todavia bonita, que no?*[234]   355

ALVARO: *Si, señor.* Still very pretty.

CLAUDIO: She is our penance. How we repay our *pecados.*[235]

ALVARO: *Nos perdona Dios los pecados.*

CLAUDIO: In English, please. I learn.

ALVARO: God forgives our sins, Don Claudio. He doesn't take them out on others.   360

CLAUDIO: Mine, he does. What happen that night?

---

[232] *Te quiero, Alvaro. Te quiero mucho*—"I love you, Alvaro. I love you so much"
[233] *Buenas noches. Disculpe si lo desperti, Tio*—"Good evening. Excuse me if I woke you up, Uncle."
[234] *¿Como si te parece? ¿Todavia bonita, que no?*—"How does she look to you? Still pretty, no?"
[235] *pecados*—"sins"

ALVARO: Sir? I don't understand. . . .

CLAUDIO: All this time, I wonder where they go. To see you, *que no?*

ALVARO: *No señor.*

CLAUDIO: They come to your house, *verdad? Rene y Cecilia. Y tu.*[236]

ALVARO: You know what happened, *Tio.*

CLAUDIO: I know what happened to *mija.* What happen to you? Why you no come see her the next day? They are going to see you, no? You are there *tambien, verdad?*[237] What do you know about this accident? You can tell me, Varo. I won't hate you. I just want to know. *¡Contestame!*[238]

ALVARO: What does it matter now? How's it going to change anything? She's not going to get better.

CECI: Oh no oh no. All my love wasted, all my wishing ruined, no chance of that cherry going boom.

ALVARO: You and me, *Tio, somos iguales.*[239] Blaming ourselves for nothin'.

[MOM, LYDIA, *and* RENE *burst through the front door with shopping bags.*]

ROSA: Alvaro! Praise the lord! What a surprise! *¡Mira, Rene, tu primo!*[240]

RENE: Hey.

ALVARO: I just came over, you know. . .

[MISHA *enters as* LYDIA *rushes to* CECI *with her shopping bags.*]

ROSA: We were shopping all day, sorry, *Viejo,* Lydia had never seen the mall, you know the new mall they put by the freeway! So I took her and you should have seen the look on her face!

LYDIA: It's the most beautiful place I have ever seen!

ROSA: We bought some things, *Viejo.*

LYDIA: I got some make-up and some perfume, see? And then I got some high-tone shampoo for my hair and conditioner, and some soap so I smell like Ali McGraw. And then at the Popular, I got these new shoes. See? *¿Les gustan mis zapatos?*[241]

CLAUDIO: How did you pay for this?

ROSA: I advanced her for the month.

CLAUDIO: A month's pay to smell like a *gringa.*

LYDIA: Like a rich *gringa.*

ROSA: On the way home, we saw Rene walking on the street. So we picked him up, Praise Jesus.

RENE: I wanted to walk.

ROSA: But look who you would miss if you did!

[LYDIA *goes to* CECI *and puts some perfume on her wrist.*]

ALVARO: For you, cuz.

[*He unzips the bag. A souvenir jacket with colored embroidery.*]

---

[236] *. . . verdad? Rene y Cecilia. Y tu*–". . . right? Rene and Cecilia. And you."

[237] *tambien*–"also"

[238] *¡Contestame!*–"Answer me!"

[239] *Tio, somos iguales*–"We're the same, Uncle."

[240] *¡Mira, Rene, tu primo!*–"Look, Rene, your cousin!"

[241] *¿Les gustan mis zapatos?*–"Do you like my shoes?"

ROSA: Oh! *¡Que bonito!* Goodness, look at the back! *Ay,* Rene . . .

> [*Sewn in gold lettering over an embroidered map of Indochina is written: "When I die, I am going to Heaven, because I've already done my time in Hell."* RENE *puts it on.*]

ALVARO: Straight outa Vietnam, *ese.* I meant to bring it last time but I was having your name sewn on the inside seam.

RENE: What can I say? It's great.

ALVARO: Over there, Rene, family is everything. That's all that kept me going. I went over 400
there for you, man. I know I made some choices in my job that don't sit well in this house, and I'm sorry. But we can't let that burn up the good times we had. I need you to accept what I am, 'cause you're my cousin and I love you.

RENE: What did you say?

ALVARO: You're my cousin. 405

RENE: No, you said something else. What did you say? Say it. Say it.

ALVARO: Rene, I'm going the best I can—

RENE: SAY IT! You fucking hypocrite!

ROSA: RENE!

> [RENE *scrambles for the door.* CLAUDIO *grabs his arm and he stops. They look at each other for the first time.* RENE *jerks his arm away and runs out.*]

CECI: Gggngng. 410

ROSA: *Lo siento.*[242] Rene just can't get used to this INS business.

ALVARO: I understand, *Tia Rosa.* He'll come around.

LYDIA: Ceci says it is best that you go.

ALVARO: Your *criada* has a wild imagination, *Tia.*[243] Ceci. [ALVARO *goes.*]

ROSA: Did you see that, *Viejo?* Did you see how Rene was? 415

CLAUDIO: I saw.

ROSA: And you're not even going to ask him why?

CLAUDIO: Already a million times I ask him!

ROSA: *¡Por Dio santo!*[244] Nobody makes sense here! Rene! Rene!

> [*She goes out after* RENE. MISHA *goes to his room.* LYDIA *and* CLAUDIO *regard each other in silence.*]

LYDIA: Are you going to stand there? He's your son, *viejo.* 420

CLAUDIO: Don't call me that. Only *Rosa* calls me that.

> [CLAUDIO *stalks to the stereo and gets his headphones.*]

LYDIA: He needs you.

CLAUDIO: [*putting them on and sitting in front of the TV*] Leave me alone.

LYDIA: Look at you. Locked inside your pride, while your family suffers. [*She rips the cord out of the stereo.*] Talk to him, Claudio! 425

CLAUDIO: How! How to take back all that time of not talking to him?

LYDIA: By talking to him. You men are so stubborn!

CLAUDIO: He look at me like I am a stranger.

---

[242] *Lo siento*–"I'm sorry"
[243] *criada*–"maid"
[244] *¡Por Dio santo!*–"For God's sake!"

LYDIA: You're his father.

CLAUDIO: All week, *sofocando*.[245] I can't breathe, I'm dying. 430

LYDIA: You're not dying. The opposite.

CLAUDIO: You call this living?

LYDIA: She does. Your life is here, *hombre*.

[CLAUDIO *grabs his coat in agitation and starts out.*]

Are you going for Rene?

CLAUDIO: I'm going to work. 435

[*He goes. She starts picking up the shopping bags.*]

CECI: Gggggg.

LYDIA: *¿Ves, chica? Tanto desmadre aqui*.[246] *Oye*, you know why we were out so late? Your *mami* couldn't say it in front of your cousin. We went to see someone in her building who is going to get me papers. She wants me to be legal.

CECI: *Ghhyyn?* 440

LYDIA: She wants my name in the passport to be Flores.

[*She smiles and then goes. The lights change, brightening over* CECI.]

CECI: Flores is a name that goes all the way back to Spain, all the way back to the origin of flowers, which is what the name means. And the Flores that live in this town, all of them come from the first Flores that ever made love to an *India*.[247] He gave her flowers for a name and she wore them for the next one and the next one wore them 445 for the next one after that. All the way down to me. The pink icing on my cake said Flores. My wrist band said Flores. The red and white blooms in my head are Flores.

[*The lights are out in the living room where* CECI *lies.* MISHA *enters sheepishly.*]

MISHA: Ceci?

CECI: Gggnh, ggnh. 450

MISHA: I went in your room. It's all different now. She took your Bobby Sherman poster down. And all those Barbies you used to have. They're gone.

CECI: Ggnhh.

[*He sits by her.*]

MISHA: Sis, remember those summers when we were little and Dad used to take us to the community pool on his days off? Remember those days? 455

[LYDIA *appears, in her bathrobe with a towel on her head, holding a manuscript.*]

There was this one afternoon, when Rene was going up on the diving board and taking these big dives, and even at twelve, he was so graceful. And Dad's just standing in the water watching him like he's this god, and he says to me: I swam the Rio for this boy, I swam and ran straight to the hospital where your mother was giving birth and made sure his name was Claudio Rene Flores. I go, you can't swim, Dad. And he just 460 goes, I know.

LYDIA: The shower is free if you need.

MISHA: I know. I heard Ceci and . . . I should let you get dressed.

---

[245] *sofocando*–"suffocated"

[246] *¿Ves, chica? Tanto desmadre aqui*–"See, girl? So much mess here"

[247] *India*–an Indian; a native woman

LYDIA: Did *Señora* find your brother?

MISHA: Not yet. 465

LYDIA: You left this on my bed.

MISHA: You asked for my poems.

LYDIA: [*looking over them*] *Gracias.* Your sister and you, very close, no? You tell each other secrets?

MISHA: I do, anyway. 470

LYDIA: I bet she has some of her own. Read me this one. *Sombra.*[248]

> [*She passes the notebook of poems back to him.*]

MISHA: She is the shadow on my wall
When I am alone and needing
Unspeakable things, alone
With only my hands to catch me 475
She is *la sombra* I cast
In my sleep, lip to *labio*[249]
Against the pillow
And her shadow legs as long
as mine, as dark, as 480
smooth, drape over mine
and give me shadow
solace, shadow peace
in headphone whispers.

LYDIA: Are you in love, young boy? 485

MISHA: I don't know what to do with girls. I never have.

LYDIA: You'll learn.

MISHA: Lydia, who are you? Why did you come here?

LYDIA: 'Cause I need work.

MISHA: But you're here for something else. I know. 490

LYDIA: You want my secrets now?

MISHA: I want to know everything about you. You're so far from your home and—

LYDIA: My home, Misha, *sinceramente,*[250] is nowhere. What I had back in Mexico. It's all gone. I am hardly even here.

MISHA: What do you mean? 495

> [*She shows him a small mark on her chest.*]

LYDIA: I died, Misha. Like Ceci, I died but I came back.

MISHA: Jesus. What is that?

LYDIA: My eyes were closed for a long time. When I opened them, I was an orphan.

MISHA: What happened?

LYDIA: It doesn't matter. This says I'm here now. This says I can't never go back. 500

MISHA: Are you a *mojada*? A wetback?

LYDIA: Uh-huh, but that's 'cause I just took a shower.

MISHA: Your English is getting better all the time.

---

[248] *Sombra*—"Shadow"
[249] *labio*—"lip"
[250] *sinceramente*—"sincerely"

LYDIA: *Gracias, guapo.*[251] I practice with your sister all day.

MISHA: You're good with her. She needs you. 505

LYDIA: It's you she needs. *En serio.*[252] She counts on your poetry. *Un dia*, when you are alone, look into her *ojitos* and hold her hand tight,[253] don't let go, no matter what.

MISHA: I don't understand.

LYDIA: I'm saying give her love and she will give you all the *poemas* of her life. *Para siempre.* Can I keep? 510

MISHA: They're all for you.

> [*He slowly moves in to kiss her. She lets him.*]

LYDIA: Misha.

> [*He kisses her again. His hand slides into her bathrobe. She likes it, but has to resist it.*]

See how quickly you learn.

MISHA: I'm just down the hall.

LYDIA: That's how it has to stay, sweet boy. 515

> [*She kisses his cheek, then he goes.* LYDIA *reads his poems, tears welling in her eyes.*]

CECI: *Ay Lydia.* All the want of before, dilating my *corazón*, it's dilating yours. You speak the *idioma* of ants and miscarried love. The cards of *La Vida Cecilia* falling into place. Some *desmadre* is coming into view and I'm gonna need you, *loca.*[254] I'll need you when I fall.

LYDIA: *¿Que ves, pajarita?*[255] 520

CECI: A new card. *Las Gemelas.* The twins.

> [LYDIA *goes. Darkness descends on the living room.* ROSA *sits on the sofa in her nightgown.*]

ROSA: Dear Jesus. I know Rene won't amount to much, that's what I believe, that's my sin, to dismiss my oldest so easily. He'll be a loyal son if he lives to be twenty. But he wasn't make a difference in the world. I know it, he knows it and You know it too. But that don't mean I don't love him. Bring him home tonight dear Father— 525

> [RENE *can be heard roaring outside, crashing against garbage cans.*]

RENE: [*off*] *¡Chinga la verga! ¡Pinchi puto cabron!*[256] Who do you think you are! I got every right to be here!

> [ALVARO *enters pushing* RENE *inside. He drunkenly staggers in, his hands cuffed behind him.*]

Let go of me! I said, LET ME GO!

ALVARO: Shut up, Rene! You're gonna wake the whole block!

RENE: You can't treat me like this! I ain't your wetback! You don't get rid of me that easy, you shit! 530

ALVARO: I know what you're trying to do. It's not gonna work.

---

[251] *Gracias, guapo*–"Thank you, handsome"

[252] *En serio*–"seriously"

[253] *Un dia . . . ojitos*–"one day . . . little eyes"

[254] *desmadre*–a spectacular and potentially chaotic event/*loca*–girl

[255] *¿Que ves, pajarita?*–"What do you see, little bird?"

[256] *¡Chinga la verga! ¡Pinchi puto cabron!*–"Fucking shit! Fucking bitch faggot!"

RENE: You don't get it, do you! You drivin' to the levee, right by the same fuckin' pole! That's why you joined *la Migra*!

ALVARO: What do you want from me! 535

RENE: I want you to talk to me! Jesus Christ, just talk to me!

ALVARO: There's nothin' to talk about! I'm through, that's all!

RENE: Then why did you give me your jacket? If you hate my guts so much, why!

ALVARO: Listen up, you fuck! You were part of my war! The whole time I was there, so were you! What we had, *ese*, nobody's ever gonna touch that, nobody's ever gonna 540 come that close! That was it, *ese*. That was my shot.

RENE: Then why won't you see me, goddammit!

ALVARO: 'Cause when I think of us, I see her! I hear those words!

RENE: What are you sayin', asshole? I live with her! I hear them every day!

ROSA: Rene. *¿Que es esta locura?*[257] 545

ALVARO: He was up on the levee, *Tia*. He's drunk. He taunted us while we were doing our job.

RENE: Oh my god! You were buying me off! This jacket's to buy me off!

ALVARO: He's talking like a crazy man.

ROSA: *Mijo*, please don't be like this. . . . 550

RENE: Get the fuck away! I'm done with you.

[MISHA *enters in his tee-shirt and shorts.*]

MISHA: Mom, back away.

ROSA: *¡Pero, mijo, mira que locura!*[258]

RENE: *¡Carnalito!*[259]

MISHA: Do as I say. Back away. 555

[ROSA *retreats in sobs as* RENE *grows more glowering and furious.* CECI *becomes agitated.*]

RENE: That's right! Back away from the Fag Basher!

MISHA: What the hell are you doing, man?

RENE: Don't look at me like that, Meesh! I'll fuckin' bust your head open! Like I busted Ceci!

MISHA: What can I do, Rene? *Te quiero ayudar.*[260] Tell me what to do. 560

CECI: GGNNGAYAAYYY!!

RENE: Hypocrites and liars! I fuckin' hate you all!

ALVARO: Misha, he just needs to sleep it off. [*to* RENE] You gotta get a grip.

RENE: FUCK YOU! TAKE THESE OFF AN' LEMME KICK YOUR ASS, YOU FUCKING COWARD! 565

[LYDIA *appears.*]

LYDIA: *¿Que pasa aqui?*[261]

---

[257] *¿Que es esta locura?*–"What is this madness?"
[258] *¡Pero, mijo, mira que locura!*–"But, son, look that's crazy!"
[259] *¡Carnalito!*–"Little Bro!"
[260] *Te quiero ayudar*–"I want to help you"
[261] *¿Que pasa aqui?*–"What's going on here?"

RENE: *Orale*.[262] You want an illegal? You wanna do your fuckin' job, *migra*?

MISHA: Go back to your room.

LYDIA: Let me take Ceci out.

ROSA: Take her to your room. *Andale*.   570

RENE: Don't put your dirty hands on her. *Mojada*.

MISHA: Rene . . .

RENE: I'm telling you, cuz, this one's trouble. This one think she knows our shit. She's gone real deep with us, *verdad, criada*?

MISHA: Back away from her. I mean it.   575

RENE: It's sad, *ese*. You giving your heart to a wetback. She's using you!

MISHA: I don't care. I'm not letting you say whatever you want about her.

ROSA: ¡*Misha, cuidado, mijo!*[263]

RENE: You think she's *toda India Mexicana*.[264] But I've seen Dad banging this whore!

ROSA: Lydia . . .   580

[MISHA *pounds him in the gut and he falls.*]

ROSA: Misha!

MISHA: I TOLD YOU TO WATCH YOUR MOUTH!

RENE: I saw them!

MISHA: Liar! [*He grabs* RENE *by the collar and threatens to hit him.*]

ALVARO: STOP IT!   585

RENE: C'mon, bro. C'mon. Just lemme have it. Just pound on me, man.

[MISHA *lets him go.*]

¡*Andale, Miguel! ¡Dale gas!*[265] Hit me, motherfucker! I want you to hit me!

MISHA: No way . . .

RENE: [*collapsing in tears*] ALVARO! ANY A YOU! I'M BEGGIN' YOU! JESUS, SOME-BODY FUCKIN' HIT ME!   590

ALVARO: Jesus, Rene, quit this now please. . . .

[CECI *convulses in terror and* LYDIA *runs to hold her tightly.* MISHA *looks at* ALVARO.]

MISHA: Are you going to tell us what is going on here? Will somebody tell us?

CECI: Ghhhn.

LYDIA: She will.

ALVARO: What?   595

MISHA: What are you talking about?

CECI: Ghghggn.

LYDIA: She knows. She was there.

CECI: Ghgn.

LYDIA: She is there now.   600

ROSA: She is?

---

[262] *Orale*—"Alright"

[263] ¡*Misha, cuidado, mijo!*—"Misha, be careful, son!"

[264] *toda India Mexicana*—"all Mexican Indian;" connotatively a shy, ignorant, innocent country girl

[265] ¡*Andale, Miguel! ¡Dale gas!*—"Go on, Miguel! Give it gas!"

CECI: Gghfnhsss
LYDIA: She says, Rene and me
CECI: Ggffeggh-ghfhn
LYDIA: Driving in the middle of the night   605
CECI: GghaaggG
LYDIA: To Alvaro's house
CECI: Ttte-ttteee
LYDIA: Delirious as ants
CECI: Ghhhngnn   610
LYDIA: Rene is driving
CECI: Hhghhhh.
LYDIA: But I'm hiding in the backseat. Crouched in the floor of the backseat.
CECI: 'Cause I wanna surprise them! I wanna see the look on Alvaro's face when he sees
    me again! Party!   615
LYDIA: She says
CECI: I hear the radio playing and I feel the wind rushing in through his open window and
    I'm tingling with excitement! I'm gonna trip 'em out!
LYDIA: She says
CECI: I hear the car stop and Alvaro getting in and I'm about to jump out, but he's like on   620
    Rene, kissing him, and my heart stops and
LYDIA: She says
CECI: I can't think I can't move but the car does. It rolls along at Roadrunner speed to
    nowhere and I can hear them talking Rene's like where you wanna go and Alvaro's
    like where we always go, cuz, the border   625
LYDIA: She says
CECI: I'm *toda* dizzy, But soon, I feel the car stopping. The engine stops and it's quiet
    as death
LYDIA: *Quiet as death*
CECI: I feel the beautiful dream of Varo and me slipping away as I hear this moaning and   630
    kissing and crying
LYDIA: She says
CECI: This moaning and kissing and crying
LYDIA: She says
CECI: And then I see Alvaro throw his head back and cry out   635
LYDIA: *¡Ay Rene!*
CECI: I see *carnal* rise up and kiss him and I can't believe it
LYDIA: She says
CECI: Alvaro was mine all these years I dreamed of kissing him like that and now
LYDIA: She says   640
CECI: Right there, right there, this ugliness inside takes over. YOU FAGS. YOU HOMOS.
    YOU DIRTY FILTHY HOMOS
LYDIA: She says
CECI: They scream, they're so shocked but the ugly keeps yelling You *Jotos*, Damn *Maricones*.
    Rene starts the car and says over and over   645
RENE: Please don't tell Dad, Ceci, please don't tell Dad
CECI: And Varo's face turned away saying
ALVARO: We weren't doing nothing, I swear

CECI: And the car is racing and I'm screaming in the backseat YOU DISGUST ME YOU MAKE ME SICK YOU LYING SHITS   650

LYDIA: She says

CECI: I'm beating on Rene, I am so mad at Rene. And he's yelling No and Alvaro is yelling Stop, Ceci! But my fists keep hitting his head and the car is swerving like crazy, and Rene reaches back and tells me right to my face

LYDIA: I'm sorry!   655

CECI: But he's not looking and the curve is right there and the pole wants the Pontiac. And there in the rear-view mirror I see you, so pale and sad, the face of death willing the car into the pole

LYDIA: Just as I see yours in my mirror

CECI: And I am pure bird soaring with the moon stretching out like *chicle* toward the red   660
card with the inscription: Now Look What You Done, Stupid

LYDIA: She says

CECI: It was me! ME! This *mierda* was me! You didn't do nothing wrong! It was all my shit my fucking shit making it wrong. The words in my heart fall out the crack in my head. The words I never meant this. Not in a million. I love you Rene. I love you   665
both. I'm ssghggngn..ggngn.

LYDIA: *Eso es lo que dice.*[266]

> [*Silence.* ALVARO *takes the cuffs off* RENE.]

ROSA: Is it true? Alvaro.

ALVARO: No, *Tia.*

ROSA: Rene? Is it true, Rene?   670

RENE: Yeah. All true.

ROSA: Get out. Get out of this house.

MISHA: Mom, you can't just—

RENE: *Alivián ate, carnal.*[267] I'm done here.

> [*He takes off the jacket and throws it at* ALVARO's *feet. Then he goes to* CECI *to make his goodbye. Intimate and silent. Then he gets up and walks out of the house forever.*]

LYDIA: [*as she gets up and starts to her room*] She wants to rest now. I'm tired too.   675

MISHA: Were you . . . did you and my dad . . . ?

LYDIA: What importance is that now, Misha?

> [*She goes.* MISHA *looks at* ROSA.]

ROSA: I always say nothing happened in this house without me knowing. But really, all I knew was nothing.

MISHA: Mom, you can't let him go like that.   680

ROSA: Go to bed, *mijo.*

> [MISHA *goes.* ALVARO *makes to go but* ROSA *stops him.*]

Sobrino.

---

[266] *Eso es lo que dice*—"That's what she says"
[267] *Alivián ate, carnal*—"Chill, bro"

[ROSA *goes to him and whispers something to him as* CECI *cowers on her mattress.*]

CECI: This *noche* nobody sleeps. This *noche* the words slam against the walls like angry little birds again and again. Faggot. Whore. *Mojado. Migra. Mijo.* Love. All those words on razor wings looking for something to cut. Slashing at the walls of what we used to call family.   685

[ALVARO *nods gravely to* ROSA. *He goes down the hall.* ROSA *sits with* CECI.]

ROSA: What does the word *madre* mean in this country? Does it mean idiot? Does it mean pretending? Does it mean living like nothing's changed? Everything's changed. I'm old. I'm a stranger to my own children. My husband won't touch me. You were going to be my partner, but look at you.   690

CECI: Gnnghg.

[*There is an awful lull, then screaming and yelling off.*]

LYDIA: [*off*] AAAYYY! AAAAAYYYY!

[ALVARO *enters dragging* LYDIA *out behind him.*]

ALVARO: That's the way it is. Now come on!

LYDIA: *AYYY! AYY! Help me!*

[MISHA *comes out.*]

MISHA: Whoa! What the fuck are you doing?   695

LYDIA: *Misha*! He's taking me away!

ALVARO: She's got no proof of residence, cuz.

MISHA: What! Where are you taking her?

ALVARO: Where do you think? *El Corralón.*

LYDIA: *Señora*! Tell him I'm American! He won't listen to me! I'm American!   700

ROSA: *Es una mojada.* I don't hire *mojadas.*

ALVARO: *Vamonos.*

MISHA: Mom, you can't do this. I won't let you.

ROSA: You dare defend her in my presence? *Esta desgraciada se abusó de mi marido,*[268] my husband!   705

LYDIA: *Señora*, please, don't be this way! I love this family! Misha!

MISHA: Let her go, Varo. C'mon, for family, cuz.

ALVARO: *Misha, con esto, familia no vale madre.*[269]

LYDIA: *¡Misha, por favor!* I don't want to go back! If I go back, I'll die! I know I will. I'll die!

ROSA: Alvaro Fernandez. TAKE THIS *PUTA* OUT OF MY HOUSE NOW!   710

ALVARO: C'mon.

LYDIA: Wait! My poems! Let me get my poems! Misha!

ROSA: *Espera.*

[ROSA *violently strips off* LYDIA'*s top.*]

LYDIA: NOO!

ROSA: This is *mija's blusa.*[270]   715

---

[268] *Esta desgraciada se abusó de mi marido*—"This ingrate took advantage of my husband"
[269] *Misha, con esto, familia no vale madre*—"Misha, with this, family doesn't mean shit"
[270] *mija's blusa*—"my daughter's blouse"

LYDIA: CECI! CECI!

> [ALVARO *pushes* LYDIA, *ravaged and half-naked, out the door.*]

MISHA: I love her.

ROSA: *Mira nomas.* Her little *pendejito.* Writing *mierda* to her with my pen.[271]

> [MISHA *runs after* LYDIA. ROSA *sits in exhaustion. The lights collapse around* CECI.]

CECI: I flew that night to a village in Jalisco; through a window, this girl sitting at a dresser brushing her hair. She looks in the mirror, sees me and smiles like she's always known me, this tragic girl brushing her hair at the break of day. 720

> [*Later in the morning.* CLAUDIO *enters. He finds* CECI *and* ROSA *sleeping together on the mattress.*]

CLAUDIO: *Vieja.* Rosa.

ROSA: Hmm? [ROSA *wakes.*]

CLAUDIO: *¿Que haces? ¿Por que duermes aqui?*[272]

ROSA: I got lonely. 725

CLAUDIO: I brought you some *menudo.*[273]

ROSA: *Gracias.*

CLAUDIO: *¿Esta todo bien?*[274] [*She nods.*] *¿Y Rene?* Did *mijo* come back home?

ROSA: He's still out.

CLAUDIO: I will wait to him. *Pos,* you better have some before it gets cold. 730

> [*She opens the container of menudo.* CLAUDIO *takes a beer from his bag and pops off the pull-tab.*]

CECI: Gghnf.

CLAUDIO: *Qiubolé, mija.*[275] Are you ever going to change out of that thing? Uh?

CECI: Da..hh . . . da..ghgntttee.

CLAUDIO: *Querida.*[276] The only English I want to know is yours.

> [*He kisses her forehead, but forgets the pull-tab on her blanket.*]

ROSA: I love when they put extra *tripas. Menudo* is always good for the morning-after. 735

CLAUDIO: Are you hung-over?

ROSA: *Hombre,* this headache like a devil with a claw hammer. I think I'm staying in today.

CLAUDIO: Then lie down for a while. *¿Y Lydia?*

ROSA: *Se fue.*[277]

CLAUDIO: *¿Como que se fue?*[278] Where is she? 740

ROSA: *Con la Migra.*[279]

CLAUDIO: *¿Que chingados dices, mujer?*[280] You turn her over to *La Migra?*

---

[271] *Mira nomas . . . pendejito . . . mierda*–"Just look"/"little dumbass"/"crap"

[272] *¿Que haces? ¿Por que duermes aqui?*–"What are you doing? Why are you sleeping here?"

[273] *menudo*–a Mexican soup or stew made with tripe (cow stomach)

[274] *¿Esta todo bien?*–"Is everything okay?"

[275] *Qiubolé, mija*–"Wassup, son"

[276] *Querida*–"Beloved"

[277] *Se fue*–"She left"

[278] *¿Como que se fue?*–"What do you mean, she left?"

[279] *Con la Migra*–"With immigration"

[280] *¿Que chingados dices, mujer?*–"What the fuck are you saying, woman?"

ROSA: If you want her, *vete*. If you miss that fucking country so much, go. Let me remind you who also needs papers.

> [*They glare at each other. Then* CLAUDIO *retreats to his bedroom. He stops at the threshold.*]

CLAUDIO: Rene and Cecilia . . . *y* Alvaro. Why?   745
ROSA: There is no why. There is never any why.

> [MISHA *enters dressed. He goes straight to* CECI *and begins her physical therapy.*]

CLAUDIO: Miguel . . . Miguel . . . [*No response. He turns to* ROSA.] Come to bed. Bring the *menudo* with you.

> [CLAUDIO *goes.* ROSA *can stomach no more soup. She goes to* MIGUEL. *She looks at* CECI.]

ROSA: ¿*Y tu que ves?*[281] What other *cochinadas* are locked in those pretty eyes of yours?[282]

> [*She walks solemnly down the hall.*]

CECI: Gggighg.   750
MISHA: It's okay, sis. I know you didn't mean it.
CECI: Mmmm . . . Meeesh shhhhhah!
MISHA: Sis, did you just—?
CECI: Mmmeeshishhhh. Aaah.

> [*He goes to her and she kisses his hand.*]

MISHA: Oh my god. Ceci. You're talking.   755

> [*She guides his hand under her dress.*]

Wait . . . what are you . . . no . . . let go. Please, Ceci. Let go! I'm sorry. No.

> [*He breaks away. She curls up and cries softly. He tries to leave but stops at the threshold of the room. He turns and crawls along invisible trails toward his sister.*]

In ant-language, teetee means sister. In ant, teeteetee means touch. I wish I knew the word for Ceci.
CECI: Tee-teeeh.
MISHA: I hear you. [*He crawls to her.*] In my dream, you had a key in your mouth.   760

> [CECI *finds the pull-tab and shows it to him.*]

CECI: My magic key out of ant-prison.
MISHA: I love you, Ceci.
CECI: Aayyyhhh.

> [*He grits his teeth as she moves his hand into her. She begins to feel him as he cries.*]

The last card. Inscribed, *Ay Te Watcho*. Which is Godspeed in Chicano. So wave bye to me, little brother, and reach inside and spell the word love in a girl that's never   765
felt it with your fingers push back the veil *ay, asi, carnal, asi,*[283] find the poems in me

---

[281] ¿*Y tu que ves?*–"And what are you looking at?"
[282] *cochinadas*–"dirty things"
[283] *ay, asi, carnal, asi*–"oh, like that bro, like that"

'cause I hid them all for you, *asi, asi*, poems of your hunger your shame your secret loves, *ay*, got them right here, Misha, your *versos*—[284]

CECI/MISHA:—dancing in me, drowning in my blood—

MISHA:—reaching all the way up to your heart, I'll find the Ceci you'll never be, give you wings with my pen, make you fly, I'll be your poet forever, *con safo, retacho, asi asi Ceci dame la vida Cecilia asi.*[285]   770

CECI: *hhhhhhg.*

> [MISHA *cries.* CECI, *in a spasm of ecstacy, sets the pull-tab gingerly on her tongue and swallows it. He watches her slowly slip away. Lights fade.*]

END OF PLAY

---

[284] *versos*–"verses"

[285] *con safo, retacho, asi asi Ceci dame la vida Cecilia asi*–This line seems the culmination of the longer exchange between Ceci and Misha which begins with Ceci's line, "push back the veil." In this exchange, Ceci gives to Misha the poetry stored inside her and Misha gives her the physical love she craves. His line here, *con safo, retacho* . . ., conveys this exchange.